Ultimate Full-Stack Web Development with MEVN

Learn From Designing to Deploying Production-Grade Web Applications with MongoDB, Express, Vue, and Node.js on AWS, Azure, and GCP

Bhargav Bachina

www.orangeava.com

First published: July 2024

Published by: Orange Education Pvt Ltd, AVA™

Address: 9, Daryaganj, Delhi, 110002, India

275 New North Road Islington Suite 1314 London,
N1 7AA, United Kingdom

ISBN: 978-81-97651-17-5

Scan the QR code to explore our entire catalogue

www.orangeava.com

Dedicated To

My Beloved Parents and Wife

Veeranjaneyulu Bachina,

Nagalaxmi Bachina,

Srividya Pullela

My Strength and Support System

About the Author

Bhargav Bachina is an eminent figure in the IT industry, celebrating a 12-year career distinguished by innovative leadership and advanced software architecture. With deep expertise spanning front-end, back-end development, and cloud computing, Bhargav's versatility shines through his mastery of Java, JavaScript, Python, and Node.js. His role as a visionary software architect is highlighted by his ability to craft comprehensive end-to-end solutions, with a commitment to excellence that has propelled numerous projects to success and established him as a pivotal thought leader.

Currently serving as the CTO of an educational startup, Bhargav is poised to launch a groundbreaking project that promises to add another achievement to his already impressive career. His role extends beyond company leadership, serving as a fractional CTO where his guidance is invaluable to emerging startups seeking his expertise, particularly those he mentors through LinkedIn.

Bhargav is also a prolific writer with a significant online presence. Over the past five years, he has authored over 700 articles on Medium, reaching a global audience of 8 million and gaining a substantial following of 22,000 readers. His insightful contributions continue to make waves on LinkedIn and provide valuable resources on GitHub, where he manages 431 repositories that frequently garner attention from the tech community.

Recently, Bhargav was honored with the 2024 Global Recognition Award for his substantial contributions to the technology and education sectors. Recognized for his strategic leadership and technical prowess in developing cutting-edge solutions for web and mobile platforms, Bhargav Bachina continues to be a beacon of industry excellence and a source of inspiration for IT professionals worldwide.

Beyond his professional life, Bhargav has a passion for watching movies, writing books, strength training, investing in real estate, and building tech things. These hobbies not only provide him with relaxation and enjoyment but also fuel his creativity and innovative thinking in his professional endeavors.

About the Technical Reviewer

Kiarash Bahrami brings over half a decade of expertise in full-stack development. He is adept in both legacy and modern frontend frameworks such as jQuery, React, and Vue.js. He possesses extensive experience in backend frameworks, including Laravel, Next.js, and Django. His proficiency extends to various database systems, encompassing SQL, NoSQL, and document-based databases like PostgreSQL, Oracle SQL, and MongoDB. Kiarash excels in cross-platform development, leveraging solutions like Electron and Capacitor.js to streamline source code deployment. Additionally, his skills encompass network-related operations and system administration.

Currently, Kiarash specializes in B2B and B2C SaaS and Cloud Solutions development, capitalizing on his diverse skill set to deliver reliable and scalable solutions tailored to client needs.

Acknowledgements

Embarking on the journey of writing *Ultimate Full-Stack Web Development with* MEVN has been an enriching and fulfilling experience, and I am deeply grateful to all those who have played a pivotal role in bringing this book to life. This endeavor wouldn't have been possible without the unwavering support, guidance, and expertise generously shared by many.

Firstly, my heartfelt thanks go to my family—my mother, Nagalaxmi Bachina, and my father, Veeranjaneyulu Bachina, for their love and encouragement. To my wife, Srividya Pullela, whose support and understanding have been my pillars of strength, and my brother, Sandeep Bachina, who has always stood by me. Their collective support has been a constant source of motivation throughout this writing journey. Additionally, a special thanks to my children, whose inspiration is the spark behind my endeavors.

I extend my gratitude to Khanna Kakarla for his support in the initial days of my software engineering career, setting the foundation upon which I built my skills. His guidance was crucial in shaping my early professional path.

I am also immensely thankful to the Node.js community and the VueJS documentation. These resources have been invaluable in the creation of this book, providing detailed insights and reliable guidance that enriched the content significantly.

Special thanks are due to Dhanunjaya Sir, whose mentorship during my college days has had a lasting impact on my career. His encouragement and advice have been instrumental in my Career.

To all those at the publication house who have contributed to various capacities, your efforts have significantly enriched this endeavor. I appreciate the collaborative spirit that has fueled the creation of *Ultimate Full-Stack Web Development with* MEVN.

Finally, to the readers, thank you for choosing this book as your guide. It is my sincere hope that it serves as a valuable resource on your journey to mastering the MEVN stack and navigating the dynamic world of web development.

Preface

In the swiftly advancing world of web development, harnessing a framework that integrates robustness with flexibility is essential. Welcome to *Ultimate Full-Stack Web Development with* MEVN–a journey that takes you beyond the basics into the sophisticated realms of the MEVN stack, comprising MongoDB, ExpressJS, VueJS, and Node.js. This book is crafted to guide you through mastering these technologies, creating dynamic full-stack web applications that stand out in today's tech landscape.

This book unfolds across 16 detailed chapters, each a focused module designed to enhance your understanding and skills in a specific area of MEVN stack development. From newcomers eager to get their hands dirty with modern web technologies to seasoned developers aiming to broaden their expertise in full-stack development, this book offers valuable insights and learning for all.

Chapter 1. Introduction: This introductory chapter serves as your gateway into the MEVN stack, explaining its components–MongoDB, ExpressJS, VueJS, and Node.js–and their roles in modern web development. By understanding the synergy between these technologies, you will appreciate their combined power in building dynamic web applications. This chapter lays the groundwork for the deeper exploration of each technology in subsequent chapters.

Chapter 2. Prerequisites: This chapter focuses on setting up the development environment essential for MEVN applications. It guides you through installing and configuring Node.js, MongoDB, VueJS, and supportive tools like Visual Studio Code and Docker. The chapter ensures that you have a solid base to start developing, including setting up a MongoDB Atlas account and preparing an example project that will be developed throughout the book.

Chapter 3. Exploring VueJS: This chapter dives deep into VueJS, showcasing its capabilities to build responsive interfaces. You will learn about VueJS's core features such as the reactive system, components, directives, and the Vue CLI. Practical examples will help you understand how to effectively use the Options API, Composition API, and other advanced features to build scalable front-end applications.

Chapter 4. Node.js Modules and Components: In this chapter, we will explore

Node.js in depth, focusing on its modules and components that are essential for backend development. The chapter covers the file system, events, streams, and the HTTP module, among others. You will learn how Node.js handles asynchronous operations with callbacks and promises, setting a strong foundation for building robust server-side applications.

Chapter 5. Setting Up Development Environment: This chapter elaborates on configuring a development environment that enhances productivity and supports efficient development workflows. You'll learn about using Vite CLI for frontend development, setting up a Node.js backend, and other tools like Nodemon for automatic reloading.

Chapter 6. Backend Development With TypeScript: Transitioning into backend development, this chapter introduces you to using TypeScript with Node.js and ExpressJS. It guides you through setting up a TypeScript project, defining routes, and building a structured API. This chapter also covers integrating MongoDB using the Mongoose library, emphasizing type safety and scalable application architecture.

Chapter 7. Getting Familiar With MongoDB and Integration: This chapter focuses on database operations, from basic CRUD operations to more complex queries and the use of aggregation pipelines. You will learn how to design effective models and use the repository pattern to encapsulate database interactions.

Chapter 8. UI Development: This chapter is dedicated to advancing your skills in UI development with VueJS. It covers the design and implementation of user interfaces, using Bootstrap for styling, and how to handle state management with Pinia. You will also learn about best practices for structuring your projects and building reusable components.

Chapter 9. Logging Options in Node.js API: Logging is crucial for monitoring and debugging applications. This chapter explores different logging frameworks like Winston, Pino, and Bunyan. You will understand how to implement a common logging interface across your application, which is essential for maintaining large-scale applications in production.

Chapter 10. Building MEVN Stack for Production: This chapter covers everything from minifying and bundling your code with Webpack or Gulp to setting up HTTPS and securing your API. You will also explore how to handle environment variables and automate tasks using npm scripts.

Chapter 11. Running MEVN Stack on Docker: This chapter guides you through creating Docker images, managing containers with Docker Compose, and best practices for multi-stage builds. This knowledge is crucial for deploying applications that require high reliability and scalability.

Chapter 12. Unit Testing: This chapter introduces tools like Jest and Vue Test Utils, teaching you how to write reliable unit tests that ensure your code behaves as expected before it goes live. We will learn to develop robust testing strategies for both frontend and backend components of your MEVN application.

Chapter 13. End-to-End Testing: This chapter covers the importance of automated browser testing and how it fits into modern development pipelines, ensuring your application functions correctly from start to finish. You will expand your testing suite to include end-to-end tests with Cypress, TestCafe, and Playwright.

Chapter 14. MEVN Stack Container Options on Google Cloud: This chapter explores Google Cloud Run and Kubernetes services, providing insights into container management and deployment strategies. You will learn how to push images to the Artifact Registry and manage applications at scale.

Chapter 15. MEVN Stack Container Options on AWS: This chapter dives into deploying your Dockerized MEVN application on AWS using services like AWS App Runner and Elastic Kubernetes Service. It covers configuring the AWS CLI, pushing Docker images to Amazon ECR, and strategies for effective cloud deployment.

Chapter 16. MEVN Stack Container Options on Azure: In this chapter, we will learn how to prepare your MEVN application for production. It covers everything from minifying and bundling your code with Webpack or Gulp to setting up HTTPS and securing your API. We will also explore how to handle environment variables and automate tasks using npm scripts.

This book is not just a technical guide, but a practical companion filled with real-world examples and expert insights. Each chapter is meticulously designed to build on the knowledge gained in the previous ones, culminating in a comprehensive understanding of full-stack development with the MEVN stack.

Prepare to embark on a transformative learning experience! *Ultimate Full-Stack Web Development with* MEVN equips you to build innovative and scalable web applications and elevates your skills in the competitive field of web development. Let's begin this exciting adventure into full-stack development. Happy coding!

Get a Free eBook

We hope you are enjoying your recently purchased book! Your feedback is incredibly valuable to us, and to all other readers looking for great books.

If you found this book helpful or enjoyable, we would truly appreciate it, if you could take a moment to leave a short review with a 5 star rating on Amazon. It helps us grow, and lets other readers discover our books.

As a thank you, we would love to send you a free digital copy of this book, and a **30%** discount code on your next cart value on our official websites:

www.orangeava.com

www.orangeava.in (For Indian Subcontinent)

☑ **Here's how:**

Leave a review for the book on Amazon.

Take a screenshot of your review, and send an email to **info@orangeava.com** (it can be just the confirmation screen).

Once, we receive your screenshot, we will send you the digital file, within 24 hours.

Thank you so much for your support – it means a lot to us!

Downloading the code bundles and colored images

Please follow the links or scan the QR codes to download the
Code Bundles and Images of the book:

https://github.com/ava-orange-education/Ultimate-Full-Stack-Web-Development-with-MEVN

The code bundles and images of the book are also hosted on
https://rebrand.ly/f66994

In case there's an update to the code, it will be updated on the existing GitHub repository.

Errata

We take immense pride in our work at **Orange Education Pvt Ltd,** and follow best practices to ensure the accuracy of our content to provide an indulging reading experience to our subscribers. Our readers are our mirrors, and we use their inputs to reflect and improve upon human errors, if any, that may have occurred during the publishing processes involved. To let us maintain the quality and help us reach out to any readers who might be having difficulties due to any unforeseen errors, please write to us at :

errata@orangeava.com

Your support, suggestions, and feedback are highly appreciated.

DID YOU KNOW

Did you know that Orange Education Pvt Ltd offers eBook versions of every book published, with PDF and ePub files available? You can upgrade to the eBook version at **www.orangeava.com** and as a print book customer, you are entitled to a discount on the eBook copy. Get in touch with us at: **info@orangeava.com** for more details.

At **www.orangeava.com**, you can also read a collection of free technical articles, sign up for a range of free newsletters, and receive exclusive discounts and offers on AVA™ Books and eBooks.

PIRACY

If you come across any illegal copies of our works in any form on the internet, we would be grateful if you would provide us with the location address or website name. Please contact us at **info@orangeava.com** with a link to the material.

ARE YOU INTERESTED IN AUTHORING WITH US?

If there is a topic that you have expertise in, and you are interested in either writing or contributing to a book, please write to us at **business@orangeava.com**. We are on a journey to help developers and tech professionals to gain insights on the present technological advancements and innovations happening across the globe and build a community that believes Knowledge is best acquired by sharing and learning with others. Please reach out to us to learn what our audience demands and how you can be part of this educational reform. We also welcome ideas from tech experts and help them build learning and development content for their domains.

REVIEWS

Please leave a review. Once you have read and used this book, why not leave a review on the site that you purchased it from? Potential readers can then see and use your unbiased opinion to make purchase decisions. We at Orange Education would love to know what you think about our products, and our authors can learn from your feedback. Thank you!

For more information about Orange Education, please visit **www.orangeava.com**.

Table of Contents

1. Introduction **1**

Introduction 1

Structure 1

Understanding MEVN Stack 2

Use Cases of MEVN Stack 2

Introduction to MongoDB 4

Evolution of MongoDB 4

Key Features 4

Use Cases 5

Key Differences with Traditional SQL 5

Getting Started with MongoDB 6

Introduction to Node.js 14

timers 16

Pending Callbacks 16

Idle, prepare 16

Poll 17

Check 17

Close Callbacks 17

Key Features of Node.js 17

Use Cases of Node.js 18

Node.js REPL 19

Introduction to ExpressJS 20

Key Features 20

Use Cases 21

Getting Started with Express.js 23

Express Application Generator 25

Introduction to VueJS 25

Key Features 25

Conclusion 26

Further Reading ... 26

2. Prerequisites ... 27

Introduction ... 27

Structure ... 27

Installing Node.js Through NVM ... 28

Installing Node.js Through NVM on Windows ... 29

Installing Node.js Through NVM on Mac ... 30

Installing Specific Versions of Node.js ... 31

Switching Between Node.js Versions ... 32

Listing All the Versions ... 32

Uninstalling Specific Version of Node.js ... 32

Installing VSCode ... 33

Installing Vite Globally for Creating VueJS Project ... 33

Understanding Vite ... 33

Installing Docker ... 36

MongoDB Setup on Local Machine ... 41

Installing and Downloading MongoDB Community Edition ... 41

Running MongoDB Through Docker ... 43

Setting Up MongoDB Atlas Account ... 44

Example Project We are Building ... 48

Conclusion ... 52

3. Exploring VueJS ... 53

Introduction ... 53

Structure ... 54

Need for VueJS ... 54

Understanding Reactivity in VueJS ... 56

Reactivity in Action ... 57

Understanding Components ... 58

Component Structure ... 58

Communication: Props and Events ... 59

Advanced Communication Patterns ... 60

Options API ... 60

Basics of the Options API 61

Vue Component with Options API 61

Advantages and Use Cases 62

Limitations 63

Composition API 63

Basics of the Composition API 63

Vue Component with Composition API 63

Advantages and Use Cases 65

Lifecycle Hooks 66

Key Lifecycle Hooks 66

`onBeforeMount` 66

`onMounted` 67

`onBeforeUpdate` 67

`onUpdated` 68

`onBeforeUnmount` 68

`onUnmounted` 69

Options API versus Composition API 69

Applying Styles 70

Inline Styles 71

Class Bindings 71

Scoped Styles 72

Global Styles 72

Custom Directives 73

Basics of Custom Directives 73

Local Custom Directives 74

Directive Hook Arguments 74

Dynamic Directives 75

Slots 75

Basics of Slots 75

Default Slot 75

Named Slots 76

Scoped Slots 76

Slot Fallbacks and Defaults 77
Destructuring Slot Props 77
Template Refs 78
Basics of Template Refs 78
Refs with Vue Components 78
Reactivity and Refs 79
Using Refs with Reactivity 79
Understanding Forms 80
Basics of Form Handling 80
Handling Form Submission 81
Form Validation 81
Using Custom Components in Forms 82
Conclusion 83
4. Node.js Modules and Components 84
Introduction 84
Structure 85
Buffer 85
Creating Buffers 86
Manipulating Buffer Data 88
Advanced Buffer Operations 88
Understanding Cluster Module and Child Process 89
Child Processes 89
Creating and Managing Child Processes 90
spawn() 90
exec() 91
execFile() 92
fork() 93
Cluster Module 94
Implementing Cluster 94
REPL 95
Advanced Usage of Core REPL 96
Streams 98

Types of Streams ... 99
Readable Streams ... 99
Types of Readable Streams ... 99
Creating a Readable Stream ... 99
Consuming Data from Readable Streams ... 100
Writable Streams ... 101
Types of Writable Streams ... 101
Creating a Writable Stream ... 101
Duplex Streams ... 103
Creating Duplex Streams ... 103
Reading from Duplex Streams ... 104
Writing to Duplex Streams ... 104
Handling Backpressure ... 104
Error Handling and Cleanup ... 105
Transform Streams ... 105
Creating Transform Streams ... 106
Using Transform Streams ... 106
Error Handling ... 107
Working With File System ... 107
Synchronous versus Asynchronous ... 108
Asynchronous Methods ... 108
Synchronous Methods ... 108
Choosing Between Synchronous and Asynchronous Methods ... 109
Reading and Writing Files ... 109
Working With Directories ... 110
File Streams ... 111
Understanding Events ... 112
Creating a `EventEmitter` ... 113
Working With Events ... 113
Emitting Events ... 113
Listening for Events ... 113
Error Handling Events ... 114

Removing Listeners 114

HTTP Module 115

Creating an HTTP Server 115

Basic Server Setup 115

Request and Response Objects 116

Handling HTTP Requests 116

Parsing Request URL 116

Handling Different Request Methods 117

Building an HTTP Client 118

Error Handling 119

Understanding Callbacks and Promises 120

Understanding Callbacks 120

Handling Errors in Callbacks 120

Callback Hell 121

Overcoming Callback Hell 121

Understanding Promises 122

Creating Promises 122

Consuming Promises 122

Chaining Promises 123

Async/Await Syntax 123

Exception Handling 124

Types of Exceptions 124

Standard JavaScript Errors 124

System Errors 124

User-Defined Errors 125

Promise Rejections 125

Assertion Errors 125

Handling Synchronous Code Exceptions 125

Handling Asynchronous Code Exceptions 126

Callbacks 126

Promises and `Async/Await` 126

Unhandled Exception Handling 127

Conclusion....128
5. Setting Up Development Environment....129
Introduction....129
Structure....129
Creating a Typescript Template Project Using Vite CLI....130
Understanding the Project Structure....133
Using Vite CLI for Watching Frontend....135
Setting Up Node.js Backend....138
Nodemon Installation and Setup....144
Conclusion....147
Further Readings....148
6. Backend Development With TypeScript....149
Introduction....149
Structure....150
Understanding API Structure....150
Introduction to REST Architecture....151
Uniform Interface Constraints....152
HTTP Methods....153
Advantages of REST....153
Understanding Express.js Middleware....154
Setting Up Express Server....156
Introduction to Webpack....163
Key Features....163
Use Cases....164
Setting Up Webpack for Building TypeScript Files....164
Defining Routes....168
Building API Structure....175
Request Validation....184
Joi....185
Express-validator....186
Implementation of Joi....188
Conclusion....193

7. **Getting Familiar With MongoDB and Integration 194**

Introduction 194

Structure 194

Different Ways to Connect to MongoDB Instance 195

Exploring Atlas CLI to Query the MongoDB 197

Understanding Mongo Aggregation Pipelines 199

Configuring MongoDB Connection in the Express API 201

Mongoose 201

Advantages of Using Mongoose in Development 203

Implementing Models 208

Implementing Repository Pattern 210

Advantages 210

Implementing CRUD Operations 218

Testing APIs with Postman 222

Testing with User Routes 223

Testing with todos Routes 225

Exploring Mongo Compass to Visualize the Data 230

Conclusion 235

8. **UI Development 237**

Introduction 237

Structure 237

Understanding Example Project 238

Understanding Project Structure 238

Defining Routes and Creating Layouts 240

Adding Bootstrap CSS Framework 244

Writing Containers and Components for UI Screens 248

Implementing Login Module 250

`Signin` Presentational Component 251

Sign up Presentational Component 253

Implementing Dashboard Module 256

Header and `NoTasksAvailable` Presentational Components 257

Tasks Presentational Component 260

Implementing Create Task Modal 262
Implementing Edit and Delete Task Modal 265
Writing Services and Proxy Setup for API Calls 270
Setting Up Pinia Store for State Management 281
Set Up Pinia Store 282
Side Effects Like API calls 284
Implementing Pinia Store for Login Module 285
Implementing Pinia Store for Dashboard/Tasks Module 290
Implementing Pinia Store for Task Detail Module 297
Rehydrating State with Pinia 300
Implementation 301
Understanding the Final UI structure 305
Conclusion 307
9. Logging Options in Node.js API 308
Introduction 308
Structure 308
Understanding the Importance of Logging 309
Importance of Logging 309
Implementing Effective Logging Strategies 309
Tools and Best Practices 310
Implementing Common Logger Service 311
Reasons for Implementing a Custom Logger Service 311
Class Definition 312
Public Logging Methods 313
Console Logging 313
Setting Up Logger Service with Pine Library 316
Setting Up Logger Service with Pino Library 319
Setting Up Logger Service with Bunyan Library 323
Setting up Logger Service with Winston Library 328
Conclusion 333
10. Building MEVN Stack for Production 334
Introduction 334

Structure....334
Building Frontend and Serving Through API....335
Serving UI Assets Through API....337
Externalize Environment Variables....340
Using the `dotenv` Library....341
Building Backend with Webpack....347
Build Once and Deploy Everywhere....347
Build for Each Environment....354
Running MEVN Stack on HTTPS....357
Step1: Generate a Self-Signed SSL Certificate....358
Step2: Configure Your Node.js Server for HTTPS....359
Step 3: Access Your Application Over HTTPS....360
Securing API....362
Implementing Helmet....363
Implementing CORS....365
Implementing CSRF....367
Implementing Rate Limiting....368
Applying Global....368
Applying Specific Route Rate Limiting....370
Global Exception Handler....373
Linting....376
Linting UI....377
Linting API....381
Configure `husky` for Pre-Commit Hooks....383
Step 1: Install Husky....383
Step 2: Enable Git Hooks....383
Step 3: Add a Pre-commit Hook....383
Step 4: Make the Hook Executable....384
Step 5: Test and Commit....384
Introducing Task Runners....385
Benefits to Use Gulp or Grunt in MEVN Stack Development....386
Generate a Final Build Zip File with npm Scripts....386

Conclusion....389
11. Running MEVN Stack on Docker....390
Introduction....390
Structure....391
Introduction to Docker and Containerization....391
Understanding Containerization....392
Embracing the Container Revolution....392
The Essence of Containerization....392
Consistency Across Environments....392
Resource Efficiency and Destiny....392
Isolation and Security....392
The Role of Docker in Containerization....393
Portability: A Docker Imperative....393
Continuous Integration and Deployment....393
Container Orchestration and Management....393
Core Concepts of Docker....393
Docker Images....393
Docker Containers....393
Dockerfile....394
Docker Registries....394
Docker Daemon....394
Docker Client....394
Docker Compose....394
Docker Networks....394
Docker Volumes....394
Getting Started with an Example....395
Building the Docker Image....398
Running the Docker Image....399
Introduction to Docker Compose....400
Simplifying Complex Applications....400
Consistent Development Environments....400
Key Features of Docker Compose....401

Writing a Docker Compose File....402
Understanding Docker Compose with Example Project....403
Best Practices with Docker Compose....407
Building and Running MEVN Stack Docker Image....409
Building and Running Image with Multi-Stage Builds....416
Understanding the Need....416
Interaction with Running Container....420
Running MEVN Stack on Docker Compose....421
Publishing the Docker Image....428
Best Practices....432
Containerization Best Practices....432
Docker Compose Best Practices....433
Publishing Docker Images Best Practices....435
Conclusion....437
12. Unit Testing....438
Introduction....438
Structure....439
Introduction to Unit Testing....439
Importance of Unit Testing....439
Best Practices for Unit Testing....439
Chapter Overview....440
Introduction to Vue Test Utils....440
Testing Vue Components with Vue Test Utils....440
Introduction to Jest....440
Setup Jest for Unit Testing Backend....441
Introduction to Mocha and Chai....441
Set Up Mocha and Chai for Unit Testing Backend....441
Introduction to Vue Test Utils....441
Practical Examples....443
Mounting a Vue Component....443
Accessing Component Data....443
Simulating User Interaction....443

Testing Props and Emits 444

Introduction to Jest 445

Best Practices 446

Jest Along with Vue/test-utils 447

Testing Frontend 448

Testing API 452

Other Unit Testing Libraries 456

Mocha and Chai 457

Best Practices 458

Tap Library 459

Best Practices 459

Conclusion 460

13. End-to-End Testing 461

Introduction 461

Structure 462

Introduction to End-to-End Testing 462

Importance of End-to-End Testing 462

Challenges in E2E Testing 463

Best Practices 463

Introduction to TestCafe 464

Key Features of TestCafe 464

Writing the First Test with TestCafe 465

Running TestCafe Tests 465

Advanced Topics and Best Practices 465

Using TestCafe for E2E Tests 466

Introduction to Cypress 471

Key Features of Cypress 471

Writing the First Test with Cypress 471

Running Cypress Tests 472

Advanced Topics and Best Practices 472

Using Cypress for E2E Tests 473

Introduction to Playwright 477

Key Features of Playwright 477
Writing the First Test with `Playwright` 478
Running Playwright Tests 478
Advanced Topics and Best Practices 478
Using `Playwright` for E2E Tests 479
Conclusion 482
14. MEVN Stack Container Options on Google Cloud 483
Introduction 483
Structure 484
Introduction to Google Cloud 484
Core Components and Services 485
Getting Started with Google Cloud 488
Different Ways to Interact with GCP 490
Configure and Set Up gcloud CLI 492
Container Options on GCP 494
Google Kubernetes Engine (GKE) 494
Cloud Run 495
Compute Engine 496
App Engine Flexible Environment 497
Pushing Docker Image to Artifact Registry 498
Running MEVN Stack on Cloud Run 506
Running MEVN Stack on Google GKE 511
Key Features of GKE 511
GKE Architecture 512
Conclusion 519
15. MEVN Stack Container Options on AWS 521
Introduction 521
Structure 522
Introduction to AWS 522
Core Components and Services 523
Advantages of Using AWS 524
Getting Started with AWS 526

Different Ways to Interact with AWS 529
AWS Management Console 529
AWS Command Line Interface (CLI) 530
AWS Software Development Kits (SDKs) 530
AWS `CloudFormation` 531
AWS Tools for PowerShell 531
Third-Party Tools and Integrations 531
Configure and Setup AWS CLI 532
Container Options on AWS 535
Amazon Elastic Container Service (ECS) 535
Amazon Elastic Kubernetes Service (EKS) 536
AWS Fargate 537
Amazon LightSail 538
AWS App Runner 538
Pushing Docker Image to Amazon ECR 539
Running MEVN Stack on AWS App Runner 543
Conclusion 549
16. MEVN Stack Container Options on Azure 551
Introduction 551
Structure 552
Introduction to Microsoft Azure 552
Core Components and Services 553
Advantages of Using Microsoft Azure 554
Getting Started with Azure 556
Different Ways to Interact with Azure 562
Azure Portal 562
Azure CLI (Command-Line Interface) 562
Azure PowerShell 563
Azure SDKs (Software Development Kits) 563
Azure Cloud Shell 564
Terraform for Azure 564
Configure and Set Up Azure CLI 565

Container Options on Azure ... 567
Azure Kubernetes Service (AKS) ... 568
Azure Container Instances (ACI) ... 568
Azure Web App for Containers ... 569
Azure Service Fabric ... 570
Azure Functions ... 571
Pushing Docker Image to Azure Container Registry ... 572
Running MEVN Stack on Azure App Service ... 577
Conclusion ... 584
Index ... 585

CHAPTER 1
Introduction

Introduction

This opening chapter lays the foundation for our exploration into the MEVN stack, detailing the essential tools and technologies that we will employ throughout this book. We begin by defining MEVN and the critical technologies required to implement this stack effectively. As the backbone of any web application, MongoDB is our chosen database. We will delve into its capabilities and discuss the pros and cons of utilizing a NoSQL database like MongoDB.

We will also explore ExpressJS, a streamlined Node.js framework, which serves as the middleware layer of our stack, enabling us to construct a robust backend. For the frontend, we turn to VueJS – a progressive framework that not only facilitates the development of the user interface but also introduces us to the main concepts of Single Page Applications (SPAs) and the VueJS library.

Node.js is pivotal as our server-side technology, enabling you to install all key technologies on your local machine and kickstart your full-stack development journey with the MEVN stack.

In addition to these foundational topics, this chapter will also guide you through the deployment of the MEVN stack on major cloud platforms such as AWS, Azure, and Google Cloud Platform (GCP). This will prepare you to leverage the cloud's scalable infrastructure to enhance and deploy your applications seamlessly.

Structure

In this chapter, the following topics will be covered:

- Understanding MEVN Stack
- Introduction to MongoDB
- Introduction to Node.js
- Introduction to ExpressJS
- Introduction to VueJS

Understanding MEVN Stack

The MEVN stack is an ensemble of four pivotal technologies that are essential for developing full-stack web applications. This acronym stands for MongoDB, ExpressJS, VueJS, and Node.js, making it a popular choice for building high-performance web applications. The trend toward a JavaScript-centric approach in application development leverages the consistency of JavaScript across both client and server sides, offering benefits like simplified development processes, reduced need for diverse programming skills, and quicker project turnarounds.

Here's a closer look at the roles each component plays within the MEVN stack:

- **MongoDB:** Serving as the database component, MongoDB is a NoSQL database renowned for its flexibility and scalability, making it ideal for managing large volumes of diverse data. Unlike traditional databases that store data in tables, MongoDB uses a JSON-like format, enhancing the ease with which data can be accessed and manipulated by clients. MongoDB can be deployed in various environments, whether via Docker, on a virtual machine, or through a cloud-based service like MongoDB Atlas, with the Mongoose library commonly used to interact with the database from the API layer.
- **Express.js:** As the backend framework of the stack, Express.js is a minimalistic and flexible Node.js web application framework designed for building robust features for web and mobile applications. Known for its simplicity and efficiency, Express.js facilitates numerous server-side tasks such as routing, middleware integration, error handling, request parsing, and sending JSON responses.
- **Vue.js:** In the frontend framework role, Vue.js is a progressive framework tailored for building user interfaces. Its adaptability, ease of integration with other technologies, reactivity, and high performance make Vue.js a favored choice for developers. The component-based architecture of Vue.js simplifies the development of large-scale applications, making it suitable for projects ranging from startups to enterprise-level deployments.
- **Node.js:** As a server-side JavaScript runtime environment, Node.js allows for the execution of JavaScript code on the server, eliminating the need for alternative server-side languages. This unification under JavaScript simplifies development across the stack, particularly within the MEVN architecture, where Node.js is pivotal for creating API layers that communicate with MongoDB to fetch, process, and serve data via REST APIs.

Use Cases of MEVN Stack

The MEVN Stack represents a robust and flexible assembly of technologies, ideal for a broad spectrum of web development endeavors. This stack is applicable to numerous scenarios, including but not limited to the following use cases:

- **E-Commerce Applications:** The MEVN Stack can be used for creating dynamic and scalable online stores with rich user experience and efficient backend processing.
- **Content Management Systems (CMS):** Developing customizable and user-friendly CMS platforms such as blogs, corporate websites, and so on.
- **Real-Time Applications:** Node.js has excellent support for web sockets, and with the Vue.js reactivity system, MEVN Stack is an excellent choice for real-time chat and live updates applications.
- **Social Media Platforms:** Building platforms that require real-time data updates, user interaction, and content management capabilities.
- **Single Page Applications (SPAs):** Creating fast and responsive SPAs, where Vue.js handles the frontend and Node.js with Express.js manages the backend operations.
- **Enterprise Web Applications:** Utilizing VueJS, a progressive framework, for building large-scale systems, and MongoDB as a database.
- **Dashboard and Analytics Tools**: Building interactive and data-intensive dashboards for data visualization.
- **Project Management Tools:** Building project management tools that require real-time tracking and updates. We can build these tools with this stack with ease.
- **Educational Platforms:** Building learning management systems with dynamic content and so much interactivity.
- **Healthcare Applications:** This stack can be used for managing patient information, scheduling appointments, and secure data handling.
- **Financial Services Applications:** Creating applications for banking, trading, or financial planning that require secure processing of financial data.
- **IoT Applications:** Node.js can handle asynchronous data efficiently and Vue.js is good for building user interfaces that make it a right choice for IoT applications.
- **Travel and Booking Platforms:** Building travel and booking websites with interactivity and live updates of the traffic data.
- **Event Management and Ticketing Systems:** For creating platforms where it needs seamless experiences for event listing, booking, and managing tickets.
- **Streaming Services:** Real-time data is crucial for building streaming platforms. Node.js single-threaded non-blocking execution and VueJS reactivity system make them ideal choices.

As you can see, the MEVN Stack is highly adaptable and suitable for diverse applications. The usage of JavaScript for both frontend and backend makes it a more popular choice for both seasoned developers and beginners.

Introduction to MongoDB

MongoDB is a leading NoSQL database, and it gained rapid adoption throughout the tech world for its innovative approach to data storage. MongoDB stores data in documents, unlike the traditional counterparts where the data is stored in tables. MongoDB stores data in Binary JSON format (BSON), and it is based on JSON. JSON is widely popular and used as a standard for data interchange on the web. JSON, a JavaScript object notation, is a subset of JavaScript, but it is entirely independent of any language and can be used to exchange data among different systems. The difference between JSON and BSON is that BSON supports more data types when compared to JSON and its binary format and can be read only by machines. For example, BSON documents may contain Date or Binary objects, which are not supported by JSON. This enables MongoDB to handle large volumes of unstructured data, making it an ideal choice for modern web applications.

Evolution of MongoDB

MongoDB was developed by MongoDB Inc. (formerly, 10gen) and was first released in 2009. It emerged as a part of the NoSQL movement, which began as a response to the growing need for a database that could handle the scalability and agility demands of big data and real-time web applications. Over the years, MongoDB has evolved significantly, adding features like text search, data aggregation, and ACID transactions, making it not only powerful but also versatile.

Key Features

There are so many advantages of MongoDB over traditional databases. Here are some of the key features:

- **Scalability:** MongoDB offers high scalability through features such as sharding and horizontal scaling across multiple servers.
- **Flexible Document Model:** One of the main advantages of MongoDB document model is flexibility in data storage. You don't have to save the same data structure across the documents. Those documents can grow based on your data, providing a rich and expressive data model.
- **High Performance:** MongoDB delivers high performance, especially for read and write operations with the help of features such as indexing, replication, and a robust query engine.

- **Aggregation Framework:** This is a powerful feature that allows you to process data and compute aggregated results, and it provides a way to transform and combine data in complex ways. This can be used for data analysis, transforming data, real-time analytics, and so on.

Use Cases

MongoDB is used in so many places from startups to big enterprises. Here are some of the common use cases:

- Real-time analytics and big data applications.
- Content management systems and e-commerce applications.
- Mobile applications that require flexible and scalable databases.
- IoT applications that need to handle large amounts of diverse data.

Key Differences with Traditional SQL

If you are coming from the traditional SQL or are new to MongoDB, understanding key differences between MongoDB and traditional SQL would be beneficial for the application development.

Here is a comprehensive comparison between them:

Feature	MongoDB Documents	Traditional SQL Databases
Data Structure	Stores data in JSON-like documents (BSON format)	Stores data in tables with rows and columns
Schema	Schema-less, documents in the same collection can have different structures	Fixed schema, all rows in a table must have the same columns
Query Language	Uses MongoDB Query Language (MQL), which is more focused on object-oriented and document-based queries	Uses Structured Query Language (SQL), which is powerful for complex queries involving joins and subqueries
Data Normalization	Generally favors denormalization; embedding related data in a single document is common	Highly normalized data structures with relationships represented using foreign keys
Transactions	Supports ACID transactions, but traditionally less emphasized; better suited for eventual consistency	Strong support for ACID transactions, ensuring data integrity and consistency
Scalability	Designed for horizontal scalability with sharding across multiple servers	Traditionally scaled vertically by increasing the power of the hardware. Horizontal scaling (sharding) is more complex

Indexing	Supports indexing on document fields for faster query performance	Supports comprehensive indexing strategies, including primary and foreign keys
Data Handling	Better suited for handling unstructured or semi-structured data with varied formats	Ideal for structured data with well-defined schemas
Flexibility	Highly flexible, allowing for easy modifications to data structures	Less flexible; schema changes can be complex and require database migrations
Relationships	Supports relationships, but they are typically data references or embedded documents	Relationships are a core feature, using primary and foreign keys
Use Cases	Ideal for big data applications, content management, mobile apps, and real-time analytics	Well-suited for applications requiring complex transactions, data integrity, and reporting

Table 1.1: *Comparison between MongoDB and Traditional SQL*

As you can see from the preceding table, you can choose MongoDB for more flexibility and scalability and scenarios in which applications deal with large volumes of diverse data or require rapid development cycles. Traditional databases are more suited for scenarios that demand complex queries, transactional integrity, and structured data handling.

Getting Started with MongoDB

Setting up MongoDB is quite straightforward, with multiple installation options available whether you are working in a local environment or on the cloud. MongoDB can be set up locally by installing the community edition or running in containers using Docker. Alternatively, for those preferring cloud-based solutions, MongoDB offers a Database as a Service called MongoDB Atlas, which simplifies management and scalability.

To connect to a MongoDB instance from your application, you will need to configure your database using a driver specific to your programming language. Here, we discuss both local and cloud installation methods, offering a basic comparison to help you choose the best setup for your needs. You can download the community edition suitable for your operating system from the following link:

https://www.mongodb.com/docs/manual/installation/

Once you follow the aforementioned instructions to install MongoDB on your local machine based on your operating system, we need to create a data directory and start the MongoDB. The Command Prompt, also known as `cmd` or Command Line Interface (CLI), is a powerful tool used to execute commands on Windows operating systems.

It allows users to perform tasks and manage the system settings via text-based commands, making it a crucial skill for system administrators and power users.

```
// create a data directory
md "\data\db"
// start the MongoDB
"C:\Program Files\MongoDB\Server\7.0\bin\mongod.exe" --dbpath="c:\data\db"
```

Figure 1.1: *Running MongoDB logs*

In the preceding logs, if you notice carefully, you can see messages regarding **`tsl connection`**, **`bind ip address`**, **`access control`**, and so on. We don't have to worry about those now; we will discuss them in the next chapters. When installing MongoDB, it's important to understand the distinction between MongoDB Server and MongoDB Shell, as well as why both are essential components of MongoDB's architecture.

MongoDB Server is the core component that manages data storage, performs operations, and handles all data management tasks. It is responsible for storing all the actual data and executing operations, including data queries, updates, and administrative commands. The server part of MongoDB runs as a service on your machine, listening for connections from clients.

MongoDB Shell, often referred to as mongo shell, is an interactive JavaScript interface to MongoDB. It allows you to manage, query, and manipulate data in MongoDB. With the shell, you can execute complex operations, run scripts, and evaluate JavaScript expressions directly against your MongoDB database.

Now that MongoDB is running, and if you want to connect to it, you need to download **`mongosh`** by following the link based on your operating system:

https://www.mongodb.com/try/download/shell

All you need to do is download the zip file, add this to the path, and run the following command to connect to the MongoDB instance already running with the previous command prompt or terminal. Remember, you need to open a new terminal to run this command:

```
// run the mongosh
"C:\Users\<usr directory>\mongosh-2.1.0-win32-x64\bin\mongosh.exe"
```

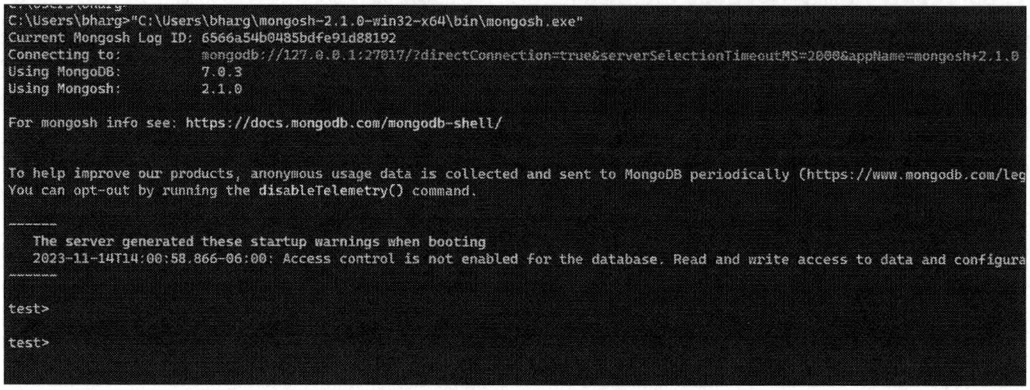

Figure 1.2: *Connecting to MongoDB*

In the preceding screenshot, you can observe that the connection is established with MongoDB running on the local machine at the IP address **`127.0.0.1`**, which is designated for localhost, on port **`27017`**. This is the default setting, but you have the option to specify different settings if you wish to connect to another MongoDB instance located elsewhere. The initial database in use is named "**`test`**." To view all available databases within your MongoDB installation, use the following command. Note that there are a few default databases included with every MongoDB setup.

The IP address **`127.0.0.1`** represents localhost, which refers to the local computer where the MongoDB server is running. Using this IP address means that the application will attempt to connect to a MongoDB instance that is hosted on the same machine as the client application itself, making it ideal for development and testing environments where the server and the client run on the same device:

```
show dbs
```

Figure 1.3: *Show dbs*

Each of these databases serves a specific purpose. Understanding these databases is very important when you configure and manage a MongoDB cluster or replica set.

Admin Database: This is the most privileged database and is almost equal to a root-level database. These are the key features:

- **User Authentication**: If you create a user in the admin database, then that user can be granted roles that apply across all the databases.
- **Server Administration**: Operations like managing users and roles, replication, sharding settings, and other administrative tasks are done in the context of this database.
- **High-Level Operations**: Commands that impact the entire MongoDB instance are run in the admin database.

Config Database: The config database stores configuration information about the MongoDB cluster. This is particularly important in sharded clusters. These are the key features:

- **Shard Configuration**: It contains collections, such as chunks, databases, shards, and collections, that MongoDB uses to manage a sharded cluster.
- **Metadata Storage**: It keeps track of the cluster's metadata, such as the mapping of the cluster's data to various shards.
- **Internal Use**: The collections in the config database is typically manipulated by MongoDB itself and are not meant for direct user interaction.

Local Database: The local database stores data specific to a single MongoDB server. These are the key features:

- **Replica Set Information**: In a replica set, the **local** database holds replication data. This includes the **`oplog`** **(oplog.rs)**, which is a capped collection that keeps a rolling record of all operations that modify the data stored in your databases.
- **Node-specific Data**: Data in the local database is not replicated to other members of the replica set. It's unique to a single server.
- **Backup and Restore**: The local database is not included when you perform backup and restore operations, as its data is relevant only to specific servers in the cluster.

Now that we have covered the default databases, you can create your own database using the following command. Keep in mind that this new database will not appear in the list until you add some collections to it:

```
use tasks
```

Figure 1.4: *Creating a Database*

We will perform some CRUD operations using the CLI. Start by creating a collection named **`'tasks'`** within the **`'tasks'`** database using the following commands. We will also insert two documents into this collection. Once these documents are created, you will be able to see the new database:

```
// creating collections
db.tasks.insertMany([
  {taskId: 1, description: 'getting groceries', status: 'New'},
  {taskId: 2, description: 'Creating an alarm', status: 'New'}
])
```

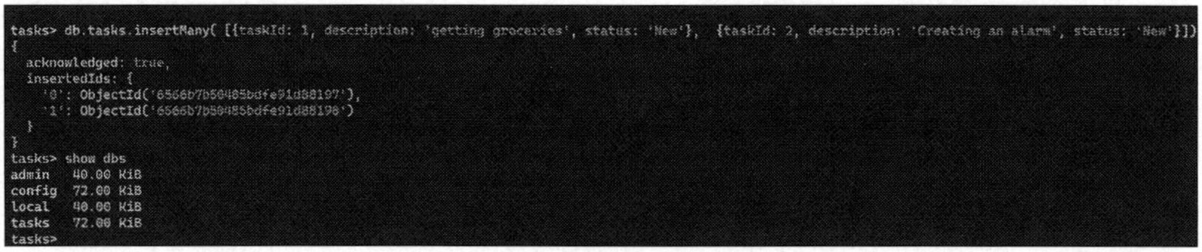

Figure 1.5: *Inserting Documents*

Let's query these documents that we just saved by running the following commands:

```
// Querying all documents
db.tasks.find()
// Querying specific documents
    db.tasks.find({taskId: 1})
```

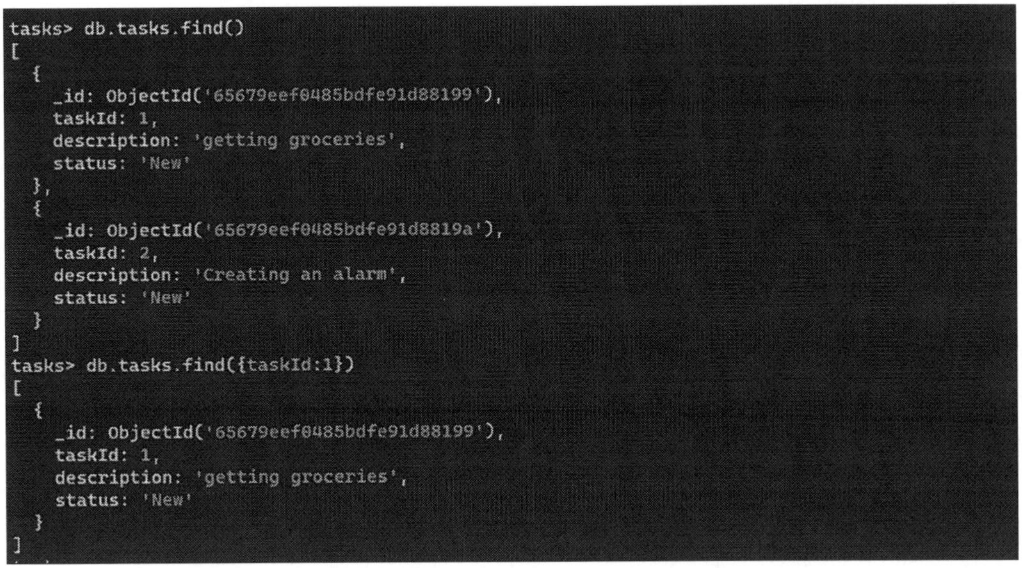

```
tasks> db.tasks.find()
[
  {
    _id: ObjectId('65679eef0485bdfe91d88199'),
    taskId: 1,
    description: 'getting groceries',
    status: 'New'
  },
  {
    _id: ObjectId('65679eef0485bdfe91d8819a'),
    taskId: 2,
    description: 'Creating an alarm',
    status: 'New'
  }
]
tasks> db.tasks.find({taskId:1})
[
  {
    _id: ObjectId('65679eef0485bdfe91d88199'),
    taskId: 1,
    description: 'getting groceries',
    status: 'New'
  }
]
```

Figure 1.6: *Querying Docs*

The following command updates a document by initially locating it using the **`taskId`**. Observe the acknowledgment response in the subsequent figure, which indicates the number of documents updated:

```
// Updating the Document
db.tasks.updateOne({taskId: 1}, {$set: {status: 'Done'}})
```

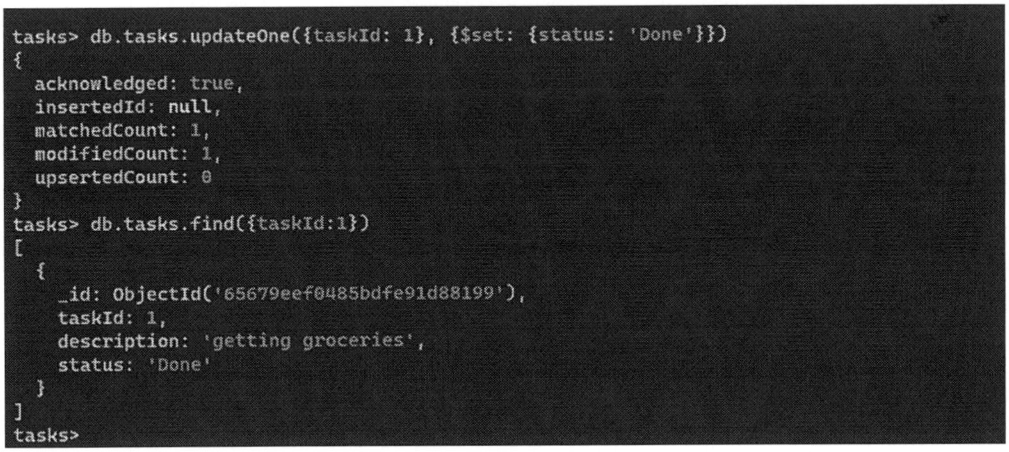

```
tasks> db.tasks.updateOne({taskId: 1}, {$set: {status: 'Done'}})
{
  acknowledged: true,
  insertedId: null,
  matchedCount: 1,
  modifiedCount: 1,
  upsertedCount: 0
}
tasks> db.tasks.find({taskId:1})
[
  {
    _id: ObjectId('65679eef0485bdfe91d88199'),
    taskId: 1,
    description: 'getting groceries',
    status: 'Done'
  }
]
tasks>
```

Figure 1.7: *Updating Documents*

The following command deletes the document by finding the document first by **`taskId`**.

```
// deleting the Document
db.tasks.updateOne({taskId: 1}, {$set: {status: 'Done'}})
```

```
tasks> db.tasks.deleteMany({taskId: 1})
{ acknowledged: true, deletedCount: 1 }
tasks> db.tasks.find({taskId:1})

tasks>
```

Figure 1.8: *Deleting Documents*

The preceding commands demonstrate how to insert and update data in MongoDB, serving as just a glimpse of the numerous other commands available, including those for utilizing the aggregation pipeline framework, which we will delve into in later chapters.

Additionally, there are various UI tools available that facilitate connection to your MongoDB instance, enabling you to visualize data and manage your database more effectively. These tools support tasks like query building and data visualization. You can explore these tools further by downloading and installing them on your computer.

MongoDB Compass:

- Official GUI from MongoDB.
- Offers a visual representation of your database schema, run queries, view query performance, and index management.

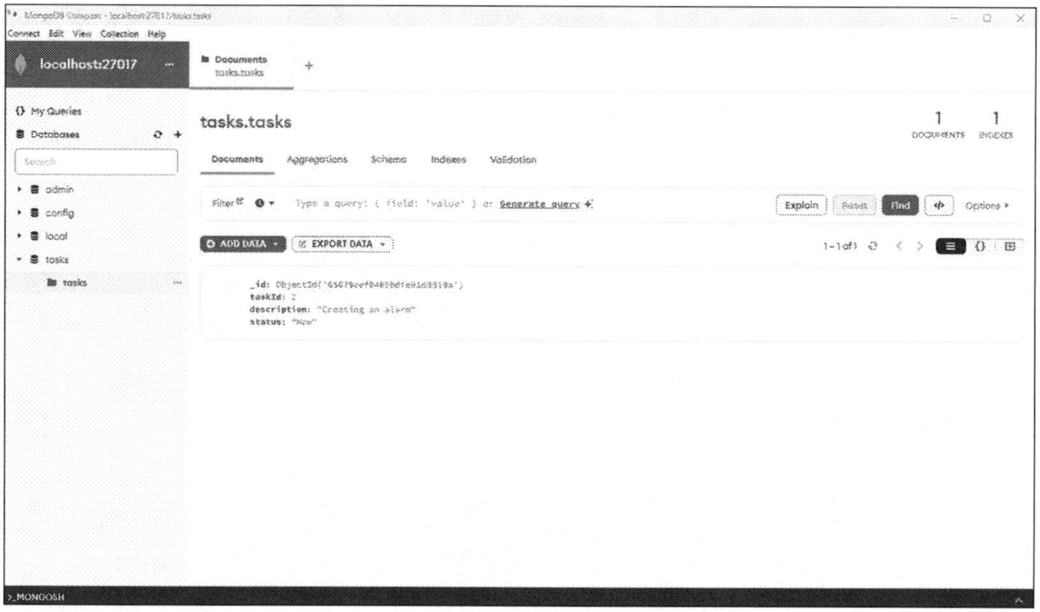

Figure 1.9: *MongoDB Compass connected to the local server*

Studio 3T:

- Offers a full range of features needed for MongoDB development and administration.
- Includes SQL query support, data import/export, and query profiling tools.

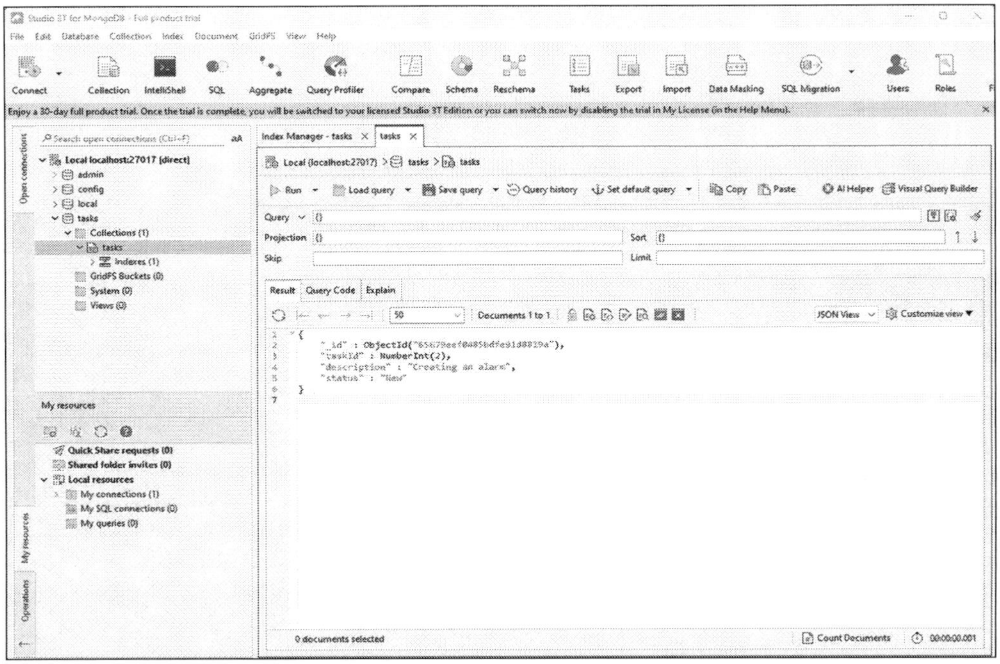

Figure 1.10: *Studio 3T connected to the local server*

NoSQLBooster for MongoDB:

- Feature-rich and cross-platform GUI tool.
- Supports SQL query, server monitoring, ES6 syntax, and more.

Figure 1.11: NoSQLBooster *connected to the local server*

MongoDB for VSCode:

- An extension for Visual Studio Code.
- Allows you to connect to MongoDB and work with your data directly from your code editor.

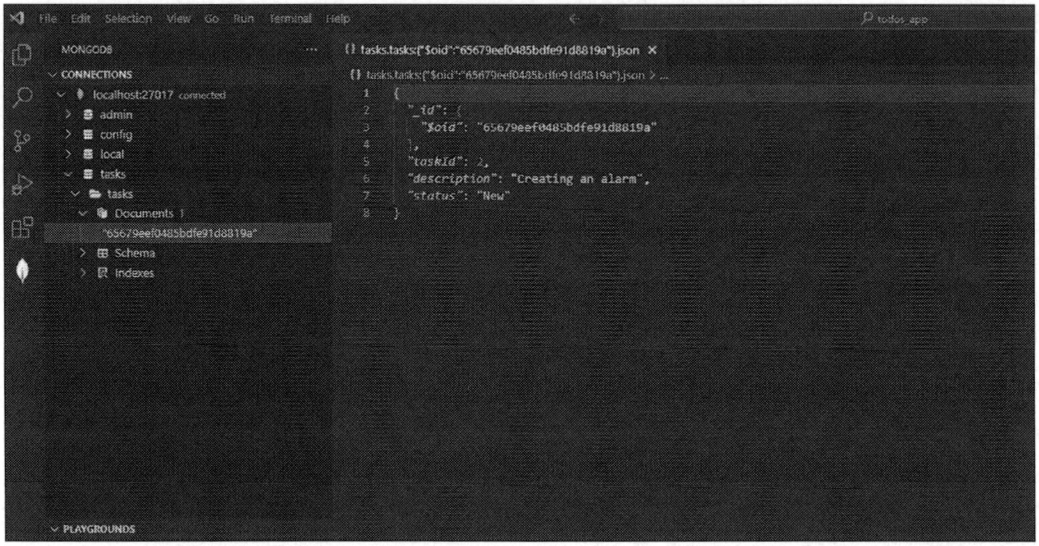

Figure 1.12: *MongoDB for VSCode connected to the local server*

Here are a few more you can try installing on your own:

Navicat for MongoDB:

- Provides a highly intuitive interface for database management.
- Features include data transfer, data synchronization, backup, and more.

MongoDB Atlas Data Explorer:

- Part of MongoDB Atlas, MongoDB's cloud service.
- Offers the ability to query, aggregate, and analyze your data in the cloud.

AdminMongo:

- Open-source, web-based tool to manage MongoDB databases.
- Provides basic features for database management.

Introduction to Node.js

Node.js is an open-source, cross-platform JavaScript runtime environment that executes JavaScript code outside a web browser. Traditionally, JavaScript was used primarily for client-side scripting, but Node.js enables JavaScript to be used for server-side scripting and runs scripts server-side to produce dynamic web page content before the page is sent to the user's web browser.

Node.js was created by Ryan Dahl in 2009, influenced by his dissatisfaction with the limited possibilities of the most popular web server at the time, Apache HTTP Server, to handle a lot of concurrent connections. Node.js was built on the V8 JavaScript runtime and aimed to optimize throughput and scalability in web applications and has since become a foundational element of the "*JavaScript everywhere*" paradigm, allowing web application development to unify around a single programming language, rather than rely on a different server-side scripting language.

Node.js is best known for its use in building scalable network applications. This contrasts with older web application frameworks that require multiple threads, where each new user or connection creates a new thread, taking up system RAM and eventually maxing out the amount of RAM available. Node.js operates on a single thread, using non-blocking I/O calls, which allows it to support tens of thousands of concurrent connections held in the event loop. *Figure 1.13* depicts the simplified overview of the event loop in Node.js, where the event loop is initialized whenever the Node.js starts or is invoked by input script or opens a REPL.

As you can see in the following figure, each box represents a phase in which we have a FIFO (first in first out) queue of callbacks to execute. Each phase has its own purpose, which is explained in detail further down. When Node.js enters each phase, it performs that phase's operations first and then executes callbacks in that phase's queue until the queue is exhausted or the maximum number of callbacks has been executed, and the event loop moves to the next phase.

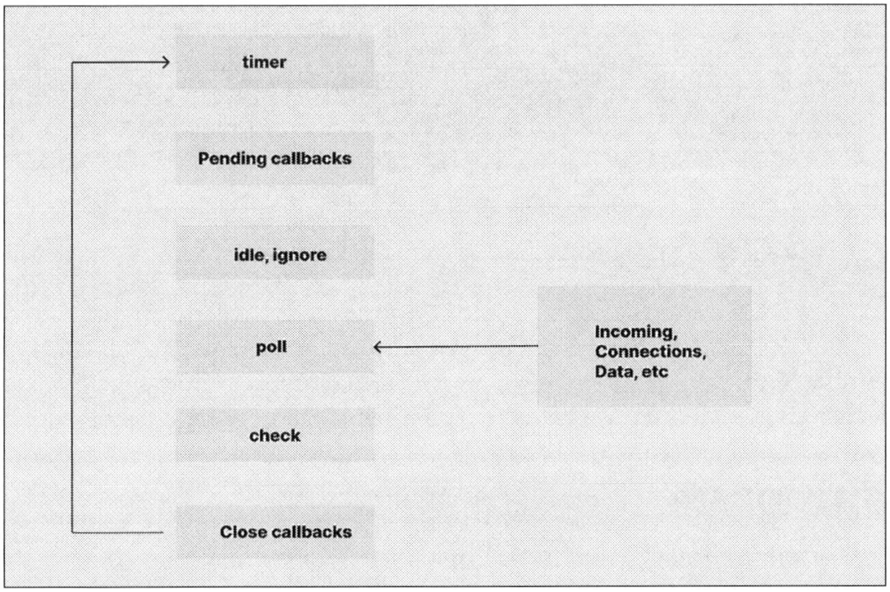

Figure 1.13: *Node.js event loop*

timers

This phase takes care of all the processes that have been set using **`setTimeout()`** and **`setInterval()`** functions. Here is the example block you can execute on REPL. A timer sets a minimum threshold before a given callback can be executed, rather than guaranteeing execution at a precise moment. The callback for timers is scheduled to run as soon as possible once the specified duration has elapsed.

Here is an example in which we have two functions: one is being executed after 3 seconds and another is being executed every 2 seconds after all the synchronous operations are completed, in this case, print statements.

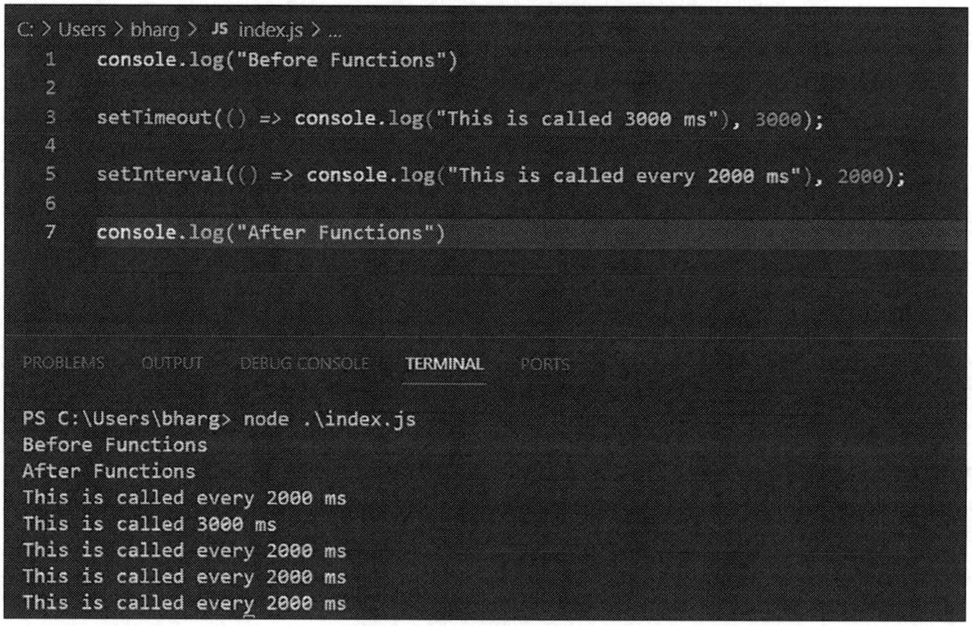

***Figure 1.14**: Timers phase*

Pending Callbacks

In this phase, callbacks for certain system operations, like specific TCP errors, are executed. For instance, if a TCP socket encounters an **`ECONNREFUSED`** error during a connection attempt, some Unix-based systems may delay reporting this error. Such callbacks are then scheduled to be executed during the pending callbacks phase.

Idle, prepare

These are used internally, and it is highly recommended not to use these for performance issues.

Poll

This phase calculates how long it should block and poll for I/O operations, and it processes events in the poll queue. There are no timers scheduled in this phase. The event loop executes all the callbacks synchronously until the queue has been exhausted or the limit is reached when the poll queue is not empty.

One more thing it does is to check the poll queue. If the poll queue is empty, it depends on the tasks scheduled by **`setImmediate()`**. If any tasks are scheduled by the **`setImmediate`** function, the event loop continues to the check phase by ending the current poll phase. If there are no scripts scheduled by the **`setImmediate()`** function, it continues to be in the poll phase and waits for the callbacks to be added and executes them immediately.

Check

This phase enables the execution of callbacks right after the completion of the poll phase. If the poll phase becomes idle and scripts are queued using **`setImmediate()`**, the event loop might proceed to the check phase instead of waiting.

`setImmediate()` functions as a unique type of timer that operates in its own phase within the event loop. It employs a **`libuv`** API to schedule callbacks for execution once the poll phase is finished. Typically, while executing code, the event loop reaches the poll phase, where it pauses to wait for an incoming connection, request, or similar events. However, if a callback is scheduled using **`setImmediate()`** and the poll phase is idle, the event loop will not wait for poll events. Instead, it will conclude the poll phase and move directly to the check phase.

Close Callbacks

This phase handles callbacks added to the message queue by a socket's close event. Essentially, any code designated to run upon the closure of a socket is queued in the message queue and executed during this phase.

Key Features of Node.js

Here are some of the key features of Node.js:

- **Asynchronous and Event Driven:** All APIs of Node.js library are asynchronous or non-blocking. This means a Node.js-based server never waits for an API to return data; it moves to the next API after calling it. The notification mechanism of Events of Node.js helps the server to get a response from the previous API call.
- **Single-Threaded but Highly Scalable:** Node.js uses a single-threaded model

with event looping. This event mechanism helps the server to respond in a non-blocking way and makes the server highly scalable as opposed to traditional servers that create limited threads to handle requests.

- **No Buffering:** Node.js applications never buffer any data. These applications simply output the data in chunks.

Use Cases of Node.js

Here are some of the use cases of Node.js:

- **Web Applications:** Building lightweight and scalable web applications, especially Single-Page Applications (SPAs), where server-side rendering and API interactions are essential.
- **Real-Time Applications:** Ideal for real-time collaborative applications like chat apps, live streaming platforms, and online gaming, due to its non-blocking and event-driven architecture.
- **API Development**: Creating RESTful and GraphQL APIs for web and mobile applications, leveraging its efficient handling of I/O operations and JSON processing.
- **Microservices Architecture**: Developing microservices, thanks to its lightweight nature and support for handling multiple concurrent requests efficiently.
- **Internet of Things (IoT):** Suitable for IoT applications where managing multiple concurrent connections and real-time data flows are crucial.
- **Data Streaming Applications:** Handling data streaming efficiently, as Node.js can process files while they are still being uploaded, reducing overall processing time.
- **Server-Side Web Applications**: Building server-side components of web applications, especially in conjunction with frontend frameworks like Angular, React, or Vue.js.
- **Command Line Tools:** Creating command-line tools and utilities, as Node.js can easily handle I/O, interact with the operating system, and run on various platforms.
- **Backend for Mobile Applications:** Serving as a backend for mobile apps, providing services like authentication, data storage, and push notifications.
- **Network Applications:** Developing network-heavy applications, such as web servers and TCP/UDP servers, due to its efficient handling of parallel connections.

Node.js REPL

Node.js REPL (Read-Eval-Print Loop) is an interactive shell that allows you to execute JavaScript code and evaluate its results in real time. REPL is a powerful tool for experimenting with Node.js code, debugging, and quickly testing snippets without the need to create a full-fledged application. Here's a brief overview of Node.js REPL:

Accessing REPL is very simple; all you need to do is to run **`node`** on your terminal or command-line tool after the installation of Node.js on your machine. You can do a lot of things with the REPL, and some of its features are as follows:

- **Execute JavaScript Code:** You can type any valid JavaScript code at the REPL prompt, and it will execute and display the result immediately.
- **Variable and Function Declaration:** You can declare variables and functions directly in the REPL environment, which will be available throughout the session.
- **Multiline Input:** If a statement isn't complete, REPL allows you to continue on the next line (for example, in the case of functions or loops).
- **Built-in Node.js Modules:** You can require and use Node.js core modules (like **`fs`** for file system, **`http`** for HTTP server) directly in the REPL.
- **History:** Node.js REPL keeps a history of your commands, which you can navigate using the arrow keys.
- **Autocompletion:** It supports autocompletion of JavaScript keywords, variable names, function names, and more.
- **Special REPL Commands:** These commands start with dot (**`.`**) such as **`.help`**, **`.exit`**, **`.save`**, **`.load`** to perform some actions.

The following is the Node.js REPL in action:

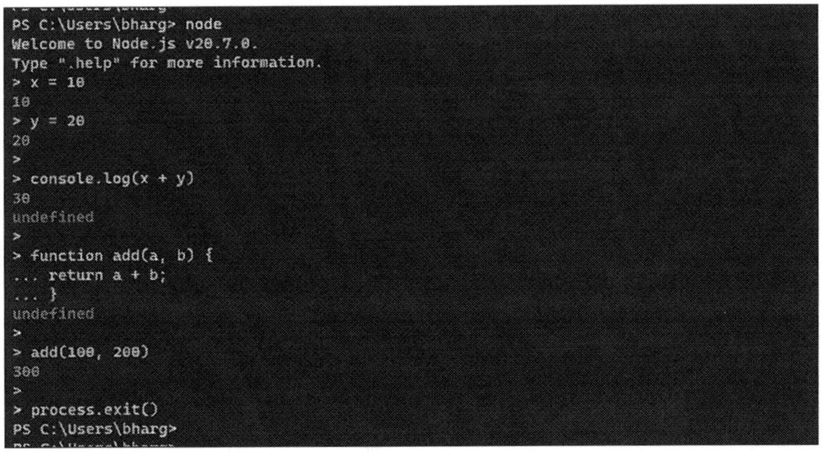

Figure 1.15: Node REPL

Here are some of the use cases of REPL:

- **Quick Prototyping**: You can quickly test small code or functions before using them in an existing project that you are working on without the need for setting up.
- **Learning and Experimenting**: Great tool for beginners to learn JavaScript and Node.js.
- **Debugging**: Useful for debugging purposes, especially in combination with Node.js's debugger.

Introduction to ExpressJS

Express is a minimal and adaptable framework for Node.js web applications, offering a comprehensive array of features suited for both web and mobile applications. With an abundance of HTTP utility methods and middleware available, constructing a strong API becomes a fast and straightforward process. Express offers a basic layer of essential web application functionalities while preserving the Node.js features you are familiar with and appreciate. Many frameworks that you know and use daily are based on this framework.

Key Features

The combination of simplicity, flexibility, and powerful features make it an ideal choice for building web applications and APIs, ranging from small projects to large-scale enterprise applications. Here are some of the key features of this framework:

- **Middleware Architecture**

  Express uses middleware functions that have access to the request object (`req`), the response object (`res`), and the next middleware in the application's request-response cycle. This allows the execution of code, modification of request and response objects, ending the request-response cycle, and calling the next middleware in the stack.

- **Routing**

  It provides a robust routing mechanism to perform different actions based on the HTTP method and URL. This feature helps in organizing the application into modular and manageable pieces with different routes.

- **Simplicity and Minimalism**

  Express is designed to be minimal and flexible, providing a thin layer of fundamental web application features without dictating any specific structure for the application. This allows developers to build applications and services as they see fit.

- **Template Engines**

  Supports various template engines like Pug, Mustache, EJS, and so on, enabling the creation of dynamic HTML content on the server side.

- **Error Handling**

  Provides a straightforward mechanism for central error handling in the application.

- **Integration with Databases**

  Express can be integrated with a variety of databases like MongoDB, MySQL, PostgreSQL, and so on, making it a versatile choice for building applications with different database requirements.

- **Performance**

  As it's built on Node.js, it inherits its performance benefits. Node's non-blocking and event-driven architecture ensures efficient handling of concurrent requests, making Express applications fast and scalable.

- **Community and Ecosystem**

  Being one of the most popular Node.js frameworks, Express has a large community of developers and a rich ecosystem of middleware and plugins, offering reusable components for a wide range of functionalities.

- **Easy to Learn and Use**

  Its straightforward and unopinionated approach makes it easy for beginners to learn and start building web applications quickly.

- **HTTP Helpers and Utilities**

  Provides numerous helper methods and utilities to simplify common web development tasks, such as handling cookies, form data, file uploads, and so on.

Use Cases

Known for its effectiveness and adaptability, Express.js is an excellent fit for a diverse array of web development endeavors. Following are some of the primary applications:

- **API Development**

  Express.js is ideal for building RESTful APIs that interact with client-side applications, mobile applications, or other services.

- **Single Page Applications (SPAs)**

  It can serve as the backend for SPAs, managing HTTP requests, and delivering data to frontend frameworks like Angular, React, or Vue.js.

- **Web Application Framework**

  Express can be used to develop full-fledged web applications, supporting features like template rendering, form processing, and session management.

- **Real-time Applications**

  Coupled with technologies like WebSocket, Express is suitable for building real-time applications like chat applications or live notification systems.

- **Middleware and Routing Solutions**

  Its extensive middleware support allows for creating sophisticated routing mechanisms and handling various HTTP operations efficiently.

- **Content Management Systems**

  It can be used to create custom CMS for websites, where content changes frequently, and a dynamic presentation is necessary.

- **E-Commerce Sites**

  Express's ability to handle complex applications makes it a good choice for developing e-commerce platforms with functionalities like product listings, shopping carts, and payment processing.

- **Authentication Services**

  Express, in combination with Passport.js or similar libraries, can efficiently handle user authentication and authorization.

- **Proxy Server Creation**

  It can be used to develop a proxy server, which can be placed in front of a web service to manage requests, logging, load balancing, and so on.

- **IoT Applications**

  For IoT applications requiring a lightweight server to collect, process, and respond to data from devices, Express is a practical choice.

- **Microservice Architecture**

  Express is well-suited for building individual microservices in a larger microservices architecture, thanks to its minimalistic nature.

- **Server-Side Rendered Applications (SSR)**

  It can be used for server-side rendering of applications built with React, Vue, or Angular for improved SEO and initial load performance.

- **Custom Application Development**

  Express's unopinionated nature makes it an excellent choice for custom application development, where specific architecture or technology choices are required.

Getting Started with Express.js

Getting started with Express.js is straightforward, and you need to install Node.js installed on your machine. We have already discussed Node.js in the previous section. Since Express.js is a Node.js framework, Node.js is necessary. The first step is to initialize the Node.js project by following these commands.

```
// make a directory
mkdir sample-express
// change the directory
cd sample-express
// initialize the Node.js project
npm init -y
```

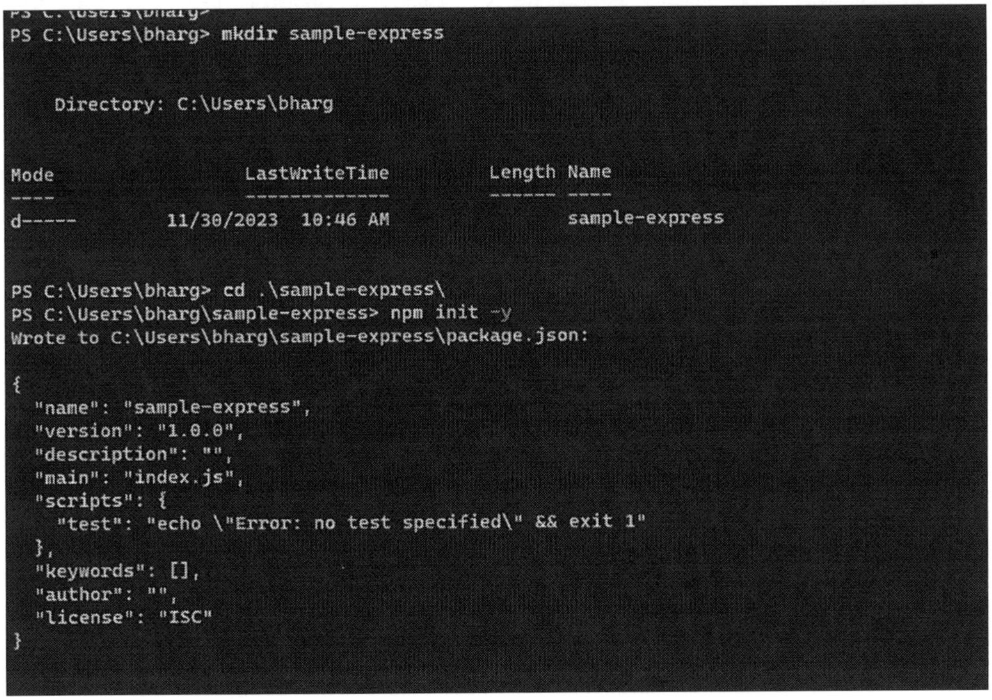

Figure 1.16: *Initializing Sample express Project*

Let's import that into your favorite IDE and install Express so that we can create a simple server and see Express.js in action:

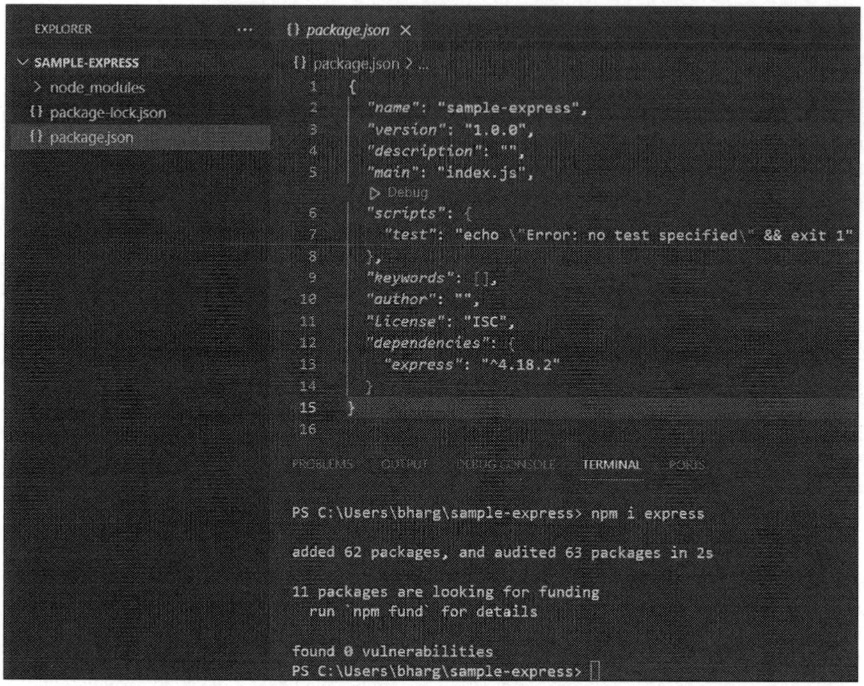

Figure 1.17: *Installing express*

Now, we can create a small file called **`index.js`** and put the following code. We can run the following command to start the express server on port **`4050`**:

```
// run the express server
node index.js
```

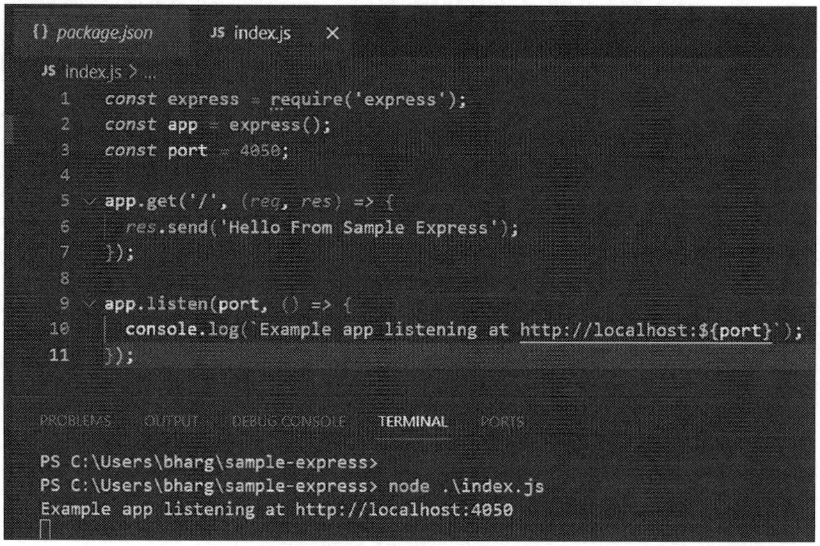

Figure 1.18: *index.js*

We can open the browser, hit the following URL, and see the message that the Express app is sending at line number 6:

```
// open it in the browser
http://localhost:4050
```

Figure 1.19: *Testing Express app*

Express Application Generator

We have an Express application generator if you want to use Express for full-stack development. You can check it out at the following link. It allows you to configure stylesheets, view engines, and more:

https://expressjs.com/en/starter/generator.html

Introduction to VueJS

Vue.js is an innovative and progressive JavaScript framework used for building user interfaces and single-page applications. Created by Evan You in 2014, Vue.js has rapidly gained popularity due to its gentle learning curve, versatility, and efficient rendering capabilities. Its core library focuses on the view layer only, making it easy to integrate into existing projects, but it is also powerful enough to build sophisticated Single-Page Applications when combined with modern tooling and supporting libraries.

Vue.js is designed to be incrementally adoptable. The core library is focused on the view layer only, and it's easy to pick up and integrate with other libraries or existing projects. Vue is also perfectly capable of powering sophisticated Single-Page Applications when used in combination with modern tooling and supporting libraries.

Key Features

Here are some of the key features of this framework:

- **Reactive and Composable Data Binding:** Vue.js provides a reactive data binding system that allows a seamless way to manipulate and display data within the UI.

- **Component-Based Architecture:** It uses a component-based architecture that helps in building reusable and maintainable codebases.
- **Virtual DOM Rendering:** Vue.js utilizes a virtual DOM to provide optimal performance by re-rendering only those components that actually change.
- **Ease of Integration:** Its design makes it simple to integrate with other projects and libraries.
- **Developer Tools:** Vue offers a set of tools for development and debugging, such as Vue Devtools, which enhance the development experience.

Conclusion

As we conclude our introductory exploration of the MEVN stack, it becomes evident that the synergy of MongoDB, Express.js, Vue.js, and Node.js provides a formidable toolkit for crafting contemporary web applications. Each component of the MEVN stack contributes unique advantages, enhancing the stack's efficiency and adaptability. This integration offers a seamless and robust framework well-suited to the dynamic and evolving demands of modern web development. The stack's focus on performance, flexibility, and user-friendliness positions it as a prime choice for developers eager to innovate in the web space.

Moving forward, the upcoming chapters will delve into each technology in depth, revealing how to harness their collective power effectively. We will embark on constructing a comprehensive example project, detailing how to dockerize the application for consistent deployment environments and deploy it across multiple cloud platforms such as Google Cloud Platform (GCP), Microsoft Azure, and Amazon Web Services (AWS). This practical application will not only demonstrate the MEVN stack's capabilities but also equip you with the knowledge to utilize these technologies cohesively in real-world scenarios.

Further Reading

- MongoDB Official Docs: https://docs.mongodb.com/
- Express.js Official Docs: https://expressjs.com/
- VueJS Official Docs: https://vuejs.org/v2/guide/
- Node.js Official Docs: https://node.js.org/en/docs/
- MEVN Stack Vue.js with MongoDB: https://www.mongodb.com/languages/mern-stack-tutorial

CHAPTER 2
Prerequisites

Introduction

This chapter provides a comprehensive guide to setting up all the necessary prerequisites for developing an MEVN Stack application on local systems. We begin by installing Node.js through NVM, allowing for streamlined management of Node.js versions, including simple installation, uninstallation, and swapping capabilities. Additionally, we will globally install the Vite tool to efficiently initiate a VueJS project tailored for the UI layer. Incorporating Docker into our setup, we will guide you through installing and executing your first container locally.

Understanding the pivotal role of databases in full-stack applications, we choose MongoDB for its robust features and flexibility. We will demonstrate how to configure MongoDB on your local machine both independently and using Docker, along with instructions for creating a MongoDB Atlas account for cloud database management. For coding and project development, VSCode is our editor of choice, recognized for its powerful features and integration capabilities. Finally, we will introduce the example project intended for this course, meticulously designed to be deployable across multiple cloud platforms, providing a practical approach to modern web development.

Structure

In this chapter, the following topics will be covered:

- Installing Node.js Through NVM
- Install VSCode
- Install Vite Globally for Creating VueJS Project
- Install Docker
- MongoDB Setup on Local
- Setup MongoDB Atlas Account
- Example Project We are Building

Installing Node.js Through NVM

The initial step in setting up our development environment is to install Node.js, as it is essential for installing subsequent tools. Node.js can be conveniently installed directly from its official website. This installation serves as the foundational component, enabling us to utilize Node Package Manager (NPM) for managing and installing additional necessary tools and libraries for our projects. By starting with Node.js, we ensure that our system is properly equipped to handle a wide range of development tasks. You can download Node.js from its official website: https://node.js.org/en/download

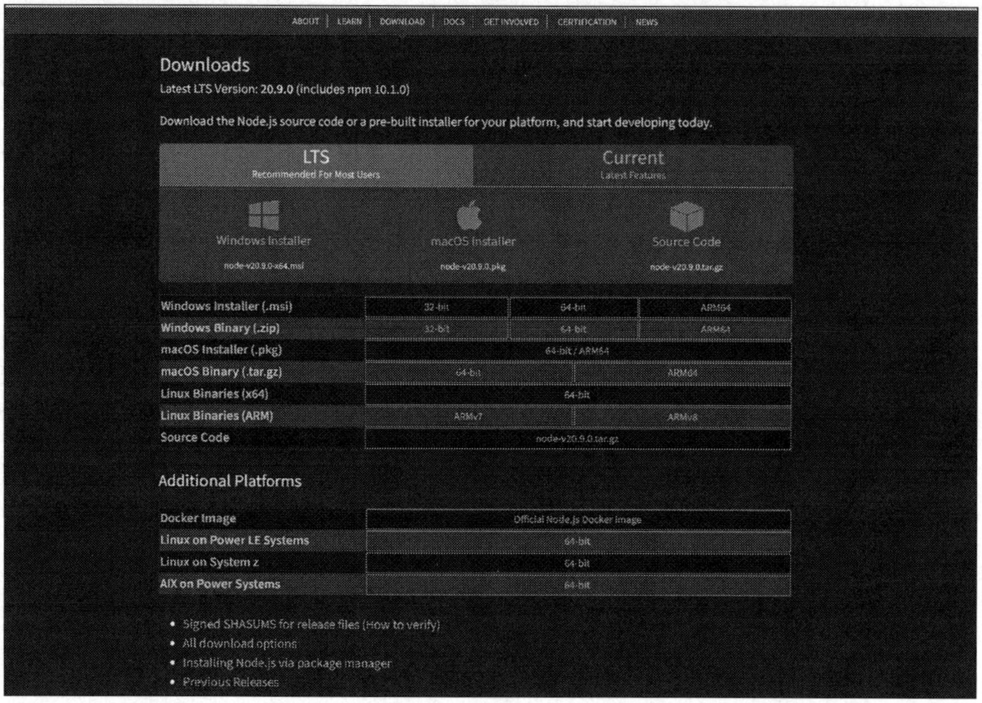

Figure 2.1: *Node.js Download Page*

Using Node Version Manager (NVM) to install Node.js offers a more efficient and flexible approach, especially for developers managing multiple projects that may require different Node.js versions. With NVM, you can seamlessly install, uninstall, and switch between Node.js versions, catering to the specific needs of each project. For example, you might use Node.js version 14 for maintaining a legacy application while employing version 20 for a new and cutting-edge development.

In this section, we will cover the following essential tasks to optimize your development environment with NVM:

- **Installing Node.js through NVM on Windows**: We will guide you through the process of setting up NVM on a Windows environment and using it to manage Node.js installations.

- **Installing Node.js through NVM on Mac**: Similar to Windows, we will demonstrate how to install and configure NVM on macOS to handle Node.js versions effectively.
- **Installing specific versions of Node.js**: Learn how to precisely install the required versions of Node.js for different projects directly through NVM.
- **Switching between Node.js versions**: We will show you how to quickly switch from one version of Node.js to another, ensuring compatibility and functionality across various projects.
- **Listing all installed Node.js versions**: Discover how to view all Node.js versions installed on your system with NVM, helping you manage your development environment more efficiently.
- **Uninstalling specific Node.js versions**: Finally, we will provide steps to remove any unnecessary or outdated Node.js versions from your system to keep your development setup clean and organized.

By mastering these steps, you will enhance your productivity and adaptability, enabling you to handle multiple projects with varying requirements effortlessly.

Installing Node.js Through NVM on Windows

Let's install NVM by going to the following GitHub Page; you can select nvm-setup.zip to download. Once downloaded, you can double-click and install it, as shown in the following figures:

https://github.com/coreybutler/nvm-windows/releases

Figure 2.2: *nvm setup*

After clicking **`nvm setup`**, an installation wizard opens, as shown in *Figure* 2.3:

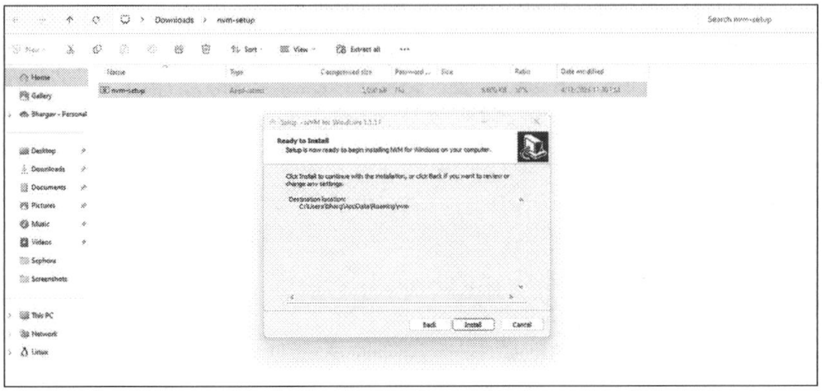

Figure 2.3: *Install Wizard*

You can check the installation of NVM by going to the Command Prompt and just typing **`nvm`**. It gives you the following output, and we can use the **`nvm install`** command from it to install any version of Node.js:

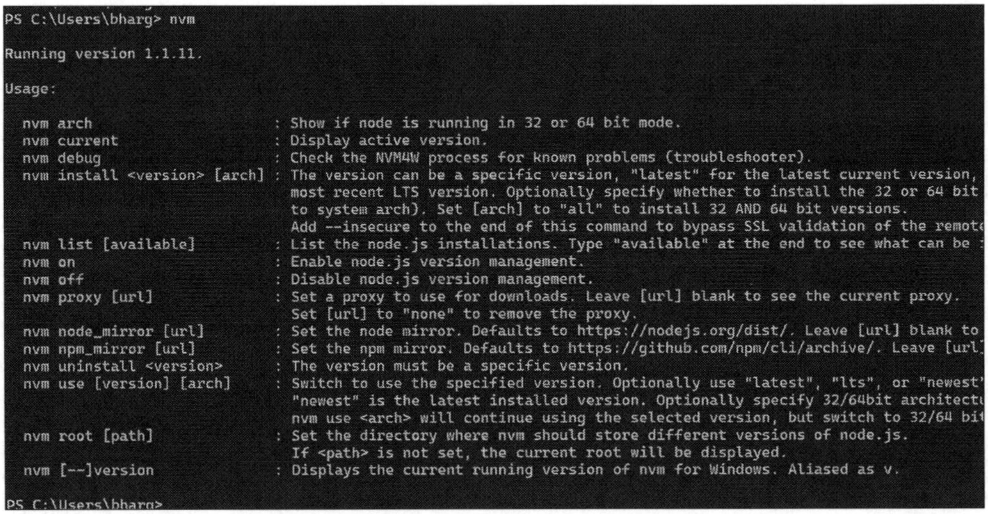

Figure 2.4: *Checking NVM on Windows*

Installing Node.js Through NVM on Mac

Installing Node.js on a Mac using the Node Version Manager (NVM) is an efficient approach that allows you to manage multiple versions of Node.js easily. To begin, open the Terminal application on your Mac. First, install NVM by running the curl command:

```
curl -o- https://raw.githubusercontent.com/nvm-sh/nvm/v0.39.1/install.sh
| bash
```

```
// If we use wget, we can run the following command
wget -qO- https://raw.githubusercontent.com/nvm-sh/nvm/v0.39.1/install.
sh | bash
```

These commands download and execute the installation script from the nvm repository. After installation, you'll need to close and reopen Terminal or run source **`~/.bash_profile`** to apply the changes and enable **`nvm`**. To install Node.js, type **`nvm install node`** for the latest version, or **`nvm install [version_number]`** to install a specific version. You can switch between installed versions using **`nvm use [version_number]`**. Finally, verify the installation with node **`-v`**, which will display the currently active Node.js version.

Installing Specific Versions of Node.js

Since the current LTS version of Node.js, nvm installs it by default when you use the following command. Let's run this command to test it:

```
nvm install node
```

As you can see in *Figure* 2.5, when we **`install node`**, the tool installs the latest version by default. We need to use the command **`nvm use <version>`** to use it:

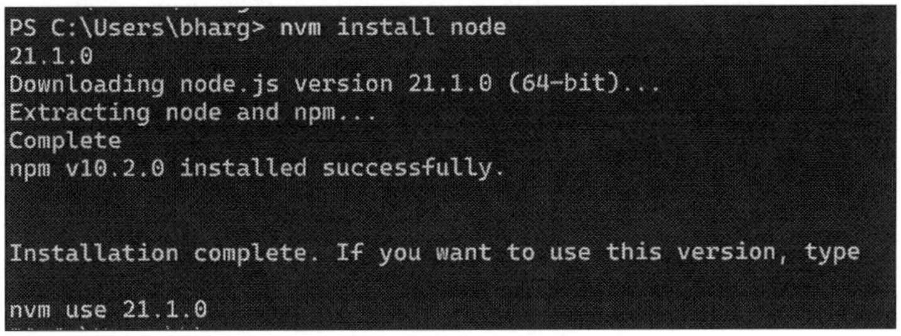

Figure 2.5: *nvm install node*

Let's install versions 16 and 18 and list the versions. When you list the versions, it lists all the versions currently available on the local machine:

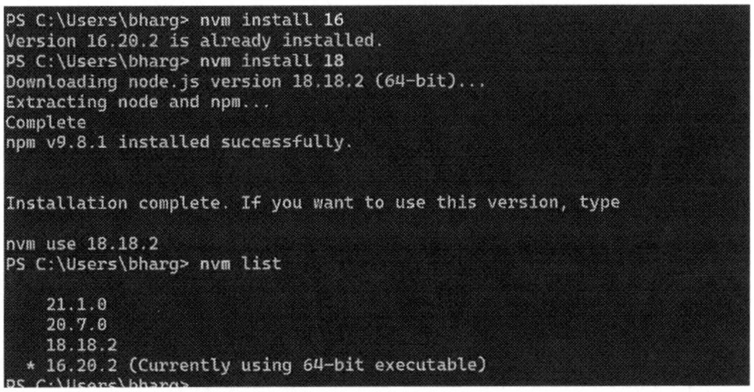

Figure 2.6: *Install specific version*

It does not install if that version is already installed on your machine, as shown in *Figure 2.6.*

Switching Between Node.js Versions

When you list the versions, there is an asterisk beside the currently used Node.js version. If you want to switch or use another version, all you need to do is use the following command. For example, the current version of Node.js is 16, and if we want to use 20, we need to use the following command:

```
nvm use 20.7.0
```

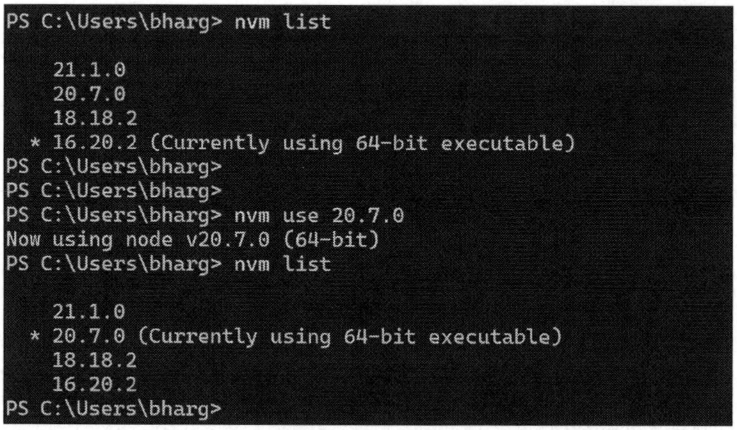

Figure 2.7: *Switching Node.js Versions*

The current version of the Node.js on your local machine is 20 after running the preceding commands.

Listing All the Versions

We have already seen how to list the Node.js versions currently available on your local machine in the preceding commands.

Uninstalling Specific Version of Node.js

If you want to uninstall a specific version of Node.js, you can do it with the following command. For example, if we are uninstalling version 18, use the following command:

```
nvm uninstall 18.8.2
```

As you can see in *Figure* 2.8, when you uninstall a specific version, that version is no longer listed among the currently available versions of Node.js on our local machine. This is one of the advantages of using NVM over directly installing Node.js from the

Node.js download page. We strongly recommend using NVM whenever you install Node.js on your local machine.

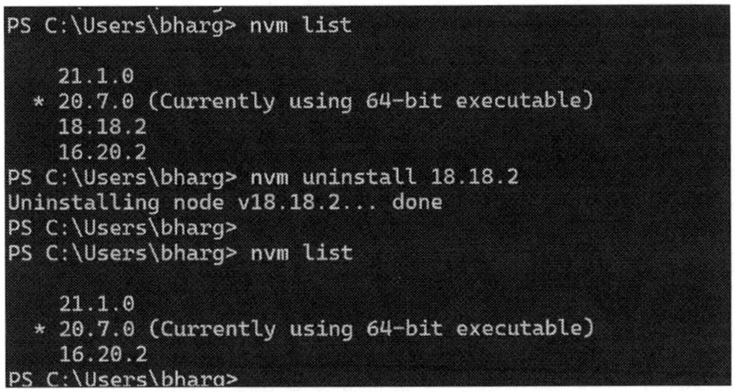

Figure 2.8: *Uninstall Node.js Version*

Installing VSCode

For full-stack web development, we recommend installing VSCode, an open-source code editor backed by Microsoft. The following is the download page where you can download based on your OS:

https://code.visualstudio.com/Download

Installing Vite Globally for Creating VueJS Project

Now, we have installed Node.js on our machine. It's time to install Vite globally so that we can create a project template with it. You can go to the following URL for the Homepage of the Vite Project:

`https://vitejs.dev/`

Understanding Vite

As we build hundreds and hundreds of components, it takes a lot of time to build the application and deploy it on the server so that users can access it. Vite aims to solve this slowness in building the application as it grows bigger by using native ES modules in the browser.

If we use webpack or any other bundler, it builds the entire application before loading it in the browser. In contrast, Vite builds dependencies and source code separately so that it uses the browser to load dynamically as the modules are needed. Vite improves the startup time that way.

The following command can be used to install Vite globally and create a VueJS template project for you. We can choose to create the template either in JavaScript or Typescript:

```
// Javascript
npm create vite@latest sample-app -- --template vue
// Typescript
npm create vite@latest sample-app -- --template vue-ts
```

We are using the second command as we are building the UI layer in TypeScript. Let's create a folder called **`mevn-stack-book`** and run the preceding command inside that folder:

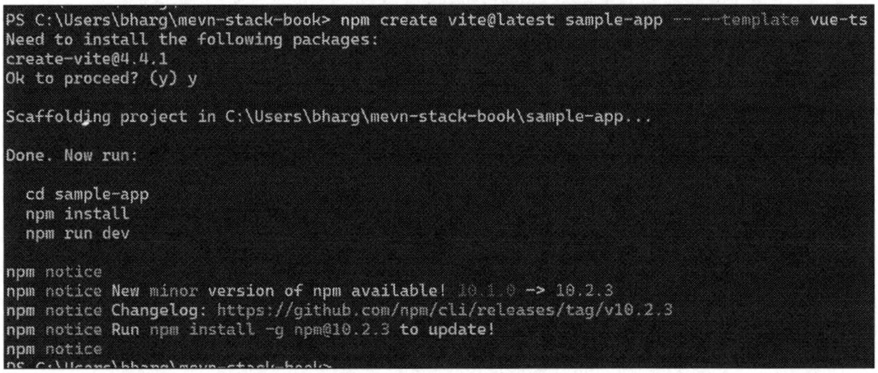

Figure 2.9: Creating Vue Project

It creates a complete project template in TypeScript. You can import this in the VSCode and see the project structure. You can notice that all the files are in TypeScript with **`.ts`** extension.

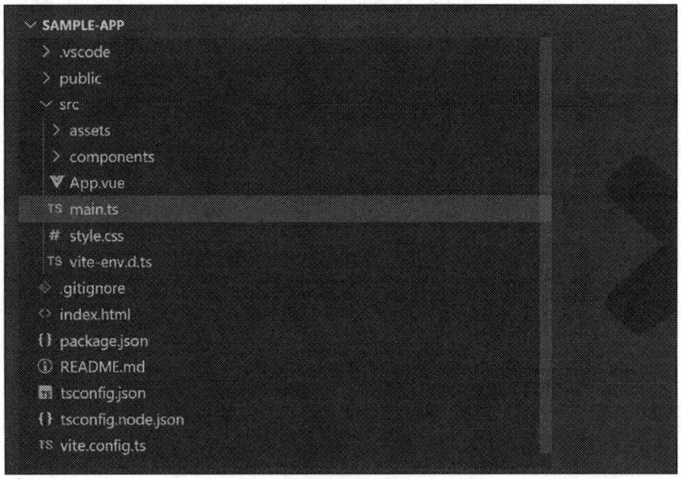

Figure 2.10: Vue Project

Once created and imported, you can run the following commands to install the dependencies and run the project in development mode:

```
cd sample-app
npm install
npm run dev
```

When you run the preceding commands, the sample project will be running on port **5173**:

Figure 2.11: *npm run dev*

Let's copy the URL and hit it in the browser so you can see the app up and running. It's that easy to create a VueJS Project using the tool Vite. You can change the App Component and see the results instantly in the browser.

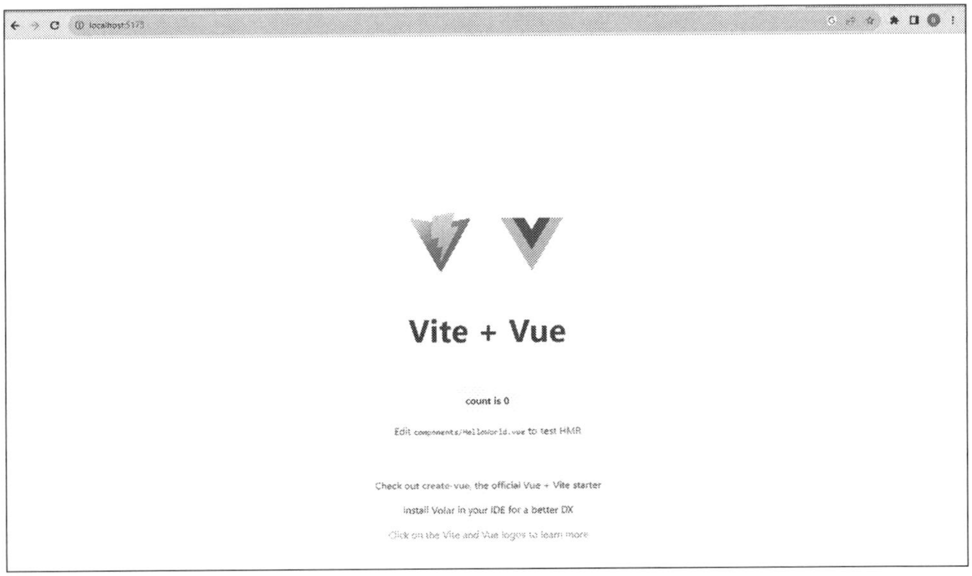

Figure 2.12: *Example Project using Vite*

Installing Docker

Docker Desktop is one of the options to install Docker on your machine. Let's go to their download page and install it based on your OS. Once you click on the **`download`** button, it will be downloaded, and you can go over the list of options to install on your machine. Here is the download page:

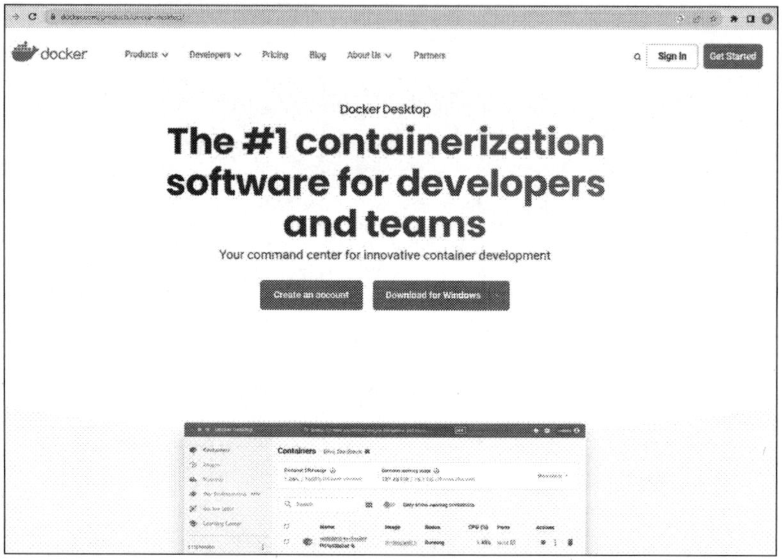

Figure 2.13: *Docker Desktop*

It takes some time to install, as shown in *Figure 2.14*:

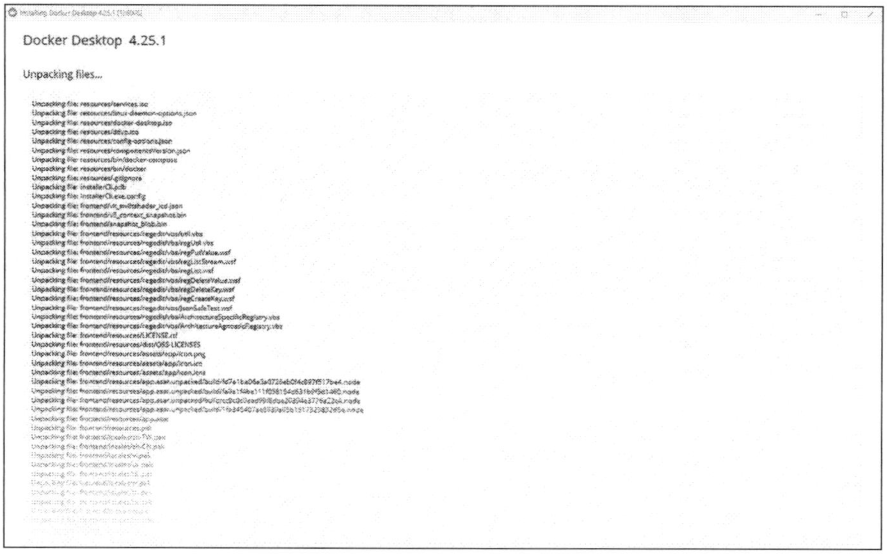

Figure 2.14: *Installing Docker*

Once installed, you can sign up for an account, or you can use it without creating one.

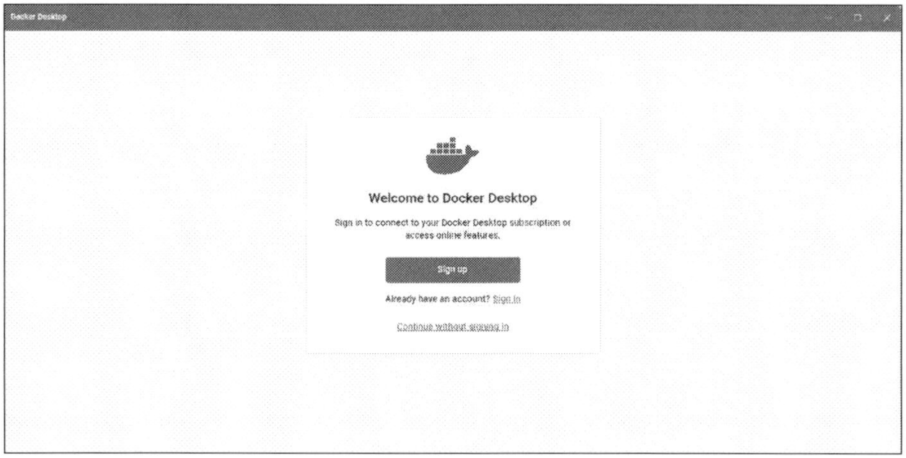

Figure 2.15: *Welcome to Docker Desktop*

Here is the Docker Desktop running on your machine. Currently, there are no images and containers. We can create some and see how it looks, as shown in *Figure* 2.16:

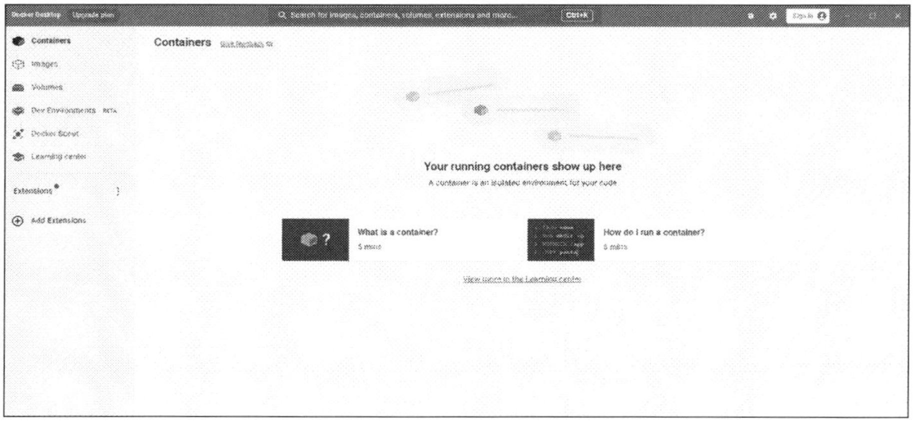

Figure 2.16: *Docker Desktop*

If you open the command prompt or terminal in case of Mac and run the following command to list the Docker images, you will get an empty list as we don't have any images created or pulled from the Docker Hub:

```
docker images
```

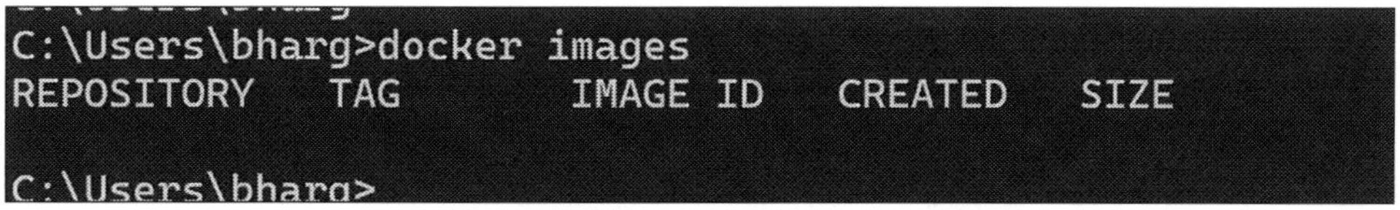

Figure 2.17: *Docker images*

Docker Hub is the world's largest library and community for container images. You can create an account and push your own images as well. We can pull the **nginx** Docker image and run that container for the sake of this tutorial. If you open Docker Hub and search for **nginx** images, you can get a lot of options and tags that you can choose from.

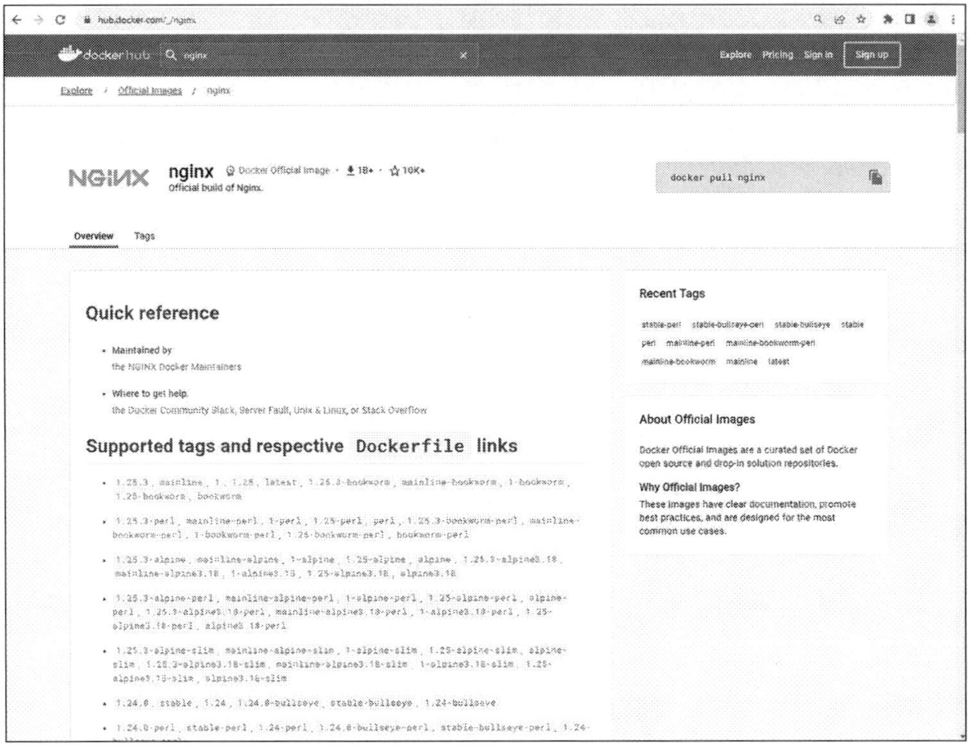

Figure 2.18: *nginx image on Docker Hub*

You can select any tag and use the following command to pull the docker image on your local machine. It pulls the latest tag if the tag is not specified in the **pull** command:

```
docker pull nginx:<tag>
```

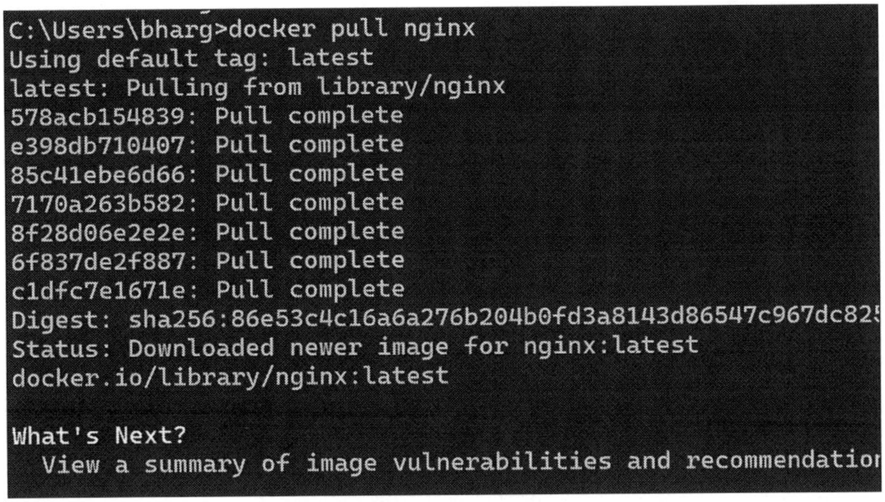

Figure 2.19: *docker pull nginx*

As mentioned earlier, it uses the default tag latest while pulling down the **nginx** image if the tag is not specified. If you now list the images with the preceding command, you will see the **nginx** image listed with the tag and other information:

Figure 2.20: *docker images*

Now that we have the image pulled, let's create a container so that it can run on your machine. Run the following command in your command prompt to run the **nginx** container:

```
docker run -d -p 8083:80 –name nginx-web nginx
```

The preceding command instructs the Docker daemon to run the container from the Docker image **nginx** in detached mode and mapping port **8083** of the host network to port **80** of the docker container with the name **nginx-web**. Once the preceding command is successful, you can list the Docker containers with the command **docker ps**. We will see the name of the container and the port is successfully mapped to port 8083 of the host network:

Figure 2.21: *docker run*

Let's go to the following URL on your browser and verify the **nginx** container is running successfully:

`http://localhost:8083/`

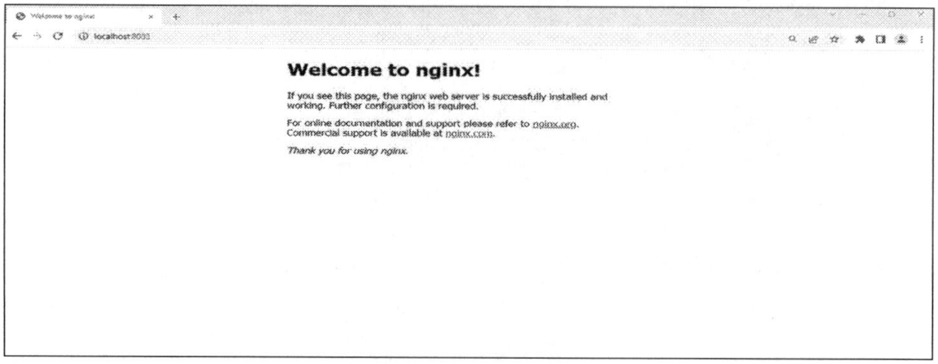

Figure 2.22: *nginx running from Docker Image*

You can see these images and containers on the Docker Desktop as well. You can even **start** and **stop** the container from here:

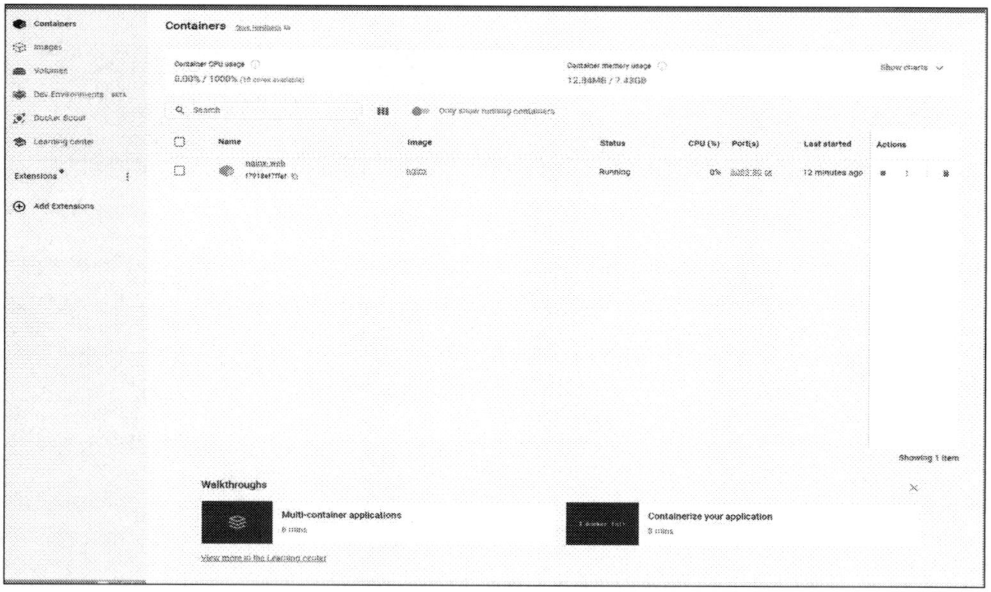

Figure 2.23: *Docker Desktop*

Use the following commands to **stop** and remove the containers and images from your local machine:

```
// start the container
docker start <container name>
// stop the container
```

```
docker stop <container name>
// remove the container
docker rm <container id>
//remove images
docker rmi <image id>
```

MongoDB Setup on Local Machine

Setting up MongoDB on your local machine can significantly speeds up your application development. In this section, we will see how to set up MongoDB and explore the different options available for setting up MongoDB on a local machine.

We will cover the following options for setting up MongoDB:

- Installing and downloading MongoDB Community Edition
- Running MongoDB through Docker
- MongoDB Atlas

Installing and Downloading MongoDB Community Edition

As shown in *Figure* 2.23, you can go to the MongoDB download page and download the community edition package:

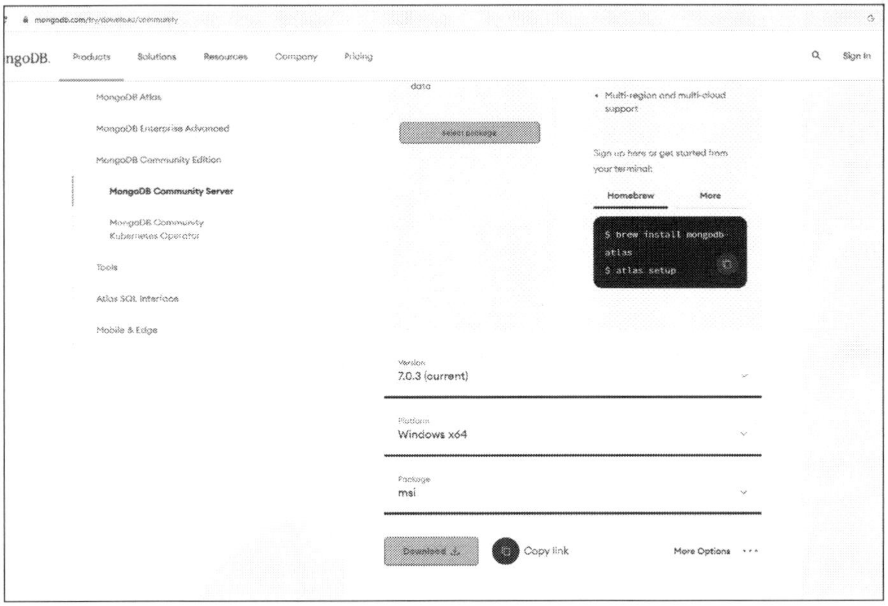

Figure 2.24: *MongoDB Community Edition*

Once downloaded, you can see the setup wizard popup and follow the steps to complete the installation:

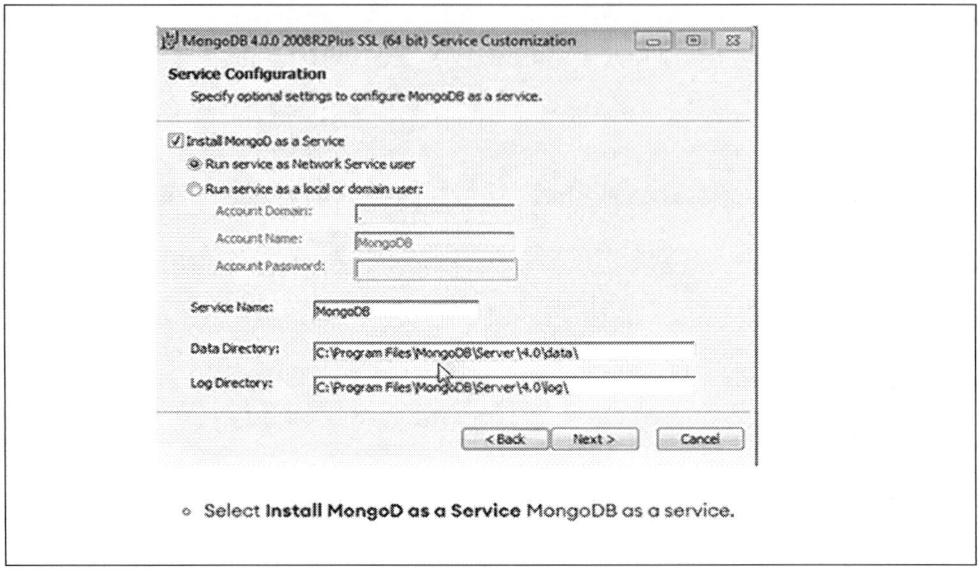

Figure 2.25: *MongoDB Install Setup*

Here is a MongoDB Compass, a GUI tool you can use to connect to a MongoDB instance you started on your local machine or you can connect to any instance as long as you have a connection URL.

You can connect to the local MongoDB server with the following connection URL:

```
// local MongoDB Connection URL
mongodb://localhost:27017/
```

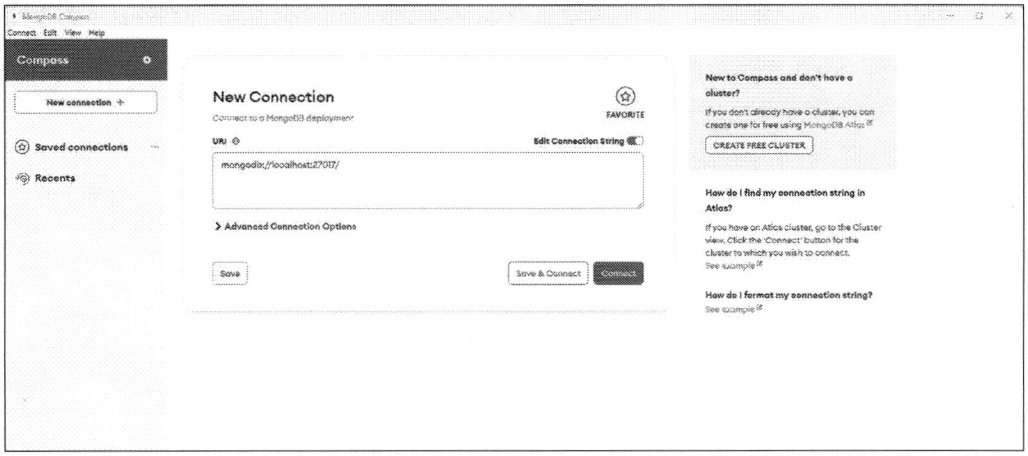

Figure 2.26: *MongoDB Compass GUI*

Once connected, you can see default databases such as admin, local, and config, as we covered in the first chapter.

Figure 2.27: *Connected to Local MongoDB Instance*

Running MongoDB Through Docker

In the earlier section, we learned how to download and install MongoDB manually. Alternatively, we can run MongoDB on your machine using Docker. We have already covered downloading and installing Docker Desktop in the previous section.

```
// pull the docker MongoDB image

docker pull mongodb/mongodb-community-server

// Run the image as Container

docker run --name mongo -d mongodb/mongodb-community-server:latest

// list the container

docker container ls
```

You can run the preceding commands to pull the MongoDB Docker image and run it as a container. Once it is running as a container, you can access it and connect to it with your MongoDB Compass.

Setting Up MongoDB Atlas Account

We have installed and set up MongoDB on our local machine in several ways. You can do the same thing on any server when deploying in production. Another option for using MongoDB is to use it through any cloud provider by creating a MongoDB Atlas Account. The following are the advantages of using a MongoDB Atlas Account:

- **Managed Service**

  MongoDB Atlas is a fully managed service you can use immediately after creating an account and cluster. Many administrative tasks, such as scaling, monitoring, backups, and more, are handled by MongoDB Atlas, so that you can focus more on application development.

- **Automatic Scaling**

  There are scenarios where your application meets heavy demand, and we have to scale the MongoDB as well in response to the demand. MongoDB Atlas provides horizontal scaling that automatically scales your cluster by adding or removing shards and replica sets.

- **High Availability**

  High availability is such a crucial design factor in modern web applications. MongoDB ensures high availability by deploying the cluster in multiple availability zones.

- **Security Features**

  MongoDB Atlas provides all these security features such as VPC peering, IP Whitelisting, RBAC, encryption at rest, encryption in transit, and so on. These features ensure secure access to the database and your data.

- **Monitoring and Alerts**

  Monitoring is one of the primary things you should do when you are running your application in a production environment. MongoDB Atlas provides built-in monitoring for all the key performance metrics of the database. You can even receive emails about these notifications so that you are always alerted to how the database is performing.

- **Backup and Restore**

  MongoDB provides automatic daily backups so that you can avoid any accidental deletion of your data. Its point-in-time recovery options help you recover any data deletion that happens in your production deployment.

- **Ease of Use**

  Setting up MongoDB Atlas is straightforward and easy through the web interface. It offers multiple connection methods to connect to the database.

- **Cost Management**

  MongoDB Atlas provides different tiers to choose from and can estimate your monthly costs. It also allows you to optimize the costs to change the cluster size based on your needs.

- **Global Distribution**

  MongoDB Atlas allows you to choose from different cloud providers, such as Google, AWS, and Azure, so that you can deploy the cluster in multiple regions. This enables you to distribute the data geographically and reduce the latency for your application users.

- **Data Migration Tools**

  MongoDB Atlas provides tools that can easily import or export data from the existing deployment to the MongoDB Atlas Account.

We have seen the advantages of using MongoDB Atlas over traditional deployments, and it's very easy to get started with MongoDB Atlas. First, we need to go to the following URL and sign up using your Google account or provide your information to create a new account:

https://www.mongodb.com/cloud/atlas/register

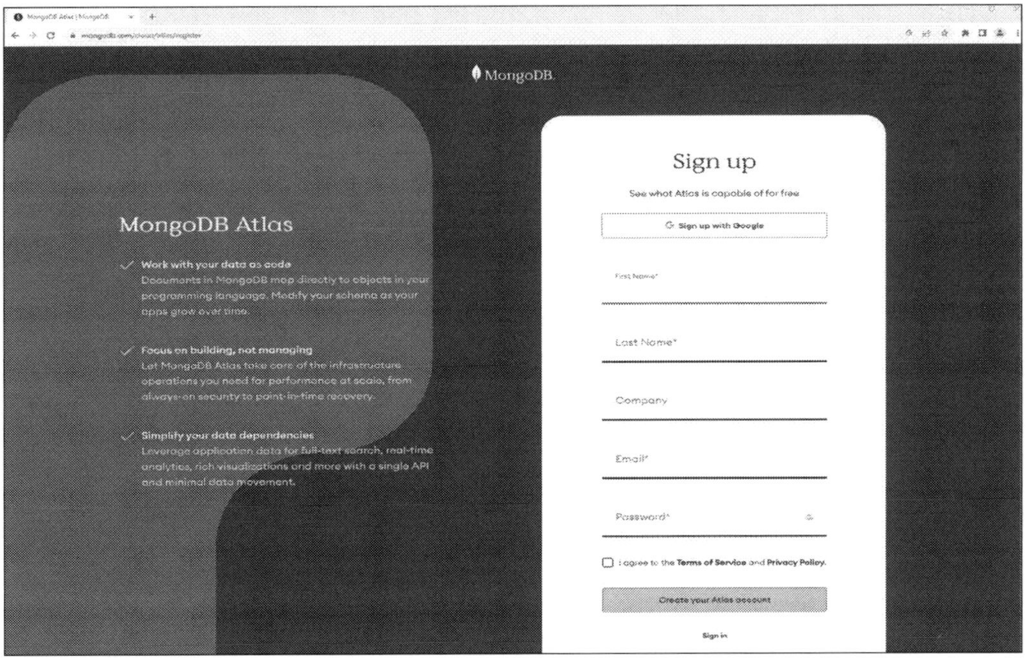

***Figure 2.28**: MongoDB Atlas Account Sign-Up Page*

You will be asked several questions during the sign-up process. Answer these questions and click the **`Finish`** button:

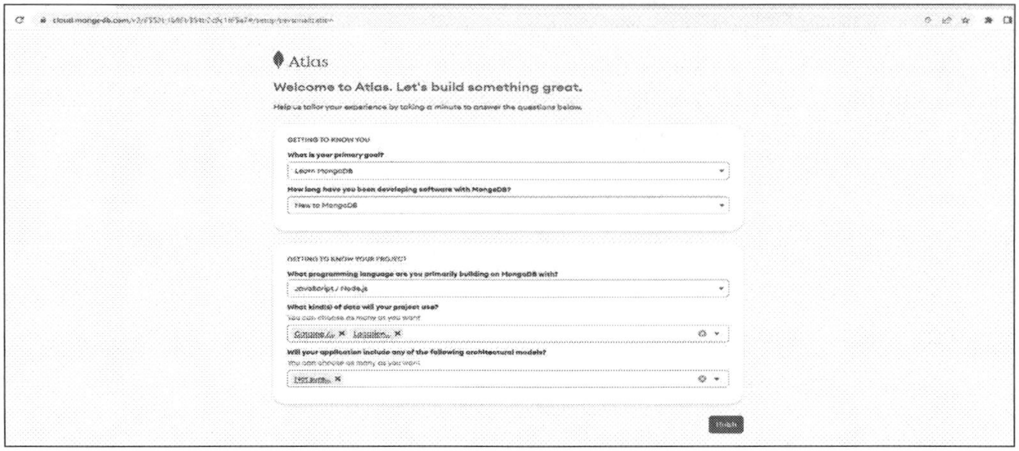

Figure 2.29: *MongoDB Atlas Account Sign-Up Process*

The next step is to create a cluster by choosing the configuration. Since we are in development, you can choose the free one, which is the **`M0`** one. We have named the cluster **`todos`** to match the developing project called **`todos`**.

You can choose any cloud provider based on your experience. Once you select all the following options, you can create this deployment. On the next screen, you will be asked to create a user and select an IP access list so that this cluster can be accessed only on the specified Ips:

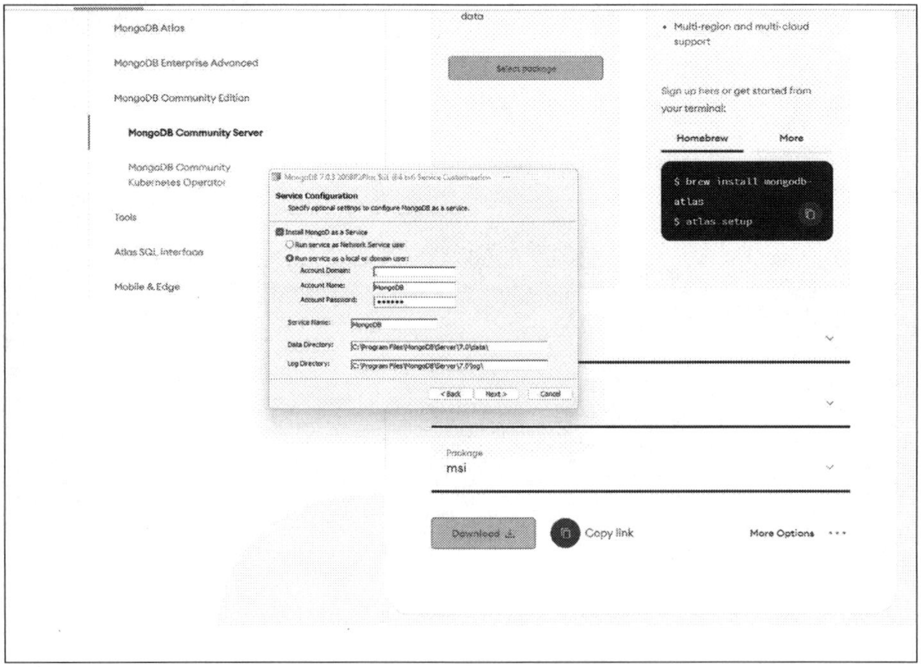

Figure 2.30: *MongoDB Atlas Deploying*

After completing all the setup steps, you can see the following screen. If you want to change the configuration, you can click the **`EDIT CONFIGURATION`** button and change it accordingly. You can also load the sample data by clicking the **`Load Sample Data`** button to get hands-on experience and start querying immediately.

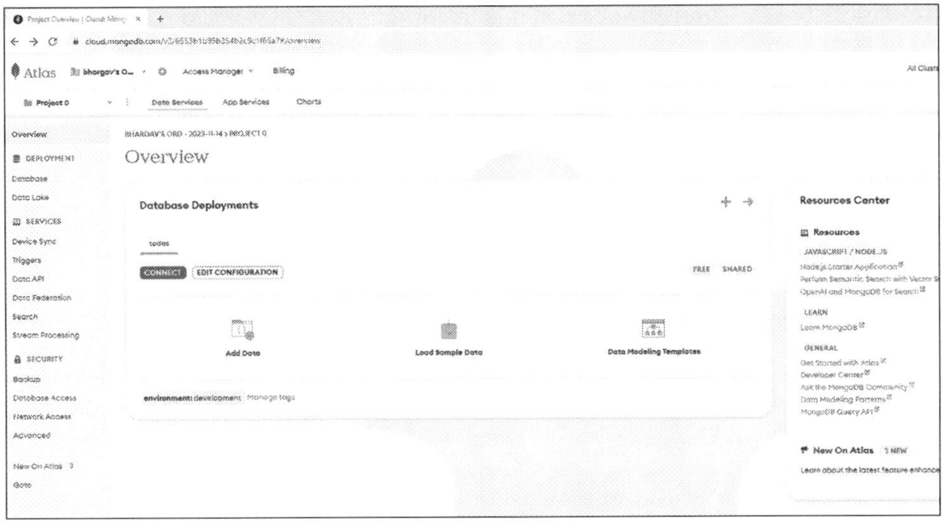

Figure 2.31: *Database Deployments*

It takes some time for the database to be created. You can load the sample data by clicking **`Load Sample Data`** to test some queries, or you can add the data manually. There are a number of ways to connect to the MongoDB instance, and you can see those options by clicking on the **`Connect`** button. You will see the following screen and select based on your connection needs:

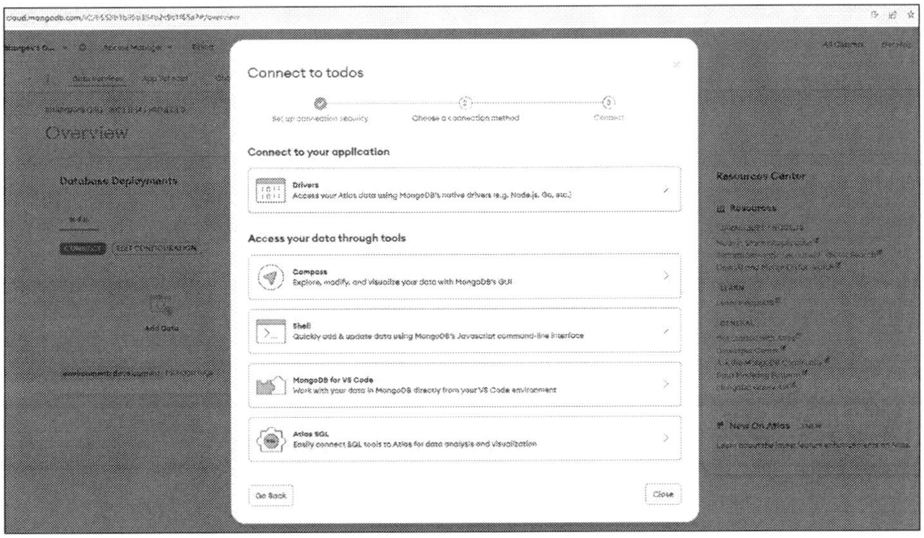

Figure 2.32: *Different ways of connecting*

Example Project We are Building

We have installed all the prerequisites so far, and it's time to see what we are going to build as an example project that covers all the important concepts for both VueJS and Node.js. Building this example project not only makes you a full-stack developer but also makes you understand all the SDLC concepts as well.

We are building a tasks project where users can create their accounts and track their tasks. The project is designed to be simple, so that we can concentrate on important concepts of building a full-stack web application.

The first screen we build is the sign-up screen, where we can enter an email and password to create an account. We can learn how to build forms in VueJS, collect the data from it, and send it to the backend via HTTP call. Building this end-to-end process helps us learn the following things:

- Understand how to build VueJS components
- Understand how to build VueJS forms and frontend `validationAPI`
- Understand how user passwords are saved at the backend
- Understand how to make an API call from VueJS to the backend
- Understand how to do backend validation before saving this info into the database.

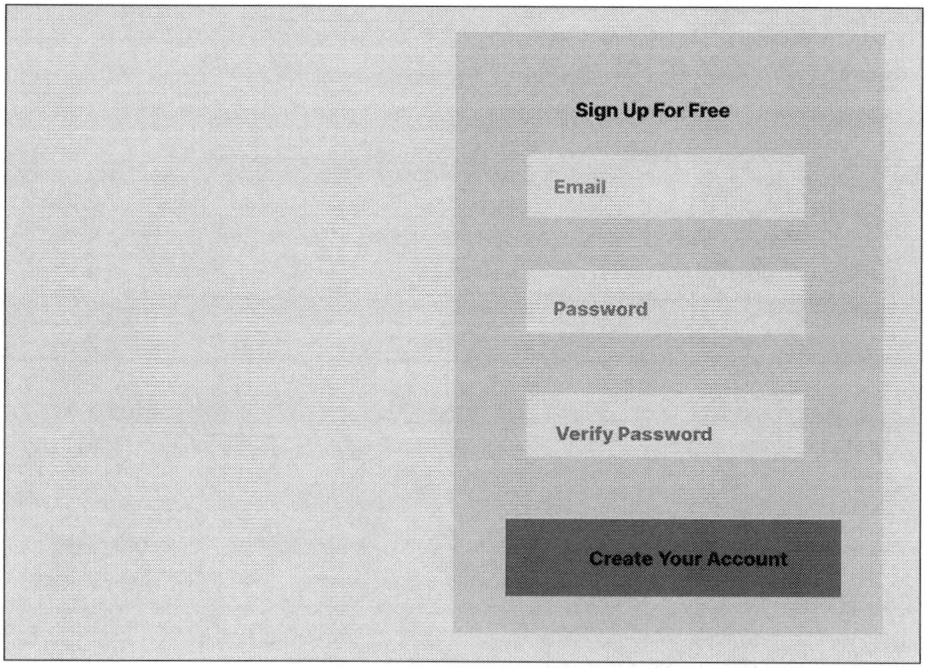

Figure 2.33: *Sign-Up Screen*

The second screen we build is the sign-in screen, where we can enter email and password to log in. We can learn how to build forms in VueJS, collect the data from it, and send it to the backend via HTTP call. Building this end-to-end process helps us learn the following things:

Users were created with the signup screen and those users can log in with this screen.

- Understand how to build VueJS components
- Understand how to build VueJS forms and frontend **`validationAPI`**
- Understand how user passwords are validated at the backend
- Understand how to make an API call from VueJS to the backend
- Understand how to do backend validation before querying this info from the database
- Understand the store management to store the user info using Pinia library
- Understand how to proxy API calls from frontend to backend

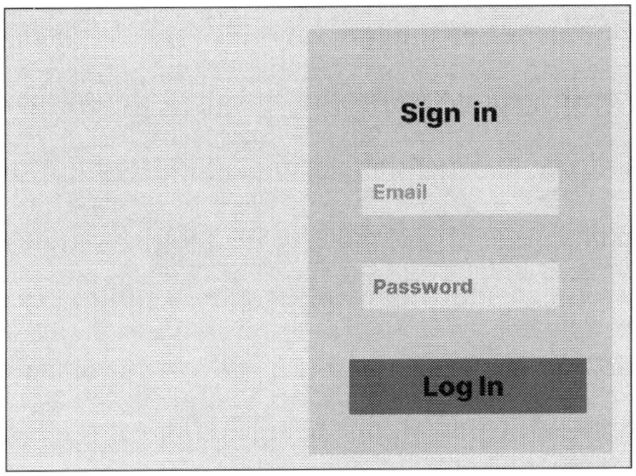

***Figure 2.34**: Sign-In Screen*

The third screen we develop is the dashboard screen, where logged-in users can view existing tasks or create new ones. This section demonstrates how to combine various components to form a cohesive dashboard. We create individual components for the header, tasks, user profile, and logout button, and integrate these to build the dashboard (see *Figure* 2.35).

Additionally, we learn how to fetch data from the Node.js backend API and render content conditionally based on the returned data. This comprehensive process teaches us the following:

- How to build Vue.js components
- How to construct a dashboard using multiple components
- How to make API calls from Vue.js to the backend and retrieve data

- How to perform backend validation before querying the database
- How to manage state to store user information using the Pinia library
- How to proxy API calls from the frontend to the backend

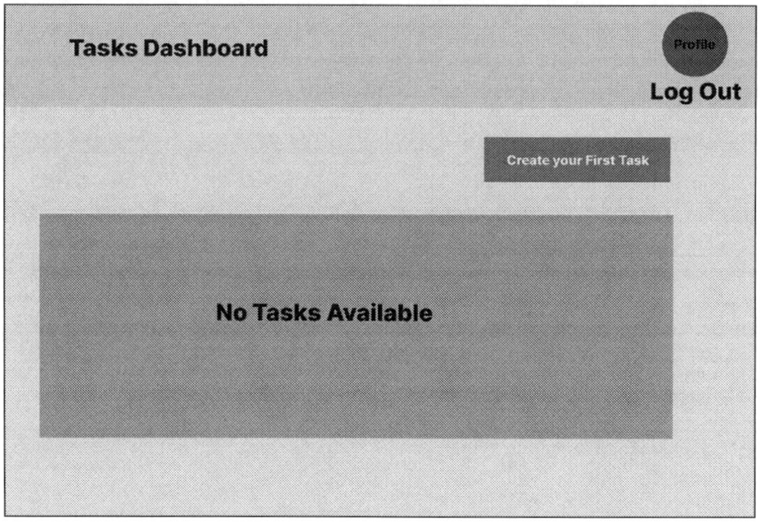

Figure 2.35: *Tasks Dashboard*

When you click the **`Create your first task`** button on this page, it opens up a new page with a form in which you enter all the task details. That's how you create a task by calling the create task backend API.

The fourth screen we built is the dashboard screen, where we can see the tasks available or can create new tasks under the logged-in user. We can learn how to use different components together to form a dashboard here. We build separate components for the header, tasks, user profile, and logout buttons and use all these components to create the following dashboard (*Figure* 2.36).

We can learn how to fetch data from the Node.js Backend API and conditionally render based on the result array. The following things we can learn building this end to end.

- Understand how to build VueJS components
- Understand how to build a dashboard using different components
- Understand how to make an API call from VueJS to the Backend and fetch the data
- Understand how to do backend validation before querying this info from the database
- Understand the store management to store the user info using pina library
- Understand how to proxy API calls from frontend to backend
- Understand how to create modal windows in VueJS

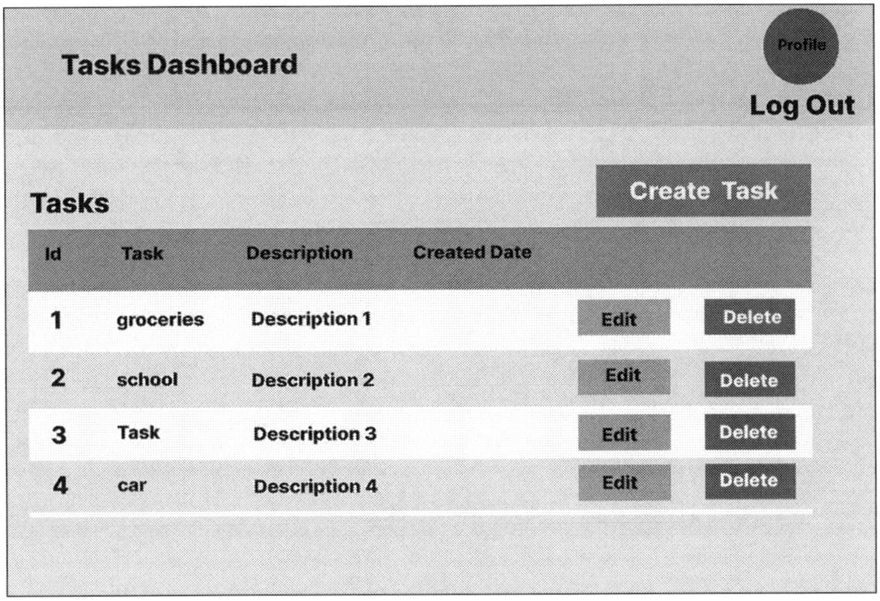

Figure 2.36: *Tasks Dashboard with Tasks*

We can edit the existing task or delete the task by clicking on the corresponding buttons on each task. When editing, we can open up a modal window to allow the user to edit the description and task name, and to confirm deletion.

The fifth screen we build is the details screen, where we can see the specific task details by clicking on a certain row on the dashboard. We can learn how to use routing to navigate from one page to another page.

We also learn how to fetch data from the Node.js Backend API and conditionally render based on the result array. Building this end-to-end process helps us learn the following things:

- Understand how to do routing in VueJS
- Understand how to use guards and fetch the data from the API before navigating to another page
- Understand how to make an API call from VueJS to the backend and fetch the data
- Understand how to do backend validation before querying this info from the database
- Understand the store management to store the user info using Pinia library
- Understand how to proxy API calls from frontend to backend

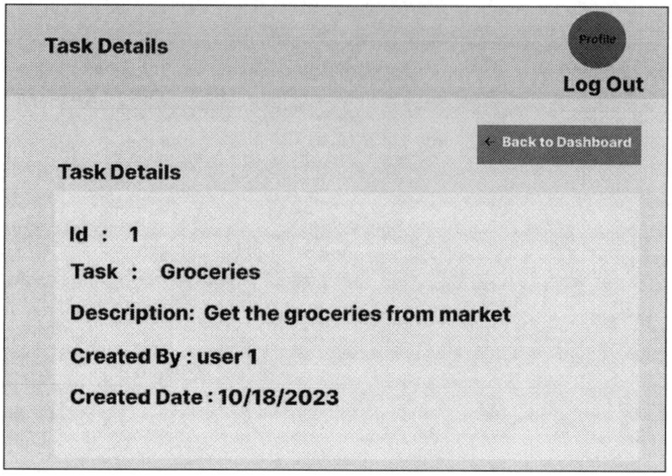

Figure 2.37: *Task Details*

Conclusion

In this chapter, we have covered all the prerequisites necessary for constructing a full-stack web application utilizing the core technologies of MongoDB, Express.js, Vue.js, and Node.js. We also introduced the example project that we will develop throughout this book. To effectively follow along and participate in the hands-on exercises, it's essential to ensure that all these prerequisites are properly installed on your system. Hands-on experience is invaluable in learning and mastering new skills. In the forthcoming chapters, we will delve deeper into the fundamental concepts of Vue.js and Node.js, and we will begin the practical development of our example project. This step-by-step approach will help solidify your understanding and application of these powerful technologies in real-world scenarios.

In the next chapter, we will explore Vue.js in depth, examining its architecture, components, and how it integrates within our full-stack application. This exploration will include practical examples and detailed explanations to enhance your understanding and skills in using Vue.js effectively in real-world projects. By the end of the next chapter, you should be well-prepared to implement Vue.js in our ongoing example project and beyond, leveraging its capabilities to create dynamic and responsive web applications.

CHAPTER 3
Exploring VueJS

Introduction

In this chapter, we'll embark on an enlightening journey through the core concepts and essentials of VueJS, laying the foundation you need to commence development effectively. As a full-stack developer, grasping the significance of a progressive framework like VueJS is paramount. We do not just aim to acquaint you with another tool; our objective is to delve into the '*why*' behind VueJs popularity and utility in modern web development. This framework stands out for its progressive nature, meaning it's designed to be incrementally adoptable and can easily integrate or coexist with other libraries or existing projects.

We'll navigate through the vital concepts of VueJS, ensuring that even if you are new to this framework, you will gain a comprehensive understanding of its features and capabilities. This chapter is meticulously structured to offer you insights and a deep understanding of VueJS, equipping you with the knowledge to tackle full-stack development challenges confidently.

To enhance your learning experience, we will not just be discussing theories. We will set up a simple, yet illustrative project. This hands-on approach is designed to solidify your understanding of VueJS's concepts in a practical setting. By working through this project, you'll gain not only theoretical knowledge but also practical skills that will be immensely beneficial as you progress to the more complex aspects of the book's main project.

The focus of this chapter is to ensure that by the end, you're not only familiar with VueJS but also comfortable using it in real-world scenarios. Whether it's understanding the Vue instance, component system, reactivity, or the Vue CLI, this chapter is your stepping stone into the world of VueJS and full-stack development. Prepare to dive into an engaging and comprehensive learning experience that will set you up for success in the following chapters.

Structure

In this chapter, the following topics will be covered:

- Why VueJS
- Understanding Reactivity in VueJS
- Understanding Components
- Options API
- Composition API
- Lifecycle Hooks
- Applying Styles
- Custom Directives
- Slots
- Template Refs
- Understanding Forms

Need for VueJS

In the landscape of modern web development, a myriad of frameworks and libraries are vying for attention, each offering unique features and benefits. Among them, VueJS has emerged as a standout choice for many developers. This section delves into the '*why*' of VueJS - understanding its advantages, ecosystem, and how it fits into the spectrum of web development needs.

VueJS, created by Evan You, was first released in 2014. It was developed to take the best parts of Angular and React, two of the most popular frameworks, and improve upon them. VueJS stands out for its simplicity, flexibility, and efficiency. Here, we'll explore its journey from a relatively unknown library to one of the most starred projects on GitHub. Here are some of the concepts.

- **Simplicity and Ease of Learning:** One of VueJS's most significant selling points is its simplicity and gentle learning curve. Unlike some of its counterparts, VueJS is easy to integrate into existing projects, making it a popular choice for developers of all skill levels. Its straightforward syntax and clear documentation mean that even newcomers to web development can quickly start building applications.
- **Reactive and Composable:** VueJS's reactivity system is a core feature, enabling efficient data binding and state management. This system makes it easier for developers to understand and predict the behavior of their code. Moreover, Vue's component-based architecture allows for building reusable and maintainable code that is essential for larger applications.

- **Robust Tooling and Ecosystem:** VueJS is accompanied by a rich ecosystem, including the Vue CLI, Vuex for state management, and Vue Router for navigation. The availability of these tools streamlines the development process, from project initiation to deployment. Additionally, a vast array of plugins and community contributions further enhance Vue's capabilities.
- **Performance and Optimization:** Performance is where VueJS shines. Its lightweight nature, combined with a virtual DOM implementation, ensures applications are fast and responsive. Vue also offers advanced features like lazy loading and code splitting, which are critical for optimizing large-scale applications.
- **Community and Support:** VueJS has a vibrant and growing community. The framework's popularity ensures a wealth of resources, from tutorials to plugins, and an active community for support. Regular updates and contributions from the community keep VueJS modern and relevant.

By the end of this section, you'll have a comprehensive understanding of why VueJS has become a favored choice in the web development community. Whether you are a beginner or an experienced developer, VueJS offers a blend of simplicity, flexibility, and power, making it a worthy contender for your toolkit in building modern web. Let's go through some advantages and disadvantages as well.

Advantages of VueJS

- **Ease of Learning:** VueJS has a gentle learning curve, with a simple and clear syntax that makes it accessible for beginners. Its comprehensive documentation and supportive community further facilitate learning.
- **Reactivity and Data Binding:** VueJS's reactivity system simplifies the process of building dynamic interfaces. Its two-way data binding ensures seamless synchronization between the model and the view.
- **Component-based Architecture:** Vue encourages the use of components, promoting code reusability, and maintainability. This is particularly beneficial for large-scale applications where managing code efficiently is crucial.
- **Performance:** VueJS is known for its high performance. Its efficient update mechanism and lightweight size contribute to faster page load and smooth dynamic interactions.
- **Flexibility and Integrability:** VueJS can be easily integrated into existing projects, and it works well with various libraries and frameworks. This flexibility makes it a versatile choice for many web development projects.
- **Ecosystem and Tooling:** Vue comes with a strong ecosystem, including tools like Vue CLI, Vuex, and Vue Router, which streamline the development process and enhance productivity.

- **Community and Support:** The VueJS community is vibrant and growing, offering a wealth of resources, plugins, and support, ensuring that developers have access to the help and tools they need.

Disadvantages of VueJS

- **Less Market Share Compared to Rivals:** Vue.js, while a popular framework, has a smaller market share compared to giants like React and Angular, which can lead to certain disadvantages. Notably, its smaller community results in fewer third-party resources, such as libraries and tools, potentially hindering development options. Additionally, job opportunities for Vue.js developers are not as plentiful as for those proficient in more widely used frameworks. This lesser prevalence can also make enterprises cautious about adopting Vue.js for large-scale projects, favoring more established technologies with robust support networks.
- **Language Barrier in Community Resources:** Some of Vue's early and extensive development and adoption were in non-English speaking countries. This can lead to some resources, plugins, or community support being in languages other than English.
- **Risk of Over Flexibility:** Vue's flexibility can sometimes lead to inconsistent coding practices among different developers or teams, potentially making the codebase harder to manage or scale.
- **Limited Resources for complex projects:** While there are ample resources for beginners, developers might find less available material for advanced or very specific use cases compared to more established frameworks.
- **Integration challenges with Larger Teams or Projects:** In large-scale projects or when working in large teams, the simplicity of Vue might pose challenges, especially if strict conventions and coding standards are not established.
- **SEO Challenges in Single Page Applications:** As with most JavaScript frameworks, VueJS-based SPAs can face challenges with SEO, although solutions like server-side rendering (with Nuxt.js) can help mitigate this.
- **Dependence on the Ecosystem:** For advanced features, developers often rely on third-party libraries. This dependency can be a concern if libraries are not well-maintained or become outdated.

In conclusion, VueJS stands out for its simplicity, performance, and flexibility, making it an excellent choice for a wide range of projects. However, its market presence, resource availability, and challenges in specific scenarios should be considered when choosing it for a project.

Understanding Reactivity in VueJS

At the heart of Vue.js is its reactivity system. This system allows your app to react to changes in data and update the view automatically. In Vue 3, this reactivity is achieved through a powerful API based on ES6 Proxies, which represents a significant improvement over the **`Object.defineProperty`**-based system used in Vue 2.

When you define a data property inside a Vuc component, Vue wraps this property with getters and setters using its reactivity system. This process is transparent to you, the developer. When the data changes, Vue knows precisely which components depend on that data and updates them automatically. This model simplifies the development process, as you do not need to track and update the DOM when the state changes manually.

Reactivity in Action

Consider a simple Vue component with a data property **`message`**. When you modify a message, any part of the template that references this property updates to reflect the new value. This automatic and immediate update is the essence of Vue's reactivity.

In Vue 3, reactivity is further enhanced with the Composition API, introducing **`ref`** and **`reactive`** functions for creating a reactive state. The **`ref`** function is used for primitive values, turning them into a reactive and mutable object, while **`reactive`** is used for making an entire object reactive.

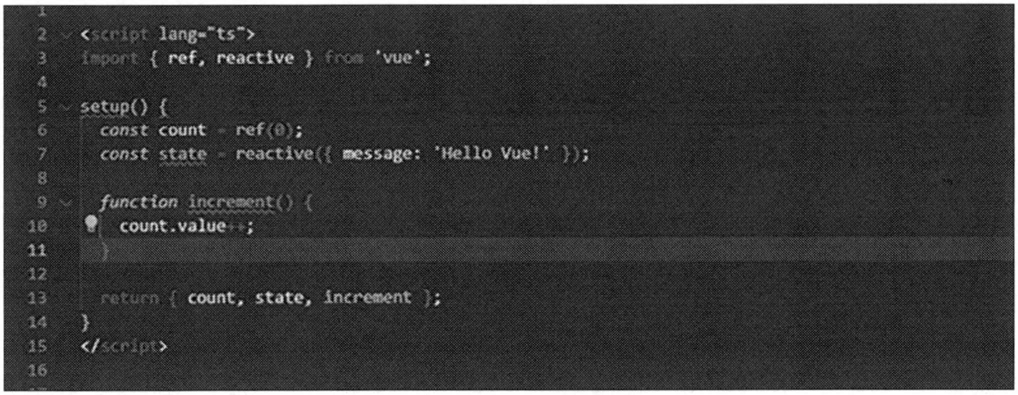

***Figure 3.1**: Reactivity in action*

In this example, changes to **`count`** or **`state.message`** will be tracked and updated in the view automatically.

While Vue's reactivity system provides a strong foundation for app development, understanding its nuances can help you avoid common pitfalls, such as ensuring reactivity when dealing with arrays and objects or distinguishing between **`ref`** and **`reactive`.** Moreover, understanding how to structure reactive data can lead to more efficient and maintainable code.

Vue's documentation offers an in-depth look at the reactivity system, including advanced topics like reactivity caveats and the new **`reactive`** APIs introduced in Vue

3. As you grow more comfortable with Vue, delving into these areas will help you leverage the full power of the framework's reactivity model.

Understanding Components

Components are the building blocks of Vue 3 applications. They help you organize and reuse code, making your projects more modular, maintainable, and scalable. Each component is a self-contained unit that manages its own state, presentation, and behavior. In Vue 3, components have been enhanced to provide better performance and more flexible composition.

Component Structure

A Vue component typically consists of three parts:

- **`Template`**: This is the HTML structure of the component, where you define the markup. Vue extends standard HTML with its own directives (like **`v-if`**, **`v-for`**, **`v-model`**, and more) to provide powerful data binding and conditional rendering capabilities.
- **`Script`**: This section is where the JavaScript logic of the component lives. It defines the component's properties, data, methods, and other options using the Options API or the Composition API.
- **`Styles`**: The style section allows you to define CSS specifically for this component. Using the **`scoped`** attribute, you can ensure that the styles apply only to this component, avoiding unwanted side effects elsewhere.

```
<template>
  <div>{{ message }}</div>
</template>

<script lang="ts">
export default {
  data() {
    return {
      message: 'Hello, Vue 3!'
    };
  }
}
</script>

<style scoped>
div {
  color: blue;
}
</style>
```

***Figure 3.2**: Component structure*

Communication: Props and Events

Components are essential in Vue 3 for creating modular and maintainable user interfaces. An equally important aspect of working with components is understanding how they communicate, especially through events and props, enabling a dynamic and interactive application structure.

- **`Props`:** allow parent components to pass data down to child components. This one-way data flow ensures that child components remain decoupled and reusable. Props are defined in the child component and are assigned values by the parent:

```
// Child Component
<template>
  <div>{{ userMessage }}</div>
</template>

<script lang="ts">
export default {
  props: ['userMessage']
}
</script>

// Parent Component
<template>
  <ChildComponent :userMessage="parentMessage" />
</template>

<script>
export default {
  data() {
    return {
      parentMessage: 'Hello from parent'
    };
  }
}
</script>
```

Figure 3.3: *Communication with props*

- **`Events`:** enable child components to communicate back to their parent components. Vue instances provide an event system to enable this communication. A child component can emit an event, and the parent component can listen to that event and respond accordingly:

```
// Child Component
<template>
  <button @click="$emit('enlargeText')">Enlarge Text</button>
</template>


// Parent Component
<template>
  <ChildComponent @enlargeText="handleEnlargeText" />
</template>

<script>
export default {
  methods: {
    handleEnlargeText() {
      // Handle the event
    }
  }
}
</script>
```

Figure 3.4: *Communication with events*

Advanced Communication Patterns

While props and events cover a lot of communication needs in Vue applications, more complex scenarios may require advanced communication patterns. Vue 3 provides several mechanisms to facilitate these patterns, improving the overall structure and maintainability of your applications.

- **Provide/Inject:** The `provide` and `inject` feature in Vue 3 allows for a direct line of communication between ancestor and descendant components, bypassing the need to prop drill through every layer of components. This pattern is particularly useful in deeply nested component structures or when implementing dependency injection.
- **Vuex for State Management:** For large-scale applications, managing state across multiple components can become complex. Vuex is a state management library designed specifically for Vue, providing a centralized store for all your applications' state. It follows the Flux architecture pattern and helps you write predictable and maintainable code.
- **`EventBus` Replacement: `Mitt or TinyEmitter`:** Vue 3 removed the built-in event bus system, recommending the usage of dedicated libraries for global event handling. Libraries like `mitt` or `tiny-emitter` provide lightweight solutions to facilitate communication between any components, regardless of their relationship.
- **Teleport:** Vue 3 introduced the `<Teleport>` component, which allows you to render content in a different location than where a component is called in the template. This is particularly useful for modals, notifications, or any component that needs to break out of its regular DOM flow.

Understanding events and communication among components is crucial for building interactive and well-structured Vue 3 applications. Proper use of props for parent-to-child communication and events for child-to-parent communication helps maintain a clear and predictable data flow, making your application easier to develop and debug.

Advanced communication patterns like provide/inject, Vuex, external event libraries, and Teleport enhance the capability of Vue applications, especially as they grow in complexity. By leveraging these patterns, developers can build scalable, maintainable, and highly decoupled components, leading to more robust and efficient Vue applications. As you delve deeper into Vue development, exploring these advanced patterns equips you with the tools necessary to tackle a wide array of development challenges.

Options API

Vue.js is a progressive JavaScript framework used for building user interfaces. The Options API is one of the core concepts in Vue, providing a straightforward and organized way of creating component logic. In Vue 3, the Options API continues to be a fundamental part of the framework, enabling developers to define components using an options object.

Basics of the Options API

The Options API allows you to structure your component logic by grouping related properties. Each property in the component's options object serves a specific purpose:

- **`data`:** A function that returns the reactive state of the component.
- **`props`:** An object defining the props the component receives from its parent.
- **`methods`:** An object containing methods that can be bound to user input events or used as utilities.
- **`computed`:** An object of getter functions for creating computed properties, which are reactive and cached based on their dependencies.
- **`watch`:** An object where keys are expressions to watch, and values are corresponding callback functions that execute when the watched value changes.
- **Lifecycle Hooks:** Options, such as **`mounted`**, **`created`**, and **`updated`** allow you to run code at different stages of the component lifecycle.

Vue Component with Options API

Here is a basic example of a Vue component defined using the Options API. In the HTML, the **`#appdiv`** serves as the mounting point for the Vue application. Vue's template syntax is used to bind the **`count`**, **`message`**, and **`reversedMessage`** from the component's state to the DOM:

- **`{{ count }}`**,**`{{ message }}`**, and **`{{ reversedMessage }}`** dynamically display the values of **`count`**, **`message`**, and the computed **`reversedMessage`** respectively.
- The **`<button>`** tag uses the Vue event directive **`@click`** to bind the **`incrementCount`** method to the button's click event. When the button is clicked, **`incrementCount`** is executed, incrementing the value of **`count`**.
- **`Props`:** In the Vue component, **`props`** are defined to specify that the component expects to receive a **`welcomeMessage`**. This message is a string and is marked as required. In the HTML template, you can see the prop being used within a **`<h1>`** tag to display the welcome message. However, note that in our plain HTML example, we're not passing **`props`** from a parent component since we're directly mounting to an application instance. In a real-world scenario, this prop would be passed from a parent component.

```
<div id="app">
  <!-- Display the welcome message prop -->
  <h1>{{ welcomeMessage }}</h1>

  <!-- Existing bindings and event listeners -->
  <p>{{ count }}</p>
  <p>{{ message }}</p>
  <p>{{ reversedMessage }}</p>
  <button @click="incrementCount">Increment</button>
</div>

<!-- Vue 3 inclusion and Vue application code -->
<script src="https://unpkg.com/vue@next"></script>
<script>
  // Updated Vue component from above
  const app = Vue.createApp({
    // Define props the component accepts
    props: {
      welcomeMessage: {
        type: String,
        required: true
      }
    },
    // Data function for reactive state
    data() {
      return {
        count: 0,
        message: 'Hello Vue!'
      };
    },
    // Methods for user interaction
    methods: {
      incrementCount() {
        this.count += 1;
      }
    },
    // Computed properties for deriving state
    computed: {
      reversedMessage() {
        return this.message.split('').reverse().join('');
      }
    },
    // Watchers for reacting to state changes
    watch: {
      count(newCount) {
        console.log(`The count has changed to ${newCount}`);
      }
    }
  });

  app.mount('#app');
</script>
```

***Figure 3.5**: Options API*

- **`Watch`:** The **`watch`** property is used to observe changes to the **`count`** property. Whenever **`count`** changes (for instance, when the button is clicked and **`incrementCount`** is invoked), the watch handler logs the new count to the console. This is useful for performing actions in response to state changes, such as fetching data, validating input, or logging.

This structure exemplifies the core features of the Options API: reactive data, computed properties, and methods, all integrated within a cohesive component. This setup is ideal for creating interactive and dynamic web interfaces with Vue 3.

Advantages and Use Cases

The Options API is highly readable and organized, making it suitable for smaller components or applications and for those who prefer an object-oriented style of code.

It's especially convenient when working with a team of developers with various levels of experience with Vue or JavaScript.

Limitations

While the Options API is powerful, it can become unwieldy as components grow in complexity. Recognizing different aspects of a component (like **`data`**, **`methods`**, **`computed`** properties) might require scrolling through the entire options object, which can affect maintainability and readability.

The Options API remains a fundamental and approachable way to build Vue components in Vue 3. It provides a structured and intuitive approach to defining component options and behavior. For developers transitioning from Vue 2 or those who prefer a more structured object-oriented approach, the Options API offers a familiar and straightforward way to build reactive components in Vue 3.

Composition API

Vue 3 introduced a new and innovative feature known as the Composition API, which provides an alternative way to compose and reuse logic in Vue components. This API is designed to improve code organization and readability, particularly in complex components, by leveraging JavaScript functions. It's an addition to the existing Options API, not a replacement.

Basics of the Composition API

The Composition API centers around the **`setup()`** function, a new component option. This function serves as the entry point for composition logic, allowing you to define reactive states, computed properties, and functions using a more flexible and organized approach.

- Reactive References (**`ref`**): Allows you to make any variable reactive.
- Reactive State (**`reactive`**): Turns an object into a reactive object.
- Computed Properties (**`computed`**): Creates computed references from functions.
- Watchers (**`watch`**, **`watchEffect`**): Allows you to apply side effects in response to reactive changes.
- Lifecycle Hooks: Specific functions like **`onMounted`, `onUpdated`**, allows you to hook into component lifecycle events within **`setup()`.**

Vue Component with Composition API

Below, we present the component as reimagined through the lens of the Composition API, following our exploration of its counterpart constructed using the Options API.

This shift provides an opportune moment to delve into the nuanced differences and deepen our comprehension of how each API influences the structure and functionality of Vue components.

By examining the components in both forms, we aim to illuminate how each API facilitates the articulation of component logic, state management, and reactivity. The comparative analysis not only aids in understanding the specific mechanics and syntax differences but also provides insight into the strategic advantages each API brings to different scenarios within Vue application development. Through this exploration, you are equipped with a clearer understanding and practical knowledge of both the Options and Composition APIs, enabling you to make informed decisions about which approach best suits your development style and project requirements.

- **Setup Method**: This is the entry point for our Composition API logic. Instead of defining **`data`**, **`methods`**, **`computed`**, and **`watch`** as separate options, we define them inside the **`setup()`** function.
- **Reactive References (`ref`):** We use **`ref()`** to create reactive references for **`count`** and **`message`**. These are equivalent to **`data`** properties in the Options API. To access or modify their values, we use **`.value`**.
- **Computed Properties (`computed`):** We create computed properties using the **`computed()`** function. This is similar to the Options API but is now inside **`setup()`**.
- **Methods:** Functions like **`incrementCount`** are defined directly inside **`setup()`** and returned so they can be accessed in the template.
- **Watchers (`watch`):** We use the **`watch()`** function to observe changes in **`count`** and perform actions in response. This replaces the **`watch`** option in the Options API.
- **Lifecycle Hooks (`onMounted`):** Lifecycle hooks such as **`onMounted`** are used directly inside **`setup()`**. They provide the same functionality as in the Options API but are integrated into the Composition logic.
- **Props (`props`):** Component props are accessed through the **`setup()`** function's first parameter. They remain reactive and can be used directly or passed into other Composition API functions.

```
<div id="app">
    <!-- Display the welcome message prop -->
    <h1>{{ welcomeMessage }}</h1>

    <!-- Existing bindings and event listeners -->
    <p>{{ count }}</p>
    <p>{{ message }}</p>
    <p>{{ reversedMessage }}</p>
    <button @click="incrementCount">Increment</button>
</div>

<!-- Vue 3 inclusion -->
<script src="https://unpkg.com/vue@next"></script>
<script>
const { ref, computed, watch, onMounted } = Vue;

const app = Vue.createApp({
  props: {
    welcomeMessage: String
  },
  setup(props) {
    // Reactive state
    const count = ref(0);
    const message = ref('Hello Vue!');

    // Computed property
    const reversedMessage = computed(() => {
      return message.value.split('').reverse().join('');
    });

    // Method
    const incrementCount = () => {
      count.value += 1;
    };

    // Watcher
    watch(count, (newCount) => {
      console.log(`The count has changed to ${newCount}`);
    });

    // Lifecycle hook: onMounted
    onMounted(() => {
      console.log('Component has been mounted!');
    });

    // Return everything that should be available in the template
    return { count, message, reversedMessage, incrementCount };
  }
});

app.mount('#app');
</script>
```

***Figure 3.6**: Composition API*

This structure helps to group related logic and reuse logic across components, improving the maintainability and readability of large Vue applications.

Advantages and Use Cases

The Composition API is particularly beneficial for:

- **Large Components:** Improves organization and reusability in large, complex components.

- **Reusable Logic:** Simplifies the extraction and reuse of logic across components.
- **TypeScript Support:** Offers better integration with TypeScript for improved type inference and composition.

The Composition API offers a flexible and powerful way to build and organize Vue components. By leveraging JavaScript functions, developers can improve code reuse, maintainability, and scalability, especially in complex applications. While it introduces new concepts and requires a shift in thinking from the Options API, the Composition API provides a robust set of tools for modern web development with Vue 3.

Lifecycle Hooks

Lifecycle hooks in Vue.js are an integral part of working with components. They are special functions that allow you to hook into different stages of a component's life, from its creation to its destruction. In Vue.js 3, these hooks play a pivotal role in controlling and managing the behavior of components throughout their lifecycle. This section delves into these hooks, providing practical examples to illustrate their usage.

Key Lifecycle Hooks

Vue.js 3 offers several lifecycle hooks that you can use to perform actions at specific stages.

`onBeforeMount`

Triggered right before the initial rendering of the component. This hook is called after the component is created but before it's added to the DOM.

Use Case: Preparing any required data or conditions before the component is rendered. This hook is ideal for non-DOM-dependent setups, such as initializing non-reactive data or configuring settings that don't rely on the DOM.

```
<script lang="ts">
import { onBeforeMount } from 'vue';

export default {
  setup() {
    onBeforeMount(() => {
      console.log('Component is about to be mounted');
    });
  }
};

</script>
```

Figure 3.7: *onBeforeMount Hook*

onMounted

This hook is called after the component had been mounted to the DOM. This is where you would perform any DOM-dependent setup.

Use Case: This hook is crucial for any tasks that require interaction with the DOM or need to ensure the component is fully rendered. Common use cases include:

- Accessing or manipulating the DOM directly.
- Integrating third-party libraries that need to interact with the DOM.
- Starting AJAX requests to fetch data that the component requires after it is visible.

```
<script lang="ts">
import { onMounted } from 'vue';

export default {
  setup() {
    onMounted(() => {
      console.log('Component has been mounted');
    });
  }
};

</script>
```

Figure 3.8: *onMounted Hook*

onBeforeUpdate

Invoked when the data used by the component changes, just before the DOM is re-rendered and patched. Useful for performing operations before an update.

Use Case: It is useful for performing actions right before the DOM is re-rendered based on reactive data changes. Suitable scenarios include:

- Validating user inputs or form fields before updating the view.
- Logging previous states for debugging purposes.
- Performing calculations or preparations before the reactive changes take effect.

```
<script lang="ts">
import { onBeforeUpdate } from 'vue';

export default {
  setup() {
    onBeforeUpdate (() => {
      console.log('Component is about to update');
    });
  }
};

</script>
```

Figure 3.9: *onBeforeUpdate Hook*

onUpdated

This is called after the component and its children have been updated. This hook runs after the DOM has been updated.

Use Case: Ideal for operations that occur after the component re-renders due to data changes. Use cases include:

- Updating the DOM in response to changes in component data.
- Refreshing or reapplying JavaScript plugins that are dependent on the rendered DOM.
- Acting upon changes that have just been reflected in the rendering.

```
<script lang="ts">
import { onUpdated } from 'vue';

export default {
  setup() {
    onUpdated(() => {
      console.log('Component has been updated');
    });
  }
};

</script>
```

***Figure* 3.10**: *onUpdated Hook*

onBeforeUnmount

Invoked right before a component is unmounted from the DOM. Ideal for cleanup activities.

Use Case: This hook is best suited for cleanup activities before removing the component from the DOM. Common use cases are:

- Removing event listeners or unsubscribing from observables.
- Stopping timers, intervals, or cancelling network requests initiated by the component.
- Saving state or persisting changes before the component disappears.

```
<script lang="ts">
import { onBeforeUnmount   } from 'vue';

export default {
  setup() {
    onBeforeUnmount  (() => {
      console.log('Component is about to be unmounted');
    });
  }
};

</script>
```

Figure 3.11: *onBeforeUnmount Hook*

`onUnmounted`

This is called after a component has been removed from the DOM. It is the last hook in the lifecycle of a component.

Use Case: Used for final cleanup after the component has been destroyed, such as:

- Cleaning up any remaining resources that were set up in **`onMounted`**
- Final logging or dispatching events to signal the component's removal
- Completing pending asynchronous tasks associated with the component

```
<script lang="ts">
import { onUnmounted    } from 'vue';

export default {
  setup() {
    onUnmounted   (() => {
      console.log('Component has been unmounted');
    });
  }
};

</script>
```

Figure 3.12: *onUnmounted Hook*

Options API versus Composition API

There's a distinction in how these hooks are used between the Options API and the Composition API. We've explored example components using both the Composition API and the Options API, showcasing their distinct styles. It's equally crucial for developers to grasp the application of lifecycle hooks within these frameworks.

In the Options API, lifecycle hooks are properties of the component's options object. Each hook corresponds to a particular stage in the lifecycle of the component. You define them as methods with the names of the lifecycle events, and Vue will call them at the appropriate time.

In the Composition API, lifecycle hooks are used differently. Instead of defining them as options in an object, you use lifecycle hook functions inside the **`setup()`** function. These functions from Vue's composition API include **`onBeforeMount`**, **`onMounted`**, **`onBeforeUpdate`**, **`onUpdated`**, **`onBeforeUnmount`**, and **`onUnmounted`**. Each of these can be imported from Vue and called directly within the **`setup()`** function, often used alongside reactive state or other composition functions.

When using the Composition API, you typically won't define lifecycle hooks in the traditional Options API manner because the Composition API is designed for composability and reusability. The setup method and lifecycle-specific hooks within it provide a more flexible way to organize and reuse logic across different components, which is a different approach from the Options API's organization method based on the component's options object.

To summarize, the Options API provides a structured, declarative approach to using lifecycle hooks, making it intuitive for developers familiar with Vue's component structure. The lifecycle hooks are part of the component definition and are directly tied to the component's options. This contrasts with the Composition API, where lifecycle hooks are used more imperatively within the **`setup()`** function.

Best Practices

- **Initialization**: Use **`onMounted`** for tasks that require the DOM, like manipulating the DOM or initializing plugins that need DOM elements.
- **Cleanup:** Always perform necessary cleanup in **`onBeforeUnmount`** and **`onUnmounted`** to avoid memory leaks.
- **Reactivity:** Use **`onBeforeUpdate`** and **`onUpdated`** judiciously, as they are called every time a reactive dependency changes.

Each lifecycle hook in Vue.js addresses specific aspects of a component's lifecycle, from initialization to teardown. By leveraging these hooks appropriately, developers can effectively manage tasks related to rendering, updates, and cleanup, ensuring the smooth operation and performance of Vue.js applications. Understanding and utilizing these hooks according to their intended use cases is the key to building responsive and efficient Vue.js applications.

Applying Styles

Styling is a crucial aspect of web development, contributing significantly to the user interface and experience. Vue 3 provides several approaches to apply styles to your components, enhancing the visual appeal and user interaction. This section explores different methods to apply styles in Vue 3 applications.

Inline Styles

Vue allows the binding of styles directly to HTML elements using the **v-bind** directive. This method is particularly useful for dynamic styling based on component state.

This approach allows styles to be defined directly within template tags, with values computed from the component's reactive data properties.

```
<template>
  <div :style="{ color: activeColor, fontSize: fontSize + 'px' }">Hello Vue!</div>
</template>

<script lang="ts">
export default {
  data() {
    return {
      activeColor: 'red',
      fontSize: 30
    };
  }
};
</script>
```

Figure 3.13: *Inline styles*

Class Bindings

Vue simplifies the dynamic application of CSS classes using the **v-bind:class** directive (or **:class** for shorthand), enabling you to toggle classes based on the component's state.

```
<template>
  <div :class="{ active: isActive, 'text-danger': hasError }">Hello Vue!</div>
</template>

<script lang="ts">
export default {
  data() {
    return {
      isActive: true,
      hasError: false
    };
  }
};
</script>
```

Figure 3.14: *Class Bindings*

Here, the **active** class is applied when **isActive** is **true**, and **text-danger** when **hasError** is **true.** This method is highly effective for toggling states like **active**, **disabled**, or **highlighted**.

Scoped Styles

Vue offers a unique feature called scoped styles that make it easy to apply CSS to a single component, avoiding global style conflicts.

Adding the **`scoped`** attribute to a **`<style>`** tag ensures that the styles only affect the current component. This encapsulation helps in maintaining styling consistency without unintended side effects. By adding **`MessageComponent`** to the parent component's template, you can render the styled message wherever needed in your application. The scoped CSS ensures that the styling of the message will remain consistent and isolated from other components, maintaining the encapsulation of component styles.

```
<template>
  <div class="message-container">
    Hello, this is a scoped style example!
  </div>
</template>

<script lang="ts">
export default {
  name: 'MessageComponent'
}
</script>

<style scoped>
1 reference
.message-container {
  padding: 20px;
  border-radius: 8px;
  background-color: lightblue;
}
</style>
```

Figure 3.15: *Scoped Styles*

Global Styles

Global styles can be applied via external stylesheets or within the main entry file of the Vue application, typically used for defining universal styles, themes, or resets.

```
// main.js or main.ts
import { createApp } from 'vue';
import App from './App.vue';
import './assets/global.css'; // Adjust the path based on where you placed the file

createApp(App).mount('#app');
```

Figure 3.16: *Global Styles*

Global CSS files should be imported to the entry file of the application (for example, **main.js** or **App.vue**) to ensure they're applied across the entire application.

Applying styles in Vue 3 can be accomplished in various ways, each suitable for different scenarios, from inline styling for dynamic changes to scoped styles for component-specific designs. Understanding these methods allows developers to create more engaging and responsive user interfaces while maintaining the application's overall aesthetic coherence.

Custom Directives

Vue.js offers the ability to create custom directives to extend the functionality of HTML elements. While Vue provides a set of built-in directives like **v-model** and **v-show**, you may encounter scenarios where you need specific, reusable functionality that isn't covered by the existing directives. This is where custom directives come in.

Basics of Custom Directives

A custom directive in Vue is defined by an object with several hook functions you can provide to add custom behavior to the DOM elements. These hooks include **created**, **beforeMount**, **mounted**, **beforeUpdate**, **updated**, **beforeUnmount**, and **unmounted**, mirroring component lifecycle hooks but applied to directives.

Custom directives can be defined globally or locally within Vue components. Here's how you can define a simple global custom directive:

```
// main.js
import { createApp } from 'vue';
import App from './App.vue';

// Define a global custom directive called 'focus'
createApp(App).directive('focus', {
  // When the bound element is inserted into the DOM...
  mounted(el) {
    // Focus the element
    el.focus();
  }
}).mount('#app');

```

***Figure 3.17**: Custom directives*

Once defined, you can use your custom directive similarly to how you would use any standard Vue directive. This input element will be automatically focused when rendered.

```
<input v-focus>
```

Local Custom Directives

While global directives are useful, sometimes you need a directive that's only relevant to a particular component. Here's how you can define a custom directive locally:

```
<template>
  <input v-local-focus>
</template>

<script lang="ts">
export default {
  directives: {
    localFocus: {
      mounted(el) {
        el.focus();
      }
    }
  }
}
</script>
```

***Figure 3.18**: Local Custom Directives*

Directive Hook Arguments

Directive hooks receive several arguments:

- **el**: The element the directive is bound to. This can be used to manipulate the DOM directly.
- **binding:** An object containing information such as the passed value and the argument.
- **vnode:** The virtual node produced by Vue's compiler.
- **prevVnode:** The previous virtual node, available only in **beforeUpdate** and **updated** hooks.

Here's a directive that changes the background color based on the binding value:

```
createApp(App).directive('background', {
  beforeMount(el, binding) {
    el.style.backgroundColor = binding.value;
  }
});

<div v-background="'yellow'">Colored Background</div>
```

***Figure 3.19**: Custom directive*

Dynamic Directives

Custom directives can also react to changes in their binding values. This is particularly useful for responding to data changes:

```
createApp(App).directive('dynamic-background', {
  beforeUpdate(el, binding) {
    el.style.backgroundColor = binding.value;
  }
});
```

***Figure 3.20**: Dynamic directives*

Custom directives in Vue 3 provide a powerful tool for direct DOM manipulations and abstracting reusable functionality. By defining global or local directives, developers can extend the capabilities of standard HTML elements and components, tailoring them to their specific project needs. Whether it's focusing an input, changing colors dynamically, or adding custom event listeners, custom directives offer a flexible way to enhance your Vue applications.

Slots

Slots are a powerful feature in Vue 3 that allows you to compose components more flexibly. They provide a method to inject content into a component from the parent scope, enabling complex and reusable component structures. This section delves into the usage and capabilities of slots in Vue 3.

Basics of Slots

In Vue, slots are placeholders inside components that can be filled with any template code from a parent component, including HTML, text, or other components. This allows for more flexible and reusable components by providing a way to mix and match different content.

Default Slot

The simplest form of a slot is the default slot, which captures any content not targeted to a named slot.

```
// Child Component
<template>
  <div>
    <slot></slot> <!-- Default slot -->
  </div>
</template>

// Parent Component

<template>
  <ChildComponent>
    <p>This will go into the default slot.</p>
  </ChildComponent>
</template>
```

Figure 3.21: *Default Slots*

Named Slots

For more control, you can use named slots to define multiple slots in a single component. Content is distributed to the same-named slots accordingly.

```
// Child Component
<template>
  <div>
    <slot name="header"></slot>
    <slot></slot> <!-- Default slot -->
    <slot name="footer"></slot>
  </div>
</template>

// Parent Component
<template>
  <ChildComponent>
    <template v-slot:header>
      <h1>Here is the header content.</h1>
    </template>

    <p>This is some default slot content.</p>

    <template v-slot:footer>
      <p>Here is the footer content.</p>
    </template>
  </ChildComponent>
</template>
```

Figure 3.22: *Named Slots*

Scoped Slots

Scoped slots allow child components to pass data back to the slot content in the parent. This is useful for creating components that are reusable and adaptable to different content structures.

```
<template>
  <ul>
    <li v-for="item in items" :key="item.id">
      <slot name="item" :item="item">{{ item.defaultText }}</slot>
    </li>
  </ul>
</template>

<script lang="ts">
export default {
  data() {
    return {
      items: [{ id: 1, defaultText: 'Item 1' }, { id: 2, defaultText: 'Item 2' }]
    };
  }
};
</script>


// Parent Component
<template>
  <ChildComponent>
    <template v-slot:item="{ item }">
      <span>{{ item.defaultText }} - Customized</span>
    </template>
  </ChildComponent>
```

***Figure 3.23**: Scoped Slots*

Slot Fallbacks and Defaults

Slot fallbacks or default content are used when no content is provided for the slot from the parent. This can be useful for defining placeholder content or default layouts.

```
<template>
  <div>
    <slot name="header">Default header content</slot>
    <slot>Default main content</slot>
    <slot name="footer">Default footer content</slot>
  </div>
</template>
```

***Figure 3.24**: Fallbacks and Defaults*

Destructuring Slot Props

In Vue 3, when using scoped slots, you can destructure slot props directly in the template, making the syntax cleaner and more concise.

```
<template>
  <ChildComponent>
    <template v-slot:item="{ item }">
      <span>{{ item.text }}</span> <!-- Destructured from the slot props -->
    </template>
  </ChildComponent>
</template>
```

***Figure 3.25**: Destructuring Slot Props*

Slots in Vue 3 offer a powerful mechanism for creating flexible and reusable components. By understanding and utilizing default slots, named slots, and scoped slots, developers can construct complex component structures that are easily maintainable and adaptable to different content needs. Whether building a simple layout component or a complex data-driven list, slots provide the necessary tools to keep components decoupled and coherent.

Template Refs

Template refs are a feature in Vue 3 that allows you to directly access DOM elements or child component instances defined in your templates. This is particularly useful for tasks that require direct access to the DOM, such as focusing an input or integrating with third-party DOM libraries.

Basics of Template Refs

In Vue, the **`ref`** attribute on an element within a template creates a reference to that element. Once a reference is established, you can access the corresponding DOM element or component instance in your JavaScript code, typically within lifecycle hooks or methods.

To use a template ref, add the **`ref`** attribute to an element in your template:

```
<template>
  <input ref="myInput">
</template>

<script lang="ts">
export default {
  mounted() {
    this.$refs.myInput.focus(); // Automatically focus the input when the component mounts
  }
}
</script>
```

Figure 3.26: *Template Refs*

In your component's JavaScript, you can then access this element using **`this.$refs.myInput`** after the component has been mounted.

Refs with Vue Components

Template refs can also be used to reference child components. This is useful for calling methods directly on a child component or accessing its data properties. Similarly, you can interact with the child component.

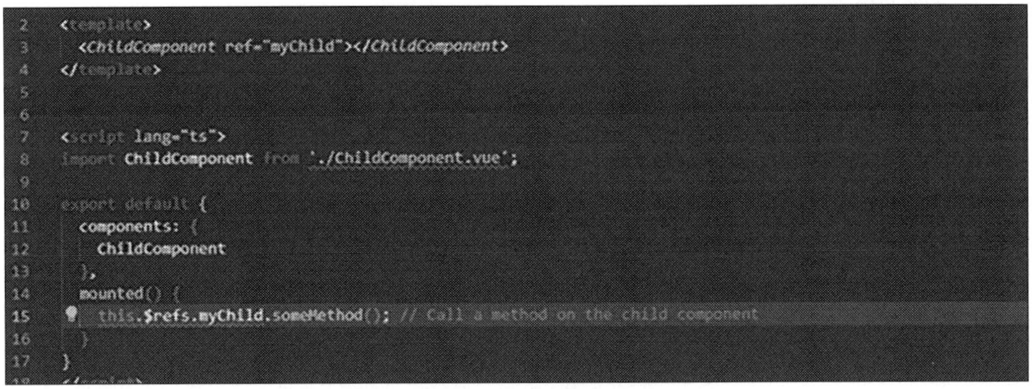

***Figure 3.27**: Refs with components*

Reactivity and Refs

In Vue 3, **`ref`** is also a function from the Composition API that creates a reactive and mutable reference to a value. However, this is distinct from template refs, although they share the same name. Template refs within the Composition API are used within the **`setup()`** function:

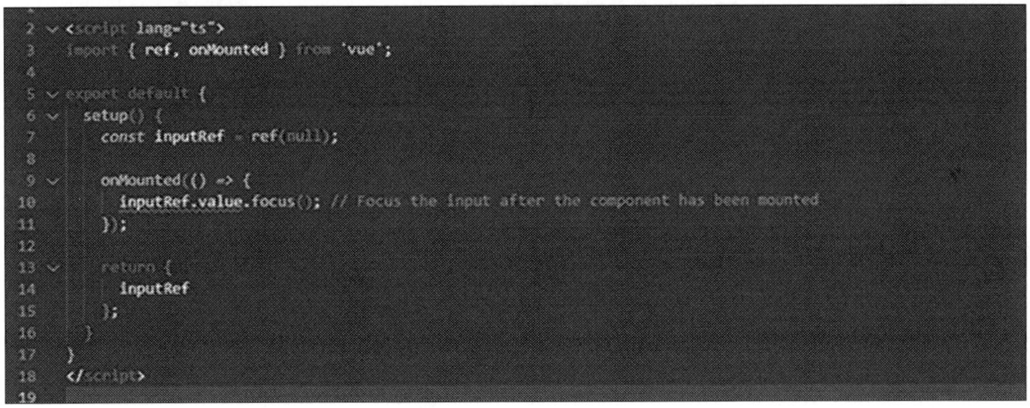

***Figure 3.28**: Reactivity*

In this Composition API context, **`inputRef`** is a reactive reference that gets assigned to the DOM element once the component mounts.

Using Refs with Reactivity

While direct DOM manipulation should be used sparingly in Vue, template refs provide a bridge to interact with the DOM directly when necessary. They are particularly useful for:

- Focusing on an input or text area.

- Triggering animations.
- Integrating with third-party libraries that require DOM access.

Best Practices and Limitations

- **Sparingly Use:** Avoid overusing refs for data that should be reactive. Vue's reactivity system is usually the best approach for most updates.
- **Lifecycle Awareness:** DOM elements referenced with `ref` are only available after the component has been mounted. Therefore, accessing refs in the `mounted` hook or later is essential.
- **Null Safety:** Always check if the `ref` is not null before accessing its properties or methods, especially when dealing with conditional rendering.

Template refs in Vue 3 provide a practical way to directly interact with DOM elements and child components within your Vue application. By understanding how to use them effectively, you can enhance your application's interactivity and integrate seamlessly with the DOM when necessary. However, it's crucial to apply them wisely and in sync with Vue's reactive data flow, ensuring your component structure remains clear and optimized.

Understanding Forms

Handling forms is a fundamental aspect of web development, enabling user interactions and data collection. Vue 3 simplifies form handling, offering a reactive approach that enhances user experience and ensures data consistency. This section explores form handling-techniques in Vue 3, emphasizing reactivity and validation.

Basics of Form Handling

Vue 3 employs the `v-model` directive to create two-way data bindings on form elements. This directive ensures that the input's value is both displayed from and updated to the component's state seamlessly.

```
<template>
  <input v-model="message">
</template>

<script lang="ts">
export default {
  data() {
    return {
      message: ''
    };
  }
}
</script>
```

Figure 3.29: *Basic form*

In this example, the **`v-model`** directive binds the input to the **`message`** data property. Any changes to the input field will automatically update the message, and any changes to **`message`** will reflect in the input field.

Handling Form Submission

Handling form submissions in Vue 3 typically involves preventing the default form submission behavior and defining a method to process form data.

The **`@submit.prevent`** modifier on the form tells Vue to prevent the default form submission behavior, allowing the **`handleSubmit`** method to handle the submission instead.

```
<template>
  <form @submit.prevent="handleSubmit">
    <input v-model="username" placeholder="Username">
    <button type="submit">Submit</button>
  </form>
</template>

<script lang="ts">
export default {
  data() {
    return {
      username: ''
    };
  },
  methods: {
    handleSubmit() {
      alert(`Username: ${this.username}`);
      // Further processing...
    }
  }
}
</script>
```

***Figure 3.30**: Form submission*

Form Validation

Client-side validation in Vue 3 can be achieved through computed properties or watchers that observe form inputs and set validation states accordingly.

```
<template>
  <form @submit.prevent="handleSubmit">
    <input v-model="email" placeholder="Email">
    <div v-if="emailError">{{ emailError }}</div>
    <button type="submit" :disabled="!isFormValid">Submit</button>
  </form>
</template>

<script lang="ts">
export default {
  data() {
    return {
      email: '',
      emailError: ''
    };
  },
  computed: {
    isFormValid() {
      return this.email.includes('@');
    }
  },
  watch: {
    email(value) {
      this.emailError = value.includes('@') ? '' : 'Invalid email';
    }
  },
  methods: {
    handleSubmit() {
      alert(`Email: ${this.email}`);
      // Further processing...
    }
  }
}
</script>
```

***Figure 3.31**: Basic form validation*

In this form, **v-model** is used to bind the input field to the **email** data property. The **isFormValid** computed property checks if the email is valid, and the form can only be submitted when it is valid. The **watch** on **email** updates **emailError** based on the validity of the email, providing immediate feedback to the user.

Using Custom Components in Forms

Vue 3 allows you to integrate custom form components, such as date pickers or color selectors, using **v-model** for seamless data binding and reactivity.

```
<Datepicker v-model="selectedDate"></Datepicker>
```

Here, **Datepicker** is a custom component, and **selectedDate** is a data property in your Vue component. The **v-model** directive ensures that **selectedDate**is updated whenever the user selects a date.

Forms are a crucial part of web applications, and Vue 3 offers a comprehensive and intuitive approach to handling them. By leveraging Vue's reactivity system through **v-model**, managing form submissions, and implementing client-side validation, developers can create efficient and user-friendly forms. Understanding these principles is essential for effective Vue application development, ensuring data integrity and enhancing user interactions.

Conclusion

In this chapter, we explored various foundational concepts and features of VueJS, a progressive JavaScript framework known for its simplicity, flexibility, and efficiency. We began by understanding the core reasons behind choosing VueJS, highlighting its reactivity system, which provides a straightforward approach to managing state changes. We delved into VueJS components, illustrating how they encapsulate functionality and promote reusable code. Both the Options API and the Composition API were discussed, showcasing different styles of organizing and composing component logic. We covered Lifecycle Hooks, which allow developers to hook into key moments in a component's life. The chapter also touched upon applying styles to Vue components, creating custom directives for extended functionality, utilizing slots for content distribution, leveraging template refs for direct DOM access, and handling forms effectively.

Throughout the chapter, we emphasized the importance of understanding these concepts to harness the full potential of VueJS. While we've covered essential topics, this represents just a portion of what VueJS offers. Developers are encouraged to dive deeper into the VueJS ecosystem and explore its extensive documentation for a more comprehensive understanding.

As we transition to the next chapter, *Node.js Core Modules and Components*, we will shift our focus from client-side frameworks to server-side development, exploring how Node.js's core modules and architectural components form the backbone of scalable and efficient web applications. This transition will highlight the versatility required in modern web development and the seamless integration between client and server-side technologies.

CHAPTER 4
Node.js Modules and Components

Introduction

Node.js, a critical player in server-side technology, forms the backbone of our MEVN stack's backend. Its role is indispensable, offering the flexibility and power necessary for efficient backend development. As we embark on this journey of building the backend with TypeScript, a deep understanding of Node.js's core concepts and modules is essential. This chapter is dedicated to unpacking these elements, providing detailed explanations and practical examples to cement your understanding.

In the initial chapters, we laid the groundwork by introducing Node.js and guiding you through its installation using Node Version Manager (NVM). Now, as we progress to this chapter, our focus shifts towards the exploration of Node.js's vital modules. These modules are the building blocks of Node.js, each serving specific functionalities that contribute to the robustness and versatility of Node.js applications.

To ensure a comprehensive grasp of these concepts, we will undertake a hands-on approach. We'll set up a sample project that will serve as a practical playground for experimenting with and understanding these modules in action. This project-based approach aims not just to familiarize you with theoretical aspects but also to build your confidence in applying these concepts in real-world scenarios.

As you journey through this chapter, you'll find yourself becoming more adept at utilizing Node.js's capabilities. The goal is to equip you with the knowledge and skills needed to comfortably tackle the backend development of the MEVN stack. Whether it's managing data flow, setting up APIs, or integrating with databases, this chapter will lay a solid foundation for you to build upon as you progress further into backend development with Node.js and TypeScript.

Structure

In this chapter, the following topics will be covered:

- Buffer
- Understanding Cluster Module and Child Process
- REPL
- Streams
- Working With File System
- Understanding Events
- HTTP Module
- Understanding Callbacks and Promises
- Exception Handling

Buffer

In Node.js, one of the core concepts that stand out for its utility and power is the Buffer. Buffers are crucial in handling binary data, a common requirement in various scenarios like file processing, network communication, or working with streams. This section aims to provide an in-depth exploration of Buffers in Node.js, enriched with practical examples to enhance your understanding.

Node.js operates primarily in JavaScript, a language initially designed for textual data and not binary streams. This is where Buffers come into play. A Buffer is a raw memory allocation outside the V8 JavaScript engine, which can store arbitrary binary data. We'll start by understanding why Buffers are necessary for Node.js and how they differ from regular text data handling.

The use of Buffer in Node.js is a crucial aspect for handling binary data. Unlike many other JavaScript environments, Node.js needs to interact with things outside the typical browser context, including files, network streams, and binary protocols. Here's a breakdown of the primary uses and significance of Buffer in Node.js:

- **Handling Binary Data:** JavaScript was originally designed to deal with textual data, not binary streams. Buffers in Node.js provide a way to handle raw binary data.
- **Interacting with Files:** When reading from or writing to files, especially binary files like images, audio, or any non-text content, Buffers are essential. They enable efficient processing and manipulation of this binary data.
- **Network Communication:** Buffers are used extensively in network communication. When receiving data over TCP or HTTP, the data is often

in a binary format, which Buffer can efficiently handle. This is important for building various network applications like HTTP servers, TCP socket servers, and more.

- **Streams Integration:** Buffers integrate seamlessly with Node.js streams. Streams are a collection of data – like arrays or strings, but they might not be available all at once and don't have to fit in memory. This makes Buffers a fundamental component in stream processing for handling data chunks efficiently.
- **Performance Efficiency:** Buffer instances represent memory allocated outside of V8's JavaScript engine heap. This allocation is faster for large amounts of binary data and improves the performance of the application.
- **Binary Data Manipulation:** Buffers allow manipulation of binary data. They provide a range of methods to modify and interact with the data, like slicing, reading, and writing in different formats.
- **Encoding and Decoding:** Buffers support encoding and decoding various data formats. For example, you can convert data from UTF-8, Base64, ASCII, and other formats to binary data and vice versa.
- **Interfacing with Native Libraries:** For applications that require interaction with native libraries or system calls, Buffers act as a bridge. They can handle the data exchange between Node.js and native operations.

Next, we will delve into the practical aspects of Buffers:

Creating Buffers

The **`Buffer`** class provides various methods to create new buffer instances. Three commonly used methods are **`Buffer.from()`**, **`Buffer.alloc()`**, and **`Buffer.allocUnsafe()`**. Each serves a different purpose and is used based on the specific requirements of your application. Here's an explanation of each:

`Buffer.from()` is used to create a new buffer from an existing data source. This method is safe and does not require manual initialization as it creates a new buffer containing a copy of the provided data. It can take various types of input: **`string`**, **`array`**, **`buffer`**, and **`arraybuffer`**.

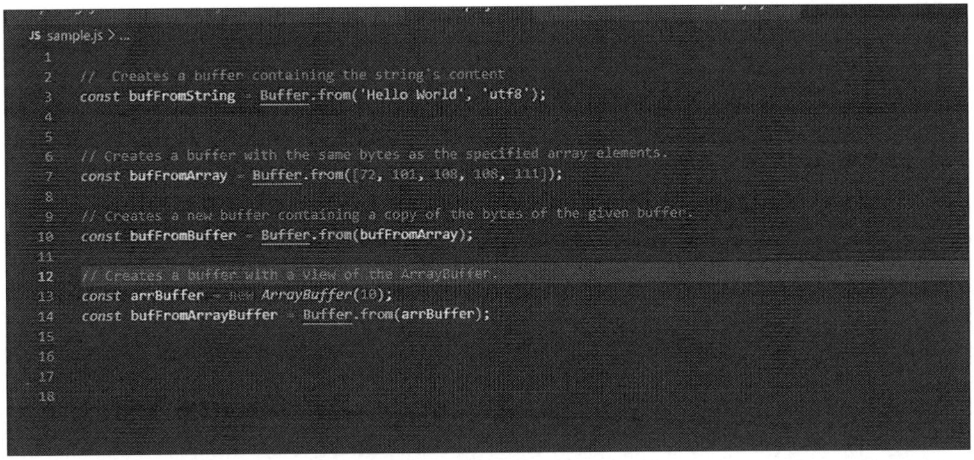

Figure 4.1: *Creating a buffer*

`Buffer.alloc()`creates a new buffer of a specified size and initializes it with zeros, ensuring that no old and potentially sensitive data is present in the buffer. This method is safer compared to **`Buffer.allocUnsafe()`** but slightly slower due to the initialization step.

Size Initialization: Creates a buffer of a specified size, filled with zeros.

Figure 4.2: *Size initialization*

`Buffer.allocUnsafe()`creates a buffer of a specified size without initializing the space in the memory that it occupies. This makes it faster than **`Buffer.alloc()`** as it skips zero-filling. However, the created buffer can contain old data from memory, which could potentially lead to sensitive data exposure if not handled correctly.

Size Initialization: Creates a buffer of a specified size. The content in the buffer is not initialized (that is, the buffer may contain random memory contents).

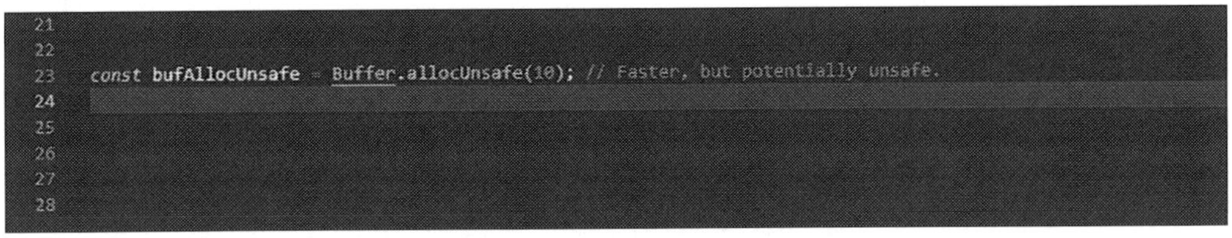

Figure 4.3: *size initialization*

It's important to choose the right method based on the need for speed and data security. **`Buffer.alloc()`** is recommended for handling sensitive data or when the content of the buffer is unknown. For non-sensitive data, or when you plan to overwrite the content immediately, **`Buffer.allocUnsafe()`** can be a faster alternative. **`Buffer.from()`** on the other hand, is best for creating buffers from existing data sources.

Manipulating Buffer Data

Understand how to manipulate data within Buffers, including reading from and writing to Buffers, and manipulating data using methods like **`slice()`** and **`copy()`**.

- The **`slice()`** method creates a new buffer that references the same memory as the original but with the specified start and end indices. It does not create a new buffer object.

```
const buffer = Buffer.from('Hello World');
const slicedBuffer = buffer.slice(0, 5); // Creates a slice with 'Hello'
```

Figure 4.4: *Manipulating Buffer Data*

- The **`copy()`** method allows you to copy data from one buffer to another. You can specify the source start and end positions, as well as the target start position.

```
const buffer1 = Buffer.from('Hello');
const buffer2 = Buffer.alloc(11);

buffer1.copy(buffer2, 0); // Copies 'Hello' into buffer2 at position 0
Buffer.from(' World').copy(buffer2, 5); // Copies ' World' into buffer2 at position 5
```

Figure 4.5: *Copying data*

There are so many other methods, you can effectively manage and manipulate binary data in Node.js. Buffers are a powerful tool in Node.js for handling a variety of tasks that involve raw data manipulation.

Advanced Buffer Operations

Buffers are often used with streams in Node.js. We'll explore how these two concepts interplay, particularly in file operations and network communications.

- **Reading and Writing Files with Buffer:** Reading and writing files with buffers in Node.js is a fundamental operation, especially when dealing with binary data or when performance is a key concern. Buffers provide a direct way to work with binary data, making them ideal for handling files at a low level.

- **Handling Network Data with Buffer:** Handling network data efficiently is a critical aspect of developing robust Node.js applications, particularly when dealing with raw binary data over the network. Buffers play a vital role in this scenario. They provide a mechanism to efficiently manage the binary data that is typically received or sent over the network.
- **Buffer Pooling**: Buffer pooling in Node.js refers to the practice of reusing a single, pre-allocated memory space for multiple buffer instances, instead of creating a new buffer and allocating new memory space each time a buffer is needed. This concept is significant in terms of performance optimization, especially when dealing with many buffer operations.
- **Interacting with Operating System:** Interacting with the operating system is a fundamental aspect of server-side programming, and Node.js provides various mechanisms to perform these interactions effectively. Leveraging Node.js, you can execute a wide range of operations, from running shell commands to interacting with the file system, managing processes, and handling network communications. These capabilities are crucial for creating applications that are not just limited to the Node.js runtime environment but are also integrated deeply with the underlying system.

Understanding Cluster Module and Child Process

Node.js is renowned for its non-blocking, event-driven architecture, making it an excellent choice for building efficient and scalable applications. However, Node.js runs in a single thread by default, which can be a limitation on multi-core systems. To leverage the full potential of modern hardware and handle the increasing load of applications, understanding clustering and child processes in Node.js is essential.

Before diving into clustering and child processes, it's important to understand the default operational model of Node.js. It is single-threaded and uses a single thread to execute your code. This design simplifies the development of applications, as developers don't need to deal with the complexity of thread management. However, this also means that a standard Node.js application doesn't automatically take advantage of multiple CPU cores. We have already gone through the event loop in the previous chapter.

Child Processes

A child process in Node.js is a new process created by the main application process. This new process can run concurrently with the main process, allowing for parallel execution of tasks. Here are some of the use cases:

- **CPU-bound Tasks:** For CPU-intensive operations, child processes ensure that the main event loop isn't blocked, maintaining the application's responsiveness.
- **Executing Shell Commands:** They allow Node.js to execute shell commands, run scripts, or invoke executables.
- **Separation of Concerns:** Different tasks can be isolated in separate processes, improving manageability and security.

Creating and Managing Child Processes

In Node.js, the **`child_process`** module is a built-in module used to spawn new processes. It provides various ways to create and manage child processes. The four primary methods provided by this module are **`spawn()`**, **`exec()`**, **`execFile()`**, and **`fork()`**. Each of these methods serves different use cases and has its own set of features.

`spawn()`

It is used to launch a new process with a given command. It's particularly suited for processes that return large amounts of data, as it streams the data through buffers. This method doesn't create a shell to execute the command, making it slightly more efficient than **`exec()`** in terms of resource usage. This is ideal for tasks that need to process large volumes of data in real time, such as reading from a file or querying a database.

Here is a simple example of creating a child process and the output when we run it.

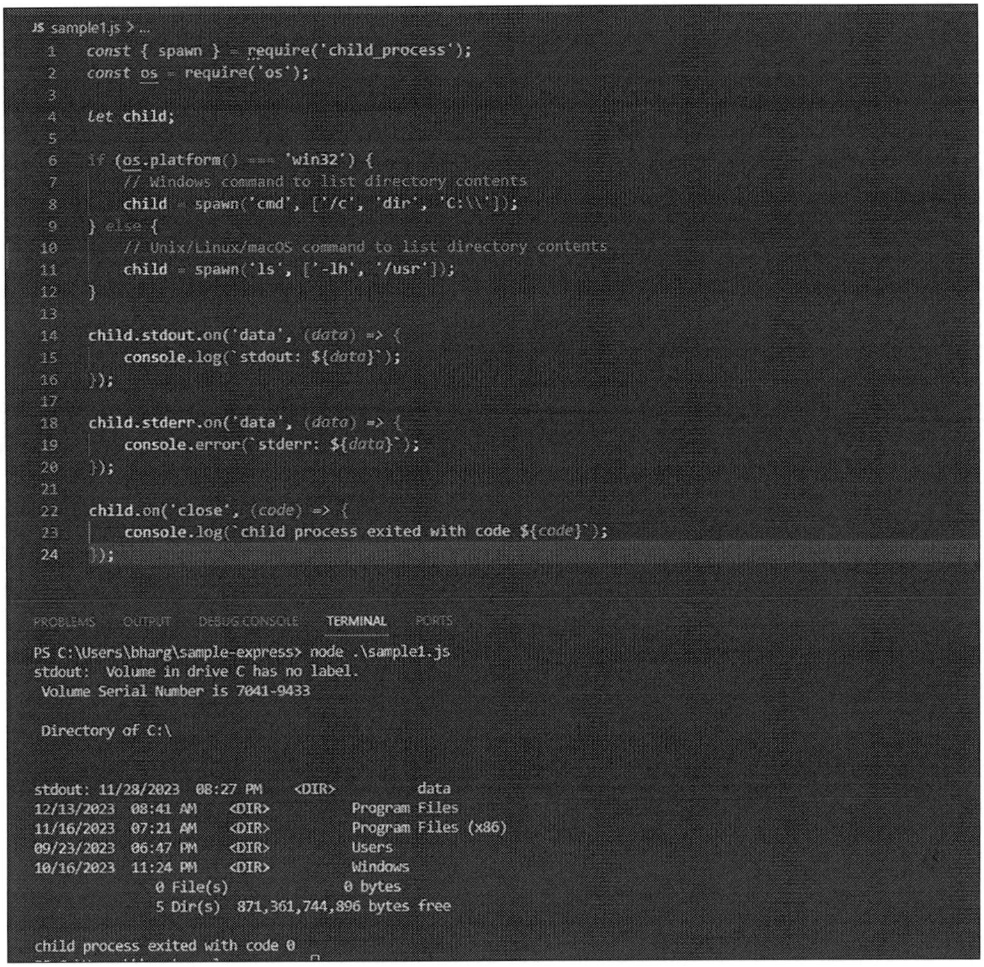

Figure 4.6: *Spawn example*

We first import the **`os`**module to detect the operating system. Then, we use an if-else statement to determine the command to run based on the operating system. For Windows, we use **`cmd /c dir C:\\`** to list the contents of the C drive. For Unix-like systems, we retain the original **`ls -lh /usr`** command.

`exec()`

It is used to execute a command in a shell and buffer the output. It returns the whole output at once after the command execution is complete. This is useful for running shell commands, but it's not suitable for commands that produce large amounts of output as it buffers the output. This is ideal for running shell scripts or commands that do not generate a lot of output.

Here is a simple example of creating a child process and the output when we run it.

```
JS sample1.js > ...
const { exec } = require('child_process');
const os = require('os');

// Determine the command based on the operating system
const command = os.platform() === 'win32' ? 'cd' : 'pwd';

exec(command, (error, stdout, stderr) => {
    if (error) {
        console.error(`exec error: ${error}`);
        return;
    }
    console.log(`Current directory: ${stdout}`);
    if (stderr) {
        console.error(`stderr: ${stderr}`);
    }
});

PROBLEMS   OUTPUT   DEBUG CONSOLE   TERMINAL   PORTS

PS C:\Users\bharg\sample-express> node .\sample1.js
Current directory: C:\Users\bharg\sample-express
```

Figure 4.7: *exec example*

We import the required modules: **child_process** for executing the command and **os** to determine the operating system. The command is set to **cd** if the platform is Windows (**win32**), and **pwd** for other operating systems. The **exec** function runs the command. If there's an error, it logs the error message. Otherwise, it prints the current directory path. Any standard error output (**stderr**) is also logged.

execFile()

It is similar to **exec()** but runs a specific file directly without spawning a shell. It's more efficient than **exec()** and should be used when you don't need a shell's features (like shell piping). It is suitable for running executables or scripts without shell overhead.

Here is a simple example of creating a child process and the output when we run it.

```
JS sample1.js > ...
const { execFile } = require('child_process');

execFile('script.sh', (error, stdout, stderr) => {
  if (error) {
    throw error;
  }
  console.log(stdout);
});
```

Figure 4.8: *execFile example*

This code snippet uses the **execFile** function from the **child_process** module to execute an external shell script named **script.sh**. The **execFile** function is designed to run a specified file directly as a new process, which can be more efficient than a shell command. In this code:

- **execFile('script.sh', callback):** It attempts to execute **script.sh**. When the execution completes, a callback function is called.
- **callback(error, stdout, stderr):** This function is executed after **script.sh** runs. It receives any error that occurred, the standard output **(stdout)**, and the standard error output **(stderr)** from the script.
- **Error Handling:** If an error occurs during the execution of the script (like the file not found or execution errors within the script), it's thrown and can be handled appropriately.

fork()

fork() is a special case of **spawn()** that creates Node.js child processes. The primary use case for **fork()**is to create a separate V8 instance for running heavy JavaScript tasks in parallel. It also provides a built-in IPC (Inter-Process Communication) channel to communicate between the parent and child processes. This is ideal for running heavy Node.js scripts in parallel and when communication between the parent and child process is required.

Here is a simple example of creating a child process and the output when we run it.

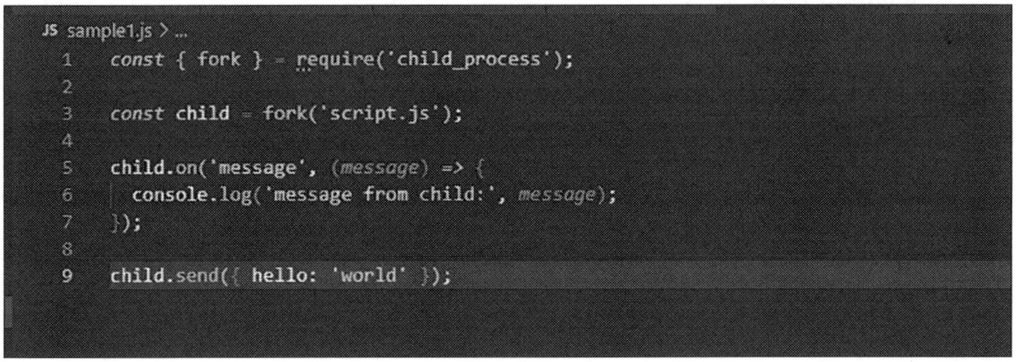

Figure 4.9: *fork example*

The preceding code uses the **fork** method from the **child_process** module to create a child process that runs a separate script (**script.js**). It demonstrates inter-process communication (IPC) between the parent and child processes:

- The **fork** method spawns a new Node.js process executing **script.js**. This child process runs independently but can communicate with the parent process.

- The parent sets up an event listener (`child.on('message', ...)`) to handle messages sent from the child process. When a message is received, it's logged to the console.
- The parent sends a message (`child.send({ hello: 'world' })`) to the child process, which the child can respond to or process accordingly.

In Node.js, child processes and clustering are powerful tools for optimizing the performance and scalability of applications. While child processes are great for offloading CPU-bound tasks and executing separate operations, clustering allows applications to run across multiple CPU cores, enhancing performance and reliability. However, it's important to understand the complexities and best practices associated with these features to effectively leverage them in your applications.

Cluster Module

The cluster module in Node.js allows you to create multiple worker processes that share the same server port. It enables the setup of a master-worker architecture, where the master process can distribute incoming network connections among the worker processes.

Here are some of the benefits of the Cluster Module:

- **Full Utilization of CPU Cores**: By spawning multiple instances of the application across different CPU cores, clustering maximizes resource utilization.
- **Improved Reliability:** If one worker dies, others continue to handle requests, enhancing fault tolerance.

Implementing Cluster

Implementing a cluster in Node.js involves using the `cluster` module to create multiple worker processes, which can handle server requests concurrently. This approach is particularly beneficial for taking advantage of multi-core systems and enhancing the performance and reliability of Node.js applications. Let's implement a cluster module.

- **Master Process:** The master process is responsible for initiating worker processes and managing them. It doesn't handle actual client requests but focuses on monitoring and controlling the workers.
- **Worker Processes:** These are the child processes created by the master process. Each worker runs an instance of the Node.js application and handles client requests.

Here is the implementation of the sample code and output of it.

It starts by importing necessary modules - `cluster` for managing child processes, `http` for creating a server, and `os` for determining the number of CPU cores.

- **Master Process Logic:** The script first checks if it's running in the master process. If so, it logs that the master process is running and then forks worker processes equal to the number of CPU cores. It also sets an event listener to log a message whenever any worker process exits, which is useful for monitoring and potentially restarting workers.
- **Worker Process Logic:** If the current process is a worker (not the master), it logs that the worker process is running. Each worker creates an HTTP server that listens on port 8000 and responds with '`Hello world`' for every request.

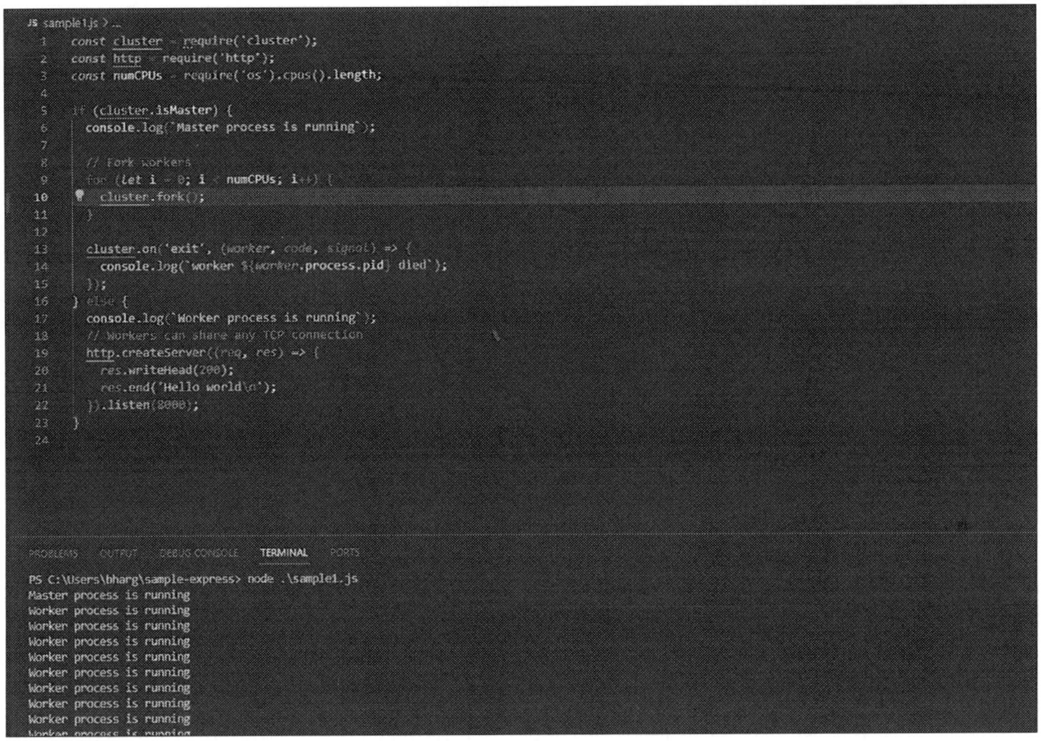

Figure 4.10: *cluster example*

As you can see from the output, this setup allows the application to handle more requests simultaneously by utilizing all available CPU cores, making it well-suited for high-load environments.

REPL

Node.js REPL (Read-Eval-Print Loop) is an interactive shell that processes Node.js expressions. The environment allows for quick testing, debugging, and experimenting with Node.js code. REPL is a powerful tool in a developer's toolkit for trying out Node.js snippets without having to create a full-fledged application.

To start the REPL, simply run **node** without any arguments in your command line interface. This action initiates an interactive shell where you can type and execute Node.js code.

Figure 4.11: *REPL example*

Core features of Node.js REPL are as follows:

- **Read:** REPL reads the input provided by the user. It parses the input into JavaScript data structures and then stores it in memory.
- **Eval:** REPL evaluates the parsed JavaScript data structures. It executes the code and returns the result. This feature is particularly useful for quick calculations or executing functions.
- **Print:** After evaluating the input, REPL prints the result onto the user's console. This immediate feedback is useful for learning and debugging.
- **Loop:** REPL loops back to the reading phase after executing the code. This loop continues until the user exits the REPL session, allowing continuous interaction.

Advanced Usage of Core REPL

This section delves into various ways to customize Node.js REPL, making it more powerful and tailored to specific development needs.

Accessing and Modifying REPL

Node.js provides the `repl` module, which is the key to customizing the REPL environment. You can create a customized REPL instance programmatically using this module.

First, import the `repl` module and start a new REPL instance:

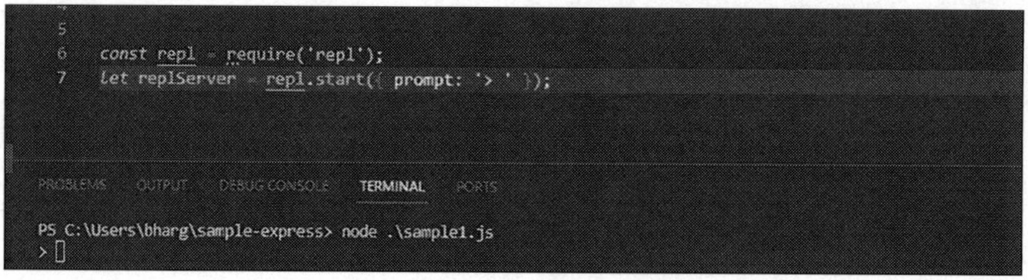

Figure 4.12: *Accessing repl*

Here, **`repl.start()`** initializes a new REPL server, and you can customize the prompt by passing an options object.

Customizing the REPL Environment

You can set a custom prompt to make your REPL instance more distinctive:

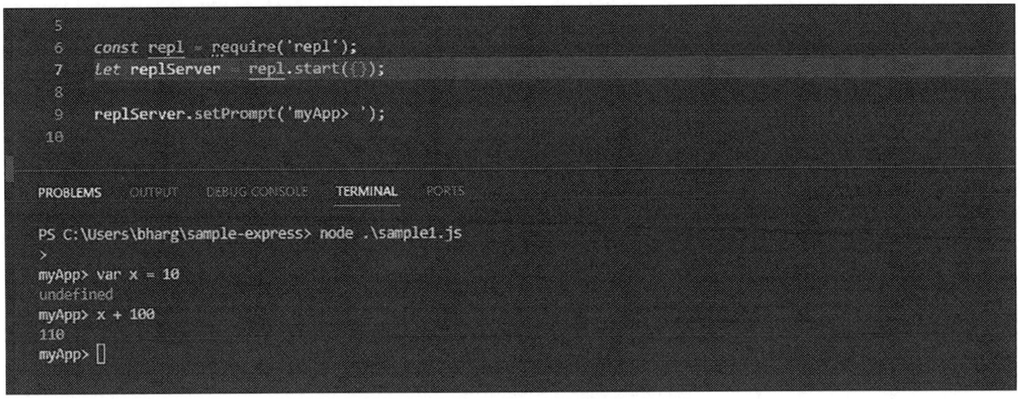

Figure 4.13: *Setting prompt*

Adding Custom Commands

Node.js REPL allows adding custom commands, which can execute specific functions. In this example, typing **`.sayhello`** followed by a name prints a personalized greeting.

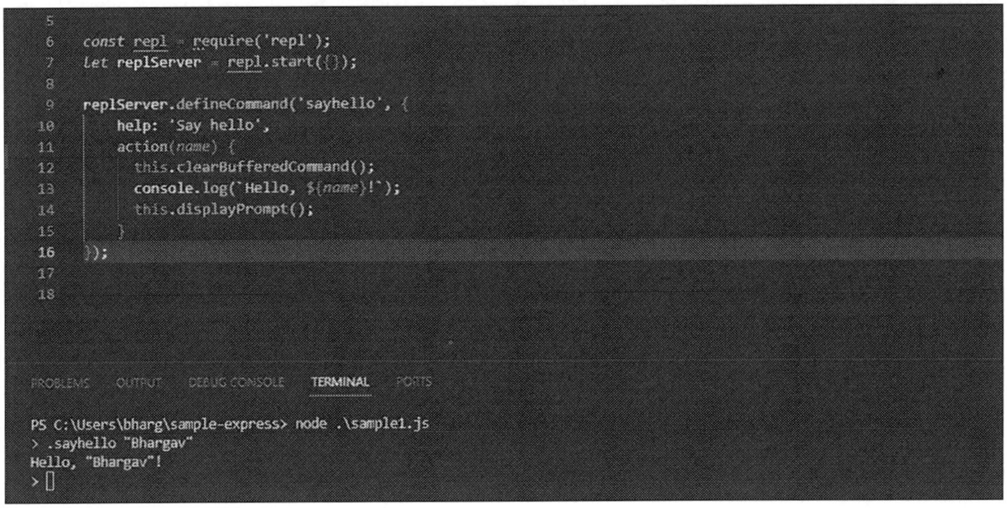

Figure 4.14: *Adding custom commands*

Adding Custom variables and Functions

You can inject custom variables or functions into the REPL context. Now, the **add** function can be used directly in the REPL. We don't have to define this function again.

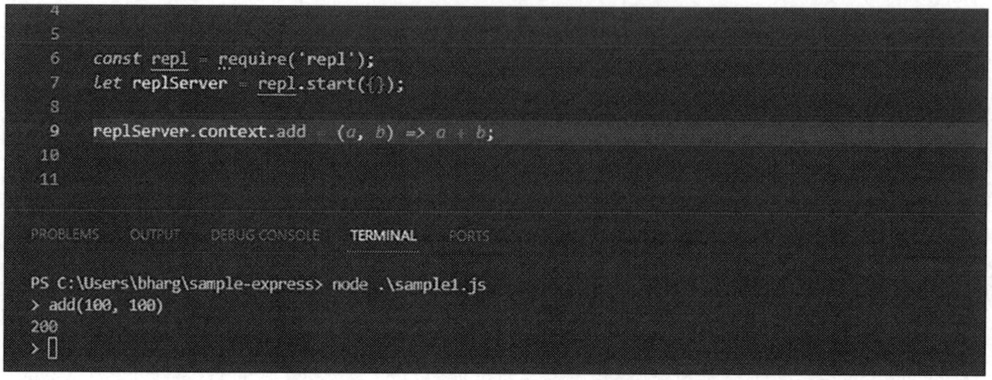

***Figure 4.15**: Custom variables and functions*

Saving and Loading Sessions

REPL sessions can be saved to and loaded from a file, which is useful for persisting state or preparing pre-configured environments.

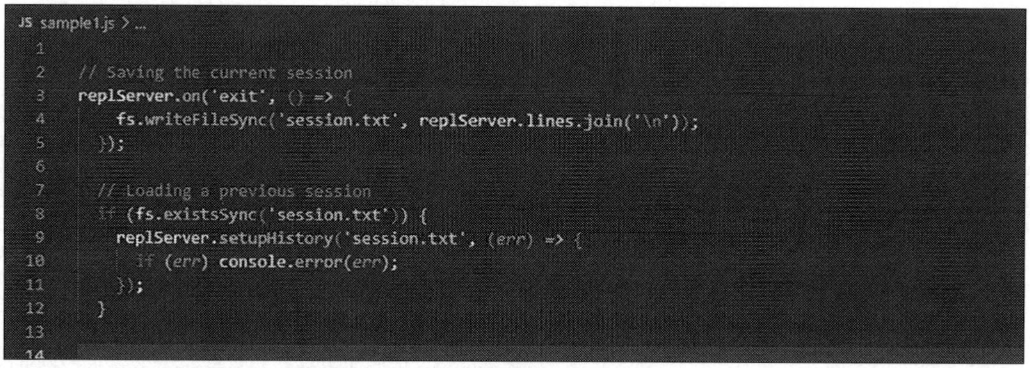

***Figure 4.16**: Saving and loading sessions*

Customizing Node.js REPL can significantly boost productivity and make the development process more efficient. Whether it's by adding custom commands, handling asynchronous operations, or persisting sessions, these customizations can adapt the REPL to fit specific workflows. With the **`repl`** module, the possibilities for customization are extensive, enabling developers to create a uniquely tailored interactive programming environment.

Streams

Node.js streams are an essential part of the platform, enabling efficient handling of data flows. They are powerful tools for reading and writing data in a continuous flow, rather than loading it all at once into memory. This section will explore Node.js streams in-depth, covering their types, usage, and practical applications.

Streams are collections of data that might not be available all at once and don't need to fit in memory. This makes streams a powerful abstraction for handling large amounts of data, like files or network transmissions.

Types of Streams

Node.js offers four primary types of streams, including:

- **Readable Streams**: These are streams from which data can be read. Example: reading data from a file.
- **Writable Streams:** These streams allow data to be written to them. Example: writing data to a file.
- **Duplex Streams:** These can both read and write data. For example, a TCP socket.
- **Transform Streams:** A type of duplex stream where the output is computed from the input. Example: a Zlib compression stream.

Readable Streams

In Node.js, readable streams is an essential construct, part of the Streams API, which is used for reading data sequentially. Understanding how to work with readable streams is crucial for efficiently handling large amounts of data, such as files, network communications, or any data source that can be consumed in chunks.

Readable streams in Node.js are abstractions for a source from which data can be consumed. They follow the producer-consumer model, where the stream (producer) generates data that the consumer can then process. Unlike traditional methods that require loading the entire data into memory, streams allow you to process data in smaller chunks, optimizing memory usage and enhancing performance.

Types of Readable Streams

Readable streams can operate in following two modes:

- **Flowing Mode (Non-Paused):** Data is read from the source automatically and provided to the application as soon as it's available.
- **Paused Mode (Buffered):** The stream reads data from the source and stores it in an internal buffer. The application must explicitly command the stream to send data.

Creating a Readable Stream

Node.js provides various ways to create a readable stream. The most common method is through the File System (`fs`) module, which allows you to read data from files.

```
JS sample1.js > ...

const fs = require('fs');
const readableStream = fs.createReadStream('example.txt');
```

Figure 4.17: *Creating a readable stream*

Consuming Data from Readable Streams

Readable streams emit events that make it possible to handle the reading process effectively.

- **`data`:** Emitted when data is available to read.
- **`end`:** Emitted when there is no more data to read.
- **`error`:** Emitted in case of any error during reading data.

Here is the complete example of using readable streams with an example:

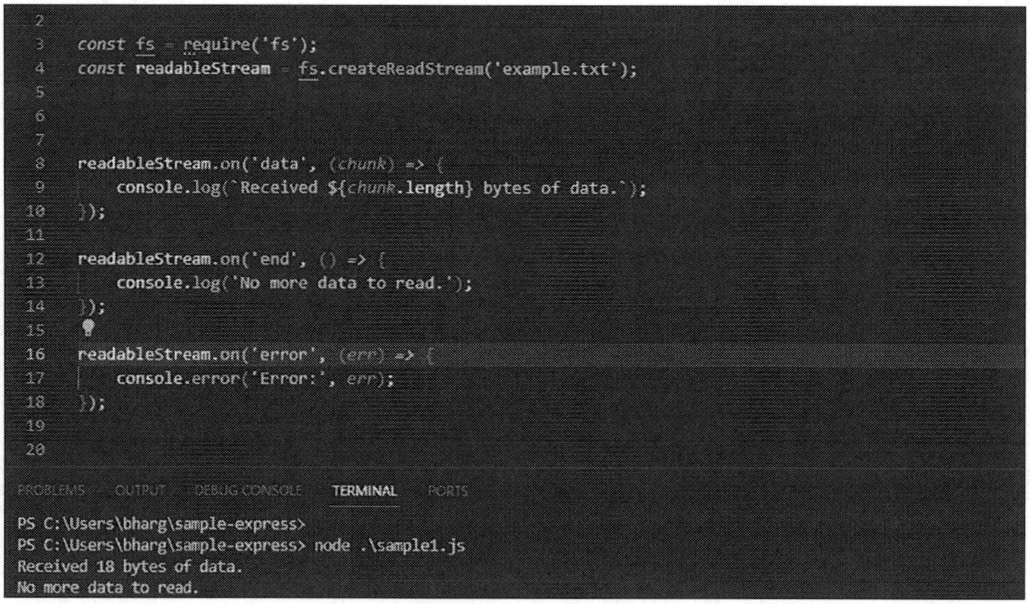

```
const fs = require('fs');
const readableStream = fs.createReadStream('example.txt');



readableStream.on('data', (chunk) => {
    console.log(`Received ${chunk.length} bytes of data.`);
});

readableStream.on('end', () => {
    console.log('No more data to read.');
});

readableStream.on('error', (err) => {
    console.error('Error:', err);
});
```

```
PROBLEMS   OUTPUT   DEBUG CONSOLE   TERMINAL   PORTS

PS C:\Users\bharg\sample-express>
PS C:\Users\bharg\sample-express> node .\sample1.js
Received 18 bytes of data.
No more data to read.
```

Figure 4.18: *Consuming streams*

Streams start in paused mode. When a **`'data'`** event handler is added, they switch to flowing mode. To pause a stream, you use **`readable.pause()`**, and to resume, you use **`readable.resume()`**.

Here are some of the practical use cases:

- **File Processing**: Efficiently reading large files.
- **HTTP Requests:** Handling incoming request data in web servers.
- **Data Streaming**: Real-time data processing, like log file monitoring.

Readable Streams are a powerful feature in Node.js, offering an efficient way to handle data reading operations. By breaking down data into manageable chunks and allowing for asynchronous processing, they provide a means to build high-performance and scalable applications, especially those dealing with large datasets or requiring real-time data processing.

Writable Streams

Writable streams in Node.js form a core component of the Stream API, which is crucial for handling write operations efficiently. They allow for writing data sequentially in chunks, making them ideal for handling large data transfers without overwhelming memory. This section offers an in-depth look at writable streams, their mechanisms, and practical implementations.

Writable streams are abstractions representing destinations to which data can be written. This could be a file, a network socket, or even another stream. The key advantage of writable streams is their ability to handle data incrementally, thereby optimizing resource usage and improving performance for large data writes.

Types of Writable Streams

Like readable streams, writable streams operate in two primary modes, including:

- **Buffered Mode:** Data written to the stream is buffered until the underlying system is ready to handle more.
- **Drain Mode:** If the stream's buffer becomes full, it will temporarily stop accepting data until it is emptied again (drained).

Creating a Writable Stream

One common way to create a writable stream in Node.js is through the File System (`fs`) module, used for writing data to files.

```
const fs = require('fs');
const writableStream = fs.createWriteStream('output.txt');
```

Figure 4.19: *Creating a writable stream*

The following code demonstrates the process of writing data to a file using a writable stream, part of the File System (**fs**) module. It begins by importing the **fs** module and creating a writable stream that points to **output.txt**. This stream is used to write data to the specified file.

The code then attempts to write the string **'Hello, World!\n'** to **output.txt** through the stream. After the write operation, it checks if the stream's internal buffer is full, which is indicated by the **write** method returning **false**. If the buffer is indeed full, a message stating **'Stream is full. Waiting for drain.'** is logged, indicating that the stream cannot accept more data until some of it is flushed to the file.

To handle this situation, known as backpressure, the code listens for the **drain** event. This event is emitted when the buffer has been emptied, meaning more data can be written to the stream. Upon the emission of this event, the code logs **'Buffer drained. Can write more data.'**, signaling that it is safe to resume writing data to the stream.

Finally, the code concludes by calling **writableStream.end()**, which closes the stream. This method is used to signal that no more data will be written to the stream, allowing Node.js to finalize the write operation and properly close the file.

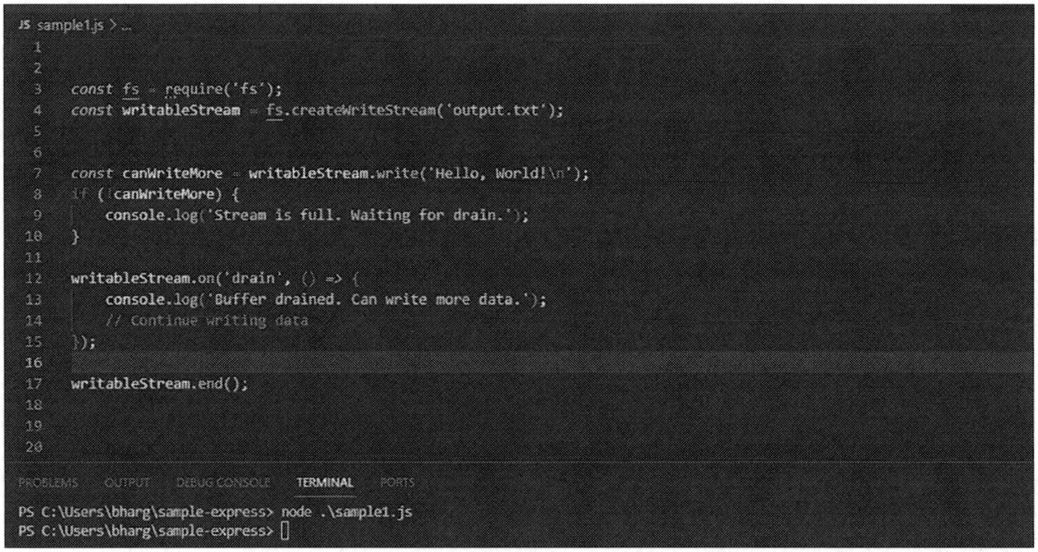

Figure 4.20: *Writable stream*

Here are some of the practical use cases:

- **File Operations:** Writing data to files, especially larger files.
- **Network Communication:** Sending data over HTTP or TCP/IP protocols.
- **Logging:** Writing logs to files in real-time.

Writable streams are a fundamental part of Node.js, providing a robust and efficient way to handle writing operations. They play a critical role in applications that require handling large data outputs, offering a way to manage such operations with minimal memory footprint and optimal resource utilization.

Duplex Streams

In Node.js, duplex streams are a special type of stream that can both read data (like a readable stream) and write data (like a writable stream). They are part of the core stream module and are particularly useful in scenarios where a continuous two-way communication is required, like in the TCP sockets or file transformations. Duplex streams combine the functionalities of both Readable and Writable streams. This dual capability makes them versatile for various applications.

Key characteristics of duplex streams are:

- **Two-way Communication**: They can handle both incoming and outgoing data streams simultaneously.
- **Independent Channels:** The read and write channels operate independently. The state of one does not affect the state of the other.

Creating Duplex Streams

Creating duplex streams in Node.js involves using the `Duplex` class from the `stream`module. A duplex stream is a type of stream that can both read data (like a readable stream) and write data (like a writable stream), making it suitable for scenarios where two-way data processing is needed.

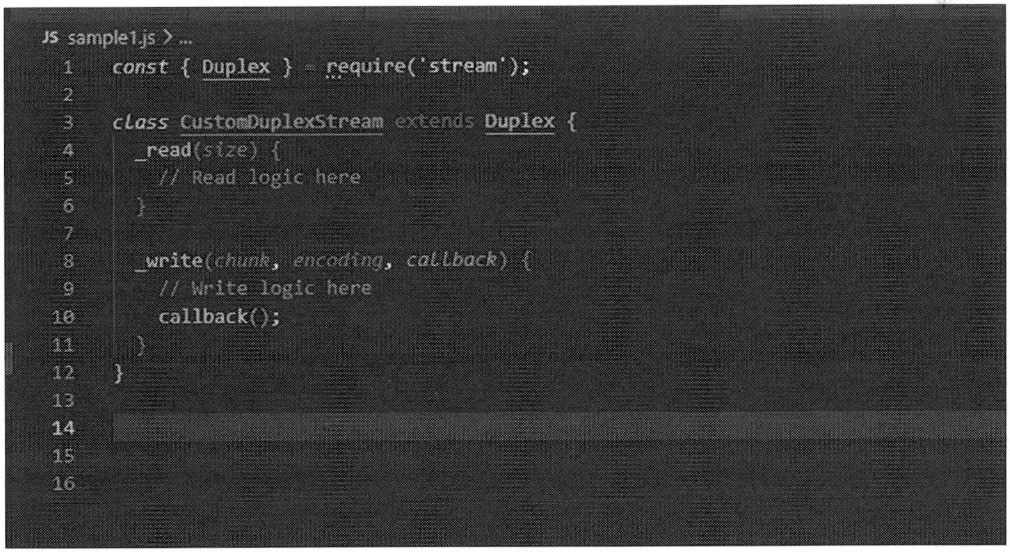

```
JS sample1.js > ...
const { Duplex } = require('stream');

class CustomDuplexStream extends Duplex {
  _read(size) {
    // Read logic here
  }

  _write(chunk, encoding, callback) {
    // Write logic here
    callback();
  }
}
```

Figure 4.21: *Creating a duplex stream*

In the custom class, you implement the **_read** and **_write** methods, which handle the read and write functionalities, respectively.

Reading from Duplex Streams

Reading from a duplex stream is like reading from a readable stream. You listen to events like **data** and **end** to process incoming data.

```
duplexStream.on('data', (chunk) => {
    console.log(`Received: ${chunk.toString()}`);
});

duplexStream.on('end', () => {
    console.log('No more data to read.');
});
```

Figure 4.22: *Duplex stream*

Writing to Duplex Streams

Writing to a duplex stream is analogous to writing to a writable stream. You use the **write** method to send data.

```
duplexStream.write('Hello, World!');
duplexStream.end();  // Close the stream
```

Figure 4.23: *Duplex stream*

Handling Backpressure

Backpressure management is crucial in duplex streams to balance the read and write operations, ensuring that neither side overwhelms the other.

- Monitor the drain event to know when the buffer is empty and it's safe to write more data.
- Use flow control methods like **pause()** and **resume()** to manage the data flow.

Error Handling and Cleanup

Error handling in duplex streams involves listening to the **error** event. Additionally, ensure proper cleanup of resources when the stream ends or encounters an error.

```

duplexStream.on('error', (err) => {
    console.error('Stream error:', err);
});

```

Figure 4.24: *Handling error*

Here are some of the practical use cases:

- **TCP Socket Communication:** Duplex streams handle bidirectional communication over TCP sockets.
- **File Transformations:** Useful in scenarios where a file needs to be read, transformed, and written back, like in compression or encryption tasks.
- **Proxy Servers:** Duplex streams implement proxy servers where incoming data needs to be processed and relayed.

Duplex streams in Node.js offer a powerful way to handle two-way data processing tasks. Their ability to read and write data makes them suitable for a wide range of applications, especially those requiring real-time data handling and transformations. Understanding and effectively utilizing duplex streams can significantly enhance the capabilities of Node.js applications in handling complex data flow scenarios.

Transform Streams

Transform streams in Node.js represent a special type of duplex stream that can modify or transform data as it is written and read. They are an integral part of the Stream API, serving a crucial role in a wide range of applications where data needs to be transformed during the streaming process.

A transform stream is a type of duplex stream but with a distinct characteristic: it applies a transformation to the data as it passes through the stream. This makes them particularly useful for tasks, such as compression, encryption, or modifying data formats.

Here are some of the key characteristics:

- **Data Transformation:** They allow you to modify data as it flows through the stream.
- **Dual Nature:** Like duplex streams, transform streams can both read and write data. However, the output is directly related to the input.

Creating Transform Streams

You can create a transform stream by extending the **Transform** class from the **stream** module. This requires implementing the **_transform** method, which handles the transformation logic.

```
const { Transform } = require('stream');

class CustomTransformStream extends Transform {
    _transform(chunk, encoding, callback) {
        // Transformation logic here
        this.push(transformedChunk);
        callback();
    }
}
```

Figure 4.25: *Creating transform stream*

In the **_transform** method, **chunk** is the data to be transformed, and **callback** is a function that you call when the transformation for the current chunk is complete.

Using Transform Streams

Suppose you want to create a stream that converts all incoming data to uppercase.

```
class UppercaseTransformStream extends Transform {
    _transform(chunk, encoding, callback) {
        const uppercased = chunk.toString().toUpperCase();
        this.push(uppercased);
        callback();
    }
}
```

Figure 4.26: *Transform streams*

You can then use this stream in a pipeline.

```
const upperCaseTr = new UppercaseTransformStream();
process.stdin.pipe(upperCaseTr).pipe(process.stdout);
```

Figure 4.27: *Use streams in a pipeline*

This setup takes input from the standard input (**`process.stdin`**), transforms it using **`UppercaseTransformStream`**, and writes it to the standard output (**`process.stdout`**).

Just like other streams, transform streams must also handle backpressure. This involves monitoring how much data is buffered and pausing the input if necessary.

Error Handling

Error handling in transform streams is critical. Listen to the **`error`** event to capture and handle any errors during the transformation process.

```
transformStream.on('error', (err) => {
    console.error('Error in Transform Stream:', err);
});
```

Figure 4.28: *Error handling*

Here are some of the practical use cases:

- **Data Compression/Decompression:** Implementing gzip or other compression formats.
- **Data Encryption/Decryption:** For secure data transmission.
- **Parsing or Formatting Data:** Similar to converting CSV to JSON.

Transform streams in Node.js offers a powerful and flexible way to handle data transformations in streaming processes. They are, particularly useful in scenarios where data needs to be modified on the fly, such as in real-time data processing or streaming file manipulations. Understanding and effectively utilizing transform streams can greatly enhance the capabilities of Node.js applications in managing complex data transformation tasks.

Working With File System

Node.js provides a powerful and versatile module, **`fs`** for interacting with the file system. This module is crucial for reading from and writing to files, making directory manipulations and handling various file system operations. This section explores the capabilities of the **`fs`** module in Node.js and demonstrates how to work with files and directories effectively.

The **`fs`** module in Node.js is a core module that provides a lot of functionalities for accessing and interacting with the file system. It can be used for operations, such as reading files, writing files, creating directories, and more.

Synchronous versus Asynchronous

The `fs` module in Node.js offers two types of methods for interacting with the file system: synchronous and asynchronous. Understanding the differences between these methods is crucial for effective Node.js programming.

Asynchronous Methods

Asynchronous methods in the `fs` module perform non-blocking operations. They allow Node.js to continue executing other code while the file operation is being processed. Callback functions are used to handle the results of these operations.

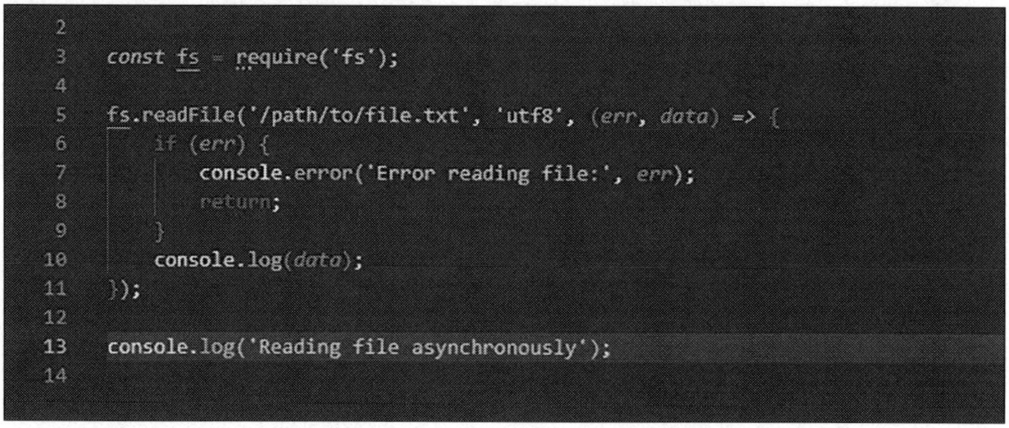

Figure 4.29: *Asynchronous file reading*

In this example, `fs.readFile` is used to read a file asynchronously. The program doesn't wait for the file read to complete and immediately executes the next line of code (`console.log ('Reading file asynchronously')`). When the file read is complete, the callback function is invoked with the file data or an error.

Synchronous Methods

Synchronous methods, on the other hand, block the Node.js event loop until the operation completes. The program execution waits for the file operation to finish before moving to the next line of code. These methods usually end with `Sync`.

```
const fs = require('fs');

try {
    const data = fs.readFileSync('/path/to/file.txt', 'utf8');
    console.log(data);
} catch (err) {
    console.error('Error reading file:', err);
}

console.log('Reading file synchronously');
```

Figure 4.30: *Synchronous file reading*

Here, **`fs.readFileSync`** reads a file synchronously. The program execution will wait at this line until the entire file is read. Only after the read operation completes, the next line of code (**`console.log ('Reading file synchronously')`**) is executed.

Choosing Between Synchronous and Asynchronous Methods

- **Asynchronous Methods** are generally preferred in a Node.js environment, especially for I/O-bound operations. They adhere to Node.js's non-blocking philosophy, allowing for better performance and scalability.
- **Synchronous Methods** can be simpler to write and understand, making them sometimes more suitable for scripts or simple applications where the blocking nature does not pose a problem. They are also commonly used during the initial setup phase of an application, where asynchronous operations might complicate the startup sequence.

The choice between synchronous and asynchronous methods in the **`fs`** module should be based on the specific needs of your application and the context in which these methods are used. Asynchronous methods align with Node.js's non-blocking model and are typically better suited for most applications, whereas synchronous methods might be appropriate for certain scenarios where simplicity and sequential operation are more important than non-blocking I/O.

Reading and Writing Files

To read a file in Node.js, you have two primary options using the **`fs`** (File System) module: **`fs.readFile`** for asynchronous file reading and **`fs.readFileSync`** for synchronous file reading. The choice between these two methods depends on how you wish to handle I/O operations within your application.

```javascript

const fs = require('fs');

// Asynchronous read
fs.readFile('/path/to/file.txt', 'utf8', (err, data) => {
    if (err) throw err;
    console.log(data);
});

// Synchronous read
const data = fs.readFileSync('/path/to/file.txt', 'utf8');
console.log(data);



```

Figure 4.31: *reading files*

Similarly, when you need to write data to a file, the **`fs`** module provides two primary methods: **`fs.writeFile`** for asynchronous writing, and **`fs.writeFileSync`** for synchronous writing. The choice between these two methods depends on how you manage I/O operations in your application.

JS sample1.js > fs.writeFile('/path/to/output.txt', 'utf8') callback

```javascript
const content = "Hello, World!";

// Asynchronous write
fs.writeFile('/path/to/output.txt', content, 'utf8', (err) => {
    if (err) throw err;
    console.log('File written successfully');
});

// Synchronous write
fs.writeFileSync('/path/to/output.txt', content, 'utf8');
console.log('File written successfully');

```

Figure 4.32: *writing files*

Working With Directories

When you need to create new directories, the **`fs`** module provides two methods: **`fs.mkdir`** for asynchronous creation and **`fs.mkdirSync`** for synchronous creation. Each method serves a different use case depending on how you manage file system operations in your application.

```
// Asynchronous directory creation
fs.mkdir('/path/to/newDir', (err) => {
    if (err) throw err;
    console.log('Directory created');
});

// Synchronous directory creation
fs.mkdirSync('/path/to/newDir');
console.log('Directory created');
```

Figure 4.33: *making directories*

When you need to read the contents of a directory, such as listing all files and subdirectories within it, you can use the **`fs`** module's **`fs.readdir`** for asynchronous operations or **`fs.readdirSync`** for synchronous operations. Each method is suited to different scenarios depending on the requirements of your application.

```
// Asynchronous
fs.readdir('/path/to/dir', (err, files) => {
    if (err) throw err;
    console.log(files);  // Array of file names
});

// Synchronous
const files = fs.readdirSync('/path/to/dir');
console.log(files);  // Array of file names
```

Figure 4.34: *reading directories*

File Streams

When dealing with large files in Node.js, using streams, specifically **`fs.createReadStream`** for reading files and **`fs.createWriteStream`** for writing files, offers a more memory-efficient approach compared to reading or writing the entire file content at once. This section elaborates on why and how streams are advantageous in such scenarios.

Reading or writing large files in a single operation can be highly memory intensive. When you attempt to read a large file using **`fs.readFile`** or write using **`fs.writeFile`**, the entire file content is loaded into memory. This leads to significant memory usage, which is inefficient and causes performance issues, especially in environments with limited memory resources.

```
const readStream = fs.createReadStream('/path/to/largeFile.txt');
const writeStream = fs.createWriteStream('/path/to/output.txt');

readStream.pipe(writeStream);
```

Figure 4.35: *file streams*

Streams in Node.js offer a solution to this problem by processing data in chunks, rather than loading the entire file into memory at once.

Advantages of Using Streams for Large Files

- **Reduced Memory Usage**: Streams significantly reduce memory usage by handling data in smaller chunks instead of loading everything into memory.
- **Increased Efficiency:** Allows data processing to start immediately as the first chunk is available, rather than waiting for the entire data set to be ready.
- **Better Performance:** Helps in enhancing overall performance for larger files as they prevent memory bottlenecks and allow smoother data processing.
- **Scalability:** More scalable streaming data, especially in environments where resources are limited or when dealing with multiple large files simultaneously.

Node.js's `fs` module is a comprehensive toolset for working with the file system. Understanding its synchronous and asynchronous methods, along with streams for handling large files is essential for developing robust Node.js applications. Whether it's for reading configuration files, writing logs, or managing directories, the `fs`module provides the necessary functionalities to interact with the file system efficiently and effectively.

Understanding Events

Node.js is designed around an event-driven architecture where various objects can emit events and listeners or callbacks can respond to these events. This model is fundamental to Node.js's non-blocking, asynchronous nature and is extensively used in handling all sorts of asynchronous operations. Understanding events and the `EventEmitter` class is crucial for working effectively with Node.js.

At the core of Node.js's event system is the `EventEmitter` class, a part of the `events` module. This class is the key to working with events in Node.js, as it provides the functionality to emit and listen to events. Most of the built-in Node.js modules, such as streams and the HTTP server, inherit from `EventEmitter`.

Creating a `EventEmitter`

The following code demonstrates the initialization of Node.js's event-driven architecture using the **`EventEmitter`** class from the **`events`** module. This class is fundamental to creating and managing custom events in a Node.js application.

```
JS sample1.js > ...
const EventEmitter = require('events');

const myEmitter = new EventEmitter();
```

Figure 4.36: *Creating an event emitter*

The second line creates a new instance of **`EventEmitter`** named **`myEmitter`**. This instance can now be used to emit and listen to custom events in your application.

Working With Events

In Node.js, the **`EventEmitter`** class handles events in an asynchronous, event-driven architecture. This concept is central to many Node.js applications, from handling HTTP server requests to streaming data. Let's delve deeper to know how events are identified and handled in this system.

Emitting Events

You can emit events using the **`emit`** method passing the event name and any data you want to pass to the listeners:

```
myEmitter.emit('event', { name: 'some event name' });
```

Figure 4.37: *Emitting an event*

Listening for Events

Listeners are functions that are called whenever the specified event is emitted. You can add listeners using the **`on`** or **`once`** methods:

- **`on`** adds a listener for the event. The listener will be invoked every time the event is emitted.

```
myEmitter.on('event', (data) => {
    console.log('An event occurred!', data);
});
```

Figure 4.38: *Listening with on method*

- **`once`** adds a one-time listener for the event. The listener is invoked only the first time the event is emitted.

```
myEmitter.once('event', (data) => {
    console.log('This will only listen once', data);
});
```

Figure 4.39: *Listening with once method*

Error Handling Events

It's crucial to handle errors correctly when working with events. By default, if an error event is emitted and there are no listeners attached, Node.js will print a stack trace and exit. To prevent this behavior, attach an error listener to your **`EventEmitter`** instances:

```
myEmitter.on('error', (err) => {
    console.error('An error occurred:', err);
});
```

Figure 4.40: *Error Handling*

Removing Listeners

You can remove specific listeners or all listeners for a given event using the **`removeListener`** or **`removeAllListeners`** methods:

```
// Remove a specific listener
myEmitter.removeListener('event', listenerFunction);

// Remove all listeners for 'event'
myEmitter.removeAllListeners('event');
```

Figure 4.41: *Removing events*

Here are some of the practical use cases:

- **Handling HTTP requests** in a web server.
- **Stream handling** where data and end events signal when data is available and when the stream ends.
- **Managing custom asynchronous operations** in applications, where various parts of the app might emit and listen to custom events.
- **File System** operations can emit events for reading and writing asynchronously.

Understanding and effectively utilizing events and the `EventEmitter` class is fundamental to Node.js programming. It allows the creation of highly scalable and efficient applications that can respond to a multitude of asynchronous scenarios. Mastery of events will undoubtedly enhance your ability to develop robust Node.js applications.

HTTP Module

Node.js includes a built-in module called `http` that allows you to create HTTP servers and clients. This module is fundamental for building web applications, RESTful APIs, and interacting with other web services. Understanding the HTTP module is crucial for web development with Node.js.

Creating an HTTP Server

The primary use of the HTTP module is to create an HTTP server that listens to server ports and gives a response back to the client.

Basic Server Setup

Here is the code to create a basic HTTP Server. In this example, `http.createServer()` is used to create a new HTTP server. The server is set to listen on port 3000. Every time a request is made to this server, it responds with `"Hello World"`.

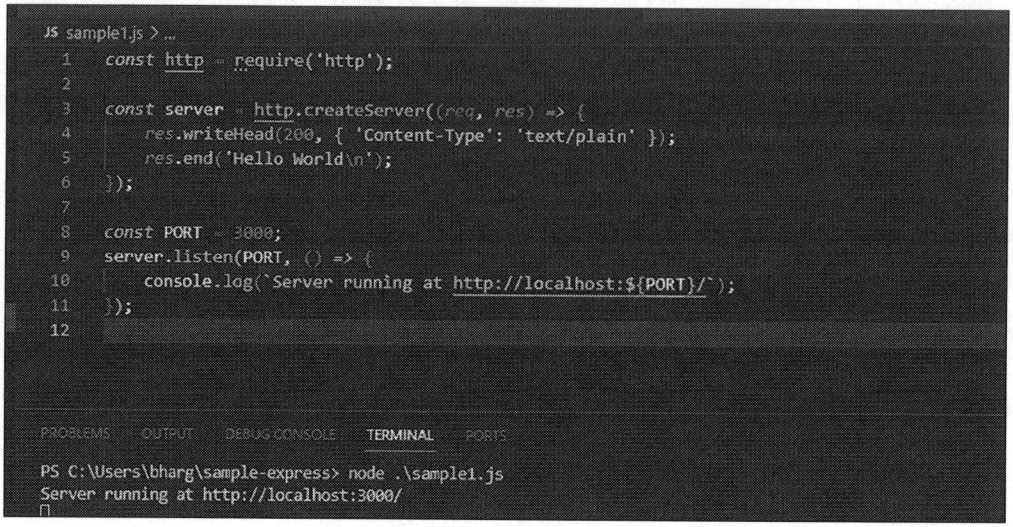

Figure 4.42: *Creating a http server*

Request and Response Objects

The callback function in **`createServer`** takes two arguments: **`req`** (the request object) and **`res`** (the response object).

- **Request Object (`req`):** An instance of **`http.IncomingMessage`**. It provides request details such as the request URL, headers, and method.
- **Response Object (`res`):** An instance of **`http.ServerResponse`**. Used to send back headers and the body of the response.

Handling HTTP Requests

When creating an HTTP server, handling different types of requests (such as GET, POST, PUT, DELETE) is essential.

Parsing Request URL

To handle different URLs or paths, you can use the URL module in conjunction with the HTTP module. It starts by importing necessary modules: **`http`** for creating the server and **`url`** for parsing request URLs. Using **`http.createServer()`**, a server is created. This server listens on port 3000 and handles incoming HTTP requests. For each request, it uses the **`url`** module to parse the request URL and extract the pathname.

The server responds based on this pathname. If the pathname is '**`/`**', it responds with "**`Home Page`**." If the pathname is '**`/about`**', it responds with "**`About Page`**." For all other pathnames, it responds with "**`Not Found`**." This basic routing mechanism allows the server to return different responses for different URL paths.

```
JS sample1.js > ...
const http = require('http');
const url = require('url');

http.createServer((req, res) => {
    const pathname = url.parse(req.url).pathname;

    if (pathname === '/') {
        res.end('Home Page');
    } else if (pathname === '/about') {
        res.end('About Page');
    } else {
        res.end('Not Found');
    }
}).listen(3000);
```

Figure 4.43: *Parsing request url*

Finally, by calling **`.listen(3000)`**, the server starts listening for incoming connections on port 3000, making it accessible to clients that request resources from this port. This code forms the foundation for a basic web server in Node.js, demonstrating essential concepts like HTTP server creation, request handling, and simple routing based on URL paths.

Handling Different Request Methods

You can differentiate request methods within the request handler. It starts by using Node.js's built-in **`http`** module to create a server. In the server's callback function, the request object **`req`** is used to determine the type of HTTP request received. This is achieved by checking the **`method`** property of the **`req`** object. If the method is **`'POST'`**, the server responds with a message indicating that a **`POST`** request was received. Similarly, if it's a GET request, the server responds with a message confirming the receipt of a GET request.

```
JS sample1.js > ...
const http = require('http');
const url = require('url');

http.createServer((req, res) => {
    if (req.method === 'POST') {
        res.end('Received POST request');
    } else if (req.method === 'GET') {
        res.end('Received GET request');
    }
}).listen(3000);
```

Figure 4.44: *Handling request methods*

The server is set to listen on port 3000, which means it can be accessed using **`http://localhost:3000`** in a web browser or through any HTTP client. This setup allows the server to handle basic routing based on the HTTP method, a fundamental requirement in web applications and APIs. This example serves as an introductory demonstration of handling HTTP methods in Node.js, showcasing the platform's capability to build web servers with customized responses based on the type of request.

Building an HTTP Client

The HTTP module can also be used to create an HTTP client to send requests to HTTP servers. It uses the **`http`** module to make a GET request to an external API. The script begins by calling the **`http.get`** method, targeting the URL **`'http://api.example.com/data'`**. This method is designed to send an **`http get`**request to the specified URL.

When the server responds to the request, the callback function is executed with the response object **`resp`**. This object is a stream, meaning that the data from the response might not be received all at once but rather in smaller chunks over time.

```
JS sample1.js > ...
const http = require('http');

http.get('http://api.example.com/data', (resp) => {
    let data = '';

    // A chunk of data has been received.
    resp.on('data', (chunk) => {
        data += chunk;
    });

    // The whole response has been received.
    resp.on('end', () => {
        console.log(data);
    });

}).on("error", (err) => {
    console.log("Error: " + err.message);
});
```

Figure 4.45: *Building an HTTP Client*

The script sets up two event listeners on the response object: one for the **`'data'`** event and another for the **`'end'`** event. The **`'data'`** event is triggered each time a chunk of data is received. In the corresponding event handler, the received chunk (represented by **`chunk`**) is appended to the **`data`** variable. This process continues until all chunks of the response are received. Once the entire response has been received, the **`'end'`** event is emitted. The event handler for **`'end'`** then logs the accumulated **`data`** to the console, showing the complete response body.

In addition, there is an error handler attached to the request. If an error occurs during the request (such as a network error or if the server is unreachable), the **`'error'`** event is emitted, and the corresponding event handler logs the error message.

Error Handling

Proper error handling is crucial when working with network operations. Listen to error events on both the server and client objects.

```
JS sample1.js > ...
const http = require('http');

const server = http.createServer((req, res) => {
    res.writeHead(200, { 'Content-Type': 'text/plain' });
    res.end('Hello World\n');
});

const PORT = 3000;
server.listen(PORT, () => {
    console.log(`Server running at http://localhost:${PORT}/`);
});

server.on('error', (error) => {
    console.error(`Error occurred: ${error.message}`);
});
```

Figure 4.46: *Error handling*

Error handling is a critical part of developing robust applications. By listening to the `'error'` event on an HTTP server, you can ensure that your application reacts appropriately to unexpected issues, potentially logging them for further analysis or taking corrective actions, thereby improving the application's reliability and user experience.

The HTTP module in Node.js stands as a foundational and versatile tool in web development, offering the capabilities to create both web servers and HTTP clients. This module is instrumental in enabling developers to build and manage complex web applications and services from the ground up. It provides the basic building blocks for handling various aspects of web development, such as creating servers, processing requests, and establishing client-server communication.

However, while the HTTP module is powerful and essential for understanding the underlying mechanisms of web interactions in Node.js, it is often not used directly in production applications. In real-world scenarios, developers usually prefer higher-level frameworks like Express.js or Nest.js. These frameworks provide additional abstractions and utilities, making it easier and more efficient to develop complex applications. They offer extended functionalities, such as middleware support, routing, and templating, which streamline the development process and enhance application structure and maintainability.

Therefore, while a deep understanding of the HTTP module is crucial for grasping the fundamentals of web interactions in Node.js, leveraging frameworks like Express.js or Nest.js is a common practice in the industry for building robust, scalable, and production-ready web applications. These frameworks not only simplify the development process but also incorporate best practices and design patterns, thereby elevating the overall efficiency and quality of web applications.

Understanding Callbacks and Promises

In Node.js, callbacks and promises are fundamental concepts for handling asynchronous operations. They are essential tools in a Node.js developer's arsenal, allowing the management of non-blocking I/O operations effectively. This section provides an in-depth understanding of these concepts, illustrating their importance, usage, and best practices with examples.

Understanding Callbacks

Callbacks are functions that are passed as arguments to other functions and are executed after some operations have been completed. A callback function is often used in asynchronous functions, for example, when reading a file asynchronously.

```
JS sample1.js > ...
const fs = require('fs');

fs.readFile('example.txt', 'utf8', (err, data) => {
    if (err) {
        console.error('Error reading file:', err);
        return;
    }
    console.log(data);
});
```

Figure 4.47: *Understanding callback*

Here, the third argument to **`fs.readFile`** is a callback function that gets executed once the file reading is complete or if an error occurs.

Handling Errors in Callbacks

In Node.js, it is a common pattern for callbacks to have an error as their first argument. This convention allows you to check for errors at the beginning of the callback.

```
function callback(err, result) {
    if (err) {
        // Handle error
    }
    // Process result
}
```

Figure 4.48: *Handling errors*

Callback Hell

Callback hell, also known as "*Pyramid of Doom*," is a phenomenon in Node.js (and JavaScript in general) where multiple levels of nested callbacks lead to complex, hard-to-read, and hard-to-maintain code. This typically arises in situations involving several asynchronous operations that depend on the results of previous ones.

Here are some of the characteristics of callback hell:

- **Deeply Nested Code:** As you add more asynchronous operations, the code gets deeply nested, forming a pyramid-like structure.
- **Difficult Error Handling:** Managing errors becomes complicated, as each callback might require its own error handling.
- **Readability Issues:** The logical flow of the program gets harder to follow due to the nesting.
- **Maintenance Challenges:** Making changes in one part of the code can affect other parts, increasing the risk of introducing bugs.

Here is an example of callback hell. Consider a scenario where you need to read multiple files in sequence. In this example, each file read depends on the completion of the previous one, leading to multiple nested callbacks.

```
JS sample1.js > ...
const fs = require('fs');

fs.readFile('file1.txt', 'utf8', (err, data1) => {
    if (err) throw err;
    console.log(data1);

    fs.readFile('file2.txt', 'utf8', (err, data2) => {
        if (err) throw err;
        console.log(data2);

        fs.readFile('file3.txt', 'utf8', (err, data3) => {
            if (err) throw err;
            console.log(data3);
            // The nesting can continue...
        });
    });
});
```

Figure 4.49: *callback hell*

Overcoming Callback Hell

Several approaches can help avoid or resolve callback hell, including:

- **Modularization:** Breaking down callbacks into separate, named functions can reduce nesting.
- **Promises:** They encapsulate the result of an asynchronous operation, allowing chaining instead of nesting.

- **Async/Await:** A syntactic feature in ES2017 that allows writing asynchronous code in a synchronous manner, making it easier to read and maintain.

Understanding Promises

In Node.js, promises represent the eventual completion (or failure) of an asynchronous operation and its resulting value. They provide a cleaner and more robust way of handling asynchronous operations compared to traditional callbacks. Understanding how to consume promises is crucial for writing efficient and readable asynchronous code.

A promise is an object that can be in one of the following three states:

- **Pending**: Initial state, neither fulfilled nor rejected.
- **Fulfilled:** The operation completed successfully.
- **Rejected:** The operation failed.

Creating Promises

A promise is created using the **`Promise`** constructor which takes a function with two parameters: **`resolve`** and **`reject`**. Once the operation is successful, resolve method will return that response. The reject method returns when there is a failure.

```
JS sample1.js > ...
const myPromise = new Promise((resolve, reject) => {
    // Asynchronous operation
    if (/* operation successful */) {
        resolve('Success');
    } else {
        reject('Failure');
    }
});
```

Figure 4.50: *Creating promises*

Consuming Promises

Consuming a promise means reacting to its resolution (fulfillment or rejection).

- **`.then()`:** Used for handling the fulfillment of the promise. It takes up to two arguments: a callback for success (fulfillment) and optionally, one for failure (rejection).
- **`.catch()`:** Used for handling rejection of the promise.

```
myPromise
    .then((result) => {
        console.log(result); // Success
    })
    .catch((error) => {
        console.error(error); // Failure
    });
```

Figure 4.51: *Consuming promises*

Chaining Promises

Promises can be chained, allowing for a sequence of asynchronous operations to be handled in a linear, more readable manner.

Here, **`doFirstThing`**, **`doSecondThing`**, and **`doThirdThing`** are functions that return promises. The output of one is used as input for the next.

The **`.finally()`** method is used to execute a block of code after the promise is settled, regardless of its outcome (fulfilled or rejected). It's useful for cleanup actions.

```
doFirstThing()
    .then((result) => doSecondThing(result))
    .then((newResult) => doThirdThing(newResult))
    .catch((error) => console.error(error));
```

Figure 4.52: *Chaining promises*

Async/Await Syntax

`async/await` is a syntactic feature in ECMAScript 2017 that simplifies the way we write and read asynchronous code that uses Promises.

- **`async`function**: An **`async`** function is a function that implicitly returns a promise and can contain **`await`** expressions.
- **`await`expression**: The **`await`** keyword is used to pause the execution of an **`async`** function and wait for the passed Promise's resolution.

In this **`async`** function, **`await`** is used to wait for the **`getDataPromise`** promise to resolve. If the promise is rejected, the error is caught in the **`catch`** block.

Callbacks and promises in Node.js provide powerful mechanisms for handling asynchronous operations. While callbacks are fundamental and form the basis for Node.js's non-blocking nature, promises, along with **`async/await`**, offer a more readable and manageable way to work with asynchronous code. Understanding these concepts is vital for any Node.js developer, as they play a critical role in building efficient and maintainable applications.

Exception Handling

Exception handling is a critical aspect of developing robust and reliable Node.js applications. In Node.js, exceptions are errors or unexpected events that disrupt the normal flow of program execution. Proper handling of these exceptions is essential to ensure that your application runs smoothly, prevents crashes, and provides meaningful error information to developers and users.

An exception in Node.js can be any error condition or unexpected behavior encountered during the execution of the program. It could be a runtime error, a rejected promise, a syntax error, or any other type of issue that prevents the program from continuing its normal execution path.

Types of Exceptions

The exceptions in Node.js can be broadly categorized into several types:

Standard JavaScript Errors

These are common errors that can occur in any JavaScript environment, not just in Node.js:

- **`SyntaxError`**: Occurs when there is a syntax mistake in the code, making it impossible to parse, for example, missing a bracket or a semicolon.
- **`ReferenceError`**: Happens when a code refers to a variable that is not in scope.
- **`TypeError`**: Arises when an operation is performed on a value of the wrong type, like trying to call a non-function or accessing a property on **undefined**.
- **`RangeError`**: Occurs when a value is not within the expected range, such as calling a function with fewer arguments than expected.

System Errors

System errors are specific to Node.js and occur when Node.js's underlying system operations fail. They typically involve operations related to the file system, network, or operating system.

- **`EACCES`**: Indicates a permission denied error.
- **`ENOENT`**: Means "*Error NO ENTry*" or "*Error NO ENTity*", commonly seen when a file or directory is not found.
- **`EADDRINUSE`**: Happens when a network address is already in use, like trying to listen on a port that is already being used.

System errors are usually presented as objects with additional information, such as an error code (**`err.code`**), system-specific error number (**`err.errno`**), and more.

User-Defined Errors

Developers can create custom errors to represent specific error conditions in their application logic. These are typically implemented by extending the built-in Error class.

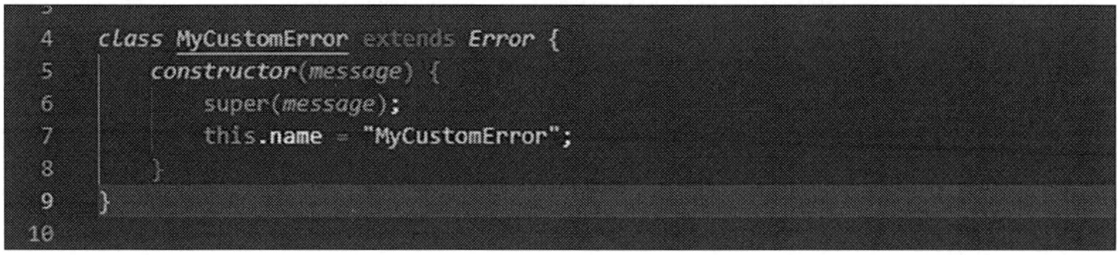

Figure 4.53: *User defined error*

Promise Rejections

Promises in Node.js are used to handle asynchronous operations. A rejection in a promise occurs when something goes wrong in an asynchronous operation and the promise transitions to the "**`rejected`**" state.

Unhandled promise Rejections: These occur when a promise is rejected, but there is no **`.catch()`** handler to handle the rejection, leading to potential runtime issues.

Assertion Errors

Assertion errors occur when a condition expected to be true is not met, often used in testing. Node.js provides the **`assert`** module for such checks.

Understanding various types of exceptions is vital for effective error handling in Node.js. By correctly identifying and managing these errors, developers can ensure more stable and reliable Node.js applications, especially in scenarios where high availability and robustness are crucial.

Handling Synchronous Code Exceptions

Synchronous code exceptions in Node.js can be handled using the traditional **`try...catch`** statement.

Wrap the code that may throw an exception in a **`try`** block and handle the exception in the **`catch`** block. Optionally, use a **`finally`** block to execute code after the **`try`** and **`catch`** blocks, regardless of whether an exception was thrown.

```
try {
    // Code that may throw an exception
} catch (error) {
    // Handle the exception
} finally {
    // Code that will run regardless of try / catch outcome
}
```

Figure 4.54: *Handling synchronous code exceptions*

Handling Asynchronous Code Exceptions

Asynchronous exceptions, particularly in operations like file reading/writing, database operations, and so on, can be more challenging to handle.

Callbacks

In traditional Node.js callbacks style, errors are usually passed as the first argument to the callback function.

```
fs.readFile('/path/to/file', (err, data) => {
    if (err) {
        // Handle error
        console.error(err.message);
        return;
    }
    // Process data
});
```

Figure 4.55: *Handling asynchronous code exceptions*

Promises and `Async/Await`

Promises and **`async/await`** syntax offer a cleaner way to handle asynchronous exceptions.

Promises: Use **`.catch()`** method or **`catch`** handler in **`then`**.

```
doAsyncOperation()
    .then(data => {
        // Process data
    })
    .catch(error => {
        // Handle error
        console.error(error.message);
    });
```

Figure 4.56: *Exception handling with promises*

`Async/Await`: Use **`try...catch`** within an **`async`** function.

```
async function fetchData() {
    try {
        const data = await doAsyncOperation();
        // Process data
    } catch (error) {
        // Handle error
        console.error(error.message);
    }
}
```

Figure 4.57: *Exception handling with async/await*

Unhandled Exception Handling

Unhandled exceptions can crash a Node.js application. Therefore, it's crucial to handle them appropriately.

Node.js provides the **`uncaughtException`** event on the process object to catch exceptions that weren't handled by any **`try...catch`**.

```
process.on('uncaughtException', (error) => {
    console.error(`Uncaught Exception: ${error.message}`);
    // Graceful shutdown or cleanup
    process.exit(1);
});
```

Figure 4.58: *Handling uncaught exception*

Similarly, handle unhandled promise rejections using the **`unhandledRejection`** event.

```
process.on('unhandledRejection', (reason, promise) => {
    console.error(`Unhandled Rejection at: ${promise}, reason: ${reason}`);
    // Graceful shutdown or cleanup
    process.exit(1);
});
```

Figure 4.59: *Handling unhandled exception*

Exception handling in Node.js is an integral part of developing reliable and fault-tolerant applications. It involves understanding different types of errors, using **`try...catch`** for synchronous code, handling errors in callbacks, and managing promises correctly. Additionally, catching unhandled exceptions and promise rejections is crucial to avoid unexpected application crashes. Effective exception handling ensures that applications behave predictably in error scenarios and helps maintain application stability and reliability.

Conclusion

As we reach the conclusion of this comprehensive exploration of key Node.js concepts, it's clear that Node.js is a powerful and versatile platform for building a wide range of applications. From handling binary data with Buffers, and managing multiple processes through the Cluster Module and Child Processes, to utilizing the interactive REPL environment, Node.js offers a rich set of features that cater to various development needs.

Streams in Node.js allow for efficient data handling, which is crucial in applications dealing with large volumes of data. The File System module provides a robust interface for interacting with the file system, enabling applications to read, write, and manipulate files and directories with ease.

A fundamental understanding of Events is pivotal in grasping Node.js's event-driven architecture, which is at the heart of its non-blocking I/O model. The HTTP module provides the necessary tools to create web servers and clients, laying the foundation for web application development in Node.js.

The concepts of Callbacks and Promises, and their evolution in the form of async/await, revolutionize the way asynchronous operations are handled, making the code more readable and maintainable. Exception handling, a critical aspect of any robust application, is effectively managed in Node.js, ensuring that applications are stable and reliable even in the face of unexpected errors or issues.

As we conclude this chapter, your understanding of these essential Node.js concepts empowers you to construct robust and dynamic MEVN (MongoDB, Express.js, Vue.js, Node.js) stack applications. With this knowledge at your disposal, you are adept at orchestrating the backend logic with Node.js, managing data with MongoDB, creating seamless APIs with Express.js, and building responsive user interfaces with Vue.js. These concepts are not just theoretical knowledge; they are practical tools that enhance your ability to develop everything from straightforward scripts to complex, high-traffic web applications and interactive real-time systems within the MEVN stack framework. Remember, the true power of Node.js, and by extension the MEVN stack, is amplified by its vibrant community and expansive ecosystem. As you continue your development journey, keep engaging with this community, enriching your knowledge, and contributing back to this continually evolving platform.

The next chapter will explore various methods for operating frontend and backend systems during development.

CHAPTER 5
Setting Up Development Environment

Introduction

Establishing a robust development environment is crucial for any developer. This chapter delves into various methods for operating frontend and backend systems during development. It also discusses strategies for accelerating the development process through the use of different tools and techniques.

In this chapter, we will start by setting up the frontend with Vite and initiate a VueJS project using a TypeScript template. This setup allows us to observe how the system monitors files and automatically refreshes the browser page when modifications are made to the components. For the backend, we employ a tool called Nodemon to track changes during development, enhancing our ability to expedite the development workflow.

Structure

In this chapter, the following topics will be covered:

- Creating a Typescript Template Project Using Vite CLI
- Understanding the Project Structure
- Using Vite CLI for Watching Frontend
- Setting Up Node.js Backend
- Nodemon Installation and Setup

Creating a Typescript Template Project Using Vite CLI

We covered all the essential VueJS concepts with examples, and discussed our example project in the previous chapters. Now, it's time to dive into the actual development. In this section, we'll install the Vite CLI and set up a TypeScript project template.

We previously explained how to create projects using Vite CLI. As our project is a todo application, we'll start by creating a directory named **'todos-app'**. Since this is a full-stack application, we will organize it into two separate directories: one for the frontend and another for the backend. Let us name the frontend directory **'ui'** and the backend **'api'** as outlined here. Keeping these in separate folders offers several benefits: it simplifies potential migrations to different implementations, avoids **node_modules** conflicts, and clearly separates concerns—keeping all frontend components in one folder and backend components in another.

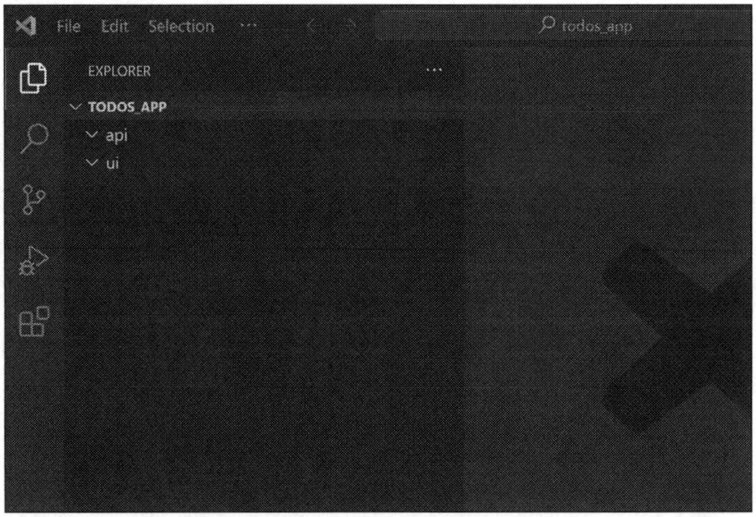

***Figure 5.1**: Folder structure*

After establishing the folder structure, we are set to begin working on the UI. To install Vite globally and initiate a VueJS template project, use the following command. You have the option to create the template in JavaScript or TypeScript. We will proceed with TypeScript, so execute the following command. First, navigate to the **todos_app** directory and then run the command provided.

```
// JavaScript

npm create vite@latest ui -- --template vue

// Typescript

npm create vite@latest ui -- --template vue-ts
```

After executing the preceding command, it will generate the basic project structure within the **'ui'** folder.

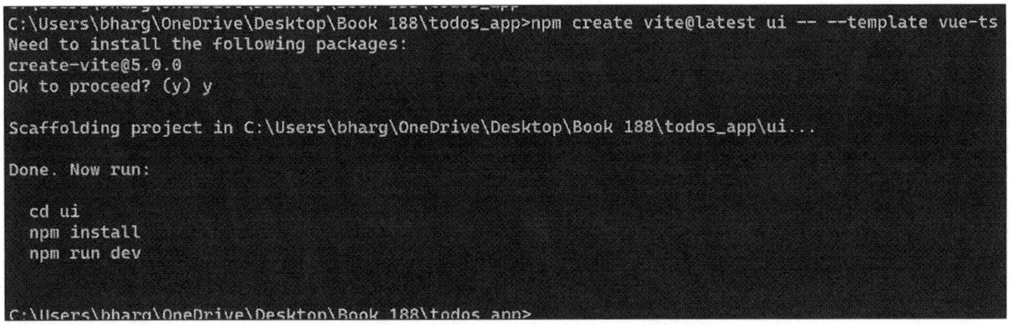

***Figure 5.2**: Creating VueJS project*

The entire project structure is visible within the **'ui'** folder. Although **'ui'** is the name used here to distinguish between frontend and backend within the '**todos_app**', any other name could also be used in its place.

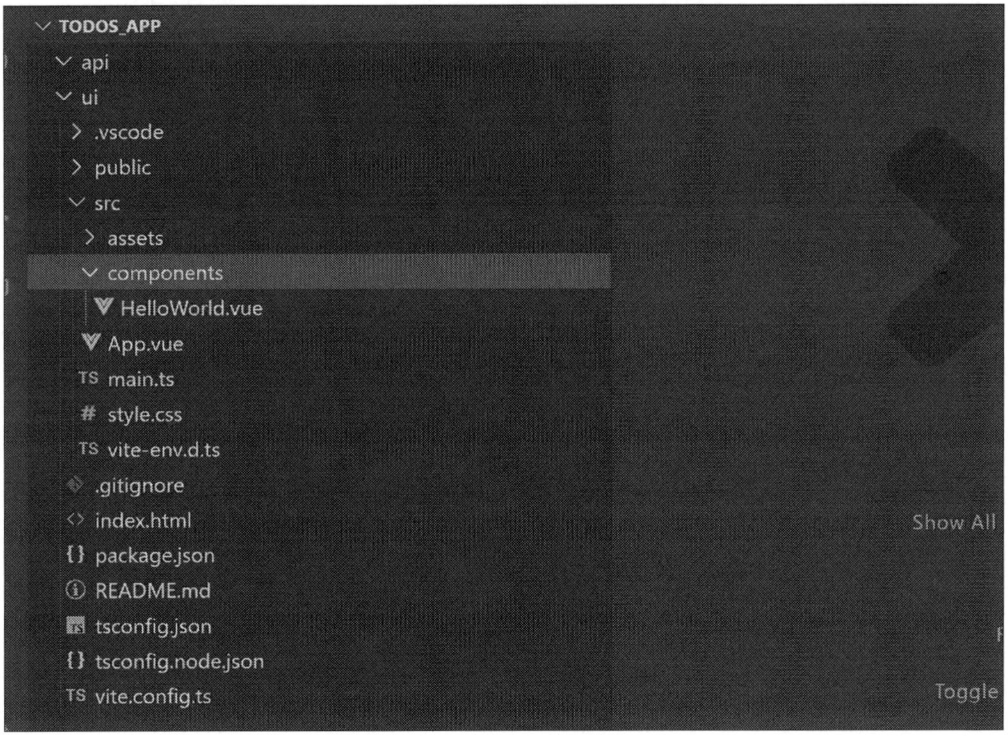

***Figure 5.3**: UI project structure*

After importing the project into VSCode, navigate to the **'ui'** directory and execute the following commands to start the project.

```
// Install Dependencies
npm install
// Run the application
npm run dev
```

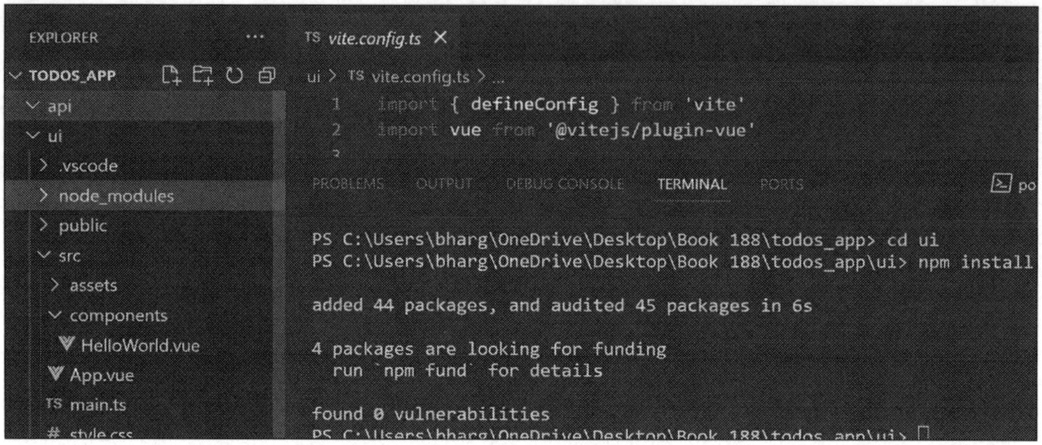

Figure 5.4: *Installing Dependencies*

Once you run the first command **npm install**, it installs all the dependencies and creates a folder called **node_modules** under the folder **ui.**

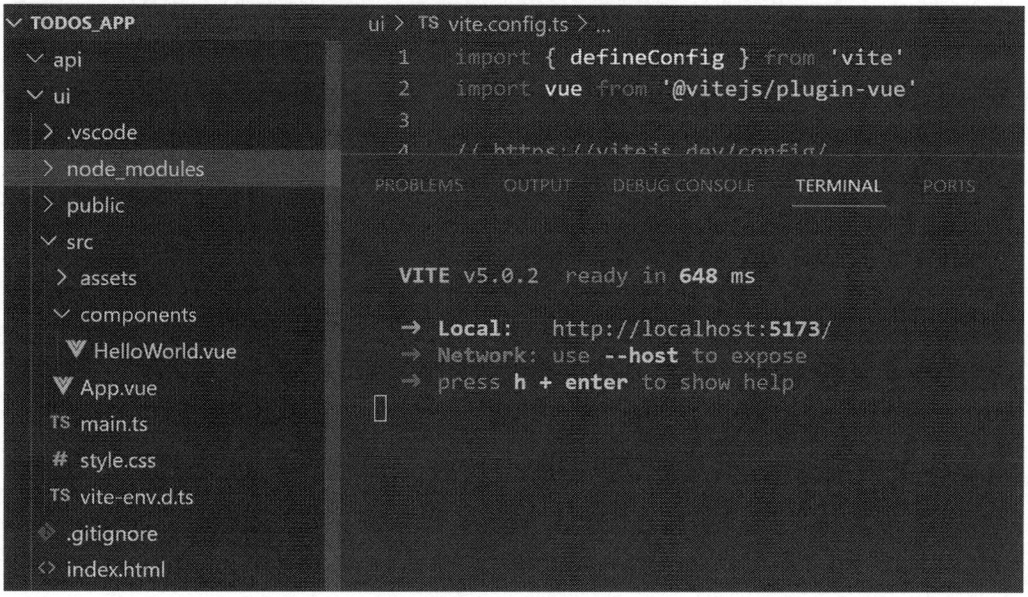

Figure 5.5: *npm run dev*

To launch the application, use the command **npm run dev**. By default, Vite serves the application on port **5173**. By entering the URL in your browser, you will be directed to the default page provided by the Vite CLI template project. This page is a basic application included with the template.

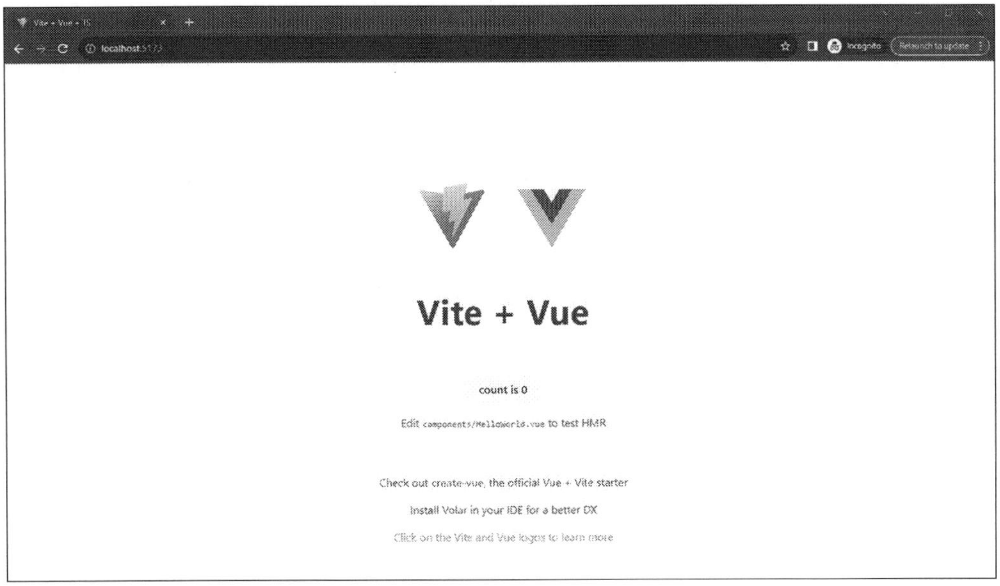

***Figure* 5.6**: *Running the sample application*

Understanding the Project Structure

We explored how to set up and launch the UI using the Vite CLI. Now, let's delve into the project structure generated by the CLI to facilitate easier configuration during subsequent development stages.

It's crucial to recognize that all the source code resides within the **`'src'`** folder. Every single-page application managed by this setup includes two key files.

The primary file is '**`index.html`**', which is essential as it loads into the browser upon building and running the application. Pay attention to lines 9-12 in this file, where you'll find the **`'div'`** element with the ID **`'app'`** and a script section. This script section dynamically loads all the JavaScript required for the application into the browser.

```
index.html ×
ui > index.html > ...
<!doctype html>
<html lang="en">
  <head>
    <meta charset="UTF-8" />
    <link rel="icon" type="image/svg+xml" href="/vite.svg" />
    <meta name="viewport" content="width=device-width, initial-scale=1.0" />
    <title>Vite + Vue + TS</title>
  </head>
  <body>
    <div id="app"></div>
    <script type="module" src="/src/main.ts"></script>
  </body>
</html>
```

***Figure** 5.7: index.html*

If you examine the **`main.ts`** file, depicted in *Figure* 5.8, you will notice that the entire application is mounted using that ID. For instance, if you alter the ID name from **`'app'`** to a different one and then attempt to launch the application, the app will not be displayed in the browser.

```
TS main.ts ×
ui > src > TS main.ts
import { createApp } from 'vue'
import './style.css'
import App from './App.vue'

createApp(App).mount('#app')
```

***Figure** 5.8: main.ts*

From the above mentioned file, it is evident that any CSS placed in the **`style.css`** file will apply to the entire application, and the first component to load is **`App.vue`**. You have the freedom to add additional components to the components folder and organize them into a distinct folder structure tailored to your project's needs. All images and other assets should be stored in the **`assets`** folder.

Vite.config.ts

All the configuration related to your application can be added to this file. For example, if you want to proxy all the API calls from the UI to the backend API while developing the application, should be added in this file.

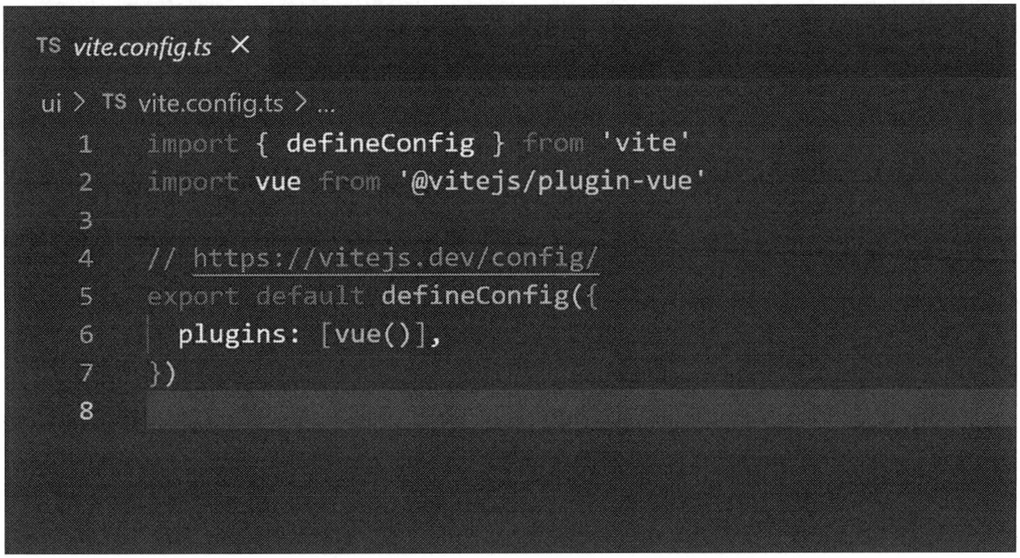

***Figure 5.9:** vite.config.ts*

There are so many other configuration options such as conditionally applying configuration based on the environment, externalizing environment variables, and so on. You can use these options based on your project need; you can go through all that in the following URL.

`https://vitejs.dev/config/`

Using Vite CLI for Watching Frontend

We understand the project structure and it's time for us to get started on our example project and see how we can leverage Hot Module Replacement (HMR) to watch files, as we change and reload automatically. We are going to build the whole UI in the next chapter, but we will understand the HMR in this chapter, as we clean up the components.

Let's remove all the styles from style.css and see how it looks. We would like you to remove and see the results in the browser immediately. You can see the HMR in action in the following image as you remove the styles. To initiate the app in development mode, simply execute the command **`npm run dev`** to start the app in development mode.

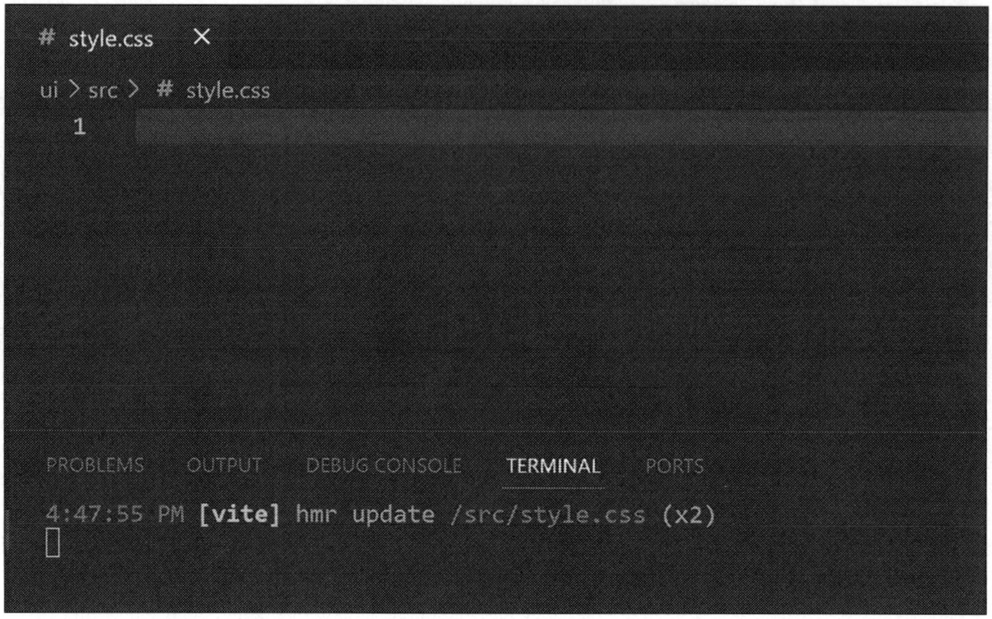

***Figure 5.10**: Removing styles*

This is how it looks now if we remove all the styles. We don't need all that styles as we are building out **`todos`** app.

***Figure 5.11:** Sample app without styles*

The next thing we need to do is remove the **`HelloWord`** component and remove all the HTML that came from the template project in the **`App.vue`** component, as shown in *Figure* 5.12. You can notice HMR in action again.

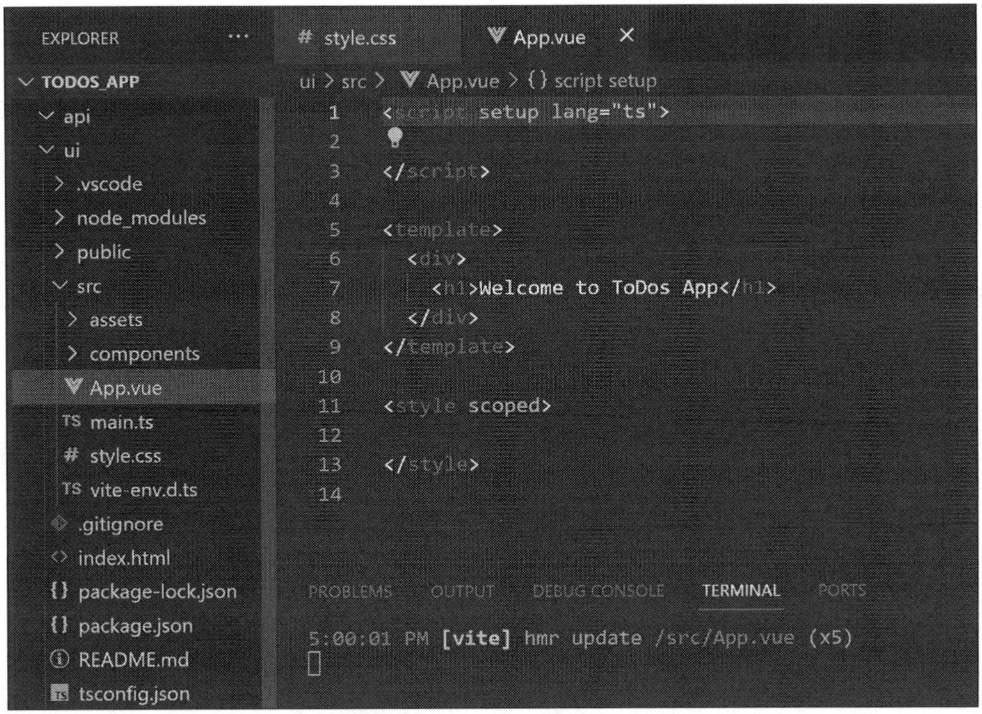

Figure 5.12: *Cleaning components*

Once you make all these changes, you'll see the updated version of your app, as shown in *Figure 5.13*.

Figure 5.13: *Updated app*

Setting Up Node.js Backend

We are maintaining two separate folders for frontend and backend. We have seen how to set up the frontend in the previous sections, it's time to set up the backend in the folder API. We need to create a Node.js project under the folder API and this Node.js project serves as an API for the application we are building.

Let's change the directory to API and do the following command to initialize the **`npm`** project. When you run the following command, it asks you a bunch of questions such as author info, GitHub info, version, name of the repo, and so on.

```
npm init
```

```
PS C:\Users\bharg\OneDrive\Desktop\Book 188\todos_app\api> npm init
This utility will walk you through creating a package.json file.
It only covers the most common items, and tries to guess sensible defaults.

See `npm help init` for definitive documentation on these fields
and exactly what they do.

Use `npm install <pkg>` afterwards to install a package and
save it as a dependency in the package.json file.

Press ^C at any time to quit.
package name: (api) todos_api
version: (1.0.0)
description: API Backend for todos application
entry point: (index.js) index.ts
test command: npm test
git repository:
keywords: API NodeJS TypeScript MongoDB
author: Bhargav Bachina
license: (ISC)
```

Figure 5.14: *npm init*

The following are the general info that you need to give while setting up the Node.js project:

- **Package Name:** This is the name that you can give to your project. Since we're building a backend API for a **`todo`** application, we've chosen a simple name **`todos_api`**. This clearly indicates the project's purpose. **`todos_api`**.
- **Version:** Every Node.js project has a version that follows semantic versioning **`major.minor.patch`**. This is useful when you are ready to publish or when you are ready to put your code into production. Whenever you push new changes, you change this version according to the following criteria. Since this is a new project, we are starting with the initial version 1.0.0.
    - **`MAJOR`**: You update this when you have breaking or incompatible changes.

  - `MINOR`: You update this when you add functionality in a backward compatible manner.
  - `PATCH`: You update this when you make backward compatible bug fixes.

- **Description:** This describes your project and we have given relevant information, as this is a backend api.
- **Entry point:** This is the entry point for your Node.js Project which means when the command npm starts, it automatically looks for the file given here and runs it with the following node command. Since we are building the entire backend with the typescript, we have given the name **`index.ts`**. It translates to main when the **`package.json`** file is created. You can check the following screenshot once.

  ```
  npm start   →  node index.ts
  ```

- **test command:** The test command is given here when you have unit tests or integration tests. We just gave the command **`npm test`** as an example. This command is put into the scripts section of the **`package.json`** as this is the script you often run to test your application.
- **Git repository:** This is the repository where your code resides and we gave it a blank for now. If you are following and creating, you can create a git repository and give that URL as a value to this.
- **Keywords:** These are keywords that are relevant to your Node.js project. You can give any words that make sense and will be helpful to search your package when it is published in the npm registry. We are not going to publish this as a npm package yet.
- **License:** This is the license you want to have with your project. Since this is a demo project that comes with this book, we have given ISC which is a permissive free software license published by the Internet Software Consortium, now called Internet Systems Consortium (ISC).

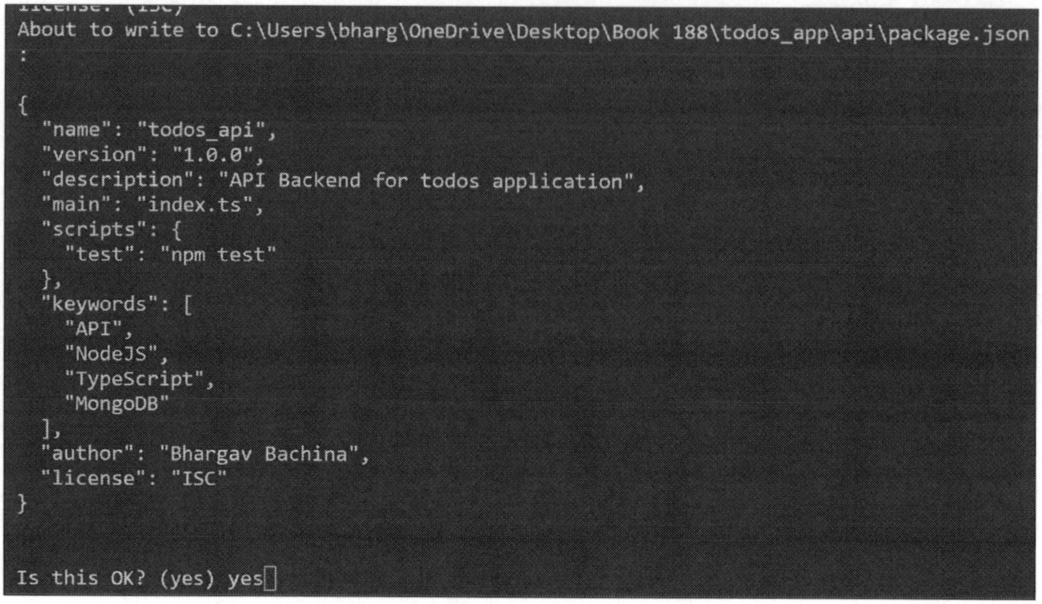

Figure 5.15: *Creating package.json*

Once you answer all the questions, you are asked to confirm and the **`package.json`** is created with all the given answers (refer to *Figure 5.16*). You can leave these blank as well. You don't have to answer every question here.

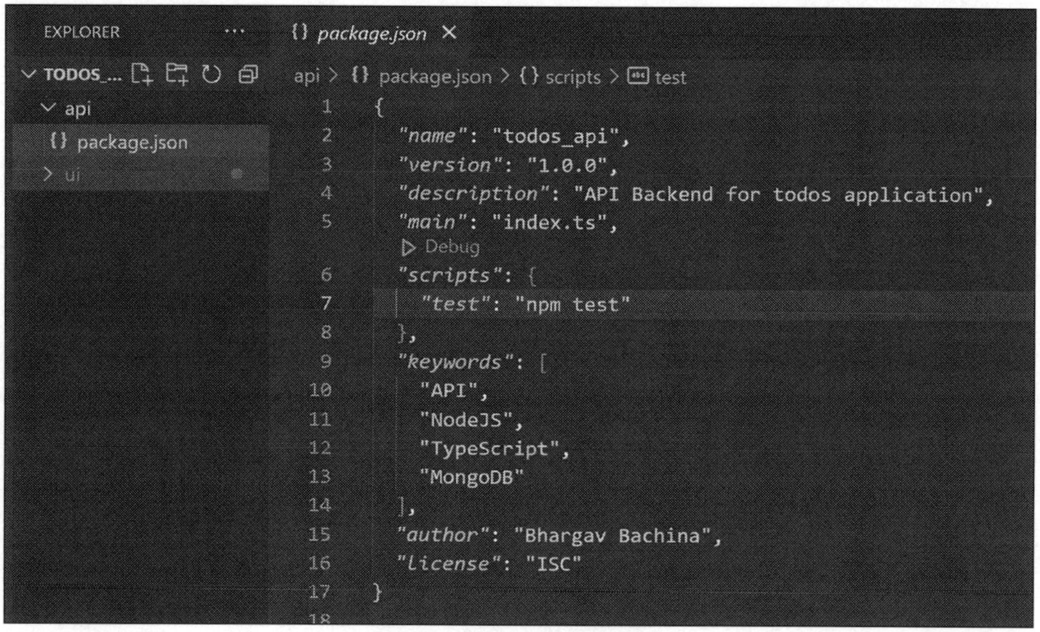

Figure 5.16: *package.json*

Now, we have a **package.json** file and it's time to create our first file called **index.js** and add a small console statement to test it out, as shown in *Figure* 5.17. It's very simple to create a file and run that with the node command if it's written in JavaScript. But we are building our backend with TypeScript and there is no out of the box solution to run the TypeScript files. We will see how to run typescript files in the next sections.

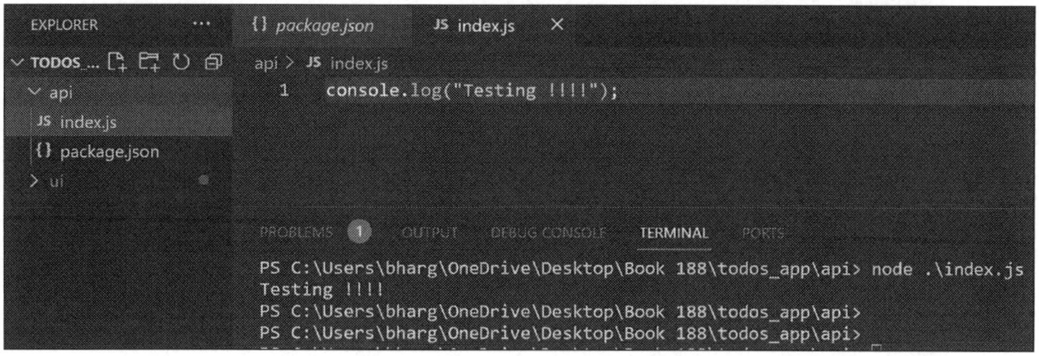

***Figure* 5.17**: *Testing index.js*

Let's try to change the file extension to **.ts** and run the command again and see what happens. Node is able to compile it and run it as the other file, why is that?

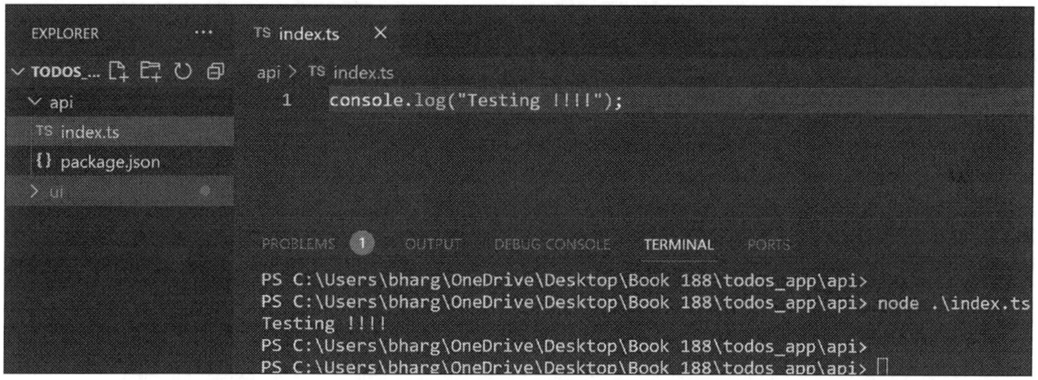

***Figure* 5.18**: *index.ts*

The reason that the node is able to run the **.ts** extension is because it contains only JavaScript code. As you start adding TypeScript syntax to the file, it won't be compiling and running it. Let's test that as well.

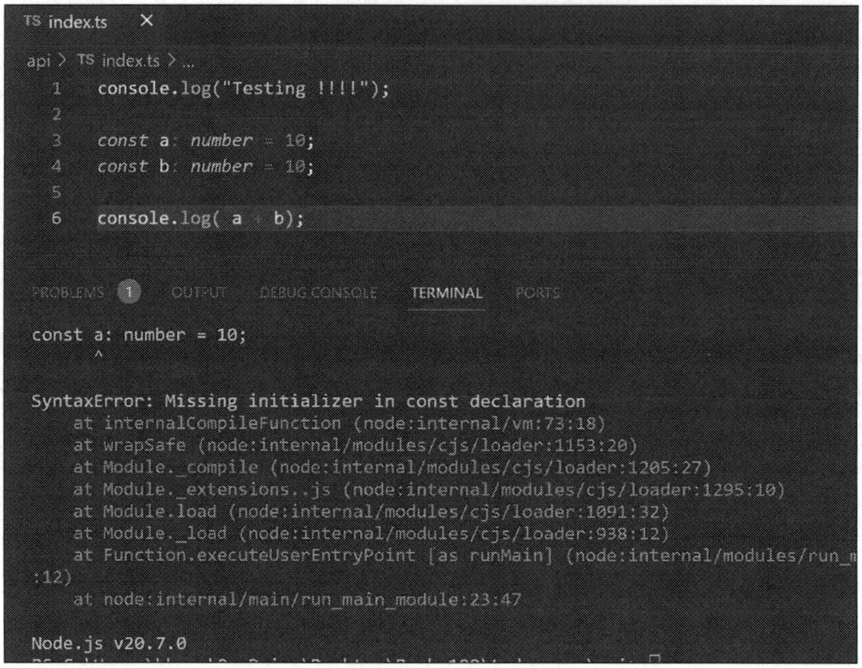

Figure 5.19: *Testing index.ts*

As you can see in *Figure* 5.19, the Node.js is giving the error for the simple type declarations. We have just added type declarations to two variables and try to do the addition. To compile the typescript files, we need to install a package called **`ts-node`** and typescript as a dev dependency.

```
npm install -D ts-node typescript @types/node
```

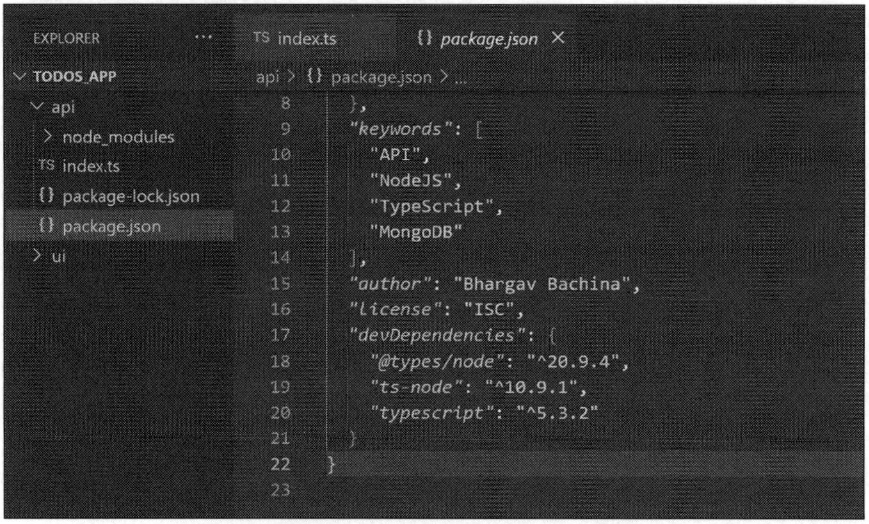

Figure 5.20: *Installing dev dependencies*

Once you run the preceding command, all those dependencies are added to the **devDependencies** portion of the **package.json** file. We can now add the following line to the scripts section of the **package.json** so that we can run the application with this command **npm start**.

```
"start": "ts-node index.ts"
```

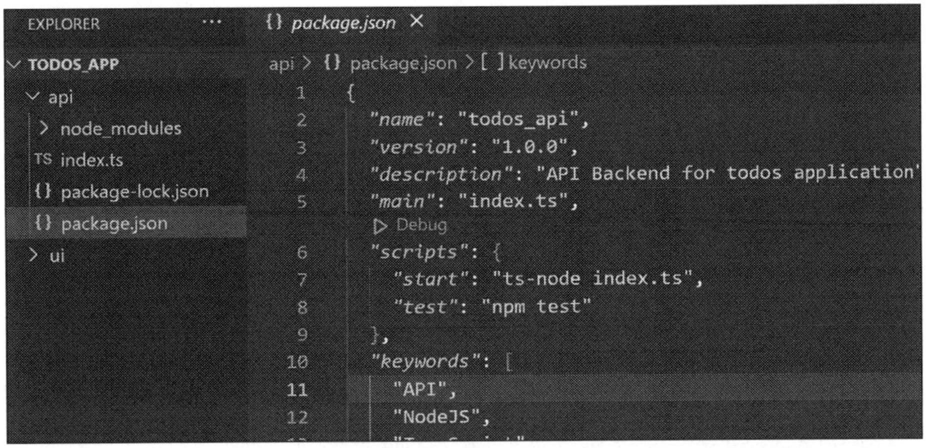

Figure 5.21: *npm start*

It's always better to add your scripts to this section of the **package.json** so that you don't have to remember every time you run these commands. We can now run the following command and our application will be compiled and run successfully, as shown in *Figure* 5.22.

```
npm start
```

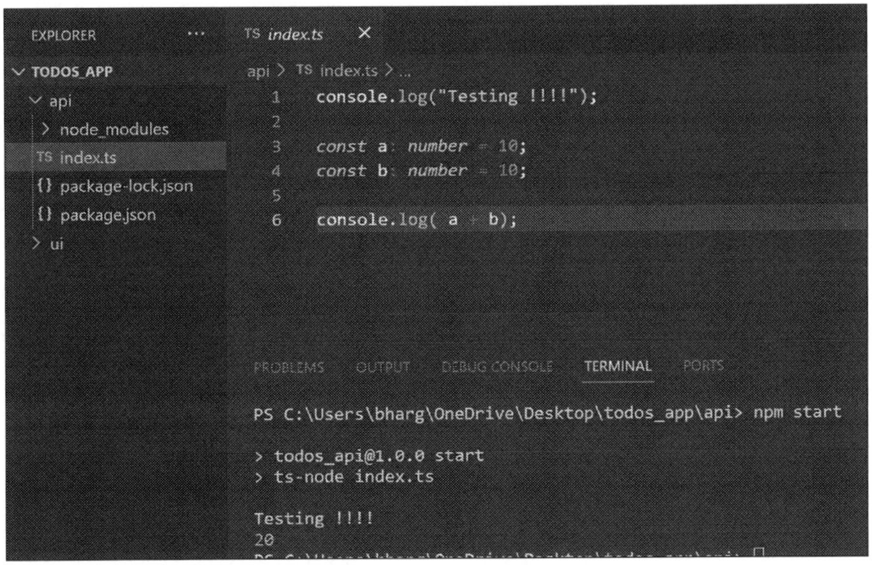

Figure 5.22: *Compiled successfully*

As you can see here, we have successfully compiled the typescript file with Type declarations with the **ts-node** package. We will see how we can watch files and run the files automatically in the next sections.

Nodemon Installation and Setup

We have successfully run our TypeScript Node.js Project. The problem is that whenever you make any changes to the files you must restart the application to see those changes. This is not a big issue when you are working with few changes but, when you are actually starting a project in a rapid development phase, starting every time to see changes is a little bit frustrating. Nodemon comes to the rescue as it watches files and automatically restarts the application as you are editing files.

Let's install this package with the following command, it should be added as a **dev** dependency as we are using this only in the development phase.

```
npm install nodemon -save-dev
```

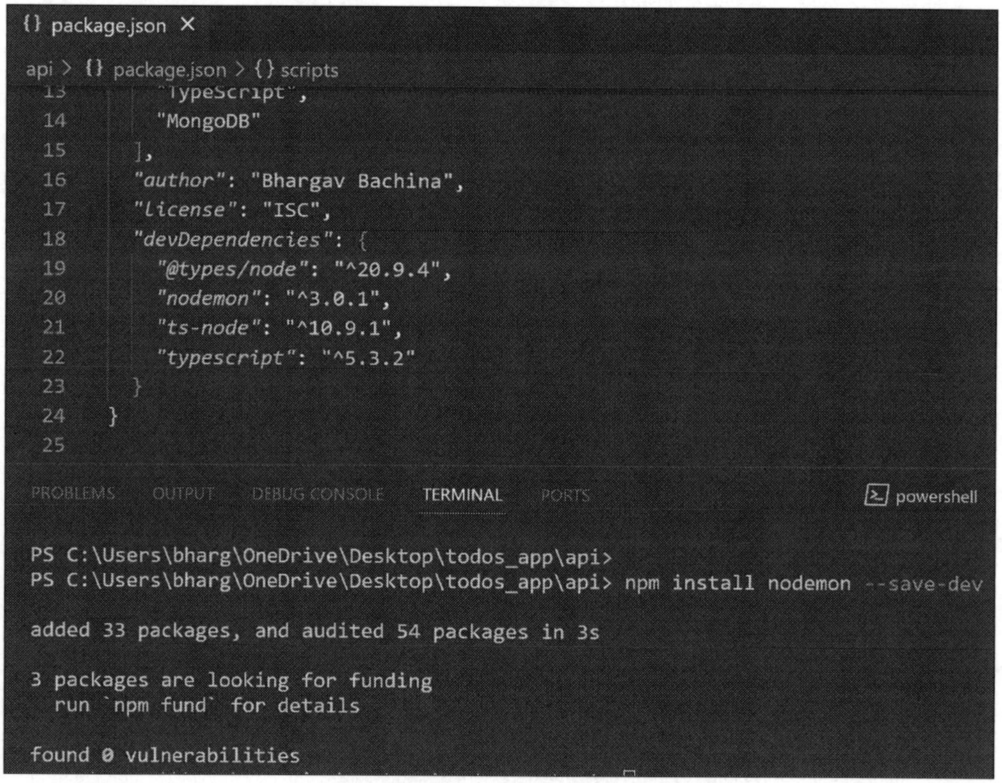

Figure 5.23: *Installing nodemon*

Once the package is installed, we can add the following script to the scripts section and run the following command to watch the file as you edit. Notice that you should use the word run to execute any commands other than start.

```
// add below to the scripts section
"dev": "nodemon index.ts"
// run this command
npm run dev
```

As you can see in the following image, **nodemon** is watching all the files with extensions ts and json by default. You can try to edit the file and see the **nodemon** in action. You can see all the options this package provides in the following URL.

https://www.npmjs.com/package/nodemon

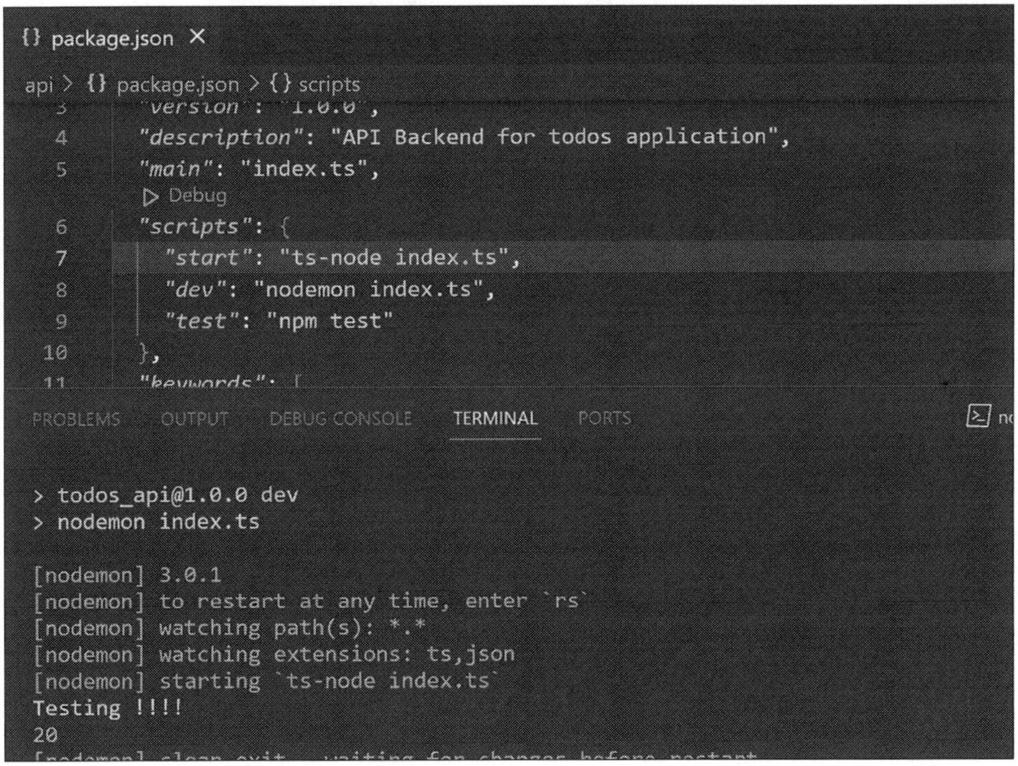

***Figure 5.24**: Running with nodemon*

We can add options to the **nodemon** command, for example, let's add a delay option so that it doesn't restart the application immediately, it waits until the delay. There are so many other options you can configure with the **nodemon.json** file, as shown in *Figure* 5.25. You can add this file at the root of the application.

nodemon.json

```
{
    "watch": ["./"],
    "delay": "5000",
    "ignore": ["node_modules", "package.json"]
}
```

We are watching all the files at the root location with a delay of 5 seconds and ignoring the **node_modules** directory and **package.json** file. You can configure other options in this file based on your need. If we have this file at the root location, all you need to run the command **nodemon**, it actually picks up this file and watch the application.

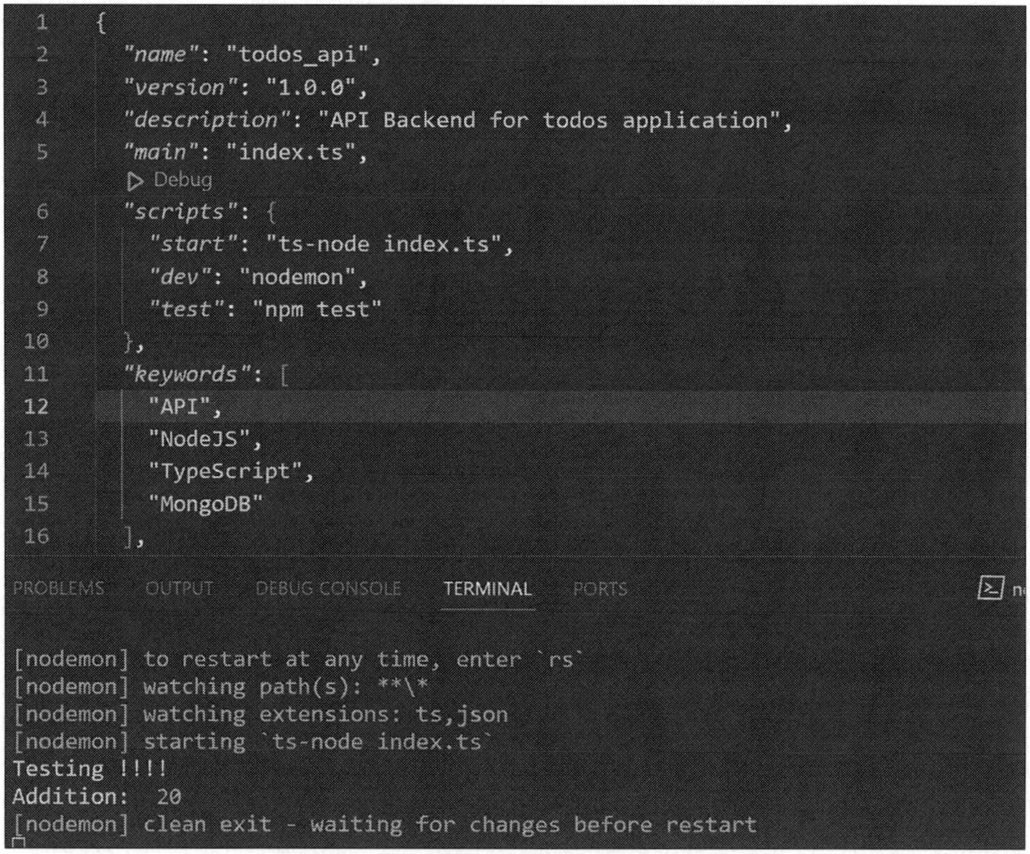

Figure 5.25: *nodemon.json*

If the **nodemon.json** file is not in the root location, you must specify the path with that command where the file is located.

The following screenshot depicts the final project structure. We are maintaining two separate folders: one for the frontend and another for the backend. This is just a basic project structure and we are going to develop on top of this in the upcoming chapters.

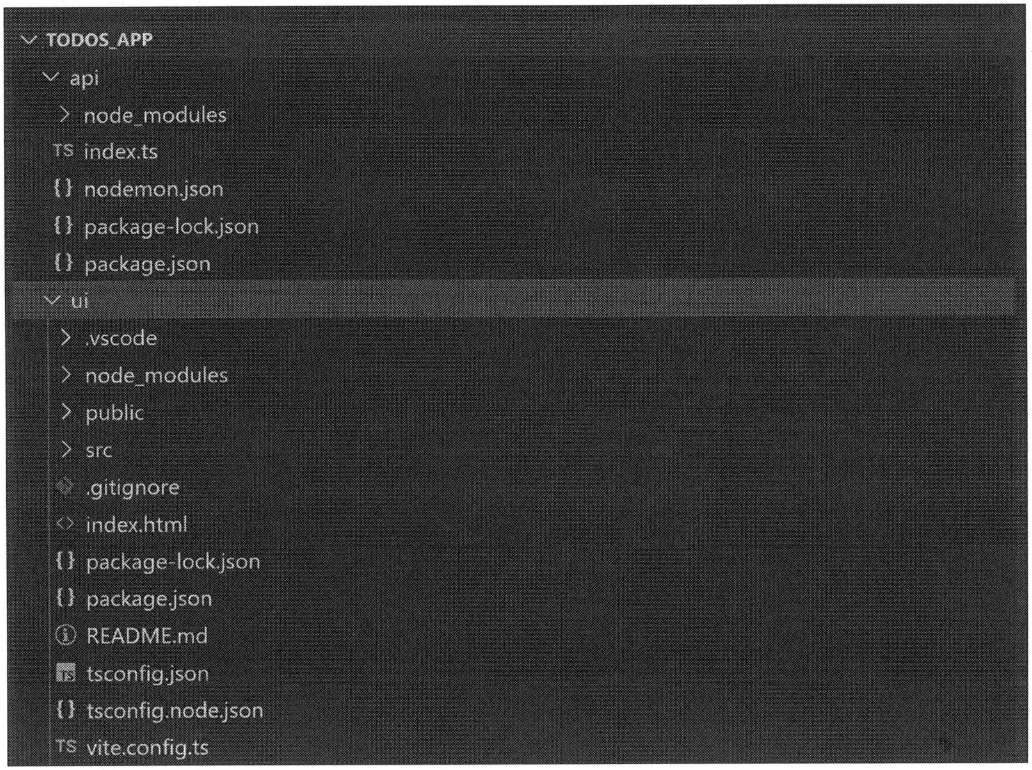

Figure 5.26: *Project structure*

Conclusion

In this chapter, we established a foundational project structure and demonstrated how to utilize Vite CLI and Nodemon to monitor changes in the frontend and backend respectively during development. These tools significantly enhance the efficiency of the development process by eliminating the need for constant application restarts to reflect changes.

In the forthcoming chapter, we will further develop both the frontend and backend components based on the initial structure we set up. For the frontend, we will construct routes, components, and utilize the Pinia store for state management, among other tasks. On the backend, we will develop an Express server that interfaces with MongoDB to serve data via REST API.

Further Readings

- About Nodemon: https://github.com/remy/nodemon
- About Vite: https://vitejs.dev/
- About MEVN Stack: https://medium.com/bb-tutorials-and-thoughts/how-to-develop-and-build-mevn-stack-10b6e8ff7f7c
- Typescript: https://www.typescriptlang.org/
- About SPA: https://developer.mozilla.org/en-US/docs/Glossary/SPA

CHAPTER 6
Backend Development With TypeScript

Introduction

In this chapter, we will embark on a comprehensive journey through the foundational aspects of building and structuring a robust API using Express. Our exploration begins with a deep dive into understanding the API structure, where we'll unravel the architectural design and organization that makes an API both scalable and maintainable. Next, we'll guide you through setting up an Express server, laying down the groundwork for your API's backend environment.

As we progress, we will introduce Webpack, a powerful module bundler that plays a crucial role in modern web development. You'll learn how to set up Webpack specifically for handling TypeScript files, enabling a more streamlined development process through bundling and optimizing assets. This optimized setup allows us to delve into defining routes, an essential step in building the skeleton of our API structure. Through carefully designed routes, we ensure that our API can handle various requests effectively, directing them to the appropriate logic for processing.

Building upon our routes, we will then construct the API structure in detail. This involves organizing our codebase into logical sections, making it easier to develop, manage, and scale our application. An integral part of this process is request validation, where we will implement checks to ensure that incoming data meets our expectations, thereby safeguarding our application from invalid data and potential security vulnerabilities.

By the end of this chapter, you will have gained a solid foundation in API development with Express and TypeScript, enhanced by the efficiency and flexibility offered by Webpack. You'll be well-equipped to build a structured, efficient, and secure API, ready to serve as the backbone for web applications. This foundational knowledge sets the stage for the subsequent phases of development and integration.

Structure

In this chapter, the following topics will be covered:

- Understanding API Structure
- Setup Express Server
- Introduction to Webpack
- Setup Webpack for Building TypeScript Files
- Defining Routes
- Building API Structure
- Request Validation

Understanding API Structure

In the previous chapters, we installed necessary tools to build the API and created folder structure for the application. We also set up the Nodemon to monitor changes during development. In this chapter, we will build the API with the Express.js framework in TypeScript. Let's understand the APIs we will be building for this example project and delve into some API techniques.

Here is the project structure we are building in this chapter. It represents a typical project structure for a Node.js backend using the Express framework, often adopted for its modular and clean separation of concerns.

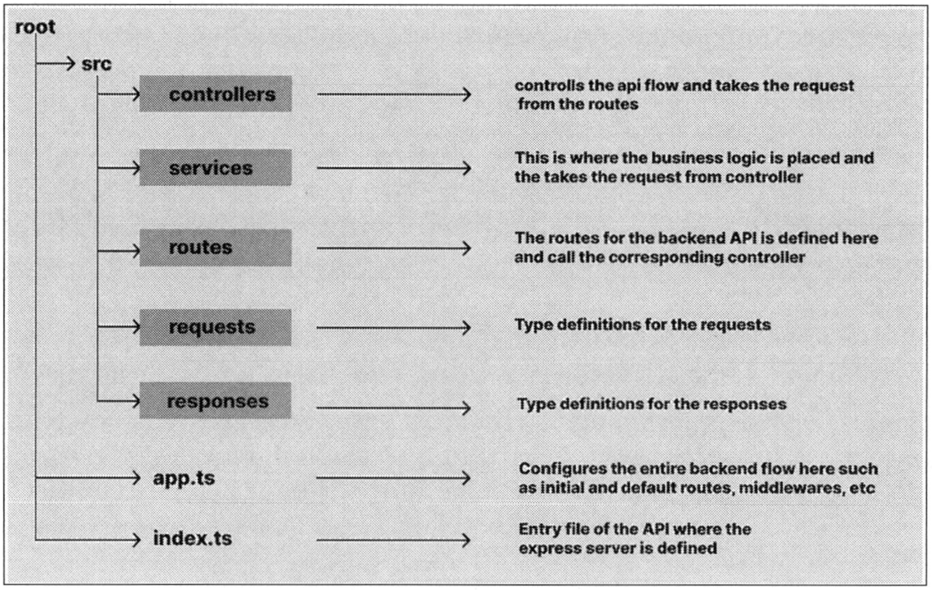

Figure 6.1: *Project structure*

Each directory within the **src** folder serves a specific purpose, including:

- **controllers**: This directory contains controller files that handle the incoming HTTP requests. Controllers receive requests from the routes, invoke the necessary services, and send back the responses.
- **services**: The services directory is where the core business logic of the application resides. Services are called by controllers to perform the main operations of the application, such as interacting with a database or performing calculations.
- **routes**: Here, the application's routes are defined. Each route is associated with a controller action that will handle the request. The routes direct the incoming HTTP requests to the appropriate controller based on the URL and HTTP method.
- **requests**: This contains type definitions or interfaces for the structure of incoming requests. It helps to validate and document the expected request format, such as the body, query parameters, or headers.
- **responses**: Like requests, this directory would include type definitions or interfaces for the API responses. This ensures consistency in the responses sent back to the client and helps with generating API documentation.

In addition to the directory, the following two files are the main files of the application:

- **app.ts**: The **app.ts** file typically initializes and configures the Express application, setting up global middleware, error handling, and connecting the routes to the Express application.
- **index.ts**: Often the entry point of the application, **index.ts** is where the Express server is set up and started. It imports the configured Express app from **app.ts** and listens on a specified port.

This structure is designed to promote a clean separation of concerns, making the codebase easier to manage, test, and scale. It follows an Model-View-Controller (MVC)-like pattern. However, in API-centric applications, views are usually not present, and their role is taken by the response types sent to the client.

Understanding REST principles and HTTP methods is essential for designing RESTful APIs. These principles provide a guideline that helps in creating web services that are easy to understand, well-structured, and maintainable. Let's understand these in the following section.

Introduction to REST Architecture

Representational State Transfer (REST) is an architectural style that governs the design and interaction of web services. It provides a set of guidelines that, when followed, lead to the development of scalable and maintainable web applications. REST was introduced by Roy Fielding in his doctoral dissertation in 2000 and has since become the standard for designing networked applications.

Core Principles of REST

RESTful systems adhere to four key architectural constraints that define their uniform interface:

- **Client-Server Separation**: The client-server architecture separates the user interface concerns from the data storage concerns, improving the portability of the user interface across multiple platforms and scalability by simplifying server components.
- **Stateless**: Each request from the client to the server must contain all the information necessary to understand and complete the request. The server should not store session information; rather, the session state is kept entirely on the client.
- **Cacheable**: The system should be designed to cache responses where possible. Well-managed caching partially or eliminates some client-server interactions, further improving scalability and performance.
- **Uniform Interface**: To obtain a uniform interface, several architectural constraints are needed to guide the behaviour of components. These constraints, which are detailed in the next section, are critical to the RESTful architecture.
- **Layered System**: A client cannot ordinarily tell whether it is connected directly to the end server or to an intermediary. Intermediary servers can improve system scalability by enabling load-balancing and providing shared caches.
- **Code on Demand (optional)**: Servers can extend client functionality by transferring executable code, such as scripts or compiled code. This constraint is the only optional one, as it can reduce visibility.

Uniform Interface Constraints

The uniform interface that any RESTful system should provide is defined by four constraints:

- **Resource-Based:** Individual resources are identified in requests using URIs. The resources themselves are conceptually separate from the representations returned to the client.
- **Manipulation of Resources through Representations:** When a client holds a representation of a resource, it has enough information to modify or delete the resource's state on the server, provided it has permission to do so.
- **Self-Descriptive Messages:** Each message includes enough information to

describe how to process the message. It can be achieved using media types and other HTTP headers.

- **Hypermedia as the Engine of Application State (HATEOAS):** Clients deliver state via body contents, query-string parameters, request headers, and the requested URI. Services deliver state to clients via body content, response codes, and response headers. This constraint decouples client and server in a way that allows the server functionality to evolve independently.

HTTP Methods

The Hypertext Transfer Protocol (HTTP) is the foundation of data communication for the World Wide Web. It's a stateless protocol that operates via a request-response model between a client and a server.

HTTP defines a set of request methods, also referred to as HTTP verbs, which indicate the desired action to be performed for a given resource. The main HTTP methods are:

- **GET:** Requests data from a specified resource. GET requests should only retrieve data and have no other effect.
- **POST**: Submits data to be processed to a specified resource. POST requests often result in a change in state or side effects on the server.
- **PUT**: Replaces all current representations of the target resource with the uploaded content.
- **DELETE**: Removes all current representations of the target resource given by a URL.
- **PATCH:** Applies partial modifications to a resource.
- **HEAD:** Like GET, the HEAD method requests a response without the response body. It is useful for retrieving meta-information written in response headers, without having to transport the entire content.
- **OPTIONS:** Describes the communication options for the target resource.

Each method has specific semantics and expected behaviours, which are crucial in RESTful API design. They help clients interact with the server in a standard way and are integral in defining the operations of any RESTful API.

Advantages of REST

The following are the advantages of RESTful APIs:

- **Scalability**: The stateless nature of RESTful APIs means that the server does not need to retain client session information. This simplifies the architecture and allows for better scaling to handle more clients.

- **Simplicity**: REST uses standard HTTP methods and is based on the ubiquitous HTTP protocol, which is familiar to developers and can be easily understood and used.
- **Flexibility**: RESTful APIs can serve multiple types of clients from a single endpoint. They return data in various formats such as JSON, XML, HTML, and so on, according to the needs of the client.
- **Portability**: With the separation of client and server, the client-side user interface can be developed independently and can be easily ported to different platforms.
- **Independence**: With the client and server separated, the client-side user interface can be developed independently, enabling it to be easily adapted and deployed across various platforms.
- **Standards-Based**: Since it is based on HTTP, RESTful APIs follow worldwide standards, which allows developers to use off-the-shelf libraries and tools for development, leading to faster development cycles.
- **Easier Communication**: Many APIs built with REST are based on resources that can be easily understood by developers, leading to fewer communication issues.
- **Debugging and Development Tools**: A plethora of tools are available for testing, developing, and interacting with RESTful APIs, which can significantly speed up development and troubleshooting.

The combination of these advantages makes RESTful APIs a popular choice for public web services and internal corporate systems alike. They facilitate a structured approach to organizing interactions between distributed systems, leading to systems that are easier to maintain, extend, and scale.

Understanding Express.js Middleware

Middleware in Express.js refers to a series of functions that have access to the request object (`req`), the response object (`res`), and the next middleware function in the application's request-response cycle. These functions can execute any code, modify the request and response objects, end the request-response cycle, or call the next function in the stack.

Here's a more detailed look at the middleware and its components:

- **Request Object (`req`):** This represents the HTTP request and has properties for the request query string, parameters, body, HTTP headers, and so on.
- **Response Object (`res`):** Represents the HTTP response that an Express app sends when it receives an HTTP request.
- **Next Function (`next`):** A function that passes control to the next middleware

function. If not called, the request will be left hanging or will need to be closed by ending the response.

Middleware functions can perform a variety of tasks, such as:

- Execute any code.
- Make changes to the request and response objects.
- End the request-response cycle.
- Call the next middleware in the stack.

If the current middleware function does not end the request-response cycle, it must call **`next()`** to pass control to the next middleware function. Otherwise, the request will be left hanging.

Middleware can be categorized into several types, including:

- **Application-level Middleware**: Bind it to an instance of **`express`** using **`app.use()`** and **`app.METHOD()`**, where **`METHOD`** is the HTTP method of the request that the middleware function handles (such as GET, PUT, or POST).
- **Router-level Middleware**: Works in the same way as application-level middleware, but it is bound to an instance of **`express.Router()`**.
- **Error-handling Middleware**: Defined in the same way as other middleware functions, except that it has four arguments instead of three, specifically with the signature **`(err, req, res, next)`**.
- **Built-in Middleware**: Express has a set of built-in middleware functions like **`express.static`**, which serves static files, and **`express.json`**, which parses incoming requests with JSON payloads.
- **Third-party Middleware**: You can install third-party middleware modules for tasks like parsing cookies, sessions management, logging, and so on.

Here's an example of a simple middleware function:

```
const exampleMiddleware = (req, res, next) => {
    console.log('Middleware executed!');
    next(); // Pass to the next middleware or route handler
};

app.use(exampleMiddleware);
```

***Figure 6.2:** Middleware Example*

Express.js applications are essentially a series of middleware function calls, creating a powerful and flexible method to handle HTTP requests.

With the preceding information, it's time for us to start implementing the backend and build this project structure.

Setting Up Express Server

As covered in the previous section, our first step is to install Express. Since we're using it as our Node.js framework for building APIs, run the following command in your api directory.

```
npm install express
```

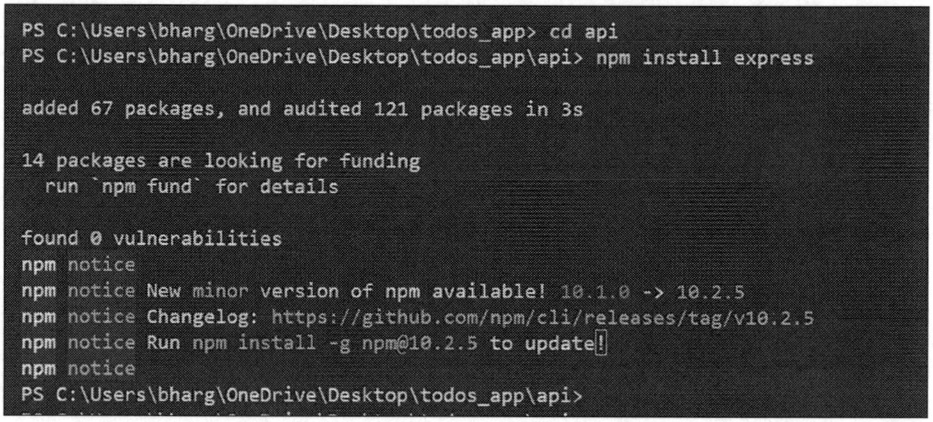

Figure 6.3: *Installing Express*

Once you run the preceding command, the Express dependency is added to the **`package.json`** along with the installation, as shown in *Figure* 6.4.

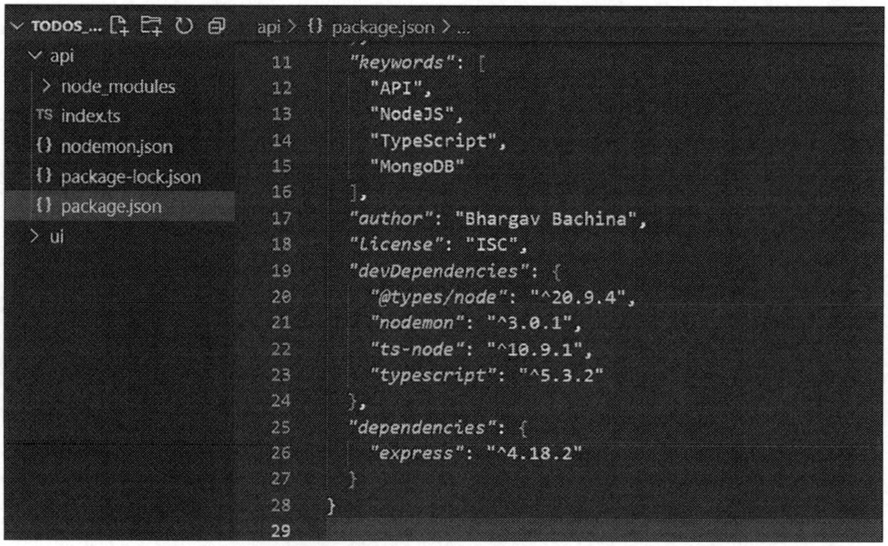

Figure 6.4: *Express installed*

As you can see, we have installed the Express version of 4.18.2. The Node.js packages maintain semantic versioning with major, minor and patch numbers. You can learn more about it here:

https://semver.org/

Since we're building the backend in TypeScript, we'll also need to install type definitions for Node.js. Let's run the following command to install this as dev dependency as we won't be shipping this for production.

```
npm install -D @types/node @types/express
```

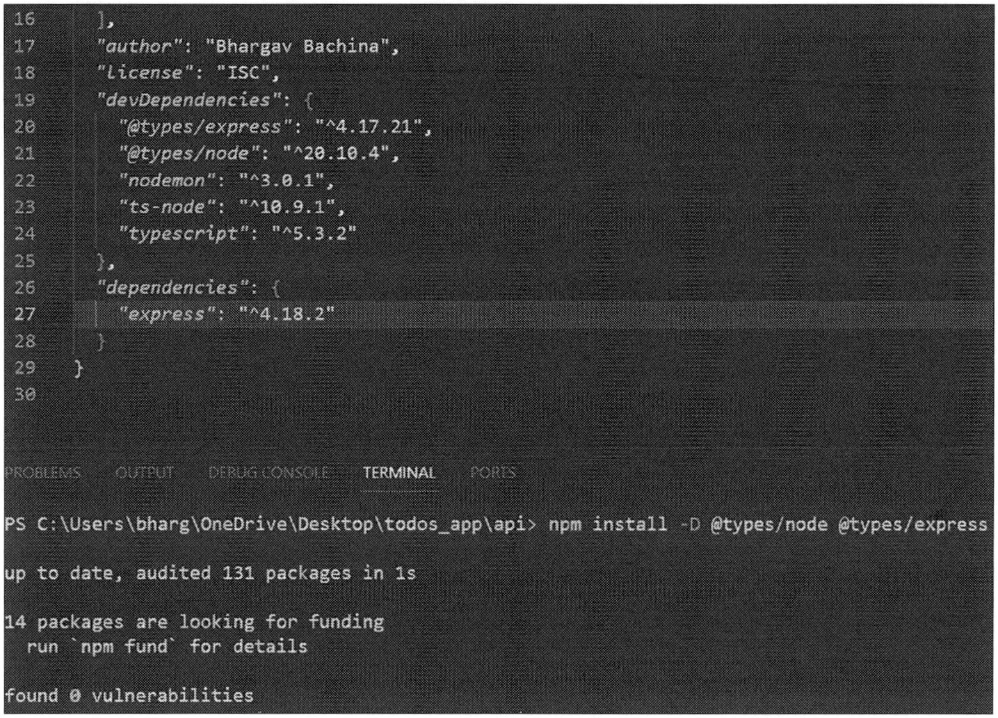

Figure 6.5: *dev dependencies*

The next thing we need to do is to add the **`tsconfig.json`** file, which is a crucial component when working with TypeScript, especially in large projects or when integrating TypeScript into existing JavaScript projects. This file is very important and the backbone of any TypeScript project because it allows you to do the following things:

- **Specifies the Root of a TypeScript Project:** By default, the presence of a **`tsconfig.json`** file in a directory indicates that the directory is the root of a TypeScript project. This helps tools and IDEs recognize the project structure and handle the files accordingly.

- **Configures TypeScript Compiler Options:** It allows you to configure various compiler options for your project. These options include the ECMAScript target version, module system, strictness levels, and more. By setting these options, you can control how the TypeScript compiler transpiles your code into JavaScript.
- **Enhances Code Quality and Consistency:** With options like `strict`, you can enforce a higher level of type-checking and other strictness features, which leads to more robust and error-resistant code. This is particularly important in large projects where code consistency is key.
- **Project-Specific Settings:** Different projects might require different compiler settings due to varying dependencies and architecture choices. `tsconfig.json` allows you to tailor TypeScript's behavior to the specific needs of each project.
- **Improves Development Experience:** Many IDEs and editors use the `tsconfig.json` file to provide a better development experience, offering features such as auto-completion, code navigation, and advanced refactoring tools.
- **Defines Included and Excluded Files:** You can specify which files should be included in or excluded from the compilation process. This is useful for ignoring certain directories (like `node_modules`) or including only specific folders.
- **Supports Advanced Features:** Features like paths aliases, decorators, and JSX support can be configured in `tsconfig.json`, enabling you to use advanced TypeScript and JavaScript features in your project.
- **Integration With Build Tools:** Build tools and bundlers often rely on `tsconfig.json` to determine how to process TypeScript files. This is crucial for integrating TypeScript into complex build pipelines.
- **Facilitates Code Sharing and Reusability:** By having standardized configurations, teams can ensure consistency across different environments and among different developers, making it easier to share and reuse code.

Here is the file we are going to add to our project.

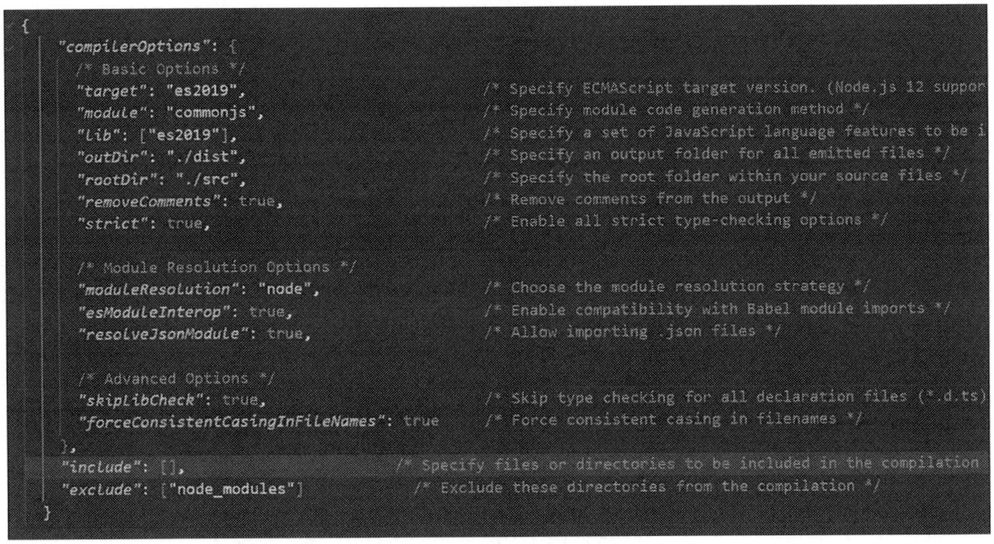

Figure 6.6: *ts.config.json*

You can see the comments in the file about what each option does and here is the high-level configuration.

- Targets ES2019, which is compatible with Node.js version 12 and later.
- Uses **`CommonJS`** modules, which are standard in Node.js.
- Outputs compiled files to the **`./dist`** directory.
- Consider. **`/src`** as the root directory for source files.
- Enables strict type-checking options for better code quality.
- Includes settings for module resolution that are compatible with Node.js.
- Skips type checking for declaration files to speed up the compilation process.
- Enforces consistent file naming to avoid issues on case-sensitive file systems.

With the necessary dependencies and configuration in place, let us set up our Express server. This is a TypeScript class with the constructor, and we call middleware and routes methods in the constructor. We will import Express as a dependency and set up a route in the routes method.

The **`use`** method is a way to register middleware functions in your Express application. The body-parser middleware parses incoming request bodies in a middleware before your handlers, available under the **`req.body`** property. The **`json()`** function specifically parses requests with JSON payloads. This is crucial for applications that need to process JSON data sent from the client, such as in a REST API where clients send JSON data to the server. The **`urlEncoded`** parser incoming request bodies that are sent with the **`Content-Type`** header set to **`application/x-www-form-urlencoded`**. This content type is commonly used by HTML forms.

```
import * as bodyParser from "body-parser";
import express from "express";

class App {

    public express: express.Application;


    constructor() {
        this.express = express();
        this.middleware();
        this.routes();
    }

    // Configure Express middleware.
    private middleware(): void {
        this.express.use(bodyParser.json());
        this.express.use(bodyParser.urlencoded({ extended: false }));
    }

    private routes(): void {

        this.express.get("/", (req, res, next) => {
            res.send("<h1> API Works !!!</h1>");
        });
    }
}

export default new App().express;
```

Figure 6.7: *app.ts*

These two lines of code in the middleware method are configuring the Express application to automatically parse JSON and URL-encoded form data from incoming requests. This parsed data is then easily accessible in your route handlers via **`req.body`**

Here is another file **`index.ts`** in which we are defining the server .**`http`** module is a Node. js's native HTTP module, which can be used to create an HTTP server. **`Createserver()`** method from the **`http`** module that creates a new HTTP server instance. We have imported the App from the **`app.ts`** and this is typically an instance of an Express application. This **`App`** handles incoming HTTP requests and sends responses based on your application's logic. When the HTTP server receives a request, it passes the request to this **`App`** for handling. The created server is stored in a constant named **`server`**. The **`server.listen()`** method is called on the created server instance to start listening for incoming network requests. When **`server.listen(port)`** is called, the server starts listening on the specified port. For example, here the default port number is **`3080`**, your server will listen for requests at **`http://localhost:3080`**.

```
import * as http from "http";
import App from "./app";

const port = process.env.PORT || 3080;

const server = http.createServer(App);
server.listen(port);

server.on("listening", function(): void {
    const addr = server.address();
    const bind = (typeof addr === "string") ? `pipe ${addr}` : `port ${addr?.port}`;
    console.log(`Express Server Listening on ${bind}`);
});

module.exports = App;
```

Figure 6.8: *index.ts*

The preceding code in the **`index.ts`** file creates an HTTP server that uses your Express application (**`App`**) to handle requests and responses. The server then starts listening on a specified port, making it possible for clients to connect to your application through that port. This is a common pattern for setting up a Node.js server with Express.

We have already configured **`nodemon`** in the previous chapter, with these files in place you can run either of these commands: one with **`nodemon`** that watches files if any changes happen, you don't have to restart the server to see those changes and another without **`nodemon`** which manual restarts are needed.

```
{
  "name": "todos_api",
  "version": "1.0.0",
  "description": "API Backend for todos application",
  "main": "index.ts",
  ▷ Debug
  "scripts": {
    "start": "ts-node index.ts",
    "dev": "nodemon",
    "test": "npm test"
  },
  "keywords": [
    "API",
    "NodeJS",
```

Figure 6.9: *npm scripts added*

```
// with nodemon
npm run dev
// without nodemon
npm start
```

When you run those commands, you can see the following message in the console which Express server is listening on a certain port, in this case, **3080**.

```
Express Server Listening on port 3080
```

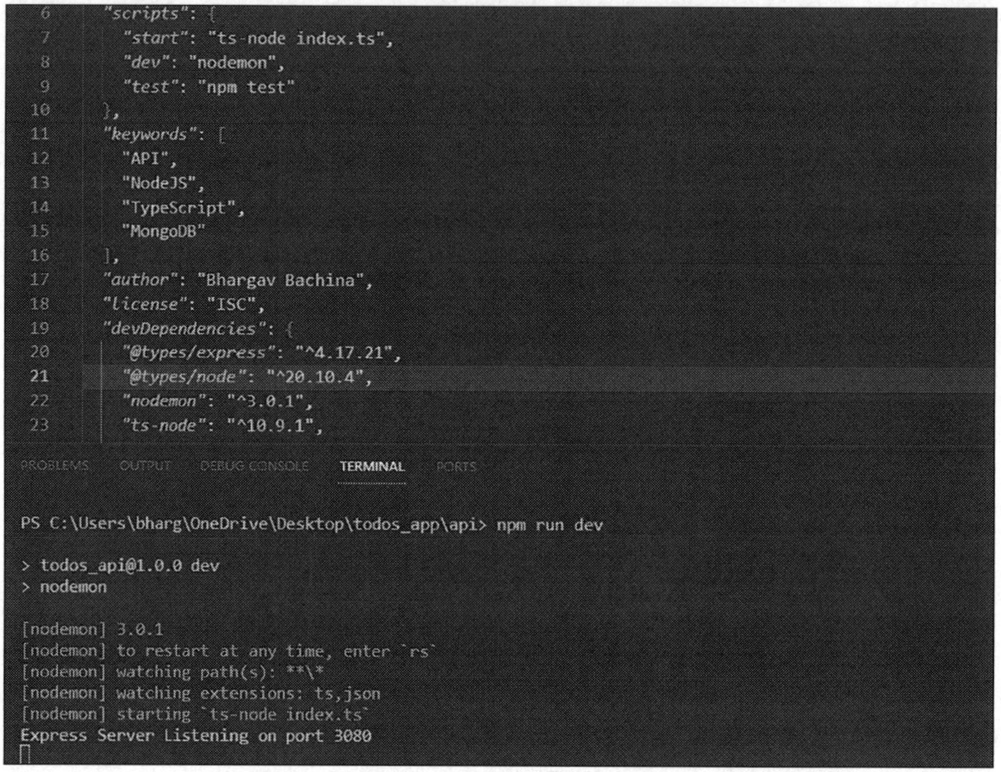

***Figure 6.10**: Express Server Listening on 3080*

As Express Server Listening on port, we have already defined the default route and you should see the message when you hit this URL in the browser.

```
this.express.get("/", (req, res, next) => {
    res.send("<h1> API Works !!!</h1>");
});
```

You can even send the file instead of this text and use **res.sendFile** method instead of **res.send**. You can explore more about this on Express website.

Figure 6.11: *API Works*

Introduction to Webpack

Webpack is a powerful and popular open-source JavaScript module bundler. It processes applications by recursively building a dependency graph that includes every module your application needs, then packaging all those modules into one or more bundles. Initially released in 2012, Webpack has become a key tool in modern web development for its ability to transform, bundle, and package web assets. Here's a closer look at what Webpack does and its features:

- **Module Bundling**: Webpack takes modules along with dependencies as an input and generates static assets to represent those modules. These output assets can be JavaScript files, CSS, images, fonts, and so on.
- **Dependency Graph**: We usually give the starting point of the applications as an input to the webpack bundler and webpack analyses the files starting from that file and their interdependencies and bundles them together.
- **Loaders and Plugins**: Loaders in Webpack transform the source code of a module. For instance, they can transform JSX into JavaScript, or SASS into CSS. Plugins can be used to perform a wider range of tasks such as bundle optimization, asset management, and environment variable injection.

Key Features

The following are the key features of Webpack:

- **Code Splitting:** Webpack allows you to split the code and generate bundles and these bundles can be loaded on demand. This feature improves the load time of the application.
- **Loaders:** There are so many different types of files when you are building the application. We need to process these files and webpack supports various loaders to process these files. This means you can write your modules in different languages or styles like ES6, TypeScript, SASS, and Webpack will compile them to JavaScript and CSS.

- **Plugins:** Webpack doesn't come with all the features we might need. That's why we have plugins to extend the functionality of the webpack. Plugins can be used for a wide variety of tasks like bundle optimization, asset management, and more.
- **Development Server:** There is a configuration called development server which can be useful for real-time development. This feature speeds up your development process.
- **Hot Module Replacement:** HMR allows modules to be updated in-place while the application is running, without a full reload.
- **Optimization:** Offers various optimization features like minifying code, tree shaking to remove unused code, and more.
- **Customizable:** Highly configurable to fit different project needs.

Use Cases

Here are some of the use cases of Webpack:

- **Single Page Applications (SPAs):** Efficiently manage and bundle the numerous scripts and assets.
- **Large Web Applications:** Handle complex dependencies and assets management.
- **Transpiling:** Convert modern JavaScript (ES6, TypeScript) or other resources (SASS, LESS) into browser-compatible formats.

Setting Up Webpack for Building TypeScript Files

As discussed earlier, the webpack revolutionized web development by simplifying the complexity of large web applications. It also streamlined the frontend application development by providing the dev server, HMR, and so on. Its extensive ecosystem and community support make it a staple in modern web development toolkits. With that said, let's get started and implement webpack on our application. We are using webpack 4 for this book and need to run the following command to install on our project. Since we only use webpack for building or developing the application, we need to install these dev dependencies.

```
npm install -D webpack@4 webpack-cli@4
```

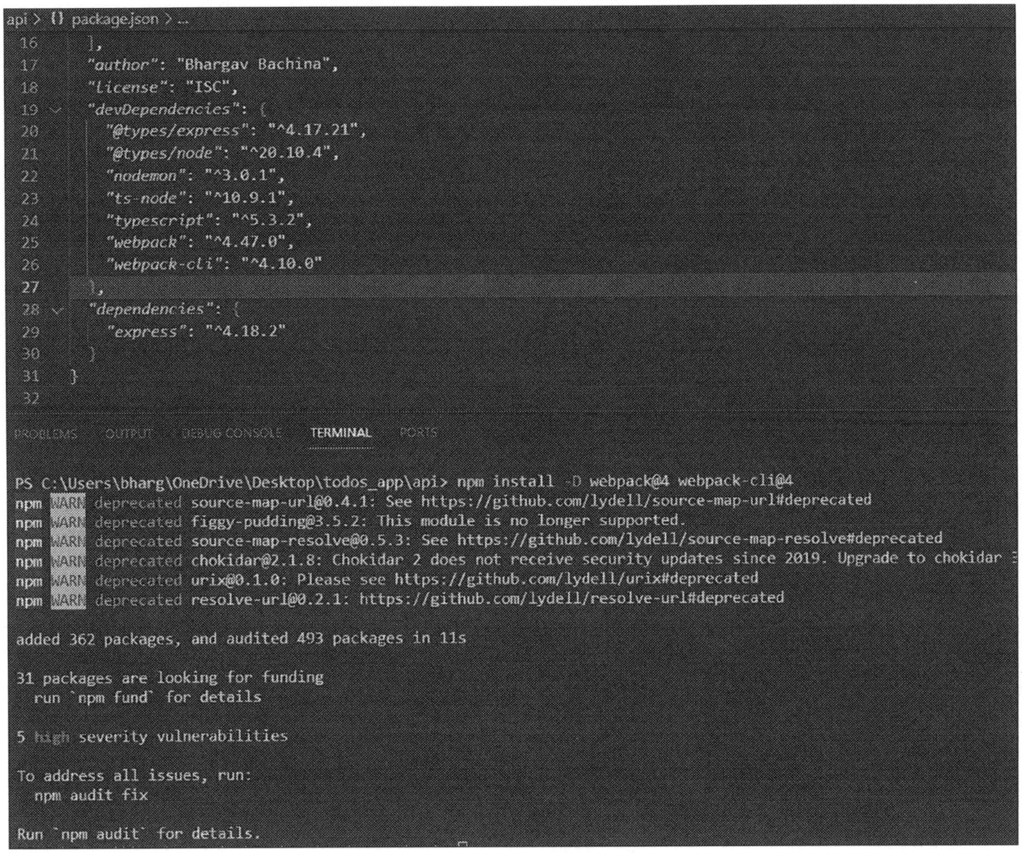

***Figure 6.12**: webpack installed*

Once installed, we need to add a file called **`webpack.config.ts`** in which we define what is the starting file of our application and the output file name where the bundler places the generated static assets. Here is the breakdown of key components in the file:

- **Modules: `path`** and **`webpack`**: These are Node.js modules. **`path`** is a core Node.js module used to handle and transform file paths, and **`webpack`** is the module bundler itself.

api > webpack.config.ts > ...

```
const path = require('path');
const webpack = require('webpack');

module.exports = {
  entry: './index.ts',
  output: {
    path: path.resolve(__dirname, 'dist'),
    filename: 'api.bundle.js'
  },
  resolve: {
    // Add `.ts` and `.tsx` as a resolvable extension.
    extensions: [".ts", ".tsx", ".js"]
  },
  module: {
    rules: [
      // all files with a `.ts` or `.tsx` extension will be handled by `ts-loader`
      { test: /\.tsx?$/, loader: "ts-loader" }
    ]
  },
  target: 'node',
  mode: 'development',
  plugins: []
};
```

Figure 6.13: *webpack.config.ts*

- **Webpack Configuration: `module.exports`**: This is a CommonJS pattern used in Node.js to export the module, in this case, the configuration object for Webpack.
- **Entry Point**: **entry: `'./index.ts`'**: This specifies the entry point of the application, which in this case is **`index.ts`**, a TypeScript file.
- **Output: output**: This property tells Webpack where to output the bundled files and what to name them. **`path: path.resolve(__dirname, 'dist')`**: The output directory for the bundle is set to a **`dist`** folder in the current directory **`(__dirname)`. `filename: 'api.bundle.js`'**: The output file for the bundled code will be named **`api.bundle.js`**.
- **Resolve: `resolve.extensions`**: This allows Webpack to resolve files with **`.ts`**, **`.tsx`**, and **`.js`** extensions, meaning it can process TypeScript and JavaScript files.
- **Module Rules (Loaders): `module.rules`**: Defines an array of rules that tell Webpack how to process different types of modules. **`{ test: /\.tsx?$/, loader: "ts-loader" }`**: This rule tells Webpack to use **`ts-loader`** to process files with **`.ts`** or **`.tsx`** extensions (TypeScript files).
- **Target: `target: 'node'`**: This specifies that the bundle is intended to be used in a Node.js environment, not in a browser.
- **Mode: `mode: 'development'`**: Sets Webpack to development mode, which optimizes the build for development, including more readable output and better debugging support.
- **Plugins: `plugins: []`**: Currently empty, but this array can be filled with Webpack plugins to extend its functionality.

The setup is optimized for development with easy-to-read output and debugging capabilities. You can enhance this configuration with additional loaders, plugins, and options as needed for our project. Make sure you run the following command to install **`ts-loader`** to process the TypeScript files. We are using the specific version as it is compatible with the Webpack version 4.

```
npm install -D ts-loader@8.2.0
```

Once you have installed this, we can add the script in the scripts sections of the **`package.json`** file and execute the following command to build the project.

```
npm run build
```

The preceding command runs the webpack and the webpack picks the **`webpack.config.ts`** at the root level by default. If you change the name, you should give that name and location of the file with the flag **`-config`** as follows:

```
webpack -config custom-folder/custom.config.ts
```

As you can see in *Figure 6.14*, it generates the output file called **`api.bundle.js`** and places that file under the folder named dist. Take a look at the file, it is a JavaScript file and contains all the necessary code and dependencies to run the application.

Figure 6.14: *build successful*

Now you can run the following command to run the application with the generated output file. Since the file extension is **.js** and **node.js** can easily execute it without any loaders such as **ts-node**, and so on.

```
node dist/api.bundle.js
```

Figure 6.15: *running the built file*

The application started and running on port **3080**. You can check and hit the URL http://localhost:3080 to test the application.

Defining Routes

We have defined the default route for the backend as shown in *Figure* 6.16, but what happens when you put something that is not defined in the routes in the URL.

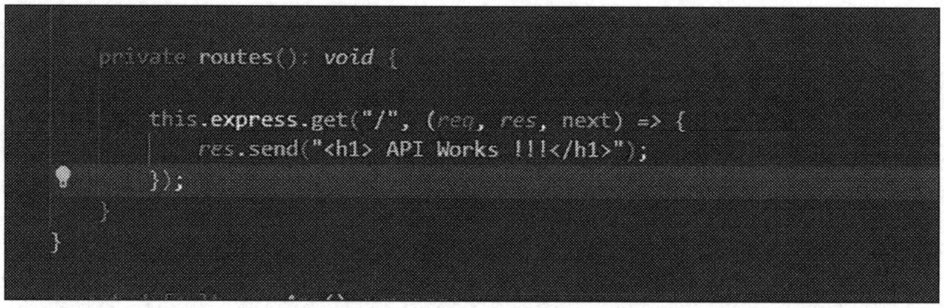

Figure 6.16: *default route*

As mentioned earlier, the preceding default route sends the message API Works. However, if you enter anything in the URL path that doesn't match a defined route, you'll receive the following response because we haven't set up specific routes yet.

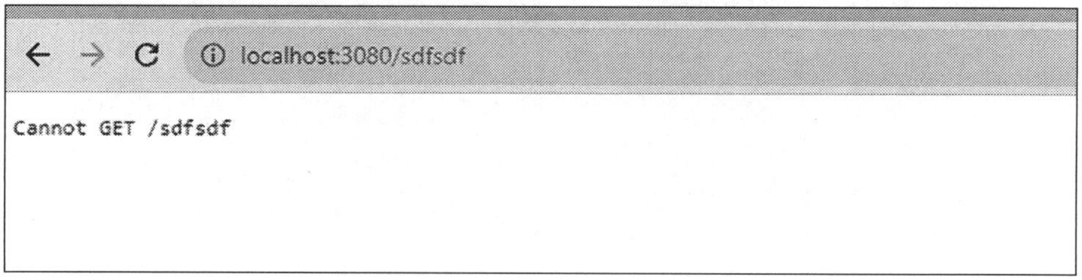

Figure 6.17: *unhandled routes*

We need to define an unhandled route for these scenarios which could take care of any route which is not defined. This wildcard route (*) catches all requests that don't match any of the defined routes and sends back a 404 Not Found status with a message. It's typically placed at the end of all route definitions.

```
private routes(): void {

    this.express.get("/", (req, res, next) => {
        res.status(200).send("<h1> API Works !!!</h1>");
    });

    // handle undefined routes
    this.express.use("*", (req, res, next) => {
        res.status(404).send("<h1 style='color:red'>Make sure url is correct!!!</h1>");
    });
}
```

Figure 6.18: *Defining unhandled routes*

Defining an unhandled route is very important for the following reasons:

- **User Feedback:** When users or clients request an endpoint that does not exist, providing a clear message about the route being incorrect or unavailable is a good practice.
- **Security:** Catch-all handlers for undefined routes can prevent exposing information about the server. Without such handlers, some servers may send default responses that could reveal sensitive details about the backend infrastructure, potentially leading to security vulnerabilities.
- **Error Handling:** Defining a behavior for unhandled routes allows you to control the error handling process. You can log these events, which might indicate a problem in the frontend or a malicious attempt to access unauthorized parts of the API.
- **API Reliability:** It ensures that your API behaves predictably. Clients of your API will receive consistent responses, whether they hit a valid endpoint or not.
- **Maintainability:** It improves the maintainability of the application. Developers can quickly identify routes that are not intentionally exposed and might need to be implemented or fixed.
- **Analytics and Monitoring:** Handling unhandled routes can be useful for analytics and monitoring. By logging these requests, you can gain insights into how your API is being used or misused.
- **Professionalism:** It contributes to the professionalism of your API. A well-handled error response is a sign of a mature and robust API.

If you put any route which is not defined, you can see the following output with status **`404`**.

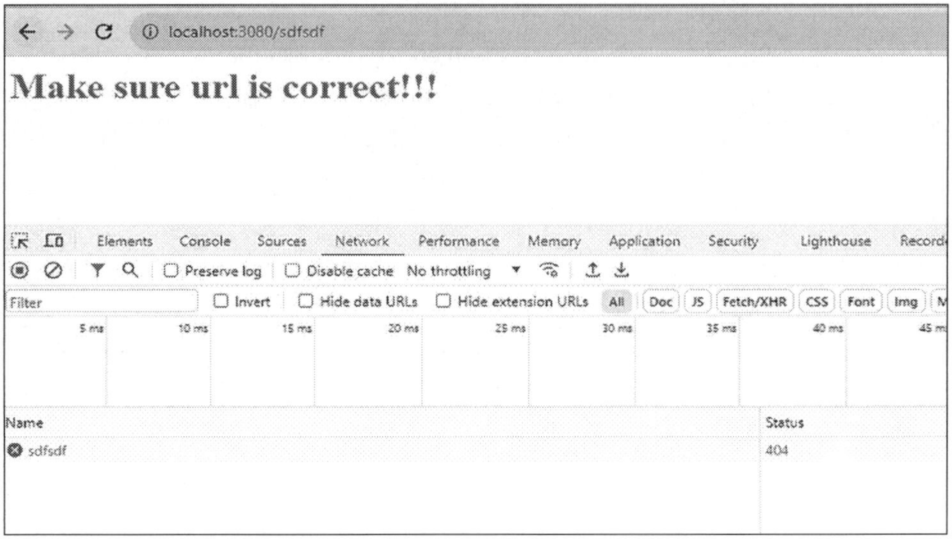

Figure 6.19: *Testing unhandled routes*

It's time to implement all the APIs as we are done with the default and unhandled routes. We have two modules: one user module in which we are defining sign in and sign-up APIs and another module for the tasks (all CRUD operations). Let's define two routes for these two modules.

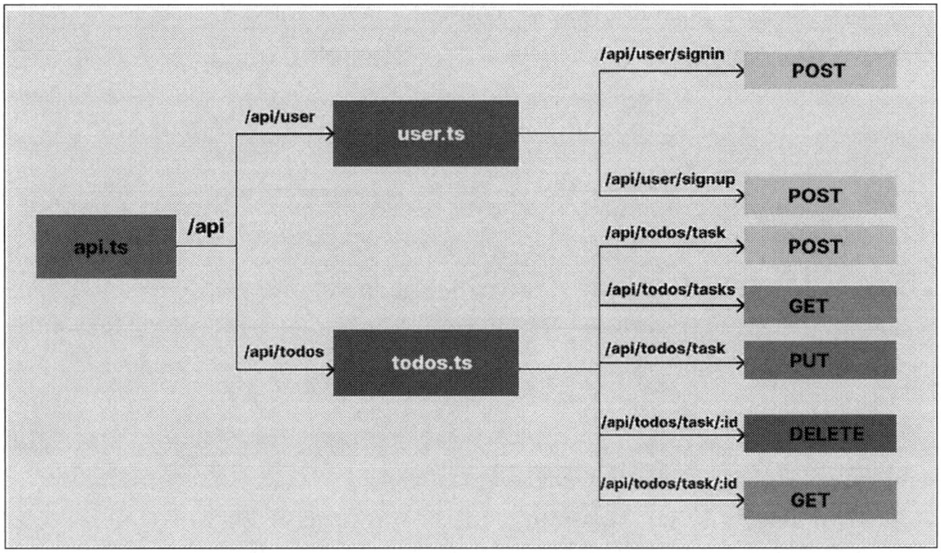

Figure 6.20: *Routing structure*

Figure 6.20 outlines the routing structure of our Express.js Node.js backend application. It visually represents how different URL paths (endpoints) correspond to different files in the backend codebase and how these paths are associated with different HTTP methods for CRUD (Create, Read, Update, Delete) operations. Here's the breakdown of the diagram:

`api.ts` (Red Box)

- This file likely acts as the central hub for routing in the application. It's common to have a main file that imports and uses router modules from other parts of the application.

Routing to Modules (Purple Boxes)

- The two main routes: **`/api/user`** and **`/api/todos`**. These routes are directed towards separate files: **`user.ts`** and **`todos.ts`**.
- This implies that **`api.ts`** delegates the handling of these routes to the respective modules. This kind of modular routing helps in organizing the codebase by domain, which is a common practice in RESTful API design.

User Routes

- **`/api/user/signin`** (Green Box with POST): This endpoint is for users to sign in. The **`POST`** HTTP method indicates that this route expects data (such as username and password) to process the sign-in.
- **`/api/user/signup`** (Green Box with POST): This endpoint is for users to create a new account. It also uses **`POST`**, as it expects data to register a new user.

Todo Routes

- **`/api/todos/task`** (Green Box with POST): This is likely used to create a new task in a todo list. It accepts **`POST`** requests with the task details.
- **`/api/todos/tasks`** (Orange Box with GET): This endpoint retrieves a list of tasks, indicated by the **`GET`** method, which is typically used for reading data.
- **`/api/todos/task`** (Pink Box with PUT): This endpoint is for updating an existing task. The **`PUT`** method is often used for updating resources.
- **`/api/todos/task/:id`** (Red Box with DELETE): This endpoint deletes a task specified by its **`id`**. The **`DELETE`** method is used for removing resources.
- **`/api/todos/task/:id`** (Green Box with GET): This gets a specific task by its **`id`**. It's another **`GET`** route, but this time it's expected to return a single task detail.

The following file defines a **`User`** class in TypeScript for an Express.js application. This class initializes an Express application and sets up two POST routes for user sign-in and sign-up functionality. Both routes log the requested URL to the console and respond with a JSON object that echoes back the **`user`** from the request body. Finally, an instance of the **`User`** class is created, and the **`express`** application is exported for use elsewhere in the application.

api > src > routes > user.ts > User

```
import express from "express";

class User {

    public express: express.Application;

    constructor() {
        this.express = express();
        this.routes();
    }

    private routes(): void {

        // user signin
        this.express.post("/signin", (req, res, next) => {
            console.info("url:::::::" + req.url);
            res.status(200).json({user: req.body.user});
        });

        // user signup
        this.express.post("/signup", (req, res, next) => {
            console.info("url:::::::" + req.url);
            res.status(200).json({user: req.body.user});
        });
    }
}

export default new User().express;
```

Figure 6.21: *user route*

The following file defines a TypeScript class named **`Todos`** that encapsulates routing logic for a **`todos`** resource within an Express.js application. The class initializes an Express application and sets up various routes to handle CRUD operations for todo items. Each route is associated with an HTTP verb (GET, PUT, POST, DELETE) corresponding to the CRUD operation it represents.

At the end of the file, the **`Todos`** class is instantiated, and the **`express`** property of that instance is exported. This means that when this module is imported elsewhere, it provides an Express application that's already configured with the routes defined in the **`Todos`** class.

```
api > src > routes > TS todos.ts > Todos > constructor
import express from "express";

class Todos {

    public express: express.Application;

    constructor() {
        this.express = express();
        this.routes();
    }

    private routes(): void {

        // GET Tasks
        this.express.get("/tasks", (req, res, next) => {
            console.info("url:::::::" + req.url);
            res.status(200).json({message: "/tasks GET called"});
        });

        // PUT Task
        this.express.put("/task", (req, res, next) => {
            console.info("url:::::::" + req.url);
            res.status(200).json({message: "/task PUT called"});
        });

        // POST Task
        this.express.post("/task", (req, res, next) => {
            console.info("url:::::::" + req.url);
            res.status(200).json({message: "/task POST called"});
        });

        // DELETE Task
        this.express.delete("/task/:id", (req, res, next) => {
            console.info("url:::::::" + req.url);
            res.status(200).json({message: "/task DELETE called"});
        });

        // GET Task detail
        this.express.get("/task/:id", (req, res, next) => {
            console.info("url:::::::" + req.url);
            res.status(200).json({message: "/task GET called"});
        });
    }
}

export default new Todos().express;
```

Figure 6.22: *todos route*

We defined two routes and it's time to add these routes in the **`app.ts`** file. We need to set up middleware for routing different HTTP requests to their respective route handlers based on the request path.

The line number 29 in *Figure* 6.23 registers a middleware with the path **`/user`**. This means that any request whose path begins with **`/user`** will be forwarded to the **`User`** middleware. The **`User`** object is likely another router or a module that contains more specific routes and handlers related to user operations, such as signing up, logging in, and user profile management.

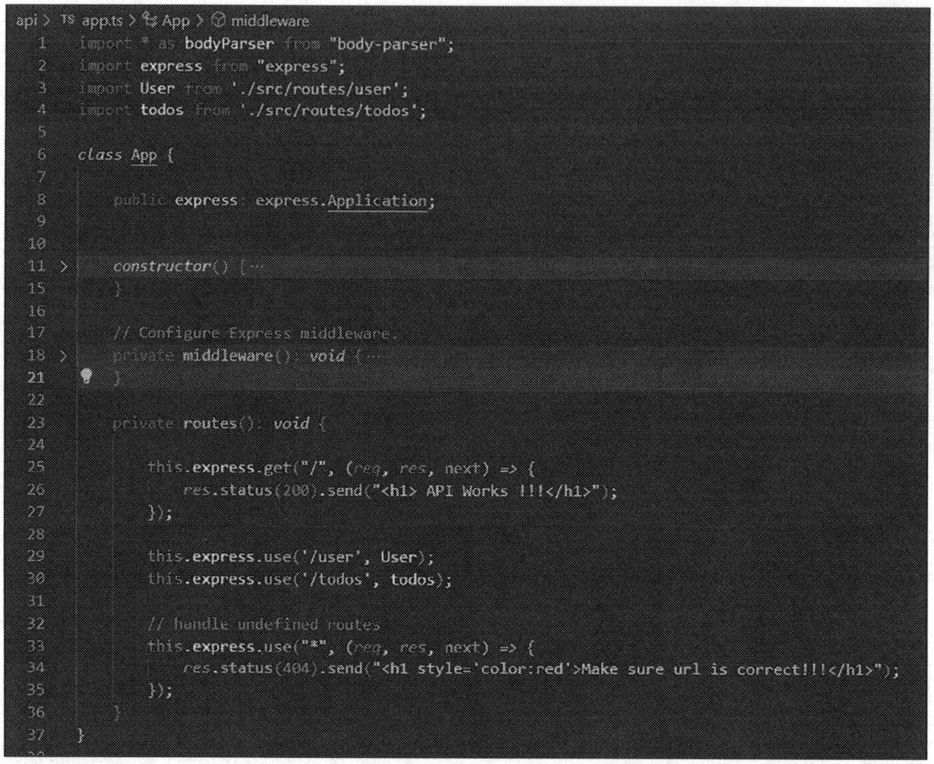

Figure 6.23: *app.ts*

Similarly, the line number 30 in *Figure* 6.23 registers a middleware with the path **`/todos`**. All requests starting with **`/todos`** will be handled by the **`todos`** middleware. The **`todos`** object could be a router that defines routes for operations related to todo items, such as creating a new todo (**`POST`**), fetching all todos (**`GET`**), updating (**`PUT`**), or deleting a todo (**`DELETE`**). In Express.js, routes are matched in the order they are defined. Thus, any request to **`/user`** or **`/todos`** will first pass through any global middleware defined before these lines, and then to the specific route handlers defined in the **`User`** and **`todos`** modules.

We can test the URLs with the postman since some of them are **`POST`**, **`PUT`**. You can do it on your own. Here is the sample GET URL testing we have done so far.

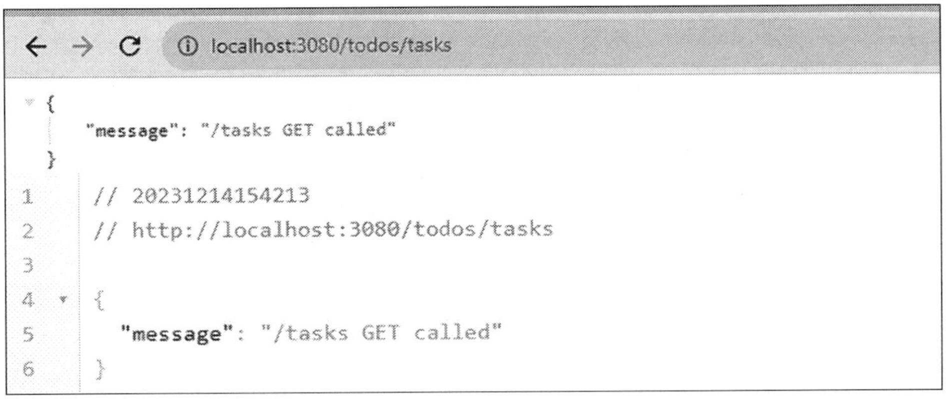

Figure 6.24: *testing api*

Building API Structure

We have set up the routes, we will build the API structure in this section. We have seen how we must maintain controllers and services for the maintainability of the code. Let's build controllers and services to handle all the endpoints properly. We are not going to plug in the database in this chapter, but we will set up the backend API for it.

The first thing we need to build is services. We are going to use dummy data in the services as we are not integrating the MongoDB in this chapter. Since we have two modules, we'll create the following two services.

The following **`UserService`** class in the provided code simulates user sign-in and sign-up processes for a Node.js application. It contains:

- A hardcoded array of users for demonstration purposes.
- A **`signin`** method that checks if a user exists with the given credentials and returns a user object if found.
- A **`signup`** method that adds a new user to the array and returns the added user object.

Both methods return a standardized **`UserResponse`** with status codes, demonstrating basic user authentication and registration flows. The implementation is simplified for illustrative purposes and lacks the security measures required for a production environment. We will make it production-ready by the end of the book.

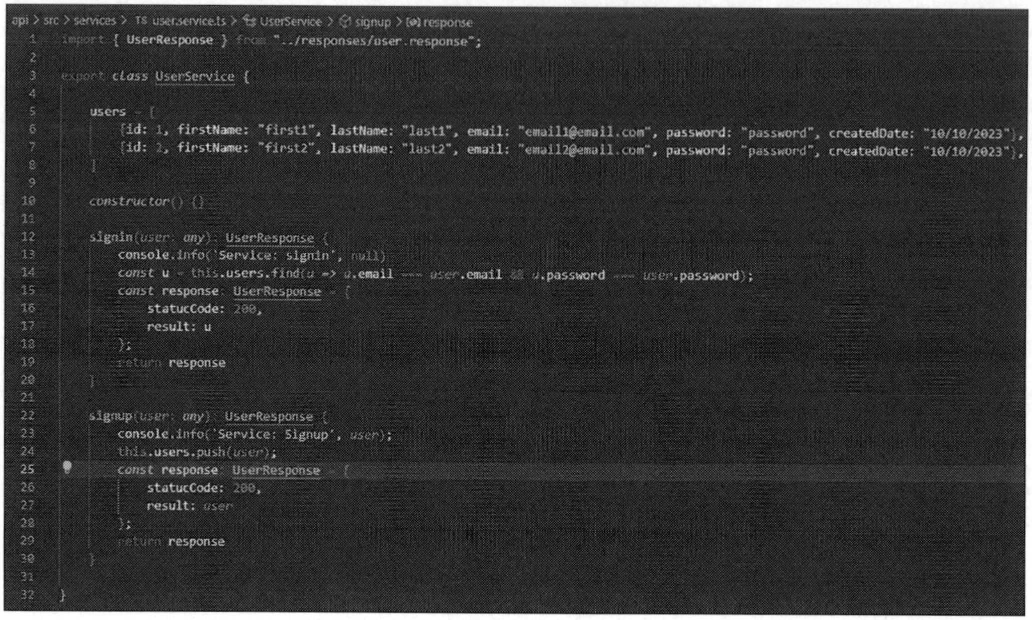
api > src > services > TS user.service.ts > UserService > signup > response

```
import { UserResponse } from "../responses/user.response";

export class UserService {

    users = [
        {id: 1, firstName: "first1", lastName: "last1", email: "email1@email.com", password: "password", createdDate: "10/10/2023"},
        {id: 2, firstName: "first2", lastName: "last2", email: "email2@email.com", password: "password", createdDate: "10/10/2023"},
    ]

    constructor() {}

    signin(user: any): UserResponse {
        console.info('Service: signin', null)
        const u = this.users.find(u => u.email === user.email && u.password === user.password);
        const response: UserResponse = {
            statucCode: 200,
            result: u
        };
        return response
    }

    signup(user: any): UserResponse {
        console.info('Service: Signup', user);
        this.users.push(user);
        const response: UserResponse = {
            statucCode: 200,
            result: user
        };
        return response
    }

}
```

***Figure 6.25**: user service*

The following **`TodosService`** class in the provided code simulates tasks processes for a Node.js application. It contains:

- **`Tasks Array`**: This array serves as an in-memory storage of tasks. Each task is an object with properties such as **`id`**, **`task`**, **`assignee`**, **`description`**, and **`createdDate`**.
- **`Constructor`**: The class has an empty constructor. This is where you could potentially initialize some values or services if needed.
- **`Methods`**: These are CRUD operations that simulates the database operations.
- **`TodoResponse` Type:** This is a custom type (presumably defined elsewhere) used to standardize the response format of each method. It includes a **`statusCode`** (which seems to be a typo and should be **`statusCode`**) and a **`result`** which varies depending on the method.

The service interacts with a simple in-memory array, which will be replaced with a database in a more complex application in the next chapter.

api > src > services > todos.service.ts > TodosService > createTask

```typescript
import { TodoResponse } from "../responses/todos.response";

export class TodosService {

    tasks = [
        {id: "1", task: "task1", assignee: "user1", description: "this is task1", createdDate: "10/10/2023"},
        {id: "2", task: "task2", assignee: "user2", description: "this is task2", createdDate: "10/10/2023"}
    ]

    constructor() {}

    getTasks(): TodoResponse {
        console.info('Service: getTasks', null)
        const response: TodoResponse = {
            statucCode: 200,
            result: this.tasks
        }
        return response;
    }

    createTask(task: any): TodoResponse {
        console.info('Service: createTask', task);
        task.createdDate = new Date();
        this.tasks.push(task);
        const response: TodoResponse = {
            statucCode: 200,
            result: this.tasks
        }
        return response;
    }

    updateTask(task: any): TodoResponse {···
    }

    deleteTask(taskId: string): TodoResponse {···
    }

    getTaskDetails(taskId: string): TodoResponse {···
    }
}
```

Figure 6.26: *todo service*

Here is the todos controller class, which acts as the controller layer in a typical MVC architecture for a to-do list application.

```
api > src > controllers > TS todos.controller.ts > TodosController > getTasks
import { Task } from '../requests/todos.request';
import { TodoResponse } from '../responses/todos.response';
import { TodosService } from '../services/todos.service';

export class TodosController {

    private todosService: TodosService;

    constructor() {
        this.todosService = new TodosService();
    }

    getTasks(): TodoResponse {
        console.info('Controller: getTasks', null)
        return this.todosService.getTasks();
    }

    createTask(task: Task): TodoResponse {
        console.info('Controller: createTask', task);
        return this.todosService.createTask(task);
    }

    updateTask(task: Task): TodoResponse {
        console.info('Controller: updateTask', task);
        return this.todosService.updateTask(task);
    }

    deleteTask(taskId: string): TodoResponse {
        console.info('Controller: deleteTask', taskId);
        return this.todosService.deleteTask(taskId);
    }

    getTaskDetails(taskId: string): TodoResponse {
        console.info('Controller: getTask Details', null)
        return this.todosService.getTaskDetails(taskId);
    }
}
```

Figure 6.27: *todo controller*

The **`UserController`** acts as a controller layer in the application, interfacing between the client-side requests and the service layer. It simplifies the request handling by delegating complex operations to **`UserService`**, following a common pattern in server-side application development to maintain separation of concerns.

- **`Signin` Method:** This method takes a user object as an argument and calls the **`signin`** method of the **`userService`**. The result (presumably a **`UserResponse`**) is then returned. This method is meant to handle user sign-in operations.
- **`Signup` Method:** Similar to **`signin`**, this method takes a user object and delegates the signup operation to the **`userService`** by calling its **`signup`** method. The result is then returned. This method is for handling user registration or sign-up.

api > src > controllers > user.controller.ts > UserController > constructor

```typescript
import { UserResponse } from '../responses/user.response';
import { UserService } from '../services/user.service';

export class UserController {

    private userService: UserService;

    constructor() {
        this.userService = new UserService();
    }

    signin(user: any): UserResponse {
        console.info('Controller: signin', user)
        return this.userService.signin(user);
    }

    singup(user: any): UserResponse {
        console.info('Controller: signup', user);
        return this.userService.signup(user);
    }

}
```

Figure 6.28: *user controller*

There is a common practice in TypeScript to enforce type safety and data integrity throughout the application, particularly useful in scenarios including form submissions or API requests. This interface is a contract that specifies the structure of an object for a sign-in request in an application.

api > src > requests > signin.request.ts > SignInRequest

```typescript
export interface SignInRequest {

    email: string;
    password: string;
}
```

Figure 6.29: *signin request*

This interface outlines the structure for a sign-up request within an application, specifying the required fields and their types.

- **`firstName`:** A **`string`** type field expected to hold the first name of the user who is signing up.
- **`lastName`:** Also a **`string`**, this field is for the last name of the user.
- **`email`:** This **`string`** field is intended to contain the user's email address.
- **`password`:** Another **`string`** field, used for the user's chosen password.

```
api > src > requests > TS signup.request.ts > SignUpRequest
export interface SignUpRequest {

    firstName: string;
    lastName: string;
    email: string;
    password: string;
}
```

Figure 6.30: *signup request*

The following TypeScript code defines an interface **`Task`** and two other interfaces **`CreateTaskRequest`** and **`UpdateTaskRequest`** that extend **`Task`**.

```
api > src > requests > TS todos.request.ts > UpdateTaskRequest
export interface Task {
    id: string;
    task: string;
    assignee: string;
    description: string;
}

export interface CreateTaskRequest extends Task{}

export interface UpdateTaskRequest extends Task{}
```

Figure 6.31: *todos request*

The following file is the response type definition. It's designed to standardize the format of responses in a to-do application. Here's a breakdown of its components.

```
api > src > responses > TS todos.response.ts > TodoResponse
export interface TodoResponse {

    statucCode: number;
    message?: string;
    result: any
}
```

Figure 6.32: *todos response*

Here is the **UserResponse** for the user module.

```
api > src > responses > TS user.response.ts > UserResponse
export interface UserResponse {

    statucCode: number;
    message?: string;
    result: any
}
```

Figure 6.33: *user response*

The following TypeScript code defines the routing module for our application. This module is responsible for handling HTTP POST requests related to user operations, specifically sign-in and sign-up.

- A POST route for **/signin**, which logs the request URL, calls the **signin** method of **userController** with the request body (assumed to contain sign-in credentials), and sends back the result as a JSON response with a 200 HTTP status code.
- A POST route for **/signup**, similarly, logs the request URL, calls the **signup** method of **userController** with the request body (assumed to contain sign-up information), and sends back the result as a JSON response with a 200 HTTP status code.

```
api > src > routes > TS user.ts > ...
import express from "express";
import { UserController } from '../controllers/user.controller'
import { SignInRequest } from '../requests/signin.request';
import { SignUpRequest } from '../requests/signup.request';
import { UserResponse } from '../responses/user.response'

class User {

    public express: express.Application;
    private userController: UserController;

    constructor() {
        this.express = express();
        this.routes();
        this.userController = new UserController();
    }

    private routes(): void {

        // user signin
        this.express.post("/signin", (req: express.Request<any, any, SignInRequest>, res: express.Response<UserResponse>, next: express.NextFunction) => {
            console.info("url:::::::" + req.url);
            const result = this.userController.signin(req.body);
            res.status(200).json(result);
        });

        // user signup
        this.express.post("/signup", (req: express.Request<any, any, SignUpRequest>, res: express.Response<UserResponse>, next: express.NextFunction) => {
            console.info("url:::::::" + req.url);
            const result = this.userController.singup(req.body);
            res.status(200).json(result);
        });
    }
}

export default new User().express;
```

Figure 6.34: *updated user route*

This TypeScript code for our application, defining an **express.Router** with route handlers for a to-do module:

- **GET /tasks**: This route is for retrieving all tasks. When a **GET** request is made to the **/tasks** endpoint, it logs the request URL, calls the **getTasks** method on the **todosController**, and sends the result back with a 200 HTTP status code in JSON format.
- **PUT /task**: This route is for updating a task. When a **PUT** request is made to the **/task** endpoint, it logs the request URL, expects the request body to match the **UpdateTaskRequest** interface, calls the **updateTask** method on the **todosController** with the request body, and sends the result back with a 200 status code in JSON.
- **POST /task**: This route is for creating a new task. On a **POST** request to the **/task** endpoint, it logs the request URL, expects the request body to match the **CreateTaskRequest** interface, calls the **createTask** method on the **todosController** with the request body, and sends the result back with a 200 status code in JSON.
- **DELETE /task/:id**: This route handles the deletion of a task. When a DELETE request is made to the **/task/:id** endpoint, it logs the request URL, extracts the **id** from the request parameters, calls the **deleteTask** method on the **todosController** with the task **id**, and sends back the result with a 200 status code in JSON.
- **GET /task/:id**: This route is for retrieving the details of a specific task. On a GET request to **/task/:id**, it logs the request URL, extracts the **id** from the request parameters, calls the **getTaskDetails** method on the **todosController** with the task **id**, and sends the result back with a 200 status code in JSON.

Each route handler also uses TypeScript generics to indicate the type of the request and response objects, thereby enforcing type safety and consistency throughout the application. For instance, **express.Request<any, any, UpdateTaskRequest>** specifies that the request body should conform to the **UpdateTaskRequest** interface, and **express.Response<TodoResponse>** specifies that the response should conform to the **TodoResponse** interface.

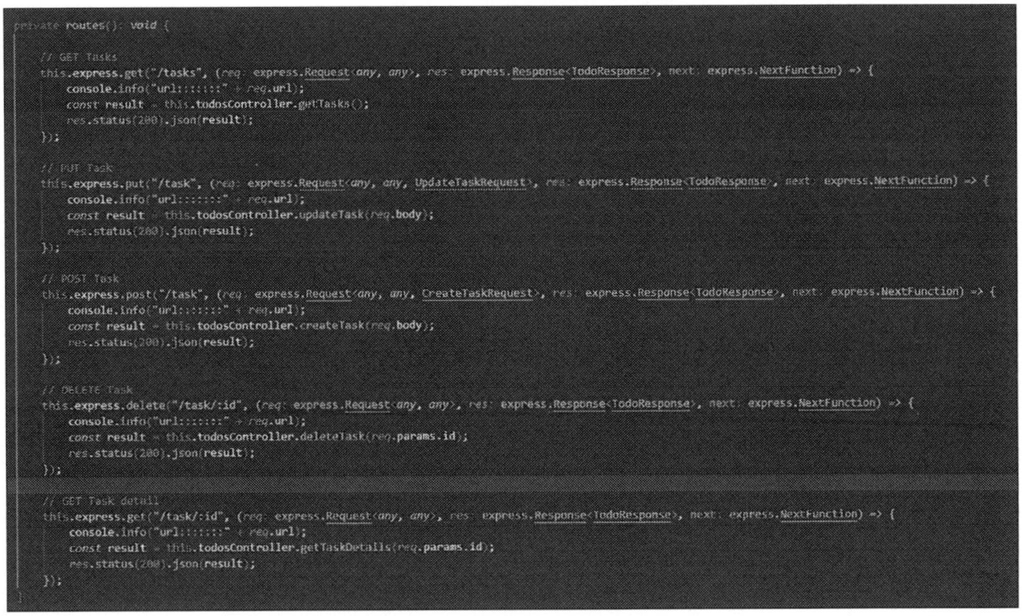

Figure 6.35: *Updated todos route*

At this stage, the application is ready to be executed and can be evaluated using Postman. While we won't cover testing every endpoint in this book, you're encouraged to conduct your own tests if you've been following along with the setup thus far.

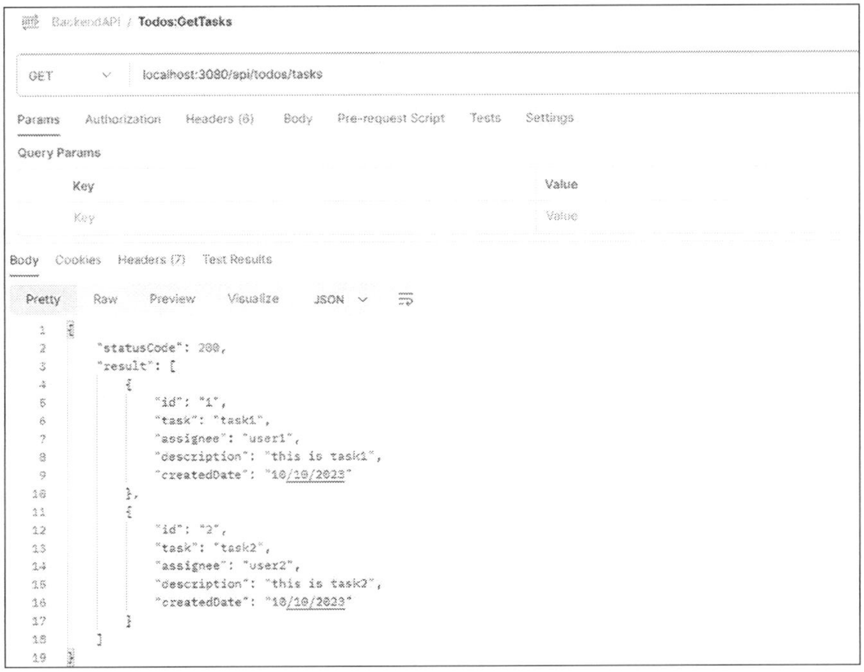

Figure 6.36: *testing apis*

We have successfully established the project structure for a backend application using Node.js, TypeScript, and Express. This setup includes a well-organized directory hierarchy that houses controllers, services, request handlers, response utilities, and routing mechanisms, among other components. Each controller is linked to corresponding service classes that encapsulate the business logic, while the request and response directories contain typed interfaces to ensure data integrity and facilitate clear communication between the client and server. The routing configuration utilizes Express to define endpoints, providing a robust and maintainable framework that is ready to handle various business requirements effectively. This architecture not only streamlines development by segregating concerns but also enhances code readability and scalability for future expansion.

Request Validation

Request validation in the context of a Node.js Express.js backend API is the process of checking that the incoming requests have the expected format, type, and content before the application processes them. It involves verifying the various parts of the request, such as the query parameters, route parameters, and body content, to ensure they meet the criteria set out by the application's business logic.

The importance of request validation in a Node.js Express.js backend API cannot be overstated, and it includes the following aspects:

- **Data Integrity**: Validation ensures only well-formed data enters the system, which helps maintain the integrity of the data throughout the application.
- **Security**: By validating input, you can prevent malicious data that could lead to security vulnerabilities, such as SQL injection or cross-site scripting (XSS) attacks, from entering the system.
- **Error Handling**: Detecting errors early in the request cycle makes error handling more manageable. It allows the application to send back meaningful error messages to the client, which can improve the client's ability to debug issues.
- **Preventing Resource Misuse**: Unvalidated requests could lead to unnecessary processing and waste server resources. Validation at the entry point prevents such misuse.
- **User Experience**: Proper validation with clear error messages can significantly improve the end-user experience by preventing invalid data submission and providing immediate feedback.
- **Business Logic Assurance**: Validation enforces the business rules of your application right at the point of entry, ensuring that subsequent operations can assume the data is correct and appropriately formatted.

- **Reduce Database Errors:** Validation can prevent database errors that would occur from trying to insert invalid data into a database.
- **Compliance**: For many applications, particularly in fields such as healthcare or finance, data validation is a legal requirement for compliance with standards and regulations.
- **Ease of Maintenance**: Validated data ensures that the rest of the application can work with a known, validated dataset, which simplifies the logic and maintenance of the code.

In an Express.js application, validation can be implemented using middleware that checks the request before it reaches the route handler. If the validation fails, the middleware can send a response with an error, preventing the route handler from executing with invalid data. There are several libraries available to facilitate request validation in Express.js, such as Joi, express-validator, and celebrate, which provide a rich set of tools for defining validation schemas and rules.

Let's look at the examples for both validation frameworks.

Joi

Joi is a powerful schema description language and data validator for JavaScript. It's particularly well-suited for Node.js and Express applications, as it allows developers to describe the data structures they expect in an expressive, readable format. Joi can validate both client-submitted data, such as form inputs and query parameters, and data constructed on the server, ensuring it meets certain criteria before being processed or passed along.

With Joi, you can construct blueprints or schemas for JavaScript objects (an object schema) to ensure validation of key information. For instance, you might define a user object requiring a string as a username with certain length constraints, a valid email address, and a complex password. Joi not only checks that these fields are of the right type but can also apply advanced validations, including regular expressions.

Joi's validation system comes with a wide range of customizable options, making it an essential tool for backend development, especially when dealing with APIs that need to validate data from various sources. It provides clear error messages that can be returned to the client, helping to debug requests that contain invalid data. As such, Joi is a staple in many Node.js RESTful service stacks, providing a layer of security and confidence in the integrity of the data being handled.

First, you will need to install Joi using npm:

```
npm install joi
```

Then, we can validate the request objects as follows. We need to import Joi and add validations to the request object. Once the request comes in and call the validate method on the request.

```
import express from 'express';
import Joi from 'joi';

const app = express();
app.use(express.json());

const userSchema = Joi.object({
  username: Joi.string().alphanum().min(3).max(30).required(),
  password: Joi.string().pattern(new RegExp('^[a-zA-Z0-9]{3,30}$')),
  email: Joi.string().email({ minDomainSegments: 2 })
});

app.post('/signup', (req, res) => {
  const { error, value } = userSchema.validate(req.body);

  if (error) {
    res.status(400).json({ error: error.details[0].message });
    return;
  }

  // Handle valid case
  res.status(200).json({ message: 'User created successfully', user: value });
});

const PORT = process.env.PORT || 3000;
app.listen(PORT, () => console.log(`Server running on port ${PORT}`));
```

***Figure 6.37:** Joi example*

If validation fails, the error is sent back in the response with a 400 Bad Request status code, along with the error message from Joi. The **`error.details[0].message`** provides the first validation error message, which is typically enough to inform the client what went wrong.

If validation is successful (that is, no error), the server responds with a 200 OK status and a success message. It also returns the validated value, which contains the sanitized user input data according to the schema.

Express-validator

`Express-validator` is a middleware library for Express.js, a popular Node.js web framework. It simplifies the process of validating and sanitizing request data in Express applications. Built on top of validator.js, a library for string validation and sanitization, express-validator provides a rich set of validations and customizations that can be easily integrated into any Express.js application.

The primary purpose of express-validator is to ensure that data coming into your server via requests (such as POST or PUT requests) is valid, correctly formatted, and secure. This includes checking for the presence of required fields, verifying that data types are as expected (such as strings, numbers, or dates), and ensuring data conforms to specific formats (such as email addresses or URLs).

Express-validator is widely used in the Node.js ecosystem for its ease of use, flexibility, and comprehensive feature set. It helps developers create more robust, secure, and reliable web applications by ensuring that incoming data is properly validated and sanitized before being processed or stored.

We need to install **`express-validator`** with **`npm`**:

```
npm install express-validator
```

We can import body and **`validationResult`** from the **`express-validator`** and add validations to the request object.

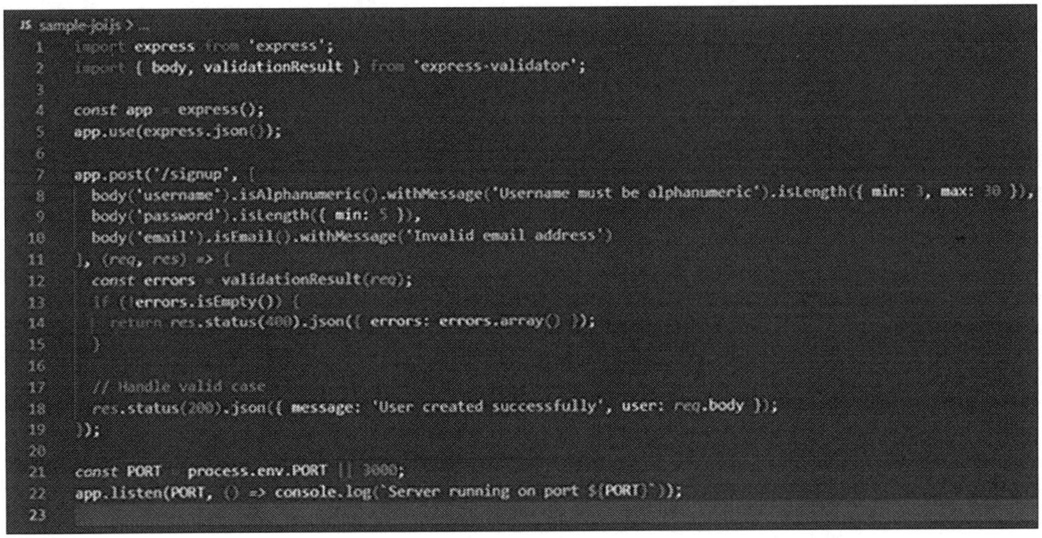

```
JS sample-joi.js > ...
import express from 'express';
import { body, validationResult } from 'express-validator';

const app = express();
app.use(express.json());

app.post('/signup', [
  body('username').isAlphanumeric().withMessage('Username must be alphanumeric').isLength({ min: 3, max: 30 }),
  body('password').isLength({ min: 5 }),
  body('email').isEmail().withMessage('Invalid email address')
], (req, res) => {
  const errors = validationResult(req);
  if (!errors.isEmpty()) {
    return res.status(400).json({ errors: errors.array() });
  }

  // Handle valid case
  res.status(200).json({ message: 'User created successfully', user: req.body });
});

const PORT = process.env.PORT || 3000;
app.listen(PORT, () => console.log(`Server running on port ${PORT}`));
```

Figure 6.38: *express-validator example*

After the request passes through the validation middleware, **`validationResult(req)`** is used to gather any validation errors. If there are errors (**`errors.isEmpty()`** is **`false`**), the function sends a 400 Bad Request response with the validation errors.

The express-validator middleware is used in the route definition as an array of validation checks. Each validator acts on a specific field in the request body and checks for certain conditions (such as length, format, and more). If any of these checks fail, the **`validationResult`** will contain details of these failures, which are then sent back to the client. This approach helps in ensuring that only valid data is processed in the route handler.

Implementation of Joi

We have seen both framework examples in the previous section, let's implement the Joi framework in our application. We need to install Joi with the following command:

```
npm install joi
```

The first thing we need to do is create a validation schema for the request objects. We can maintain these in separate files for maintainability.

```
api > src > validations > TS user.validation.ts > signupSchema
import Joi from 'joi';

export const signinSchema = Joi.object({
    password: Joi.string().pattern(new RegExp('^[a-zA-Z0-9]{3,30}$')),
    email: Joi.string().email({
        tlds: { allow: true } // This will validate top-level domains
      }).required() // Use .required() if the email is a mandatory field
});

export const signupSchema = Joi.object({
    firstName: Joi.string().alphanum().min(2).max(30).required(),
    lastName: Joi.string().alphanum().min(2).max(30).required(),
    password: Joi.string().pattern(new RegExp('^[a-zA-Z0-9]{3,30}$')),
    email: Joi.string().email({
        tlds: { allow: true } // This will validate top-level domains
      }).required() // Use .required() if the email is a mandatory field
});
```

Figure 6.39: *user validations*

A schema for the sign-in process is defined using **`Joi.object()`**. The schema requires two fields:

- **`email`**: A string that must be a valid email format and is required.
- **`password`**: A string that must match the given regular expression, enforcing a password with 3 to 30 alphanumeric characters.

The schema for the sign-up process is also defined. The **`signupSchema`** includes additional fields for **`firstName`** and **`lastName`**, both of which must be alphanumeric strings with a minimum length of 2 and a maximum of 30 characters, and both are required fields. The **`password`** and **`email`** fields have the same requirements as in the **`signinSchema`**.

The following defines two Joi validation schemas for task management operations in an application. The **updateTaskSchema** is for validating data when updating a task, and the **createTaskSchema** is for validating data when creating a new task. Both schemas ensure that the **id**, **task**, **assignee**, and **description** fields are alphanumeric strings with specific length requirements and are mandatory for the operation to proceed.

```
api > src > validations > TS todos.validation.ts > ...
import Joi from 'joi';

export const updateTaskSchema = Joi.object({
    id: Joi.string().alphanum().min(2).max(30).required(),
    task: Joi.string().alphanum().min(2).max(30).required(),
    assignee: Joi.string().alphanum().min(2).max(30).required(),
    description: Joi.string().alphanum().min(2).required()
});

export const createTaskSchema = Joi.object({
    id: Joi.string().alphanum().min(2).max(30).required(),
    task: Joi.string().alphanum().min(2).max(30).required(),
    assignee: Joi.string().alphanum().min(2).max(30).required(),
    description: Joi.string().alphanum().min(2).required()
});
```

***Figure 6.40:** todos validations*

Once you define validation files, we need to import these into our routes to validate the request.

For the sign-in endpoint, **signinSchema.validate(req.body)** is called to validate the request body against the **signinSchema**. If the validation fails, an error response is sent back with a 400 status code along with the validation error message and the input value.

Similarly, for the sign-up endpoint, **signupSchema.validate(req.body)** checks the request body against the **signupSchema**. Again, if there's an error, a 400 response with the validation error message and the input value is returned.

In both cases, if validation is successful (no error), the respective controller method (**signin** or **signup**) is called to proceed with the request handling, and the result is sent back with a 200-status code. This Joi validation ensures that only correctly formatted and valid data is passed to the controller methods.

By maintaining separate validation files, we can have following advantages:

- **Reusability:** Schemas defined in separate files can be easily imported and reused across different parts of the application, avoiding duplication of validation logic.

- **Separation of Concerns**: It keeps validation logic separate from business logic and route handling, leading to cleaner and more focused code within each module.
- **Maintainability:** When validation logic needs to be updated, it can be done in a single location, without searching through route handlers or controller functions.
- **Readability:** Having a dedicated place for schemas makes it easier for developers to find and understand the expected structure of the data.
- **Testing:** Independent schema files can be more easily unit tested, ensuring that the validation logic works as expected without the need to mock requests or responses.

Now, we will import these files into our routes and validate the request.

```
private routes(): void {

  // user signin
  this.express.post("/signin", (req: express.Request<any, any, SignInRequest>, res: express.Response<UserResponse>, next: express.NextFunction) => {

    const { error, value } = signinSchema.validate(req.body);

    if (error) {
      res.status(400).json({ message: error.details[0].message, statucCode: 400, result: value });
      return;
    }

    const result = this.userController.signin(req.body);
    res.status(200).json(result);
  });

  // user signup
  this.express.post("/signup", (req: express.Request<any, any, SignUpRequest>, res: express.Response<UserResponse>, next: express.NextFunction) => {

    const { error, value } = signupSchema.validate(req.body);

    if (error) {
      res.status(400).json({ message: error.details[0].message, statucCode: 400, result: value });
      return;
    }

    const result = this.userController.singup(req.body);
    res.status(200).json(result);
  });
}
```

Figure 6.41: *user routes updated with validations*

For the **PUT /task** endpoint, it uses the **updateTaskSchema** to validate the request body. If validation fails, it returns a 400 status code with the validation error message and the input value.

For the **POST /task** endpoint, it employs the **createTaskSchema** to validate the request body. Similarly, if validation fails, a 400 status code and error details are sent back to the client.

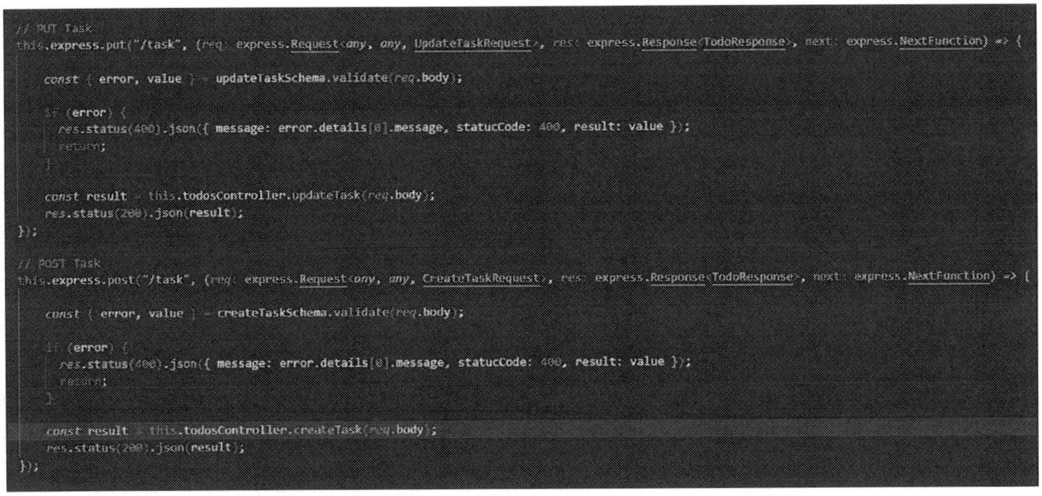

Figure 6.42: *todos routes updated with validations*

When validation passes for either endpoint (no errors), the code proceeds to call the respective controller method to handle the task update or creation, followed by a 200-status code response with the result.

Let's test one endpoint by passing an empty task, we would get a validation error with the status code 400, which is a bad request. We can confirm that with *Figure* 6.43.

Figure 6.43: *testing validations*

Figure 6.44 depicts the final project structure we built in this chapter. This modularization aligns with the principles of the Model-View-Controller (MVC) design pattern, a tried-and-true methodology for dividing an application into distinct sections based on their roles.

This architecture ensures a clear separation of concerns, where each part of the system has a single responsibility and operates independently. It enhances maintainability as developers can focus on specific areas without affecting others, facilitates easier and more targeted testing, and allows the application to scale, as components can be independently scaled to match demand.

By adopting this approach, Node.js APIs become more organized, with each route defining clear paths to the corresponding controllers and models. This allows for the logic to be abstractly separated, making the codebase cleaner, more coherent, and more straightforward to navigate and refactor when necessary.

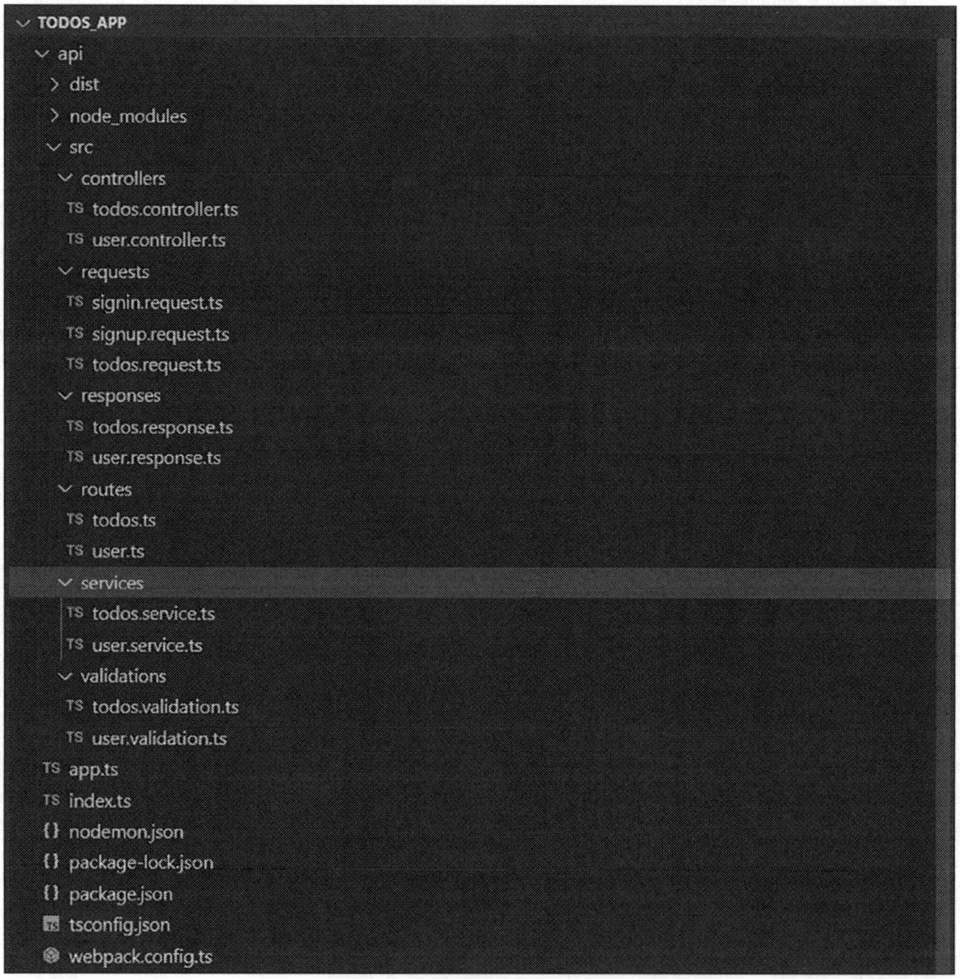

Figure 6.44: API structure

Conclusion

Throughout this chapter, we embarked on a journey through the foundational elements of creating a robust backend API using Express.js. We began with understanding the API structure, emphasizing the importance of a well-thought-out architecture that can support scalability and maintainability. Our next step involved setting up the Express server, a critical component that forms the backbone of our API, allowing us to handle requests and serve responses.

We then turned our attention to Webpack, exploring its utility in bundling and optimizing our TypeScript files. We pieced together our API structure, carefully assembling the controllers, services, and models to form a coherent and functional system. Request validation was our safeguard, ensuring that the data entering our API met the necessary criteria, thereby protecting the integrity of our application and enhancing user experience.

As we move forward, our next chapter will introduce MongoDB, a powerful NoSQL database that pairs exceptionally well with Node.js and Express. We will delve into the configuration of MongoDB within our Express.js environment, understand its role in persisting and retrieving data, and learn how to leverage its flexibility to enhance our API's capabilities.

We will cover schema design, CRUD operations, and effective ways to integrate MongoDB's features into our Express routes. By the end of the next chapter, you will be equipped with the knowledge to incorporate a database into your API, transforming it into a dynamic platform ready to interact with the vast world of data.

CHAPTER 7
Getting Familiar With MongoDB and Integration

Introduction

In the realm of modern web development, understanding the intricacies of database interaction is crucial. This comprehensive chapter embarks on a journey through the diverse methods of connecting to a MongoDB instance, a fundamental step in leveraging the power of this popular NoSQL database. Whether you are working on a simple application that requires a straightforward connection or a complex system necessitating advanced configurations, the chapter caters to a broad spectrum of needs. From utilizing basic connection strings to exploring more intricate connection pooling options, this section is designed to provide a thorough understanding of the various approaches to establish a robust connection with MongoDB. Such knowledge is vital for developers looking to optimize the database interactions of their applications, thus ensuring both efficiency and reliability.

Further enriching this exploration, we delve into the capabilities of the Atlas Command Line Interface (CLI), a potent tool in the arsenal of MongoDB users. The Atlas CLI offers a streamlined and powerful means to interact with MongoDB, allowing developers to execute queries, manage data, and perform administrative tasks directly from the command line. This segment not only enhances your skill set in database management but also opens new possibilities for efficient and effective data manipulation using MongoDB.

Structure

In this chapter, the following topics will be covered:

- Different Ways to Connect to MongoDB Instance

- Exploring Atlas CLI to Query the MongoDB
- Understanding Mongo Aggregation Pipelines
- Configuring MongoDB Connection in the Express API
- Implementing Models
- Implementing Repository Pattern
- Implementing CRUD Operations
- Testing APIs with Postman
- Exploring Mongo Compass to Visualize the Data

Different Ways to Connect to MongoDB Instance

In the dynamic world of web development, establishing a connection to a database is a foundational step, often dictating the efficiency and reliability of the application. MongoDB, as a popular choice for modern applications, offers a variety of methods to establish connections, catering to different use cases and deployment scenarios. In this section, we will explore these diverse methods to connect to a MongoDB instance, providing insights into the nuances and best use cases of each approach.

Standard Connection String (URI)

At the heart of MongoDB connectivity is the use of a standard connection string, also known as a Uniform Resource Identifier (URI). This string is a compact representation of all the necessary connection information:

```
const mongoose = require('mongoose');
const uri = 'mongodb://username:password@host:port/database';
mongoose.connect(uri);
```

Figure 7.1: *Standard Connection*

This approach is straightforward and widely used for its simplicity. It is particularly effective in environments where connection parameters remain relatively static and do not require extensive customization.

Connection with Options

For scenarios requiring more granular control over the connection, MongoDB allows the specification of an options object. This method is crucial when dealing with advanced settings like SSL/TLS configurations, connection timeouts, or specific behaviors in a distributed database setup:

```
mongoose.connect(uri, {
    useNewUrlParser: true,
    useUnifiedTopology: true,
    ssl: true,
    connectTimeoutMS: 10000,
    // Additional options as needed
  });
```

Figure 7.2: *Connection with options*

Here, each option serves a specific purpose, from ensuring the use of the latest URL parser (`useNewUrlParser`) to configuring secure connections (`ssl`) and managing connection establishment times (`connectTimeoutMS`).

Environment Variables for Security

In production environments or situations where security is paramount, embedding connection details directly in the code is not advisable. Instead, using environment variables is a best practice.

```
const uri = process.env.MONGODB_URI;
mongoose.connect(uri);
```

Figure 7.3: *Environment Variables*

By doing so, sensitive information such as database credentials are kept out of the codebase, mitigating the risk of accidental exposure and providing the flexibility to change connection details without code modifications.

Replica Set Connections for High Availability

High-availability applications often leverage MongoDB's replica set feature, requiring a slightly different approach to connection strings.

```
const uri = 'mongodb://host1:port1,host2:port2,host3:port3/database';
mongoose.connect(uri, { replicaSet: 'rs0' });
```

Figure 7.4: *Replica Set Connections*

In this setup, the URI includes multiple hosts, ensuring that the application can maintain database connectivity even if one of the MongoDB instances becomes unavailable, thus providing redundancy and improved data availability.

Connection Pooling for Performance

Connection pooling is a technique where a pool of database connections is created and managed, allowing multiple clients to share these connections. Mongoose, by default, manages a pool of connections.

```

mongoose.connect(uri, { poolSize: 10 });
```

Figure 7.5: *Connection Pooling*

Although Mongoose abstracts much of the complexity of connection pooling, understanding and appropriately configuring the pool size (**`poolSize`**) can significantly impact the application's performance, especially under high load.

Selecting the appropriate method to connect to a MongoDB instance is a crucial decision that can impact the application's performance, security, and scalability. From simple single-string connections for development environments to more complex setups involving replica sets and connection pools for production-grade applications, MongoDB offers the flexibility to cater to a wide range of requirements. Understanding these different methods enables developers to make informed choices, ensuring their applications are robust, secure, and performant.

Exploring Atlas CLI to Query the MongoDB

In the world of database management, the ability to interact with your database through a command-line interface offers a level of efficiency and control that is highly valued by developers and database administrators. The MongoDB Atlas CLI is a robust tool that brings this capability to MongoDB users, providing a direct line to MongoDB Atlas, MongoDB's fully managed cloud database service. In this section, we delve into the Atlas CLI's functionalities, focusing on how it can be utilized for querying and managing MongoDB instances.

Getting Started with Atlas CLI

The Atlas CLI is a command-line utility designed to interact with MongoDB Atlas. It enables users to perform a variety of tasks, from managing clusters and databases to querying data directly. To begin using the Atlas CLI, you first need to install it, which can be done through various package managers or by downloading it from MongoDB's official website.

After installation, the next step is to configure the CLI to connect to your MongoDB Atlas account. This typically involves setting up API keys or access tokens, ensuring a secure connection between your local environment and the MongoDB Atlas service.

Querying Data with Atlas CLI

One of the key features of the Atlas CLI is its ability to execute database queries. This function is particularly useful for quickly retrieving or manipulating data without the need for a full-fledged GUI or writing a backend script.

Fetching Data

To fetch data from a collection, you can use the Atlas CLI to run find queries. For example, to retrieve all documents from a **`users`** collection, you would use a command like:

```
atlas mongodb find myClusterName myDatabaseName users '{}'
```

This command fetches all documents in the **`users`** collection. You can also add query filters and projection parameters to refine the data you retrieve.

Inserting Data

Adding new data to your collections is just as straightforward. For instance, to insert a new document into the **`users`** collection, your command might look like:

```
atlas mongodb insert myClusterName myDatabaseName users '{"name": "John
Doe", "email": "john@example.com"}'
```

Uploading Data

The CLI also allows you to update documents. For example, updating a user's email could be achieved with

```
atlas mongodb update myClusterName myDatabaseName users '{"name": "John
Doe"}' '{"$set": {"email": "john.newemail@example.com"}}'
```

Deleting Data

Similarly, removing documents is a simple command away. To delete a user, you might use:

```
atlas mongodb delete myClusterName myDatabaseName users '{"name": "John
Doe"}'
```

Advanced Features and Automation

Beyond basic CRUD operations, the Atlas CLI supports more complex tasks like index management, which is crucial for optimizing query performance. Additionally, the CLI's compatibility with scripting makes it an excellent tool for automating routine database tasks such as backups, data imports/exports, and regular maintenance operations.

The Atlas CLI is a powerful asset for anyone working with MongoDB, especially within the Atlas ecosystem. It provides a quick, scriptable way to interact with your database, making tasks that would typically require a graphical interface or backend code, both straightforward and efficient. Whether you are a developer needing to perform ad-hoc queries, a database administrator managing multiple clusters, or anyone in between, the Atlas CLI is an invaluable tool, streamlining your MongoDB experience and enhancing your productivity.

Understanding Mongo Aggregation Pipelines

The MongoDB Aggregation Framework is a powerful feature that allows for complex data processing and transformation within MongoDB collections. It operates through a concept known as aggregation pipelines, which are essentially a series of data processing stages. Each stage in the pipeline transforms the data as it passes through, enabling a flexible and powerful approach to data manipulation and analysis. This section explores the intricacies of MongoDB's aggregation pipelines, providing examples to illustrate their capabilities.

The Basics of Aggregation Pipelines

An aggregation pipeline in MongoDB is a series of stages, each performing a specific operation on the data. The output of one stage is passed as input to the next stage in the pipeline. This sequence of operations can include filtering, grouping, sorting, or transforming data.

For example, consider a **`sales`** collection where each document represents a sale and contains fields like **`item`**, **`price`**, and **`quantity`**.

Example: Grouping and Summing

A basic aggregation task could be to calculate the total sales for each item. The pipeline for this operation might include a **`$group`** stage to group documents by the **`item`** field, and a **`$sum`** operator to sum up the sales.

```
db.sales.aggregate([
    {
      $group: {
        _id: "$item",
        totalSales: { $sum: { $multiply: ["$price", "$quantity"] } }
      }
    }
  ]);
```

Figure 7.6: *Aggregation Pipeline Example*

In this pipeline, the **`$group`** stage groups the documents by the **`item`** field and calculates the total sales for each item by summing the product of **`price`** and **`quantity`**.

Example: Filtering and Projecting

Suppose you want to analyze sales for items that sold more than 100 units. You can first filter the documents using **`$match`** and then project the desired fields using **`$project`**.

```
db.sales.aggregate([
  { $match: { quantity: { $gt: 100 } } },
  { $project: { item: 1, total: { $multiply: ["$price", "$quantity"] } } }
]);
```

Figure 7.7: *Filtering and Projecting*

Here, the **`$match`** stage filters documents where **`quantity`** is greater than 100, and the **`$project`** stage projects the **`item`** and calculates the total sales.

Advanced Aggregations: Pipeline Composition

Aggregation pipelines can be composed of multiple stages, allowing for complex data transformations. For instance, you can combine matching, grouping, and sorting in a single pipeline:

```
db.sales.aggregate([
  { $match: { date: { $gte: new Date("2021-01-01") } } },
  { $group: { _id: "$item", totalSales: { $sum: "$quantity" } } },
  { $sort: { totalSales: -1 } }
]);
```

Figure 7.8: *Pipeline Composition*

This pipeline filters sales from 2021, groups them by item, sums their quantities, and then sorts the results in descending order of total sales.

Aggregation and Performance

While MongoDB's aggregation framework is powerful, it is essential to consider performance implications, especially when dealing with large datasets. Proper indexing, pipeline optimization, and understanding the memory limitations of certain stages (like **`$group`** and **`$sort`**) are crucial to maintaining efficient operations.

MongoDB's aggregation pipelines provide a flexible and powerful toolset for data analysis and transformation within the database itself. They enable the execution of complex data processing tasks, which can be invaluable for business intelligence, reporting, or data science applications. By mastering aggregation pipelines, developers and data analysts can unlock deep insights into their data, directly within MongoDB.

Configuring MongoDB Connection in the Express API

Throughout our exploration, we have uncovered various approaches to establish a connection between an Express API and a MongoDB instance. The choice of connection method hinges on the specific requirements and structure of our application. Within the scope of our text, we have opted to utilize a MongoDB Atlas account, which provides a cloud-hosted database solution, offering scalability and ease of use.

Our application architecture is thoughtfully designed, with distinct modules that separate different areas of concern, thereby promoting a clean and maintainable codebase. To facilitate this, we will be setting up our MongoDB connection within an isolated configuration file. This practice not only enhances security by centralizing sensitive connection details but also streamlines the management of our database settings.

Furthermore, we will employ the mongoose library, a robust tool that significantly simplifies the process of defining schemas, interacting with the database, and handling data models. Mongoose also comes with built-in connection pooling capabilities, which is a highly efficient way to manage database connections. This feature maintains a pool of database connections that our application can reuse, avoiding the overhead of establishing a new connection for each database operation. It is a strategy that greatly improves performance, especially under high load, by reducing latency and resource consumption.

In the upcoming section, we will delve into the specifics of configuring our MongoDB connection using Mongoose. We will demonstrate how to leverage Mongoose's features to define our data models succinctly and how to interact with our MongoDB Atlas database effectively, ensuring our application benefits from the robustness and efficiency of connection pooling.

Mongoose

Mongoose is an Object Data Modeling (ODM) library for MongoDB and Node.js that manages the relationship between data, offers schema validation, and is used to translate between objects in code and their representation in MongoDB. It acts as a front-end to MongoDB, an open-source NoSQL database that uses a document-oriented data model and a non-structured query language.

Here is a more detailed look at what Mongoose provides:

Schema Definition

Mongoose allows developers to define schemas for their collections. A schema maps to a MongoDB collection and defines the shape of the documents within that collection. These schemas are not just for defining structure but also for defining validation rules, default values, and even methods to extend the document's functionality.

Model Creation

Models are constructor functions created from a schema definition. They represent documents that can be saved and retrieved from the database. All document creation and retrieval from the MongoDB database are handled by these models.

Validation

Mongoose provides built-in validators, such as required fields, maximum and minimum values, and unique values. It also allows custom validation rules to be defined easily, ensuring data integrity.

Instance Methods

Developers can define methods that apply to individual document instances. These can be used to write business logic that applies to a single document, such as instance-based transformations or calculations.

Static Methods

Static methods can be defined that apply to all instances of a model, allowing for broader operations or queries on the collection level.

Middleware (Hooks)

Mongoose supports pre and post middleware (hooks) for operations. Middleware allows developers to write plugins and to set up functions to run before or after calls to, for example, save documents, delete them, or run queries.

Population

Mongoose supports document population, which is a powerful feature that lets you reference documents in other collections and, when querying, replace the reference with the actual document. This is akin to a JOIN in a relational database system.

Query Building

Mongoose provides a rich query building API, allowing developers to compose queries without needing to write complex MongoDB query syntax.

Transactions

Mongoose supports MongoDB transactions, which allow several database operations to be executed in isolation and rolled back if any operation fails, ensuring data integrity.

Plugins

The Mongoose ecosystem includes a wide array of community-created plugins that can add additional features to schemas, such as adding complex validation rules, virtual properties, or hooks.

Connection Pooling

Mongoose manages a pool of connections to MongoDB, keeping several connections open simultaneously so they can be reused for future requests, improving performance.

Advantages of Using Mongoose in Development

The following are the advantages of using Mongoose in development:

- **Streamlines the Object Mapping:** Directly maps objects in your code to MongoDB documents.
- **Reduces Boilerplate Code:** Automates the conversion of data types and the validation of data formats.
- **Improves Readability and Maintainability:** Through schemas, methods, and middleware, it makes code easier to read and maintain.
- **Facilitates Development:** With its rich API and plugins, makes common database operations straightforward.

In essence, Mongoose provides a layer of features on top of the MongoDB driver that makes database programming in Node.js easier, safer, and more productive.

Let us install mongoose and its type definitions with the following command:

```
// install mongoose
npm install mongoose
// install type definitions
npm install -D @types/mongoose
```

The following dependencies are updated accordingly in the **`package.json`** file. We have to install type definitions as we are using TypeScript to develop the backend API.

```
  "license": "ISC",
  "devDependencies": {
    "@types/express": "^4.17.21",
    "@types/mongoose": "^5.11.97",
    "@types/node": "^20.10.4",
    "nodemon": "^3.0.1",
    "ts-loader": "^8.2.0",
    "ts-node": "^10.9.1",
    "typescript": "^5.3.2",
    "webpack": "^4.47.0",
    "webpack-cli": "^4.10.0"
  },
  "dependencies": {
    "express": "^4.18.2",
    "joi": "^17.11.0",
    "mongoose": "^8.0.3"
  }
}
```

Figure 7.9: *Installing mongoose*

The MongoDB configuration defines the following connection URL. We must replace the password in the URL.

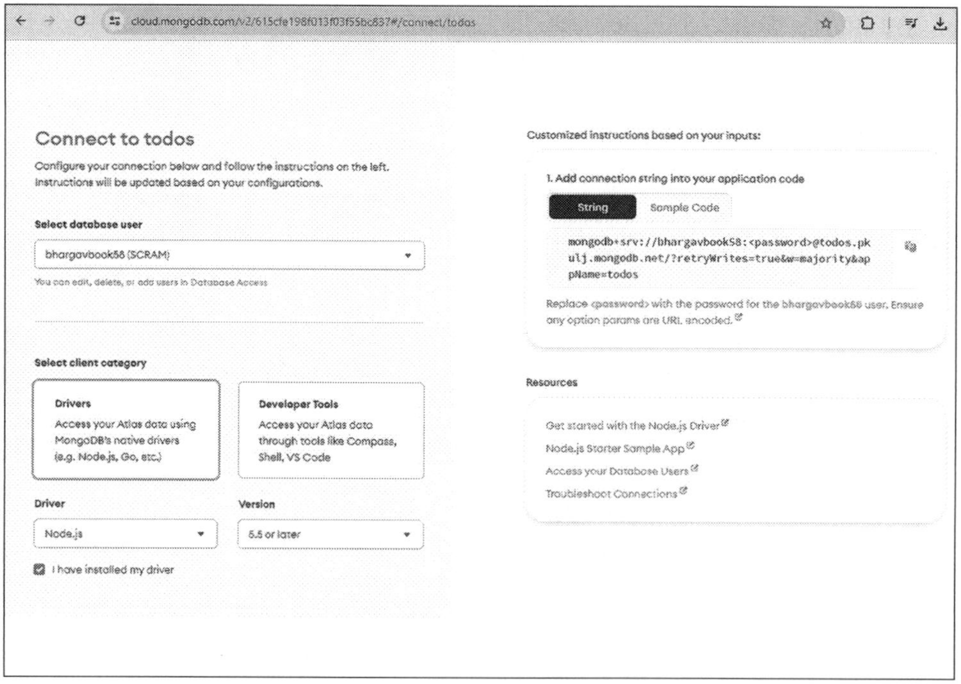

Figure 7.10: *Connecting with MongoDB Driver*

```
// MongoDB Connection URL

mongodb+srv://bhargavbook58:<password>@todos.usujbgr.mongodb.net/?retry-Writes=true&w=majority
```

Before integrating the following code to establish a connection to the database from your application, it is imperative to configure your MongoDB instance to recognize your IP address or to enable connections from all locations. While allowing connections from any IP can be convenient for initial development or testing, it is strongly advised to employ more secure connection strategies. Broadly permitting access is not a best practice for a production environment due to potential security risks. In a production setting, you should specify and restrict IP addresses that are permitted to connect to ensure the security of your database.

There are two methods provided by Mongoose and it is very important to understand the difference between them. **`mongoose.connect`** and **`mongoose.createConnection`** are two methods provided by Mongoose, a popular Object Data Modeling (ODM) library for MongoDB and Node.js. Both methods are used to establish a connection to a MongoDB database, but they have some key differences in their usage and behavior.

mongoose.connect

- **Global Connection:** **`mongoose.connect`** creates a default global connection to the MongoDB database. It sets up the default connection which is managed by the Mongoose module itself.
- **Singleton Pattern:** When using **`mongoose.connect`** all models created through **`mongoose.model`** will use this default connection. It essentially follows the singleton pattern, meaning that the same connection instance is reused across the entire application.
- **Usage:** It is used in simpler applications where a single database connection suffices, or where all models will connect to the same database.

Here is an example code where the connection is established, and all the models are created using the default connection.

```
JS index.js > ...
// connecting to the database
mongoose.connect('mongodb://localhost/myapp', { useNewUrlParser: true });

// creating model
const TestModel = mongoose.model('Test', new Schema({ name: String }));

// TestModel is automatically associated with the default connection
```

Figure 7.11: *Connecting with mongoose.connect*

mongoose.createConnection

- **Multiple Connections: `mongoose.createConnection`** returns a fresh connection to the MongoDB database, allowing you to create multiple different connections to different databases or the same database.
- **No Singleton Pattern:** Each connection created by **`mongoose.createConnection`** is distinct and not shared globally. Models are created directly from a connection and are bound to that specific connection.
- **Usage:** It is preferred in more complex applications, like those requiring connections to multiple databases, or where different sets of models should use different database connections.

Here is an example code where the connection is established, and all the models are created with that connection, not the default one.

```
JS index.js > ...
// connecting to the database
const connection = mongoose.createConnection('mongodb://localhost/test', { useNewUrlParser: true });

// creating model
const TestModel = connection.model('Test', new Schema({ name: String }));

// TestModel is associated specifically with 'connection', not the default connection

```

***Figure* 7.12:** *Connecting with mongoose.createConnection*

Since we are using only one database, and all the models are connected to the same database. We need to use the method **`mongoose.connect`**. We are going to create a separate folder called config and place the following file there for the database related connection details. This class is designed for efficient management of MongoDB connections in a Node.js environment using Mongoose. This class plays a crucial role in establishing and maintaining database connectivity, a foundational aspect for any data-driven application.

At the core of this setup is the **`MONGO_OPTIONS`** constant, which defines critical parameters for the MongoDB connection. These parameters, including the minimum and maximum sizes for the connection pool and the socket timeout duration, are key to optimizing the performance and reliability of the database interactions. By configuring these options, the application can manage its database connections more efficiently, ensuring robustness even under varying load conditions.

The **`DBConfiguration`** class itself, with its private properties **`connection`** and **`connectionURL`**, serves as the central point for database connectivity management. The **`connection`** property is meant to hold the active Mongoose connection, ensuring that this crucial resource is easily accessible and manageable throughout the application's lifecycle. The **`connectionURL`**, on the other hand, contains the necessary information to establish a connection to the MongoDB database, including credentials and the database's network address.

Key to the class's functionality are two asynchronous methods – **`connectToDB`** and **`closeConnection`**. The **`connectToDB`** method is intelligently designed to establish a connection to the MongoDB server only if it does not already exist, thereby avoiding unnecessary reconnections and fostering efficient use of resources. It utilizes Mongoose's **`connect`** method with the specified **`connectionURL`** and **`MONGO_OPTIONS`**, setting the **`connection`** property upon successful connection. This method is also robustly equipped to handle and report any errors during the connection process, ensuring that such issues are properly communicated and managed.

Figure 7.13: *DB Configuration file*

The **`closeConnection`** method complements **`connectToDB`** by providing a mechanism to gracefully close the active database connection. This is particularly important for ensuring that the application cleans up its resources properly, which is a best practice in software development. The method attempts to close the existing connection and resets the **`connection`** property, thereby maintaining the integrity and consistency of the class's state. Similar to **`connectToDB`**, it is designed to handle and report errors during the disconnection process.

Finally, the **`DBConfiguration`** class is instantiated and exported as a singleton, ensuring that a single, shared instance is used throughout the application. This approach is critical in preventing the creation of multiple database connections, which can be resource-intensive and lead to complications in connection management.

In summary, the **DBConfiguration** class encapsulates all the necessary logic for handling MongoDB connections in a Node.js application using Mongoose. Its well-thought-out design and robust error handling make it an indispensable part of the application architecture, especially in scenarios where efficient and reliable database connectivity is paramount.

Following the establishment of the DB configuration, the subsequent phase involves creating models. These models will leverage the database connection set up by the **DBConfiguration** class to interact with the database. With these models in place, we will be able to execute queries and perform various operations on the database, harnessing the connection infrastructure we have just configured.

Implementing Models

Implementing models in Mongoose, a popular ODM library for MongoDB and Node.js, involves several steps. These models are crucial as they define the structure of the documents within a MongoDB collection and provide an interface to interact with the database.

Implementing models in Mongoose effectively abstracts a lot of direct database interaction and provides a more structured and organized way to handle data in a Node.js application. It also leverages JavaScript's object-oriented programming features, making it more intuitive to work with MongoDB.

We need to define two models – one for the user, and another for tasks. First, you need to define a schema. A schema represents the structure of a document in MongoDB, like how a table defines the structure of records in relational databases. It specifies the types of fields, their validation, and default values.

Here is the user model. The code snippet provided is a TypeScript implementation for defining a Mongoose model in a Node.js application. It includes an **IUser** interface extending Mongoose's **Document** to ensure type safety, and a **userSchema** defining the structure and rules for a user document in MongoDB. This schema includes fields like **firstName**, **lastName**, **email**, and **password**, with appropriate data types and constraints (such as **required** and **unique** for email). Additionally, the schema is configured to automatically include **createdAt** and **updatedAt** timestamps. Finally, a Mongoose model **UserModel** is created from this schema, representing the **users** collection in MongoDB, and enabling operations like create, read, update, and delete on user documents.

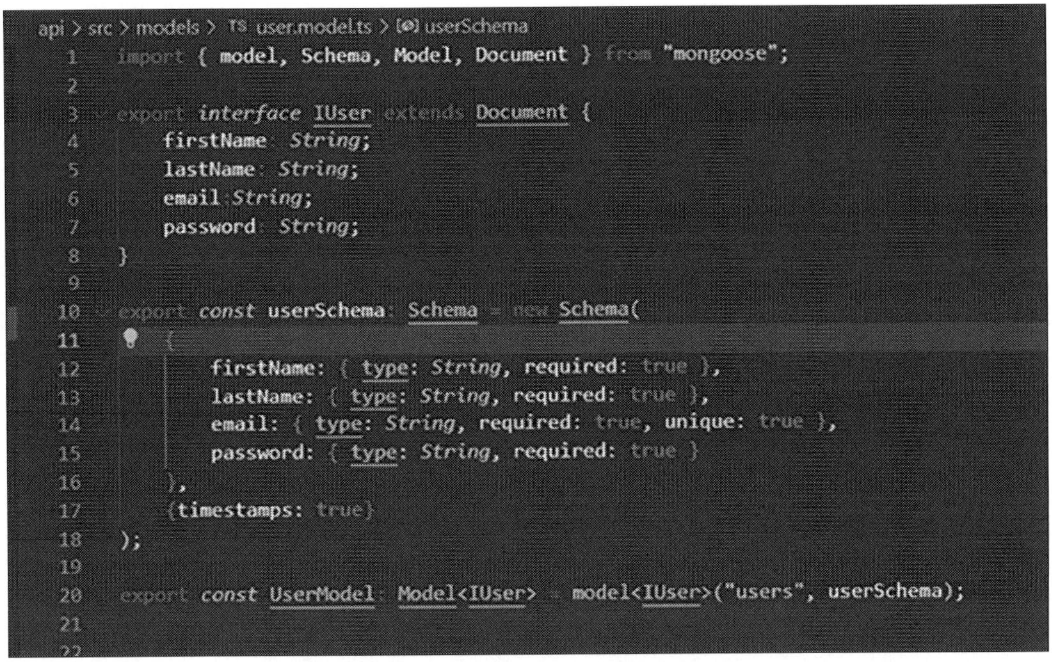

```
api > src > models > TS user.model.ts > [@] userSchema
import { model, Schema, Model, Document } from "mongoose";

export interface IUser extends Document {
    firstName: String;
    lastName: String;
    email:String;
    password: String;
}

export const userSchema: Schema = new Schema(
    {
        firstName: { type: String, required: true },
        lastName: { type: String, required: true },
        email: { type: String, required: true, unique: true },
        password: { type: String, required: true }
    },
    {timestamps: true}
);

export const UserModel: Model<IUser> = model<IUser>("users", userSchema);
```

Figure 7.14: *User Schema*

With this setup, you can create, read, update, and delete user documents in your MongoDB database while benefiting from TypeScript's type checking. For example, when creating a new user, TypeScript will enforce that you provide an object that conforms to the **`IUser`** interface. This integration enhances the robustness and maintainability of your code by leveraging both Mongoose's powerful data modeling capabilities and TypeScript's strong typing system.

Here is another file called **`tasks.model.ts`**. The code snippet is a TypeScript implementation for defining a Mongoose model in a Node.js application, tailored for managing task-related data. It features an **`ITask`** interface that extends Mongoose's **`Document`**, ensuring type-safe interaction with task documents. The **`tasksSchema`** defines the MongoDB schema for tasks, including fields like **`task`**, **`description`**, **`assignee`**, **`status`**, and **`createdBy`**, all marked as required. The **`assignee`** field is uniquely indexed, meaning each task must have a distinct assignee. The schema also configures automatic timestamping for each document. Finally, the **`TasksModel`** is a Mongoose model created from this schema, representing the **`tasks`** collection in MongoDB and allowing CRUD operations on task documents while adhering to the defined schema structure and TypeScript interface.

```
api > src > models > TS tasks.model.ts > tasksSchema
import { model, Schema, Model, Document } from "mongoose";

export interface ITask extends Document {
    task: String;
    description: String;
    assignee: String;
    status: String;
    createdBy?: string;
    updatedBy?: string;
}

export const tasksSchema: Schema = new Schema(
    {
        task: { type: String, required: true },
        description: { type: String, required: true },
        assignee: { type: String, required: true, unique: true },
        status: { type: String, required: true } ,
        createdBy: { type: String, required: false },
        updatedBy: { type: String, required: false }
    },
    {timestamps: true}
);

export const TasksModel: Model<ITask> = model<ITask>("tasks", tasksSchema);
```

***Figure* 7.15:** *Tasks Schema*

This setup allows for CRUD operations on task documents in MongoDB with the assurance of TypeScript's type checking. The model provides methods to create, read, update, and delete tasks, adhering to the structure and rules defined in the **`tasksSchema`**.

Having established both the Models and the DB configuration, we are now poised to develop repositories. These repositories will utilize the models and the established database connection to execute queries. Implementing a repository pattern is crucial for enhancing the maintainability and flexibility of our application, as it provides a structured approach to data access and manipulation.

Implementing Repository Pattern

The repository pattern is a design pattern that abstracts data access and manipulation in an application. It acts as a middle layer between the business logic and data access layers, effectively separating the two. This pattern is particularly useful in large applications or those that may need to switch databases in the future.

Advantages

Some advantages of implementing repository pattern are as follows:

- **Separation of Concerns**: Isolates data access logic, making the application more organized.

- **Maintainability**: Simplifies the maintenance of the application by centralizing the data access logic.
- **Testability**: Easier to mock database interactions for testing purposes.
- **Flexibility:** Facilitates changing the database or ORM without impacting the business logic.

Let us implement the repository pattern in our API. First, we need to create an interface as shown in *Figure* 7.16. This interface defines the methods to access the data and will be implemented by a concrete class to interact with the database. Interfaces in TypeScript are used to define the shape of an object or the contract of a class or function. We have two interfaces – user interface and tasks interface.

```
api > src > repositories > TS user.interface.ts > IUserRepository
export interface IUserRepository<T> {

    getByEmailAndPassword(email: string, password: string): Promise<T | null>;

    create(item: T): Promise<T>;

}
```

Figure 7.16: *User Repository Interface*

`IUserRepository`

- The **`I`** prefix is commonly used in many programming languages to denote an interface. It is a naming convention to help distinguish interfaces from classes or other types.
- **`<T>`**: This indicates that the interface is generic. It can work with any type **`T`**, which is specified when implementing the interface. This makes the interface flexible and reusable for various data types.
- **`getByEmailAndPassword(email: string, password: string): Promise<T | null>`**: This method retrieves an entity of type **`T`** (like a user) based on the provided email and password. It returns a **`Promise`** that either resolves to the entity or **`null`** if not found. It is asynchronous, likely involving database queries.
- **`create(item: T): Promise<T>`**: This method creates a new entity of type **`T`**. It takes an entity as input and returns a **`Promise`** that resolves to the newly created entity. This method is also asynchronous, typically used for database insertions.

ITasksRepository

```
api > src > repositories > TS tasks.interface.ts > ITasksRepository
import { ITask } from "../models/tasks.model";

export interface ITasksRepository<T> {

    getAll(): Promise<T[]>;

    getById(id: string): Promise<T | null>;

    create(item: T): Promise<T>;

    update(id: string, item: ITask): Promise<T | null>;

    delete(id: string): Promise<boolean>;
}
```

Figure 7.17: *Tasks Repository Interface*

This interface **`ITasksRepository`** with generic type **`T`**, which includes five methods for handling tasks. Here is a brief description of each method:

- **`getAll(): Promise<T[]>`**: Retrieves all tasks, returning them as an array.
- **`getById(id: string): Promise<T | null>`**: Fetches a single task by its ID, returning the task or **`null`**.
- **`create(item: T): Promise<T>`**: Creates a new task, returning the created task.
- **`update(id: string, item: ITask): Promise<T | null>`**: Updates a task by its ID, returning the updated task or **`null`**.
- **`delete(id: string): Promise<boolean>`**: Deletes a task by its ID, returning **`true`** for success or **`false`** for failure.

We have defined the interfaces and it is time to create repositories that implement these interfaces. This class will handle the data access logic using an ORM like Mongoose for MongoDB.

UserRepository

The **`UserRepository`** class in TypeScript is designed to implement the **`IUserRepository<T>`** interface, indicating that it conforms to a specific set of methods for user-related data operations. This class is generic, denoted by **`<T>`**, allowing it to work with various types of data, most commonly user data in this context.

```
api > src > repositories > TS user.repository.ts > UserRepository
import { Model } from "mongoose";
import { IUserRepository } from "./user.interface";

export class UserRepository<T> implements IUserRepository<T> {

    private model: Model<T>;

    constructor(model: Model<T>) {
        this.model = model;
    }

    getByEmailAndPassword(email: string, password: string): Promise<T | null> {
        return this.model.findOne({email, password}).exec();
    }

    create(item: T): Promise<T> {
        return this.model.create(item);
    }

}
```

***Figure* 7.18:** *User Repository*

A key feature of this class is its use of the **`Model<T>`** from Mongoose, a popular tool for MongoDB object modeling in Node.js applications. The **`private model: Model<T>`** property within the class signifies that **`UserRepository`** is specifically geared towards database operations, leveraging the capabilities of Mongoose to interact with MongoDB. This model is passed to the class through its constructor, **`constructor(model: Model<T>)`**, allowing the **`UserRepository`** to perform operations on the database using this model. This approach provides a high level of flexibility and reusability, as different models can be injected depending on the needs of the application.

The **`UserRepository`** class implements two key methods from the **`IUserRepository`** interface. The first method, **`getByEmailAndPassword(email: string, password: string): Promise<T | null>`**, is used to retrieve a user by their email and password. This method utilizes Mongoose's **`findOne`** method, returning a **`Promise`** that resolves to the user object if found, or **`null`** if not. This method is particularly useful for authentication purposes where user credentials need to be verified.

The second method, **`create(item: T): Promise<T>`**, handles the creation of new users. It uses Mongoose's **`create`** method to add a new user to the database and returns a **`Promise`** that resolves to the newly created user object. This method simplifies the process of adding new users to the database, encapsulating the complexity of database interactions within the repository layer.

Overall, the **`UserRepository`** class serves as a concrete implementation of a user data repository, abstracting the complexities of direct database interactions and providing a clean, modular way to handle user data in a Node.js application using MongoDB.

TasksRepository

The **TasksRepository** class in TypeScript is an implementation of the **ITasksRepository<T>** interface, designed to handle task-related data operations. This class is a part of a system that likely uses Mongoose, a MongoDB object modeling tool for Node.js. The use of generics (**<T>**) in this context indicates that the class is flexible and can be used for various data types, although it's primarily focused on tasks.

The core of this class revolves around the **Model<T>** from Mongoose. The private property **model: Model<T>** holds the Mongoose model, which is used for performing database operations. This model is injected into the repository through the constructor **constructor(model: Model<T>)**, enabling the class to interact with a MongoDB database using the Mongoose library. This setup is quite versatile as it allows for different models to be used, making the repository adaptable for different data structures.

The **TasksRepository** class implements several methods as per the **ITasksRepository** interface:

- **create(item: T): Promise<T>**: This method is responsible for creating new tasks. It uses the **create** method of Mongoose and returns a **Promise** that resolves to the newly created task. This simplifies adding new tasks to the database.
- **getAll(): Promise<T[]>**: This method retrieves all tasks stored in the database. It uses Mongoose's **find** method to fetch all documents and returns them as an array, encapsulated in a **Promise**.
- **getById(id: string): Promise<T | null>**: This method fetches a specific task by its ID using Mongoose's **findOne** method. It returns a **Promise** that resolves to the task if found, or **null** otherwise.

```
api > src > repositories > TS tasks.repository.ts > TasksRepository > getById
import { Model } from "mongoose";
import { ITask } from "../models/tasks.model";
import { ITasksRepository } from "./tasks.interface";

export class TasksRepository<T> implements ITasksRepository<T> {

    private model: Model<T>;

    constructor(model: Model<T>) {
        this.model = model;
    }

    create(item: T): Promise<T> {
        return this.model.create(item);
    }

    getAll(): Promise<T[]> {
        return this.model.find({}).exec();
    }

    getById(id: string): Promise<T | null> {
        return this.model.findOne({_id: id});
    }

    update(id: string, item: ITask): Promise<T | null> {
        return this.model.findOneAndUpdate({_id: id}, {...item});
    }

    delete(id: string): Promise<any> {
        return this.model.deleteOne({_id: id});
    }

}
```

Figure 7.19: *Tasks Repository*

- **`update(id: string, item: ITask): Promise<T | null>`**: This method updates a task identified by its ID. It uses Mongoose's **`findOneAndUpdate`** method, where the task's new data is passed in the **`item`** parameter. The method returns a **`Promise`** that resolves to the updated task or **`null`** if the update fails.
- **`delete(id: string): Promise<any>`**: This method removes a task from the database based on its ID. It employs Mongoose's **`deleteOne`** method and returns a **`Promise`** that indicates the success or failure of the deletion operation.

Overall, the **`TasksRepository`** class abstracts the database interactions for tasks, providing a clean and modular approach to handling task data in a Node.js application using MongoDB. This design promotes maintainability and scalability, as database operations are encapsulated within a dedicated repository layer.

The subsequent step involves incorporating these repositories into our service layer. This integration is crucial for establishing a seamless, end-to-end connection with MongoDB. By doing so, we enable a cohesive flow of data and operations between our application's services and the MongoDB database.

In the **UserService** class, the **UserRepository** and its related model play a central role in managing user data operations. Here is an explanation focused on those aspects:

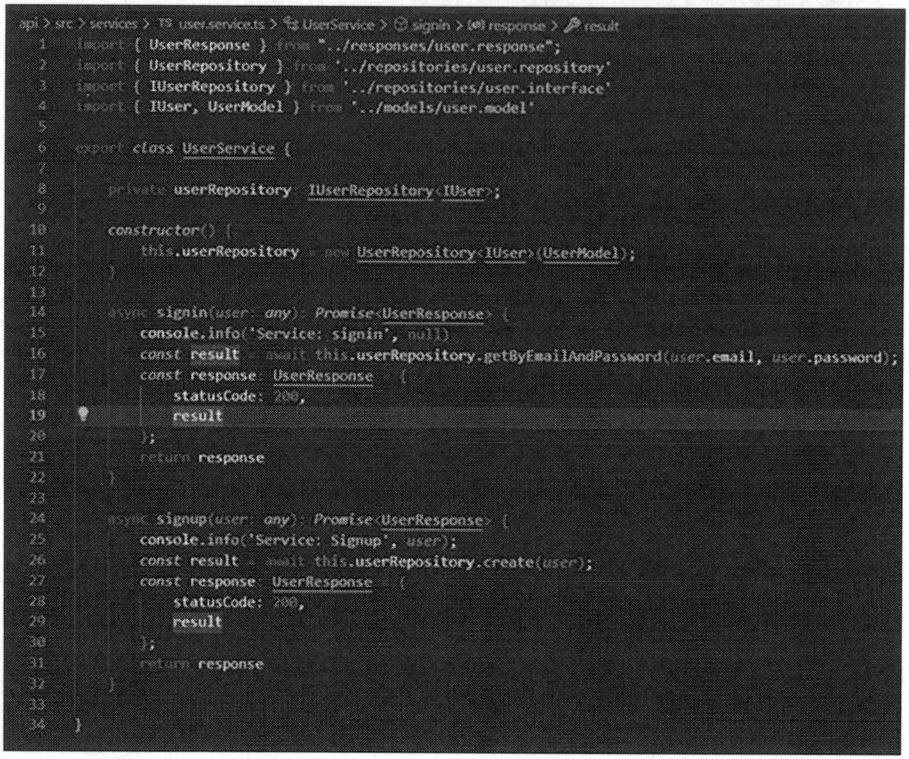

```
import { UserResponse } from "../responses/user.response";
import { UserRepository } from '../repositories/user.repository'
import { IUserRepository } from '../repositories/user.interface'
import { IUser, UserModel } from '../models/user.model'

export class UserService {

    private userRepository: IUserRepository<IUser>;

    constructor() {
        this.userRepository = new UserRepository<IUser>(UserModel);
    }

    async signin(user: any): Promise<UserResponse> {
        console.info('Service: signin', null)
        const result = await this.userRepository.getByEmailAndPassword(user.email, user.password);
        const response: UserResponse = {
            statusCode: 200,
            result
        };
        return response
    }

    async signup(user: any): Promise<UserResponse> {
        console.info('Service: Signup', user);
        const result = await this.userRepository.create(user);
        const response: UserResponse = {
            statusCode: 200,
            result
        };
        return response
    }

}
```

Figure 7.20: *User service*

`UserRepository Installation`

- Within the **UserService** class, an instance of **UserRepository<IUser>** is created and assigned to the **userRepository** private property. This instantiation is done in the constructor of **UserService**.
- **UserRepository<IUser>** indicates that the repository is specifically working with a user model, denoted by the generic **<IUser>**. This generic type ensures that the repository methods will be tailored to handle user data.

Model Integration

- The **UserRepository** is initialized with **UserModel** as an argument. **UserModel** is likely a Mongoose model, representing the structure and the methods to interact with the user data in the MongoDB database.
- By passing **UserModel** to **UserRepository**, the repository is equipped to perform CRUD (Create, Read, Update, Delete) operations specific to user data. This setup encapsulates all the database logic within the repository, abstracting it from the service layer.

Usage in `UserService`

- In the **`signin`** and **`signup`** methods of **`UserService`**, the **`userRepository`** is used to interact with the user data.
- For **`signin`**, **`userRepository.getByEmailAndPassword`** is called with the user's email and password. This method likely checks the database for a user matching these credentials, facilitating the authentication process.
- For **`signup`**, **`userRepository.create`** is used to add a new user to the database. This involves creating a new user record with the provided user data.

In summary, the **`UserRepository`** in the **`UserService`** class acts as a bridge between the service logic and the database, using the **`UserModel`** to interact with the user data in MongoDB.

In the **`TodosService`** class, the **`TasksRepository`** and its associated model play a crucial role in managing task-related data operations. Here is an explanation focused on these aspects.

```
async getTasks(): Promise<TodoResponse> {
    console.info('Service: getTasks', null)
    const result = await this.taskRepository.getAll();
    const response: TodoResponse = {
        statusCode: 200,
        result
    }
    return response;
}

async createTask(task: any): Promise<TodoResponse> {
    console.info('Service: createTask', task);
    const result = await this.taskRepository.create(task);
    const response: TodoResponse = {
        statusCode: 200,
        result
    }
    return response;
}

async updateTask(task: any): Promise<TodoResponse> {
    console.info('Service: updateTask', task);
    const result = await this.taskRepository.update(task._id, task);
    const response: TodoResponse = {
        statusCode: 200,
        result
    }
    return response;
}

async deleteTask(taskId: string): Promise<TodoResponse> {
    console.info('Service: deleteTask', taskId);
    const result = await this.taskRepository.delete(taskId);
    const response: TodoResponse = {
        statusCode: 200,
        result
    }
    return response;
}

async getTaskDetails(taskId: string): Promise<TodoResponse> {
    console.info('Service: getTasks', taskId)
    const taskDetails = await this.taskRepository.getById(taskId);
    const response: TodoResponse = {
        statusCode: 200,
        result: taskDetails
    }
    return response;
}
}
```

Figure 7.21: *Tasks Service*

`TaskRespository` Integration

- The class initializes an instance of **`TasksRepository<ITask>`** and assigns it to the **`taskRepository`** private property. This is done in the constructor of `TodosService`.
- The generic type **`<ITask>`** specifies that the **`TasksRepository`** is intended to handle data operations related to tasks. This ensures that the methods within **`TasksRepository`** are tailored for task data management.

Model Utilization

- **`TasksRepository`** is instantiated with **`TasksModel`**, likely a Mongoose model. This model defines the structure and methods for interacting with task data in a MongoDB database.
- By integrating **`TasksModel`** into **`TasksRepository`**, the repository is equipped to perform various CRUD operations on task data. This encapsulation of the model within the repository abstracts the complexities of direct database interactions.

Usage in TodosService

The **`taskRepository`** is utilized in several methods within **`TodosService`** to interact with task data:

- **`getTasks()`**: Fetches all tasks using **`taskRepository.getAll()`**.
- **`createTask(task)`**: Adds a new task using **`taskRepository.create(task)`**.
- **`updateTask(task)`**: Updates a task based on its ID using **`taskRepository.update(task._id, task)`**.
- **`deleteTask(taskId)`**: Deletes a task by its ID using **`taskRepository.delete(taskId)`**.
- **`getTaskDetails(taskId)`**: Retrieves the details of a specific task using **`taskRepository.getById(taskId)`**.

In summary, **`TasksRepository`** in **`TodosService`** serves as the conduit for all task-related data operations, leveraging **`TasksModel`** for MongoDB database interactions.

This design aligns with the Repository pattern, effectively separating the database logic from the service layer, thus enhancing modularity, maintainability, and scalability of the application.

Implementing CRUD Operations

In our Express TypeScript API, we have successfully implemented the repository pattern along with our models, paving the way for the next critical phase – implementing CRUD (Create, Read, Update, Delete) operations. To kickstart this process, our immediate task is to integrate the database configuration into the **index.ts** file. This integration is vital to ensure that a stable connection with the database is established prior to initiating any API calls. This step is particularly crucial because all subsequent operations, be they creating, reading, updating, or deleting records, rely on a seamless interaction with the database.

Here is the **index.ts** file in which we have imported DB Configuration and established the connection.

```
api > TS index.ts > ...
import * as http from "http";
import App from "./app";
import dbConfiguration from './src/config/db.config'
import mongoose, { Connection, Mongoose } from "mongoose";

const port = process.env.PORT || 3000;

const server = http.createServer(App);
server.listen(port);

server.on("listening", async () => {
    const addr = server.address();
    const bind = (typeof addr === "string") ? `pipe ${addr}` : `port ${addr?.port}`;
    dbConfiguration.connectToDB();
    console.log(`Express Server Listening on ${bind}`);
    mongoose.connection.on('connected', () =>
        console.log(`Connected to MongoDB, Connection Name ${mongoose.Connection.name}`)
    );
    mongoose.connection.on('disconnected', () =>
        console.log(`Disconnected, Connection Name ${mongoose.Connection.name}`)
    );
});

module.exports = App;
```

***Figure* 7.22:** *index.ts*

The process of connecting to MongoDB is a critical aspect of the application's initialization and is managed through several key steps in the code. At the core of the MongoDB connection setup is the **dbConfiguration** module, which is imported at the beginning of the file. This module contains the necessary configuration details and methods to establish a connection with the MongoDB database.

Once the server is created using **http.createServer(App)** and started by listening on a specified port (**server.listen(port)**), an event listener is attached to the **'listening'** event of the server. The **callback** function of this listener is where the MongoDB connection process is initiated. This approach ensures that the attempt to connect to the database occurs only after the server has successfully started, thereby maintaining a sequential and organized startup process.

The code further establishes event listeners on the Mongoose connection object for the **'connected'** and **'disconnected'** events. These listeners are set to log messages to the console when the application connects to and disconnects from MongoDB, respectively. This setup is crucial for monitoring the state of the database connection during the application's runtime. By logging the connection status, the application provides real-time feedback on the database's availability, which is essential for both development and production environments.

Once the database connection is configured and confirmed to be operational, our focus shifts to enhancing our Express routes. Given the nature of database interactions, which are inherently asynchronous, we need to employ **async/await** syntax in our route handlers. This approach allows us to handle the operations in a more efficient and error-resilient manner. By using **async/await**, we can write a code that is not only more readable and maintains a synchronous flow but also simplifies the handling of asynchronous operations, like querying the database or awaiting responses.

Incorporating **async/await** is particularly important in our case, where the API interacts with a MongoDB database through Mongoose. Each route will correspond to specific CRUD operations, facilitated by our repositories. For instance, when a request to create a new task arrives, the relevant route handler will await the **create** method of the **TasksRepository**. Similarly, for fetching tasks, the **getAll** method will be used, and so forth for update and delete operations.

```
private routes(): void {

    // user signin
    this.express.post("/signin", async (req: express.Request<any, any, SignInRequest>,
        res: express.Response<UserResponse>, next: express.NextFunction) => {

        const { error, value } = signinSchema.validate(req.body);

        if (error) {
          res.status(400).json({ message: error.details[0].message, statusCode: 400, result: value });
          return;
        }

        const result = await this.userController.signin(req.body);
        res.status(200).json(result);
    });

    // user signup
    this.express.post("/signup", async (req: express.Request<any, any, SignUpRequest>,
        res: express.Response<UserResponse>, next: express.NextFunction) => {

        const { error, value } = signupSchema.validate(req.body);

        if (error) {
          res.status(400).json({ message: error.details[0].message, statusCode: 400, result: value });
          return;
        }

        const result = await this.userController.singup(req.body);
        res.status(200).json(result);
    });
}
```

***Figure 7.23**: user routes*

In the preceding code, **async/await** is used in the Express route handlers for user sign-in and sign-up. The **async** keyword marks the route handlers as asynchronous, allowing the use of **await** for pausing execution until promises from **this.userController.signin** and **this.userController.signup** are resolved. This approach simplifies handling of asynchronous operations like database interactions, leading to cleaner and more readable code. Additionally, before these asynchronous operations, user input validation is performed, with immediate responses sent if errors are found.

In the next code snippet, **`async/await`** is employed within the Express route handlers for various task-related operations. Each route handler is marked as **`async`**, allowing for asynchronous processing within them. This is particularly important for operations that involve database interactions or other asynchronous tasks, which are common in server-side logic.

For instance, in the GET, PUT, POST, and DELETE routes for tasks, **`await`** is used to pause execution until the respective controller methods (**`getTasks`**, **`updateTask`**, **`createTask`**, **`deleteTask`**, **`getTaskDetails`**) complete their execution. This use of **`await`** ensures that the server responds only after the completion of these asynchronous operations, providing a more structured and predictable flow of execution.

Additionally, for routes that modify data (PUT, POST, DELETE), the request body is validated before proceeding with the controller method. If validation fails, an immediate response is sent with an error status code and message, preventing further execution.

Overall, the use of **`async/await`** in these route handlers enhances the readability and maintainability of the code, while effectively managing asynchronous operations.

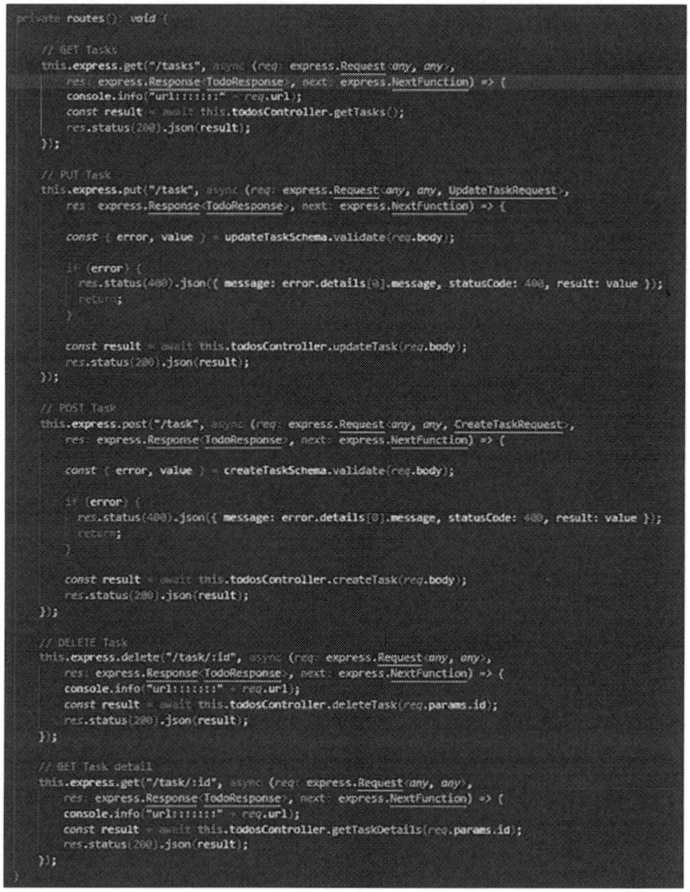

```
private routes(): void {

    // GET Tasks
    this.express.get("/tasks", async (req: express.Request<any, any>,
        res: express.Response<TodoResponse>, next: express.NextFunction) => {
        console.info("url:::::::" + req.url);
        const result = await this.todosController.getTasks();
        res.status(200).json(result);
    });

    // PUT Task
    this.express.put("/task", async (req: express.Request<any, any, UpdateTaskRequest>,
        res: express.Response<TodoResponse>, next: express.NextFunction) => {

        const { error, value } = updateTaskSchema.validate(req.body);

        if (error) {
          res.status(400).json({ message: error.details[0].message, statusCode: 400, result: value });
          return;
        }

        const result = await this.todosController.updateTask(req.body);
        res.status(200).json(result);
    });

    // POST Task
    this.express.post("/task", async (req: express.Request<any, any, CreateTaskRequest>,
        res: express.Response<TodoResponse>, next: express.NextFunction) => {

        const { error, value } = createTaskSchema.validate(req.body);

        if (error) {
          res.status(400).json({ message: error.details[0].message, statusCode: 400, result: value });
          return;
        }

        const result = await this.todosController.createTask(req.body);
        res.status(200).json(result);
    });

    // DELETE Task
    this.express.delete("/task/:id", async (req: express.Request<any, any>,
        res: express.Response<TodoResponse>, next: express.NextFunction) => {
        console.info("url:::::::" + req.url);
        const result = await this.todosController.deleteTask(req.params.id);
        res.status(200).json(result);
    });

    // GET Task detail
    this.express.get("/task/:id", async (req: express.Request<any, any>,
        res: express.Response<TodoResponse>, next: express.NextFunction) => {
        console.info("url:::::::" + req.url);
        const result = await this.todosController.getTaskDetails(req.params.id);
        res.status(200).json(result);
    });
}
```

Figure 7.24: *Tasks Routes*

This structured approach ensures that our Express TypeScript API is not only well-architected in terms of separating concerns through the repository pattern but is also robust and capable of handling real-world data operation scenarios efficiently. With this setup, we are well-prepared to handle various CRUD operations, providing a solid foundation for building a reliable and scalable web application.

Testing APIs with Postman

Testing APIs with Postman is a widely adopted practice in software development, offering a streamlined and intuitive process for verifying the functionality and reliability of APIs. Postman is a versatile tool, providing a user-friendly interface that simplifies sending requests to APIs and analyzing their responses.

When you start using Postman, the first step is to install it, which is straightforward as it is available as a desktop application for various operating systems and as a browser extension. Once installed, you can organize your API testing by creating collections. These collections are essentially groups of requests that can be structured according to your API's endpoints or specific testing requirements.

The core of Postman's functionality lies in its ability to create and configure requests. For each API endpoint you wish to test, you set up a new request in Postman. This setup involves specifying the HTTP method (such as GET, POST, PUT, DELETE), entering the API endpoint's URL, and configuring any necessary headers, query parameters, or body data. For APIs that necessitate authentication, Postman provides convenient ways to include authentication tokens or user credentials.

Sending these configured requests is where Postman truly shines. Upon sending a request, Postman presents the response from the API, including vital details like the status code, the response body, and headers. This response data is crucial for verifying whether the API is behaving as expected – for example, returning the correct data and status codes.

For more advanced testing needs, Postman allows the writing of tests in JavaScript that are executed after a request is made. These tests can assert various aspects of the response, such as checking for specific data or validating the response status code. These tests can be automated and run in sequence using Postman's Collection Runner, or externally via Newman, Postman's command-line tool, enabling comprehensive automated testing scenarios.

Lastly, Postman facilitates collaboration and sharing of API tests. Collections and environments can be shared with team members, an invaluable feature for collaborative projects. The tool offers options to export and import collections, and for those using Postman's cloud features, collections can be synced across devices, enhancing team coordination and efficiency.

In essence, Postman is a robust and comprehensive tool for API testing. Its ease of use, combined with a rich set of features for both manual and automated testing, makes it a popular choice among developers for ensuring their APIs function correctly and efficiently.

Having successfully completed all necessary configurations and modifications, we have now reached the crucial phase of testing our routes. This is an essential step to ensure that everything is functioning as intended.

Testing with User Routes

Testing the signup route is a crucial part of verifying that the user registration functionality of your application works correctly. It ensures that new users can successfully create accounts, which is fundamental for any application with user authentication.

This URL points to the signup route of your application running locally. The port **`3080`** suggests that the application's server is listening on this port. The path **`/api/user/signup`** is mapped to the signup functionality in your application.

```
// Signup URL
http://localhost:3080/api/user/signup
// Request Body
 {
    "firstName": "first1",
    "lastName": "last1",
    "email": "test@email.com",
    "password": "password"
 }
```

The screenshot that follows represents the testing of the preceding signup URL. We can notice in the response that the user is successfully created with the status code 200.

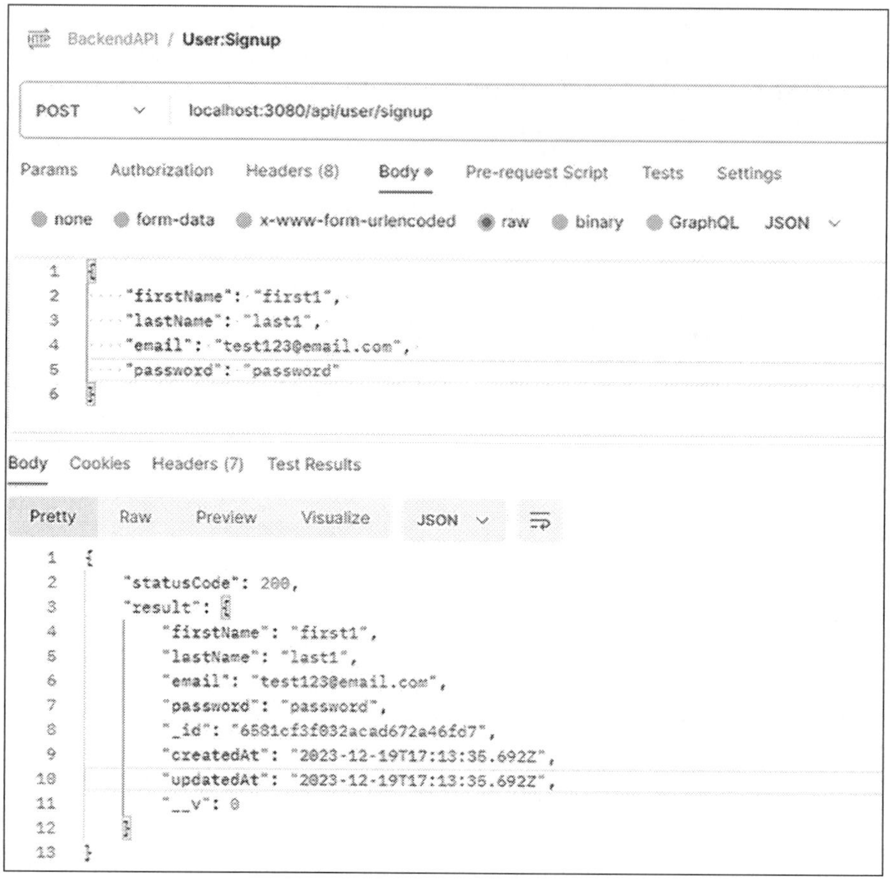

Figure 7.25: *Testing Signup URL*

The following **`Signin URL`** to authenticate users in an application, where a POST request with these credentials is sent to the server to grant access based on the validity of the provided **`email`** and **`password`**.

```
// Signin URL
http://localhost:3080/api/user/signin
// Request Body
{
    "email": "test123@email.com",
    "password": "password"
}
```

The following screenshot represents the testing of the preceding **`signin`** URL. We can notice in the response that the user is successfully authenticated with the status code 200.

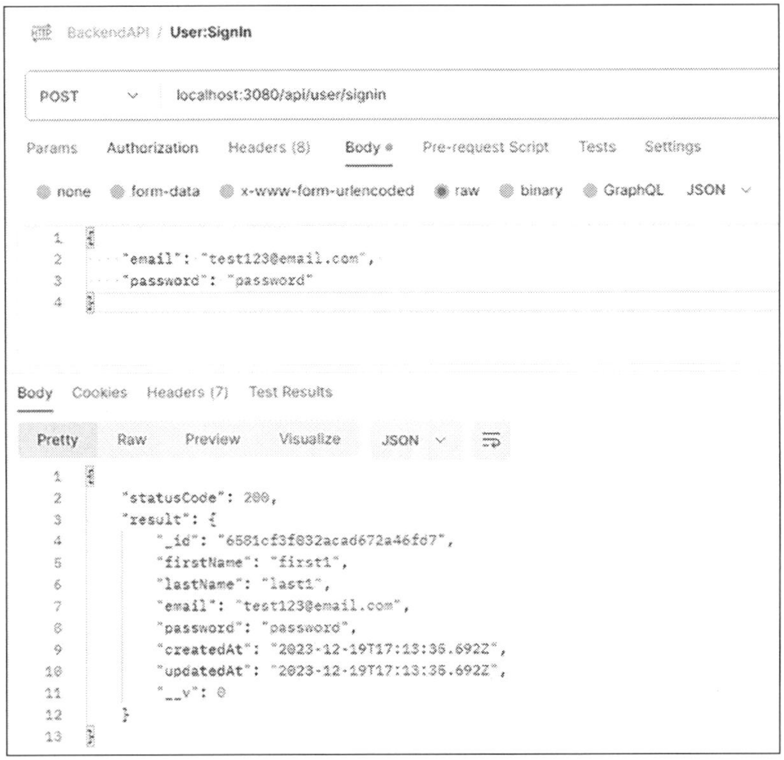

Figure 7.26: *Testing Signup URL*

Testing with todos Routes

The following POST request is sent to the provided URL with the JSON-formatted request body. The server's response can then be checked to confirm the successful creation of the task and to ensure that all the provided task details are correctly processed and stored.

```
// Create Tasks URL
http://localhost:3080/api/todos/task
// Request Body
{
    "task": "TASK1",
    "assignee": "user3",
    "description": "this is task",
    "status": "TODO",
    "createdBy": "user1"
}
```

The following screenshot represents the testing of the above URL. We can notice in the response that Task is successfully created with the status code **200**.

Figure 7.27: *Testing Creating Tasks*

The following GET request is typically sent to the URL. The expected response would be a list or collection of tasks, possibly in JSON format, representing the tasks currently managed or tracked within the application. This endpoint is essential for viewing all tasks and their details in a todo management system or a similar application.

```
// Get Tasks URL
http://localhost:3080/api/todos/tasks
```

The following screenshot represents the testing of the preceding URL. We can notice in the response that we are getting tasks with the status code **200**.

Figure 7.28: *Testing Getting Tasks*

The following is a PUT request (depending on the API design), typically sent to the specified URL with the provided JSON body. The server's response can then be observed to verify that the task has been updated correctly with the new details.

```
// Update Task URL
http://localhost:3080/api/todos/task
// Request Body
{
    "_id": "657f6d2210d6b9ed5745417a",
    "task": "task3sdfsf",
    "assignee": "user15",
```

```
    "description": "this is updated",
    "status": "DONE",
    "updatedBy": "user1"
}
```

The following screenshot represents the testing of the preceding URL. We can notice in the response that the task is updated successfully with the status code **200**.

Figure 7.29: *Testing Updating a Task*

The following is a DELETE request that is sent to the URL with the appropriate **taskId** replaced in the placeholder. For example, if the task ID is **12345**, the URL would be **http://localhost:3080/api/todos/task/12345**. The server's response after this request can be checked to confirm the successful deletion of the specified task. This feature is essential for managing and maintaining the tasks within the application, allowing for the removal of tasks that are no longer needed or relevant.

```
// Delete Task URL
http://localhost:3080/api/todos/task/<taskId>
```

The following screenshot represents the testing of the above URL. We can notice in the response that the task is deleted successfully with the status code **200**.

Figure 7.30: *Testing Deleting Tasks*

The following GET request is sent to the URL with the specific **`taskId`** substituted in place of **`<taskId>`**. For instance, if you wish to retrieve details of a task with the ID **`abc123`**, the URL would be **`http://localhost:3080/api/todos/task/abc123`**. The server's response to this request typically includes detailed data about the task, such as its name, description, assignee, status, and any other relevant information stored in the system. This functionality is crucial for viewing and managing individual tasks within the application.

```
// Get Task Details
http://localhost:3080/api/todos/task/<taskId>
```

The following screenshot represents the testing of the preceding URL. We can notice in the response that we are getting task details successfully with the status code **200**.

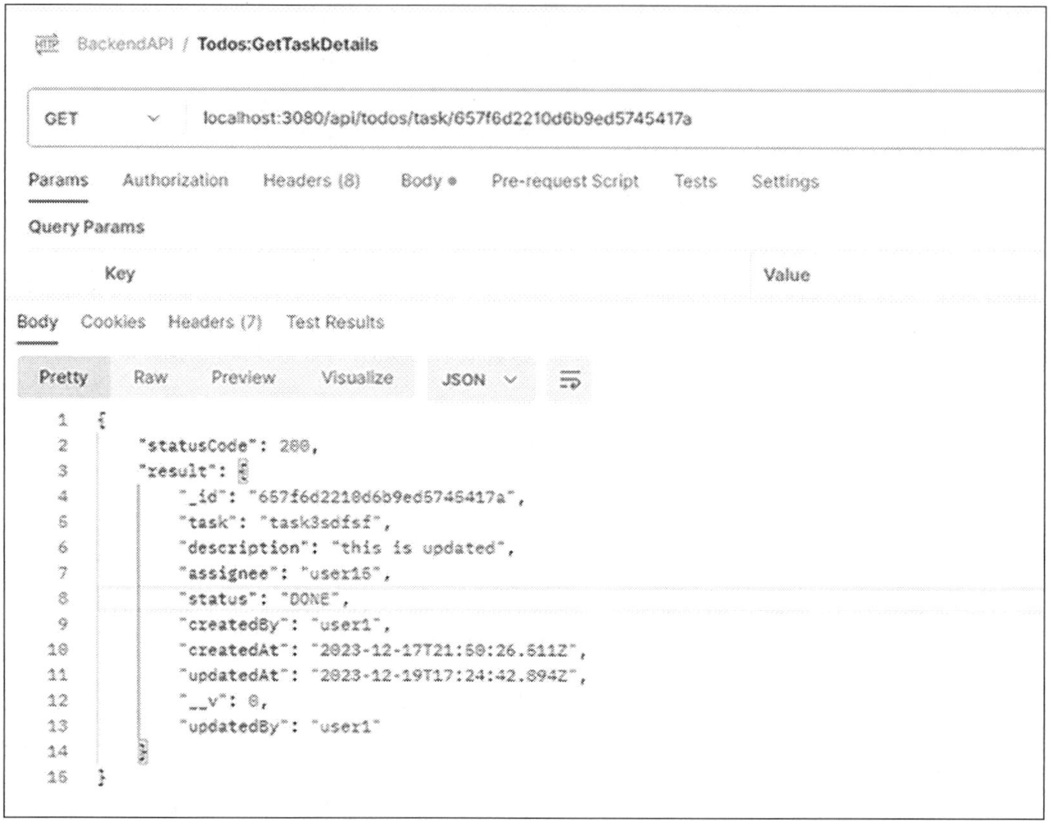

Figure 7.31: *Testing Getting Task Details*

Exploring Mongo Compass to Visualize the Data

Mongo Compass is the official GUI for MongoDB, designed to provide a straightforward and intuitive interface for interacting with your MongoDB databases. It is an essential tool for developers, especially when working with Node.js, Express, and TypeScript, as it allows you to visualize and manipulate your data more effectively. This section delves into how you can utilize Mongo Compass in your development workflow to enhance your understanding and management of the data stored in MongoDB.

Installing and Connecting Mongo Compass

Before diving into the functionalities of MongoDB Compass, the first step is its installation. Mongo Compass can be downloaded from the MongoDB website and is available for various operating systems. Once installed, connecting it to your MongoDB database is straightforward. You will need to enter your database's connection URI, which is typically provided by your MongoDB service or can be constructed based on your database set up. Once connected, you have direct access to your databases, collections, and documents.

We have already installed Mongo Compass in the previous chapters, and we have a connection URL. We need to give that URL in the box below and click on the **`Connect`** button.

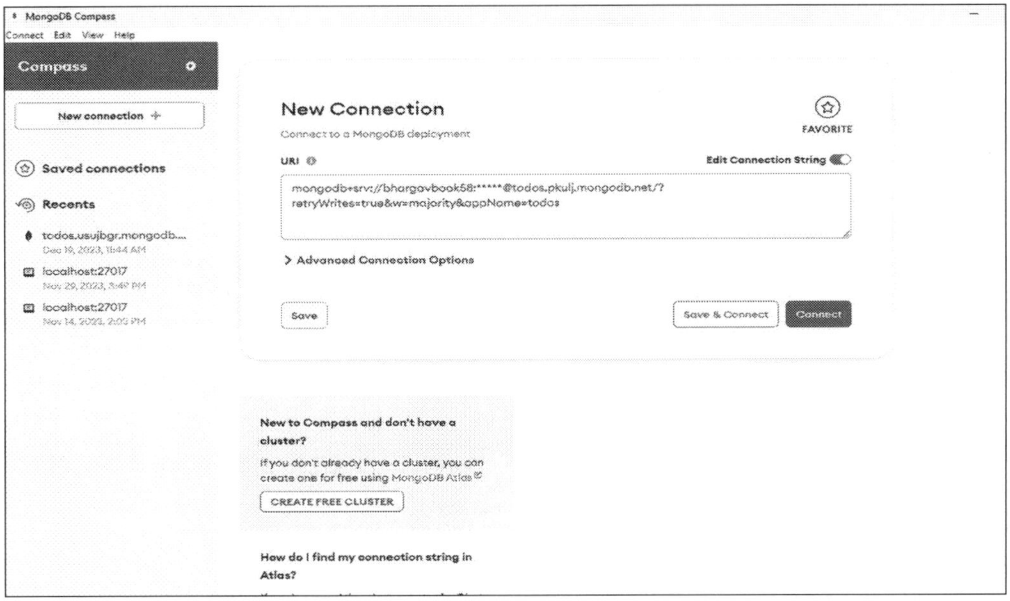

Figure 7.32: *Compass Connected*

The following figure shows the database details view:

Figure 7.33: *Viewing the database details*

Navigating the MongoDB Data Structure

Mongo Compass provides a clear and organized view of your MongoDB data structure. Upon connecting, you will see a list of databases. Clicking on a database expands it to show its collections, and further clicking on a collection displays its documents. This hierarchical view makes it easy to navigate through your data, offering a quick overview of your database's structure and contents.

Figure 7.34: *Navigating Data Structure*

Querying and Filtering Data

One of the key features of Mongo Compass is the ability to query and filter data within your collections. You can use MongoDB's query language to search for specific documents, filter results based on certain criteria, and sort data. This functionality is incredibly useful for testing queries that you will use in your Express application, allowing you to fine-tune and verify them in a more interactive environment.

Figure 7.35 shows the example of querying the tasks documents for which the status is **DONE**.

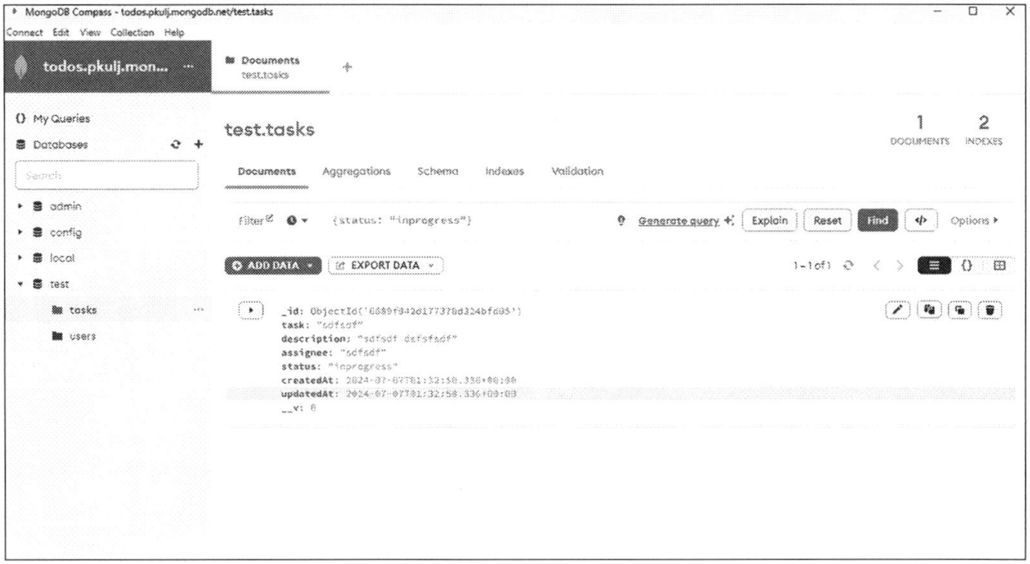

Figure 7.35: *Querying and Filtering Data*

Viewing and Editing Documents

Mongo Compass not only allows you to view your documents but also provides options to edit them directly. This feature is particularly useful for making quick modifications to your data, fixing issues, or simply experimenting with data changes. The interface offers a user-friendly way to add, delete, or modify the fields in your documents.

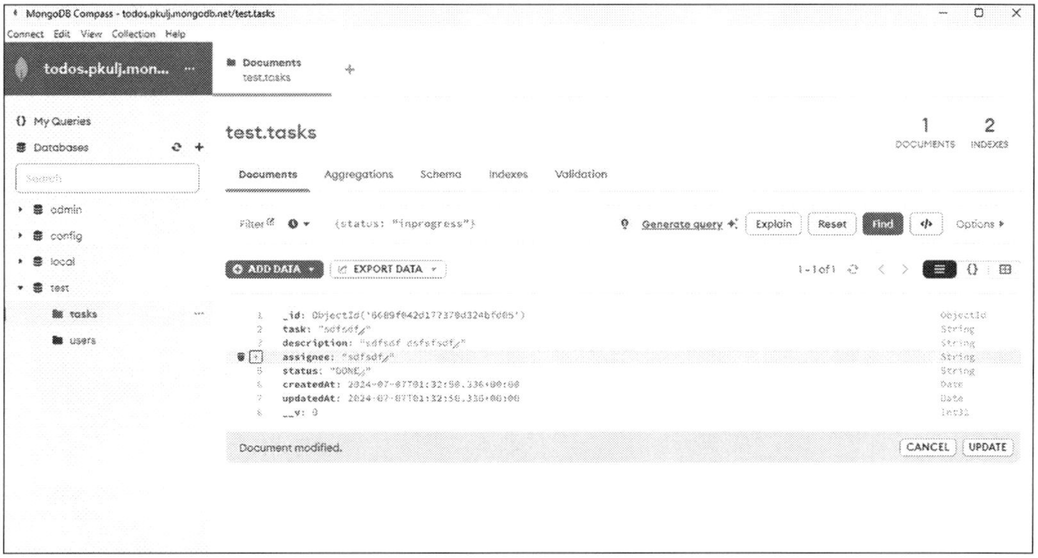

Figure 7.36: *Viewing and Editing Documents*

Analyzing Data with Aggregation Pipelines

For more advanced data analysis, Mongo Compass supports aggregation pipelines. This feature lets you process data and aggregate it in various ways, providing deeper insights into your data patterns and relationships. The aggregation pipeline builder in Compass offers a more visual and intuitive way to build complex queries and understand their results.

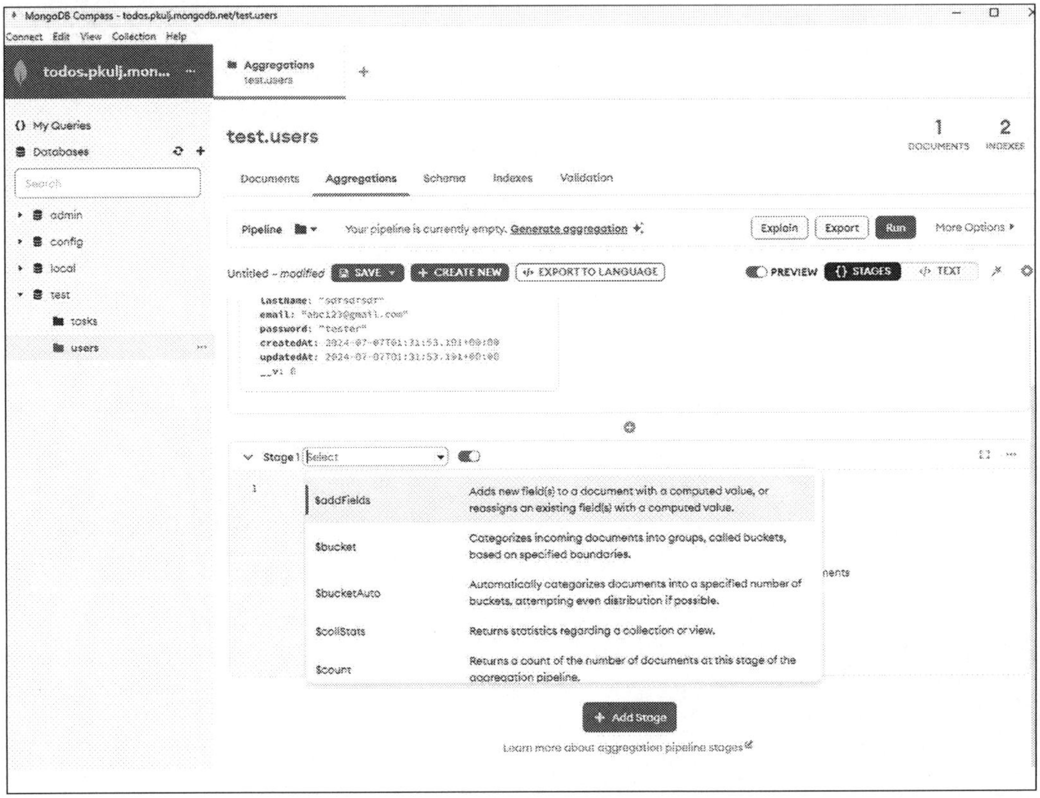

Figure 7.37: *Aggregation Pipeline Options*

Exporting and Importing Data

Mongo Compass facilitates the exporting and importing of data. This can be particularly useful for backup purposes, migrating data, or sharing datasets with team members. The tool supports various formats, making it flexible for different data handling needs.

Figure 7.38: *Exporting and Importing Data*

Conclusion

In this chapter, we have traversed a comprehensive journey through various aspects of integrating and managing MongoDB in a modern web application environment. Starting with the different ways to connect to a MongoDB instance, we laid the foundational knowledge essential for any developer venturing into the realm of database management.

The exploration of Atlas CLI offered insights into querying MongoDB, demonstrating the power and flexibility of MongoDB's tools. We then delved deeper into the intricacies of MongoDB with a focus on understanding Mongo Aggregation Pipelines, a critical feature for performing complex data transformations and analyses.

The technical walkthrough extended into the realm of application development with a detailed exposition on configuring MongoDB connections in an Express API. This is a crucial step for any full-stack or backend developer, ensuring that the application effectively communicates with the database.

Further, we explored the implementation of models and the repository pattern, key concepts in structuring and organizing database interactions in a clean, modular, and scalable way. These practices not only improve code maintainability but also enhance the overall architecture of the application.

The chapter also covered the implementation of CRUD operations, an essential part of interacting with the database, followed by a practical guide on testing these operations using Postman. This section provided valuable insights into ensuring the reliability and robustness of our API endpoints.

We concluded our journey with an exploration of Mongo Compass. This tool brings a visual dimension to database management, making it more accessible and intuitive, especially for those who prefer a GUI over command-line interactions.

This chapter offered a holistic view of working with MongoDB in a web application context. From establishing connections to visualizing data, each section was carefully crafted to equip you with the necessary skills and knowledge to proficiently manage and interact with MongoDB databases. Whether you are a beginner or an experienced developer, the concepts and practices discussed here will undoubtedly enhance your capabilities in developing efficient, scalable, and robust web applications. Having completed the integration with MongoDB, we now turn our attention to the development of the user interface. In the upcoming chapter, we will focus on crafting the UI and establishing integration with API calls for database interaction.

CHAPTER 8
UI Development

Introduction

Having established the backend for our example project, we now shift our focus to implementing the UI component, a pivotal aspect of the MEVN stack. This chapter will guide you through the essential elements and design structures that comprise a dynamic and robust web application interface.

Moving deeper into the frontend, we will discuss the process of writing containers and components, the building blocks of our UI screens. No application stands alone, and our example project is no exception. We will examine the intricacies of writing services and setting up a proxy for API calls, ensuring our frontend communicates effectively with the backend, bridging the gap between the client and the server.

State management is the conductor of our application's symphony, and with Pinia, we orchestrate a harmonious state that is both reactive and efficient. We will explore how to set up a Pinia store to centralize and manage the application's state. However, state management does not stop at initialization. We will delve into the concept of rehydrating state with Pinia, a strategy that ensures persistence and continuity of user experience across sessions and page reloads.

In conclusion, this chapter will encapsulate the essence of building an MEVN stack application from the ground up, providing you with the knowledge and confidence to craft your own applications that are scalable, maintainable, and user centric.

Structure

In this chapter, the following topics will be covered:

- Understanding Example Project
- Understanding Project Structure
- Define Routes and Creating Layouts
- Adding Bootstrap CSS Framework
- Writing Containers and Components for UI screens
- Writing Services and Proxy Setup for API Calls
- Setting Up Pinia Store for State Management

- Rehydrating State with Pinia
- Understanding the Final UI structure

Understanding Example Project

We have already written backend APIs in *Chapter 6, Backend Development With Typescript*, and it is now time to build the frontend for the following screens. We have already seen the example project that we are building in *Chapter 2, Prerequisites*. We have these two screens from which users can log in and sign up.

Once the users log in, they can see the dashboard in which they can list the tasks, edit the task, create the task, and delete the task. They can click on each task and see the complete details on the details screen.

The approach we should take is that of designing two templates based on the above screens with the help of nested routing. We will be able to explore all that in the coming sections. We have two kinds of templates – one template can be created for the sign in and the sign up screen and another template can be created for other screens after the user logs in. It will be easily maintainable and have code reusability if you want to add more screens. We have already set up the project structure in *Chapter 5, Setting Up Development Environment*. Let us now get started with writing components for these screens first.

Understanding Project Structure

Designing and understanding the project structure before we dive into its development is a very crucial aspect of web application development. *Figure 8.1* illustrates the architecture of a frontend application built with Vue.js, incorporating state management with Pinia and interaction with a Node.js API backend.

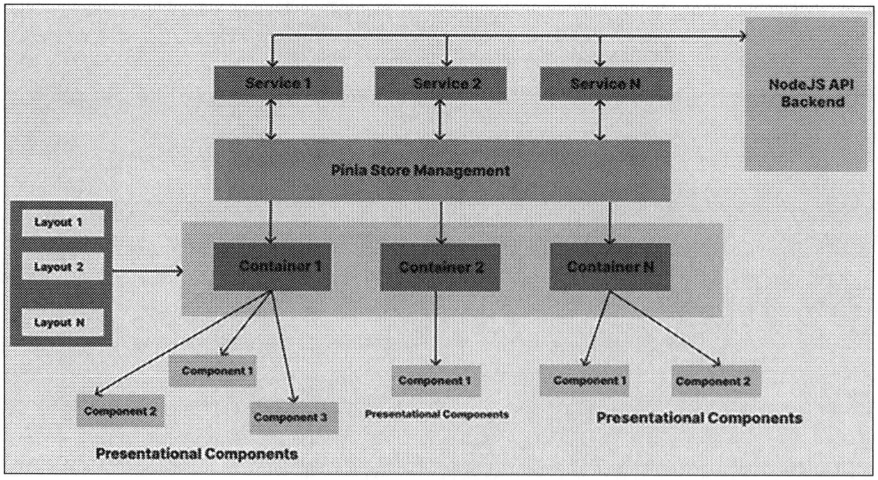

Figure 8.1: Project Structure

Here is an explanation of the different parts of the diagram:

Node.js API Backend

This represents the server-side of the application built with Node.js. It handles API requests and responses, business logic, database interactions, and more. We have developed this backend in the previous chapter. We call these backend APIs from services.

Services

These are the services that interact with the Node.js backend. They encapsulate the API calls and potentially some business logic for data transformation before passing the data to the store or components.

Pinia Store Management

Pinia is the state management library. It acts as a centralized store for all the states in the application. Components dispatch actions or commit mutations to the store to update the state, and they reactively receive new data from the store.

Containers

Containers are Vue components that are connected to the store. Their role is to fetch state from Pinia and pass it down to the presentational components. They might also dispatch actions to the store to trigger data updates or API interactions.

Layouts

Layouts define the structure of the UI. They are like templates that determine how the containers and components should be organized and displayed on the page. Each layout can be used for different parts of the application, such as a homepage layout, a dashboard layout, and more. In our case, we will create two layouts – one for login and another for the dashboard.

Components/Presentational Components

These are the building blocks of the application's UI. They receive data from their parent containers as props and are primarily concerned with how things look. They do not know where the data comes from and are often reusable across different parts of the application.

Flow of Data and Interaction

The arrows represent the data flow and interactions between different parts of the application. Layouts define the structure, containers fetch and manage state, and components render the UI. Services interact with the backend and provide data to the store, which in turn updates the containers.

In summary, the diagram shows a well-structured frontend architecture that promotes maintainability, scalability, and separation of concerns. Components are focused on UI and are kept dumb (presentational), containers manage data and state, and the store acts as a single source of truth, with services handling the server communication.

Defining Routes and Creating Layouts

We have a long way to go and it is time to install router dependency and add the routes to the application. We need to install the following dependency from the Vue ecosystem.

```
npm install vue-router
```

The first line imports the **createRouter** and **createWebHistory** functions from the **vue-router** package. **createRouter** is used to create a new router instance, and **createWebHistory** is a history mode that uses the browser's **history.pushState** API to create real URLs without reloading the page.

Here, an empty array **routes** is defined, which is meant to hold the route configurations for the application. We do not have any routes for now.

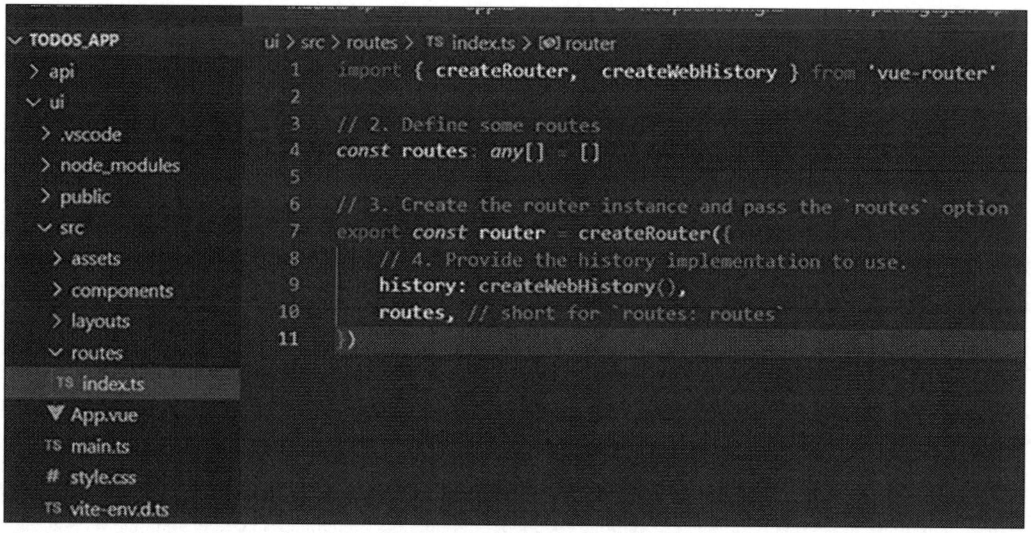

Figure 8.2: *Creating router*

The **createRouter** function is called to create a new router instance. It is passed an object with the **history** and **routes** options. **history** is set to the result of **createWebHistory()**, which means the router will use the browser's history stack and make the URL look "**normal**" (no **#** hashbang). The **routes** are set to the previously defined **routes** array. Even though it is empty, this is where you would list all your route configurations.

We are exporting the created router instance so that it can be imported and used in other parts of your Vue.js application, typically in the main entry file where you create the Vue app instance with **createApp**. This router can be imported into the **main.ts** file.

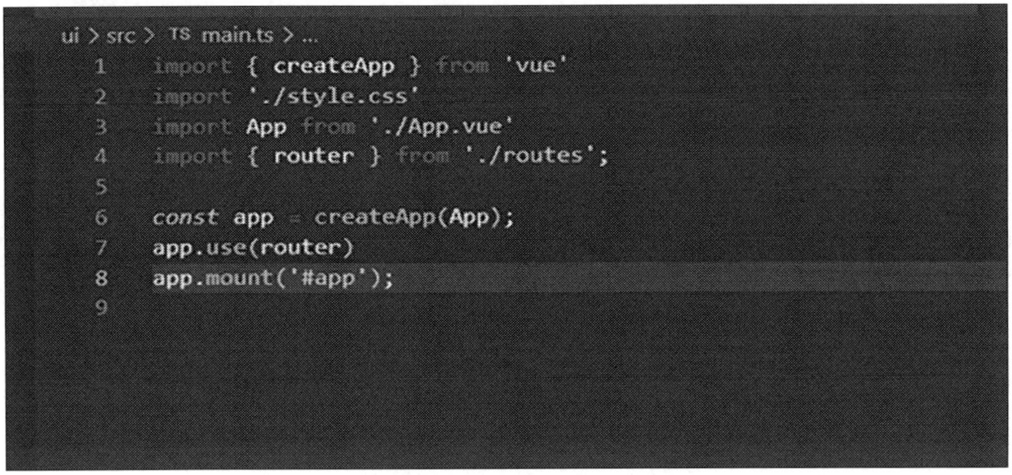
ui > src > TS main.ts > ...
```
import { createApp } from 'vue'
import './style.css'
import App from './App.vue'
import { router } from './routes';

const app = createApp(App);
app.use(router)
app.mount('#app');
```

Figure 8.3: *main.ts*

The **use** method is called on the application instance **app**. This method is used to install additional plugins into the Vue application. In this case, it installs the router instance that was previously exported from the router file. This initializes the Vue application and configures it to use Vue Router for navigation between different components based on the browser's URL. We need to define two templates based on our screens. Let us create these layouts under the folder called layouts. We will use the SFC (Single File Component). An SFC, or Single File Component, is a file with a **.vue** extension that encapsulates the structure, styling, and behavior of a component in a single file. This approach is central to Vue's design philosophy, making it easier to develop, maintain, and organize UI components.

An SFC typically consists of three types of blocks:

- **Template Block:** The **<template>** block contains the HTML markup. It describes the structure of the Vue component and can include dynamic data binding and directives to control rendering.
- **Script Block:** The **<script>** block contains the JavaScript logic of the component. In Vue 3, this often utilizes the Composition API, which provides a flexible way to compose component logic through reactive variables and functions.
- **Style Block:** The **<style>** block contains the CSS specific to this component. Styles can be scoped to the component, preventing them from affecting other elements outside the component.

The following is the first layout component: **DashboardLayout**

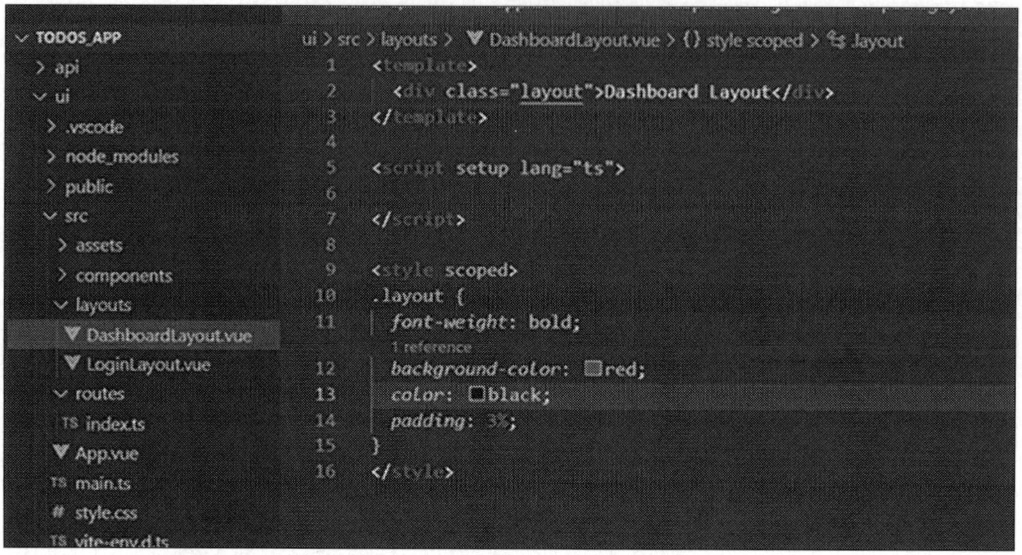

***Figure 8.4**: Dashboard Layout*

Here is the second layout component: **LoginLayout**

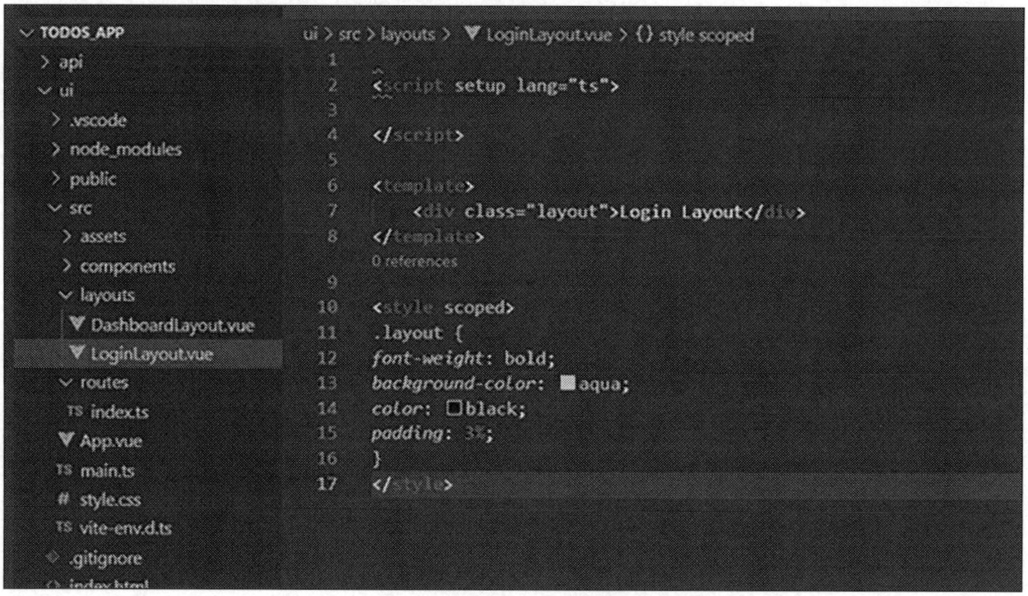

***Figure 8.5**: Login Layout*

Once our layouts are defined, we need to import these components into our router as below. We are defining paths: loading **LoginLayout** with the default path and loading dashboard layout with the path /dashboard.

ui > src > routes > TS index.ts > routes

```
import { createRouter,  createWebHistory } from 'vue-router'
import LoginLayout from '../layouts/LoginLayout.vue'
import DashboardLayout from '../layouts/DashboardLayout.vue'

// 2. Define some routes
const routes: any[] = [
    {
        path: '',
        component: LoginLayout
    },
    {
        path: '/dashboard',
        component: DashboardLayout
    }
]

// 3. Create the router instance and pass the `routes` option
export const router = createRouter({
    // 4. Provide the history implementation to use.
    history: createWebHistory(),
    routes, // short for `routes: routes`
})
```

Figure 8.6: *router*

Once defined, we must put the **App** component, which is loaded in the browser as the first component. This is where the component renders based on the path.

```
<router-view></router-view>
```

ui > src > App.vue > {} style scoped

```
<script setup lang="ts">

</script>

<template>
  <div>
    <h1>Welcome to ToDos App</h1>
    <router-view></router-view>
  </div>
</template>

<style scoped>

</style>
```

Figure 8.7: *App.vue*

Let us test these routes by running the application.

Figure 8.8: *welcome page*

The following is the **`Dashboard`** page.

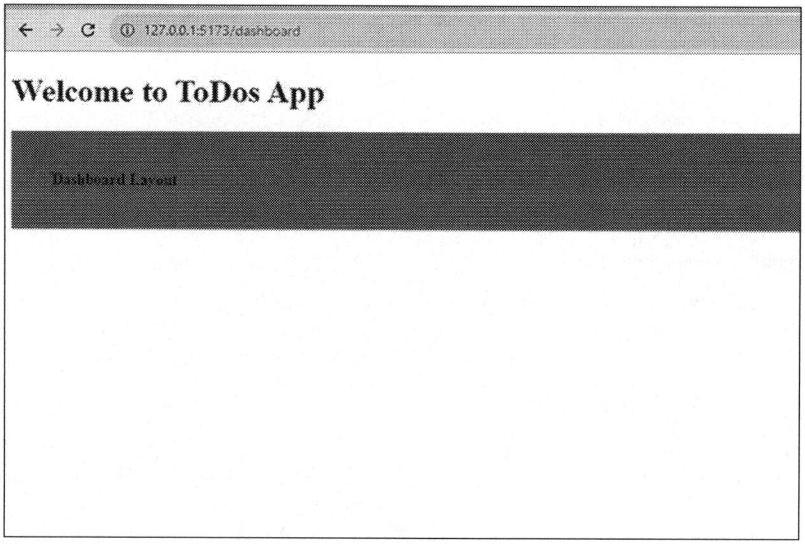

Figure 8.9: *Dashboard Page*

Adding Bootstrap CSS Framework

Bootstrap 5 is the fifth major release of the Bootstrap framework, which is an open-source and free CSS framework directed at responsive, mobile-first frontend web development. It contains CSS- and (optionally) JavaScript-based design templates for typography, forms, buttons, navigation, and other interface components.

With the release of Bootstrap 5, several significant changes were introduced:

- **jQuery Dependency Removed:** Unlike its predecessors, Bootstrap 5 does not depend on jQuery. It uses plain JavaScript, which makes it lighter and faster as it no longer needs to load the jQuery library.
- **Improved Grid System:** Bootstrap 5 comes with an enhanced grid system that offers more flexibility with gutters and allows for more complex layouts.
- **Custom SVG Icons**: Bootstrap 5 includes its own SVG icon library, which is a separate project and can be used independently of the Bootstrap framework.
- **Updated Forms**: There is an updated look and feel for form controls, which also improves their customizability.
- **Enhanced Customization:** It provides more CSS custom properties (variables) and introduces new utility classes that make customization easier without the need to compile Sass.
- **Dropped support for Internet Explorer:** Bootstrap 5 has dropped support for Internet Explorer, allowing the use of modern CSS features that are not supported in older browsers.
- **Improved Accessibility:** Bootstrap 5 focuses on improving accessibility by default, ensuring that web components are accessible to users with disabilities.
- **Updated Navbar**: The navbar component has been updated to be more customizable and versatile.
- **Dropped Card Decks:** The card deck feature has been dropped in favor of the grid system's more flexible rows and columns.
- **New Components and Utilities:** Bootstrap 5 introduces new components and utilities, expanding its toolkit for developers.

Bootstrap 5 continues to build on the foundation of its previous versions by offering a more modern and streamlined experience for developers to create responsive websites and applications quickly. It aims to provide an all-in-one solution for designing and prototyping new ideas, or for building full-fledged web applications with a standardized look and feel.

Using a CSS framework like Bootstrap 5 in a MEVN stack (MongoDB, Express.js, Vue.js, Node.js) offers several advantages:

- **Rapid Development:** Bootstrap provides a wealth of pre-styled components, such as buttons, navigation bars, modals, and so on, which can significantly speed up the development process. You do not need to write CSS from scratch; you can use Bootstrap's classes to style your application quickly.
- **Consistency:** Bootstrap enforces consistency automatically. All components follow a unified design language, which helps maintain a consistent look and feel across the entire application, regardless of who is working on it.

- **Responsiveness and Mobile-First:** Bootstrap's grid system and responsive utility classes make it easy to build applications that work on a variety of screen sizes and devices, adhering to the mobile-first philosophy.
- **Customizability:** Although Bootstrap comes with its own design defaults, it is also highly customizable. You can override the styles to match your application's design requirements without too much hassle.
- **Community and Documentation:** Bootstrap has a large community and comprehensive documentation, making it easy to find solutions to problems and get help when needed. This can be especially beneficial for teams new to the MEVN stack.
- **JavaScript Components:** Bootstrap 5 comes with a set of JavaScript components that can be easily integrated with Vue.js, such as modals, dropdowns, or carousels, which can enhance the interactivity of your application without additional dependencies like jQuery.
- **Utility Classes:** Bootstrap's utility classes for margin, padding, flexbox, and more allow for rapid layout design changes without writing custom CSS, leading to cleaner and more maintainable HTML code.
- **Cross-Browser Compatibility:** Bootstrap is tested and supported in major browsers and ensures that a website or application will be functional and look the same in all supported browsers.
- **Accessibility:** Bootstrap components are built with accessibility in mind, which helps in creating web applications that are accessible to users with disabilities.

Bootstrap's benefits help streamline the frontend development process, allowing developers to focus more on building the application's functionality with Vue.js, managing the server-side with Express.js and Node.js, and handling data with MongoDB. It is a way to ensure that the frontend is not only visually appealing and responsive but also efficient to develop and easy to maintain.

There are so many other frameworks out there and Bootstrap libraries as well, but we are going to install and add the bootstrap library without any other libraries. First, let us install these two dependencies with this command.

```
npm install -save bootstrap @popperjs/core
```

```
  "scripts": {
    "dev": "vite",
    "build": "vue-tsc && vite build",
    "preview": "vite preview"
  },
  "dependencies": {
    "@popperjs/core": "^2.11.8",
    "bootstrap": "^5.3.2",
    "vue": "^3.3.8",
    "vue-router": "^4.2.5"
  },
  "devDependencies": {
    "@vitejs/plugin-vue": "^4.5.0",

PROBLEMS 1   OUTPUT   DEBUG CONSOLE   TERMINAL   PORTS

S C:\Users\bharg\OneDrive\Desktop\todos_app\ui> npm install --save bootstrap @popperjs/core
```

Figure 8.10: *package.json*

The preceding command will add the dependencies to the dependencies section of the **`package.json`** and also add corresponding **`node_modules`**. We just need to import the dependencies in the **`main.ts`** file as follows after the installation is completed.

```
ui > src > TS main.ts > ...
import { createApp } from 'vue'
import './style.css'
import App from './App.vue'
import { router } from './routes';
import "bootstrap/dist/css/bootstrap.min.css"
import "bootstrap"

const app = createApp(App);
app.use(router)
app.mount('#app');
```

Figure 8.11: *importing bootstrap*

You can start adding bootstrap components now. Let us test out a sample component in one of the containers. We are using the alert component from the bootstrap.

```
<template>
    <div class="layout">Login Container</div>

    <div class="alert alert-primary" role="alert">
      A simple primary alert—check it out!
    </div>
</template>
```

Figure 8.12: *Testing bootstrap class*

This is how it looks in the browser. These convenient components make your development faster and easier.

Figure 8.13: *Welcome page with bootstrap*

Writing Containers and Components for UI Screens

Having completed the layout structure for our application and adding Bootstrap library, we now move towards the heart of the interface – the containers and presentational components. Containers serve as the connective tissue, binding the state management and services to the components that users interact with. They are responsible for handling data-fetching, state updates, and responding to user inputs, effectively acting as mediators between the stateful logic of our application and the visual elements.

Presentational components, on the other hand, are the building blocks of our application's user interface. Their primary role is to render data provided by the containers in a visually appealing and interactive manner. These components focus on the '*look and feel*', ensuring that the user experience is intuitive and responsive. By separating these concerns, we enable a more modular and maintainable codebase, where UI and business logic can be developed and refined independently. As we delve into containers and presentational components, we will see how they work in tandem to bring functionality and design together in a seamless user experience.

The application's user interface is structured into logical units known as layouts, containers, and presentational components.

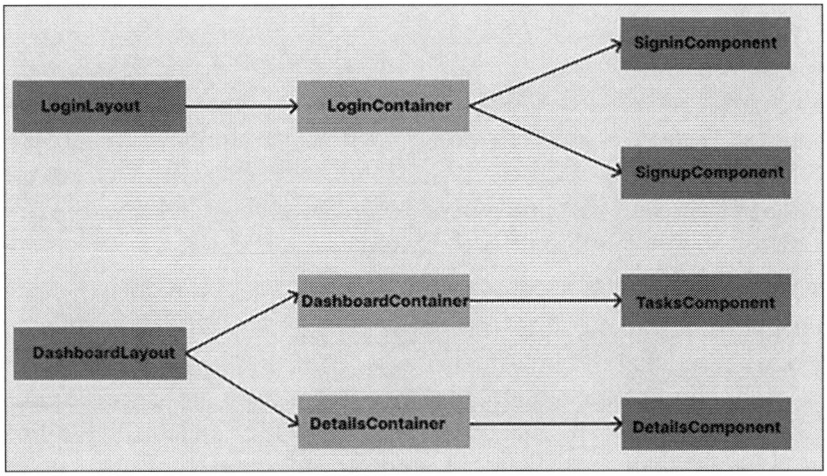

Figure 8.14: *Project Structure*

Here is an explanation in the context of the diagram.

- **`LoginLayout`:** This is a layout component that defines the overall structure and arrangement of the login-related user interface. It sets the stage for where containers and their child components will be placed.
- **`LoginContainer`:** Acting as an intermediary within the **`LoginLayout`**, the **`LoginContainer`** is responsible for orchestrating the logic behind user authentication. It manages state and behavior that will be utilized by its child components.
  - **`SigninComponent`:** This presentational component is focused on rendering the sign-in form. It is concerned with the visuals and user interactions for signing in, such as input fields for username and password, and the sign-in button.
  - **`SignupComponent`:** Similarly, this presentational component deals with the sign up process. It provides the user interface for new users to create an account, containing input fields for user details and a sign-up button.
- **`DashboardLayout`:** It is another layout component, but for the dashboard section of the application. It defines the structural framework for the dashboard's user interface.
- **`DashboardContainer`:** Within the **`DashboardLayout`**, the **`DashboardContainer`** connects the dashboard-related state and logic to its presentational components. It acts as a data provider and state manager for what the user sees and interacts with on the dashboard.
  - **`TasksComponent`:** This is a presentational component that displays the list of tasks. It is solely responsible for presenting the tasks in a user-friendly format without worrying about where the data comes from.

- **DetailsConatiner**: It is a container that might be used for managing the state and logic necessary for viewing the details of a particular task. It fetches and supplies the data to the **DetailsComponent**.
    - **DetailsComponent**: As a presentational component, it displays detailed information about a specific task when selected. It focuses on how task details are laid out and ensures the user can read and possibly interact with the information effectively.

In summary, layout components like **LoginLayout** and **DashboardLayout** define the visual structure. Containers such as **LoginContainer**, **DashboardContainer**, and **DetailsContainer** manage logic and state. In contrast, presentational components like **SigninComponent**, **SignupComponent**, **TasksComponent**, and **DetailsComponent** are dedicated to rendering the UI. This separation allows for a clear distinction between how things look (presentational components) and how things work (containers), leading to a more manageable and scalable codebase.

Implementing Login Module

We are set to develop a comprehensive login module, an integral part of our application's user interface. This module will encompass a login container, which serves as the primary component managing the state and logic of the login process. Within this container, we will incorporate two key presentational components: sign in and sign up. These components are designed to handle the user interface aspects of signing in and signing up, respectively, providing a user-friendly experience for these critical functionalities.

Our implementation plan includes not just the creation of these components but also their seamless integration into the application's routing system. This integration is vital for ensuring that users can navigate to and from the login process smoothly and intuitively. Once these components are developed and integrated into the routing, we will proceed with a thorough testing phase.

Creating a sign-in presentational component in VueJS 3 with TypeScript and using the Bootstrap CSS framework involves several key aspects. You will want to ensure that your component handles user input for email and password fields securely and efficiently. Here are the things we need to handle developing both **Sign in** and **Sign up** components.

- **Component Structure:** Use Bootstrap classes for styling and layout.
- **Form Handling:** Utilize Vue's reactive properties for form inputs.
- **Validation:** Implement basic client-side validation.
- **Event Emitting:** Emit an event with the credentials for the parent component to handle the actual sign in logic.

`Signin` Presentational Component

The functionality of the described sign-in presentational component is focused on user authentication and navigation between different user states - signing in and signing up.

In the sign in component, users are prompted to input their username and password. This is the authentication process, where the system verifies the entered credentials against stored data to grant access. Adjacent to the sign in feature, there is a sign up button. This is for users who do not have an account and wish to create one. Upon clicking this button, the user is redirected from the sign in interface to a sign up interface.

The component encapsulates both authentication (signing in) and navigation (moving to the sign up screen), streamlining the user's interaction with the application's entry points.

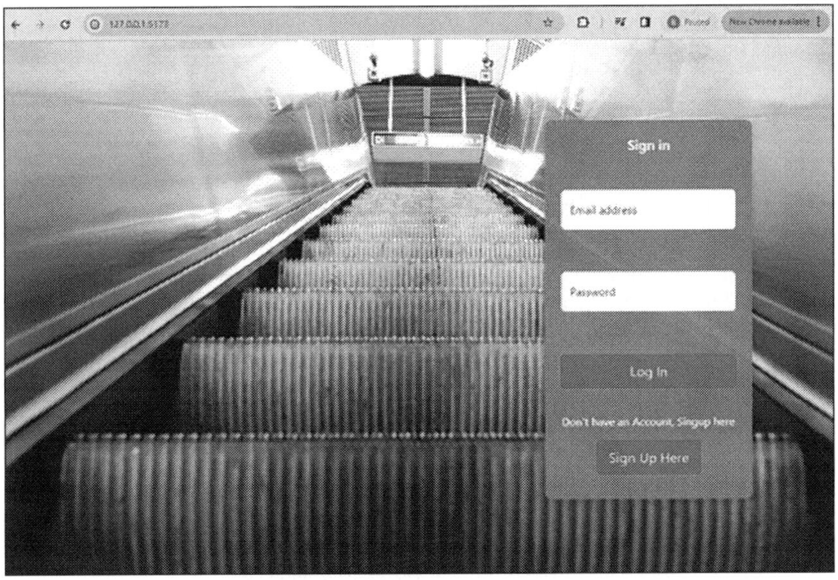

Figure 8.15: *Sign in Page*

Here is the template part of the sign in component. The Vue component is designed to create a user sign in interface with a visually appealing background and a card layout for the form elements.

Structure and Style

The component uses a full-height (`vh-100`) flexbox container to center the sign in card on the right side of the screen, with a darkened background image fetched from Unsplash. The card itself has a semi-transparent blue background, rounded corners, and a drop shadow for depth.

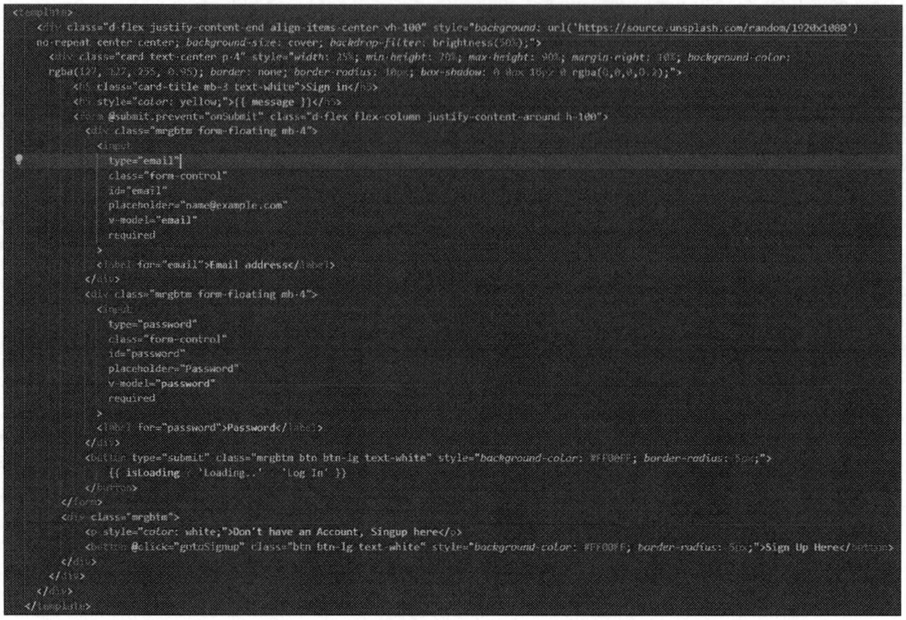

Figure 8.16: *Sign in template*

Sign In Form

Within the card, there is a form titled "**`Sign in`**" where users can enter their email address and password. Both fields are mandatory (**`required`**) for form submission. The form uses floating labels for a modern, clean aesthetic. Submission of the form is handled by the **`onSubmit`** method, which emits a custom **`signIn`** event with the email and password data.

The following is the script and style part of the sign in component.

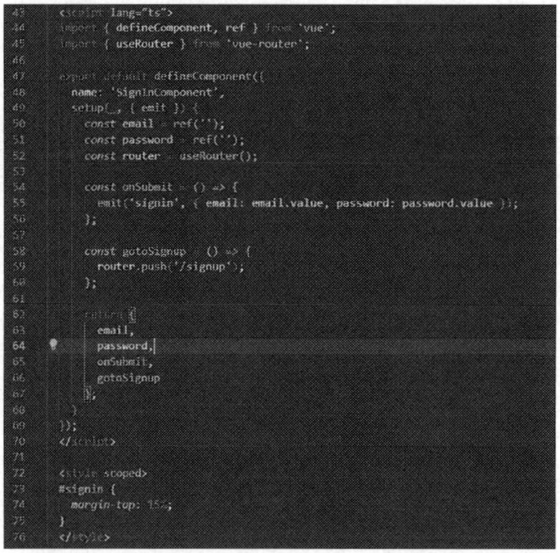

Figure 8.17: *sign in script*

Navigation

Just under the form, there is a prompt for users who do not have an account, followed by a "**Sign Up Here**" button. Clicking this button triggers the **gotoSignup** method, which uses Vue Router to navigate to the sign up page.

Scripting

The script section is written in TypeScript and uses Vue's Composition API. It defines reactive state references for the email and password, and methods for form submission and navigation. The **useRouter** hook from Vue Router enables programmatic navigation for the sign up process.

Styling

Lastly, the component includes minimal scoped CSS to add top margin spacing for the elements within the card, ensuring that the layout is evenly spaced and visually balanced.

Sign up Presentational Component

The form is encapsulated within a semi-transparent panel that floats over the image, providing a clear area for user interaction while still allowing the beauty of the background to remain visible. The form itself comprises two input fields – one for the user's email address, which serves as a unique identifier and a point of contact, and two for the user's chosen password. The dual password fields work in tandem to verify that the password entered is free of typos and errors, a crucial step for maintaining account security.

This sign up interface is not just a gateway to user registration but also a reflection of the application's attention to user experience, balancing visual elements with the practicalities of account creation.

***Figure 8.18**: Sign up Page*

Here is the template part of the sign up component. The Vue component is designed to create a user sign in interface with a visually appealing background and a card layout for the form elements.

This Vue component is a user interface for a sign up form, designed to register new users. It features a full-screen background sourced from **Unsplash**, with a centered card that houses the form elements. The sign-up form includes three fields: **Email address**, **Password**, and **Verify Password**. Each field is accompanied by floating labels that provide clear instructions for the user. The email and password data are bound to Vue's reactive variables, ensuring that the input is synchronized with the component's state.

```
<template>
  <div class="d-flex justify-content-end align-items-center vh-100" style="background: url('https://source.unsplash.com/random/1920x1080')
  no-repeat center center; background-size: cover; backdrop-filter: brightness(50%);">
   <div class="card text-center p-4" style="width: 25%; min-height: 70%; max-height: 90%; margin-right: 10%;
   background-color: rgba(127, 127, 255, 0.95); border: none; border-radius: 10px; box-shadow: 0 8px 16px 0 rgba(0,0,0,0.2);">
      <h5 class="card-title mb-3 text-white">Sign Up For Free</h5>
      <h5 style="color: yellow;">{{ message }}</h5>
      <form @submit.prevent="onSubmit" class="d-flex flex-column justify-content-around h-100">
        <div class="mrgbtm form-floating mb-4">
          <input
            type="email"
            class="form-control"
            id="email"
            placeholder="name@example.com"
            v-model="email"
            required
          >
          <label for="email">Email address</label>
        </div>
        <div class="mrgbtm form-floating mb-4">
          <input
            type="password"
            class="form-control"
            id="password"
            placeholder="Password"
            v-model="password"
            required
          >
          <label for="password">Password</label>
        </div>
        <div class="mrgbtm form-floating mb-4">
          <input
            type="password"
            class="form-control"
            id="verifypassword"
            placeholder="Verify Password"
            v-model="verifypassword"
            required
          >
          <label for="verifypassword">Verify Password</label>
        </div>
        <button type="submit" class="mrgbtm btn btn-lg text-white" style="background-color: #FF00FF; border-radius: 5px;">
          {{ isLoading ? 'Loading..' : 'Create Your Account' }}
        </button>
      </form>
    </div>
  </div>
</template>
```

Figure 8.19: *sign up template*

When the form is submitted, a **'signUp'** event is emitted, carrying the user's email and password data, which can then be handled by a parent component or a Vuex action. The **onSubmit** method prevents the default form submission to manage the process programmatically.

The component's styling is scoped, meaning it only affects this component's elements, preventing any global style conflicts. The form's submit button is styled distinctively and is designed to grab attention, encouraging users to complete their registration.

```
<script lang="ts">
import { defineComponent, ref } from 'vue';

export default defineComponent({
  name: 'SignUpComponent',
  setup(_, { emit }) {
    const email = ref('');
    const password = ref('');
    const verifypassword = ref('');

    const onSubmit = () => {
      emit('signup', { email: email.value, password: password.value, verifypassword: verifypassword.value });
    };

    return {
      email,
      password,
      verifypassword,
      onSubmit
    };
  }
});
</script>

<style scoped>
#signup {
  margin-top: 15%;
}
</style>
```

Figure 8.20: *Sign up script*

We have explored the presentational components, and following are the container components and routing configurations that seamlessly integrate the entire login module. The following login container utilizes the **<router-view>** tag, which is a placeholder element used by Vue Router. The **<router-view>** is where the matched component will be rendered, depending on the current route.

There is no script set up logic present in the script section, which implies that this component is solely responsible for rendering the appropriate view based on the URL path accessed by the user. It is a single point of entry for various components which are displayed depending on the route navigated to.

ui > src > containers > LoginContainer.vue > {} style scoped

```
<template>
    <router-view></router-view>
</template>

<script setup lang="ts">

</script>

<style scoped>
.layout {
    font-weight: bold;
    background-color: red;
    color: black;
    padding: 3%;
}
</style>
```

Figure 8.21: *Login Container*

The following is the router configuration. The configuration for the path '' defines the root route of the application. This route uses **LoginLayout** as its component, serving as a wrapper for its child routes. Within this root route, there are two child routes defined.

The first child route is for the path **signup**. When the user navigates to **/signup**, the **SignupComponentVue** is rendered within the **LoginLayout**. This component is likely designed to allow new users to create an account.

The second child route corresponds to the root path within the **LoginLayout**. It renders the **SignInComponentVue** when the user navigates to the root of the application (that is, the homepage or the base URL). This component is intended for users to log in to their existing accounts.

In essence, the root route serves as a gateway, directing users either to the sign-in page by default or to the sign-up page if they navigate to **/signup.** This setup enables a clean and organized structure for the login-related functionalities, encapsulated within the **LoginLayout**.

```
// 2. Define some routes
const routes: any[] = [
    {
        path: '',
        component: LoginLayout,
        children: [
            {
                path: 'signup',
                component: SignupComponentVue
            },
            {
                path: '',
                component: SignInComponentVue
            }
        ]
    },
    {
        path: '/dashboard',
        component: DashboardLayout
    },
```

Figure 8.22: *routes*

Implementing Dashboard Module

In the preceding section, we crafted the **Login** Module, equipping users with the ability to access their accounts. Moving forward, our focus shifts to the construction of the **Dashboard** Module. This module is central to user interaction post-login and features a header that displays a profile icon along with a logout button, allowing users to manage their session.

The **Dashboard** Module is also responsible for presenting task-related information. When a user has not yet created any tasks, a "**No Tasks Available**" message is prominently displayed, indicating the absence of actionable items. Conversely, when tasks exist for the user, a Task Table materializes, neatly listing all the tasks along with options to manage them.

Integral to this module are three pivotal buttons: "**`Create Your Task`**," "**`Edit`**," and "**`Delete`**". Each button, upon interaction, summons a corresponding modal window. These modal windows serve as interactive forms where users can input new tasks or modify existing ones. The "**`Create Your Task`**" button, specifically, launches a modal that invites the user to articulate a new task, enriching their to-do list. Conversely, the "**`Edit`**" and "**`Delete`**" buttons allow for the refinement or removal of current tasks, respectively.

As we progress, we will delve into the implementation of these components, ensuring each user action is met with a seamless and intuitive response. Let us embark on establishing these features within the Dashboard Module.

Header and `NoTasksAvailable` Presentational Components

Figure 8.23 captures the dashboard screen of a task management application, specifically tailored for a user currently logged in but who has not created any tasks yet. The top portion of the screen is dedicated to a header that not only identifies the page as the "**`Tasks Dashboard`**" but also integrates user interaction elements. On the upper right, the header features a personalized profile icon, accompanied by a **`Log Out`** button—tools that allow users to access their personal settings and securely exit their session.

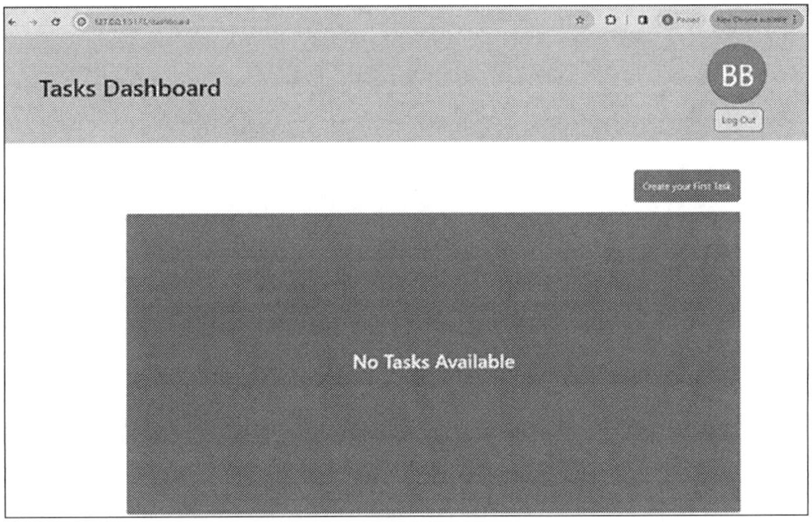

Figure 8.23: *Dashboard without tasks*

At the front and centre of the dashboard is a prominent display indicating the absence of tasks. It's a clear, unambiguous message reading "**`No Tasks Available`**," which serves as a visual cue for users who have not yet added tasks to their list. This section acts as both a status indicator and a prompt, suggesting that the user's next step might be to initiate task creation and populate this currently empty space with actionable items.

A "**`Create your First Task`**" button is available for users to initiate their first entry. By clicking this button, users can begin the process of adding their inaugural task.

Here is the header component designed for an application interface. It receives a title as a prop, which is then displayed within an h1 tag, indicating its prominence in the hierarchy of the page content.

The header is divided into two main areas – on the left, the title is presented with additional left margin space for visual balance; on the right, there is an interactive section with profile-related actions. This section includes a circular button labeled "**BB**," which, when clicked, triggers the **onProfileClick** method - presumably to open the user's profile or related settings. Following the profile button, there's a "**Log Out**" button styled distinctly to stand out as a secondary action. Clicking this button invokes the **onLogoutClick** method, likely to sign the user out of the application.

```
ui > src > components > Header.vue > {} script > default > setup
<template>
  <header class="header d-flex justify-content-between align-items-center p-3">
    <h1 style="margin-left: 50px;">{{ title  }}</h1>
    <div class="profile-actions d-flex flex-column align-items-end">
      <button class="btn btn-danger rounded-circle mb-2">
        {{ profileName }}
      </button>
      <button class="btn btn-outline-danger" @click="onLogoutClick">
        Log Out
      </button>
    </div>
  </header>
</template>

<script lang="ts">
import { computed, toRefs } from 'vue'
import { useUserStore } from '../store/userStore';
import { useRouter } from 'vue-router';

export default {

  props: {
    title: String
  },

  setup(props) {

    const { title } = toRefs(props)
    const userStore = useUserStore();
    const router = useRouter();

    const onLogoutClick = () => router.push('/');
    const profileName = computed(() => userStore.getProfileName)

    return {
      onLogoutClick,
      title,
      profileName
    }

  }
}

</script>

<style scoped>
.header {
  background-color: #afbcfa; /* Replace with the actual color code from your design */
}
```

Figure 8.24: *Header Component*

The script section of the component is written in TypeScript, utilizing Vue's Composition API. It sets up the component's reactive state and behavior. Within the **`setup`** function, two methods are declared: **`onProfileClick`** and **`onLogoutClick`**. Both methods currently log messages to the console, indicating placeholder functionality where actual logic would be implemented to handle profile viewing and user logout.

Overall, the header component is structured to provide essential user interaction points, allowing for navigation and session management within the application's user interface.

The following **`NoTasksAvailable`** component outlines a user interface component, primarily a message display. This component is structured as a column within a larger grid, prominently showcasing a "**`No Tasks Available`**" message at its center. The absence of tasks is clearly communicated to the user through this central element. The template's simplicity suggests it could be part of a task management application, ready to be integrated with additional interactive features for task creation and management. The script section is currently empty, indicating that the functionality to add tasks would be implemented elsewhere.

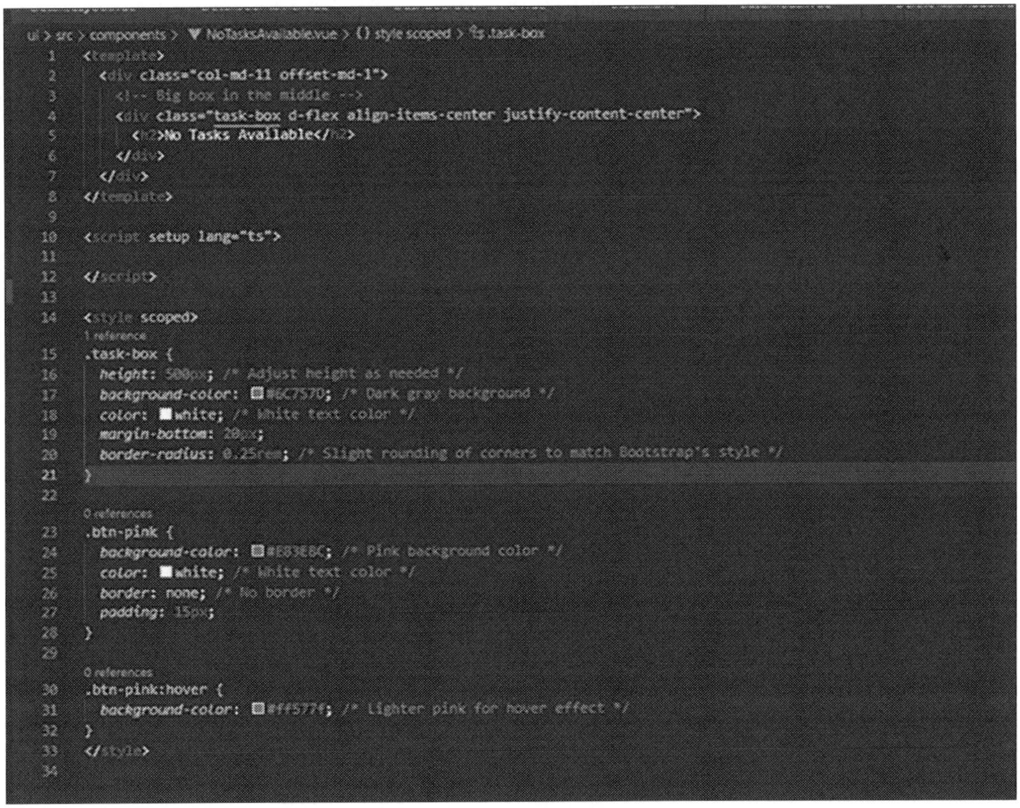

Figure 8.25: *No Tasks Available Component*

Tasks Presentational Component

Having observed the interface's appearance in scenarios where no tasks are available, we are now at a juncture where the next logical step is to introduce the tasks table into the dashboard. This implementation marks a significant enhancement, transitioning from a state of emptiness to one of functional interaction with the user's tasks.

In the segment of our application dedicated to task management, we encounter a crucial user interface component–the task table. This table is meticulously designed to display a list of tasks, each accompanied by essential details such as a unique identifier, task name, description, and the date of creation. A glance at the table reveals a structured and intuitive layout. Each task is neatly presented in its own row, making it easy for users to scan and comprehend the information. The inclusion of '`Edit`' and '`Delete`' buttons adjacent to each task is a thoughtful design choice, granting users the power to modify or remove tasks with ease. These buttons are instrumental in providing an interactive experience, as they are the gateways to updating existing tasks or purging obsolete ones.

Above the task table, there is a prominently placed button labeled `'Create your First Task'`. Despite the table already containing tasks, the presence of this button serves as a clear call-to-action, encouraging users to continue adding new tasks to their list. Its striking design ensures it stands out, guiding new users to initiate their first task creation without hesitation.

The task table's design not only prioritizes functionality but also aligns with the aesthetic coherence of the application. Its color scheme and typography are chosen to maintain visual harmony with the rest of the application, providing a seamless user experience. The `'Create your First Task'` button, with its inviting appearance, adds a touch of warmth and engagement, further enhancing the user-friendly nature of the application.

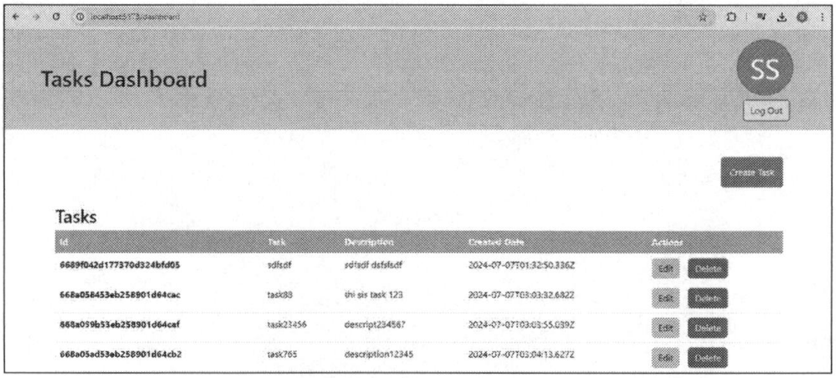

Figure 8.26: *Dashboard with tasks*

Here is the tasks component in which we are displaying the table. A prominent heading "`Tasks`" is placed above the table, giving users a clear indication of the table's content. The table itself is marked up with standard HTML table elements, styled with Bootstrap classes for consistency and aesthetics. The **<thead>** section sets the column headings, denoting the data each column will display: **'Id'**, **'Task'**, **'Description'**, '**Created Date**', and **'Actions'**.

The dynamic nature of the table is introduced through the use of the **v-for** directive, which iterates over the **tasks** array passed down as a prop. Each task's properties are bound to the respective table cells using the double curly braces syntax **{{ }}**, a feature of Vue.js's template syntax. The **'Actions'** column includes **'Edit'** and **'Delete'** buttons, providing users with the ability to modify or remove tasks. These buttons are wired to event handlers **onEditTask** and **onDeleteTask** using Vue.js's **@ click** directive, which listens for click events.

Figure 8.27: *Tasks Component*

Moving to the **<script setup>** section, this block demarcates the component's script logic, utilizing the Composition API introduced in Vue 3. The **defineProps** and

defineEmits functions are used to establish the component's interface. **defineProps** declares the **tasks** prop, allowing the parent to pass down the tasks data, while **defineEmits** sets up the component to emit custom events, in this case, **'editTask'** and **'deleteTask'**. Within the script block, two methods, **onEditTask** and **onDeleteTask**, are defined. These methods serve as the event handlers for the **'Edit'** and **'Delete'** buttons, respectively. Upon invocation, they log their action to the console and emit the corresponding event, signalling the parent component to handle the task editing or deletion.

Implementing Create Task Modal

This modal is a critical feature of the application, providing users with an intuitive and isolated space to input the details of a new task without navigating away from the current view. When the user clicks the '**Create Task**' button, typically located on the main dashboard, the modal window appears, overlaying the primary content. This modal is designed to capture attention and guide the user through the task creation process in a focused manner. The modal typically contains a form with several fields for the user to fill out, such as **'Name'**, **'Task Assignee'**, **'Description'**, and **'Status'**. These fields are essential for defining the attributes of a new task, ensuring that all the necessary information is captured in a structured format.

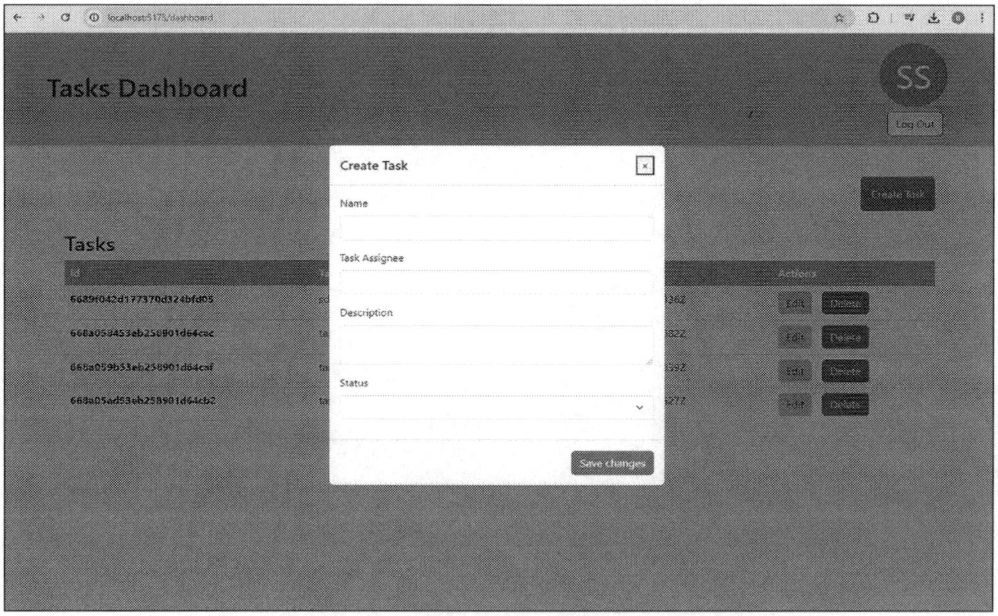

Figure 8.28: *Create Task Modal Window*

The **<BaseModal>** component is used as a wrapper for the modal content, indicating that there is a pre-defined component named **BaseModal** which is likely responsible for the common modal functionalities like displaying, positioning, and styling. The

`modalStyle="show"` attribute suggests that the modal is intended to be visible, possibly controlled by a reactive property or passed as a prop.

Within the **`<BaseModal>`** component, scoped slots are utilized to inject specific content into the modal's header, body, and footer sections. Scoped slots are a powerful feature in Vue.js that allows for more flexible and reusable components:

- **Modal Header:** The **`#modalheader`** slot is populated with the text "**`Create Task`**," serving as the title of the modal.
- **Modal Body:** The **`#modalbody`** slot contains a form with various fields allowing users to input details about the new task. Each form control is bound to a reactive property using Vue's **`v-model`** directive, enabling two-way data binding.
- **Modal Footer:** The **`#modalfooter`** slot includes a "**`Save changes`**" button, which suggests that upon clicking, the data entered the form would be processed, likely leading to the creation of a new task.

```
ui > src > modals > CreateTaskModal.vue > {} script setup > task > status
<template>
    <BaseModal modalStyle="show" @handle-close="() => emit('handleClose')">
        <template #modalheader>Create Task</template>
        <template #modalbody>
            <form>
                <div class="mb-3">
                    <label for="name" class="form-label">Name</label>
                    <input type="text" class="form-control" id="name" v-model="task.task">
                </div>
                <div class="mb-3">
                    <label for="assignee" class="form-label">Task Assignee</label>
                    <input type="text" class="form-control" id="assignee" v-model="task.assignee">
                </div>
                <div class="mb-3">
                    <label for="description" class="form-label">Description</label>
                    <textarea class="form-control" id="description" v-model="task.description"></textarea>
                </div>
                <div class="mb-3">
                    <label for="status" class="form-label">Status</label>
                    <select class="form-select" id="status" v-model="task.status">
                        <option value="pending">Pending</option>
                        <option value="inprogress">In Progress</option>
                        <option value="completed">Completed</option>
                    </select>
                </div>
            </form>
        </template>
        <template #modalfooter>
            <button type="button" @click="onSaveChanges" class="btn btn-primary">Save changes</button>
        </template>
    </BaseModal>
</template>

<script setup lang="ts">
import { ref } from 'vue'
import BaseModal from './BaseModal.vue'

const emit = defineEmits(['saveChanges', 'handleClose'])

const task = ref({
    task: '',
    assignee: '',
    description: '',
    status: ''
})

const onSaveChanges = () => {
    console.log('task  ', task)
    emit("saveChanges", task.value)
    emit("handleClose")
}
</script>
```

Figure 8.29: *Modal Window*

In the **`<script setup>`** section, the composition API's **`ref`** function is imported from Vue, and a **`task`** reactive reference is created with properties for name, assignee, description, and status. This reference holds the state for the form within the modal, and due to Vue's reactivity system, any updates to these fields will be reactively reflected in the component's state.

The script also imports the **`BaseModal`** component, indicating that this modal functionality is modularized and can be reused across different parts of the application with varying content.

Here is the Modular Base Modal Component where slots are defined.

```
ui > src > modals > BaseModal.vue > {} template
<template>
  <div class="modal" :class='modalStyle' style="padding-top: 10%;" tabindex="-1" role="dialog">
        <div class="modal-dialog" role="document">
            <div class="modal-content">
            <div class="modal-header">
                <h5 class="modal-title">
                    <slot name="modalheader"> default header </slot>
                </h5>
                <button type="button" class="close" data-dismiss="modal" @click="closeModal" aria-label="Close">
                    <span aria-hidden="true">&times;</span>
                </button>
            </div>
            <div class="modal-body">
                <slot name="modalbody"> default body </slot>
            </div>
            <div class="modal-footer">
                <slot name="modalfooter"> default Footer </slot>
            </div>
            </div>
        </div>
    </div>
</template>

<style scoped>
.show {
  display: block;
  background-color: rgba(0, 0, 0, 0.5);
}

</style>

<script lang="ts">
import { onUnmounted, toRefs} from 'vue';

export default {

  props: {
      modalStyle: String
  },

  emits: ['handleClose'],

  setup(props, { emit } ) {
    const { modalStyle } = toRefs(props)

    const closeModal = () => emit('handleClose');

    onUnmounted  (() => {
      console.log('Component has been unmounted');
      modalStyle.value = "show"
    });

    return {
      closeModal,
      modalStyle,
      emit
    }
  }
};

</script>
```

Figure 8.30: Base Modal

Implementing Edit and Delete Task Modal

This modal is a crucial component, as it provides users with the ability to modify the details of an existing task within the '**`Tasks Dashboard`**'. When the user elects to edit a task by clicking an **`'Edit'`** button associated with a task entry, the modal window is displayed. The modal is brought into focus against the backdrop of the dashboard, allowing the user to concentrate on the editing task without leaving the current context of the page.

Inside the modal, the user is presented with a form containing several fields pre-populated with the task's existing data: '**`Task ID`**', **`'Name'`**, **`'Description'`**, and **`'Status'`**. The **`'Task ID'`** is typically a non-editable field that uniquely identifies the task, ensuring that the correct item is being edited. The **`'Name'`** field allows the user to update the task's title, while the **`'Description'`** field provides a text area for additional details to be entered or revised. The **`'Status'`** field likely offers a dropdown menu with various states of task progression, such as **`'Pending'`**, '**`In Progress`**', or **`'Completed'`**.

At the bottom of the modal, a '**`Save changes`**' button suggests that upon submission, the updated data will be saved, and the task list on the dashboard will reflect these changes. This action likely triggers an event or API call to update the task information in the backend system.

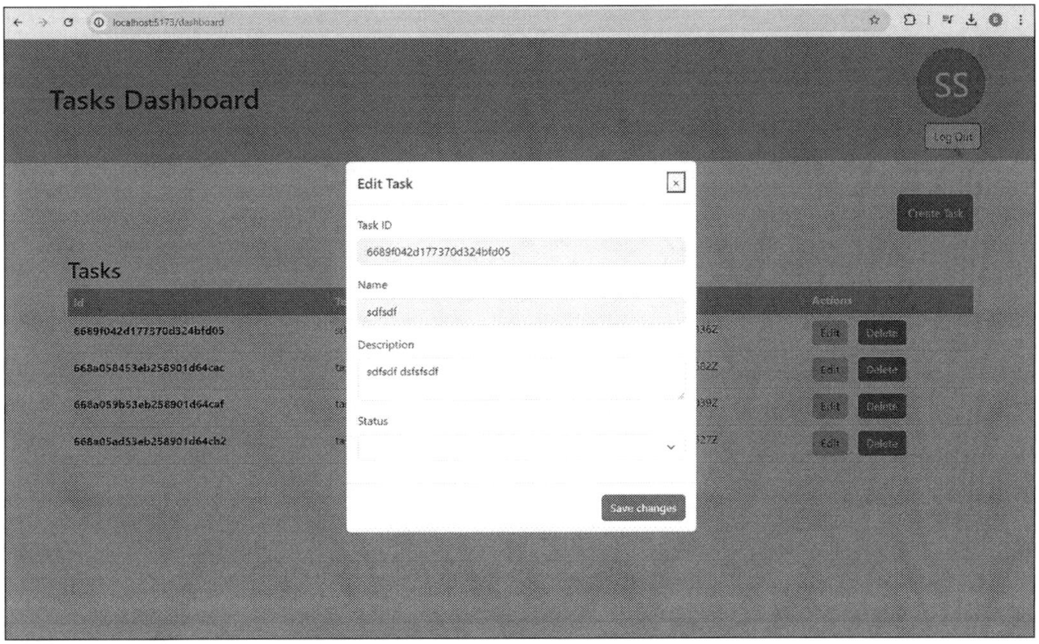

***Figure 8.31:** Edit Task Modal*

This "**`Edit Task`**" modal is a vital part of the application's functionality, enabling users to efficiently manage their tasks. It exemplifies an effective design pattern for editing data in web applications, providing a seamless and focused user experience. The modal's strategic design ensures that users can quickly and easily update tasks, which is a critical feature for maintaining productivity and ensuring the accuracy of task management within the application.

Here is the component of the **`Edit Task`** Modal. The **`<template>`** block defines the structure of the **`'Edit Task'`** modal window, utilizing a **`BaseModal`** component that likely includes common modal functionalities like open/close behavior and styling. This reusability pattern is a common best practice in Vue.js development, promoting code reuse and separation of concerns. The modal leverages Vue.js's scoped slots to insert custom content into predefined areas of the **`BaseModal`**. A scoped slot for the modal header contains a simple label indicating the modal's purpose, "**`Edit Task`**". The body of the modal comprises a form, with each field bound to the **`task`** object's properties using **`v-model`**. This two-way data binding is quintessential in Vue.js, as it allows for reactive updates between the user interface and the underlying data model.

```
ui > src > modals > EditTaskModal.vue > {} template
<template>
    <BaseModal :modalStyle="props.modalStyle" @handle-close="() => emit('handleClose')" >
        <template #modalheader>Edit Task</template>
        <template #modalbody>
            <form>
                <div class="mb-3">
                    <label for="taskId" class="form-label">Task ID</label>
                    <input type="text" disabled class="form-control" id="taskId" v-model="task._id">
                </div>
                <div class="mb-3">
                    <label for="name" class="form-label">Name</label>
                    <input type="text" disabled class="form-control" id="name" v-model="task.task">
                </div>
                <div class="mb-3">
                    <label for="description" class="form-label">Description</label>
                    <textarea class="form-control" id="description" v-model="task.description"></textarea>
                </div>
                <div class="mb-3">
                    <label for="status" class="form-label">Status</label>
                    <select class="form-select" id="status" v-model="task.status">
                        <option value="pending">Pending</option>
                        <option value="inprogress">In Progress</option>
                        <option value="completed">Completed</option>
                    </select>
                </div>
            </form>
        </template>
        <template #modalfooter>
            <button type="button" @click="saveChanges" class="btn btn-primary">Save changes</button>
        </template>
    </BaseModal>
</template>

<script setup lang="ts">
import BaseModal from './BaseModal.vue'

const props = defineProps(['modalStyle', 'task'])
const emit = defineEmits(['handleClose', 'editConfirm'])

console.log('props ', props.task)

const { task } = props

const saveChanges = () => {
    console.log('task ', props.task);
    emit("editConfirm", props.task)
    emit("handleClose")
}


</script>
```

Figure 8.32: *Edit Task Modal Component*

In the accompanying **`<script setup>`** section, we see TypeScript in action alongside Vue's Composition API. The **`defineProps`** and **`defineEmits`** functions are used to define the component's props and events, respectively. This setup script reflects the modern approach in Vue 3, where the Composition API provides a more organized and scalable way to manage component logic. The **`task`** object is deconstructed into refs using **`toRefs`**, ensuring that each property of the task remains reactive when used independently within the component. This is particularly useful when you want to pass down props from a parent component and maintain their reactivity within a child component.

The modal also includes a method, **`saveChanges`**, which is intended to be triggered when the user clicks the "**`Save changes`**" button. This method would typically handle the logic for updating the task data, such as sending a request to an API or emitting an event with the updated task data for the parent component to handle.

When you click the delete button on each row, it deletes that row and displays this modal window. This modal, labeled "**`Delete Task`**", serves a crucial role in the user experience by confirming that a task has been successfully deleted. The message "**`Task 2 Has been Deleted!!!`**" is displayed prominently within the modal, providing clear and specific feedback regarding the action's outcome. This message not only confirms the action but also specifies which task was affected, reducing the likelihood of user confusion.

A single **`'Ok'`** button within the modal suggests that the user's acknowledgement is required to proceed. Clicking this button would likely close the modal and possibly trigger a refresh of the task list, reflecting the updated state without the deleted task.

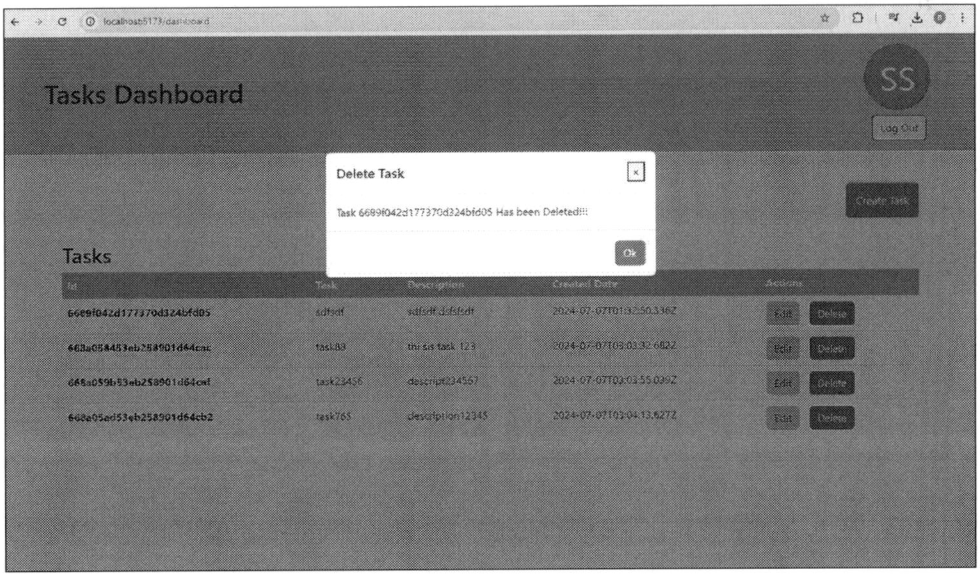

Figure 8.33: *Delete Task Modal*

Here is the delete modal component that uses **`BaseModal`** component.

```
ui > src > modals > DeleteTaskModal.vue > {} script setup
<template>
    <BaseModal :modalStyle="props.modalStyle" @handle-close="() => emit('handleClose')">
        <template #modalheader>Delete Task</template>
        <template #modalbody>Task {{ taskId }} Has been Deleted!!!</template>
        <template #modalfooter>
            <button type="button" class="btn btn-secondary" @click="onOk" data-dismiss="modal">Ok</button>
        </template>
    </BaseModal>
</template>

<script setup lang="ts">
import BaseModal from './BaseModal.vue'

const props = defineProps(['modalStyle', 'taskId'])

const emit = defineEmits(['handleClose', 'deleteConfirm'])

const onOk = () => {
    emit("deleteConfirm", props?.taskId)
    emit("handleClose")
}

</script>
```

Figure 8.34: *Delete Task Modal Component*

The use of a **`BaseModal`** component across different functionalities of the application—creating, editing, and deleting tasks - epitomizes the essence of modular design in web development. This design pattern harnesses the strength of reusability, enabling a consistent user interface and interaction model while reducing code duplication. Such a modular approach simplifies both the development and maintenance of the application by ensuring that any updates to the modal's core functionality are centralized, thus eliminating the need to replicate changes across multiple, similar components. It creates a single source of truth for the modal's behavior and styling that is beneficial for both current functionality and future enhancements.

Furthermore, the abstraction provided by a **`BaseModal`** allows for clear separation between the modal's presentation layer and the business logic of task management. This separation not only streamlines the implementation of complex user interactions but also significantly enhances the scalability of the application. As the application's requirements evolve, new modal types can be introduced with minimal effort, adhering to the established modal framework. The flexibility of this approach is evident in the ease with which developers can inject custom content and actions into the modal via scoped slots, adapting to diverse use cases while maintaining a unified user experience. Ultimately, modularizing components like **`BaseModal`** leads to a codebase that is more organized, maintainable, and adaptable, aligning perfectly with the principles of agile and scalable software architecture.

We have seen all the dashboard components so far and it is time to see the dashboard container component that holds all these components together. Here is the template part. We can see all the components are being used based on the conditions. This showcases the power of component-based architecture, where each piece of the user interface is encapsulated into reusable and composable components. This architecture enables a clear organization of the application's features, making it scalable and easy to maintain. It also illustrates the reactivity system of Vue.js, where changes to the data model such as adding or removing tasks can trigger updates to the UI without manual DOM manipulation, creating a seamless experience for the end-user.

ui > src > containers > DashboardContainer.vue > {} template

```
<template>
  <div class="container mt-5">
    <div class="row">
      <CreateTask
       @create-task="() => onCreateTask()"
       :btn-name="computedTasks.length > 0 ? 'Create Task' : 'Create Your First Task'"
      >
      </CreateTask>
    </div>
    <div class="row">
      <NoTasksAvailable v-if="computedTasks.length === 0"></NoTasksAvailable>
      <Tasks
        v-if="computedTasks.length > 0"
        :tasks="computedTasks"
        @edit-task="(task) => onEditTask(task)"
        @delete-task="(task) => onDeleteTask(task)"
        @detail-task="(id) => onDetailTask(id)"
      >
      </Tasks>
      <DeleteTaskModal
        :modalStyle="showDeleteModal ? 'show' : 'none'"
        :taskId="deleteTaskId"
        v-if="showDeleteModal"
        @handle-close="() => closeModal('delete')"
        @handle-ok="() => closeModal('delete')"
        @delete-confirm="(taskId) => onDeleteConfirm(taskId)"
      >
      </DeleteTaskModal>
      <EditTaskModal
        :modalStyle="showEditModal ? 'show' : 'none'"
        :task="editTask"
        v-if="showEditModal"
        @handle-close="() => closeModal('edit')"
        @handle-ok="() => closeModal('edit')"
        @edit-confirm="(task) => onEditConfirm(task)"
      >
      </EditTaskModal>
      <CreateTaskModal
          :modalStyle="showCreateModal ? 'show' : 'none'"
          v-if="showCreateModal"
         @handle-close="() => closeModal('create')"
         @handle-ok="() => closeModal('create')"
         @save-changes="(task: any) => onSaveTask(task)"
      >
      </CreateTaskModal>

    </div>
  </div>
</template>
```

Figure 8.35: *Dashboard Container*

Here is the script section of the dashboard container component. The **`<script setup>`** section defines the script logic for the task management interface. This section imports several components and modals, each encapsulating distinct parts of the application's functionality. **`NoTasksAvailable`**, **`Tasks`**, **`CreateTask`**, and the various modals for creating, editing, and deleting tasks are modular components that represent different aspects of the user interface, from displaying tasks to handling user interactions.

The **`tasks`** array is a hardcoded dataset, representing a typical task list that one might fetch from an API in a real-world application. It is used here to illustrate the application's functionality with sample data. The **`btnName`** variable is dynamically set based on whether there are tasks present, providing an intuitive cue to the user to create a task when none exist.

```
<script setup lang="ts">
import { ref } from 'vue';
import NoTasksAvailable from '../components/NoTasksAvailable.vue'
import Tasks from '../components/Tasks.vue'
import CreateTask from '../modals/CreateTask.vue'
import DeleteTaskModal from '../modals/DeleteTaskModal.vue'
import EditTaskModal from '../modals/EditTaskModal.vue'
import CreateTaskModal from '../modals/CreateTaskModal.vue'

const showDeleteModal = ref(false);
const showEditModal = ref(false);
const showCreateModal = ref(false);
const deleteTaskId = ref(null);
const editTask = ref(null);

const closeModal = (modalType: string) => {
  if(modalType === 'delete') {
    showDeleteModal.value = false;
  } else if(modalType === 'edit') {
    showEditModal.value = false;
  } else if(modalType === 'create') {
    showCreateModal.value = false;
  }
}

const editTask = (task: any) => {
  console.log('onEdit', task);
  showEditModal.value = true;
  editTask.value = task;
}

const deleteTask = (task: any) => {
  console.log('onDelete', task);
  showDeleteModal.value = true;
  deleteTaskId.value = task.id;
}

const createTask = () => {
  showCreateModal.value = true;
}

const tasks: any[] = [
  { id: 1, name: 'groceries', description: 'Description 1', createdDate: '2021-01-01' },
  { id: 2, name: 'groceries', description: 'Description 1', createdDate: '2021-01-01' },
  { id: 3, name: 'groceries', description: 'Description 1', createdDate: '2021-01-01' },
  { id: 4, name: 'groceries', description: 'Description 1', createdDate: '2021-01-01' },
  { id: 5, name: 'groceries', description: 'Description 1', createdDate: '2021-01-01' },
  { id: 6, name: 'groceries', description: 'Description 1', createdDate: '2021-01-01' }
];

const btnName = tasks.length > 0 ? 'Create Task' : 'Create Your First Task';
</script>
```

Figure 8.36: *Dashboard Container Script Section*

Overall, this script section showcases the use of the Composition API in Vue 3, which enhances code organization and readability, particularly in TypeScript-enabled environments. It emphasizes the power of reactive state management in building responsive interfaces and the effectiveness of component modularity for a scalable and maintainable application architecture.

Writing Services and Proxy Setup for API Calls

As we embark on the journey to explore the dynamic capabilities of the MEVN stack, a pivotal chapter awaits us - writing services in Vue.js. Services, often referred to as the heart of the application's frontend logic, are where the core business functionality resides. They act as a bridge between the user interface and the backend, managing the flow of data and encapsulating the business rules of our application.

In this section, we will delve into how to construct well-defined services within a Vue.js application. These services are the conduits through which our application interacts with server-side resources, sending and receiving data to and from a Node.js/Express backend, and communicating with a MongoDB database. We will guide you through best practices for structuring your services, ensuring they are both maintainable and scalable, aligned with the Vue.js ethos of reactivity and composability.

Understanding services in the context of the MEVN stack will not only enable you to craft a seamless data layer but also empower you to build a robust frontend architecture. Whether you are fetching lists of data, sending updates to the server, or streaming real-time interactions, services play an indispensable role. They encapsulate the logic for API calls, handle state management, and provide methods for components to interact with external systems without being burdened by the complexity of direct API communications.

First, we need to install the **axios** dependency to make API calls.

```
npm install axios
```

Choosing Axios as the HTTP client in web development projects, including those using the MEVN stack (MongoDB, Express, Vue, Node.js), is a popular decision due to several compelling reasons:

- **Ease of use:** Axios is renowned for its straightforward and readable syntax. It simplifies the process of sending HTTP requests and handling responses, making it accessible for developers at all skill levels.
- **Promise-based:** Axios relies on JavaScript promises for handling asynchronous operations. This leads to cleaner, more manageable code, especially when dealing with complex chains of requests.
- **Interceptors:** One of Axios' powerful features is its ability to intercept HTTP requests and responses. This allows developers to modify requests before they are sent and handle responses consistently. It is particularly useful for tasks like adding authentication tokens, logging, or handling errors globally.
- **Web Browser Support:** Axios has excellent compatibility with modern web browsers, ensuring that HTTP requests work consistently across different client environments.
- **Automatic JSON Transformation:** Axios automatically transforms request and response data into JSON, eliminating the need for manual parsing and stringifying. This is a significant convenience, as JSON is the predominant format for data exchange in modern web applications.
- **Timeouts:** Axios allows developers to specify how long an HTTP request should wait before automatically being terminated. This is a crucial feature for enhancing the user experience, especially in scenarios where a server might be unresponsive.

- **Cancellation:** With Axios, developers can easily cancel requests. This is useful in situations where a request is no longer needed, such as navigating away from a page before a request completes.
- **Upload Progress:** Axios makes it easy to monitor the progress of HTTP requests, which is particularly useful for tasks like file uploads.
- **Community and Ecosystem:** As a widely adopted library, Axios has a strong community and ecosystem. This means better support, more frequent updates, and a wealth of documentation and resources for troubleshooting.
- **Server-side usage:** While primarily used in the browser, Axios can also be used on the server-side with Node.js. This makes it a versatile choice for full-stack JavaScript applications.

In summary, Axios is a feature-rich, easy-to-use library that streamlines the process of making HTTP requests in web applications. Its promise-based nature, combined with a robust set of features, makes it an excellent choice for both simple and complex web development tasks.

You can see the updated **`package.json`** once you run the install command.

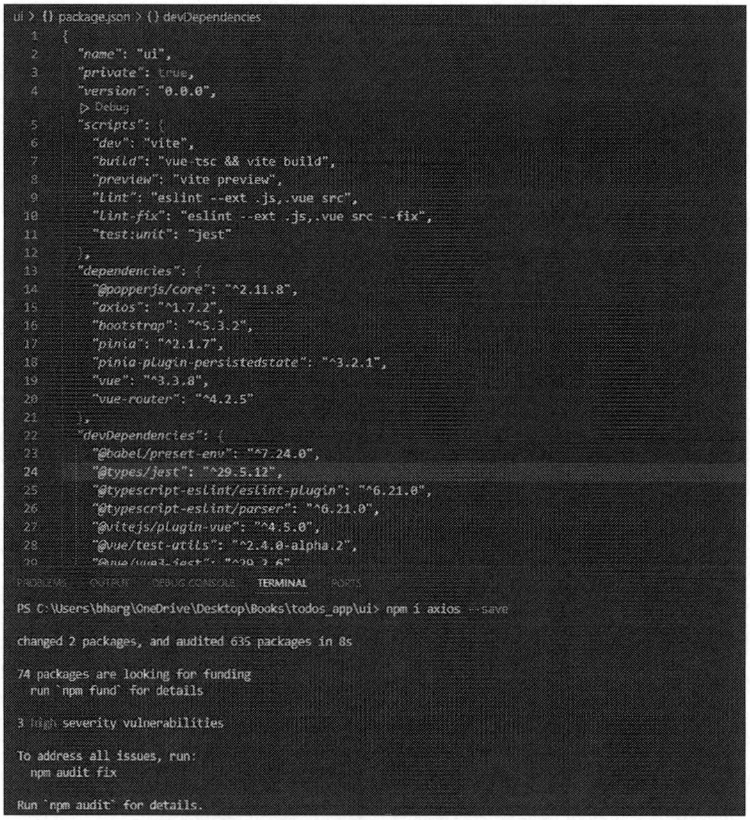

Figure 8.37: Adding Dependency

Establishing a fundamental base service class dedicated to managing the principal HTTP operations is an astute architectural decision in application development. By constructing this foundational class, we lay the groundwork for a centralized mechanism to handle HTTP requests across the application. This approach, particularly when implemented in TypeScript and utilizing Axios within a Vue.js context, ensures a robust, cohesive, and maintainable structure. The base service class is designed to encapsulate generic methods for various HTTP actions, GET, POST, PUT, DELETE, thereby abstracting the complexities of direct HTTP client interactions.

Subsequently, this base class can be seamlessly extended by more specialized service classes tailored to specific areas of the backend API. This extension pattern fosters reusability and consistency in handling API requests throughout the application. Such an arrangement is not only efficient but also pragmatic, especially when future modifications are considered. For instance, should there be a need to switch the underlying HTTP client, this can be accomplished in a single location, the base service class, without the necessity for widespread changes throughout the codebase.

Furthermore, the integration of interceptors, crucial for tasks like global error handling or setting up authentication headers, becomes a centralized operation. By configuring these within the base service class, we ensure that all HTTP requests processed through the extended services inherit this functionality, maintaining a uniform approach to request handling.

The ensuing base service class, therefore, is not just a code construct but a strategic decision in building scalable and efficient web applications. It represents a thoughtful approach to managing API interactions, ensuring that the application's network layer is both adaptable and straightforward to maintain. This methodology exemplifies best practices in modern web development, particularly in the context of the Vue.js ecosystem, fortified by TypeScript's strong typing and Axios's versatile HTTP capabilities.

Here is the base service class in which we have defined major HTTP calls.

```
ui > src > services > TS BaseService.ts > BaseService
import axios, { AxiosInstance, AxiosResponse, AxiosRequestConfig } from 'axios';

export default class BaseService<T> {

  public readonly instance: AxiosInstance;

  constructor(baseURL: string) {
    this.instance = axios.create({
      baseURL,
      // You can add your custom headers here
      // headers: { 'Content-Type': 'application/json' },
    });

    // Set the INTERCEPTORS here if you need to handle tokens or headers
  }

  public get(url: string, config?: AxiosRequestConfig): Promise<AxiosResponse> {
    return this.instance.get<T>(url, config);
  }

  public post(url: string, data?: T, config?: AxiosRequestConfig): Promise<AxiosResponse> {
    return this.instance.post<T>(url, data, config);
  }

  public put(url: string, data?: T, config?: AxiosRequestConfig): Promise<AxiosResponse> {
    return this.instance.put<T>(url, data, config);
  }

  public delete(url: string, config?: AxiosRequestConfig): Promise<AxiosResponse> {
    return this.instance.delete<T>(url, config);
  }
}
```

Figure 8.38: *Base Service*

The preceding class in TypeScript, utilizing Axios, a popular HTTP client, to handle network requests. This class is designed to be a generic, reusable foundation for making various types of HTTP requests. Upon instantiation, the **`BaseService`** class creates an Axios instance configured with a base URL, and optionally, custom headers can be added for all requests made through this instance. The class includes methods corresponding to the common HTTP methods – GET, POST, PUT, and DELETE. Each method returns a promise, allowing for asynchronous operations, and they are generic, meaning they can be adapted to handle various data types (`T`). This setup simplifies making API calls throughout an application, as it abstracts the details of configuring and using Axios for different types of requests. This approach promotes cleaner and more maintainable code, especially in applications that need to interact with various endpoints of a backend service.

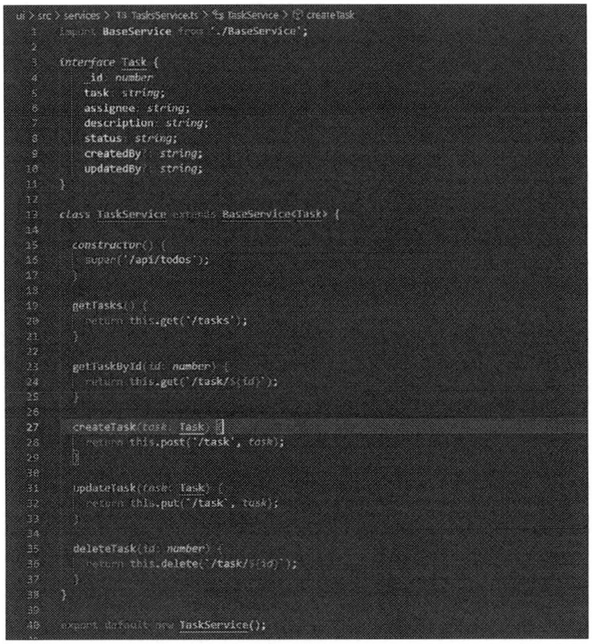

Figure 8.39: *Task Service*

The **TaskService** class, an extension of a generic **BaseService**, tailored to handle operations related to tasks in an application. This class, defined in TypeScript, manages API calls specifically for tasks, which are represented by the **Task** interface with properties like task name, assignee, description, status, and creator information. The **TaskService** class simplifies interactions with the backend API, providing methods to retrieve all tasks, fetch a single task by its ID, create a new task, update an existing task, and delete a task. Each method utilizes the corresponding HTTP method (GET, POST, PUT, DELETE) from the **BaseService**, making the class a centralized and reusable way to manage task-related data within the application.

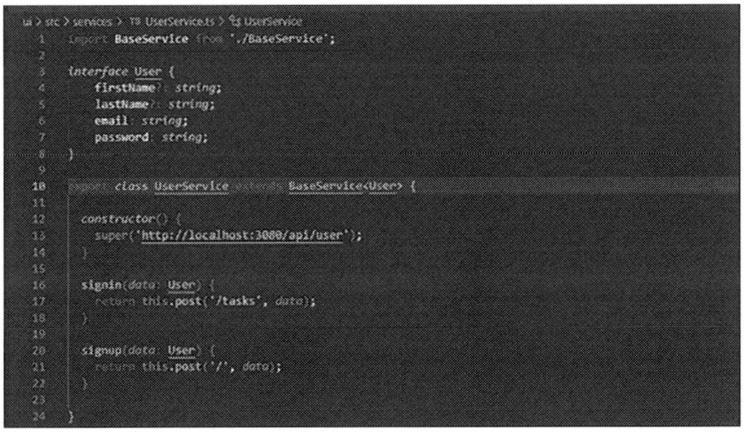

Figure 8.40: *Base Service*

Here is the **UserService** class in TypeScript, which extends a generic **BaseService** to handle user-related functionalities in a web application. The **UserService** is designed specifically for user management tasks and is built around a **User** interface that includes optional first and last names, along with required email and password fields. This service class facilitates user authentication and registration processes through its methods: **signin** and **signup.** The **signin** method handles user logins by sending data to a specified backend endpoint (**/tasks** in this case, which might be a typo and should perhaps be something like **/signin**), while the **signup** method manages new user registrations, posting the user data to the root of the user API endpoint **(http://localhost:3080/api/user)**. This setup centralizes user-related API interactions, streamlining the process of communicating with the backend for user authentication and account management.

In the realm of MEVN stack development, there are primarily two distinct approaches for initiating API calls from the frontend to the backend server. The first method involves directly embedding the complete URL of the backend server within each service class. This means that every time an API call is made, the full backend server address is specified, directing the request to the appropriate endpoint. The second, more streamlined method employs a proxy setup within the **vite.config.ts** file. This configuration allows you to specify that all requests starting with **/api** be automatically redirected to a predetermined domain. This proxy setup offers the flexibility to define multiple proxies, catering to various parts of your application or different backend services.

Let us explore the method of using the complete URL directly in our service classes. The primary distinction in this approach lies in the service class implementation. It is important to note that regardless of whether we use direct URLs or a proxy setup, the code in the component files remains consistent across both methods. This uniformity in component code, irrespective of the API call strategy, highlights the flexibility of our frontend architecture.

We previously explored the dashboard container component where the tasks data was hardcoded and used to populate the relevant sections. Moving forward, we will be modifying this container to dynamically fetch data. Specifically, we will implement an API call within the **onMounted** lifecycle hook to retrieve task data as soon as the component loads. This will ensure that the tasks table is updated with fresh data directly from the backend each time the component is rendered. Here is the updated section of the dashboard container component.

Figure 8.41: *Calling Service from onMounted Lifecycle Hook*

The **`onMounted`** lifecycle hook plays a crucial role in fetching data as soon as the component is rendered on the webpage. Within this hook, the code initializes an instance of the **`TaskService`**, a service class responsible for making API calls related to tasks. The **`getTasks`** method of this service is then invoked to fetch the list of tasks from the backend. This is an asynchronous operation, and the code uses **`await`** to pause execution until the response from the backend is received.

Once the response is obtained, the data containing the tasks (**`resp.data.result`**) is assigned to the **`computedTasks`** variable. This variable is a computed property in Vue, which means it is reactive and any changes to its value will automatically update the corresponding parts of the UI. In this case, the tasks table in the template will be updated to reflect the newly fetched tasks. By using a computed property, the application efficiently updates the UI in response to changes in the underlying data, ensuring that the displayed tasks are always current.

This approach of fetching data in the **`onMounted`** hook and using computed properties for UI updates is a common pattern in Vue applications. It leverages Vue's reactivity system to ensure that the UI stays in sync with the application's state, providing a dynamic and responsive user experience. The **`onMounted`** hook is particularly well-suited for API calls as it ensures that the data is fetched right after the component is added to the DOM, but before the user interacts with it, thus preparing the component with the necessary data from the outset.

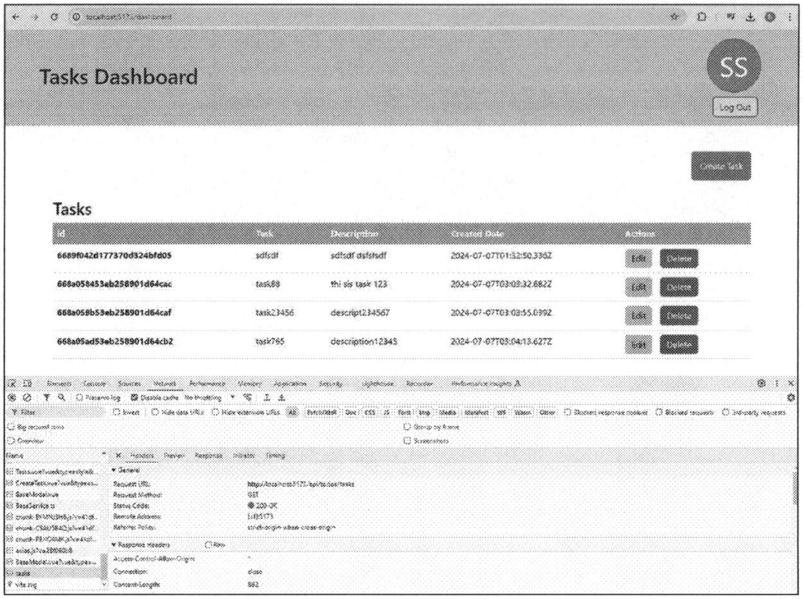

Figure 8.42: *Making API calls*

In the given figure, as the API call to fetch tasks is executed, the complete server URL used for the call is displayed within the console. This allows the developer to verify the endpoint being hit (`http://localhost:3000/api/todos/tasks` in this case), the HTTP method used (GET), and to inspect additional details like the request headers, status code returned (200 OK indicates success), and the response payload.

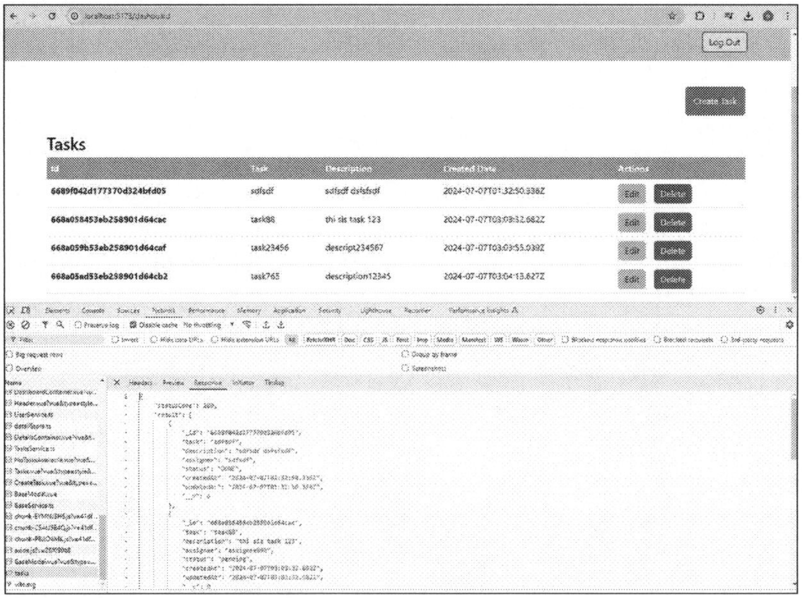

Figure 8.43: *API call response*

The figure presented illustrates the outcome of an API call within the developer console. It highlights the table within the application interface being populated with data, correlating directly with the response details observed in the console. This visual representation in the console confirms the successful retrieval and integration of data into the application's user interface.

Having explored the direct URL approach earlier, let's now turn our attention to implementing proxy configuration in a Vue 3 environment. In a Vue 3 project using Vite with TypeScript, setting up a proxy for development involves modifying the **`vite.config.ts`** file. This configuration allows you to route API requests through the Vite server, which can help avoid CORS issues when your frontend and backend are running on different ports during development.

Open or create a **`vite.config.ts`** file in the root of your Vue 3 project. Here is an example of how you can configure the proxy settings:

- **`Proxy` Configuration**: The **`proxy`** object defines how different paths are proxied to other servers. In the preceding example, requests to paths starting with **`/api`** are proxied to **`http://localhost:3080`**, which would typically be the address of your Express.js backend in a MEVN stack setup.
- **Path Rewriting**: The **`rewrite`** option is a function to rewrite the request path before sending it to the target server. In this case, it removes the **`/api`** prefix.
- **`Vite` Plugins**: The **`plugins`** array includes **`@vitejs/plugin-vue`** to enable Vue 3 support.
- **`Export` Configuration**: The configuration is exported using **defineConfig** from Vite, which enhances type support and IntelliSense in your IDE.

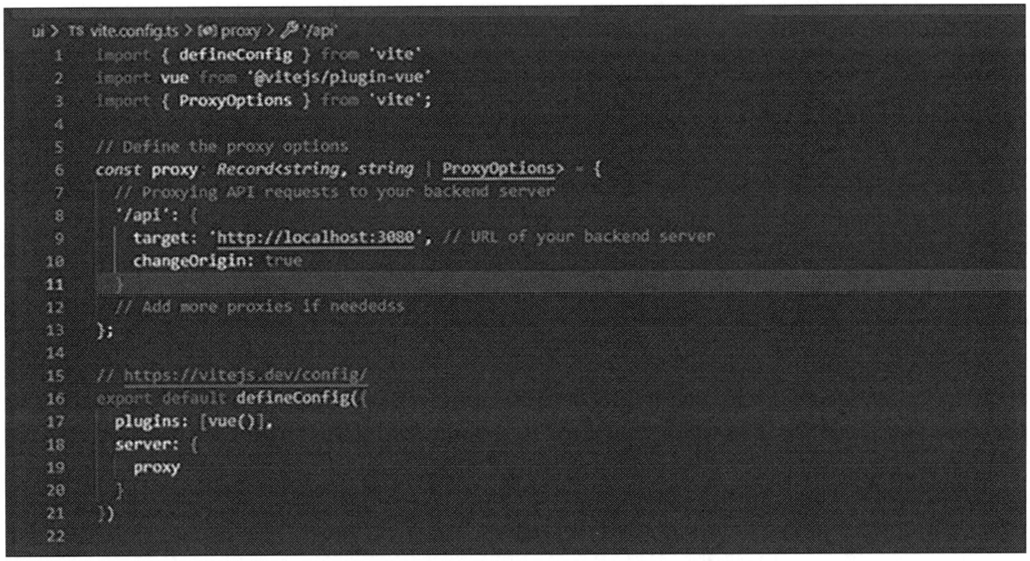

```
import { defineConfig } from 'vite'
import vue from '@vitejs/plugin-vue'
import { ProxyOptions } from 'vite';

// Define the proxy options
const proxy: Record<string, string | ProxyOptions> = {
  // Proxying API requests to your backend server
  '/api': {
    target: 'http://localhost:3080', // URL of your backend server
    changeOrigin: true
  }
  // Add more proxies if neededss
};

// https://vitejs.dev/config/
export default defineConfig({
  plugins: [vue()],
  server: {
    proxy
  }
})
```

Figure 8.44: *proxy configuration*

With this setup, when you run your Vue app in development mode (**`vite`** or **`npm run dev`**), API requests to paths starting with **`/api`** will be automatically proxied to your Express.js backend, circumventing CORS issues. Here are some additional points to remember:

- Ensure that the target URL matches the URL where your Express.js server is running.
- This proxy setup is intended for development purposes. For production, you would typically have a different setup where your frontend and backend are served from the same domain or handled via server configuration.
- Make sure to install any necessary TypeScript typings if your project requires them for Vite configuration.

With this configuration in place, we can observe a notable change in the network call within the developer console, where the web URL is displayed instead of the backend server's host address. The earlier URL was **`http://localhost:3000/api/todos/tasks`**, but we can see **`http://127.0.0.1:5173/api/todos/tasks`** with the proxy configuration.

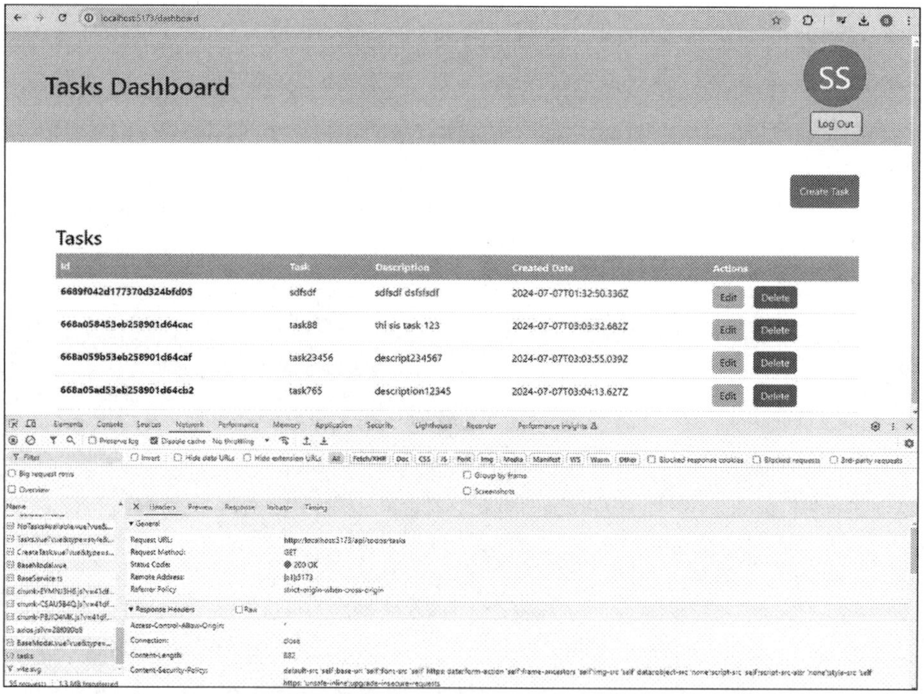

Figure 8.45: *API calls with proxy configuration*

Advantages of Using a Proxy Setup

- **Simplified Endpoint Management:** With a proxy setup, you can manage and change your backend server's URL in a single location without needing to update each service class individually. This centralization is especially beneficial in large-scale applications with numerous API calls.

- **Enhanced Development Experience:** Developers can work seamlessly in a local development environment without worrying about CORS (Cross-Origin Resource Sharing) issues, as the proxy handles cross-origin requests internally.
- **Environment Flexibility:** By using proxies, it is easier to switch between different backend environments (like development, staging, and production) by simply changing the proxy target in the configuration file.
- **Security:** A proxy setup can add a layer of abstraction to your API calls, concealing the actual backend server's URL from the frontend, thus enhancing security.
- **Performance Optimization:** Proxies can be configured to improve load times and resource management, especially when dealing with multiple backend services or microservices architecture.

Testing both methods in a MEVN stack application will provide valuable insights into their practical implications and benefits. The direct URL approach offers straightforwardness and explicit control over each request, while the proxy setup brings a more maintainable and scalable solution, particularly for complex applications. This comparison is crucial for developers to understand the best practices and make informed decisions based on the specific needs of their projects.

Setting Up Pinia Store for State Management

As modern web applications grow in complexity, managing state - information that persists between component interactions - becomes increasingly challenging. In the realm of the MEVN stack, Vue.js offers a solution through state management libraries, with Pinia emerging as a front-runner. This section will demystify Pinia, examining its role, benefits, and why a state management library is essential for your application.

Pinia is the official state management library for Vue.js. At its core, Pinia serves as a centralized store for all the components in an application. It allows for shared state management, which means that any component can access, react to, or mutate the application's state from a single, organized place.

In a Vue application, especially as it scales, components need to share and react to state changes. While Vue's reactivity system handles component-level state well, it becomes less efficient as you pass state up and down through a component tree or across unrelated components. This is where state management libraries like Pinia come in. They provide a single source of truth for the application's state, making it easier to reason about, debug, and maintain as the application evolves.

Pinia stands out for its simplicity and integration with Vue's Composition API. It is lightweight and straightforward, offering an intuitive API that aligns with the Vue ecosystem's best practices. With Pinia, you can:

- Define stores easily with a simple and powerful API.
- Access stores anywhere in your application without the hassle of prop drilling or complex event handling.
- Maintain reactivity and keep components in sync with the global state effortlessly.

Advantages of using Pinia

- **Simplicity:** Pinia offers a simple and declarative approach to managing state, making it easy for developers to use and understand.
- **Developer Experience:** It provides excellent TypeScript support, ensuring type safety and a more enjoyable development experience with autocompletion and error-checking.
- **DevTools Integration:** Pinia integrates with Vue DevTools, offering a seamless debugging experience where you can inspect and mutate the state directly from the browser.
- **Modularity:** Pinia stores can be broken down into modules, allowing for better organization and maintainability as your application's state logic grows.
- **Hot Module Replacement:** Supports hot module replacement (HMR) for rapid development and instant feedback.
- **Composition API Compatibility:** Designed to work beautifully with Vue's Composition API, allowing for a more compositional and reactive approach to state management.
- **Plugin Support:** You can extend Pinia's functionality with plugins, providing a flexible way to add global features to your stores.

In summary, Pinia offers a developer-friendly, efficient, and scalable solution for state management in Vue.js applications. As part of the MEVN stack, it ensures that your application's state is managed in an organized, predictable manner, which is crucial for maintaining a smooth user experience and reliable data flow across components. Whether you are building a simple to-do app or a complex enterprise-grade application, Pinia provides the tools necessary to manage your application's state with confidence.

Set Up Pinia Store

Setting up Pinia in a Vue 3 application involves several steps to ensure that you are adhering to industry standards and best practices. First, you need to add Pinia to your project. Use your package manager to install it.

```
npm install pinia
```

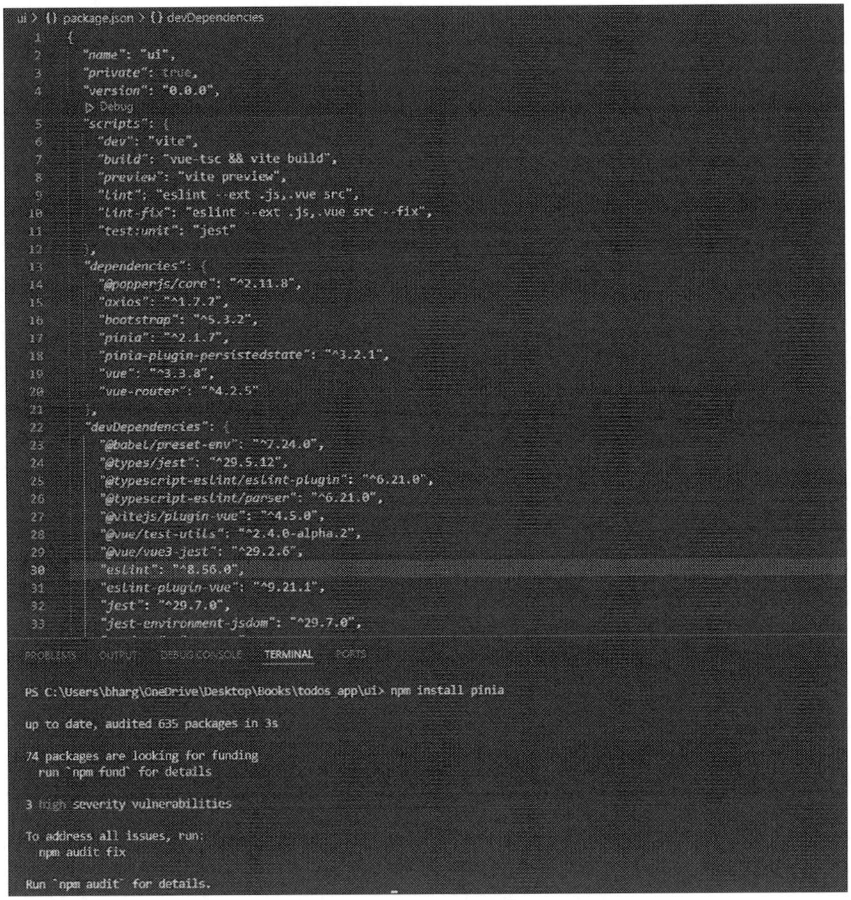

Figure 8.46: Adding Dependency

After installing Pinia, in your main entry file, usually **`main.ts`**, you need to create a Pinia instance and tell Vue to use it.

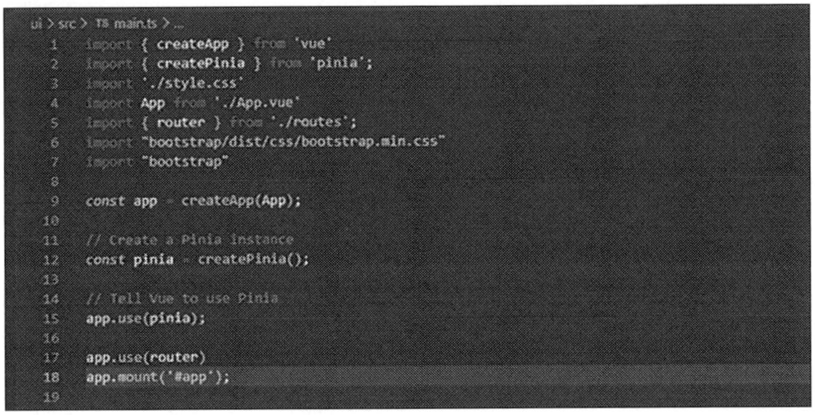

Figure 8.47: main.ts

Since we have installed and setup, here are some of the best practices we should follow:

- **Modularity:** Break down your state into multiple stores if it gets too large or if there are distinct domains within your application.
- **Naming:** Use clear, descriptive names for your stores, state properties, getters, and actions.
- **Persistence:** Consider using plugins like `pinia-plugin-persist` if you need to persist your state between page reloads.
- **Testing:** Write unit tests for your stores to ensure state management logic works as expected.
- **DevTools:** Make use of Vue DevTools to debug your state, watch for changes, and travel through state history.
- **TypeScript:** Use TypeScript for type safety. Pinia is designed to work well with TypeScript.

This is how we structure our store.

- **State:** Keep your state flat and normalized where possible. A nested state can make mutations more complex.
- **Getters:** Use getters to compute derived state. This is more efficient than doing the same in component methods.
- **Actions:** Use actions for methods that modify state. Keep them simple, and consider breaking them down into smaller functions if they get too complex.
- **Avoid Direct State Mutations:** Always use actions to mutate your state, even inside other actions.

Side Effects Like API calls

Performing side effects like API calls within a Pinia store is a common pattern, and it typically involves using actions. Actions in Pinia are functions that allow you to perform side effects, mutate the state, and handle asynchronous operations. Here are some of the best practices using side effects in Pinia:

- **Error Handling:** Always include error handling in your actions to manage API call failures gracefully.
- **Loading States:** Consider adding a `loading` state in your store to track the progress of API calls and provide feedback to the user.
- **Modularization:** If your application makes numerous different API calls, consider separating them into different service files or modules for clarity and maintainability.
- **Cancellation:** If your API calls can take a long time, consider implementing a cancellation mechanism to prevent outdated responses from affecting your application state.

By following these steps and best practices, you will set up a scalable, maintainable, and testable state management system in your Vue 3 application using Pinia. This will lead to a more organized codebase and a smoother development process as your application grows. We have three major flows – user flow, tasks dashboard, and task detail and we will set up each of these in the coming sections to wrap up this chapter.

Implementing Pinia Store for Login Module

In preparation for integrating the Pinia store with the login module of our application, it is essential to grasp the overarching architecture and the interaction flow between the sign in and sign up components. The diagram provided serves as a visual guide to this architecture. It depicts the Vue routing configuration where the **`LoginLayout`** serves as a parent container, branching into child routes for sign up and sign in, represented by **`SignupComponent`** and **`SigninComponent`**, respectively.

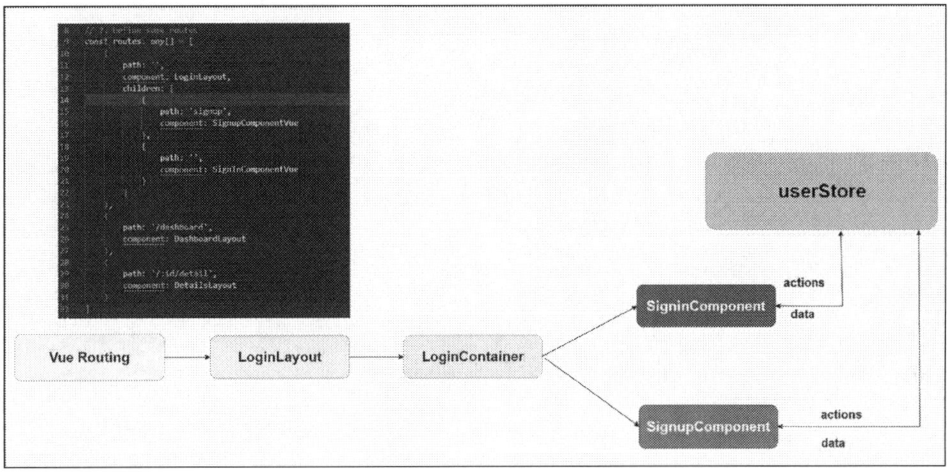

Figure 8.48: *Understanding login module structure*

These authentication components are designed to engage with the **`userStore`**. They do so by dispatching actions–such as login or registration requests–and in return, they receive necessary data from the store. This interaction is a two-way street–components send user inputs via actions to the **`userStore`**, which then processes these actions–likely involving API calls–and updates the store's state accordingly. Once updated, the components can react to these state changes, accessing the updated data to provide real-time feedback to the user, such as confirmation of a successful sign in or registration.

The design ensures a clear separation of concerns – components are responsible for handling user input and presenting data, while the store manages the state and logic of the authentication process. This modular approach not only simplifies development and enhances maintainability but also streamlines the process of scaling the application or integrating additional features in the future.

Here is the **userStore** that implements side effects like making API calls for both sign in and sign up flows. We are going to place this file under the store folder. The following defines a Pinia store for managing user state in a Vue application. The store is named '**user**' and it is set up with a state, getters, and actions to handle user data and interactions. The **UserState** interface outlines the structure of the state within the store, which includes a **userProfile** object for storing user information like first name, last name, email, and password. There are also **loading** and **status** flags to indicate whether an asynchronous operation is in progress and to represent the user's authentication status, respectively.

```
ui > src > store > TS userStore.ts > ...
import { defineStore } from 'pinia';
import userService, { User } from '../services/UserService';

interface UserState {
    userProfile: {firstName?: string, lastName?: string, email?: string, password?: string};
    loading: boolean;
    status: boolean;
}

export const useUserStore = defineStore('user', {
  // Define the state as a function that returns the object
  state: (): UserState => ({
    userProfile: {},
    loading: false,
    status: false
  }),

  persist: true,

  // Add getters for computed properties
  getters: {
    getUserProfile: (state) => state.userProfile,
    isLoading: (state) => state.loading,
    getProfileName: (state) => `${state.userProfile?.firstName?.charAt(0).toUpperCase()}${state.userProfile?.lastName?.charAt(0).toUpperCase()}`
  },

  // Add actions for functions that cause side effects and can involve asynchronous operations
  actions: {
    async signin(userData: User) {
      try {
        this.loading = true;
        const response = await userService.signin(userData);
        this.loading = false;
        if(response.data.result && response.data.statusCode === 200 && response.data.result !== null) {
          this.status = true;
          this.userProfile = response.data.result;
        }
      } catch (error) {
        // Handle the error appropriately.
        console.error('Failed to fetch users:', error);
        this.loading = false;
      }
    },

    async createUser(userData: User) {
      try {
        this.loading = true;
        const response = await userService.signup(userData);
        this.loading = false;
        if(response.data.result && response.data.statusCode === 200 && response.data.result !== null) {
          this.status = true;
          this.userProfile = response.data.result;
        }
      } catch (error) {
        console.error('Failed to create user:', error);
        this.loading = false;
      }
    },
  },
});
```

Figure 8.49: *user store*

The **state** function returns the initial state object according to the **UserState** interface, with the **userProfile** initialized as an empty object, **loading** as false, indicating no current loading operation, and **status** as false, suggesting the user is initially not authenticated. The **getters** provide computed properties based on the state. **getUserProfile** returns the user profile data, **isLoading** reflects the loading state, and **getProfileName** computes the initials from the user's first and last names, capitalizing the first letter of each.

The **actions** are methods that perform asynchronous operations. The **signin** action attempts to sign in a user by making an API call through the **userService.** During this process, it sets the loading state to true, and upon completion or failure, sets it back to false. If the sign in is successful and the server responds with a 200-status code, the user's profile data is stored in the state, and the **status** is set to true to reflect a successful sign in. Similarly, the **createUser** action handles new user registration, following the same pattern of loading indication and status updates based on the response from the server.

Error handling is present in both actions to catch any exceptions that occur during the API calls, logging the error and ensuring that the loading state is correctly reset. Overall, this store module centralizes the handling of user data and authentication-related operations, providing a clean and reactive way to manage user state within a Vue application.

This script pertains to the **SignInComponent**, where we utilize the store for user authentication. Upon successful sign in, the script facilitates redirection to the dashboard.

```
<script lang="ts">
import { computed, defineComponent, ref } from 'vue';
import { useRouter } from 'vue-router';
import { useUserStore } from '../store/userStore';

export default defineComponent({
  name: 'SignInComponent',
  setup() {

    const email = ref('');
    const password = ref('');
    const router = useRouter();
    const message = ref('')

    const userStore = useUserStore();

    const onSubmit = async () => {
      message.value = '';
      await userStore.signin({ email: email.value, password: password.value })
      if(!userStore.isLoading && userStore.status) {
        console.log(userStore.userProfile)
        router.push('/dashboard');
      } else {
        message.value = "User doesn't exist in the system"
      }
    };

    const isLoading = computed(() => userStore.isLoading);

    const gotoSignup = () => router.push('/signup');


    return {
      email,
      password,
      onSubmit,
      gotoSignup,
      userStore,
      isLoading,
      message
    };
  }
});
</script>

<style scoped>
.mrgbtm {
    margin-top: 12%;
}
</style>
```

Figure 8.50: *using user store*

Within the component's set up function, it sets up reactive references for user credentials and a message for potential feedback. It leverages the **useUserStore** to access the authentication-related state and actions. When the form is submitted, the **onSubmit** function is called, which invokes the **signin** action from the store with the user's email and password. It then checks the store's loading state and status. If the sign in is successful and the store is not in a loading state, indicating that the asynchronous sign in process has completed, the user is redirected to the dashboard route. Otherwise, an appropriate error message is set to indicate that the user does not exist in the system. Additionally, the component uses a computed property to track the loading state from the store, providing a reactive way to indicate the sign in process's status.

Here is the script portion of the **SignUpComponent** that details how it interacts with the **userStore** for registration purposes. It handles the sign up process and, if successful, navigates the user to the dashboard.

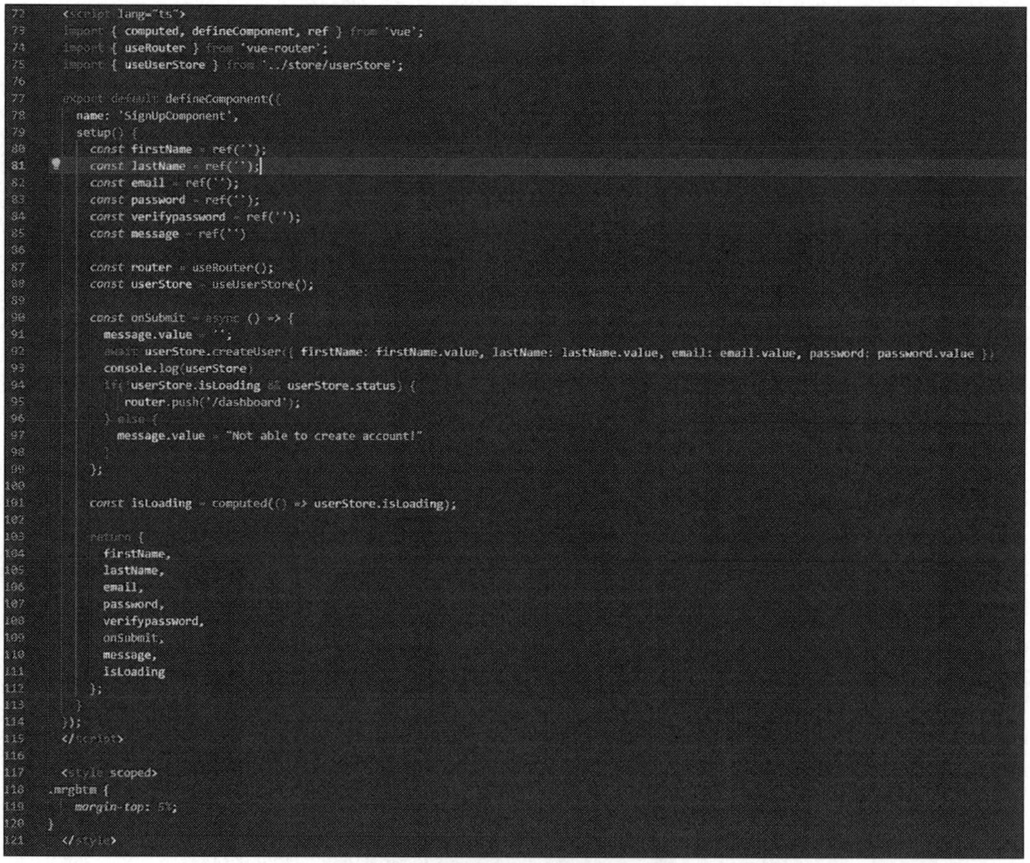

```
<script lang="ts">
import { computed, defineComponent, ref } from 'vue';
import { useRouter } from 'vue-router';
import { useUserStore } from '../store/userStore';

export default defineComponent({
  name: 'SignUpComponent',
  setup() {
    const firstName = ref('');
    const lastName = ref('');
    const email = ref('');
    const password = ref('');
    const verifypassword = ref('');
    const message = ref('')

    const router = useRouter();
    const userStore = useUserStore();

    const onSubmit = async () => {
      message.value = '';
      await userStore.createUser({ firstName: firstName.value, lastName: lastName.value, email: email.value, password: password.value })
      console.log(userStore)
      if(!userStore.isLoading && userStore.status) {
        router.push('/dashboard');
      } else {
        message.value = "Not able to create account!"
      }
    };

    const isLoading = computed(() => userStore.isLoading);

    return {
      firstName,
      lastName,
      email,
      password,
      verifypassword,
      onSubmit,
      message,
      isLoading
    };
  }
});
</script>

<style scoped>
.mrgbtm {
  margin-top: 5%;
}
</style>
```

Figure 8.51: *using user store*

The script sets up reactive state references for user details and a message for displaying feedback. It uses the **useUserStore** to access the store and perform actions related to user management.

When the user submits the registration form, the **onSubmit** function is called, which triggers the **createUser** action within the **userStore**, passing along the new user's details. It then checks the **isLoading** and **status** properties from the **userStore** to determine the outcome of the registration attempt. If the sign up is successful—indicated by **status** being true and **isLoading** being false—the user is programmatically redirected to the dashboard using Vue Router's **router.push** method. If the registration fails, the script sets an error message to inform the user that the account creation was unsuccessful. The **isLoading** property is also made available to the template as a computed property to reflect the current loading state of the sign up process.

If the sign in attempt fail, an error message will be displayed on the sign in screen to inform the user of the unsuccessful attempt.

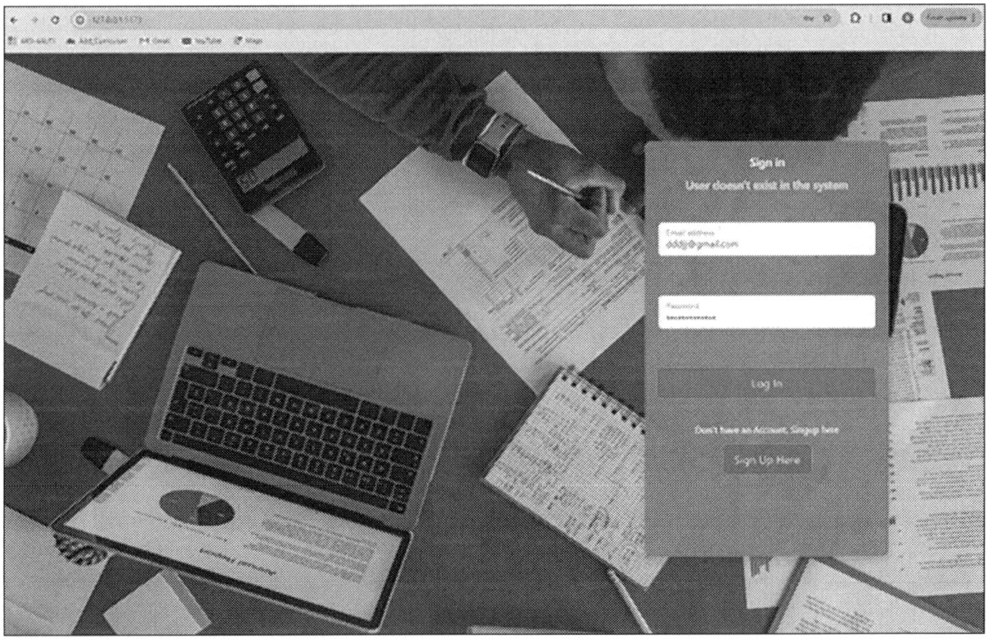

Figure 8.52: *Showing Error Message*

If the sign up process fails, an error message is presented on the sign up screen to notify the user of the unsuccessful registration.

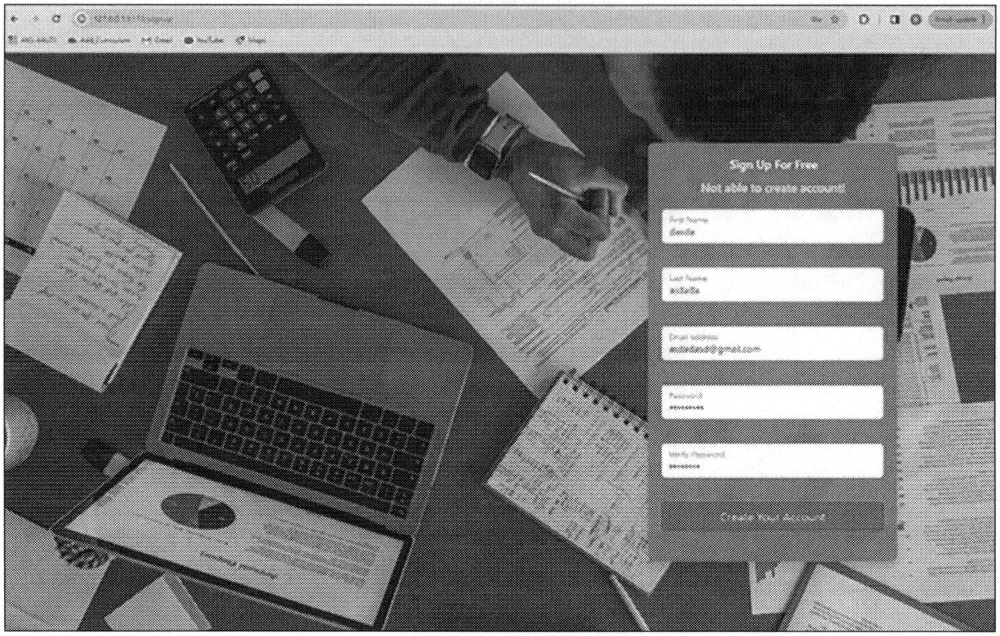

Figure 8.53: *Showing error message*

Implementing Pinia Store for Dashboard/Tasks Module

Prior to implementing the Pinia store for the dashboard module, it is crucial to have a comprehensive understanding of the overarching architecture and the data flow mechanism that renders tasks on the user interface via routing. The diagram elucidates the structure of the dashboard module's store setup. It showcases the **`Tasks`** component along with various modal components, all of which are designed to interact with the store by dispatching actions to perform operations and by receiving pertinent data.

In this system, the **`DashboardContainer`** acts as the central command unit that oversees the task management process. It coordinates the actions for fetching, creating, editing, and deleting tasks. These actions are executed within the context of the **`DashboardContainer`**, which then passes the necessary data down to the individual components like the **`Tasks`** component and various task-related modals.

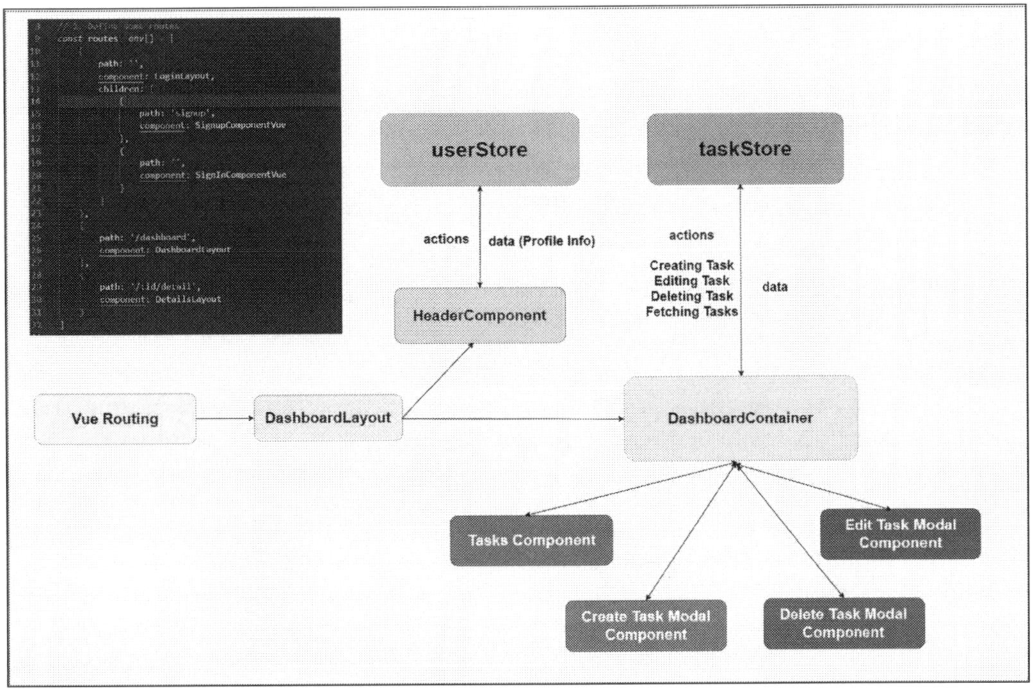

***Figure 8.54:** Understanding dashboard flow*

Each component is dependent on the **`DashboardContainer`** for its data, which it receives through a well-defined flow. This ensures that the components remain lightweight and focused on their specific roles–rendering the user interface and handling user interactions–while the store manages the state and logic of task operations. This delineation fosters a modular and maintainable codebase, where each part of the system has a clear and distinct responsibility.

The code that follows defines a Pinia store named **`task`**, responsible for managing the state related to tasks in a Vue application. The store's state is shaped by the **`TaskState`** interface, which includes an array of tasks, a loading flag to indicate ongoing operations, and a status flag to represent the success or failure of an action.

The store has several key parts:

- **State:** It initializes with an empty task list, **`loading`** set to **`false`** indicating no current operations, and **`status`** also set to **`false`**, implying no successful action has been completed yet.
- **Getters:** These are functions that return pieces of the state, acting similarly to computed properties. **`getTasks`** returns the list of tasks, and **`isLoading`** provides the current loading state.
- **Actions:** These are methods that handle side effects and asynchronous operations:

- **fetchTasks**: This action fetches tasks from a service and updates the store's state with the results. It sets the **loading** state to **true** while the operation is in progress and updates it upon completion. If successful, it populates the **tasks** array with the fetched data.
- **createTask**: It sends a new task to the service to be created. While the API call is being made, **loading** is **true**. Upon success, it resets the tasks and updates the status.
- **deleteTask:** It deletes a task by its ID using the service. It follows the same pattern of setting **loading** while the operation is in progress and updates the store based on the response.
- **editTask:** It updates a task's details. Before making the call, it removes the **createdAt** and **updatedAt** properties, since they are typically managed by the backend. If the update is successful, the tasks array is reset, and the status is updated.

Errors are caught and logged in the console, and the **loading** flag is reset to **false** in the event of an error. This structure ensures that components can react to changes in the store's state, display loading indicators, and reflect the results of task operations. The store acts as a centralized place to manage all task-related logic, making the application's data flow easier to understand and maintain.

```
ui > src > store > TS taskStore.ts > ...
import { defineStore } from 'pinia';
import tasksService from '../services/TasksService'

interface TaskState {
    tasks: any;
    loading: boolean;
    status: boolean;
}

export const useTaskStore = defineStore('task', {
  // Define the state as a function that returns the object
  state: (): TaskState => ({
    tasks: [],
    loading: false,
    status: false
  }),

  // Add getters for computed properties
  getters: {
    getTasks: (state) => state.tasks,
    isLoading: (state) => state.loading
  },

  // Add actions for functions that cause side effects and can involve asynchronous operations
  actions: {
    async fetchTasks() {···
    },

    async createTask(task: any) {···
    },

    async deleteTask(id: any) {···
    },

    async editTask(task: any) {
      try {
        this.loading = true;
        delete task.createdAt;
        delete task.updatedAt;
        const response = await tasksService.updateTask({_id: task._id, task: task.task, assignee: task.assignee,
          description: task.description, status: task.status})
        this.loading = false;
        if(response.data.result && response.data.statusCode === 200 && response.data.result !== null) {
          this.tasks = []
          this.status = true;
        }
      } catch (error) {
        // Handle the error appropriately.
        console.error('Failed to fetch users:', error);
        this.loading = false;
      }
    }
  },
});
```

Figure 8.55: *Task Store*

The script segment of the dashboard container outlines its interaction with the task store. Within this script, multiple actions are dispatched to the store, and data is subsequently retrieved to be utilized within the container and passed down to the components.

```
<script setup lang="ts">
import { computed, onMounted, ref } from 'vue'
import { useRouter } from 'vue-router';
import { useTaskStore } from '../store/taskStore'
import NoTasksAvailable from '../components/NoTasksAvailable.vue'
import Tasks from '../components/Tasks.vue'
import CreateTask from '../components/CreateTask.vue'
import DeleteTaskModal from '../modals/DeleteTaskModal.vue'
import EditTaskModal from '../modals/EditTaskModal.vue'
import CreateTaskModal from '../modals/CreateTaskModal.vue'

const router = useRouter()
const taskStore = useTaskStore();

const showEditModal = ref(false);
const showDeleteModal = ref(false)
const showCreateModal = ref(false)
const deleteTaskId = ref(null);
const editTask = ref(null);

const computedTasks = computed(() => taskStore.getTasks);

onMounted(async () => {
  await taskStore.fetchTasks();
})

const closeModal = (modalType: string) => {
  if(modalType === 'delete') {
    showDeleteModal.value = false;
  } else if(modalType === 'edit') {
    showEditModal.value = false;
  } else if(modalType === 'create') {
    showCreateModal.value = false;
  }
};

const onEditTask = (task: any) => {
  console.log('onEdit', task)
  showEditModal.value = true;
  editTask.value = {...task};
}

const onSaveTask = async (task: any) => {…
}

const onDeleteTask = async (task: any) => {
  console.log('onDelete', task);
  showDeleteModal.value = true;
  deleteTaskId.value = task._id
}

const onDeleteConfirm = async (taskId: any) => {…
}

const onEditConfirm = async (task: any) => {…
}

const onDetailTask = (id: number) => router.push(`${id}/detail`)

const onCreateTask = () => showCreateModal.value = true;

</script>
```

Figure 8.56: *Using task store*

In this container component, which serves as a dashboard container, the **`useTaskStore`** from Pinia is imported and utilized to manage the tasks' state. Upon the component mounting, the **`onMounted`** lifecycle hook is triggered, fetching the list of tasks by invoking the **`fetchTasks`** action from the task store. This store is also responsible for handling the creation, deletion, and editing of tasks through respective methods like **`createTask`**, **`deleteTask`**, and **`editTask`**.

The component has computed property **`computedTasks`**, which derives its value from the store's **`getTasks`** getter, ensuring reactivity and real-time updates to the tasks displayed on the dashboard. Actions for editing, saving, deleting, and confirming these operations are defined and tied to the corresponding modals through event listeners. These actions interact with the task store by dispatching the relevant actions and updating the tasks list based on the operations performed.

For instance, when a user initiates a task creation through the **`CreateTask`** modal, the **`onSaveTask`** method is called, which dispatches the **`createTask`** action to the store. Upon successful creation, the task list is refreshed by calling **`fetchTasks`** again. Similarly, for deleting a task, **`onDeleteConfirm`** is used to call the **`deleteTask`** action and refresh the list after the operation.

Each modal component is controlled by a reactive variable (like **`showCreateModal`**, **`showEditModal`**, and **`showDeleteModal`**), which is used to display or hide the modals based on user interactions and the completion of task operations. If the operation is successful and the store's status is confirmed, the task list is re-fetched to display the latest data. Additionally, the **`onDetailTask`** method provides navigation functionality to the task detail view using Vue Router.

The component effectively demonstrates the interaction with the Pinia store, showcasing how data flows from the store to the UI and how user actions trigger updates to the store's state.

Displayed is the dashboard screen, where tasks are neatly populated within a table under a header. Taking a closer look at the header reveals a rounded profile icon featuring the initials - specifically, the first letters of the first and last names. This detail, too, is sourced from the store, illustrating the ease of store access from any component. Direct interaction with the store from the header component allows us to retrieve this information using the designated Getters defined in the **`userStore`**.

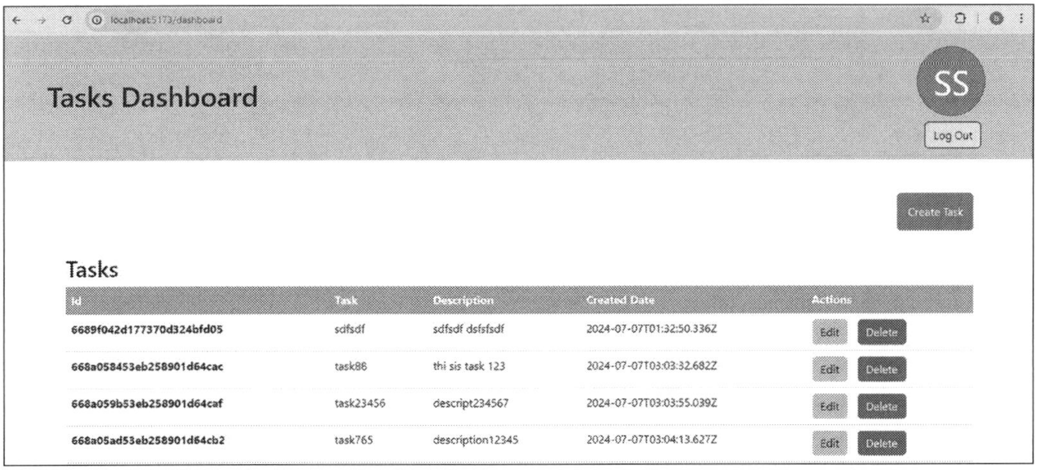

***Figure 8.57:** Dashboard with Tasks*

Here is the header component in which we are reading the profile info from the store and displaying in the header. The header of a user interface, there is a direct interaction with the **userStore** defined by Pinia. The header displays a button with the user's initials, which are obtained through a computed property named **profileName**. This computed property derives its value from a getter function called **getProfileName** within **userStore**. The getter function is responsible for compiling the initials from the user's first and last names, which are then displayed on the rounded button in the header.

Additionally, the header includes a "**Log Out**" button that, when clicked, triggers the **onLogoutClick** function. This function uses Vue Router to navigate the user back to the home page, indicating a logout action. The script tags import necessary dependencies, such as the **useUserStore** from the store directory and **useRouter** from Vue Router, establishing the necessary connections for the component to interact with the store and routing.

Overall, this set up demonstrates how components in a Vue application can interact with a global state managed by Pinia, utilizing store getters to display dynamic data, and responding to user actions with routing changes.

```
<template>
  <header class="header d-flex justify-content-between align-items-center p-3">
    <h1 style="margin-left: 50px;">{{ title  }}</h1>
    <div class="profile-actions d-flex flex-column align-items-end">
      <button class="btn btn-danger rounded-circle mb-2">
        {{ profileName }}
      </button>
      <button class="btn btn-outline-danger" @click="onLogoutClick">
        Log Out
      </button>
    </div>
  </header>
</template>

<script lang="ts">
import { computed, toRefs } from 'vue'
import { useUserStore } from '../store/userStore';
import { useRouter } from 'vue-router';

export default {

  props: {
      title: String
  },

  setup(props) {

      const { title } = toRefs(props)
      const userStore = useUserStore();
      const router = useRouter();

      const onLogoutClick = () => router.push('/');
      const profileName = computed(() => userStore.getProfileName)

      return {
          onLogoutClick,
          title,
          profileName
      }

  }
}

</script>
```

Figure 8.58: *Header Component using user store*

Implementing Pinia Store for Task Detail Module

The provided diagram serves to clarify the flow and architecture of the detail task page within the application. When a user selects a task from the table by clicking a row, they are navigated to a detailed view of that task. This transition is facilitated by Vue's routing system, where the unique identifier for each task (**`:id`**) is embedded within the URL, enabling a dynamic route to the detail page.

Once the user arrives at the **`DetailContainer`**, this component engages in direct communication with the **`detailStore`**, pulling in the required task details to be displayed on the page. Simultaneously, there is a **`HeaderComponent`** present on the detail page, which also interacts with the **`userStore`**. The header component is designed to adapt its display based on the context, showing the appropriate heading for the detail view.

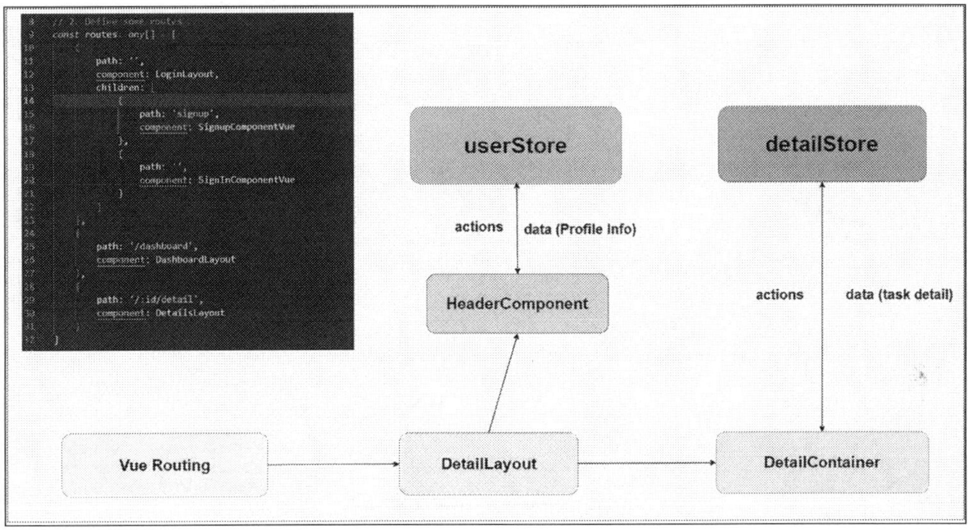

Figure 8.59: *Understanding Task Detail Flow*

The **`HeaderComponent`** is especially interactive with the **`userStore`**, extracting user information such as profile initials whenever it is available in the store. These initials are then showcased within the profile icon in the header, maintaining a consistent user experience across different views by providing personalization and recognition.

In essence, this set up illustrates a modular and well-organized structure where components are neatly aligned with the stores they interact with, ensuring a seamless data flow and user navigation experience within the application.

The following code establishes a Pinia store named **`task-detail`**, which is structured to manage the state for task details in a Vue application. Within this store, an interface called **`TaskState`** defines the shape of the state, including a **`taskDetails`** object to store the detailed information about a task, a **`loading`** boolean to indicate if a data fetch operation is in progress, and a **status** boolean that signifies the success status of fetching data.

The store's state is initialized with empty **taskDetails**, and the **loading** and **status** flags are both set to **false**. The store includes two getters – **getTaskDetails** returns the current task details, and **isLoading** provides the loading status, allowing components to reactively display loading indicators or fetched data.

A crucial part of this store is its actions, which contain an asynchronous function named **fetchTaskDetails**. This function is designed to retrieve detailed information about a task from the backend, identified by a unique **id**. When called, it sets the **loading** flag to **true**, makes an API call using the **tasksService**, and upon receiving a successful response (indicated by a status code of 200), updates the store's **taskDetails** with the fetched data and sets **status** to **true**. If there is an error during this process, it logs the error to the console and sets **loading** back to **false**.

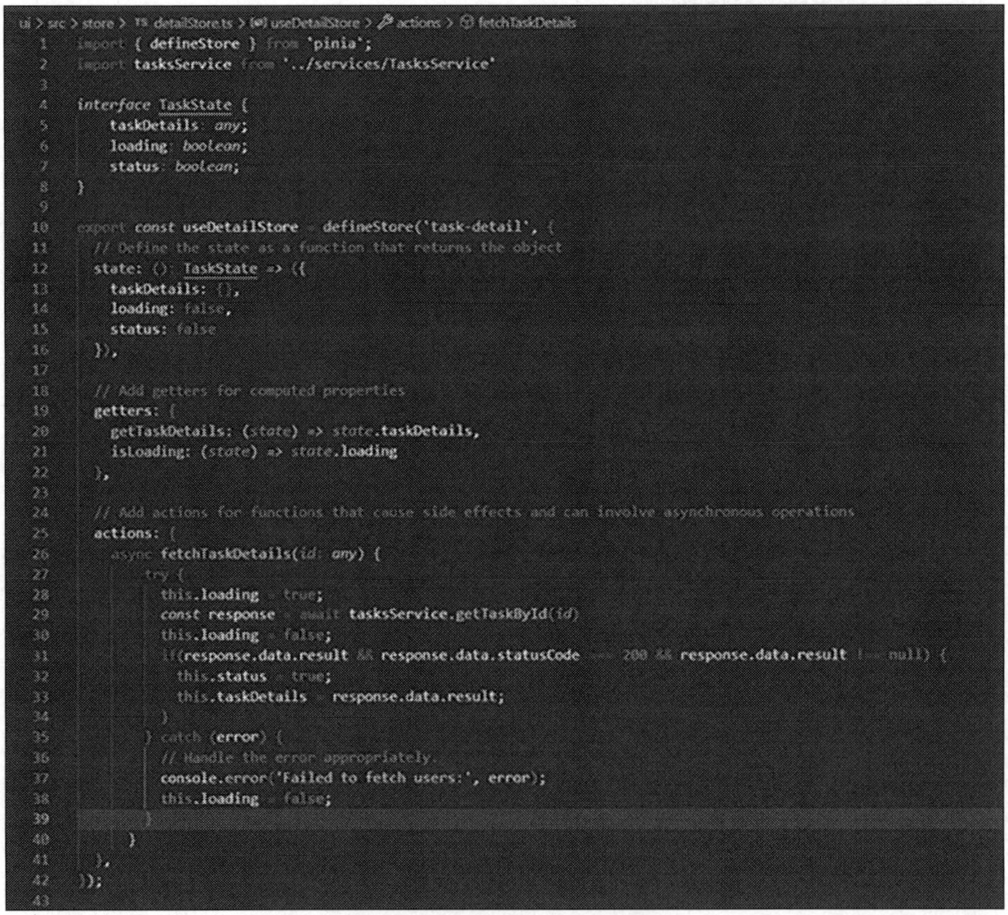

```
import { defineStore } from 'pinia';
import tasksService from '../services/TasksService'

interface TaskState {
    taskDetails: any;
    loading: boolean;
    status: boolean;
}

export const useDetailStore = defineStore('task-detail', {
  // Define the state as a function that returns the object
  state: (): TaskState => ({
    taskDetails: {},
    loading: false,
    status: false
  }),

  // Add getters for computed properties
  getters: {
    getTaskDetails: (state) => state.taskDetails,
    isLoading: (state) => state.loading
  },

  // Add actions for functions that cause side effects and can involve asynchronous operations
  actions: {
    async fetchTaskDetails(id: any) {
      try {
        this.loading = true;
        const response = await tasksService.getTaskById(id)
        this.loading = false;
        if(response.data.result && response.data.statusCode === 200 && response.data.result !== null) {
          this.status = true;
          this.taskDetails = response.data.result;
        }
      } catch (error) {
        // Handle the error appropriately.
        console.error('Failed to fetch users:', error);
        this.loading = false;
      }
    }
  },
});
```

Figure 8.60: *task detail store*

This Pinia store encapsulates all the logic and state related to fetching and displaying task details, separating concerns, and providing a maintainable approach to state management within the application.

Following is the dashboard container component. This template is part of a Vue component that displays the details of a task within a user interface. The layout includes a "**`Back to Dashboard`**" button, allowing users to easily navigate back to the main dashboard. The core of the template consists of a detailed view, where various attributes of a task - such as its ID, name, description, status, assignee, creator, and creation date - are displayed in a structured format.

In the accompanying script, Vue's Composition API is utilized along with Vue Router's **`useRouter`** and **`useRoute`** to handle routing. The script imports and sets up a **`detailStore`** using Pinia, which contains the state and actions related to the task details. When the component is mounted, it immediately fetches the task details based on the task ID obtained from the route parameters.

```
ui > src > containers > DetailsContainer.vue > {} template
<template>
  <div class="container my-4">
    <div class="row mb-4">
      <div class="col">
        <!-- Back to Dashboard button -->
        <button class="btn btn-back" @click="onBackToDashboard">
          ← Back to Dashboard
        </button>
      </div>
    </div>
    <div class="row">
      <div class="col details-section">
        <h2 class="mb-4">Task Details</h2>
        <p class="detail-item"><span class="detail-label">Id:</span> {{ taskDetails.id }}</p>
        <p class="detail-item"><span class="detail-label">Task:</span> {{ taskDetails.task }}</p>
        <p class="detail-item"><span class="detail-label">Description:</span> {{ taskDetails.description }}</p>
        <p class="detail-item"><span class="detail-label">Status:</span> {{ taskDetails.status }}</p>
        <p class="detail-item"><span class="detail-label">Assignee:</span> {{ taskDetails.assignee }}</p>
        <p class="detail-item"><span class="detail-label">Created By:</span> {{ taskDetails.createdBy }}</p>
        <p class="detail-item"><span class="detail-label">Created Date:</span> {{ taskDetails.createdDate }}</p>
      </div>
    </div>
  </div>
</template>

<script setup lang="ts">
import { computed, onMounted } from 'vue';
import { useRouter, useRoute  } from 'vue-router';
import { useDetailStore } from '../store/detailStore'

const router = useRouter();
const route = useRoute();
const detailStore = useDetailStore();

const onBackToDashboard = () => router.push('/dashboard')

onMounted(async () => {
  await detailStore.fetchTaskDetails(route.params.id);
})

const taskDetails = computed(() => {
  const details = detailStore.getTaskDetails;
  return {
    id: details._id,
    task: details.task,
    description: details.description,
    status: details.status,
    assignee: details.assignee,
    createdBy: details.createdBy,
    createdDate: details.createdAt
  }
})

</script>
```

Figure 8.61: *Detail Container*

A computed property named **`taskDetails`** is declared to reactively transform and present the task data from the **`detailStore.`** It maps the store's task detail properties to a local object, formatting them as needed for display. This ensures that any updates to the task details in the store will be automatically reflected in the component, maintaining consistency with the application's state.

The script facilitates user interaction by providing the **`onBackToDashboard`** method, which uses Vue Router to redirect the user to the dashboard when invoked. This method is tied to the "**`Back to Dashboard`**" button within the template, illustrating a clear separation of concerns between user navigation and data presentation.

The detail page presents a comprehensive view of a task's information, complete with a header. The task's unique identifier is also visible in the page's URL.

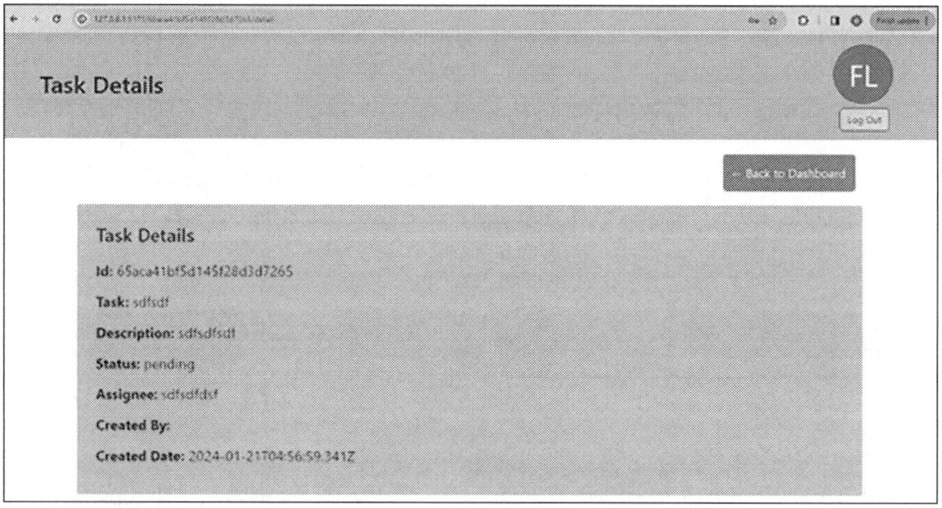

Figure 8.62: *Task Details Page*

Rehydrating State with Pinia

In the context of Single Page Applications (SPAs), state rehydration refers to the process of populating the application's state with previously saved data, often from the user's local storage or a server response. This technique is crucial in SPAs to ensure a seamless user experience, providing immediate access to a previous state after a page refresh or when revisiting the application.

Pinia, as a state management library for Vue.js, plays a pivotal role in the state rehydration process. It provides a centralized store that can be easily persisted and restored, maintaining the application's state across sessions and page reloads.

Following are the points to consider why we need to rehydrate the state.

- **User Experience:** Rehydrating state allows users to pick up exactly where they left off, without having to redo actions or re-enter data.

- **Performance:** It can improve the perceived performance of an application by reducing the need for initial data fetches after the first load.
- **Consistency:** Maintains consistency in the user's workflow by preserving the application state between sessions.
- **Offline Support:** Enables certain features of the application to be available even when the user is offline.

Implementation

To rehydrate a store in Pinia, you typically need to:

- **Persist the Store State:** Use browser storage solutions like **`localStorage`** or **`sessionStorage`**, or integrate a library like **`pinia-plugin-persist`** to automatically handle the persistence of the state.
- **Restore the state:** On application initialization, check for any existing state in storage and populate the Pinia store with this data.
- **Handle State Migrations:** If your application's state shape changes with updates, ensure you have a migration strategy for old state structures.

When navigating the dashboard, if you happen to refresh the page and have not implemented store rehydration, you will encounter an issue where the profile icon at the top right corner displays **`'undefined'`**. This occurs because the store does not inherently retain information after a page reload. Without rehydration, the store is reset to its initial state, which lacks the user's profile information, leading to the display issue with the profile icon. Implementing rehydration ensures that the user's data persists across page refreshes, maintaining a consistent and uninterrupted user experience.

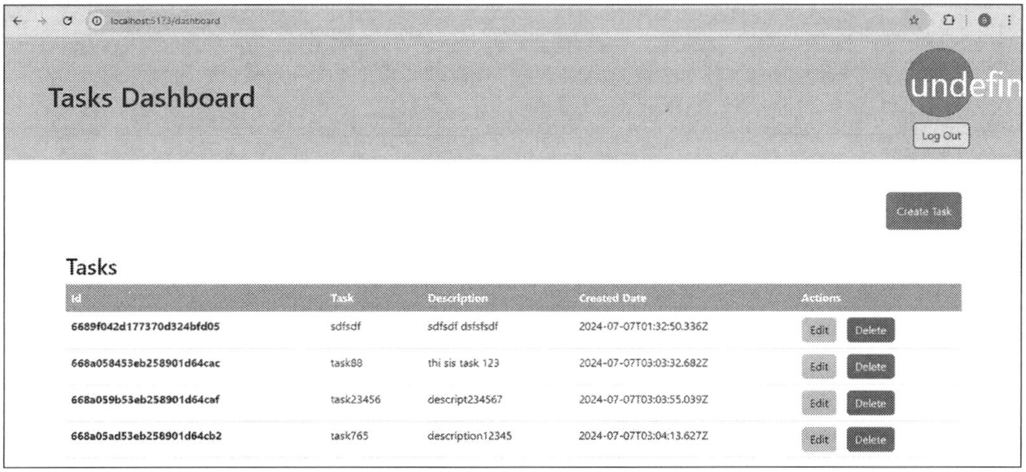

Figure 8.63: *Header without store rehydration*

The first thing we need to do is to install the following dependency. This is a plugin that takes care of state rehydration.

```
npm install pinia-plugin-persistedstate
```

We are setting up a Vue application with state persistence using a Pinia plugin. The **piniaPluginPersistedstate** is a plugin for Pinia that automatically saves the state of your stores in the browser's local storage. When you use this plugin with Pinia, it enables the state to persist across browser sessions and page reloads.

By including **piniaPluginPersistedstate**, the application ensures that the state managed by Pinia stores is preserved even after the user closes the browser tab, navigates away, or refreshes the page. This enhances the user experience by providing continuity and saving the user from having to repeat actions such as logging in every time they return to the application.

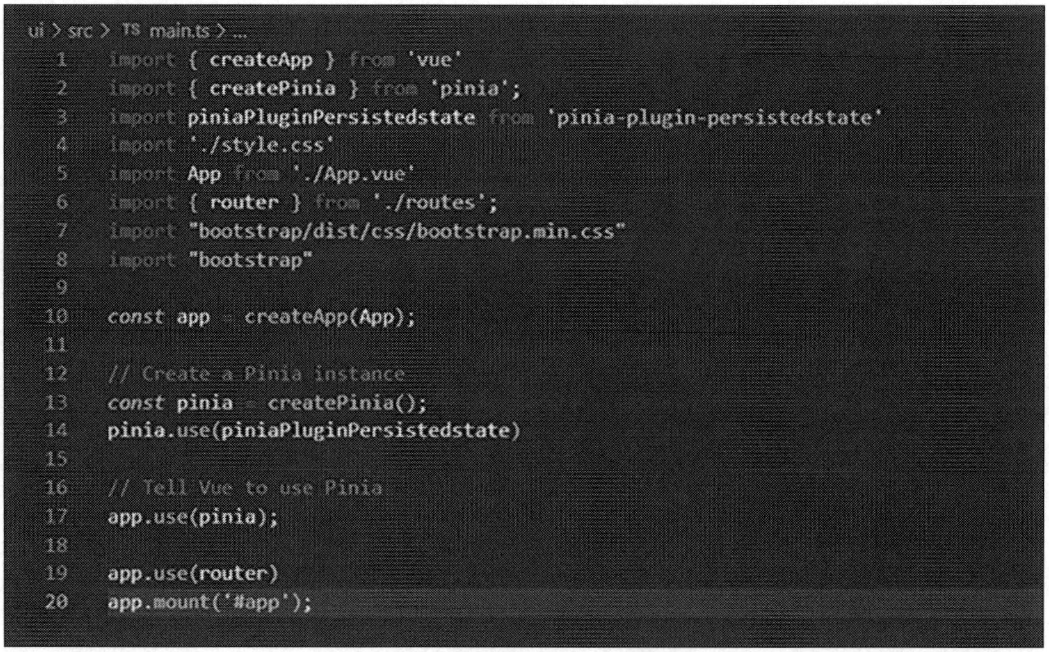

```
ui > src > TS main.ts > ...
import { createApp } from 'vue'
import { createPinia } from 'pinia';
import piniaPluginPersistedstate from 'pinia-plugin-persistedstate'
import './style.css'
import App from './App.vue'
import { router } from './routes';
import "bootstrap/dist/css/bootstrap.min.css"
import "bootstrap"

const app = createApp(App);

// Create a Pinia instance
const pinia = createPinia();
pinia.use(piniaPluginPersistedstate)

// Tell Vue to use Pinia
app.use(pinia);

app.use(router)
app.mount('#app');
```

***Figure 8.64**: Using Plugin*

Considering that our primary focus is on maintaining user information upon refreshing the page, it suffices to simply introduce the property **persist: true** within the **userStore**, as demonstrated in the following example.

```
export const useUserStore = defineStore('user', {
  // Define the state as a function that returns the object
  state: (): UserState => ({
    userProfile: {},
    loading: false,
    status: false
  }),

  persist: true,

  // Add getters for computed properties
  getters: {
    getUserProfile: (state) => state.userProfile,
    isLoading: (state) => state.loading,
    getProfileName: (state) => `${state.userProfile?.firstName?.charAt(0).toUpperCase()}${state.userPr
  },

  // Add actions for functions that cause side effects and can involve asynchronous operations
  actions: {
    async signin(userData: User) {
      try {
        this.loading = true;
        const response = await userService.signin(userData);
        this.loading = false;
        if(response.data.result && response.data.statusCode === 200 && response.data.result !== null
          this.status = true;
          this.userProfile = response.data.result;
```

Figure 8.65: *Adding Persist Flag*

With the configuration established, refreshing the page will no longer result in the loss of user information. Instead, the user's initials will persist and remain visible. This is achieved through the plugin we integrated, which automatically saves the state of the **`user`** from the store into the browser's local storage. By default, when the **`persist: true`** setting is active in the **`userStore`**, the plugin ensures that the user's state is retained across page reloads, providing a seamless experience where previously entered data, such as user initials, remains accessible and displayed correctly.

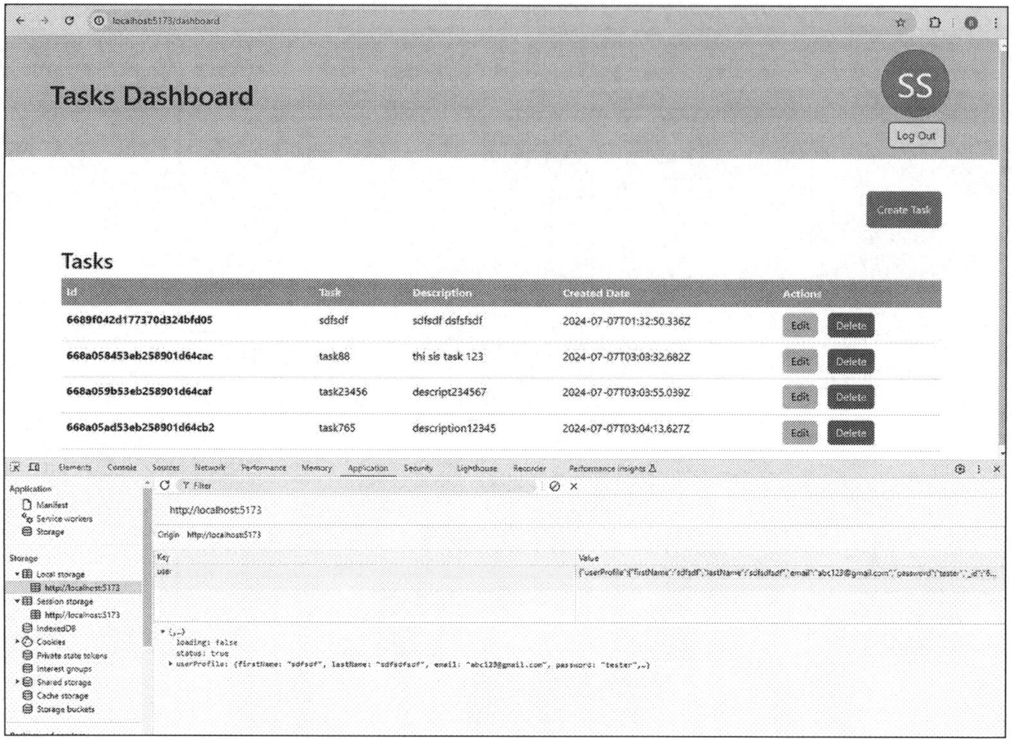

Figure 8.66: *Setting the Local Storage*

Here are some of the best practices for rehydrating state:

- **Security:** Be cautious about what data you persist as sensitive information may be at risk if stored improperly.
- **Data Validation:** Validate the rehydrated data to ensure it matches the expected shape and content to avoid application errors.
- **Selective Persistence:** Choose selectively which parts of the state to persist. Not all state needs to be saved, particularly transient data.
- **Versioning:** Version your persisted state to manage migrations and updates to the store structure.
- **Synchronization:** Ensure that the rehydrated state is synchronized with the backend to prevent conflicts or outdated data.

Rehydrating the state in an SPA using Pinia is an effective strategy to enhance user experience and application performance. When implemented with consideration for security and data integrity, state rehydration can significantly contribute to a more efficient and user-friendly application. By leveraging Pinia's capabilities, developers can provide a resilient and persistent state management solution that bridges sessions and reloads, making modern SPAs more robust and intuitive.

Understanding the Final UI structure

Having extensively developed numerous components, services, and integrated the Pinia store into our application, it is prudent to take a step back and conduct a thorough review of the UI structure. This reflective overview is not just a mere examination but an opportunity to fully grasp the intricacies and interconnections of the various elements we have implemented. Understanding the UI structure in its entirety is crucial, as it provides a holistic view of how individual components and services cohesively work together. Such a comprehensive understanding is essential for ensuring that the application functions smoothly, adheres to design principles, and delivers an optimal user experience. This final evaluation of the UI structure is a key step in validating our development efforts, identifying potential areas for improvement, and solidifying our grasp of the application's overall flow and functionality.

In the `src` folder of a Vue 3 TypeScript project, the structure is thoughtfully organized into several directories and files, each serving a specific purpose:

- **components:** This directory contains all the Vue components that are the building blocks of the UI. These are reusable elements like `CreateTask.vue`, `Header.vue`, and `SignInComponent.vue` which can be integrated into various parts of the application.
- **containers:** Here you will find components like `DashboardContainer.vue` and `DetailsContainer.vue` that typically manage a section of the application, often serving as the glue between the UI and the application logic. They may contain multiple components and provide them with the necessary data and functions they need.
- **layouts:** This directory holds layout components such as `DashboardLayout.vue` and `LoginLayout.vue`. These are higher-level components that define the overall layout of a page or a group of pages, providing a consistent structure for the user interface.

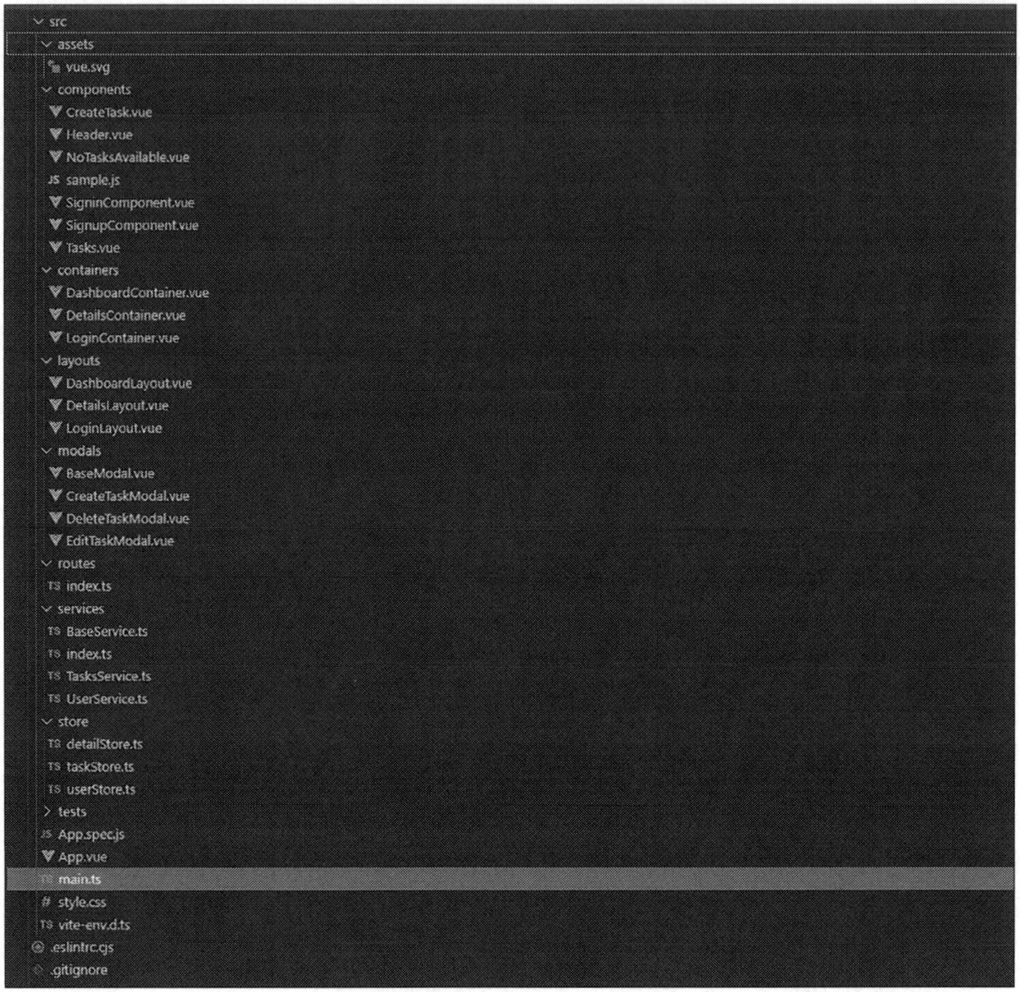

Figure 8.67: *Project Structure*

- **modals:** Modals like **`CreateTaskModal.vue`** and **`EditTaskModal.vue`** are defined here. These are overlay components that appear on top of the main content, typically used for forms, information, confirmations, or other interactions that require user attention.
- **routes:** Contains the project's routing configuration files. Routing in Vue.js is handled by the Vue Router, which defines the navigational structure of the application, mapping URLs to components.
- **services:** Service files like **`TaskService.ts`** encapsulate the logic for making API calls and handling data operations. They act as an intermediary between the frontend components and backend endpoints.
- **store:** This is where the Pinia stores are defined, such as **`detailStore.ts`** and

`taskStore.ts`. They manage and centralize the application's state, and in a TypeScript project, they also ensure that the state structure is strongly typed.

- **`App.vue`:** The root Vue component that acts as the entry point for the UI part of the application.
- **`main.ts`:** The main TypeScript file where the Vue app instance is created and plugins are initialized.

This structured approach aligns with Vue 3 and TypeScript best practices, ensuring that the project is scalable, maintainable, and easy to navigate for developers. Each piece of the application has its designated place, which simplifies both development and debugging.

Conclusion

As we conclude this chapter on implementing the UI for our example MEVN stack project, we have traversed through a journey of building a dynamic and user-friendly interface. By carefully laying out the structure, integrating a responsive design with Bootstrap, and harnessing the power of Vue for our components and containers, we have set the stage for a comprehensive and interactive user experience. Furthermore, the incorporation of services and proxy set up for API calls, along with the adept management of application state using Pinia, underscores our commitment to creating a robust and scalable web application.

The concept of rehydrating state with Pinia has prepared our application to maintain consistency and user context, proving essential for real-world applications where user experience continuity is key. Our exploration of the final UI structure has provided a clear perspective on how each component and service plays a vital role in the holistic development process.

The journey continues as we turn our attention to an often overlooked but crucial aspect of application development – that is, logging. In the next chapter, we will dive into various logging options, a critical step in preparing our application for a production environment. Effective logging strategies are not just about debugging; they are about understanding user interactions, monitoring application health, and ensuring a smooth operational flow. The chapter that follows will equip you with the necessary tools and knowledge to implement efficient logging mechanisms, further enhancing the reliability and maintainability of your MEVN stack application.

CHAPTER 9
Logging Options in Node.js API

Introduction

In this chapter, we will delve into the crucial aspect of logging in the development and maintenance of Node.js APIs. Logging is an essential part of any robust application. It not only helps in tracking the flow of operations and understanding the state of the system at any given point but also plays a critical role in diagnosing issues, monitoring application performance, and ensuring security compliance. Effective logging can be the difference between quickly resolving a production issue and wasting hours in trying to reproduce the problem.

To harness the full potential of logging in Node.js, we will explore how to implement a Logger Service, a dedicated component for handling log messages. This service is vital for centralizing log management, ensuring consistency in log formats, and simplifying log analysis. The focus then shifts to integrating various popular logging libraries with the Logger Service. Each library offers unique features and configurations, catering to different logging needs and preferences.

By the end of this chapter, you will have a comprehensive understanding of the importance of logging in Node.js applications and the practical knowledge to implement and configure a Logger Service using various renowned libraries, tailored to your application's needs.

Structure

In this chapter, the following topics will be covered:

- Understanding the Importance of Logging
- Implementing Common Logger Service
- Setting up Logger Service with Pine Library
- Setting up Logger Service with Pino Library

- Setting up Logger Service with Bunyan Library
- Setting up Logger Service with Winston Library

Understanding the Importance of Logging

Logging is a fundamental aspect of any robust Node.js Express backend API. It involves recording and storing information about the application's operations, which is essential for a variety of purposes such as debugging, monitoring, and compliance. This chapter explores why logging is indispensable in the context of Node.js Express backend development.

Importance of Logging

The following points elucidate the importance of logging:

- **Debugging and Error Tracking:** The primary function of logging is to facilitate debugging. When an error occurs, logs provide a chronological account of the events leading up to the error, making it easier to identify and fix the issue. Without adequate logging, diagnosing problems can become a time-consuming and challenging task.
- **Monitoring Application Health:** Logs play a critical role in monitoring the health and performance of an application. They provide real-time insights into the application's operational state, allowing developers to detect and address issues like slow response times, failed requests, or system downtimes promptly.
- **Performance Optimization:** Over time, logs can be analyzed to identify performance trends. This data is invaluable for optimizing database queries, load balancing, and resource allocation, leading to improved application performance and user experience.
- **Compliance and Security:** In many industries, maintaining logs is a regulatory requirement. Logs are instrumental in security audits, as they record access patterns, authentication attempts, and other security-relevant events, helping in identifying potential security breaches or vulnerabilities.

Implementing Effective Logging Strategies

Implementing effective logging strategies is essential for monitoring our application's performance and troubleshooting issues efficiently.

- **What to Log:** Deciding the scope of logging is crucial. It is important to log error messages, warnings, user activities, especially those related to authentication and authorization, and significant state changes in the system. However, logging excessive information can lead to clutter, making it difficult to find relevant data when needed.

- **Log Levels:** Effective logging systems categorize logs into different levels such as error, warning, info, and debug. This categorization helps in filtering and analyzing logs based on their severity and nature. For instance, '`error`' logs are critical and usually need immediate attention, whereas '`debug`' logs are more verbose and useful during development or detailed troubleshooting.
- **Structured Logging:** Structured logs, typically in a format like JSON, are easier to read and process, both by humans and log management systems. This format standardizes logs and makes it easier to search for specific information, analyze trends, and generate reports.
- **Correlation IDs for Debugging:** In distributed systems, using correlation IDs is a best practice. These IDs help trace and correlate log entries across different services and requests. This approach is crucial for debugging in microservices architectures where a user request might span multiple services.

Tools and Best Practices

Here are some of the tools and best practices:

- **Logging Libraries:** Libraries like Winston, Bunyan, and Pino provide powerful logging capabilities for Node.js applications. These libraries support various features like managing log levels, custom formats, and directing logs to different destinations (like console, file systems, or remote logging servers).
- **Centralized Logging:** In distributed systems or large-scale applications, centralized logging is essential. Tools like the ELK Stack or Splunk aggregate logs from various sources into a central repository, making it easier to monitor and analyze logs from all parts of the application.
- **Log Rotation and Management:** Proper log management includes log rotation to prevent logs from consuming excessive disk space and archiving old logs for compliance and historical analysis. Log rotation involves periodically archiving current logs and starting new ones, ensuring that log files remain manageable and searchable.

Logging is more than a mere tool for error recording in Node.js Express backend APIs; it is a comprehensive strategy for application oversight and improvement. Effective logging practices lead to better maintainability, performance, and security of applications. As developers, dedicating efforts towards a well-thought-out logging strategy can significantly enhance your control over the application, offering crucial insights into its behavior and performance.

Implementing Common Logger Service

In the context of a Node.js Express API, implementing a custom Logger Service is not just a matter of recording messages in the console. It is about creating a systematic way to capture, structure, and manage the information flow within your application. A well-designed Logger Service can mean the difference between hours of combing through console logs and having immediate, actionable insights into your application's performance and issues.

Reasons for Implementing a Custom Logger Service

Having previously explored the significance of logging in applications and delved into its best practices, we now turn our attention to understand the benefits that a custom logger service offers to an API. This section will highlight the unique advantages and enhancements that this specialized logger service contributes to the overall functionality and maintenance of the API.

- **Structured Logging:** A custom Logger Service allows you to implement structured logging, which organizes log messages in a consistent and readable format. This structure is essential for parsing and analyzing logs, especially when dealing with large volumes of data.
- **Controlled Log Levels:** Different situations call for different levels of logging (info, warn, error, debug). A Logger Service provides a centralized way to manage these levels, enabling you to filter and control the verbosity of your application logs based on the environment (development, staging, production) or specific needs.
- **Centralized Log Management:** In modern application architectures, especially those based on microservices, centralized logging becomes crucial. A Logger Service can be designed to integrate with centralized log management tools, providing a cohesive view of your logs across multiple services and components.
- **Performance and Scalability:** Efficient logging should not impact the performance of your application. A well-implemented Logger Service ensures that logging operations are fast and, where possible, asynchronous, minimizing their impact on the application's throughput.
- **Compliance and Security:** In many applications, especially those in regulated industries, logging is not just a best practice but a compliance requirement. A Logger Service helps in maintaining logs for audits, security reviews, and compliance checks.

As we proceed to implement the Logger Service, we will focus on these aspects, ensuring that the service is not only functional but also efficient, scalable, and compliant with best practices. We will start by defining the core structure of the Logger Service, followed by methods for different logging levels, and then discuss how to integrate this service into your Express API. The aim is to provide a comprehensive and practical approach to logging that can be tailored to the specific needs of your application.

First, we need to create a folder called logger. Let us define the class with methods corresponding to the different logging levels in the folder.

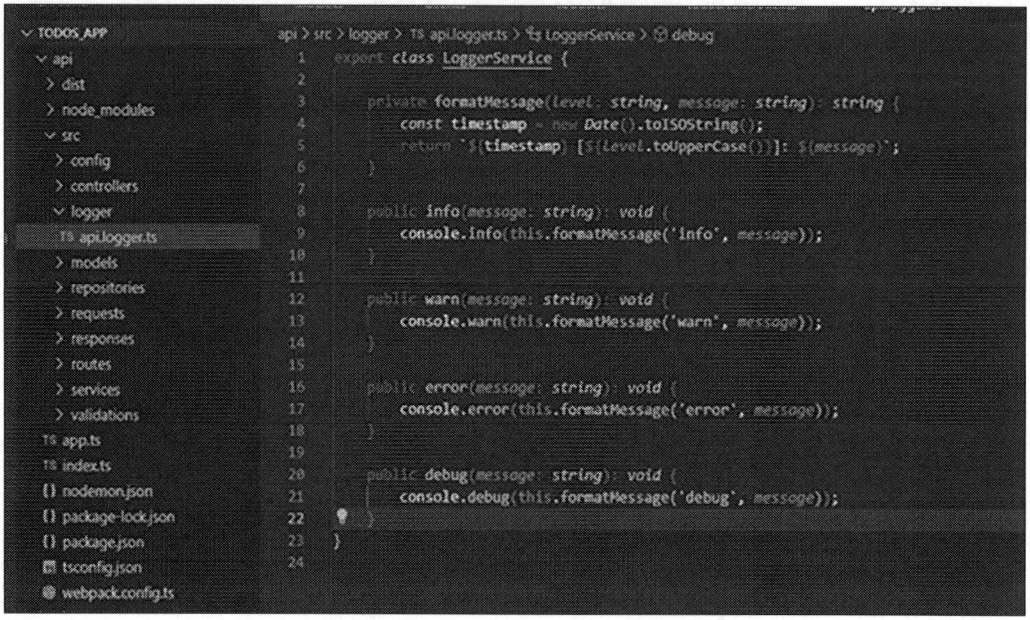

Figure 9.1: *Custom Logger Service*

This procedure defines a `LoggerService` class, which is a custom logging utility for a Node.js application. This class is structured to handle various levels of logging, such as info, warn, error, and debug, by providing dedicated methods for each.

Class Definition

The `LoggerService` is an exportable class, meaning it can be used in different parts of the application by importing it. This class encapsulates all logging functionalities.

Private `formatMessage` Method

This method is responsible for formatting the log messages. It takes two parameters – `level`, which is the severity of the log message (like `info`, `warn`, `error`, `debug`), and `message`, which is the actual log content. The method generates a timestamp in ISO format and combines it with the log level and message to create a structured and readable log entry. The log level is transformed to uppercase to standardize its format.

Public Logging Methods

The class provides four public methods – `info`, `warn`, `error`, and `debug`. Each method corresponds to a different log level:

- **`info` Method:** Used for general informational messages that are useful for tracking the flow and state of the application.
- **`warn` Method:** Intended for warning messages that indicate potential issues or unexpected events that are not necessarily errors but might require attention.
- **`error` Method:** Used for logging error messages. These are critical logs that indicate failures in the application that need to be addressed.
- **`debug` Method:** Designed for debugging purposes. These logs are typically used during development to provide detailed information about the application's state and behavior.

Console Logging

Each method utilizes the respective console method (`console.info`, `console.warn`, `console.error`, `console.debug`) to output the formatted message to the console. This choice makes the logs visible in the standard output, which is a common practice in Node.js applications.

This `LoggerService` provides a centralized and standardized way to handle logging across the application. By using this service, developers can ensure consistent log formats and easily adjust the granularity of logging output as needed. The clear separation of log levels allows for more effective monitoring and debugging, aiding in the maintenance and troubleshooting of the application.

We have defined the Logger Service, and now it is time to import it and use it wherever we want to log. Let us import it in `index.ts` file and test it out. The `LoggerService` is imported from its module, and an instance of it is created. We are using the logger. info method to send an informational message indicating that the Express server has started and is listening on a specific port or pipe. It is also employed to log database connection events. This is particularly useful for monitoring the status of the connection to the MongoDB database.

```
import * as http from "http";
import App from "./app";
import dbConfiguration from './src/config/db.config'
import mongoose, { Connection, Mongoose } from "mongoose";
import { LoggerService } from './src/logger/api.logger'

const port = process.env.PORT || 3080;

const server = http.createServer(App);
server.listen(port);

const logger = new LoggerService();

server.on("listening", async () => {
    const addr = server.address();
    const bind = (typeof addr === "string") ? `pipe ${addr}` : `port ${addr?.port}`;
    dbConfiguration.connectToDB();
    logger.info(`Express Server Listening on ${bind}`);
    mongoose.connection.on('connected', () =>
        logger.info(`Connected to MongoDB, Connection Name ${mongoose.Connection.name}`)
    );
    mongoose.connection.on('disconnected', () =>
        logger.info(`Disconnected, Connection Name ${mongoose.Connection.name}`)
    );
});

module.exports = App;
```

Figure 9.2: *Importing Logger Service*

Here is the **`app.ts`** file in which the logger is imported and used.

```
class App {

    public express: express.Application;
    private logger: LoggerService


    constructor() {
        this.express = express();
        this.middleware();
        this.routes();
        this.logger = new LoggerService();
    }

    // Configure Express middleware.
    private middleware(): void {...
    }

    private routes(): void {

        this.express.get("/", (req, res, next) => {...
        });

        this.express.use('/api/user', User);
        this.express.use('/api/todos', todos);

        // handle undefined routes
        this.express.use("*", (req, res, next) => {
            this.logger.debug(`Handling unhandled route ${req.path}`)
            res.status(404).send("<h1 style='color:red'>Make sure url is correct!!!</h1>");
        });
    }
}
```

Figure 9.3: *Importing Logger Service in app.ts*

Here is the format of the message we can see in the console after we imported and tested logger service. Note that the Nodemon logs in this screenshot appear differently because they originate from the Library.

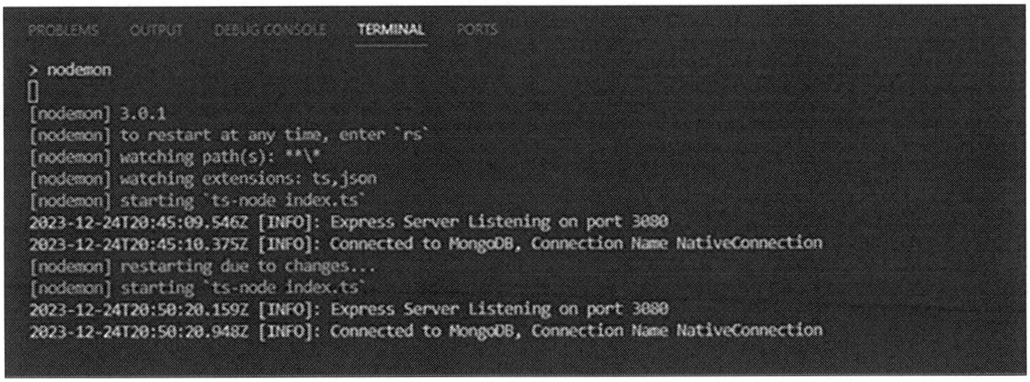

***Figure 9.4**: Console log statements*

In our exploration of the application's logging strategy, we have focused on the utilization of a centralized logger service. The primary benefit of this approach lies in its flexibility and maintainability, particularly when integrating external logging libraries. Centralized logging, as implemented through the **`LoggerService`**, offers a singular point of modification for logging operations. This means that if you decide to switch to a different logging library or change the way logs are processed and formatted, these adjustments need only be made within the **`LoggerService`** itself.

This design philosophy greatly simplifies the task of maintaining and upgrading the logging system. Instead of having to refactor logging code scattered across various parts of the application, all modifications are centralized in one location. Whether it is a shift to a more advanced logging mechanism or a need to adhere to different logging standards, these changes can be efficiently implemented without the need to comb through the entire codebase.

Moreover, by isolating the logging logic in the **`LoggerService`**, the rest of the application remains agnostic to the specifics of the logging implementation. This abstraction not only cleans up the code but also enhances its robustness. Developers can write and update application code with the assurance that logging will consistently behave as expected, regardless of the underlying logging library or mechanism being used.

In essence, the centralized logger service approach streamlines the integration and management of logging within the application, providing a scalable and adaptable logging solution that can evolve with the application's needs. We are going to implement several libraries in the upcoming sections.

Setting Up Logger Service with Pine Library

In the world of Node.js, efficient logging is crucial for tracking application performance, debugging, and monitoring. While there are numerous logging libraries available, Pine stands out for its simplicity and effectiveness. This chapter will explore how to integrate the Pine logging library into a Node.js Express application written in TypeScript, providing practical examples to illustrate its usage and benefits.

Pine is known for its lightweight and straightforward approach to logging, making it an excellent choice for applications that require a no-frills, easy-to-use logging solution. Its simplicity does not compromise on functionality, as it provides all the essential features needed for effective logging in a Node.js environment.

Before diving into the examples, you need to install Pine in your Node.js Express project. This can be done using **`npm`**:

```
npm install pine
```

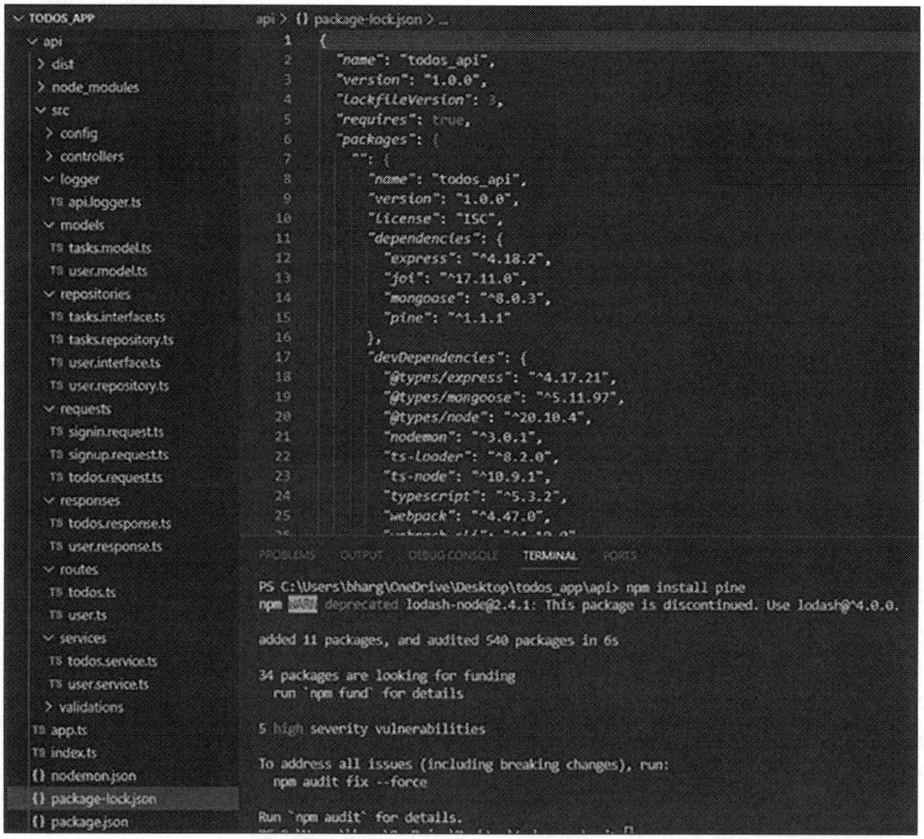

Figure 9.5: *Installing Pine Library*

We must use this library in the Logger Service class so that all the log messages are printed on the console through this library. Here is the implementation of it. This **LoggerService** encapsulates the functionality of Pine to provide a structured and flexible logging system within a Node.js application.

***Figure 9.6**: Integration of Pine Library in Logger Service*

- **Initialization:** The Pine library is imported and used to initialize a logger instance within the **LoggerService** constructor. This initialization sets up the basic configuration for the logger. In this setup, the Pine logger is configured with a specific log level and a custom format function. The log level is set to **'debug'**, which is typically the most verbose level, capturing all levels of log messages (**info**, **warn**, **error**, and **debug**).
- **Custom Format:** The custom format function defined in the Pine configuration specifies how each log message should be structured. It includes a timestamp, the log level (converted to uppercase for consistency and visibility), and the log message itself. This structured format enhances the readability and usability of the logs, especially when reviewing them for debugging or monitoring purposes.

Here are the messages in the console produced by Pine Library.

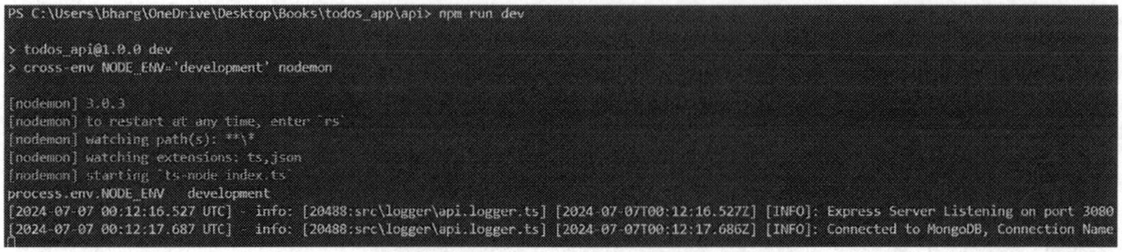

Figure 9.7: *Console Statement with Pine Library*

The Pine library in Node.js is a logging tool known for its simplicity and effectiveness. Like any library, Pine comes with its own set of advantages and disadvantages that can influence its suitability for a particular project.

Advantages of Pine Library

- **Simplicity and Ease of Use:** Pine is straightforward to set up and use, making it ideal for developers who need a no-nonsense, easy-to-implement logging solution.
- **Performance:** Being a lightweight library, Pine has a minimal impact on the performance of an application, which is crucial in high-throughput environments.
- **Customizable Log Formatting:** Pine allows customization of log formats. Developers can define how log messages are structured, which is beneficial for parsing and analyzing logs.
- **Support for Different Log Levels:** Pine supports various log levels (like `info`, `warn`, `error`, and `debug`), allowing developers to categorize log messages based on their importance and nature.
- **Integration with Node.js:** Designed specifically for Node.js applications, Pine integrates seamlessly, ensuring a smooth logging experience in Node.js environments.
- **Better Readability of Logs:** The ability to customize log formats leads to more readable logs, which is essential for debugging and monitoring applications.

Disadvantages of Pine Library

- **Limited Features Compared to Other Libraries:** Compared to more robust logging libraries like Winston or Bunyan, Pine might lack some advanced features such as custom transports, extensive configuration options, or built-in support for distributed logging.
- **Less Community Support:** Being less popular than some other logging libraries, Pine might have a smaller community, which can impact the availability of external plugins, extensions, and community support.

- **Not Ideal for Complex Logging Requirements:** For applications with complex logging needs, such as detailed log analysis, centralized logging in microservices architecture, or custom log routing, Pine might not be sufficient.
- **Lack of Built-in Log Rotation:** Unlike some other logging libraries, Pine might not offer built-in log rotation features, which can be a drawback for long-running applications that generate large log files.
- **Limited Integration with External Tools:** In cases where integration with external monitoring or log analysis tools is required, Pine's simplicity might limit its effectiveness compared to more feature-rich libraries.

Pine library offers a refreshingly simple yet powerful way to handle logging in a Node.js Express TypeScript application. Its ease of use and flexibility make it a great choice for both small-scale projects and larger applications that require straightforward logging capabilities. By integrating Pine, you ensure that your application has a reliable and efficient way to record and manage log data, which is essential for monitoring, debugging, and maintaining the health of your application.

Setting Up Logger Service with Pino Library

Among the various logging libraries available, Pino stands out for its performance and simplicity. This chapter explores the integration of Pino, a fast and low-overhead logging library, into a Node.js Express application using TypeScript. We will cover the basics of setting up Pino, delve into its key features, and provide practical examples to illustrate its usage.

Pino is designed to be as efficient as possible, which means it can handle logging at high speeds without significantly impacting application performance. This efficiency makes Pino an excellent choice for applications where performance is crucial. Additionally, Pino's API is straightforward, making it easy to use while still offering the flexibility to be customized for more complex logging needs.

Before diving into the examples, you need to install Pino in your Node.js Express project. This can be done using `npm`:

```
// install pino library
npm install pino
// install type definitions
npm install -D @types/pino
```

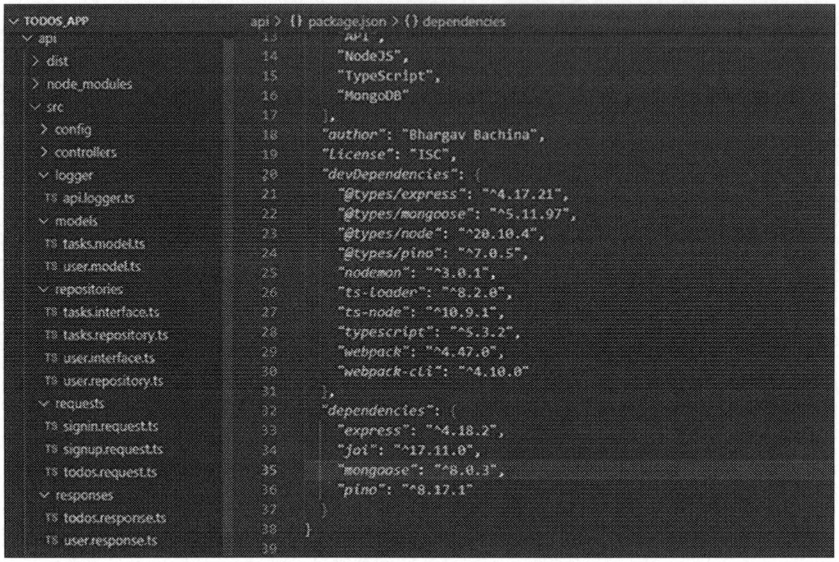

Figure 9.8: *Installing Pino Library*

We should integrate the Pino library within the Logger Service class, ensuring that all log messages within our application are processed and outputted via this library. Below is the detailed implementation of this approach. The **`LoggerService`** class, in this context, harnesses the capabilities of Pino to offer a well-structured and adaptable logging framework suitable for a Node.js environment.

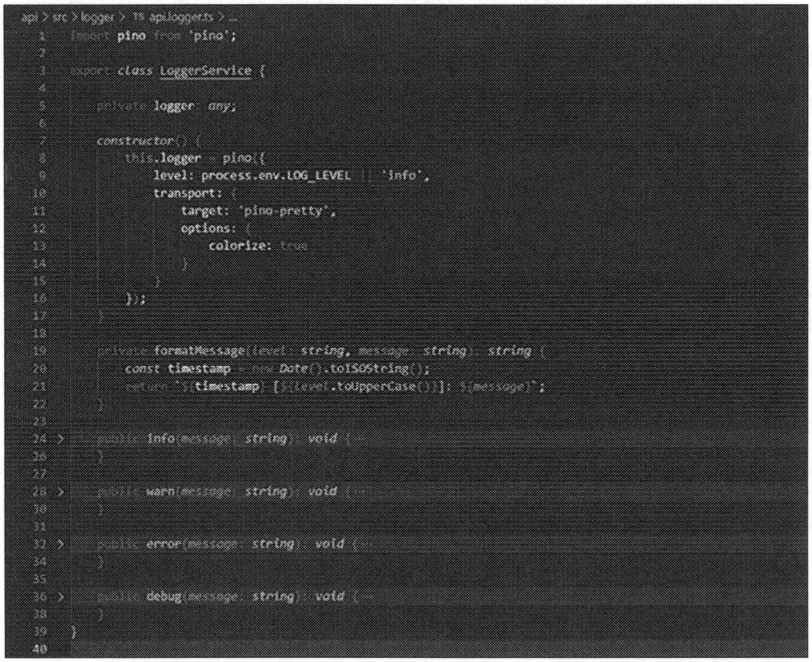

Figure 9.9: *Integration of Pino Library in LoggerService*

The above code showcases the integration of the Pino Library into a custom **LoggerService** class in our application. This class is designed to encapsulate logging functionalities and offer a structured approach to logging across the application.

Integration of Pino Library

- **Pino Import and Logger Initialization:** The Pino library is imported at the beginning of the file. In the constructor of the **LoggerService** class, a Pino logger instance is created with specific configurations. The **pino** function call initializes the logger.
- **Configuration of Pino Logger:** The logger is configured with a log level, which defaults to **'info'** but can be overridden by an environment variable (**process.env.LOG_LEVEL**). This flexibility allows for easy adjustment of logging verbosity depending on the environment (development, staging, production). Additionally, the **transport** option is set to use '**pino-pretty**', a module that formats the logs to be more human-readable, complete with colorization for better visibility and distinction of log levels.

Custom Logging Methods

- **Formatting Log Messages:** The **formatMessage** private method is designed to structure the log messages uniformly. It takes a log level and a message, prepends a timestamp to the message, and formats the level to uppercase, providing consistency across all logs.
- **Log Level Methods:** The class exposes four public methods: **info**, **warn**, **error**, and **debug**, each corresponding to a different log level. These methods utilize the formatted message from **formatMessage** and then call the appropriate logging method on the Pino logger instance (**this.logger.info**, **this.logger.warn**, and so on). This setup allows for logs to be categorized appropriately based on their severity and purpose.

Here are the messages in the console produced by Pino Library.

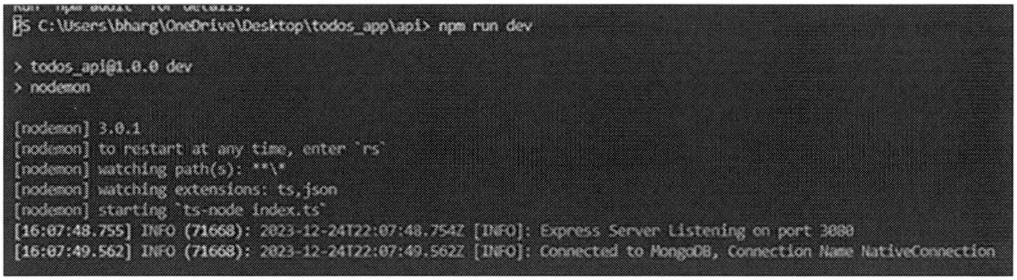

***Figure 9.10**: Console statements with Pino Library*

Pino is a widely used logging library for Node.js known for its performance and simplicity. Like any library, it has its own set of strengths and limitations. Understanding these can help determine if Pino is the right choice for a particular project.

Advantages of Pino Library

- **High Performance:** Pino is designed for speed and efficiency. It has a low overhead, making it one of the fastest logging libraries available for Node.js. This is particularly beneficial for high-load applications where logging could potentially impact performance.
- **Structured Logging:** Pino supports structured logging, which outputs logs in a JSON format. This structure is highly beneficial for modern log management solutions as it makes parsing and querying logs easier and more efficient.
- **Customizable:** Pino allows a high degree of customization. Users can define custom log levels, formats, and transports according to their application's needs.
- **Ecosystem Compatibility:** Pino is compatible with a range of Node.js frameworks and tools, making it a versatile choice for many Node.js applications.
- **Child Loggers:** Pino supports the concept of child loggers, enabling the creation of logger instances with their own configurations. This is useful for large applications where different modules or components may have distinct logging requirements.
- **Pretty Printing:** For development environments, Pino offers pretty-print capabilities, enhancing the readability of logs during the development process.

Disadvantages of Pino Library

- **Learning Curve:** While Pino is generally straightforward, its rich feature set and customization options can present a learning curve for new users, especially those unfamiliar with structured logging.
- **Limited Built-in Transports:** Unlike some other logging libraries, Pino does not come with a wide range of built-in transports. External modules or additional configurations are often required for log storage and management solutions.
- **Too Verbose in Default Setting:** Pino's structured logging (JSON format) can be overly verbose for simple debugging purposes or in situations where human-readable logs are preferred.
- **Complexity in Log Processing:** While JSON logs are excellent for machine parsing, they may require additional tools or services for log analysis, which can add complexity to the logging infrastructure.
- **No Built-In Log Rotation:** Pino does not have built-in log rotation capabilities. This means that for file-based logging, external tools or additional configurations are necessary to manage log file sizes.

Pino is a powerful logging library for Node.js applications, ideal for scenarios where performance is a critical concern. Its support for structured logging and customization makes it a flexible choice for complex applications. However, the benefits of Pino's performance and structure come with considerations around log verbosity, management, and the potential need for additional tools for log processing and rotation. As with any technology choice, it is crucial to weigh these factors against the specific requirements and context of your project.

Setting Up Logger Service with Bunyan Library

Bunyan is a popular and versatile logging library for Node.js applications. It is particularly known for its JSON logging format and its ability to create child loggers. In this chapter, we will explore how to set up a Logger Service using the Bunyan library in a Node.js Express application written in TypeScript. This set up will illustrate how to effectively utilize Bunyan's features to enhance the logging capabilities of your application.

Bunyan provides structured logging in JSON format, which is ideal for modern application logging where logs might need to be processed by various tools for monitoring, alerting, and analysis. The structured nature of Bunyan logs makes them highly queryable and suitable for large-scale applications. Furthermore, Bunyan's support for child loggers allows for more granular control over logging, making it easier to trace and debug issues in specific parts of your application.

Before diving into the examples, you need to install **Bunyan** in your Node.js Express project. This can be done using **`npm`**:

```
// install bunyan library

npm install bunyan

// install Type Definitions

npm install -D @types/bunyan
```

Incorporating the Bunyan library into the Logger Service class is a strategic approach to centralize and enhance the logging mechanism within a Node.js application. This integration ensures that all logging activities throughout the application funnel through Bunyan, leveraging its robust and versatile logging capabilities. The subsequent sections will provide a detailed implementation guide for this integration.

By utilizing **Bunyan** within the **`LoggerService`** class, we tap into a rich set of features that Bunyan offers – structured logging in JSON format, customizable log levels, and the ability to create child loggers. This integration not only standardizes the logging output across the application but also enriches it with the detailed and queryable logs that Bunyan produces.

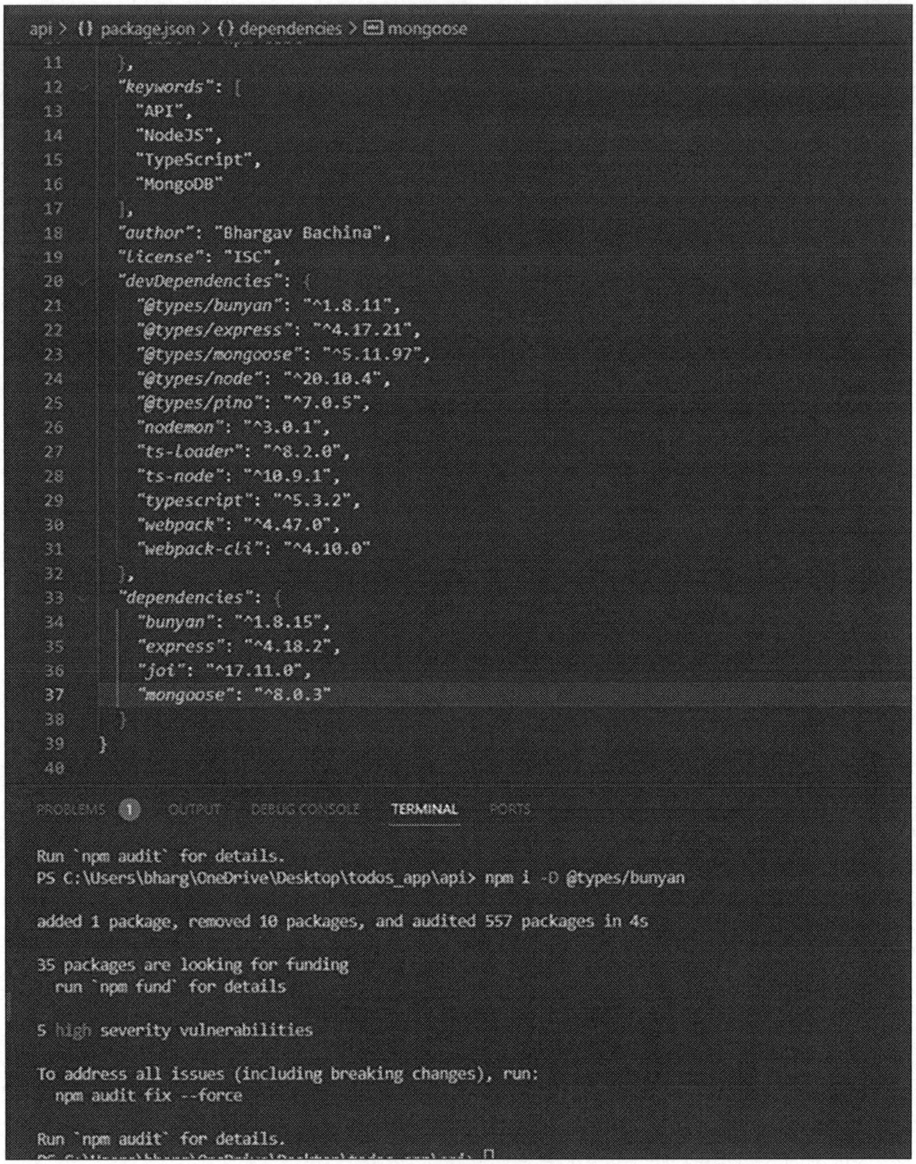

Figure 9.11: *Installing bunyan library*

Bunyan's structured approach to logging, where each log entry is a JSON object, makes logs more informative and easier to analyze. This is particularly beneficial in complex applications where understanding the context and sequence of events is crucial for debugging and monitoring. Furthermore, the `LoggerService` class acts as a wrapper around Bunyan's functionalities, providing a unified interface for logging. This encapsulation means that any change in the logging library or its configuration needs to be done only in the `LoggerService`, without affecting the rest of the application's code. It simplifies maintenance and enhances the scalability of the logging system.

In essence, the **LoggerService** class, empowered by Bunyan, becomes a powerful tool for logging in Node.js environments, offering flexibility, detailed insights, and ease of use. This setup is particularly advantageous for applications that require comprehensive logging for effective monitoring, debugging, and analysis.

```
api > src > logger > TS api.logger.ts > LoggerService > constructor > streams
import bunyan from 'bunyan';

// Custom serializer for request object
const reqSerializer = (req: any) => {
    return {
        method: req.method,
        url: req.url,
        headers: req.headers
    };
};

export class LoggerService {

    private logger: any;

    constructor() {
        this.logger = bunyan.createLogger({
            name: 'myapp',
            serializers: {
                req: reqSerializer
            },
            streams: [
                {
                    level: process.env.NODE_ENV === 'production' ? 'error' : 'debug',
                    stream: process.stdout
                },
                {
                    level: 'error',
                    path: './logs/error.log' // log ERROR and above to a file
                }
            ]
        });
    }

    private formatMessage(level: string, message: string): string {···
    }

    public info(message: string): void {···
    }

    public warn(message: string): void {···
    }

    public error(message: string): void {···
    }

    public debug(message: string): void {···
    }
}
```

Figure 9.12: *Integration of Bunyan Library in LoggerService*

The above code illustrates the implementation of a **LoggerService** class in a Node.js application, integrating the Bunyan logging library. This class is designed to manage and streamline the application's logging process, utilizing Bunyan's advanced features.

Integration and Configuration of Bunyan

- **Initialization with Bunyan:** The class initializes a Bunyan logger within its constructor. Bunyan is known for its powerful and efficient logging capabilities, particularly suitable for structured logging in JSON format.
- **Custom Serializer for Requests:** A custom serializer function **`reqSerializer`** is defined to handle the logging of HTTP request objects. This function takes a request object and returns a simplified version containing the method, URL, and headers. Such serialization is crucial for capturing relevant request details in the logs without logging unnecessary or sensitive information.
- **Logger Configuration:** The Bunyan logger is meticulously configured with several key parameters to optimize its functionality: it is named **`'myapp'`**, symbolizing the application or logger's identity; it incorporates a custom serializer, specifically for HTTP request objects, enhancing log detail and clarity; and it is set up with dual log streams for output. The first stream directs log output to the console, adapting its verbosity based on the **`NODE_ENV`** environment variable–capturing only **`'error'`** level logs in production and **`'debug'`** level logs otherwise. The second stream focuses on persistently recording **`'error'`** level logs to a file located at **`./logs/error.log`**, ensuring crucial error information is retained for thorough examination and analysis.

Logger Service Methods

- **Log Formatting:** The **`formatMessage`** method formats each log message to include a timestamp, the log level (in uppercase), and the message content. This consistent formatting enhances the readability and standardization of logs.
- **Logging Methods:** The service exposes four methods – **`info`**, **`warn`**, **`error`**, and **`debug`** – each corresponding to a different log level. These methods format the message using **`formatMessage`** and then log it using the appropriate Bunyan logging method.

Here are the messages in the console produced by Bunyan Library.

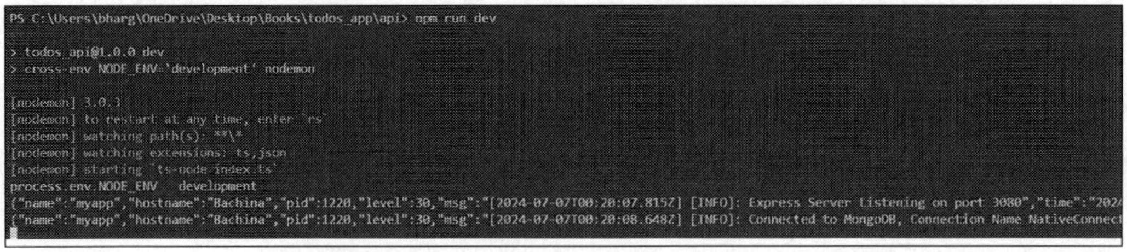

Figure 9.13: *Console Statements with Bunyan Library*

The Bunyan library offers a high degree of flexibility in tailoring log outputs to specific requirements. It enables the definition of custom serializers, allowing fine-tuned control over how certain log record properties are formatted and displayed.

Additionally, Bunyan supports the configuration of multiple streams, providing the capability to route logs to various destinations based on your logging strategy. This versatility extends to several other customizable aspects, enhancing the overall logging experience. Let us understand the advantages and disadvantages of this library.

Advantages of Bunyan Library

- **Structured Logging:** Bunyan produces log output in JSON format, which is ideal for modern logging strategies where logs need to be easily parsed and processed by various tools.
- **Highly Configurable:** It offers extensive customization options, including custom serializers, multiple logging levels, and stream configurations. This flexibility allows for detailed control over what is logged and how.
- **Child Loggers:** Bunyan supports the concept of child loggers, enabling more granular logging within different parts of an application. Each child logger can have its context and settings.
- **Integration with External Systems:** Thanks to its JSON output, Bunyan integrates well with log management and analysis systems, making it suitable for complex applications and microservices architectures.
- **Readable Logs in Development:** While Bunyan focuses on JSON logging, it also offers pretty-printing options for development, making logs more human-readable.
- **Community Support:** Bunyan has good community support, with numerous plugins and extensions available to extend its core functionality.

Disadvantages of Bunyan Library

- **Complexity:** Due to its extensive configuration options, Bunyan can be complex to set up and manage, especially for beginners or in simple applications where such configurability might be overkill.
- **Performance Overhead:** While Bunyan is efficient, the structured logging in JSON format can introduce more overhead compared to simpler logging solutions, particularly in high throughput environments.
- **Log Management Requirements:** The JSON format, while excellent for machine processing, often requires additional tools or services for log analysis and management, potentially increasing the complexity of your logging infrastructure.
- **Learning Curve:** Given its range of features and configurability, there can be a significant learning curve to effectively use all of Bunyan's capabilities.
- **File Size Considerations:** JSON logs, especially when verbose, can grow significantly in size, necessitating proper log rotation and management strategies.

Bunyan is a powerful logging library for Node.js applications that require structured logging and extensive customization. Its ability to produce detailed, machine-readable logs makes it an excellent choice for large-scale and complex applications. However, for smaller projects or scenarios where simplicity and minimal overhead are key, a lighter logging solution might be more appropriate. As with any technology choice, it is important to assess your specific requirements and constraints to determine if Bunyan is the right fit.

Setting up Logger Service with Winston Library

Winston is one of the most versatile and popular logging libraries available for Node.js. Known for its flexibility and customizability, it allows developers to log messages in various formats and transport them to different storage devices. This chapter focuses on integrating the Winston library into a Node.js Express application written in TypeScript, demonstrating how to set up a comprehensive logging service.

Winston stands out for its ability to support multiple transports, that is, different places where your logs can be stored, such as files, databases, or remote services. It also offers flexibility in log formatting and supports multiple logging levels, making it an excellent choice for both development and production environments.

Before diving into the examples, you need to install **`winston`** in your Node.js Express project. This can be done using npm with the following commands.

```
// install winston library

npm install winston
```

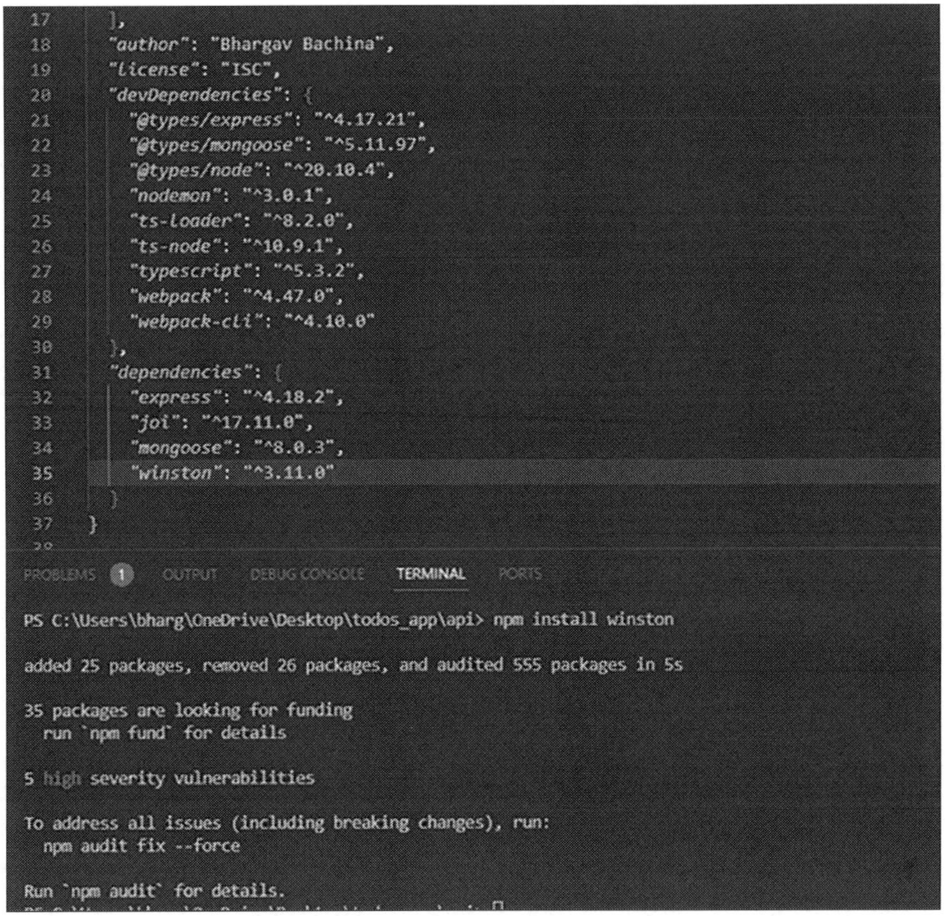

Figure 9.14: *Installing Winston Library*

Incorporating the Winston library into the **`LoggerService`** class is a strategic decision that centralizes the logging mechanism of a Node.js application, ensuring uniformity and efficiency in handling log messages. This integration guarantees that all logging within the application is funneled through Winston, taking advantage of its robust features. The sections that follow provide a comprehensive guide on how to implement this integration effectively.

By embedding Winston within the **`LoggerService`** class, the application benefits from Winston's advanced logging capabilities. Winston is known for its ability to produce well-structured, customizable logs and to support various logging levels and outputs, making it a versatile choice for diverse logging needs. The **`LoggerService`** class, equipped with Winston, becomes a powerful tool for logging, offering a cohesive and flexible logging solution.

In summary, embedding the Winston library in the **`LoggerService`** class provides a scalable and adaptable logging framework, aligning well with the needs of a

Node.js environment. This setup ensures that the application's logging system is not only effective in capturing detailed logs but also adaptable to evolving requirements, thereby enhancing the overall quality and maintainability of the application.

Figure 9.15: *Integration of Winston Library in LoggerService*

The above code demonstrates the implementation of a `LoggerService` class in Node.js, using the Winston logging library. This class encapsulates the logging functionality, providing a structured and unified way to handle logging throughout a Node.js application.

Implementation Details of the `LoggerService` Class

- **Logger Initialization with Winston:** The constructor of the `LoggerService` class initializes a Winston logger. Winston is a popular logging library in the Node.js ecosystem, known for its versatility and configurability.
- **Logger Configuration**
  - **Level:** The logger's level is set to `'info'`, which means it will capture log messages of `'info'` level and above (including `'warn'`, `'error'`, and `'debug'`).

- **Format:** The format combines a timestamp and a **`printf`** function. The timestamp is formatted as **`'YYYY-MM-DD HH:mm:ss'`**, making it readable and useful for tracking when events occur. The **`printf`** function structures each log message to include the timestamp, the log level, and the log message.
- **Transports:** Two transports are defined:
  - **Console:** Logs are output to the console, making them visible during development or when running the application.
  - **File:** Logs are also written to a file named '**`combined.log`**'. This ensures that log data is persisted and can be analyzed later.

- **`LoggerService` Methods:** The class defines four methods – **`info`**, **`warn`**, **`error`**, and **`debug`**, corresponding to different logging levels. These methods are public and can be called from anywhere in the application to log messages at the respective levels. Each method takes a message string as a parameter and logs it using the Winston logger instance.

Here are the messages in the console produced by Bunyan Library.

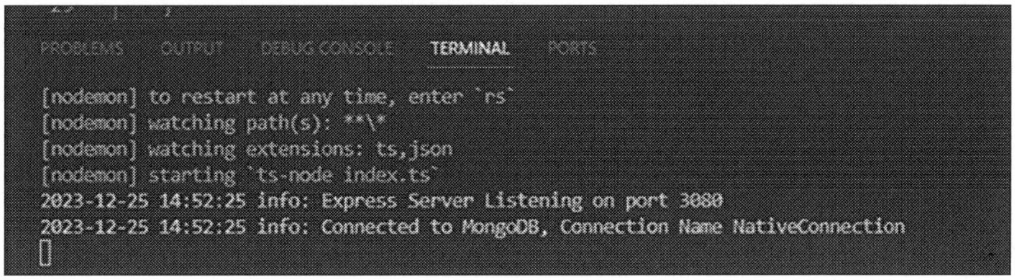

Figure 9.16: *Console Statements with Winston Library*

We can also see these messages in a separate log file called **`combined.log`** which is the name given in the **`configuration`** class.

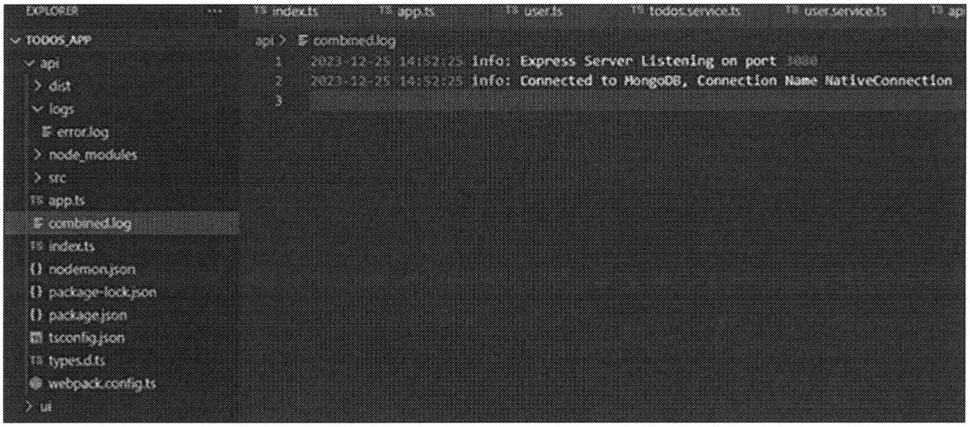

Figure 9.17: *Console Statements in combined.log*

The Winston library provides extensive adaptability in customizing log outputs to meet specific needs. It allows for the creation of custom formats, granting precise control over the presentation and structure of log record properties. Moreover, Winston is known for its ability to configure multiple transports, offering the flexibility to direct logs to a variety of destinations, aligning with diverse logging strategies. This level of customization is further complemented by various other configurable features Winston offers, significantly enriching the logging experience. In the following sections, we will delve into the benefits and drawbacks of using the Winston library.

Advantages of Winston Library

- **Versatility in Transport Management:** Winston allows logs to be transported to various destinations, including console, files, databases, or even remote endpoints. This makes it highly versatile for different logging requirements.
- **Customizable Log Levels:** It supports custom log levels, enabling developers to define and use logging levels that are best suited to their application's needs.
- **Flexible Log Formatting:** Winston offers the ability to format logs in various ways. Developers can create custom formats, making logs readable and suitable for different environments and use cases.
- **Rich Integration Options:** Being a popular library, it integrates well with many other Node.js tools and frameworks, making it a robust choice for complex applications.
- **Support for Multiple Loggers:** Winston allows the creation of multiple logger instances, each with its own configuration. This is particularly useful in large applications with varied logging needs across different modules.
- **Stream Integration:** It can be integrated with Node.js streams, offering more complex and sophisticated logging mechanisms.

Disadvantages of Winston Library

- **Complexity:** With its extensive features and configurations, Winston can be complex to set up and manage, particularly for beginners or in simple applications where such complexity is unnecessary.
- **Performance Overhead:** While Winston is efficient, its advanced features, especially when logging at a verbose level or with multiple transports, can introduce a performance overhead.
- **File Management:** In scenarios where logs are written to files, developers need to manage log rotation and to archive themselves, as Winston does not handle this out of the box.
- **Learning Curve:** Understanding and effectively utilizing all of Winston's features can require a significant learning curve, especially for those new to logging concepts.

- **Dependency Management:** As with any third-party library, using Winston introduces external dependencies into your project, which requires ongoing maintenance and updates.

Winston's powerful logging capabilities make it a top choice for Node.js developers. Its ability to log in different formats and transport logs to various locations makes it suitable for applications of any scale. By following the steps and examples in this chapter, you can effectively implement Winston in your TypeScript-based Express API, enhancing your application's logging strategy with a robust, flexible, and reliable solution. However, its complexity and potential performance impact might be overkill for smaller projects or those with simpler logging needs. It is important to assess the specific requirements of your project to determine if Winston aligns well with your logging strategy.

Conclusion

Throughout this exploration of logging in Node.js APIs, we have uncovered the pivotal role that logging plays in the development and maintenance of robust applications. From understanding the fundamental importance of logging to implementing a Logger Service in a Node.js API, each step has contributed to a deeper appreciation of this essential practice. We have journeyed through various logging libraries – **Pine**, **Pino**, **Bunyan**, and **Winston** – each offering unique features and capabilities. Pine and Pino, with their simplicity and speed, are well-suited for applications where performance is a key concern. Bunyan's structured logging in JSON format shines in scenarios requiring detailed log analysis, while Winston stands out for its versatility and rich configuration options. The selection of a logging library and the implementation of a Logger Service significantly enhance the observability, debuggability, and overall health of an application.

As we conclude this chapter on logging, it is evident that effective logging is not just a tool for developers but a cornerstone for maintaining the health and integrity of any application. It provides critical insights into the behavior of applications, aids in quick debugging, and ensures a smooth operational flow.

With a solid understanding of logging in place, we are well-equipped to move forward to the next crucial stage of our journey – building both the frontend and backend for a MEVN (MongoDB, Express.js, Vue.js, Node.js) stack geared for production. In the upcoming chapter, we will delve into the intricacies of developing and fine-tuning a full-stack application. We will explore best practices for structuring and optimizing both the client-side and server-side components, ensuring that they not only work seamlessly together but are also optimized for performance, security, and scalability in a production environment.

Chapter 10
Building MEVN Stack for Production

Introduction

In this chapter, we venture into optimizing and streamlining the development process of the MEVN stack (MongoDB, Express.js, Vue.js, Node.js). Our journey will traverse through essential tools and methodologies that elevate the efficiency and quality of your web applications. Emphasizing practicality, each section is designed to provide you with actionable insights and techniques tailored for the MEVN stack.

We begin by discussing the significance of externalizing environment variables, a crucial step for enhancing security and maintaining project scalability. The introduction of task runners like Gulp and Grunt follows, highlighting their role in automating repetitive tasks and ensuring a smooth workflow. We then delve into the intricacies of building both the frontend and backend using Webpack, demonstrating how to optimize and bundle your application's assets effectively.

The latter part of the chapter focuses on combining these elements into a cohesive unit. We explore how to use Gulp to merge frontend and backend builds into a single deployable entity and delve into the practicalities of adding NPM scripts to simplify and automate various development tasks. Lastly, we emphasize the importance of code quality and consistency, introducing Husky for implementing pre-commit hooks, ensuring that your codebase remains clean and error-free.

By the end of this chapter, you will be equipped with the knowledge to not only develop MEVN stack applications more efficiently but also to maintain a high standard of code quality and project manageability. These skills are vital in the modern web development landscape, where efficiency and reliability are paramount.

Structure

In this chapter, the following topics will be covered:

- Building Frontend and Serving Through API

- Externalize Environment Variables
- Building Backend with Webpack
- Running MEVN Stack on HTTPS
- Securing API
- Global Exception Handler
- Linting
- Configure Husky for Pre-Commit Hooks
- Introduction to Task Runners Such as Gulp, Grunt
- Generate a Final Build Zip File with npm Scripts

Building Frontend and Serving Through API

Building the frontend of an application using Vite, a modern frontend build tool, is a straightforward process. Vite is designed to offer a simpler and faster development experience for modern web projects. To compile your frontend application and prepare it for deployment, you typically need to execute a build command provided by Vite. This command processes your application's source code, optimizes it, and outputs the static assets into a directory, commonly named **`dist`**.

The command to build your frontend with **`Vite`** is as follows:

```
vite build
    or
npm run build
```

In our specific scenario, which involves a Vue 3 project built with TypeScript, the process outlined in the **`package.json`** differs slightly. When you run the second command as specified in the **`package.json`**, it takes into account the unique requirements and configurations of a Vue 3 TypeScript project.

When you run this command, Vite performs several actions:

1. **Compilation:** It compiles the source code, transforming and bundling JavaScript modules, Vue components, CSS, and other assets.
2. **Optimization:** **`Vite`** optimizes the application for production. This includes minification (to reduce file sizes), tree-shaking (to eliminate unused code), and potentially other performance enhancements.
3. **Output:** The processed and optimized files are then outputted to the **`dist`** directory. This directory contains all the static files needed to deploy your

application, such as HTML files, JavaScript bundles, CSS stylesheets, and any other assets.

4. **Ready for Deployment:** The contents of the **`dist`** folder are what you deploy to your server. These static files are optimized for fast loading and performance, making them ideal for production environments.

In this project, the frontend build process is initiated by running a specific command that compiles the application and generates the production-ready static assets into the **`dist`** directory. As illustrated in the provided figure, executing this build command via the terminal results in the creation of an **`index.html`** file along with associated JavaScript and CSS assets in the **`dist`** folder.

Upon examining the **`index.html`** file, you can observe that all the necessary scripts are properly referenced with **`<script>`** tags, and the stylesheet is linked using a **`<link>`** tag. These include the compiled JavaScript modules and the application's stylesheet, which are now optimized for production.

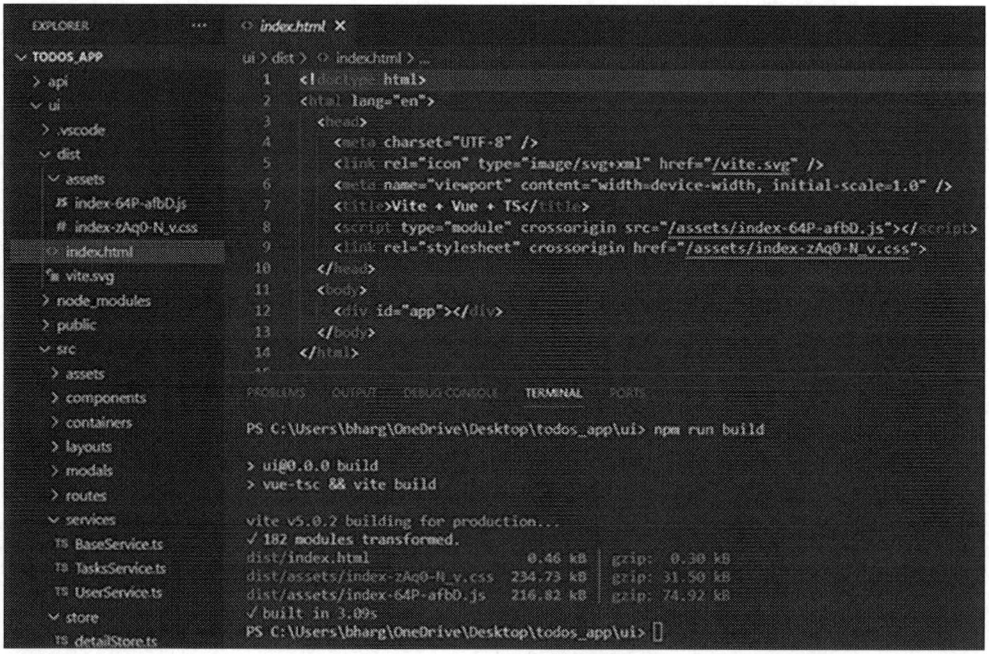

Figure 10.1: *index.html*

A noteworthy detail in the **`index.html`** is the presence of a **`<div>`** element with an **`id`** attribute on line 12. This **`id`** corresponds to the mounting point for the Vue 3 application, as specified in the **`main.ts`** file of the project. It is this exact **`id`** where the Vue application is injected, enabling the dynamic rendering of the frontend.

The output in the terminal confirms the completion of the build process, showing the paths to the generated files along with their respective sizes. This indicates a successful build, where the Vue 3 frontend is now compiled and ready to be served from the **dist** directory, demonstrating an efficient and streamlined build process facilitated by Vite for TypeScript-based projects.

In summary, building a frontend application with Vite is a simple yet efficient process. By just running the **vite build** command, you can quickly prepare your application for production, ensuring it is optimized for performance and ready for deployment. This ease of use and efficiency makes Vite an increasingly popular choice for modern web development projects.

Serving UI Assets Through API

The process of building a Vue 3 frontend with the **vite build** command has successfully compiled our application, depositing the resulting assets into the **dist** directory. In the context of constructing a MEVN stack application, our development environment involves running the frontend and backend on separate ports for ease of development and testing. However, as we transition towards production or prepare our application for deployment in higher environments, a unified approach is recommended where the static frontend assets are served through our Express backend API.

This unified approach simplifies deployment, allowing both the user interface and the API to be accessed via a single URL and port, streamlining the user experience, and reducing the infrastructure complexity. In the forthcoming section, we will delve into the specifics of configuring our Express server to serve the frontend static assets. We will explore the necessary steps to integrate the frontend and backend into a cohesive unit that can be run as a singular entity. This integration is a key step in preparing our full-stack MEVN application for a production environment, ensuring that it is optimized for performance, security, and maintainability.

The development setup is not suitable for production environments due to several important considerations. Firstly, **security** is a primary concern. Running an application on multiple ports can expose additional attack vectors. By consolidating the application to run on a single port, we minimize the exposed surface area and streamline security configurations.

Secondly, **infrastructure simplicity** is another advantage. When deploying to production, the goal is to reduce the complexity of the deployment and the number of services to manage. Serving both the UI and the API from the same port allows us to manage a single service rather than coordinating multiple services across different ports. This simplification also extends to load balancing and SSL termination, which can be managed more effectively when all traffic is routed through a single point.

Moreover, **cross-origin resource sharing (CORS)** issues are automatically handled when serving both the frontend and backend from the same domain and port. In development, different ports can lead to CORS errors, requiring additional setup to allow resources to be accessed across different origins. In production, having a single origin eliminates these concerns and streamlines the browser's security model.

Furthermore, **user experience** is enhanced when the application is served from a single port. Users can access the application through a single, clean URL without specifying different ports for different parts of the application. This setup resembles more closely the environment in which users interact with most web applications, providing a cohesive experience without the need for additional navigation or complex URL structures.

To achieve this, the Express server is configured to serve the static assets generated by Vite from the **`dist`** directory. We set up a middleware in Express that directs requests for frontend resources to these static assets. When a user accesses the main URL, they are served the Vue frontend, while API requests are handled by the appropriate Express routes on the same domain and port.

Figure 10.2: *app.ts*

Line 29 tells Express to serve the static files—such as compiled JavaScript, CSS, and HTML from your Vue.js frontend—in the **`dist`** directory, which is the output folder typically generated by frontend build tools. The **`express.static`** middleware is built into Express and is designed to serve static resources. The **`path.join`** function is used to create an absolute path to the **`dist`** directory, ensuring that Express can correctly locate and serve the files regardless of the environment it is running in.

This catch-all route handler at line number 45 is designed to respond to any requests that do not match any of the API routes. Instead of sending a 404 error, it serves the **`index.html`** file from the **`dist`** directory. This is particularly useful for single-page applications (SPAs) built with frameworks like Vue.js, as it allows the frontend routing to handle any specific route requests, ensuring that the SPA functions correctly when the user navigates directly to a URL other than the root.

After configuring our API to serve static assets, accessing the URL **http://localhost:3080**—the designated port for our API—will result in the display of the application's login page. This occurs because Express, upon receiving a request from the browser, utilizes the catch-all route handler to intercept the request. Instead of returning a 404 error for paths not matched by API routes, it serves the **`index.html`** file from our static assets. This file is the entry point for our Vue.js application, enabling the frontend to load and manage subsequent in-app navigation. Essentially, Express acts as a conduit between the client and the static files, ensuring users are presented with the correct interface when they commence their interaction with the application.

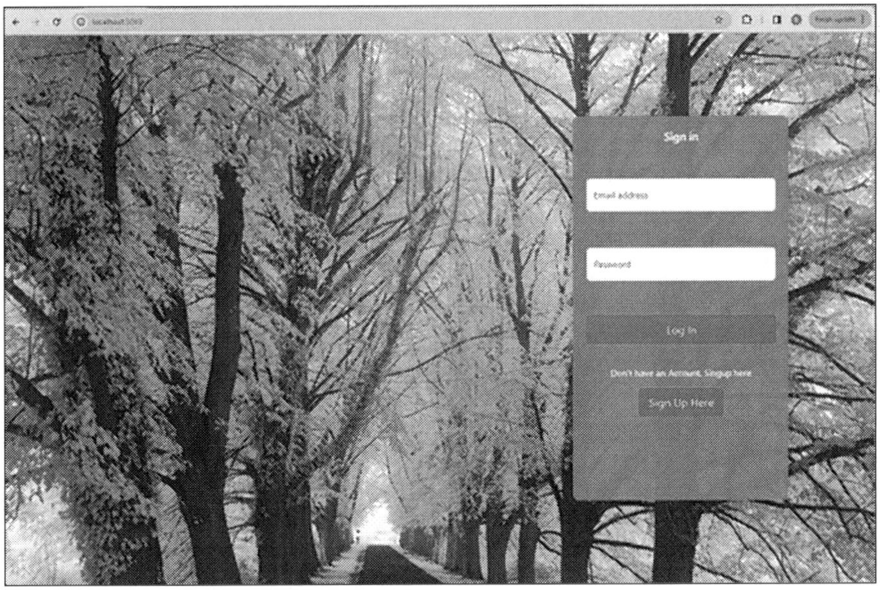

***Figure 10.3**: Serving Home Page through express*

With our Express server now configured to serve the static assets of our Vue.js application, users can interact with the app as they typically would in a production setting. Upon visiting the root URL, users are greeted with the login page. Post-authentication, they are seamlessly directed to the dashboard, where they can access the full range of app features and data.

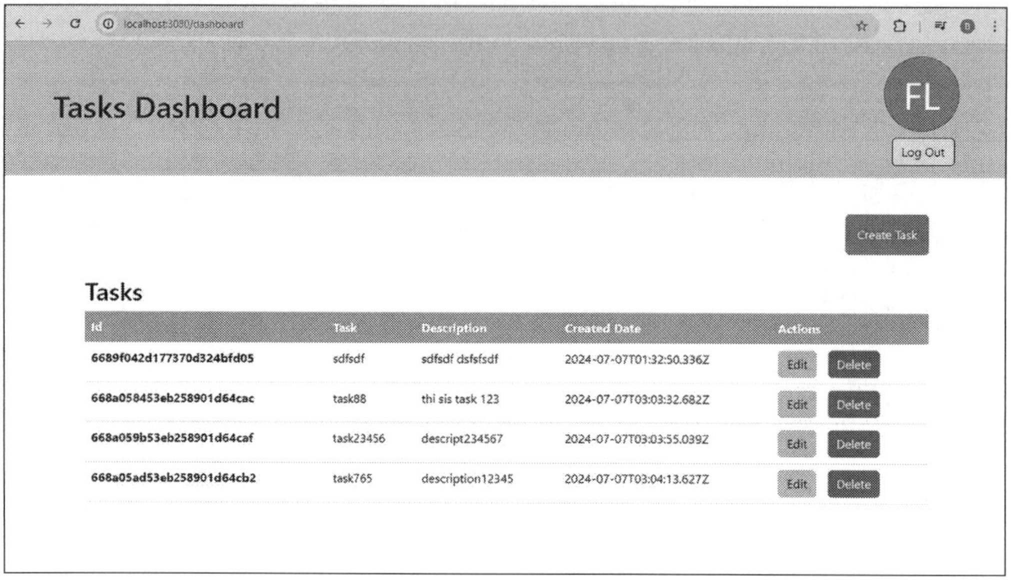

Figure 10.4: *Serving Dashboard through express*

As the users navigate the app, any API requests initiated by the frontend are correctly routed to the corresponding Express API endpoints. This seamless integration ensures that data-driven interactions, such as retrieving dashboard information or submitting forms, function as intended. The server-side logic processes these API requests and communicates back with the frontend, thereby populating the dashboard with dynamic data from the server. This cohesive flow between the frontend and backend illustrates a well-structured full-stack application, providing users with a smooth and uninterrupted experience.

In essence, the strategy of serving the entire MEVN stack on a single port in production is not just a matter of convenience–it is a deliberate decision to enhance security, reduce complexity, and provide a better end-user experience. This approach reflects best practices in deploying modern web applications and is a critical step in the journey from development to a robust production deployment.

Externalize Environment Variables

In the context of our Node.js TypeScript Express API, we encounter a common yet crucial scenario in modern web development – managing environment-specific variables. The nature of these variables is dynamic; they change based on the environment in which the API operates. Consider, for instance, our project that spans across three different environments – development (dev), staging (stage), and production. In each of these environments, certain aspects like the port number on which the API runs or the database it connects to, vary significantly.

The variability of these elements, such as the **`PORT`** and **`MONGO_CONNECTION_STR`** (MongoDB Connection String), poses a challenge. In development, we might run our API on a local port and connect to a database hosted locally. In staging, the port might differ, and the database could be an instance closer to a production-like setup for testing. Finally, in production, both the port and the database would be set to support live traffic and data integrity.

According to the 12-factor app methodology, a robust software application should be designed for continuous deployment, which mandates a build-once, deploy-anywhere approach. This principle implies that the build process should be agnostic of the environment. It means that our application's build should not be tailored specifically for development, staging, or production. Instead, it should be a uniform artifact that can be deployed in any environment without requiring changes.

To align with this methodology in our Node.js TypeScript API, we need to externalize environment-specific variables. In the previous chapter, we developed the complete API, but now we must take the crucial step of externalizing the **`PORT`** and **`MONGO_CONNECTION_STR`** variables. By doing so, we ensure that our API can be built once and then deployed seamlessly across different environments. Externalization is typically achieved through configuration files or environment variables, which can be set differently for each environment without altering the core application code.

This approach not only adheres to the 12-factor app principles but also significantly enhances the flexibility and scalability of our API. It allows us to maintain a single codebase for all environments, reducing complexity and potential for errors, while also streamlining the deployment process. As we proceed, we will explore the practical steps and best practices for externalizing these variables, ensuring our Node.js TypeScript Express API is robust, scalable, and environment-agnostic.

Using the `dotenv` Library

As said earlier, environment variables are essential in a Node.js application for managing configuration settings that should not be hard-coded in the source code, especially sensitive data like database credentials, API keys, and configuration options **`dotenv`** is a zero-dependency module that loads environment variables from a **`.env`** file into **`process.env`** making environment configuration for your development easy and secure. This chapter delves into the practical implementation of **`dotenv`** in a Node.js TypeScript Express API.

To begin integrating the **`dotenv`** library into our project, the initial step involves installing it using a specific command. Given that our focus is solely on constructing the API, and **dotenv** is primarily utilized during the development phase, it is appropriate to install it as a development dependency. This approach aligns with best practices in Node.js development, ensuring that our production environment remains lean and efficient. Installing a package as a development dependency indicates that it is not required in the production environment, but is essential for development tasks such as testing, building, and local configuration management. This distinction is crucial for maintaining an optimal balance between development flexibility and production performance.

```
npm install -D dotenv
```

Once installed, you can start using it by creating a **.env** file at the root of your project. This file should contain key-value pairs of all the environment variables. For example:

Figure 10.5: *dotenv file*

We have these two files in which we are using environment variables such as **PORT** and **Mongo Connection String**. We are using the port at line number 7.

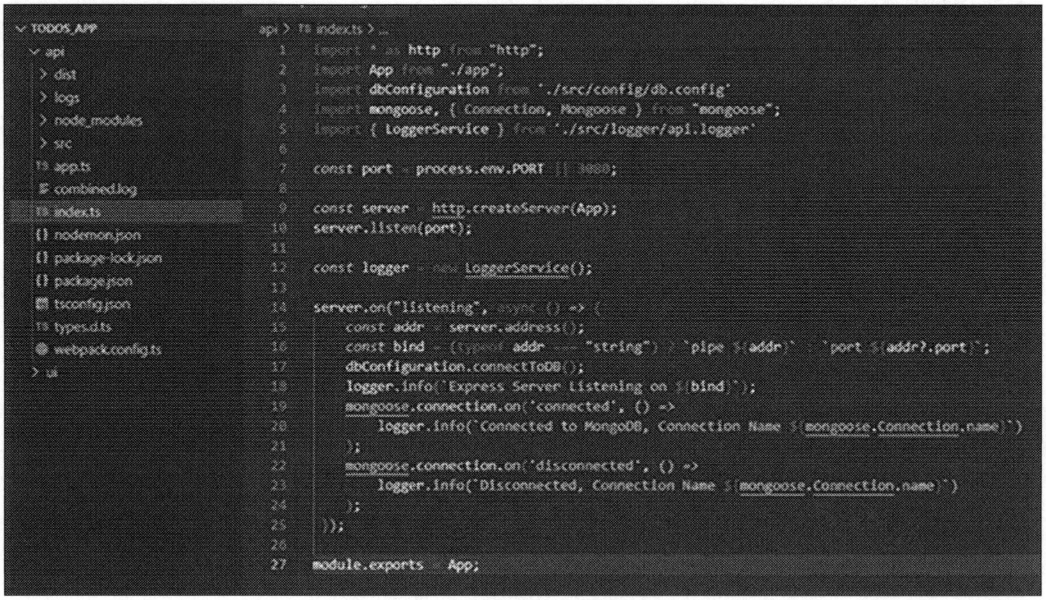

Figure 10.6: *index.ts*

Here is the DB Configuration file in which we are using Mongo Connection String. We are using that at line number 14.

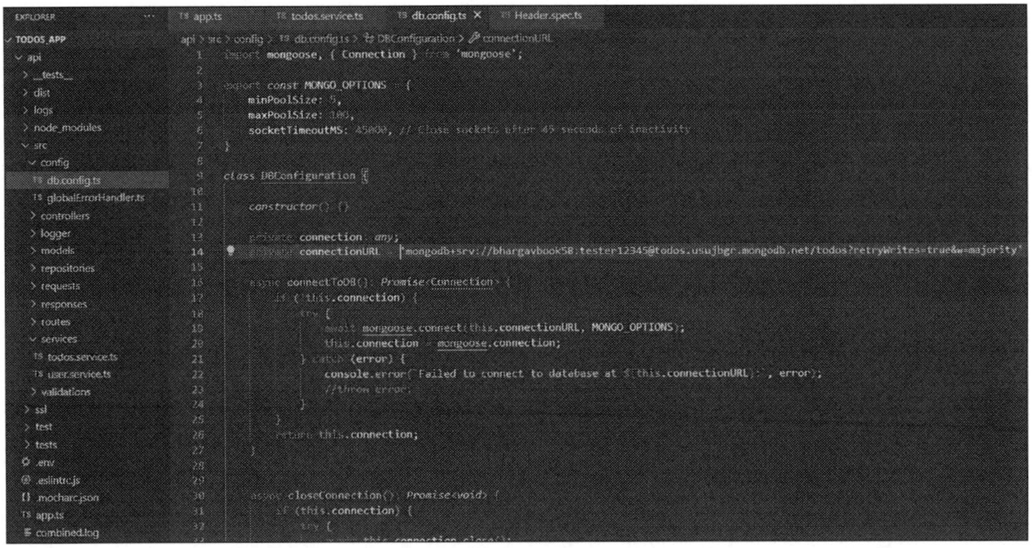

Figure 10.7: *DB Configuration*

Let us create a **.env** file at the root of the API and place these two environment variables in that file as follows.

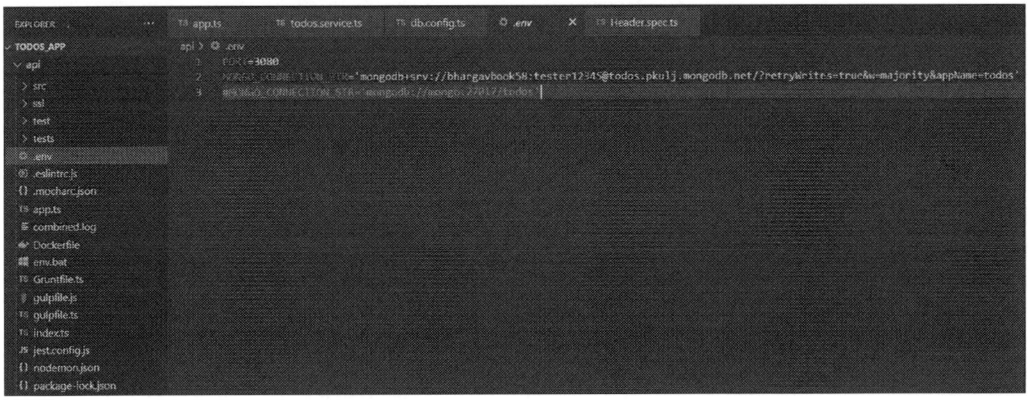

Figure 10.8: *Mongo Connection String*

Incorporating **dotenv** into your Node.js application is a straightforward yet crucial process, particularly focused on the initial set up phase of your project. The core principle here is to ensure that **dotenv** is operational right from the start of your application's lifecycle. This is typically achieved by placing the **dotenv** configuration at the very top of your main application file. In most Node.js projects structured with TypeScript, this file is often named **index.ts** or **app.ts**. In our case, we can place it in the **index.ts** file.

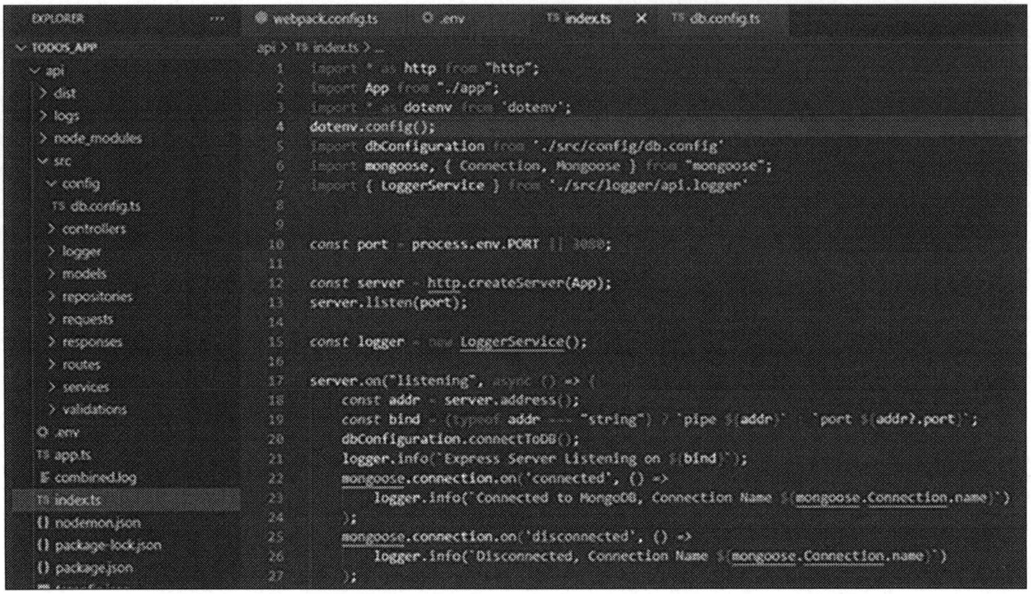

Figure 10.9: *Initializing Connection*

Why at the beginning? The reason is simple yet fundamental. By initializing **`dotenv`** early, you ensure that all environment variables from your **`.env`** file are loaded into **`process.env`** before any other part of your application code executes. This order of operations is crucial because any module or piece of code that requires these environment variables will have access to them as soon as it is imported or executed.

With these lines at the top of your main file, every subsequent import or piece of code that is executed can safely assume that the environment variables are set and accessible via **`process.env`**

Now, you can access these variables anywhere in your application using **`process.env.VARIABLE_NAME`** For instance:

```
const port = process.env.PORT || 3080
```

We are already using this in **`index.ts`**. Let us change the DB configuration file by reading the Mongo Connection String from the **`process.env`**

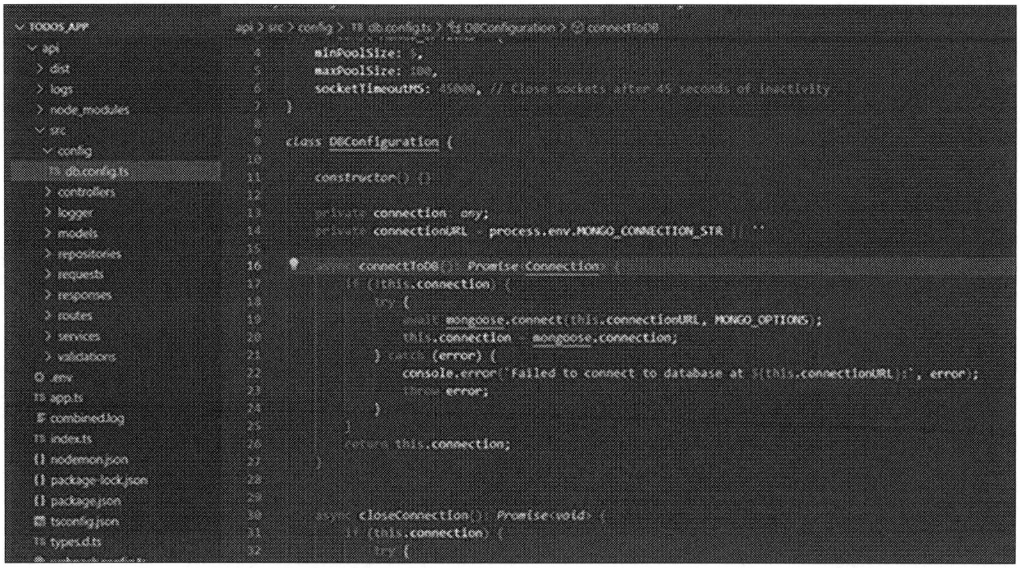

Figure 10.10: *Reading Connection String*

Let us initiate our API and verify its functionality by checking if it successfully reads the environment variables from the **`dotenv`** library. This step is crucial to confirm that the integration of **`dotenv`** is working correctly and the API is operational with the environment-specific configurations applied.

As you can see in the figure that follows, our application is reading the PORT and Mongo Connection String through **`dotenv`** library and is successfully initialized.

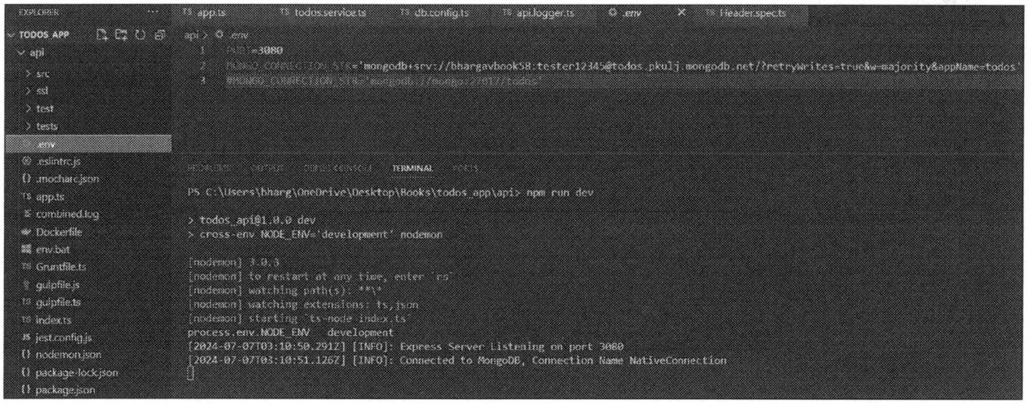

Figure 10.11: *Mongo Connection String*

Now that we have implemented the dotenv library, here are some best practices we can follow.

- **`.env` File Security:** Never commit your **.env** file to version control. Instead, add it to your **`.gitignore`** file. For deployment, use environment variables set in your hosting environment or a secure vault service.
- **`Example.env.example`:** Provide an **`.env.example`** file in your repository with dummy values or placeholders to illustrate the required environment variables without exposing sensitive information.
- **Validating Environment Variables:** Consider adding a validation step for your environment variables, ensuring all required variables are set and in the correct format. Libraries like **`joi`** can be used for this purpose.

`dotenv` is a popular library for managing environment variables in Node.js applications, but there are several other libraries and tools that offer similar functionality. Here are some alternatives:

- **`node-config`:** A configuration management library for Node.js. It lets you define a set of default parameters and extend them for different deployment environments (development, production, and so on). It is more comprehensive than **`dotenv`** as it allows for hierarchical configurations and environment-specific configurations.
- **`cross-env`:** This tool allows you to set and use environment variables across platforms. It is particularly useful if you are working in a cross-platform setting (for example, Windows, Linux, macOS) and need to ensure consistent environment variable behavior.
- **`env-cmd`:** A simple node program for executing commands using an environment from an env file. It is similar to **`dotenv`** but allows you to specify different **.env** files for different environments directly in your **`package.json`** scripts.
- **`configstore`:** This is a handy tool for developers who need to store configuration settings and other data. It is not specifically for environment variables, but it can be used for similar purposes, especially for applications that require more complex configurations.
- **`nconf`:** A hierarchical node.js configuration with files, environment variables, command-line arguments, and atomic object merging. It provides a bit more flexibility in managing configurations.
- **`convict`:** Defines a schema for your configuration and provides utilities for using that schema to load, validate, and manage the configuration in your applications. It supports environment variables and JSON files.
- **`dotenv-expand`**: An extension for **`dotenv`**, which adds the ability to expand variables already on your machine for use in your **`.env`** file.
- **`rc`:** Stands for "**`run commands`**", it is a configuration loader that supports hierarchical configurations derived from files, environment variables, and command-line arguments.

When choosing an alternative, consider the specific needs of your project. Some libraries offer more than just loading environment variables (like hierarchical configurations, type validation, and so on), while others might be simpler and more focused on the task like **`dotenv`**.

By integrating **`dotenv`** into your Node.js TypeScript Express API, you create a flexible, secure, and maintainable way to handle environment-specific settings. This approach not only facilitates local development and testing but also paves the way for scalable and secure production deployments. Remember, handling configuration wisely is key to building robust and secure applications.

Building Backend with Webpack

In the context of developing applications with the MEVN stack, a key practice we have adopted is the externalization of environment variables from the application code. This approach involves separating configuration settings that may vary between different deployment environments (like development, testing, and production) from the main codebase. Such a strategy enhances both security and flexibility. Sensitive data like API keys or database credentials are kept out of the source code, thereby reducing the risk of accidental exposure. It also allows for easier adjustments to the application's configuration without needing to modify the code itself.

When it comes to building the application using Webpack, there are two predominant methodologies:

Build Once and Deploy Everywhere

This method involves creating a singular, unified build of the application, which is then suitable for deployment across all environments. Key aspects of this approach include:

- **Uniformity:** A single, consistent artifact is generated and then moved through the various stages of the deployment pipeline, such as development, staging, and production.
- **Runtime Configuration:** In this set up, environment variables are injected at the time of running the application, rather than during the build process. This could be achieved via a server that hosts the application, or other runtime configuration management tools.

Benefits

- Streamlines the Continuous Integration/Continuous Deployment (CI/CD) process by eliminating the need for multiple builds.
- Minimizes the risk of environment-specific bugs, as the same build is used throughout.

Considerations

- It requires a mechanism to manage and inject configuration settings at runtime, which might add complexity to the deployment set up.
- Not all configurations can be externalized this way and might need additional strategies like feature flags.

Previously, we explored the '*Build Once and Deploy Everywhere*' approach and will now proceed to implement and test this method. The **dotenv** library is employed to externalize configurations like the **PORT** and **MongoDB Connection String**. It is important to note that using **dotenv** for environment configuration is primarily recommended for development purposes. In production, environment variables are typically obtained from the deployment environment itself. For this purpose, specific tools such as Ansible, Chef, or Puppet are used to automate the deployment and manage environment variables across different environments, although these tools will not be covered in this book as they fall outside its scope. Understanding and applying this distinction between development and production settings is crucial for effective application deployment.

First, we need to modify the code to load environment variables from the **.env** file only when your application is running in a development environment. In the code given in *Figure* 10.12, **dotenv** is configured to load the environment variables only if the **NODE_ENV** environment variable is not set to **'production'**. This way, in production environments where environment variables are typically set by the hosting platform or CI/CD pipeline, the **.env** file will not be used, thereby following best practices for security and configuration management.

```
api > TS index.ts > ...

import * as http from "http";
import App from "./app";
if (process.env.NODE_ENV !== 'production') {
    require('dotenv').config();
}
import dbConfiguration from './src/config/db.config'
import mongoose, { Connection, Mongoose } from "mongoose";
import { LoggerService } from './src/logger/api.logger'

console.log('process.env.NODE_ENV  ', process.env.NODE_ENV)

const port = process.env.PORT || 3080;

const server = http.createServer(App);
server.listen(port);
```

Figure 10.12: *app.ts*

In the logs provided, the appearance of '**undefined**' in the console output for the **NODE_ENV** environment variable indicates that this variable has not been set. Typically, the **NODE_ENV** variable is used to specify the environment in which a Node.js application is running, such as **'development'**, **'production'**, or **'test'**. The absence of a defined value for **NODE_ENV** means that it defaults to **'undefined'**, reflecting that it has neither been set in the code nor passed as an environment variable during the application's runtime. This is a common scenario in development environments where setting **NODE_ENV** might not be a priority, but in production, it is crucial to set this variable for proper environment-specific configurations.

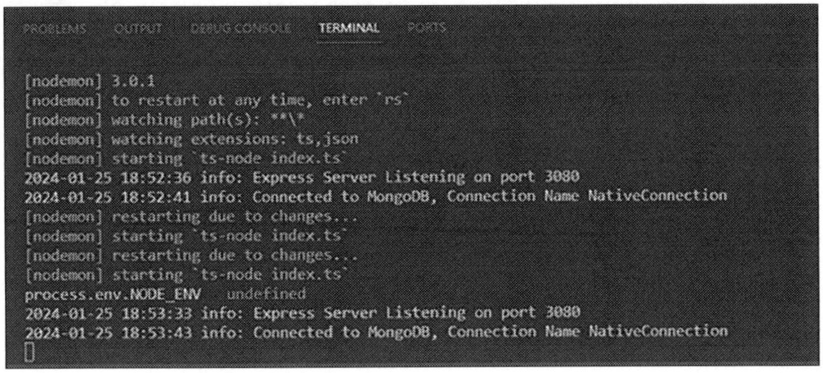

Figure 10.13: NODE_ENV *undefined*

We can set the environment variable in our script using the **cross-env** library. This tool allows us to specify environment variables in a script across different operating systems seamlessly.

Figure 10.14: *passing NODE_ENV from scripts*

Upon examining the figure provided, it is evident that the application fails to read environment variables from the **.env** file when **NODE_ENV** is set to **'production'** in the script. This results in a MongoDB connection error, due to the absence of the correct connection string. This scenario serves as a demonstration of how the **dotenv** library functions are in tandem with the appropriate setting of the node environment. It highlights the importance of correctly configuring environment variables, especially in differentiating between development and production settings.

To make the API work like before by reading all these environment variables, we need to set environment variables in the Node Environment in which the API is running like the way we set the **NODE_ENV** variable. We can do it through scripts, or we can do it manually. Although there are many ways to set the environment variables, we are just using the **set** method below.

```
// setting environment variables in Node Environment

set PORT=3080

set MONGO_CONNECTION_STR=<connection string>
```

To start the **api** with these settings in production, we can proceed as follows:

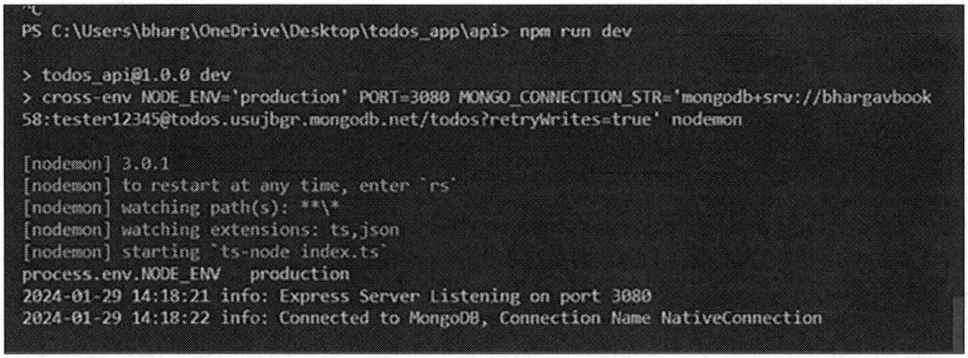

Figure 10.15: *Running API*

In previous discussions, we explored the process of setting environment variables in production environments without relying on external libraries. Initially, it is crucial to build the API using Webpack. This approach streamlines the deployment process by eliminating the need to transfer the entire set of folders and files to the production environment. Instead, with Webpack, we can compile and bundle the API into a few output files. This method not only simplifies deployment but also optimizes the application for production use.

We have already introduced Webpack in earlier chapters, outlining its significance in modern web development. Webpack serves as a powerful tool for bundling and optimizing assets and code. It plays a key role in the '*Build Once, Deploy Everywhere*' methodology, which is particularly effective for environments where consistency between development and production set ups is essential.

```
api > webpack.config.ts > output
const path = require('path');
const nodeExternals = require('webpack-node-externals');

module.exports = {
  // Set the environment for Node.js
  target: 'node',

  // Define the entry point for the application
  entry: {
    app: ['./index.ts'] // Point to your main TypeScript file
  },

  // Define output settings
  output: {
    path: path.resolve(__dirname, 'dist'),
    filename: 'api.bundle.js'
  },

  // Resolve .ts and .js files
  resolve: {
    extensions: ['.ts', '.js'],
  },

  // Exclude node_modules from the bundle
  externals: [nodeExternals()],

  // Use ts-loader to handle TypeScript files
  module: {
    rules: [
      {
        test: /\.ts$/,
        use: 'ts-loader',
        exclude: /node_modules/,
      },
    ],
  },
};
```

Figure 10.16: *webpack.config.ts*

This Webpack configuration file starts by importing necessary Node.js modules and a package to handle Node-specific externals. The configuration is set to target a Node.js environment, ensuring that the output is optimized for server-side execution. The entry point of the application is specified as **`./index.ts`**, indicating where Webpack should begin its bundling process. This is typically the main TypeScript file of the Node.js application. For the output configuration, it is defined to emit the bundled file in the **`dist`** directory, with the filename **`api.bundle.js`**. This setup directs Webpack to compile the TypeScript files, along with any JavaScript files, and bundle them into a single file in the specified directory.

To handle file resolution, the configuration is set up to recognize both **`.ts`** and **`.js`** extensions. This allows the bundler to process both TypeScript and JavaScript files, providing flexibility in using various file types within the project. Finally, the configuration includes a module section with rules for processing TypeScript files. The **`ts-loader`** is used for this purpose, and it is configured to exclude the **`node_modules`** directory to prevent bundling of external dependencies. This results in a more streamlined and efficient bundle, suitable for production deployment in a Node.js environment.

After executing the command below, Webpack compiles the code and outputs the resulting file into a directory named **`dist`.** This process is depicted in the subsequent figure, showcasing the outcome of the build operation performed by Webpack.

```
// command runs webpack
npm run build
```

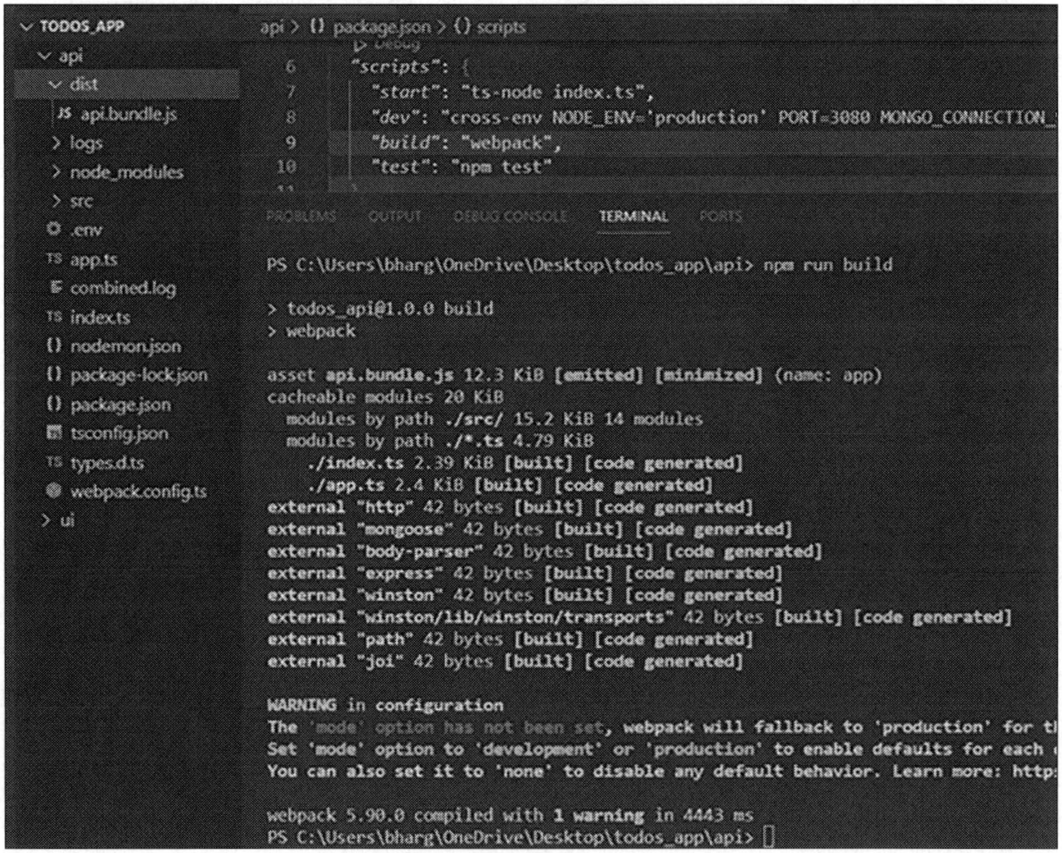

***Figure 10.17**: building with webpack*

Upon building the assets, they are stored in the **`dist`** folder. However, when attempting to run the command **`node dist/api.bundle.js`**, an error occurs indicating the absence of a connection string. This issue arises because the necessary environment variables, including the database connection string, are not being passed to the application.

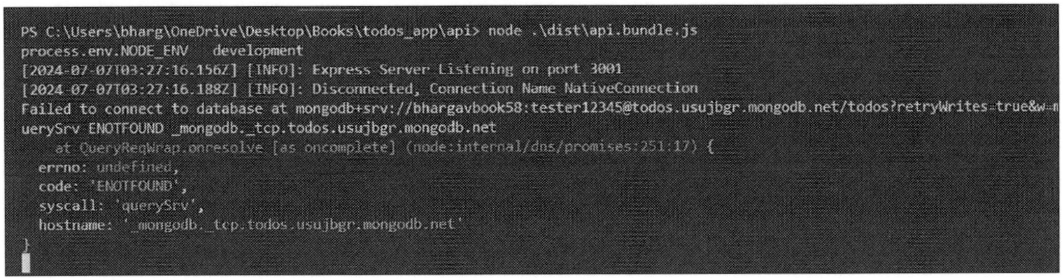

Figure 10.18: *Running without environment variables*

By including the necessary environment variables in conjunction with the **`node dist/api.bundle.js`** command, the API begins to function smoothly without encountering any errors. This ensures that all required configurations, such as the database connection string, are correctly provided to the application at runtime.

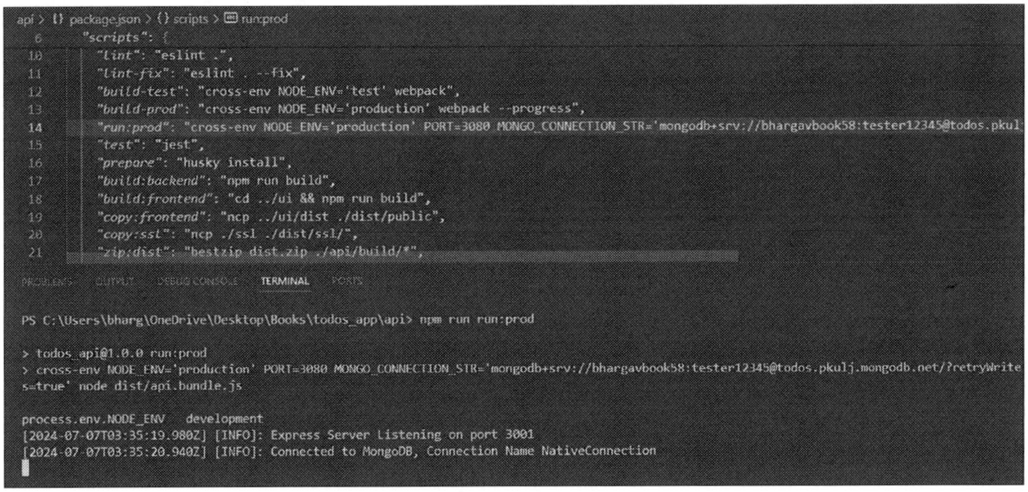

Figure 10.19: *Running with environment variables*

To conclude, our approach has been focused on building code that is not tied to any specific environment. This allows us to deploy the same build across different environments by simply passing in the relevant environment variables at the time of deployment. This strategy aligns with the "*build once, deploy anywhere*" methodology, significantly enhancing deployment flexibility.

The task of injecting these environment variables at runtime is typically handled by specialized tools like Puppet, Chef, or Ansible. These tools are designed to manage and automate the deployment process, ensuring that the correct configurations are applied based on the environment. While the intricacies of these tools are beyond the scope of this book, their role is crucial in facilitating a seamless and efficient deployment process, integral to modern software development practices.

Build for Each Environment

Alternatively, this approach involves generating distinct builds for each deployment environment, incorporating the specific configurations for each during the build phase. Characteristics of this method include:

- **Environment-Specific Artifacts:** Separate build processes are conducted for each environment, embedding the relevant environment variables during the build.
- **Compile-Time Configuration:** Here, the environment settings are integrated directly into the build at the time of compilation, necessitating distinct build processes for each environment.

Benefits

- Offers high customization for each environment, accommodating substantial differences in configurations or application behavior.
- Useful in scenarios where the differences between environments are too significant to handle with runtime configuration.

Considerations

- Introduces complexity into the CI/CD pipeline, as it requires managing multiple builds.
- Increases the potential for inconsistencies between environments, possibly leading to environment-specific issues.

Choosing between these two approaches hinges on the specific requirements and constraints of your project. The '*Build Once and Deploy Everywhere*' model is generally favored for its simplicity and consistency, especially when the variations between environments are minimal and can be managed through runtime configuration. On the other hand, the '*Build for Each Environment*' approach might be more suitable for scenarios where the environments have significant differences that need to be reflected in the application behavior or configuration.

Now that we have a clear understanding of the '*Build for Each Environment*' method, it is time to apply this knowledge to our example project. This approach involves tailoring the build process to each specific environment, ensuring that the configuration and dependencies are optimized for the characteristics of that environment. By implementing this method, we can fine-tune our application to meet the unique requirements and constraints of each deployment setting, whether it be development, staging, or production. Let us proceed to integrate this methodology into our project, demonstrating how it enhances the adaptability and performance of the application across different environments.

Webpack's **`DefinePlugin`** is a crucial tool in this method, as it allows you to define global constants at compile time which can be configured and accessed throughout your application. This is particularly useful for setting environment-specific variables that can alter the behavior of your code depending on whether it is in a development, testing, or production environment.

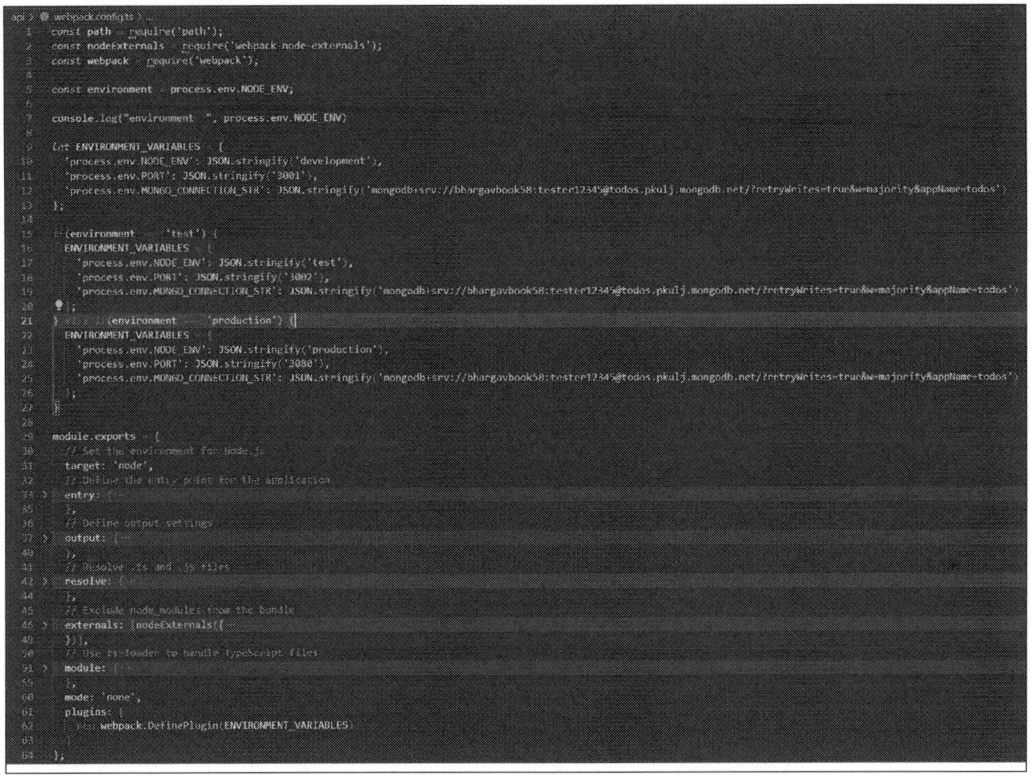

***Figure 10.20**: Defining Environment Variables*

In *Figure 10.20*, the **`webpack.DefinePlugin`** is utilized, which plays a pivotal role in setting global constants for the application at compile time. The **`ENVIRONMENT_VARIABLES`** object is first declared with a default set of environment variables, tailored for the development environment. This includes settings for **`NODE_ENV`**, **`PORT`**, and **`MONGO_CONNECTION_STR`**.

Based on the current value of **`process.env.NODE_ENV`**, the script adjusts the **`ENVIRONMENT_VARIABLES`** object. For instance, if the environment is set to **`'test'`**, the object is modified to reflect test environment settings, including a different port and possibly a different database connection string. Similarly, for a production environment, the variables are adjusted accordingly.

Finally, in the Webpack configuration object, the **`plugins`** array includes an instance of **`webpack.DefinePlugin`**, initialized with the **`ENVIRONMENT_VARIABLES`** object. This plugin effectively embeds these variables into the bundle created by Webpack. When the application is compiled, these constants are made available globally, allowing the application to access different settings based on the environment it is running in.

Having configured environment variables in the **`webpack.config.ts`**, our next step involves passing the Node environment explicitly during the build process. To facilitate this, we need to add specific scripts to the **`npm scripts`** section of our **`package.json`** file. These scripts will enable us to execute distinct build commands for each environment.

For example, we can create separate npm scripts for development, testing, and production builds. Each script will set the **`NODE_ENV`** to the appropriate environment and then execute the Webpack build as shown in the following figure. This ensures that the right set of environment variables, as defined in the **`webpack.config.ts`**, are incorporated into the build process.

When we run the application post-build, particularly after building it for a specific environment like testing, the application will reflect and operate based on the environment variables set for that environment. For instance, if we have a different database URL or server port specified for the test environment, the running application will use these test-specific configurations as we see in the following console statements (*Figure* 10.21):

Figure 10.21: *Building Code with webpack definePlugin*

Through our examples, we have delved into two distinct deployment strategies: – *Build for Each Environment* and *Build Once, Deploy Everywhere*. These methods offer different approaches to managing and deploying applications, and the choice between them depends on the specific requirements and constraints of the project.

The '*Build for Each Environment*' method involves creating separate builds for each environment (development, test, production, and so on), with each build tailored to the specific settings and configurations of that environment. This approach can be advantageous when each environment has significantly different requirements or when the highest level of optimization for each specific setting is necessary.

On the other hand, the '*Build Once, Deploy Everywhere*' strategy focuses on creating a single, universal build that can be deployed across all environments. This method is particularly useful for simplifying the deployment process and ensuring consistency across different stages of the application lifecycle. It can save time and resources, as the same build is reused, reducing the need for environment-specific adjustments.

As you decide which approach to adopt for your project, consider factors like the complexity of your application, the differences between your environments, and the resources available for maintaining multiple builds. While '*Build for Each Environment*' offers customization for each specific setting, '*Build Once, Deploy Everywhere*' streamlines and simplifies the deployment process.

In conclusion, both methods have their merits and can be effectively employed depending on your project's needs. Assessing your application's requirements and your team's workflow will guide you in choosing the most feasible and beneficial approach for your situation.

Running MEVN Stack on HTTPS

Up until this point, our MEVN Stack application has been operating over HTTP, a protocol that does not encrypt data transmitted between the web browser and the Node.js server. This lack of encryption poses a security risk, as information can be intercepted by unauthorized parties. In contrast, for production environments, it is standard practice to utilize HTTPS—a secure communication protocol that encrypts data in transit, safeguarding against potential eavesdropping and data tampering. HTTPS is the preferred and secure method for data exchange between a browser and a Node.js server.

In the forthcoming section, we are going to delve into the process of configuring our application to run over HTTPS on localhost. Although the ideal approach for a production setup involves acquiring an SSL certificate from a recognized Certificate Authority (CA) such as '*Let's Encrypt*', for the purposes of local development and testing, we will demonstrate how to generate and use a self-signed certificate. This temporary solution allows us to simulate a secure HTTPS environment on our local development machine, offering a closer approximation to the security level of the production set up.

Step1: Generate a Self-Signed SSL Certificate

To run a MEVN (MongoDB, Express, Vue, Node.js) stack application over HTTPS, we need to set up an SSL certificate and configure your Node.js server to serve content over HTTPS. Given under is a step-by-step guide to achieve this, using a self-signed certificate for development purposes. For production environments, you should obtain a certificate from a trusted CA.

First, we need to open the terminal or command prompt and navigate to your project directory or a specific directory for storing your certificates. Run the following OpenSSL command to create a private key and a self-signed certificate:

```
// Run this command on Mac terminal
openssl req -nodes -new -x509 -keyout server.key -out server.cert
```

For Windows users, the equivalent process involves using OpenSSL as well, as OpenSSL is available for Windows. However, you might need to download and install OpenSSL if it is not already installed on your system. Once OpenSSL is installed on your Windows machine, you can use the same command in the Windows Command Prompt (**`cmd`**) or PowerShell to generate a self-signed SSL certificate and private key:

Go to the official OpenSSL binaries page or a trusted source to download the OpenSSL installer for Windows. Once installed, we can run the same command to create self-signed certificates under the directory **`ssl`**.

Figure 10.22: *openssl command prompt*

This process will generate **`server.key`** (the private key) and **`server.cert`** (the self-signed certificate) files in the directory **`ssl`**.

***Figure 10.23:** openssl certificates*

Step2: Configure Your Node.js Server for HTTPS

Modify your Express server setup to use the HTTPS module along with the generated SSL certificate.

1. Install the HTTPS module if your project does not already include it. Note that the HTTPS module is built into Node.js, so you typically do not need to install anything extra.
2. Modify your server setup script **`index.ts`** to include the HTTPS module and use the generated certificate and key.

This is achieved by importing the https module from Node.js, contrasting with the http module which facilitates communication over an unencrypted channel. The application reads SSL certificate (**`server.cert`**) and private key (**`server.key`**) files from the filesystem, which are essential for establishing a secure HTTPS connection. These files are located within the **`./ssl`** directory and are loaded using Node.js's fs module. The certificate and key are then used to create HTTPS server credentials. An HTTPS server is instantiated with these credentials and the Express app (App), ensuring that all incoming and outgoing communications are encrypted. This setup is particularly crucial for environments beyond development, such as staging or production, where data security is paramount. The server is configured to listen on a port defined by the

process.env.PORT environment variable, or defaults to 3080 if the variable is not set, thereby starting the secure server and making the application accessible over HTTPS.

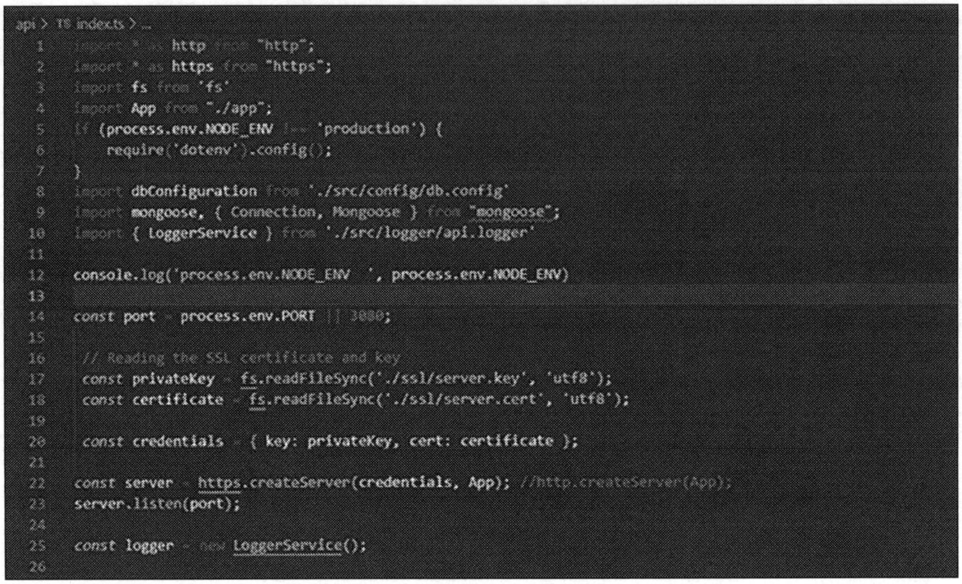

```
api > TS index.ts > ...
import * as http from "http";
import * as https from "https";
import fs from 'fs'
import App from "./app";
if (process.env.NODE_ENV !== 'production') {
    require('dotenv').config();
}
import dbConfiguration from './src/config/db.config'
import mongoose, { Connection, Mongoose } from "mongoose";
import { LoggerService } from './src/logger/api.logger'

console.log('process.env.NODE_ENV ', process.env.NODE_ENV)

const port = process.env.PORT || 3080;

 // Reading the SSL certificate and key
 const privateKey = fs.readFileSync('./ssl/server.key', 'utf8');
 const certificate = fs.readFileSync('./ssl/server.cert', 'utf8');

 const credentials = { key: privateKey, cert: certificate };

const server = https.createServer(credentials, App); //http.createServer(App);
server.listen(port);

const logger = new LoggerService();

```

Figure 10.24: *running server on https*

Step 3: Access Your Application Over HTTPS

Open your web browser and navigate to **https://localhost** or your configured domain. Since you are using a self-signed certificate, the browser will likely warn you about the site's security certificate.

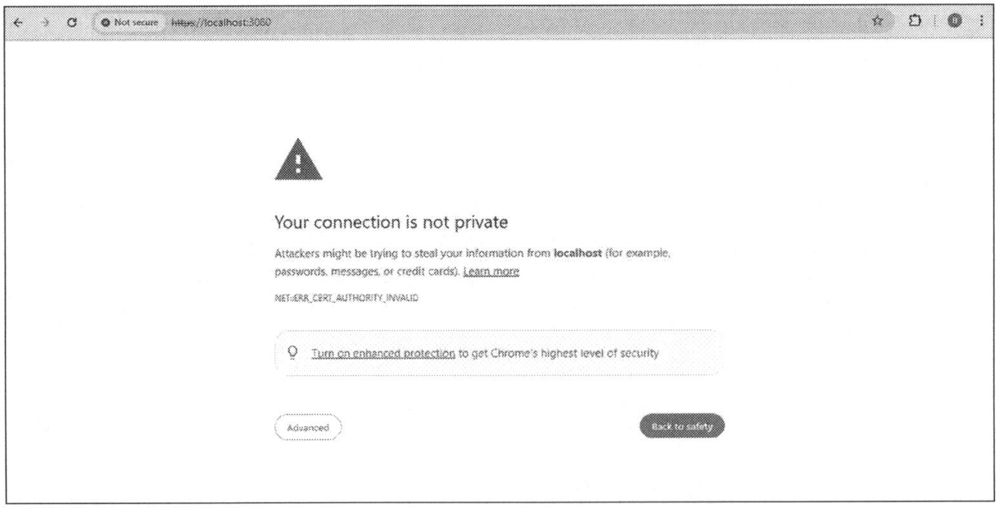

Figure 10.25: *Browser Warning*

This is expected with self-signed certificates. You can proceed by allowing an exception in your browser.

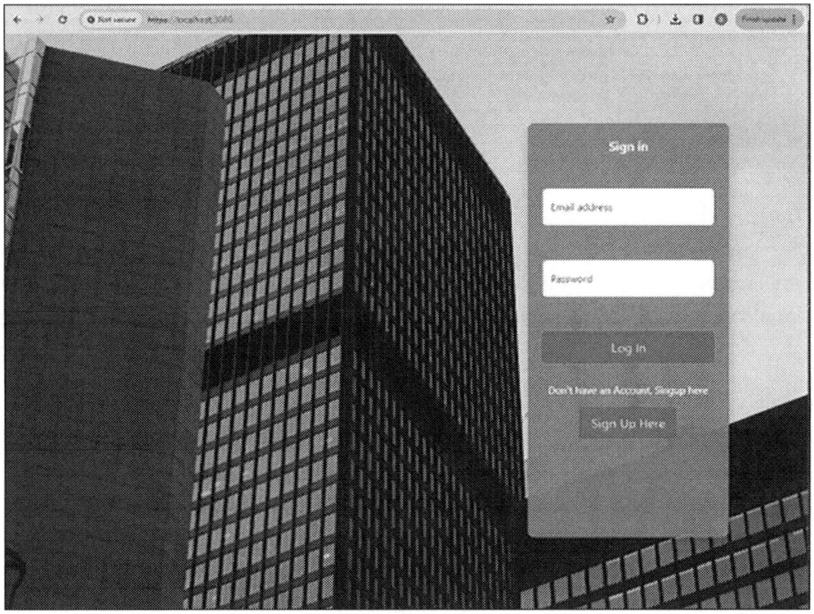

Figure 10.26: *Accessing the application on HTTPS*

Important Notes for production

- For a production environment, it is recommended to obtain an SSL certificate from a trusted CA like '*Let's Encrypt*', which offers free certificates.
- You might also consider using a web server like Nginx or Apache as a reverse proxy that handles HTTPS. This allows your Node.js app to run over HTTP locally, while Nginx/Apache manages the SSL/TLS part. This set up is common in production environments for performance and security reasons.
- Ensure to redirect HTTP traffic to HTTPS to enforce secure access.

Transitioning a MEVN (MongoDB, Express, Vue, Node.js) stack application to run over HTTPS is a significant step towards enhancing its security and protecting the data exchanged between the server and its clients. This process involves setting up an SSL/TLS certificate, configuring the Node.js server to use HTTPS, and ensuring all communications are encrypted.

To recap, the key steps to achieve this include generating or obtaining an SSL certificate, configuring the Express server to use this certificate for HTTPS communication, and adjusting any client-side configurations to ensure they respect the HTTPS protocol. For development purposes, a self-signed certificate can suffice, but for production environments, it is crucial to obtain a trusted certificate from a Certificate Authority (CA) like 'Let's Encrypt'.

Implementing HTTPS not only secures your application against eavesdropping and data tampering but also boosts user trust and potentially improves search engine rankings. It is a best practice and, increasingly, a user expectation for modern web applications. As you move forward, remember to keep your certificates updated and to monitor your application for any emerging security vulnerabilities continuously.

Securing API

In the digital age, APIs (Application Programming Interfaces) have become fundamental to software development, enabling different systems to communicate and exchange data. As APIs often expose business logic and sensitive data, they become prime targets for malicious attacks. Therefore, securing APIs is not just an option; it is an imperative.

Securing an API involves implementing measures to ensure confidentiality, integrity, and availability of the data it handles. This includes protecting the API from common security threats identified by organizations like OWASP (Open Web Application Security Project) as well as adhering to legal and regulatory requirements.

Here are some of the key areas we can focus:

- **Authentication:** Authentication is the first line of defence in securing an API. It involves verifying the identity of a client or user. Common methods include username and password, token-based authentication (like JWT - JSON Web Tokens), and OAuth.
- **Authorization:** Authorization is a crucial aspect of securing APIs, ensuring that only authorized users or systems can access protected resources and perform specific actions. It involves verifying the identity and permissions of clients attempting to interact with the API and enforcing access control based on predefined rules or policies.
- **Encryption and Hashing:** Protecting data at rest and in transit to prevent unauthorized access and ensure data integrity.
    - **Encryption** is used to protect data in transit (like HTTPS) and data at rest, ensuring that even if data is intercepted or accessed, it remains unreadable without the proper key.
    - **Hashing** is used primarily for storing passwords securely. A good hashing algorithm ensures that passwords cannot be easily reversed or decoded.
- **Helmet:** Helmet helps secure Express.js applications, an integral part of the MEVN stack. It sets various HTTP headers to mitigate common vulnerabilities, such as cross-site scripting (XSS) and clickjacking.
- **CORS (Cross-origin Resource Sharing):** CORS is a security feature that manages how resources on a web server can be requested from another domain. It is a crucial aspect of API security as it prevents unwanted cross-domain requests while allowing legitimate ones.

- **CSRF Protection (Cross-Site Request Forgery protection):** CSRF attacks trick a user into performing actions they did not intend to in a web application where they are authenticated. CSRF protection involves creating and validating tokens that accompany each client request, ensuring the request is legitimate.
- **Rate Limiting:** Rate limiting controls the number of requests a user or system can make to an API in each time frame. It is essential for preventing overuse or abuse of the API, particularly protecting against brute-force attacks and DDoS (Distributed Denial of Service) attacks.

Implementing Helmet

Implementing Helmet in a Node.js application using TypeScript is a straightforward process that enhances the security of your application by setting various HTTP headers. Helmet is a middleware for Express.js that can help protect your app from some well-known web vulnerabilities by setting HTTP headers appropriately.

Helmet is not just a single middleware, but rather a collection of several smaller middleware functions that collectively set HTTP response headers. These headers are pivotal in protecting against a range of well-known web vulnerabilities.

- **XSS Protection:** Helmet sets headers that help protect against Cross-Site Scripting (XSS) attacks, which are among the most common security threats to web applications.
- **Clickjacking Prevention:** It includes headers to mitigate clickjacking attacks, where users are tricked into clicking something different from what they perceive.
- **HSTS:** Helmet enforces strict HTTP transport security. This security measure ensures that browsers only communicate with the server over HTTPS, preventing SSL stripping attacks.

```
// install helmet
npm install helmet
// install helmet type definitions
npm install -D @types/helmet
```

Once you run the preceding commands, you should see those dependencies added to your `package.json`.

In the `middleware()` method of our `App` class, Helmet is integrated with a simple call `this.express.use(helmet())`. This line of code is deceptively simple yet significantly powerful. By invoking Helmet here, we instruct our Express application to employ the various security measures provided by Helmet.

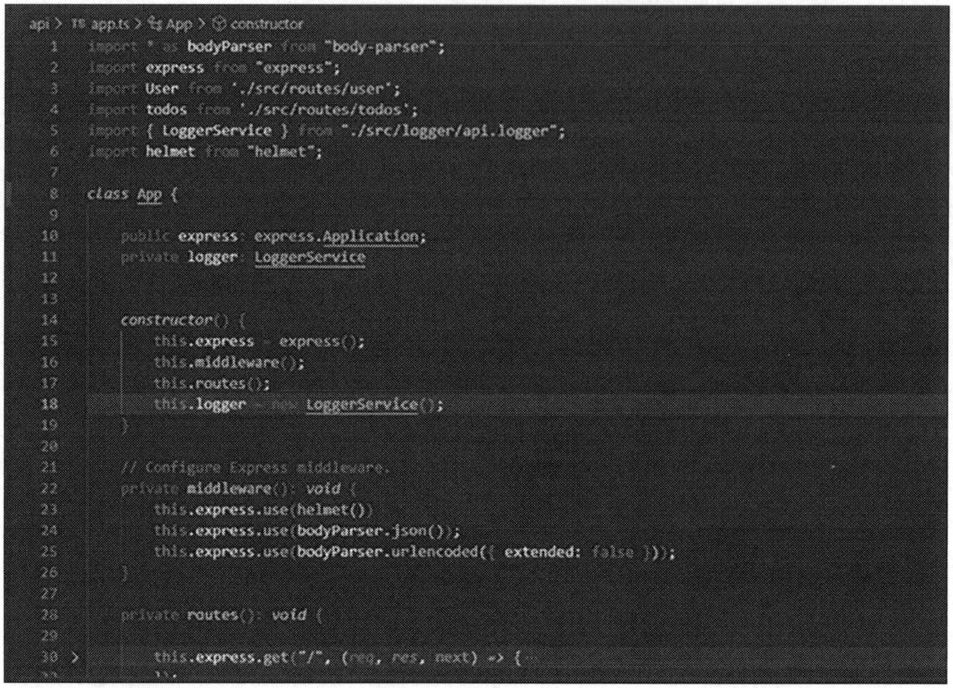

Figure 10.27: *app.ts*

Let us delve deeper into understanding the tangible impact of Helmet in our API. To appreciate its effect, we will examine the situation without Helmet and observe the response headers our API generates in its absence. In this scenario, the API responses are relatively minimal in terms of security headers. Without Helmet, the response from our API includes only seven headers. These headers typically consist of basic information like content type, cache control, and server details, but lack advanced security directives.

The absence of these additional headers leaves the application more exposed to common web vulnerabilities. Headers that Helmet would typically add, such as those for XSS protection, content security policy, and strict transport security, are missing. This lack of security-enhanced headers can make the application susceptible to a range of attacks, including cross-site scripting, clickjacking, and other exploits that leverage the headers' absence to manipulate or misuse the application.

By contrasting this bare-minimum set up with the enhanced security profile provided by Helmet, we can better understand the significant role Helmet plays in fortifying our application's defences. Helmet's ability to seamlessly integrate a set of protective measures into our API's responses is pivotal in elevating our security posture, making our application not just functional but also resilient against a variety of web-based threats.

With Helmet, we got to see 19 headers in the response. In summary, observing our API's response headers without Helmet underscores the middleware's importance in safeguarding our application. The contrast highlights Helmet's role in extending the application's native capabilities to include essential security measures, thereby ensuring a more secure and robust environment for both the application and its users.

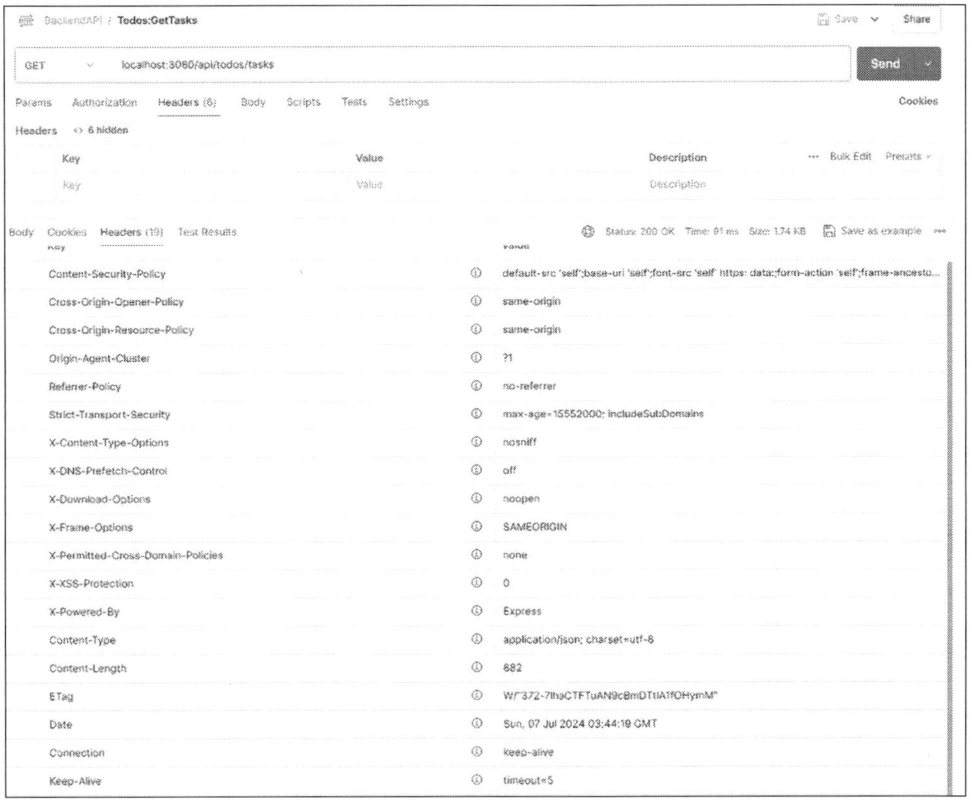

Figure 10.28: *Headers with helmet*

In summary, Helmet's inclusion in our Express application's middleware stack is a testament to its essential role in web application security. Its simplicity in implementation, coupled with the breadth of security enhancements it provides, makes Helmet an indispensable tool in our development arsenal. As we progress further in building our Express application, the presence of Helmet ensures that we are on the right track towards creating a secure and robust web application.

Implementing CORS

Implementing Cross-Origin Resource Sharing (CORS) in a Node.js application using Express and TypeScript involves a few straightforward steps. CORS is a security feature that allows you to restrict which web applications can make requests to your server.

```
// install cors
npm install cors
```

```
// install helmet type definitions
npm install -D @types/cors
```

Once you run the above commands, you should see those dependencies added to your **package.json**.

The integration of CORS is done in the **middleware()** method within the **App** class. This is a strategic placement, as middleware in Express defines functions that have access to the request object (**req**), the response object (**res**), and the next middleware function in the application's request-response cycle. The **cors()** function call adds the CORS middleware to the application, enabling CORS for all routes and endpoints defined in the application.

This setup is achieved with the line **this.express.use(cors())**, which instructs the Express application to use the **cors** package. By default, this enables CORS for all requests, allowing any domain to make requests to the API. This default behavior is often suitable for APIs that are publicly accessible and do not require restrictive cross-origin policies.

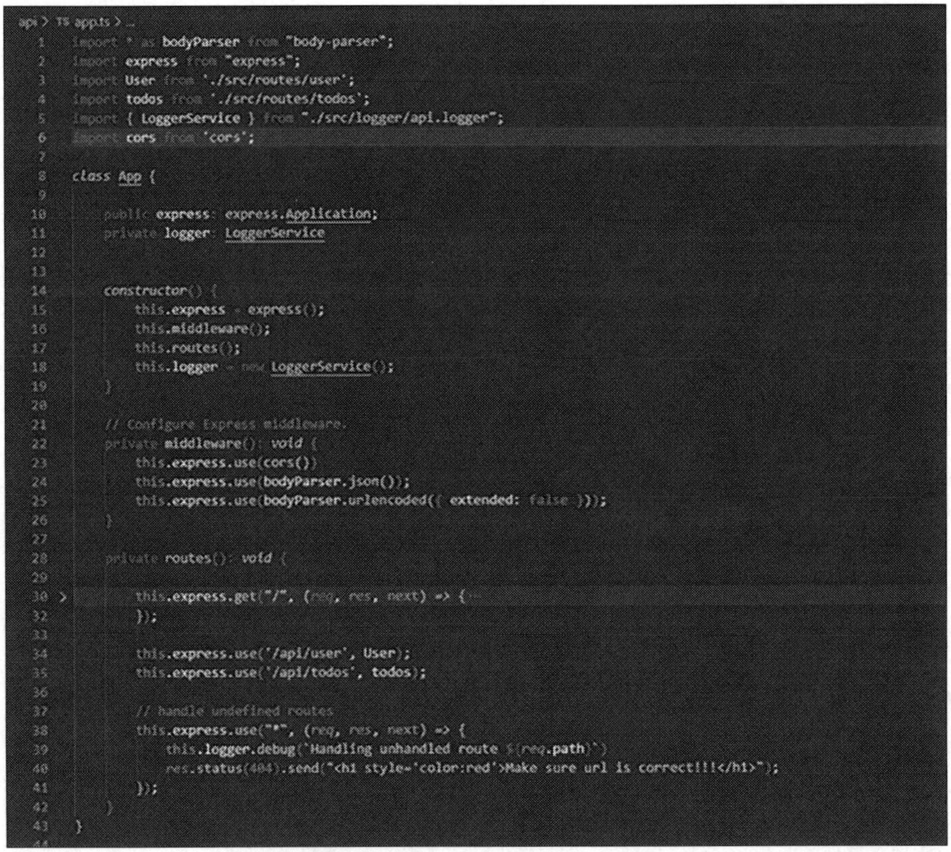

Figure 10.29: *Configuring CORS*

If you need to customize CORS settings (for example, allowing specific origins, methods, or headers), you can do so by passing options to the **`cors()`** middleware.

```
// Configure Express middleware.
private middleware(): void {

    const corsOptions = {
        origin: 'http://example.com', // Specific origin
        methods: 'GET,POST', // Allowed methods
        allowedHeaders: 'Content-Type,Authorization'
    };

    this.express.use(cors(corsOptions))
    this.express.use(bodyParser.json());
    this.express.use(bodyParser.urlencoded({ extended: false }));
}

private routes(): void {
```

Figure 10.30: *CORS Options*

By integrating CORS into your Express application using TypeScript, you can manage cross-origin requests effectively, enhancing both the security and accessibility of your application. Customizing the CORS middleware allows for fine-tuned control over how your application handles requests from different origins, making it a versatile solution for a wide range of web application scenarios.

Implementing CSRF

Implementing Cross-Site Request Forgery (CSRF) protection in a Node.js application using Express and TypeScript involves integrating a CSRF middleware. CSRF attacks involve tricking a user into unknowingly executing actions on a web application in which they are authenticated. To mitigate such attacks, a common approach is to use a token-based system where each request must include a unique token that the server verifies.

CSRF Protection is typically not required for our rest API for the following reasons:

- **Token-Based Authentication:** REST APIs often use token-based authentication mechanisms (like OAuth tokens, JWTs - JSON Web Tokens). Since these tokens are typically sent in the HTTP header and not automatically included with every request by browsers (unlike cookies), they are inherently resistant to CSRF attacks.
- **Stateless APIs:** A key principle of REST is statelessness, meaning the server does not maintain any state (like user sessions) between requests. If your REST API is truly stateless and doesn't rely on session cookies for authentication, then CSRF protection is not necessary.

In summary, whether CSRF protection is needed for your REST API primarily hinges on your API's authentication method. Stateless, token-based APIs generally do not require CSRF protection. However, if cookies, especially session cookies, are used for authentication, and if browsers are primary clients of the API, CSRF protection becomes important. Understanding the context and architecture of your API is crucial in determining the appropriate security measures.

Implementing Rate Limiting

Implementing rate limiting in a Node.js server within a MEVN stack is crucial to protect your API from excessive use and to mitigate denial-of-service attacks. A popular approach is to use middleware that can limit the number of requests a user can make to the API in each time frame. One widely used package for this purpose is **`express-rate-limit`**.

First, you need to add **`express-rate-limit`** to your project. Run the following command in your terminal:

```
// install express rate limiter
npm install express-rate-limit
```

In your Express application, import **`express-rate-limit`** and apply it as middleware to routes you wish to limit. You can apply it globally or to specific routes.

Applying Global

This mechanism is crucial for controlling the rate at which users can make requests to the server, thereby helping to protect against abuse and excessive load. As you can see in the following figure, the **`express-rate-limit`** package is imported to use its functionality for rate limiting. The defined rules are:

- **`windowMs: 15 * 60 * 1000`**: This sets the duration of the rate limiting window to 15 minutes. All requests from a single IP will be counted within this timeframe.
- **`max: 2`**: This limits each IP address to making only 2 requests per window (in this case, every 15 minutes). This limit is set to 2 for local testing purposes to easily simulate and observe the rate limiting behavior.
- **`standardHeaders`**: When set to **`true`**, the middleware adds the **`RateLimit-*`** headers to responses, providing clients with information about the rate limit, the number of requests remaining before the limit is reached, and when the window resets.
- **`legacyHeaders`**: Setting this to **`false`** disables the older **`X-RateLimit-*`** headers, preferring the newer **`RateLimit-*`** headers for conveying rate limit information.

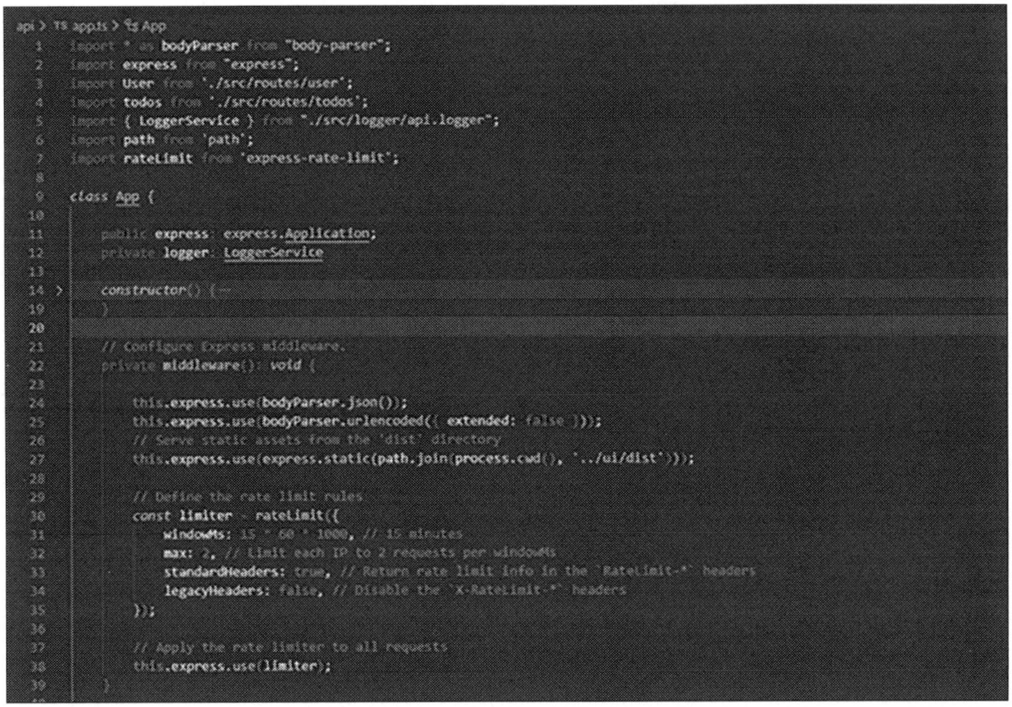

Figure 10.31: *Configuring Rate Limiter*

The rate limiter middleware is applied globally to all incoming requests to the Express application using **`this.express.use(limiter)`**. This means every request will be checked against the defined rate limit rules.

In a production environment, the **`max`** value (the number of requests allowed per window per IP) should be adjusted based on the application's specific needs and expected traffic. A typical value might be much higher than 2, to balance protecting the server against abuse while still providing a good user experience. For example, setting **`max`** to 100 or more requests per 15-minute window might be reasonable for many applications, but the optimal value depends on the nature of the API and its usage patterns.

With that in place, when we make an API call more than 2 times, The browser displays a message '**`Too many requests, please try again later`**'. This is the response sent by the server when the rate limit is exceeded.

The Network tab in the browser's developer tools is open, showing the details of an HTTP GET request to the API endpoint **`/api/todos/tasks`.** The Status Code is **`429 Too Many Requests`**, which is the HTTP status code for rate limiting responses. This confirms that the rate limiter has kicked in, as the number of requests allowed in the time window has been exceeded.

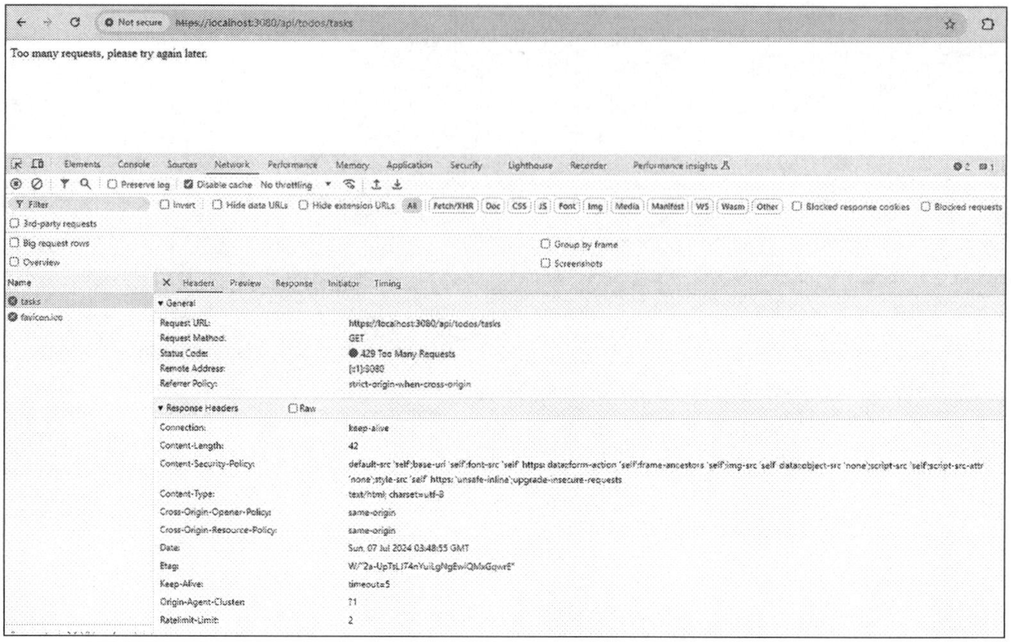

Figure 10.32: *too many requests*

It is important to carefully consider the rate limit settings to ensure they provide adequate protection without unnecessarily restricting legitimate usage. Monitoring and adjusting based on observed traffic and behavior is often necessary to find the right balance.

Applying Specific Route Rate Limiting

If you only want to apply rate limiting to specific routes, you can do so as follows. This **`loginLimiter`** applies a threshold of 2 requests per hour for each IP address, which is an intentionally low limit chosen to demonstrate the functionality and is typically set higher in a real-world scenario. After reaching this limit, any further sign-in attempts from the same IP address will receive a response indicating "**`Too many login attempts from this IP, please try again after an hour`**" on Line 30, thereby preventing excessive requests and mitigating brute-force attacks on user accounts. This targeted application of rate limiting on sensitive routes like sign-in is a critical security measure in web applications.

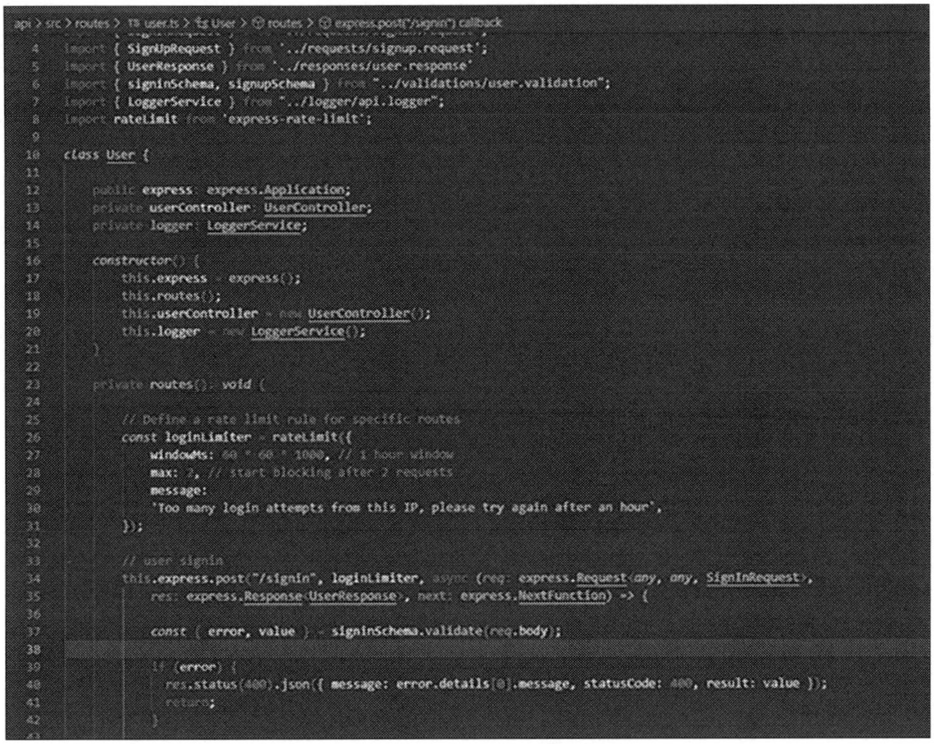

```
api > src > routes > TS user.ts > ts User > routes > express.post("/signin") callback
import { SignUpRequest } from '../requests/signup.request';
import { UserResponse } from '../responses/user.response'
import { signinSchema, signupSchema } from "../validations/user.validation";
import { LoggerService } from "../logger/api.logger";
import rateLimit from 'express-rate-limit';

class User {

    public express: express.Application;
    private userController: UserController;
    private logger: LoggerService;

    constructor() {
        this.express = express();
        this.routes();
        this.userController = new UserController();
        this.logger = new LoggerService();
    }

    private routes(): void {

        // Define a rate limit rule for specific routes
        const loginLimiter = rateLimit({
            windowMs: 60 * 60 * 1000, // 1 hour window
            max: 2, // start blocking after 2 requests
            message:
            'Too many login attempts from this IP, please try again after an hour',
        });

        // user signin
        this.express.post("/signin", loginLimiter, async (req: express.Request<any, any, SignInRequest>,
            res: express.Response<UserResponse>, next: express.NextFunction) => {

            const { error, value } = signinSchema.validate(req.body);

            if (error) {
                res.status(400).json({ message: error.details[0].message, statusCode: 400, result: value });
                return;
            }
```

Figure 10.33: *applying specific routes*

Upon conducting a test on the sign-in endpoint, the network tab in the developer console reveals that the request has encountered a **`'429 Too Many Requests'`** error. This indicates that the rate limiting mechanism has been triggered due to an excessive number of requests being sent to this endpoint. In the response headers, we observe two distinct rate limit values: the **`RateLimit-Limit`** and **`X-RateLimit-Limit`**.

The **`RateLimit-Limit`** header, displaying a value of 100, suggests a global rate limit configuration (changed from 100 to 2), which is a common threshold set for all users across the application. However, for this specific sign-in route, the **`X-RateLimit-Limit`** reflects a value of 2, underscoring a more restrictive rate limit policy has been enforced for this endpoint. This lower value is likely set to provide stringent control over sensitive actions such as user authentication attempts.

This differentiated rate limiting strategy is instrumental in enhancing the application's security posture. By imposing stricter limits on sensitive endpoints, the application can provide additional safeguards against automated attacks and other malicious activities that target user accounts, such as password brute-forcing. The headers in the response also communicate essential information about the rate limit status to the client, including how many requests remain (**`X-RateLimit-Remaining`**) and the time until the rate limit resets (**`X-RateLimit-Reset`**), enabling client-side handling strategies for rate limiting conditions.

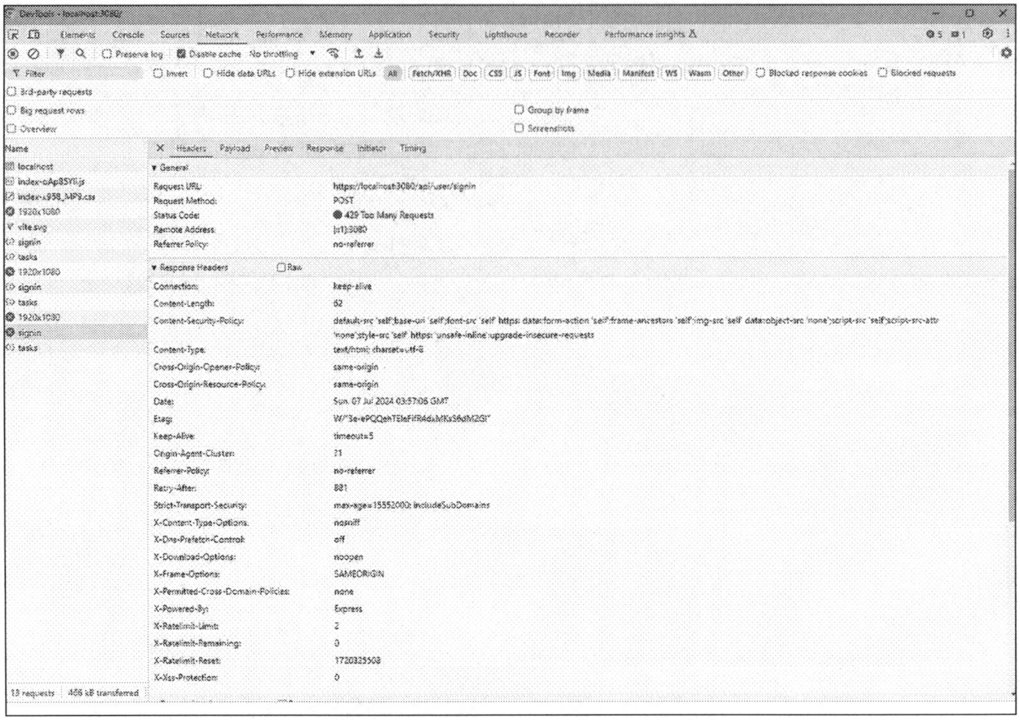

Figure 10.34: *too many requests*

The implementation of rate limiting in the application has been successfully validated through testing. When the sign-in endpoint is subjected to several requests exceeding the threshold, the server responds with a '**`429 Too Many Requests`**' error. This response is visible in the developer console's network tab, confirming the effectiveness of the rate limiting middleware.

For this specific route, the rate limit is configured to allow only 2 requests per hour per IP, a stringent limit that helps protect against password brute force attempts and other types of abusive behavior aimed at user accounts. The presence of both global and route-specific rate limit headers in the response allows for fine-grained control over request thresholds, ensuring that while general application use remains fluid, critical endpoints are afforded additional protection.

Overall, the rate limiter's role is crucial in maintaining the application's integrity and availability. It prevents individual users from making excessive requests that could lead to service degradation or outages, thereby upholding a reliable service for all users. The clear communication of rate limit status to the client also aids in creating a transparent interaction, allowing users and client-side applications to understand and adapt to the imposed limits.

As a final point, while the current limits are set with local testing in mind, for a production environment, these values would need to be carefully evaluated and set according to the application's usage patterns and security requirements. The rate limiting strategy should strike a balance between user convenience and system protection, adapting as necessary to the evolving traffic and threat landscape.

Global Exception Handler

Implementing a Global Exception Handler in an Express application is crucial for gracefully handling unexpected errors and preventing your app from crashing. It ensures that any uncaught exceptions are caught and processed in a centralized manner, allowing for better error management, logging, and potentially notifying developers or systems when critical issues occur.

Having a Global Exception Handler in your application offers numerous advantages, significantly enhancing both development efficiency and application stability. Here are some key benefits:

- **Centralized Error Management:** A Global Exception Handler centralizes error handling logic, eliminating the need to replicate error handling code across different parts of your application. This not only reduces boilerplate but also ensures consistency in how errors are processed and responded to.
- **Improved Application Stability:** By catching unexpected exceptions that may not be caught locally within `try-catch` blocks, a Global Exception Handler helps prevent your application from crashing. This contributes to the overall stability and reliability of your application, ensuring that it remains operational even when unexpected errors occur.
- **Enhanced Debugging and Diagnostics:** Centralized handling allows for systematic logging of errors and exceptions. This can be invaluable for debugging purposes, providing a clear overview of what went wrong and where, which can significantly speed up the troubleshooting process.
- **Consistent Error Responses:** Particularly important for APIs, a Global Exception Handler ensures that all error responses are consistent in structure and content. This is crucial for external systems or clients consuming your API, as it provides a predictable error handling mechanism.
- **Security Benefits:** Proper error handling can help mitigate certain security vulnerabilities, such as preventing sensitive information from being exposed to clients. A Global Exception Handler can ensure that error messages are sanitized before being sent, reducing the risk of leaking details that could be exploited.
- **Graceful Degradation**: In the face of errors, a Global Exception Handler allows your application to fail gracefully, potentially providing fallback logic or user-friendly error messages that enhance the user experience, even when things go wrong.

- **Compliance and Logging:** For applications that must comply with specific regulations, a Global Exception Handler can ensure that all errors are logged in compliance with regulatory requirements. This can include logging the necessary information for audit trails or error reporting.
- **Simplified Maintenance and Scalability:** With a single point of management for exceptions, updating your error handling logic or adapting it to new requirements becomes much simpler. This is especially beneficial as your application scales and evolves over time.

Implementing a global error handler in a TypeScript-based Express application involves creating middleware that captures any errors thrown during the request-handling process and responds appropriately.

We need to create a new TypeScript file for the error handler, for example, **`globalErrorHandler.ts`**. This file will export a function that Express can use as middleware to handle errors. The function needs to accept four arguments – the error object, the request object, the response object, and the next function in the middleware chain. The global error handler has been positioned within the **`config`** directory, reflecting its application-wide utility. However, the organization of such handlers is flexible, and you may opt to allocate a distinct folder specifically for them, based on your preference and the structure of your project. The decision on how to organize these elements is entirely yours.

This basic global error handler logs the error to the console and sends a generic "**`Internal Server Error`**" response if no response has been sent yet. You can customize this to include more sophisticated logic, such as differentiating between production and development environments to control the amount of error detail sent back to the client.

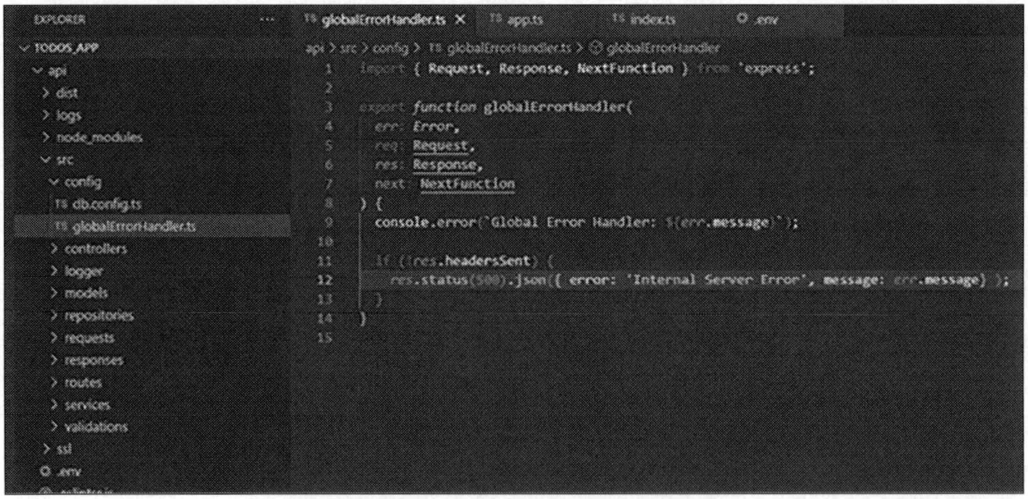

Figure 10.35: *Global Exception Handler*

Import the **globalErrorHandler** middleware into your main app file **app.ts** and use it with your Express app. This must be the last middleware you add, so that it can catch any errors that have occurred in earlier middleware or routes.

Our application is structured to include a specific route (**/error**) designed to test the functionality of a global error handler. This test route, when accessed, deliberately throws an error with the message '**Testing Global Error Handler**.' The purpose of this route is to simulate an error scenario to verify that the global error handler is correctly configured and operational. The global error handler itself is imported from a separate module (**globalErrorHandler**) and integrated into the application's middleware stack. By placing this error handler after all other middleware and route definitions, it acts as a catch-all for any unhandled errors that occur within the application, ensuring that no error goes uncaught. This set up prevents the application from crashing due to unhandled exceptions, thereby enhancing its stability and reliability. Instead of the application terminating unexpectedly, the global error handler can log the error, perform necessary cleanup, and return a controlled response to the client, maintaining a smooth user experience even in the face of errors.

Figure 10.36: *defining error route*

When you navigate to **`/error`** in your browser or use a tool like Postman to make a request to that route, the global error handler should catch the thrown error, log it, and return the "**`Internal Server Error`**" message.

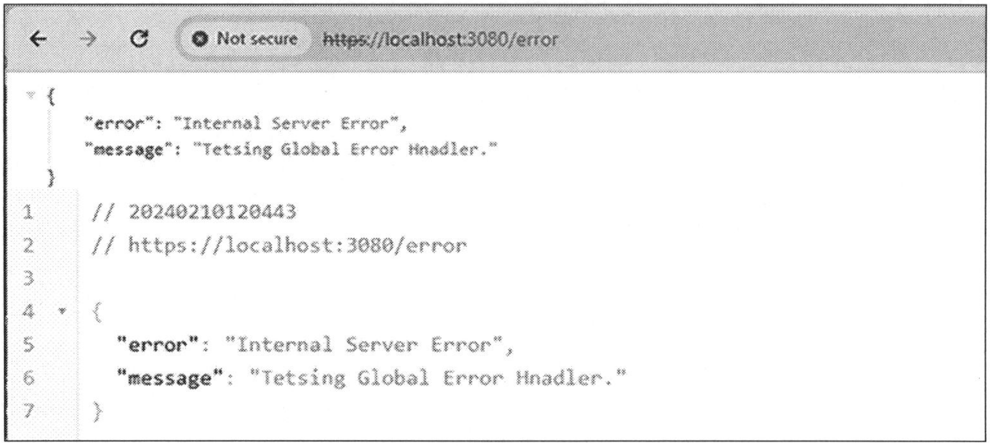

Figure 10.37: *Testing Global Exception Handler*

Concluding the section on the global error handler, it is paramount to underscore the significance of such mechanisms in ensuring the resilience and reliability of your application. A well-implemented global error handler plays a critical role in intercepting unhandled exceptions and errors that occur during the request-response cycle. Without it, your application is at risk of crashing upon encountering such exceptions, potentially leading to downtime and a degraded user experience.

The global error handler not only prevents the application from crashing but also provides a centralized place for logging errors and performing cleanup operations. This aids in monitoring and diagnosing issues swiftly, allowing for prompt responses to potential problems. Furthermore, it ensures that the application can respond gracefully to the client in the event of an error, maintaining a professional and reliable interface with users.

In collaborative and production environments, where stability and uptime are crucial, having a robust error handling strategy, including a global error handler, is indispensable. It reflects best practices in software development, contributing significantly to the maintenance of high-quality, resilient applications. By prioritizing the implementation of such error handling mechanisms, developers can safeguard their applications against unexpected failures, thereby enhancing overall application health and user satisfaction.

Linting

Linting is a fundamental practice in modern software development that involves the use of a tool called a '*linter*' to automatically check source code for potential issues.

Linters are designed to identify syntax errors, stylistic errors, and construct usage that does not adhere to best practices, all of which could lead to more serious problems down the line, such as bugs or performance issues.

In the context of a MEVN stack, where the UI and API are often developed in separate projects or folders, linting becomes especially important for several reasons:

- **Consistency:** Linting enforces a consistent coding style across both the frontend (Vue.js) and backend (Express/Node.js) codebases, which is crucial when multiple developers are working on the same project. Consistent code is easier to read, maintain, and less prone to errors.
- **Best Practices:** Linters can encourage best practices by enforcing rules that help avoid common mistakes. They help align your code with the latest standards and can educate developers on the nuances of the languages they are working with.
- **Error Prevention:** Linters analyze the code for patterns that may lead to bugs. By catching errors early in the development process, linting saves time and resources that would otherwise be spent on debugging and fixing.
- **Code Quality:** Beyond catching errors, linters can suggest improvements to the code that enhance its quality, performance, and readability.
- **Automation:** Linting can be integrated into continuous integration/continuous deployment (CI/CD) pipelines, ensuring that every commit adheres to the defined coding standards, and reducing the chance of problematic code making its way into the production environment.

For these reasons, implementing linting in both the frontend and backend parts of a MEVN stack is a best practice that supports the delivery of high-quality, maintainable, and reliable software.

Linting UI

To begin setting up `ESLint`, we start by opening the terminal and executing the following command. This command initiates a sequence of prompts that guide us through the configuration process and automatically installs the required dependencies.

```
// install express rate limiter
npm init @eslint/config
```

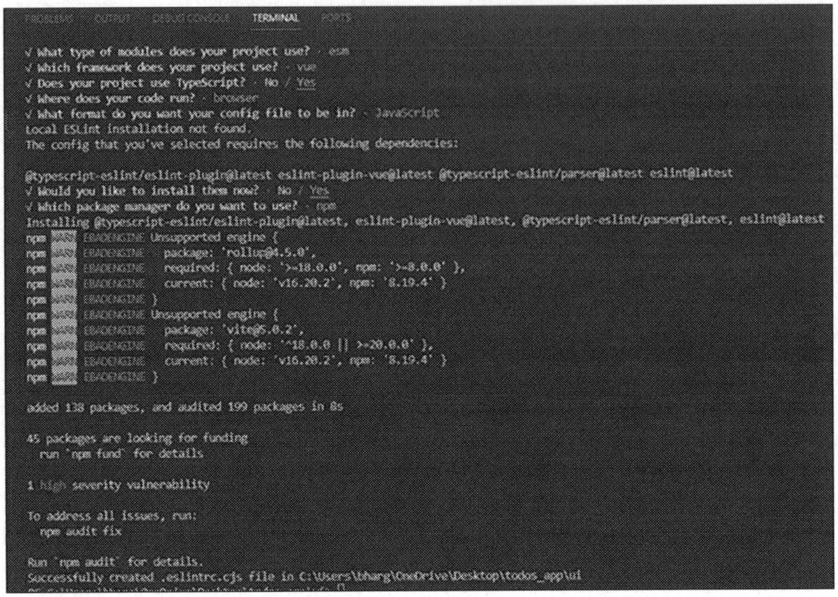

Figure 10.38: *Configuring Linting*

Additionally, the process generates a JavaScript configuration file which specifies a variety of rules for **ESLint** to enforce.

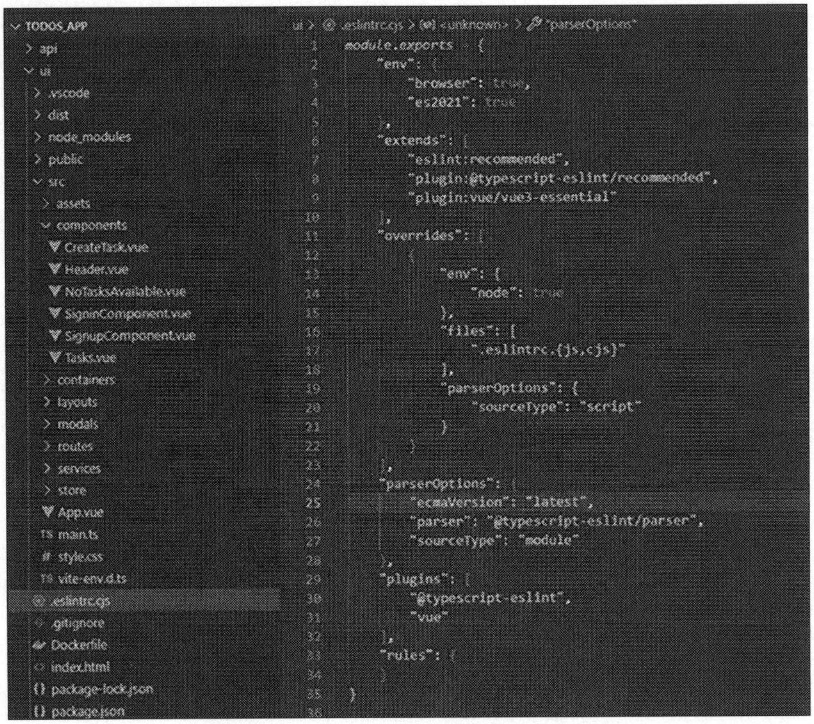

Figure 10.39: *eslint configuration file*

This JavaScript file serves as the configuration for **ESLint** in a development environment where both browser and Node.js contexts are relevant. It outlines the environments under **env**, setting them to recognize browser globals and ECMAScript 2021 features. The **extends** property pulls in a set of predefined rules from **eslint:recommended**, TypeScript-specific linting rules from **@typescript-eslint/recommended**, and Vue 3 essential rules from **plugin:vue/vue3-essential**, establishing a baseline for code quality and style. An **overrides** section is included to apply different settings to the **ESLint** configuration files themselves, treating them as Node.js scripts. The **parserOptions** define how the code is parsed, specifying the latest ECMAScript syntax version, and using a module source type by default, with **@typescript-eslint/parser** for parsing TypeScript files. It also includes **@typescript-eslint** and **vue** in the **plugins** section, allowing **ESLint** to use additional rules provided by these plugins. Lastly, the **rules** object is currently empty, indicating that no custom rules are being applied beyond what is extended, but it is available for specifying or overriding rules as needed.

After configuring the script, it is possible to incorporate **npm run lint** into the development workflow by adding it to the **scripts** section of the **package.json** file. Executing this command identifies 11 errors, which are determined by the predefined rules in the **ESLint** configuration. For errors that are automatically correctable, executing **npm run lint-fix** will adjust the code accordingly. However, some issues may require manual resolution, indicating that not all errors can be fixed through automated means and will need direct developer intervention to address them.

Figure 10.40: *Linting Errors*

To disable specific rules in your **ESLint** configuration file, you can add them to the **rules** section and set their value to **"off"**. In your case, you want to disable the rules **@typescript-eslint/no-explicit-any**, **vue/no-dupe-keys**, and **vue/multi-word-component-names**. Here is how you would modify the `rules` object in your **module.exports**:

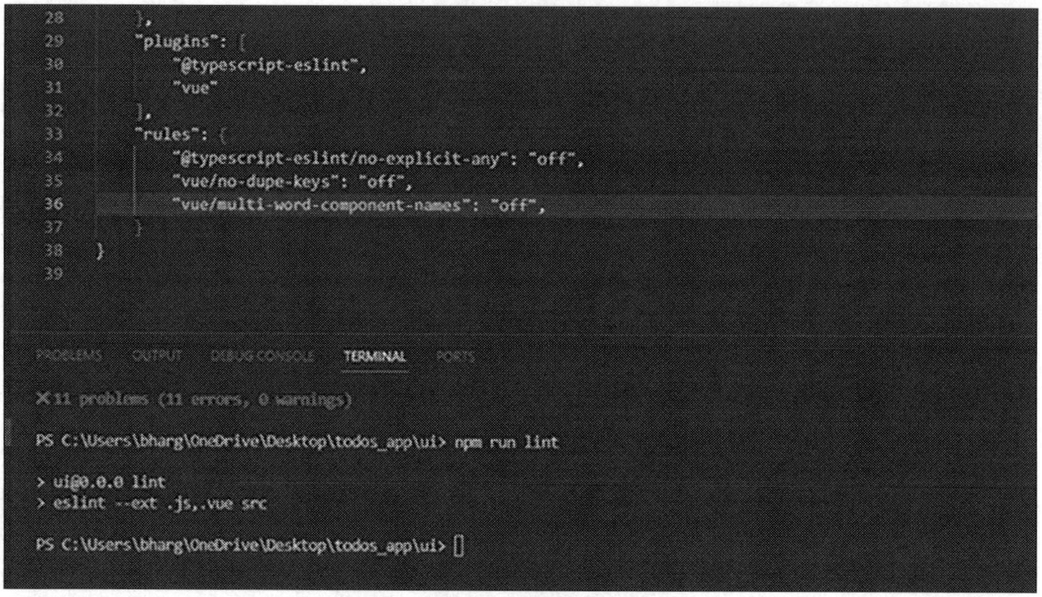

Figure 10.41: *Disabling Errors*

By setting these rules to **"off"**, you are instructing **ESLint** to ignore violations of these rules when linting your code. This allows you to use **any** in TypeScript, have duplicate keys in Vue component objects, and use single-word names for Vue components without **ESLint** reporting them as issues. Upon executing the linting process once more, the previously encountered rule violations should no longer trigger any error messages, thanks to the adjustments made to the **ESLint** configuration. This presents an excellent opportunity for readers to engage in a practical exercise– attempt to address and resolve these issues within the code as outlined in this book. It is an instructive task that reinforces understanding of best practices and the implications of disabling certain linting rules.

It is important to note, however, that bypassing these linting rules is generally not advised when preparing code for a production environment. The rules are there for a reason–to ensure code quality and maintainability–and turning them off can lead to potential pitfalls down the line. As such, while the exercise serves as a valuable learning tool, in a real-world scenario, developers should strive to adhere to these guidelines, resolving any highlighted issues to ensure robust, clean, and reliable code prior to deployment.

Linting API

The process for setting up linting in an API adheres to a similar procedure; by executing the command **`npm init @eslint/config`**, a configuration file is generated. This step involves answering a series of questions that tailor the **`ESLint`** setup to the specific needs of your project.

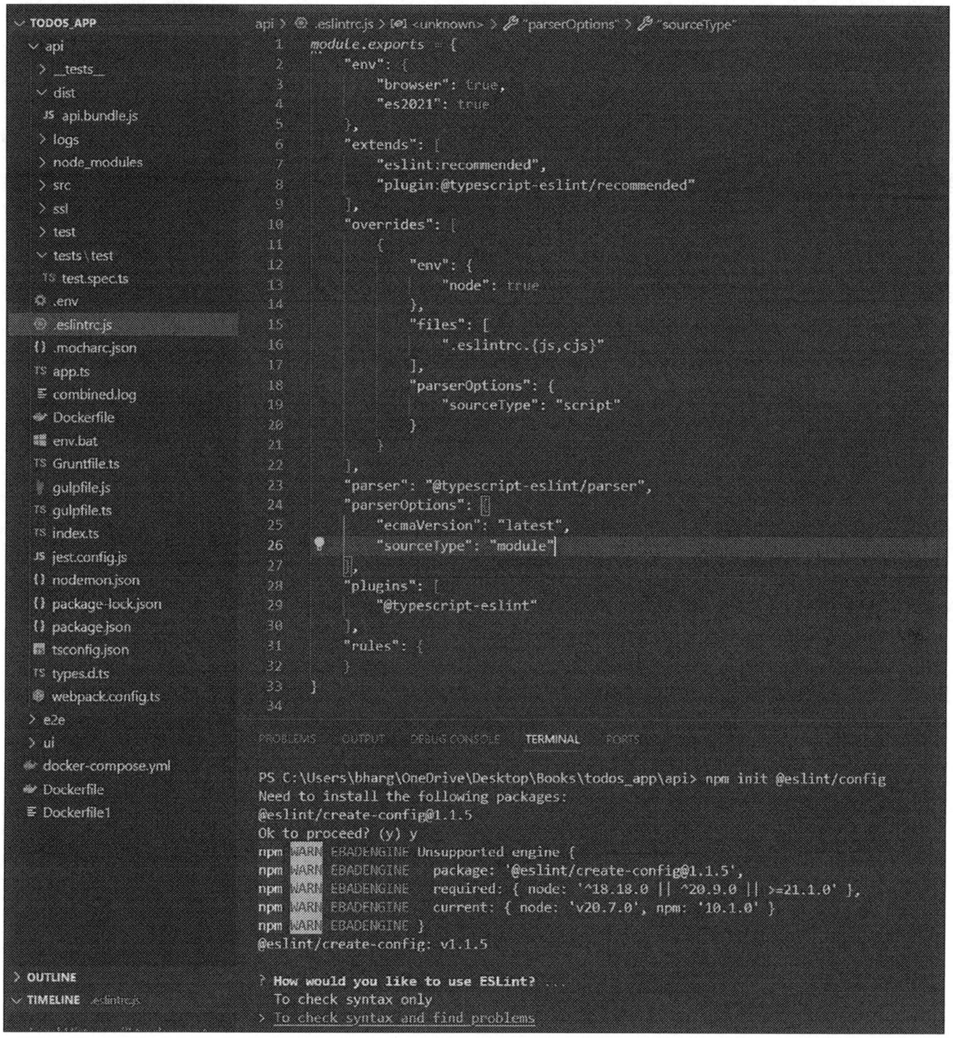

Figure 10.42: *Eslint Configuration file*

After establishing the ESLint configuration, it is possible to integrate the linting process into your project's workflow by incorporating **`npm run lint`** into the **`scripts`** section of your **`package.json`** file. Upon executing this lint command, you might encounter a total of 91 errors, with 8 being automatically rectifiable. This scenario presents an excellent opportunity for readers to engage in a practical exercise by addressing and resolving these detected issues. Furthermore, if certain **ESLint** rules are deemed too stringent or not applicable to your project's specific context, you have the option to deactivate them. This can be achieved by listing these rules within the **rules** section of your **ESLint** configuration file and setting their values to **"off"**, mirroring the approach taken for the UI component of your project. This flexibility allows for a customized linting experience that aligns with your coding standards and preferences.

Figure 10.43: *Linting Errors*

In conclusion, the role of a linter in software development, particularly within a collaborative environment, cannot be overstated. By enforcing a consistent coding style and identifying potential errors before they become problematic, linting tools like **ESLint** significantly contribute to the maintenance of code quality and readability across large codebases. This uniformity is especially crucial in team settings where developers with varying coding styles and levels of experience contribute to the same project. Linters ensure that all contributions adhere to predefined standards, facilitating easier code reviews, reducing the likelihood of bugs, and streamlining the integration of new features. Moreover, the ability to customize linting rules allows teams to tailor the linting process to their specific project requirements and preferences, further enhancing development workflows. Ultimately, the integration of linting into the development process represents a best practice that supports the delivery of high-quality, maintainable software in collaborative environments.

Configure husky for Pre-Commit Hooks

Configuring Husky for pre-commit hooks in your project involves a few straightforward steps. Husky is a tool that allows you to easily manage Git hooks, ensuring that certain tasks, like linting or tests, are automatically run before commits are made. This can help catch errors early and maintain code quality. Here is how to set it up:

Step 1: Install Husky

First, you need to install Husky in your project. Navigate to your project directory in the terminal and run:

```
// install husky

npm install husky -save-dev
```

Step 2: Enable Git Hooks

Husky requires you to enable Git hooks in your project. You can do this by adding a **`prepare`** script in your **`package.json`**:

After adding the script, run it:

```
// Run Prepare

npm run prepare
```

This command sets up Husky and creates the **`.husky/`** directory in your project, where your Git hooks will reside.

Step 3: Add a Pre-commit Hook

Now, you can add a pre-commit hook. This hook will be triggered each time you commit changes. For example, to add a hook that runs **`ESLint`** before a commit, use the following command:

```
// adding pre commit hook

npx husky add .husky/pre-commit "npm run lint"
```

Replace **`"npm run lint"`** with the command you want to run before each commit. This command creates a pre-commit file in the **`.husky/pre-commit`** directory with the specified command.

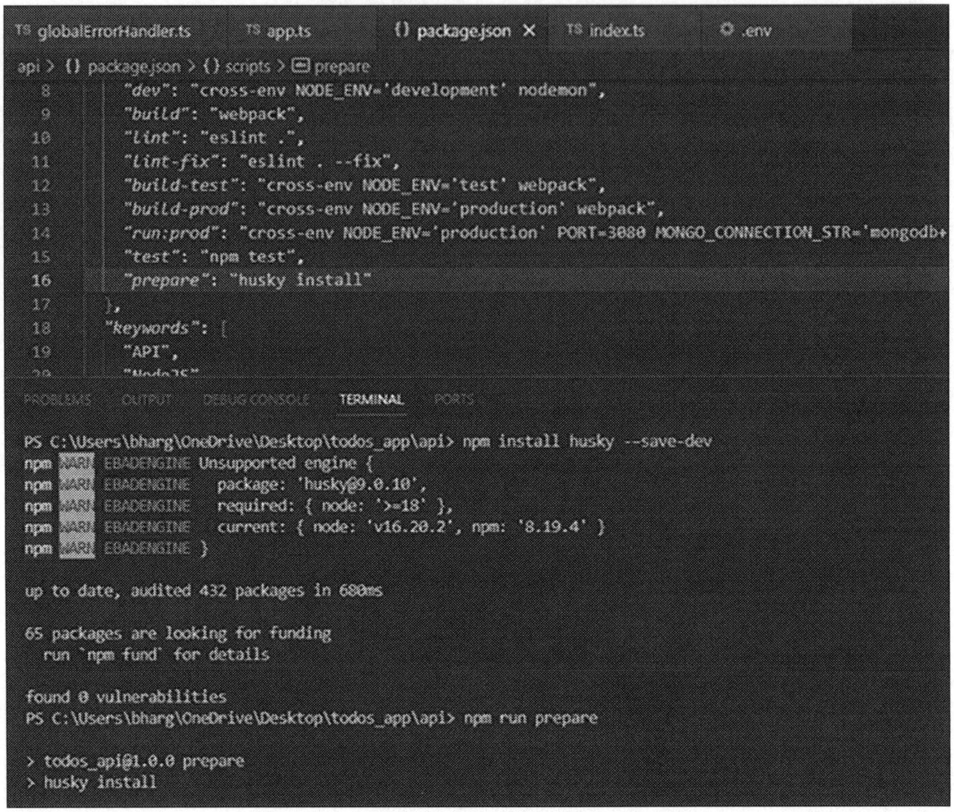

Figure 10.44: *Adding husky to npm scripts*

Step 4: Make the Hook Executable

Ensure the pre-commit hook script you have just created is executable. You can usually skip this step as **`husky add`** should make it executable automatically. However, if needed, run prepare.

Step 5: Test and Commit

To test if your pre-commit hook is working, try making a commit that would trigger an error in the script you have specified (for example, introduce a linting error if you are using **`ESLint`**). The commit should be blocked, and you will see the output of the script in your terminal. Do not forget to commit the changes made to your **`package.json`** and the newly added **`.husky/`** directory.

By following these steps, you have successfully configured Husky to use pre-commit hooks in your project, helping ensure that your codebase remains clean and error-free. Husky is a powerful tool that can run various scripts before commits, pushes, and more, making it a valuable addition to any development workflow.

The importance of Husky in collaborative environments cannot be overstated. By enforcing code quality checks and standards across all team members, Husky fosters a culture of responsibility and quality assurance. This uniformity not only streamlines the code review process but also minimizes the time spent on identifying and rectifying coding errors, allowing teams to focus more on feature development and innovation.

Moreover, Husky's flexibility in configuring pre-defined hooks tailored to specific project needs makes it an indispensable tool for projects of any scale. Whether it is ensuring that commit messages follow a particular format, code passes linting rules, or tests are green before pushing to a repository, Husky automates these checks, reinforcing best practices and facilitating a smoother, more efficient development pipeline.

In essence, Husky serves as a guardian of code quality, safeguarding projects from common pitfalls and fostering a disciplined approach to software development. Its adoption into development workflows marks a significant step towards achieving higher code quality, team collaboration, and overall project integrity, making it a valuable asset in the arsenal of modern development teams.

Introducing Task Runners

In the rapidly evolving landscape of web development, efficiency and automation are key. This is where task runners like Gulp and Grunt come into play, offering a powerful solution to streamline your development workflow. For developers working with the MEVN stack (MongoDB, Express.js, Vue.js, Node.js), incorporating task runners can significantly enhance productivity, from simplifying repetitive tasks to optimizing the overall performance of applications. This chapter introduces Gulp and Grunt, explores their significance, and discusses how they can be integrated within the MEVN stack development process.

Task runners automate mundane and repetitive tasks in software development, such as minification of JavaScript and CSS files, compiling LESS or SASS to CSS, running tests, and refreshing your browser automatically whenever a file is saved. Gulp and Grunt are two of the most popular JavaScript-based task runners, distinguished by their ease of use, flexibility, and extensive plugin ecosystems.

Gulp

Gulp is a streaming build system that emphasizes simplicity and speed. By using Node.js streams, it reads files as they are, modifies them, and then outputs the modified files. This approach minimizes the amount of temporary file handling, making Gulp faster in many scenarios. Gulpfiles, which define tasks, are written in JavaScript, allowing developers to leverage the full power of JavaScript and Node.js libraries.

Grunt

Grunt is an older task runner compared to Gulp, known for its vast plugin ecosystem. It requires configuration over code, meaning tasks are defined in a JSON-like data structure. This can make Gruntfiles verbose but also straightforward to understand. Grunt's extensive collection of plugins covers almost every task needed in a web development process, from simple file concatenation to more complex image optimization.

Benefits to Use Gulp or Grunt in MEVN Stack Development

Integrating Gulp or Grunt into your MEVN stack development process brings several benefits:

- **Automation:** Automatically compile Vue components, minify JavaScript and CSS files, or compile Sass/SCSS files to CSS. This saves time and reduces the potential for errors.
- **Performance Optimization:** Enhance application performance by compressing images, minifying files, and bundling resources, leading to faster load times.
- **Consistency:** Ensure a consistent code style and catch errors early by automating linting and formatting tasks.
- **Development Experience:** Improve the developer experience with live reloading, automatically refreshing your application as you develop.

Generate a Final Build Zip File with npm Scripts

Leverage `npm` scripts in your `package.json` to handle the build processes for both the frontend and backend, and possibly even zipping the distribution if that is a requirement. Here is how you could structure it:

Here are the steps to generate the final zip file.

1. **Build Backend**

   This script triggers the build process for the backend part of the application. It assumes that there is another npm script named `build` defined in the same `package.json` file, or within the backend project's `package.json`, responsible for compiling or preparing the backend code for production. This could involve transpiling TypeScript to JavaScript, bundling files, or performing any other necessary steps to get the backend ready for deployment.

2. **Build Frontend**

   This script navigates to the frontend project directory (assumed to be located at **../ui** relative to the backend project) and executes its build script. The frontend's build process is typically managed by a tool like Webpack, Vite, or another module bundler and involves compiling source code, optimizing assets, and generating static files to be served by the backend or deployed to a static hosting service.

```
"scripts": {
  "start": "ts-node index.ts",
  "dev": "cross-env NODE_ENV='development' nodemon",
  "build": "webpack",
  "lint": "eslint .",
  "lint-fix": "eslint . --fix",
  "build-test": "cross-env NODE_ENV='test' webpack",
  "build-prod": "cross-env NODE_ENV='production' webpack",
  "run:prod": "cross-env NODE_ENV='production' PORT=3000 MONGO_CONNECTION_STR='mongodb+srv://bhargavbook58:tester12345@todos.usujb
  "test": "npm test",
  "prepare": "husky install",
  "build:backend": "npm run build",
  "build:frontend": "cd ../ui && npm run build",
  "copy:frontend": "ncp ../ui/dist ./dist/public",
  "copy:ssl": "ncp ./ssl ./dist/ssl/",
  "zip:dist": "bestzip dist.zip ./api/build/*",
  "zip-build": "npm run build:backend && npm run build:frontend && npm run copy:frontend && npm run copy:ssl && npm run zip:dist"
},
```

Figure 10.45: *npm script final zip commands*

3. **Copy Frontend**

   After the frontend has been built, this script copies the generated static files from the frontend's **dist** directory to the **public** directory within the **dist** folder of the backend project. This is done using **ncp**, a Node.js package that provides an asynchronous recursive file and directory copying function. This step is crucial for serving the frontend assets directly from the backend server.

4. **Copy SSL**

   This script copies SSL certificates and keys from a source **ssl** directory to a target **ssl** directory inside the **dist** folder. This is important for setting up HTTPS in production environments where secure communication is required. The **ncp** tool is used here as well for the copy operation.

5. **Zipping Build**

   This command packages the contents of the **./api/build** directory into a zip file named **dist.zip**. It uses **bestzip**, a Node.js package that provides a cross-platform JavaScript API for creating zip files. This is typically used to bundle the entire application or a part of it for deployment or distribution.

6. **Combining all scripts**

   Finally, the **zip-build** script orchestrates the entire build and packaging process by sequentially executing the previously defined scripts. It starts by building both the backend and frontend parts of the application, copying the frontend build artifacts and SSL certificates to the appropriate directories within the backend's **dist** folder, and then zipping the backend build directory. This comprehensive script simplifies the build and deployment process into a single command, ensuring all steps are executed in the correct order.

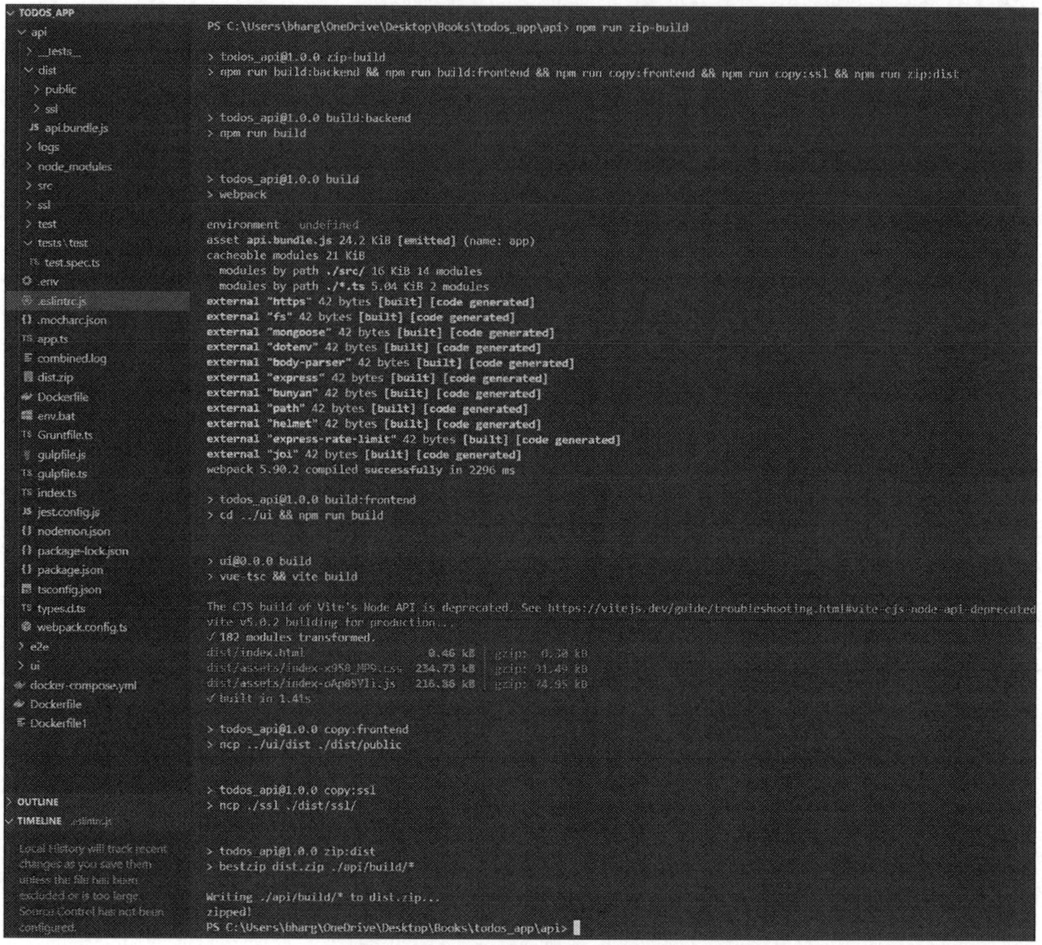

Figure 10.46: *Building Zip File*

Each of these scripts automates crucial parts of the development, build, and deployment workflow, making it easier to manage complex web applications with both frontend and backend components. We can see the build assets under the folders **dist** and **dist.zip**.

Conclusion

In this chapter, we have explored the development, enhancement, and security of a MEVN stack application. Starting with frontend construction and integration with an Express API, we ensured seamless communication between Vue.js and the backend. This integration forms the core of dynamic web applications, responding instantly to user inputs. We prioritized security by externalizing environment variables to protect sensitive data and configurations, crucial for maintaining security and adaptability across deployment environments. Additionally, we optimized backend build processes with Webpack for better performance and deployment ease.

An emphasis was placed on HTTPS implementation for secure communication, essential for safeguarding data and fostering user trust. We discussed API security strategies to fortify against threats, introducing a global exception handler to manage errors gracefully and maintain application stability. Emphasizing linting for code quality and early issue detection, we employed Husky for pre-commit hooks, automating quality checks and fostering consistency among teams. Task runners like Gulp and Grunt automated repetitive tasks, demonstrating streamlined deployment through Gulp's final build zip file generation. In the next chapter we will explore containerization with Docker, a pivotal step for simplifying deployments and enhancing scalability and portability.

CHAPTER 11
Running MEVN Stack on Docker

Introduction

Having meticulously crafted the backend and frontend of our MEVN stack application and prepared it for production in the preceding chapters, we now embark on a pivotal journey into the realm of Docker and containerization. This chapter aims to demystify the principles of Docker and how it revolutionizes the deployment and distribution of applications by encapsulating them in containers.

Containerization is a technology that encapsulates an application and its environment at a granular level, ensuring consistency across multiple development and deployment cycles. We will begin by introducing Docker, the industry-standard platform that enables developers to package applications into containers—self-sufficient units that contain everything needed to run the software.

Following the introduction to Docker, we will explore Docker Compose, a tool that simplifies the management of multi-container Docker applications. With Docker Compose, orchestrating various services that make up an application becomes manageable and reproducible. We will then dive into the practical aspects of running a MEVN stack on Docker Compose. You will learn how to define and run multi-container Docker applications, ensuring that each component of the MEVN stack works in unison within the Docker ecosystem.

The building of Docker images for the MEVN stack is up next, where we will cover how to create a Docker image that encapsulates the application and its dependencies, making it ready for deployment anywhere Docker is supported. We will then guide you through the process of running the MEVN stack on Docker, demonstrating how to launch your containerized application with all its components working seamlessly together.

We will also touch upon best practices for using Docker with the MEVN stack, ensuring that your journey with containers is not just effective but also adheres to the standards expected in professional environments.

Structure

In this chapter, the following topics will be covered:

- Introduction to Docker and Containerization
- Introduction to Docker Compose
- Building and Running MEVN Stack Docker Image
- Building and Running Image with Multi-Stage Builds
- Running MEVN Stack on Docker Compose
- Publishing the Docker Image
- Best Practices

Introduction to Docker and Containerization

In the previous chapters, we navigated through the development and production build processes for the MEVN stack. Now, we transition into deploying our application using Docker, a shift that represents the modern era of containerization in software development.

Docker is a platform that revolutionized software development and deployment by introducing containerization to the masses. It is a tool designed to make it easier to create, deploy, and run applications by using containers. Containers allow a developer to package up an application with all the parts it needs, such as libraries and other dependencies, and ship it all out as one package.

The inception of Docker dates to 2013, when it was introduced as an open-source project to the developer community. It rapidly gained popularity due to its ability to simplify the complexities of shipping and running applications. The Docker engine, the core part of Docker, is a lightweight runtime that manages containers on your machine.

While Docker is not the only container platform, it is the most widely used. A container is not much different from a virtual machine but is more portable, more resource-friendly, and more dependent on the host operating system.

At its core, Docker leverages the containerization technology provided by the Linux kernel (specifically features like namespaces and cgroups) to isolate the application's execution environment from the rest of the system. This means the application works in a sandbox, independent of others, and does not require a full-fledged operating system to run.

Understanding Containerization

Containerization provides a consistent environment for applications from development through production. It encapsulates the application's environment, ensuring that it works uniformly across different systems.

Embracing the Container Revolution

Containerization has taken the software industry by storm, transforming the way applications are developed, deployed, and managed. It represents a seismic shift from traditional deployment methods to a more efficient, scalable, and resilient infrastructure. But what exactly is containerization, and why has it become so indispensable in modern software practices? This chapter will explore the compelling reasons behind the widespread adoption of containerization and its impact on the technological landscape.

The Essence of Containerization

At its heart, containerization is about encapsulating an application and its environment into a container, which includes everything the application needs to run code, runtime, system tools, libraries, and settings. This container can be transported and run consistently across any computing environment, from a developer's laptop to a test environment, from a staging environment into production, and across on-premises and cloud providers.

Consistency Across Environments

One of the primary advantages of containerization is consistency. Developers can be assured that their applications will run the same way, regardless of where they are deployed. This consistency drastically reduces the 'it works on my machine' syndrome, a common source of frustration in software development teams.

Resource Efficiency and Destiny

Containers are more lightweight than traditional virtual machines because they share the host system's kernel, rather than requiring an OS per application. They can start up quickly and require less compute and memory resources, which allows for higher density of use on the host hardware.

Isolation and Security

While containers share the host system's kernel, they run in isolated user spaces. This means that they do not interfere with each other and can have different dependencies and environments. This isolation also provides an additional layer of security as the containers' processes and resources are isolated from the host system.

The Role of Docker in Containerization

Docker has emerged as the de facto standard for containerization, providing the tools and platform to build, ship, and run containers. It simplifies the process of container management and has built a vast community around its ecosystem.

Portability: A Docker Imperative

With Docker, applications are no longer tied to the environment they run in, making them portable and easy to deploy. This is a game-changer for teams looking to adopt a more agile and flexible approach to software delivery.

Continuous Integration and Deployment

Containerization aligns perfectly with the principles of continuous integration and deployment (CI/CD), allowing for rapid iterations and frequent releases. Docker containers can be easily integrated into CI/CD pipelines, enabling automated testing and deployment.

Container Orchestration and Management

As the adoption of containerization grows, so does the need for tools to manage and orchestrate containers at scale. Solutions like Kubernetes, Docker Swarm, and OpenShift have risen to the challenge, providing robust platforms for managing container lifecycles, scaling, networking, and more.

Core Concepts of Docker

Docker is built on a foundation of core concepts that facilitate its functionality as a containerization platform. Understanding these concepts is crucial for anyone looking to leverage Docker in their development or production workflows.

Docker Images

A Docker image is an immutable file that contains the source code, libraries, dependencies, tools, and other files needed for an application to run. An image is a snapshot of the application and its environment at a specific point in time. It is used to create Docker containers and is often built from a Dockerfile, which contains a list of instructions to automatically configure the environment.

Docker Containers

A container is a runtime instance of a Docker image. Think of it as a process with its own filesystem, networking, and isolated environment. Containers are created from images and can be started, stopped, moved, and deleted. Each container is an isolated and secure application platform, but it can communicate with other containers and the host system.

Dockerfile

A Dockerfile is a text document that contains all the commands a user could call on the command line to assemble an image. It automates the process of image creation and ensures that the build process is transparent and repeatable. Dockerfiles use a simple syntax that allows them to be lightweight and easy to understand.

Docker Registries

A Docker registry is where Docker images are stored. The Docker Hub is the default registry where Docker looks for images, but users can also create their own private registries. Registries can be public or private, with private registries typically used for proprietary images that are not meant to be shared publicly.

Docker Daemon

The Docker daemon (`dockerd`) listens for Docker API requests and manages Docker objects such as images, containers, networks, and volumes. It is a background service that manages the Docker images, containers, networks, and volumes on the host it runs.

Docker Client

The Docker client (`docker`) is the primary interface for many Docker users. When you use commands such as `docker run`, the client sends these commands to `dockerd`, which carries them out. The Docker client can communicate with more than one daemon.

Docker Compose

Docker Compose is a tool for defining and running multi-container Docker applications. With Compose, you use a YAML file to configure your application's services, networks, and volumes. Then, with a single command, you create and start all the services specified in your configuration.

Docker Networks

Docker networking allows containers to communicate with each other and with the outside world. Docker provides several networking models, and containers can be connected to one or more networks.

Docker Volumes

Docker volumes are used to persist data generated by and used by Docker containers.

They are a way to separate data from the container's lifecycle, so you can update or remove a container without losing the data.

Grasping these fundamental principles is key to effectively harness Docker's capabilities for packaging and distributing applications. With a firm grasp on these concepts, we can proceed to practically apply our knowledge by pulling and running a Docker image on our local machine. Recall from *Chapter 2, Prerequisites*, that we have already set up Docker Desktop, preparing our environment for the hands-on experiences to follow. Let us move forward by interacting with a simple Docker image and container, which will solidify our understanding through direct engagement with the Docker platform.

Getting Started with an Example

In the previous chapters, we have laid the groundwork by exploring the core concepts of Docker. Now, it is time to roll up our sleeves and dive into the practical side of Docker. This chapter will guide you through the initial steps of using Docker, setting the stage for a hands-on experience that brings those concepts to life.

Before we can use Docker, we need to ensure that it is installed on our system. Docker offers different versions for Windows, macOS, and various Linux distributions. We already went through the installation process in *Chapter 2 Prerequisites*. Once Docker is installed, you can verify the installation and check the version by running the following command in your terminal or command prompt:

```
docker --version
```

Figure 11.1: *Checking the Docker Version*

This command should return the version of Docker that is currently installed on your system, confirming that Docker is ready to use. Now that Docker is installed, let us start with the classic "`Hello World`" example to ensure everything is set up correctly.

Open your terminal or command prompt and execute the following command:

```
docker run hello-world
```

This command does two things – it pulls the "**hello-world**" image from Docker Hub (if it is not already present on your machine) and runs a container using that image. The container's sole job is to print a message confirming that Docker is installed correctly.

When you run the command, Docker checks for the "**hello-world**" image locally. If not found, it pulls it from Docker Hub. Then, Docker creates a new container from that image and runs it. The container prints a message to the console and exits.

```
PS C:\Users\bharg> docker run hello-world
Unable to find image 'hello-world:latest' locally
latest: Pulling from library/hello-world
c1ec31eb5944: Pull complete
Digest: sha256:4bd78111b6914a99dbc560e6a20eab57ff6655aea4a80c50b0c5491968cbc2e6
Status: Downloaded newer image for hello-world:latest

Hello from Docker!
This message shows that your installation appears to be working correctly.

To generate this message, Docker took the following steps:
 1. The Docker client contacted the Docker daemon.
 2. The Docker daemon pulled the "hello-world" image from the Docker Hub.
    (amd64)
 3. The Docker daemon created a new container from that image which runs the
    executable that produces the output you are currently reading.
 4. The Docker daemon streamed that output to the Docker client, which sent it
    to your terminal.
```

Figure 11.2: *Running the first Docker Container*

After executing a sample Docker image from DockerHub, we will now progress to constructing our own Docker image, featuring a basic Node.js server, and subsequently deploying it as a container.

Create a new directory for your project and add two files: `package.json`, `app.js`, and Dockerfile.

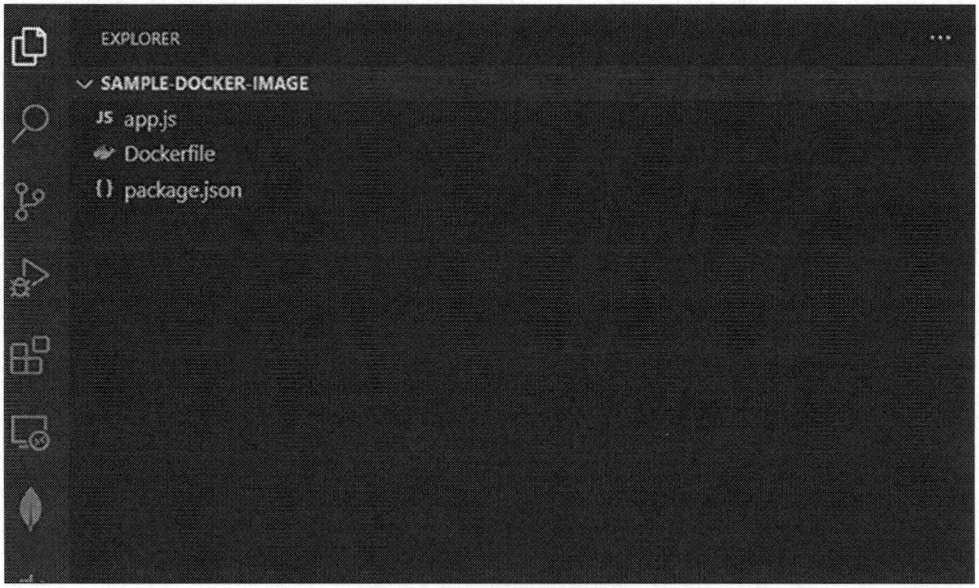

Figure 11.3: *Sample Project*

Here is a simple **package.json** file with the **start** command.

```
{
    "name": "sample-docker",
    "version": "1.0.0",
    "description": "Node.js on Docker",
    "main": "app.js",
    "scripts": {
      "start": "node app.js"
    }
  }
```

Figure 11.4: *package.json*

This is a basic **app.js** file where we set up an HTTP server that listens on port 3000. Upon executing this file, we should observe the output of the console statement.

```
const http = require('http');

const server = http.createServer((req, res) => {
  res.end('Hello Docker World!');
});

server.listen(3000, () => {
  console.log('Server running on port 3000');
});
```

Figure 11.5: *app.js*

Here is the Dockerfile that automates the building of the Docker image for this app.

```
FROM node:14

WORKDIR /app

COPY package.json package.json

RUN npm install

COPY . .

CMD ["npm", "start"]
```

Figure 11.6: *Dockerfile*

This Dockerfile is a set of instructions to build a Docker image for a Node.js application, starting with the base image **`node:14`**. It sets the working directory in the container to **`/app`** and copies the **`package.json`** file from the local directory to this location. The **`npm install`** command then installs the necessary Node.js dependencies inside the container. Following this, the **`COPY . .`** instruction transfers all other application files from the local directory into the container. Finally, the **`CMD ["npm", "start"]`** command specifies that the container will run **`npm start`** upon startup, effectively launching the Node.js application. This Dockerfile provides a self-contained environment with everything needed to run the Node.js app. In this instance, we have chosen Node version 14 for demonstration purposes. However, it is important to ensure that the version of Node that you are employing is currently supported and has not reached its End-of-Life (EOL). Using an active or maintained version of Node ensures that you receive critical security updates, bug fixes, and performance improvements, and it helps maintain the stability and security of your application. Always verify against the official Node.js release schedule to select a version that is actively supported.

Building the Docker Image

Run the following command in the same directory as your **Dockerfile**:

```
docker build -t docker-node-http-server
```

This command builds a new Docker image with the tag **`docker-node-http-server`** using the instructions from your **Dockerfile.**

Figure 11.7: *Building Docker Image*

If you run this command, you can see the image that is just built or you can directly see that on the Docker Desktop.

```
docker images
```

Figure 11.8: *Docker Desktop*

Running the Docker Image

Once the image is built, you can run a container from it:

```
docker run -d -p 3000:3000 docker-node-http-server
```

This command starts a new container and maps port 3000 from the container to port 3000 on your host machine. You can see the running container with the command **`docker ps`** and logs with the command **`docker logs <container name>`**.

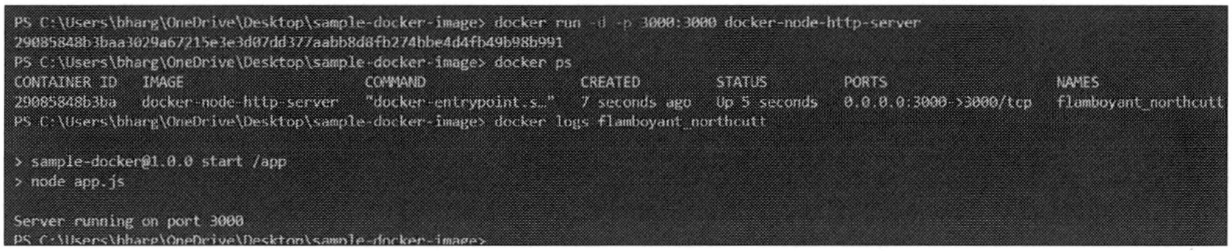

Figure 11.9: *Running Docker Container*

Navigate to **`http://localhost:3000`** in your web browser. You should see the message "**`Hello Docker World!`**".

Figure 11.10: *Testing Container*

The knowledge and skills that you have acquired till now will enable you to take on more advanced tasks. These skills include successfully installing Docker, running a basic container, building your first Docker image, and executing a simple Node.js application within a Docker container. This foundation is crucial for Docker development, ensuring a reliable and uniform environment for applications. In the upcoming sections, we will leverage this expertise to build and deploy our MEVN stack on Docker, tackling more complex images, managing multiple containers, and preparing applications that are robust, scalable, and ready for production environments.

Introduction to Docker Compose

Docker Compose is a powerful tool in the Docker ecosystem, designed to simplify the process of configuring and managing multi-container Docker applications. While Docker is excellent for running a single container, real-world applications often consist of multiple interconnected containers. Docker Compose addresses this complexity by allowing developers to define and run multi-container Docker applications using a simple YAML file.

Docker Compose plays a critical role in streamlining and simplifying the development process, especially in projects where applications consist of multiple interconnected Docker containers. In such scenarios, managing each container individually becomes cumbersome and prone to errors. Docker Compose elegantly solves this problem by enabling developers to define, run, and manage all the services of a multi-container application in a unified and coherent manner.

Simplifying Complex Applications

Modern applications often consist of several components, such as a web server, a database, and perhaps a caching service – each running in its own container. Docker Compose allows you to define these multi-container environments in a single file, making it easier to manage complex applications.

Consistent Development Environments

One of the biggest challenges in software development is ensuring consistency across different environments. Docker Compose facilitates this by allowing developers to define their environment in code. This means the same set up can be replicated across development, testing, and production environments, reducing the '*works on my machine*' problem.

Key Features of Docker Compose

Docker Compose comes packed with features that make it a preferred tool for managing containerized applications:

Service Definition and Isolation

- **Multi-Service Management:** Docker Compose allows you to define multiple services in a single `docker-compose.yml` file. Each service can represent a component of the application, and Docker Compose will manage these services as a single project.
- **Service Isolation:** While services are part of a single project, they are isolated from each other, running in separate containers. This isolation is beneficial for security and modularity.

Networking and Communication

- **Custom Networks:** With Docker Compose, you can define custom networks for your services. This is particularly useful for creating secure and efficient communication pathways between containers.
- **Service Discovery:** Services defined in a Docker Compose file can discover and communicate with each other by default. You can refer to another service by its name in the Docker network, simplifying internal communication.

Volume Management

- **Persistent Data Storage:** Docker Compose allows you to define and manage volumes for your containers. These volumes can be used for persisting data between container restarts or for sharing data between containers.

Build and Configuration

- **Build Configuration:** Docker Compose lets you build your Docker images with custom configurations, ensuring that each service is set up with the right environment and dependencies.
- **Environment Variable Support:** You can use environment variables in your `docker-compose.yml` file, which is essential for injecting configuration values that may differ between environments (like development, staging, and production).

Simplified Workflow

- **One-Command Up and Down:** With Docker Compose, you can start up your entire application stack using the `docker-compose up` command, and similarly, stop it with **`docker-compose down`**. This simplifies the workflow significantly as compared to managing each container individually through Docker.

Scalability and Extensibility

- **Scaling Services:** Docker Compose supports scaling services, allowing you to increase or decrease the number of container instances of a service.
- **Extensible and Customizable:** Docker Compose files can be extended and customized for different environments or different use cases, making it a versatile tool for complex application setups.

In conclusion, the role of Docker Compose in development is invaluable, particularly when dealing with applications that require multiple interdependent services. Its ability to define, manage, and scale these services in a unified manner drastically simplifies the development workflow and ensures consistency across various deployment environments.

Writing a Docker Compose File

Creating a Docker Compose file is a fundamental step in using Docker Compose for managing multi-container Docker applications. This file, typically named **`docker-compose.yml`**, is a YAML file that defines the services, networks, and volumes for your application. It serves as a blueprint that Docker Compose uses to create and start your application's containers.

Let us understand the structure of a Docker Compose file. A Docker Compose file is structured into several sections, each serving a specific purpose:

```yaml
docker-compose.yaml
version: '3.8'

services:
  ui:
    build: .
    ports:
      - "4000:4000"
  redis:
    image: "redis:alpine"


networks:
  my_network:


volumes:
  my_volume:

```

Figure 11.11: *Sample Docker Compose File*

- **Version:** This specifies the version of the Docker Compose file format. The version you choose determines which features of Docker Compose you can use.
- **Services:** This is where you define your application's services. Each service represents a container or a group of containers that are deployed together. For each service, you can define the Docker image to use, ports to expose, volumes for data persistence, and other configuration details.
- **Networks:** This optional section allows you to define custom networks for facilitating communication between your services. Docker Compose sets up a default network for inter-service communication, but you can define additional networks for specific requirements.
- **Volumes:** This section is used to define persistent storage for your services. Volumes are essential for data that should be kept across container restarts or for sharing data between containers.

Configuring Services

When configuring services in your Docker Compose file, you have a wide range of options:

- **Image:** Specify the Docker image to use for the service.
- **Build:** Define the path to the directory containing the Dockerfile if you want to build the image.
- **Ports:** Map ports from the container to the host.
- **Environment Variables:** Set environment variables within the container.
- **Volumes:** Mount volumes for persistent or shared data.
- **Depends On:** Specify service dependencies to control the order of service startup.
- **Command:** Override the default command to run in the container.

Understanding Docker Compose with Example Project

Let us create a simple example where two Dockerized Express apps read from and write to a shared file in a Docker volume. This demonstrates how containers can share data using Docker volumes.

In our example, we will demonstrate the power of Docker volumes in facilitating data sharing between containers. We will create two separate Express applications, each running in its own Docker container, with one app writing data to a file and the other reading from it. Both applications will interact with the same file located in a shared Docker volume. This set up exemplifies a common use case in containerized environments where different services need to share or persist data.

The shared Docker volume acts as a common storage area accessible to both containers. Since Docker volumes are managed by Docker and exist outside the lifecycle of an individual container, they provide a persistent storage solution. This means the data written to the volume by one container can be accessed by another container, even if the containers are stopped and restarted, or updated.

- **Express App for Writing (App1):** This application serves as a data writer. It exposes an endpoint **(/data),** and upon receiving a request to this endpoint, it writes or appends data to a file (**message.txt)** in the shared Docker volume. Each write operation includes a timestamp, making each entry in the file unique.

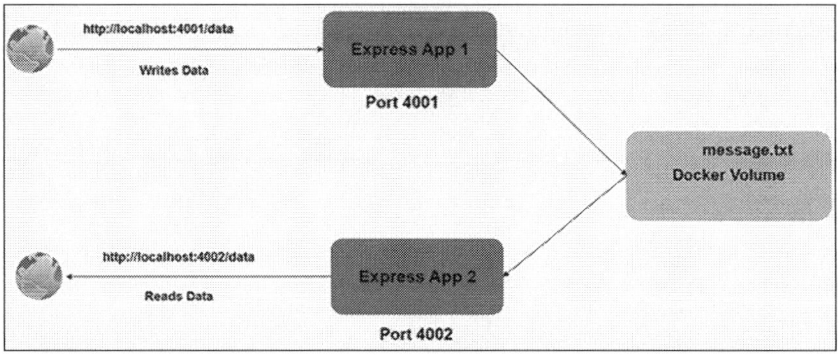

Figure 11.12: *Example Project Setup*

- **Express App for Reading (App2):** The second application functions as a data reader. It has a read endpoint (**`/data`**) that, when accessed, reads data from the same **`message.txt`** file in the shared volume and returns the content as the response.

Here is a simple **`app1/index.js`** file in which we are appending the data to the file in the volume.

```
app1 > JS index.js > app.listen() callback
const express = require('express');
const fs = require('fs');
const app = express();
const port = 4001;

app.get('/data', (req, res) => {
  const message = `Hello from App 1 at ${new Date()}\n`;
  fs.appendFileSync('/app-data/message.txt', message);
  res.send(`Message written by App 1. ${message}`);
});

app.listen(port, () => {
  console.log(`App 1 (Writer) listening at http://localhost:${port}`);
});
```

Figure 11.13: *App 1 writes data*

Here is a simple **app2/index.js** file in which we are reading the data to the file from the volume.

```
app2 > JS index.js > app.get('/data') callback > data
const express = require('express');
const fs = require('fs');
const app = express();
const port = 4002;

app.get('/data', (req, res) => {
  try {
    const data = fs.readFileSync('/app-data/message.txt', 'utf8');
    res.send(data);
  } catch (err) {
    res.status(500).send('Error reading message');
  }
});

app.listen(port, () => {
  console.log(`App 2 (Reader) listening at http://localhost:${port}`);
});
```

Figure 11.14: *App 2 reads data*

We need to define Dockerfile for each application. Here are the two Docker files that build the applications.

```
app1 > Dockerfile > ...
FROM node:14

WORKDIR /usr/src/app

COPY package*.json ./

RUN npm install

COPY . .

EXPOSE 4001

CMD [ "node", "index.js" ]
```

```
Dockerfile ×
app2 > Dockerfile > ...
FROM node:14

WORKDIR /usr/src/app

COPY package*.json ./

RUN npm install

COPY . .

EXPOSE 4002

CMD [ "node", "index.js" ]
```

Figure 11.15: *Dockerfile*

The following **docker-compose.yml** file outlines the configuration for our two services, including the shared **app-data** volume. Observe the structure of the sample project where each app maintains its individual Dockerfile. This set up illustrates how we build each application using the Docker Compose file, highlighting the integration of multiple services and shared volumes within a single project architecture.

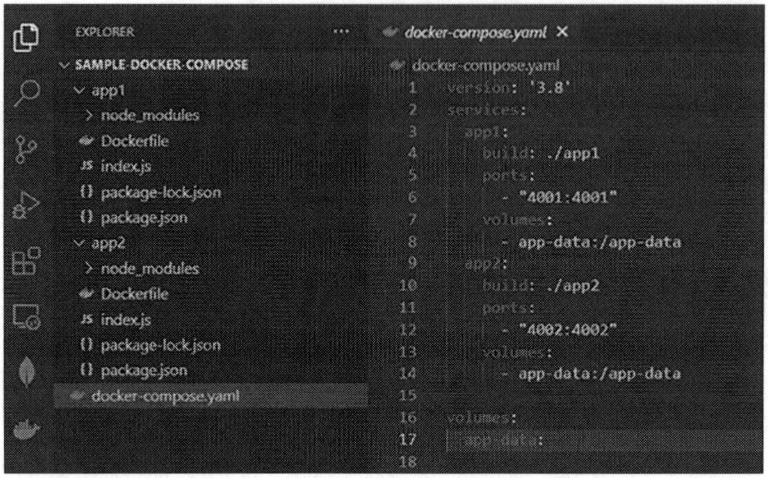

Figure 11.16: *Project Structure and docker-compose file*

Executing **`docker-compose up`** is a streamlined command that builds and launches all the containers defined in your **`docker-compose.yml`** file. This process involves automatically building Docker images from specified Dockerfiles, creating, and starting containers for each defined service, including setting up necessary networks, volumes, and port mappings. It ensures that service dependencies are respected, and containers are started in the correct order. By default, it also provides real-time log output to the console, facilitating easy monitoring and troubleshooting of your multi-container Docker application.

We can see from the below figure that App1 is running on the port 4001 that writes to the volume and App 2 is running on the port 4002 that reads from the volume.

Figure 11.17: *docker-compose up*

Once they are up and running, we can test the functionality as follows:

- **Writing**: Access **http://localhost:4001/data** in your browser or use a tool like **curl**. This will trigger `app1` to write a new message to the shared file.
- **Reading**: Access **http://localhost:4002/data** in your browser or use a tool like **curl**. This will trigger `app2` to read a message from the shared file.

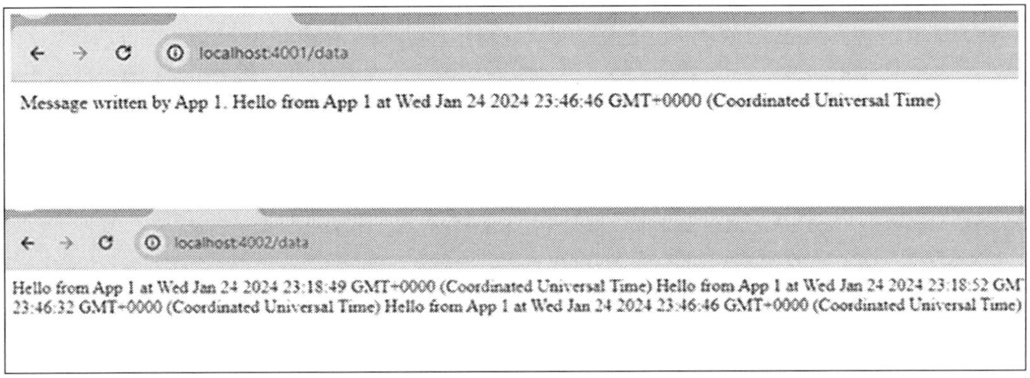

Figure 11.18: *Testing Docker Compose and Volumes*

This example underscores the integral role of Docker volumes in multi-container application set ups, particularly crucial for microservices-based architectures. Docker volumes facilitate seamless data sharing and persistence across applications running in separate containers, simplifying data management, and enhancing application modularity and scalability. When integrated with Docker Compose, this approach streamlines the orchestration of multi-container environments. Docker Compose allows for the easy configuration of services, networks, and shared volumes through a single YAML file, ensuring efficient management, consistency, and controlled service interdependencies. This combination of Docker volumes and Docker Compose not only simplifies the deployment of complex applications but also aligns perfectly with modern development workflows and team-based projects.

Best Practices with Docker Compose

Using Docker Compose effectively involves more than just writing a `docker-compose.yml` file. It requires an understanding of best practices to ensure that your Dockerized applications are efficient, secure, and easy to maintain. Below are key best practices to consider when working with Docker Compose.

- **Version Control:** Always keep your `docker-compose.yml` files under version control (such as Git). This allows you to track changes over time, revert to previous versions if necessary, and understand the evolution of your application's infrastructure. Version controlling your Docker Compose files also facilitates collaboration among team members, ensuring everyone is working with the same configurations.

- **Environment Variables for configurations:** Avoid hardcoding sensitive information like passwords or API keys in your Docker Compose files. Use environment variables or `.env` files for such data. This not only enhances security but also adds flexibility to your set up, as you can easily change configurations without modifying the Compose file itself. This practice is especially important when your application needs to run in different environments (development, staging, production), each with its own configuration.
- **Keep Services Isolated and Decoupled:** Design each service to have a single responsibility and ensure that it is loosely coupled with other services. This makes it easier to update, scale, and maintain each service independently. Use Docker Compose's networking features to enable communication between services. Define custom networks if necessary for complex applications.
- **Manage Data Persistence Carefully:** Use Docker volumes for data persistence, especially for databases or stateful services. This ensures that your data persists even when containers are stopped or restarted. Always have a backup strategy for your volumes, particularly in production environments.
- **Monitor and Log Effectively:** Set up proper logging for your containers. Docker Compose can aggregate logs from multiple containers, making it easier to monitor the health and performance of your application. Consider integrating third-party monitoring tools for deeper insights into your application's performance and health.
- **Optimize Your Compose File:** Keep your `docker-compose.yml` file modular and readable. Use Compose file overrides for different environments or scenarios. Utilize YAML anchors and extensions to avoid duplication in your Compose files.
- **Regularly Update and Maintain:** Keep Docker and Docker Compose updated to the latest stable versions to take advantage of new features, performance improvements, and security patches. Regularly update the base images and dependencies for your services to address any security vulnerabilities.
- **Leverage Compose in Development and CI/CD Pipelines:** Use Docker Compose in development to mirror your production environment as closely as possible. Integrate Docker Compose into your Continuous Integration/ Continuous Deployment (CI/CD) pipelines for consistent testing and deployment processes.

Adopting these best practices with Docker Compose will not only streamline your development and deployment processes but also ensure that your applications are secure, scalable, and maintainable. The simplicity and power of Docker Compose, when used effectively, can significantly enhance the overall quality and efficiency of your containerized applications.

Docker Compose is an indispensable tool for modern developers, particularly those working in team environments or on complex applications with multiple services. It simplifies the development process, reduces configuration errors, and ensures consistency across environments. As we progress through the book, we will delve deeper into how Docker Compose can be used to manage the MEVN stack, further illustrating its practicality and power in real-world applications.

Building and Running MEVN Stack Docker Image

Having explored Docker and Docker Compose through practical examples, we are now well-prepared to embark on the next crucial phase – building a Docker Image for our MEVN stack application. This process marks a significant step in containerizing our application, enhancing its portability, and streamlining the deployment process. In the upcoming sections, we will delve into the specifics of constructing a Docker Image tailored to our MEVN Stack, covering the necessary steps and best practices to ensure a successful build. This progression into Dockerizing our application represents a key advancement in adopting modern deployment strategies, aligning our project with industry standards for software development and deployment. Let us proceed with these focused sections to effectively containerize our MEVN stack.

One thing we need to understand before we build the Docker image is that in our Node.js Express application code, two significant features are used to serve the frontend and handle web requests: **`express.static`** and **`sendFile`** in a wildcard route handler.

Serving Static Assets with `express.static`

- The **`express.static`** middleware function is a crucial feature of Express for serving static files, such as HTML, CSS, JavaScript, and images. In this application, **`express.static(path.join(process.cwd(), '/ui/dist'))`** is used, which specifies that Express should serve the static files from the **`ui/dist`** directory. This directory typically contains the built assets of your front-end application (like a Vue.js app).
- When a request is made to the server, Express checks this directory for a file matching the request URL. If a corresponding file is found, Express serves it directly. This is particularly useful for serving the main index.html, JavaScript bundles, stylesheets, and images that are part of the frontend application.

Wildcard Route Handler with `sendFile`

- The wildcard route handler, denoted by `*`, is used to catch all other requests that do not match any of the previously defined routes (like your API endpoints). This is an essential part of integrating a Single Page Application (SPA) with a backend server.

- In the route handler, **`res.sendFile(path.join(process.cwd(), '/ui/dist/index.html'))`** is used. This instructs Express to respond to any unmatched request by sending the **`index.html`** file from the **`ui/dist`** directory. This approach is vital for SPAs where the routing is handled on the client-side by JavaScript running in the browser. The server sends the same **`index.html`** file irrespective of the requested path, and the front-end routing logic then displays the correct content.
- This set up ensures that users entering your application through various routes always receive the entry point of your SPA, allowing the frontend routing to function correctly.

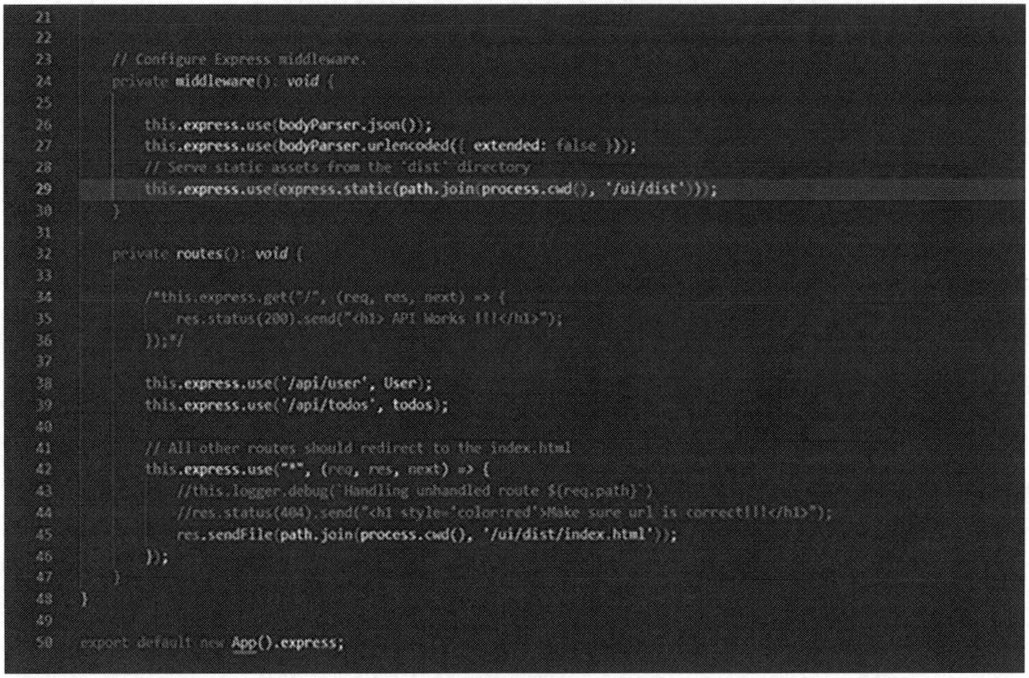

Figure 11.19: *Changes in app.ts*

Here is the Dockerfile script that outlines the steps to create a container image for a MEVN stack application, which includes both a Vue.js frontend (**`ui`**) and a Node.js/Express backend **(`api`).**

Initial Setup

- The Dockerfile begins by specifying **`node:16`** as the base image. This image includes the Node.js runtime, which is necessary for running a Node.js application.
- The **`WORKDIR`** is then set to **`/usr/src/app`** in the container. This command creates a working directory inside the container where the application files will be placed.

Preparing the Frontend

- The Dockerfile proceeds to handle the frontend part of the application first. It copies the **`package.json`** and **`package-lock.json`** files from the local **`ui`** directory to the **`ui`** directory inside the container.
- It then changes the working directory to **`/usr/src/app/ui`**.
- **`npm install`** is run to install the dependencies for the Vue.js application.
- The source code of the Vue.js application from the local **`ui`** directory is then copied into the container.
- **`npm run build`** is executed to build the frontend application. This command typically compiles the Vue.js app into static files ready for deployment.

```
# Use an official Node runtime as a parent image
FROM node:16

# Set the working directory in the container
WORKDIR /usr/src/app

# Copy package.json and package-lock.json
COPY ui/package*.json ./ui/

# change the working directory
WORKDIR /usr/src/app/ui

# Install any needed packages
RUN npm install

# Bundle app source
COPY ui/ .

# Running the build
RUN npm run build

# change the working directory
WORKDIR /usr/src/app

# Copy package.json and package-lock.json
COPY api/package*.json ./api/

# change the working directory
WORKDIR /usr/src/app/api

# Install any needed packages
RUN npm install

# Bundle app source
COPY api/ .

# Your app binds to port 3080 so you'll use the EXPOSE instruction to have it mapped by the docker daemon
EXPOSE 3080

# Running the build
RUN npm run build-prod

# change the working directory
WORKDIR /usr/src/app

# Run the application
CMD ["node", "api/dist/api.bundle.js"]
```

Figure 11.20: *Dockerfile*

Preparing the Backend

- The working directory is switched back to **/usr/src/app**.
- The Dockerfile then handles the backend part by copying the **package.json** and **package-lock.json** files from the local **api** directory to the **api** directory inside the container.
- The working directory is changed to **/usr/src/app/api**.
- **npm install** is run again, this time to install dependencies for the Node.js/Express application.
- The source code of the Node.js/Express application from the local **api** directory is copied into the container.
- **npm run build-prod** is executed to build the backend application. This typically involves transpiling the code and bundling it for production.

Finalizing the Build

- The Dockerfile exposes port **3080**, which is the port that the Express server will listen on.
- The final command in the Dockerfile, **CMD ["node", "api/dist/api.bundle.js"]**, tells Docker how to run the container. It starts the Node.js application using the bundled JavaScript file created by the **npm run build-prod** command.

This Dockerfile effectively creates a Docker image that includes both the frontend and backend of a MEVN stack application, ready to be run in a containerized environment. The process involves installing dependencies, building both parts of the application, and setting up the necessary commands to run the application within the Docker container.

After executing the specified command, Docker interprets the instructions from the Dockerfile to construct the Docker image. Once the build process is complete, you can view a list of all available Docker images on your system by using the **docker images** command.

```
docker build -t mevn-stack .
```

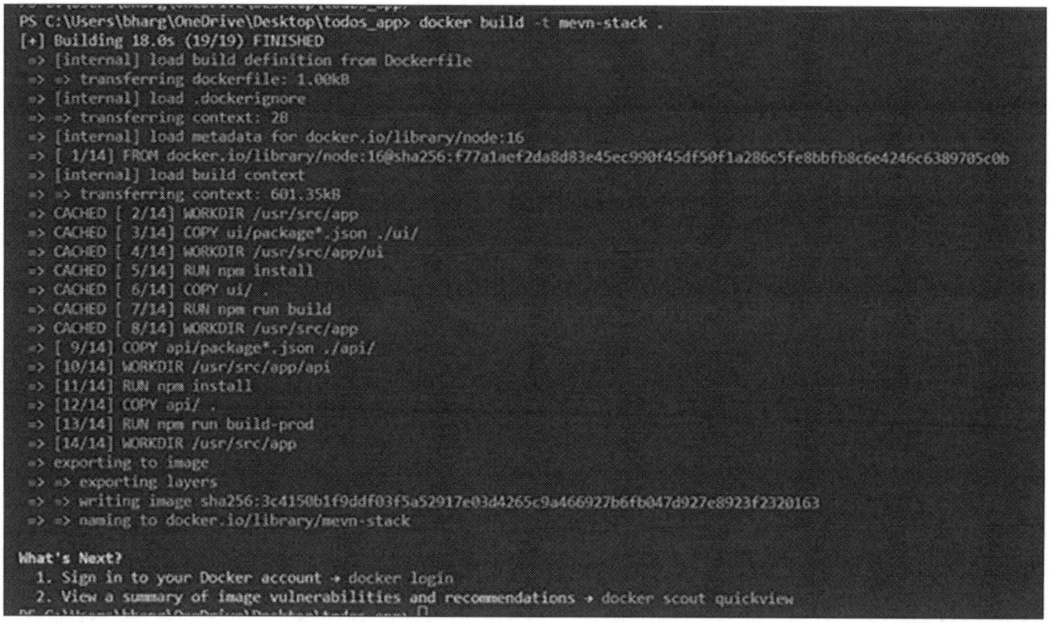

Figure 11.21: *Building Docker Image*

After successfully building the Docker image, it becomes visible not only through the command line but also on the Docker Desktop interface. An important observation here is the substantial size of the Docker image, which, in this case, is approximately 1.24GB. The reason behind this considerable size is the absence of multi-stage builds in our current Dockerfile configuration.

Multi-stage builds in Docker are a powerful feature designed to minimize the final size of Docker images. They achieve this by allowing multiple stages in the Docker build process, where each stage can use a different base image, and only the necessary artifacts from each stage are carried over to the final image. This approach avoids including unnecessary files, dependencies, and build environments in the final image, thus significantly reducing its size.

In the upcoming section, we will delve into multi-stage builds and demonstrate how to implement them. By adopting this approach, we aim to optimize our Docker image, reducing its size without sacrificing the functionality or integrity of our application. This optimization is particularly crucial for efficient storage, faster deployment, and improved performance, especially in production environments where resources and speed are paramount.

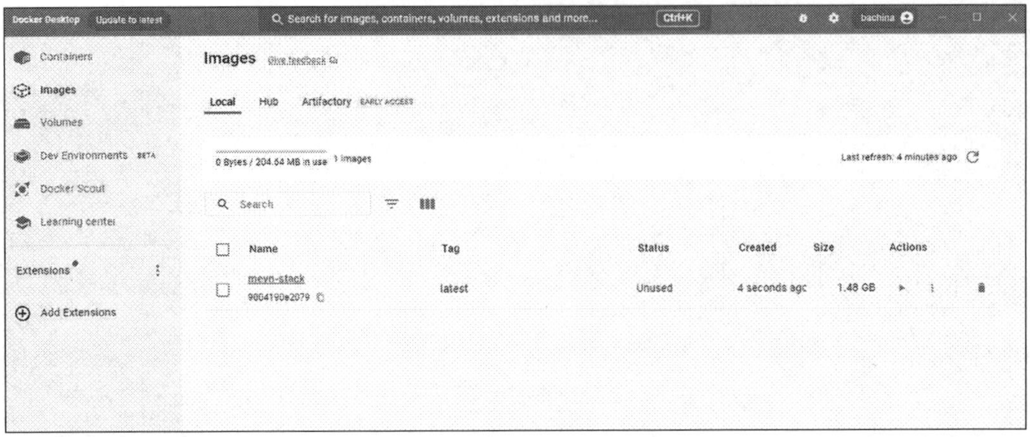

Figure 11.22: *Docker Desktop*

Let us run the following command to start and run the container.

```
docker run -d -p 3080:3080 –name mevn-stack mevn-stack
```

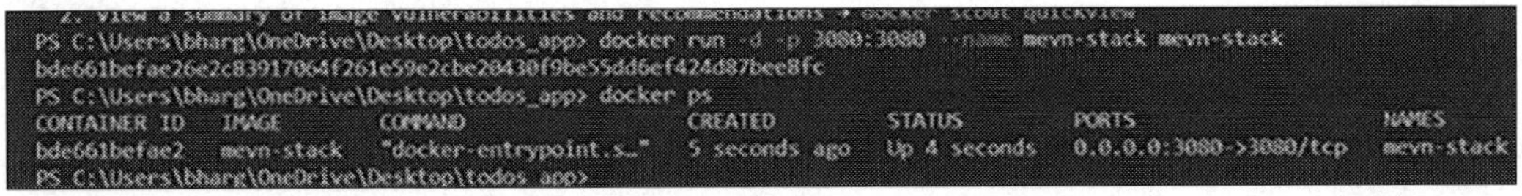

Figure 11.23: *Docker Run Command*

The **docker run** command is a fundamental instruction used in Docker for starting containers from Docker images. In this command, **docker run -d -p 3080:3080 --name mevn-stack mevn-stack**, various options and parameters are specified to control how the container is created and run.

The **-d** flag stands for "**detached mode**." This option runs the container in the background of your terminal. It allows the container to continue running without occupying the command line interface and without being tied to a specific terminal session. This mode is commonly used in production deployments where the container needs to run continuously, like a web server or a database.

The **-p 3080:3080** part of the command is about port mapping. This option tells Docker to map port 3080 of the host machine (the first **3080**) to port **3080** inside the Docker container (the second **3080**). This port mapping is crucial for web applications, as it allows external access to the services running inside the container. For instance, if your MEVN stack application's server listens on port **3080**, this setting will enable users to access it using the host machine's IP address and port **3080**.

The **--name mevn-stack** segment assigns a custom name to the running container. In this case, the container is named **mevn-stack**. Naming containers is helpful for managing and identifying them, especially when you have multiple containers running on the same host.

Finally, the last **mevn-stack** in the command specifies the name of the Docker image to use for creating the container. This should be the name of an image you previously built, which contains your MEVN stack application. When this command is executed, Docker looks for an image named **mevn-stack** in the local Docker image registry and uses it to start a new container.

The application is accessible on your local machine via port 3080, thanks to the port mapping configuration that routes this port to the external interface. This set up ensures that the application running inside the Docker container can be reached through **localhost:3080**. This functionality is illustrated in the subsequent figure.

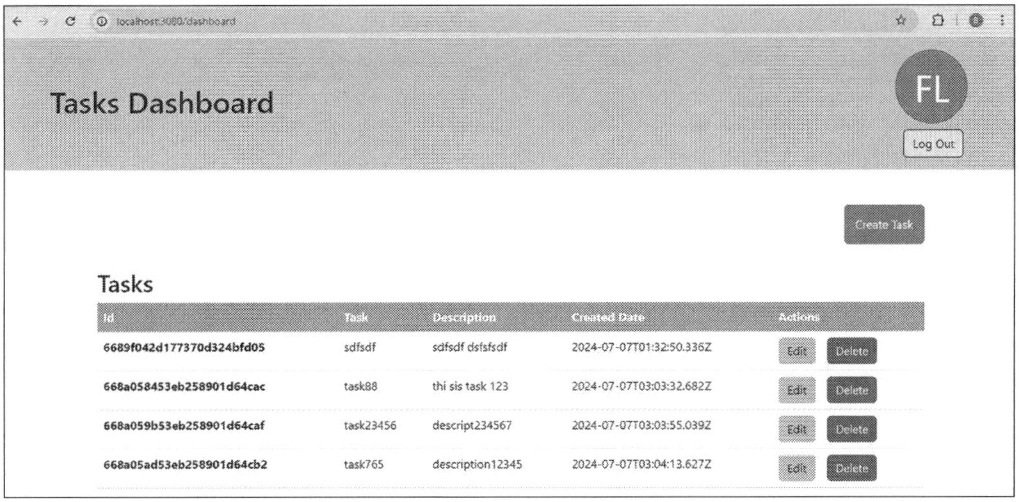

Figure 11.24: *Running Application on Docker*

We have the capability to view the logs of the running container using the **docker logs** command. To watch the logs of a running Docker container in real-time, you use the **docker logs** command with the **-f** (or **--follow**) option. This will continuously display the container's log output to the console.

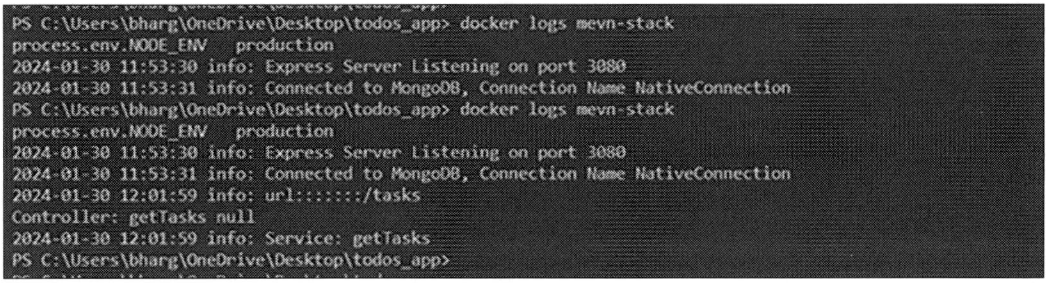

Figure 11.25: *Docker logs*

Building and Running Image with Multi-Stage Builds

In the realm of Docker containerization, multi-stage builds represent a significant advancement in optimizing Dockerfile configurations. This methodology enables the creation of leaner, more efficient Docker images by utilizing multiple stages in a single Dockerfile. Each stage can use a different base image and perform specific tasks, such as building dependencies or compiling code. The final stage assembles the necessary components, often discarding development tools and intermediate artifacts. This results in smaller, more secure, and performance-optimized images.

Understanding the Need

Traditional Docker images often contain unnecessary components like build dependencies, source code, and development tools. These elements, while crucial during the build phase, are superfluous in a production environment. Multi-stage builds address this issue by separating the build environment from the runtime environment. The process involves compiling, testing, and building the application in initial stages, followed by copying only the essential elements to the final stage. This separation ensures that the resulting image contains only what is necessary to run the application, reducing the attack surface and improving load times.

Multi-stage builds offer numerous advantages:

- **Reduced Image Size**: Smaller images are faster to deploy and require less storage.
- **Enhanced Security**: Images containing only necessary components reduce the potential attack surface.
- **Better Organization**: Separating build and production concerns leads to cleaner, more maintainable Dockerfiles.

Multi-stage builds in Docker are an essential technique for any developer or organization aiming to leverage containerization effectively. By adopting this approach, teams can ensure efficient resource utilization, improved security, and streamlined deployment processes, making it a cornerstone of modern containerized application development.

The provided Dockerfile demonstrates a multi-stage build process. Initially, the user interface (UI) is constructed in the initial stage, labeled as **`build-ui`**. Subsequently, the application programming interface (API) is assembled in the next stage, named **`build-api`**. In the final stage of the build process, only the essential assets from both the UI and API stages are selectively copied over, ensuring that the final Docker image contains only the necessary components.

Stage 1: Building the UI

The Dockerfile begins with the first stage focused on building the user interface (UI). It uses **`node:16`** as the base image to set up a Node.js environment. The process involves setting **`/app/ui`** as the working directory in the container, copying the UI's **`package.json`** and **`package-lock.json`**, and then running **`npm install`** to install the necessary UI dependencies. After this, the UI source code is copied into the container. The build command **`npm run build`** is executed to compile the UI, resulting in a set of static files typically located in a **`dist`** directory.

Stage 2: Building the API

The second stage of the Dockerfile is dedicated to building the application's API. This stage also starts with the **`node:16`** image. It sets up **`/app/api`** as the working directory. The API's **`package.json`**, **`package-lock.json`**, and **`tsconfig.json`** are then copied into this directory. Dependencies for the API are installed via **`npm install`**. Following this, the API's source code is copied into the container. The API is then built using **`npm run build-prod`**, preparing it for production deployment, typically involving the transpilation of TypeScript code.

Stage 3: Final Assembly and Execution

The final stage of the Dockerfile is where the UI and API are combined to create the runnable application image. Again, using **`node:16`** as the base, this stage sets **`/app`** as the working directory and exposes port 3080, which the API uses. It then copies the built UI assets from the **`build-ui`** stage and the API's **`package.json`** and **`package-lock.json`**. Only the production dependencies are installed to keep the image lean. Finally, the built API files from the **`build-api`** stage are copied over. The Docker container starts the application with the command **`CMD ["node", "api.bundle.js"]`**, initiating the API server.

```
Dockerfile > ...
# Stage 1: Build the UI
FROM node:16 as build-ui
# Set the working directory for the UI
WORKDIR /app/ui
# Copy UI package.json and package-lock.json
COPY ui/package*.json ./
# Install UI dependencies
RUN npm install
# Copy the rest of the UI source code
COPY ui/ .
# Build the UI
RUN npm run build

# Stage 2: Build the API
FROM node:16 as build-api
# Set the working directory for the API
WORKDIR /app/api
# Copy API package.json and package-lock.json
COPY api/package.json ./
COPY api/tsconfig.json ./
# Install API dependencies
RUN npm install
# Copy the rest of the API source code
COPY api/ .
# Build the API
RUN npm run build-prod


# Stage 3: Final stage - Combine UI and API
FROM node:16
# Expose the port the API is running on
EXPOSE 3080
# Set the working directory to where API is copied
WORKDIR /app
# Copy built UI assets from the UI build stage
COPY --from=build-ui /app/ui/dist /app/ui/dist
# Copy package.json and package-lock.json
COPY /api/package*.json /app
# Install production dependencies
RUN npm install --only=production
# Copy built API files from the API build stage
COPY --from=build-api /app/api/dist /app


# Run the API
CMD ["node", "api.bundle.js"]
```

Figure 11.26: *Multistage Docker File*

This multi-stage Dockerfile efficiently separates the build environments for the UI and API, resulting in a cleaner, more optimized final Docker image. By only including what is necessary for running the application in the final stage, the Dockerfile ensures a leaner image, beneficial for storage, faster deployments, and improved performance.

To build the Docker image, you can use the same command as previously mentioned.

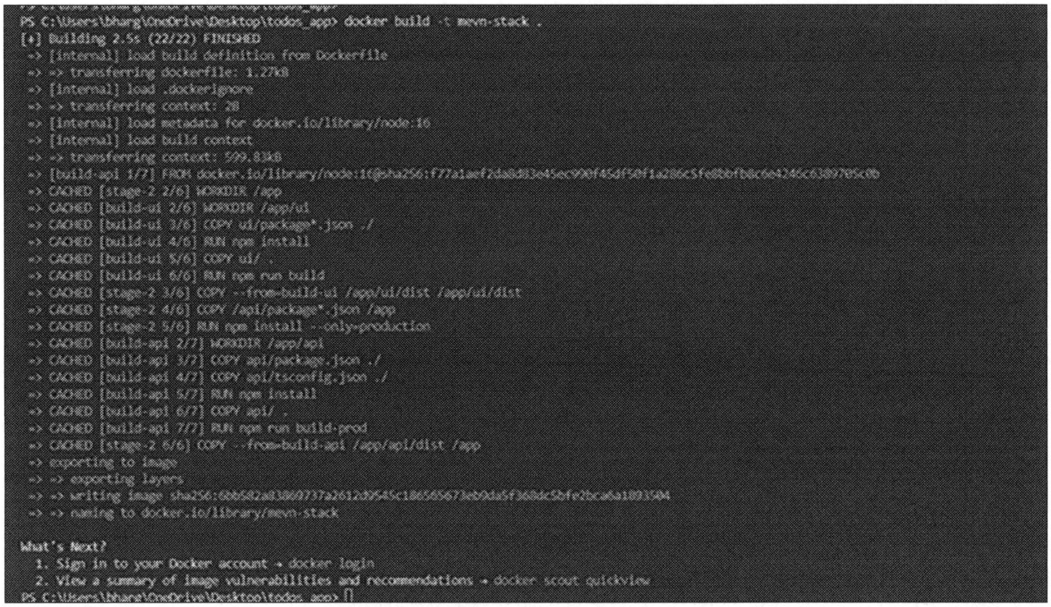

Figure 11.27: *Building Docker Image*

The size of the Docker image has now been reduced, which is evident from the information displayed on Docker Desktop.

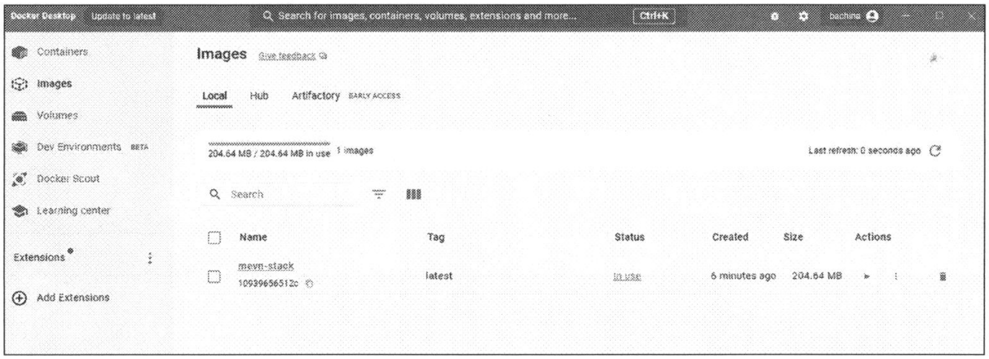

Figure 11.28: *Docker Desktop*

Just like the approach detailed in the preceding section, you can launch the Docker image using the same set of commands to get your application up and running inside a Docker container. This process involves utilizing the **`docker run`** command with appropriate options to start a container based on the newly built Docker image. Once the container is running, it hosts your application, making it accessible and functional within the Docker environment. This method provides a consistent and isolated set up, allowing you to interact with your application as it would operate in a production-like environment. By following these steps, you can verify the correct set up and functionality of your application, ensuring that it behaves as expected in the containerized context provided by Docker.

Interaction with Running Container

In the context of Docker, **`docker exec`** is a command used to run a specific command in an already running container. If you want to interact with a container that is already up and running, **`docker exec`** allows you to start a new command in a running container. This can be particularly useful for debugging purposes, for executing one-off commands, or for interacting with an application that is running inside a Docker container.

```
PS C:\Users\bharg\OneDrive\Desktop\Books\todos_app> docker ps
CONTAINER ID   IMAGE        COMMAND                  CREATED          STATUS          PORTS                    NAMES
48e44a36b66d   mevn-stack   "docker-entrypoint.s…"   13 seconds ago   Up 12 seconds   0.0.0.0:3080->3080/tcp   mevn-stack
PS C:\Users\bharg\OneDrive\Desktop\Books\todos_app> docker exec -it mevn-stack /bin/sh
/app # ls
api.bundle.js      node_modules       package-lock.json  package.json       public             ssl                ui
/app # cd ui
/app/ui # ls
dist
/app/ui # cd dist
/app/ui/dist # ls
assets      index.html  vite.svg
/app/ui/dist # cd ..
/app/ui # cd ..
/app # ls
api.bundle.js      node_modules       package-lock.json  package.json       public             ssl                ui
/app # cat package.json
{
  "name": "todos_api",
  "version": "1.0.0",
  "description": "API Backend for todos application",
  "main": "index.ts",
  "scripts": {
    "start": "ts-node index.ts",
    "dev": "cross-env NODE_ENV='production' nodemon",
    "build": "webpack",
    "lint": "eslint .",
    "lint-fix": "eslint . --fix",
    "build-test": "cross-env NODE_ENV='test' webpack",
    "build-prod": "cross-env NODE_ENV='production' webpack --progress",
    "run:prod": "cross-env NODE_ENV='production' PORT=3080 MONGO_CONNECTION_STR='mongodb+srv://bhargavbook58:tester12345@tod
    "test": "jest",
    "prepare": "husky install",
    "build:backend": "npm run build",
    "build:frontend": "cd ../ui && npm run build",
    "copy:frontend": "ncp ../ui/dist ./dist/public",
    "copy:ssl": "ncp ./ssl ./dist/ssl/",
    "zip:dist": "bestzip dist.zip ./api/build/*",
    "zip-build": "npm run build:backend && npm run build:frontend && npm run copy:frontend && npm run copy:ssl && npm run zi
  },
  "keywords": [
    "API",
    "NodeJS",
    "TypeScript",
    "MongoDB"
```

***Figure 11.29:** Interacting with Docker Container*

In the given scenario, depicted through the command execution in the image, one can observe the utilization of **`docker exec -it mevn-stack /bin/sh`**. This command initiates an interactive shell session within the running container identified as **`mevn-stack`**. The options **`-it`** are critical; **`-i`** ensures that the session is interactive, allowing the user to enter commands, while **`-t`** allocates a pseudo-terminal, emulating a terminal interface within the context of the container. This setup is indispensable for developers or system administrators who require a direct command-line interface to manage the container's internal environment effectively.

This series of commands demonstrates how a user can interact with the file system within a Docker container, checking the structure and contents, much like navigating the file system on their own local machine. This can be essential for verifying that files are placed correctly during the Docker build process and for troubleshooting any issues related to file paths and access within the container.

Running MEVN Stack on Docker Compose

In earlier sections, we have explored the functionalities and advantages of Docker Compose. Now, we shall demonstrate its practical application by deploying our MEVN stack application using Docker Compose. This will illustrate the capability of Docker Compose to streamline the development process by encapsulating all the necessary components within containers, thereby eliminating the need for individual installations on a developer's workstation. Let us proceed to witness Docker Compose in action, facilitating the orchestration of our application's services with minimal set up requirements.

Before proceeding to write the **`docker-compose.yml`** file for our services, it is essential to first establish Dockerfiles for each component of our application. Although it is technically possible to include all necessary commands directly within the Docker Compose file, this approach is generally not advised due to concerns of maintainability and clarity. In our case, where the application is structured with two distinct layers – the User Interface (UI) and the Application Programming Interface (API) – we need to create separate Dockerfiles for each. These Dockerfiles act as blueprints for building the respective Docker images. Ideally, these Dockerfiles should be placed at the root of their respective directories, **`api`** and **`ui`**. This organization ensures a clear separation of concerns and makes the build process more intuitive and manageable, especially in a development environment where different teams or individuals might be responsible for different components of the application.

This Dockerfile describes the process for creating a Docker image for an API built with Node.js. It begins by specifying **`node:16`** as the base image, ensuring that the container has the Node.js runtime environment. The **`build-api`** tag identifies this stage of the build. The working directory within the container is set to **`/usr/src/app`**, where the application's files will reside. The **COPY** command then transfers **`package.json`** and **`package-lock.json`** into the container to manage dependencies. **npm install** is executed to install these dependencies. After this, the **`COPY . .`** command copies the rest of the application's source code into the container. The **`EXPOSE`** instruction informs

Docker that the application listens on port 3080. Following this, **`npm run build`** is used to build the application, compiling the source code into a distributable format located in the **`dist`** directory. Finally, the **`CMD`** instruction sets the default command to run the built application (**`node dist/api.bundle.js`**), which starts the API server when the container is launched.

```
api > Dockerfile > ...
# Use an official Node runtime as a parent image
FROM node:16 as build-api

# change the working directory
WORKDIR /usr/src/app

# Copy package.json and package-lock.json
COPY package*.json .

# Install any needed packages
RUN npm install

# Bundle app source
COPY . .

# Your app binds to port 3080 so you'll use the EXPOSE instruction to have it mapped by
EXPOSE 3080

RUN npm run build

# Running the build
CMD ["node", "dist/api.bundle.js"]
```

Figure 11.30: API *Dockerfile*

This Dockerfile outlines the process for building a Docker image for a Node.js-based User Interface (UI). It uses **`node:16`** as the parent image to provide the Node.js runtime environment, and tags this build stage as **`build-ui`**. The working directory is set to **`/usr/src/app`** within the container, which serves as the main directory for the application's files. The **`COPY package*.json`** command transfers the **`package.json`** and **`package-lock.json`** files into the container, which contain the project's dependency information. The **`RUN npm install`** command then installs these dependencies. Following this, the **`COPY . .`** instruction copies the rest of the application's source code into the container. Finally, the **`CMD ["npm", "run", "dev"]`** command is set as the default command to be executed when the container starts, triggering the **`dev`** script defined in **`package.json`**. This script typically starts a development server for the UI, making it accessible for development and testing purposes.

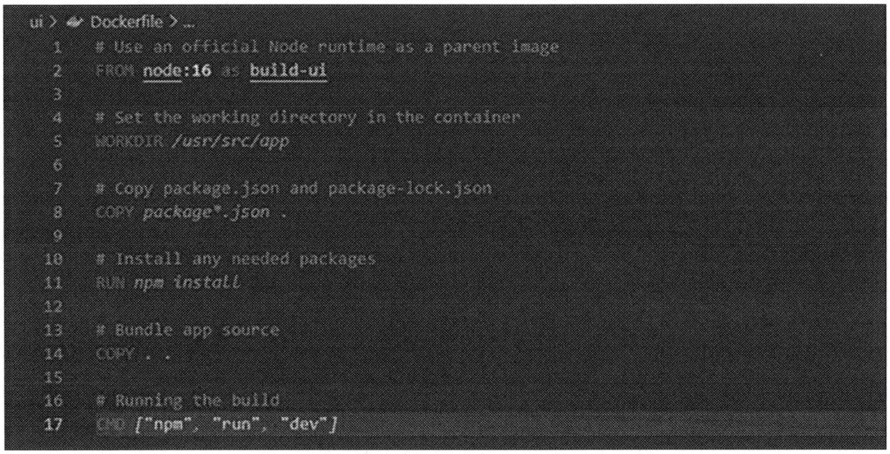

ui > Dockerfile > ...

```
# Use an official Node runtime as a parent image
FROM node:16 as build-ui

# Set the working directory in the container
WORKDIR /usr/src/app

# Copy package.json and package-lock.json
COPY package*.json .

# Install any needed packages
RUN npm install

# Bundle app source
COPY . .

# Running the build
CMD ["npm", "run", "dev"]
```

Figure 11.31: *UI Dockerfile*

In the illustrated architecture, we have articulated a three-tiered service structure for the MEVN stack application using Docker Compose. This structure includes a Vue.js front-end user interface, an Express.js API as the server-side layer, and a MongoDB database. The Vue UI is accessible through **`http://localhost:5173/`,** which is mapped to the **`vue-ui`** container running the front-end code. It communicates with the backend Express API via **`http://node-api:3001`**, where **`node-api`** corresponds to the service name defined in Docker Compose, facilitating seamless inter-container communication on the Docker network. For database operations, even though the MEVN stack typically utilizes MongoDB Atlas for cloud-based data storage, for local development, a MongoDB instance is run as a **`mongo-db`** service container. It can be interacted through the URL **`mongodb://mongo:27017/todos`**, where **`mongo`** is the alias for the MongoDB container specified within the Docker Compose file. This set up ensures that the entire application stack can be run and managed locally using Docker Compose, providing a simplified and isolated development environment that closely mirrors production settings.

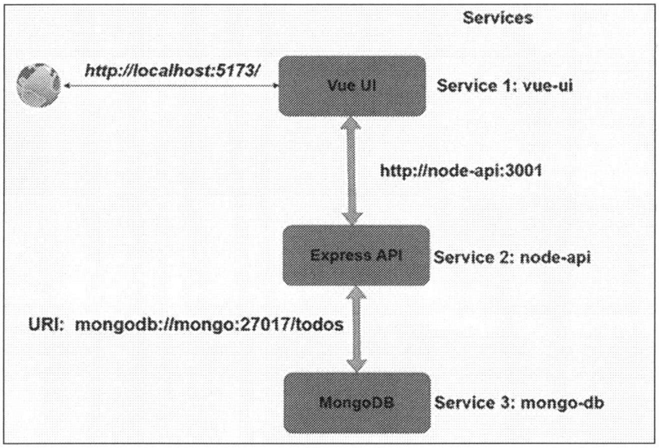

Figure 11.32: *Docker Compose Setup*

Due to the switch to a local MongoDB instance, it is necessary to modify the MongoDB connection string found within the **.env** file to reflect this change. This adjustment ensures that the application correctly interacts with the MongoDB service hosted within the local Docker environment instead of an external cloud-based database, thereby aligning the development environment more closely with the production set up.

Figure 11.33: *Dotenv Configuration*

Adjusting the backend service URL in our Vue application necessitates an update to the **vite.config.ts** configuration file. This file's **proxy** settings are crucial for local development, particularly when working within a Docker Compose network. The **proxy** option reroutes API requests from the frontend server to the backend service, ensuring that calls to **/api** are directed to **http://node-api:3001**, which is the new backend service URL specified within our Docker Compose setup. By setting **host: true** within the server configuration of our Vite set up, we are ensuring that the development server is accessible to the host network, a necessary change for it to operate correctly when encapsulated in a Docker environment. This makes it possible for the Dockerized Vue UI to communicate with the backend service through Docker's internal networking capabilities, closely mimicking the conditions of a deployed environment while developing locally.

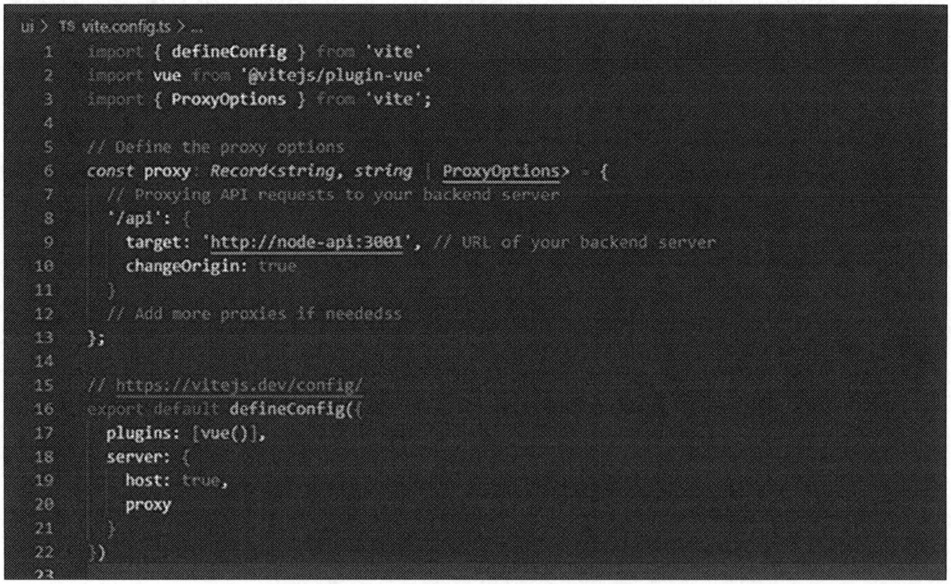

Figure 11.34: *vite configuration file*

Here is the complete Docker compose file that defines a multi-service application using version **3.8** of the Compose file format. There are three services: **`api`**, **`ui`**, and **`mongo`**.

- The **`api`** service builds from a **`Dockerfile`** located in the **`./api`** directory, specifically targeting the **`build-api`** stage. It sets the container's name to **`node-api`** and maps the host's port **`3001`** to the container's port **`3001`**, enabling access to the API. It also mounts the **`./api`** directory into the container at **`/app`** for development purposes, allowing changes to be reflected immediately. This service depends on the **`mongo`** service, ensuring the database is available before the API starts.
- The **`ui`** service also builds from a **`Dockerfile`**, found in the **`./ui`** directory, targeting the **`build-ui`** stage. The container is named **`vue-ui`**, and the service binds the host's port **`5173`** to the container's port **`5173`**. The **`./ui`** directory is mounted to **`/app`** inside the container, facilitating hot-reloading during development.
- The **`mongo`** service uses the official **`mongo:latest`** image from Docker Hub without building from a **`Dockerfile`**. It names the container **`mongo-db`** and exposes port **`27017`** to match the default MongoDB port, allowing other services or host systems to connect to the database. It uses a named volume, **`mongo-data`**, to persist the database data even if the container is removed.

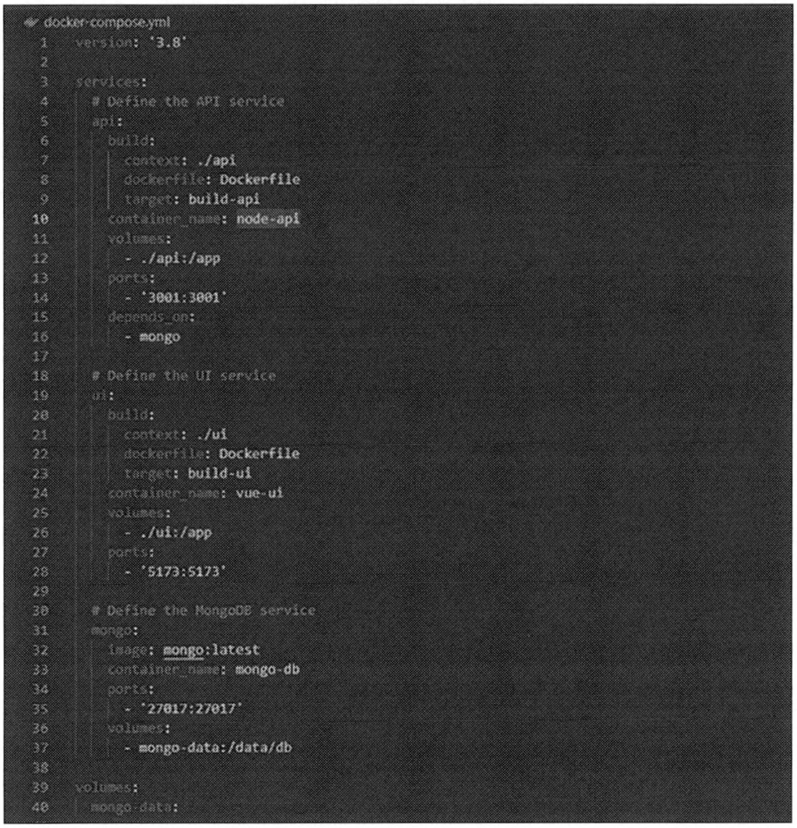

docker-compose.yml

```yaml
version: '3.8'

services:
  # Define the API service
  api:
    build:
      context: ./api
      dockerfile: Dockerfile
      target: build-api
    container_name: node-api
    volumes:
      - ./api:/app
    ports:
      - '3001:3001'
    depends_on:
      - mongo

  # Define the UI service
  ui:
    build:
      context: ./ui
      dockerfile: Dockerfile
      target: build-ui
    container_name: vue-ui
    volumes:
      - ./ui:/app
    ports:
      - '5173:5173'

  # Define the MongoDB service
  mongo:
    image: mongo:latest
    container_name: mongo-db
    ports:
      - '27017:27017'
    volumes:
      - mongo-data:/data/db

volumes:
  mongo-data:
```

Figure 11.35: *Docker Compose File*

The **volumes** section at the end of the file declares **mongo-data**, which is a Docker-managed volume where MongoDB stores its data files. This ensures that the database data is kept intact across container restarts and removals.

Using this **docker-compose** file, one can build and run a full-stack MEVN application with each service running in its isolated environment but able to communicate with each other as required.

After you have implemented the necessary modifications and ensured that Docker Desktop is operational, the next step is simply to execute the commands provided below.

```
// start the docker compose
docker-compose up -d
// list services
docker ps
// stop the services
docker-compose down
```

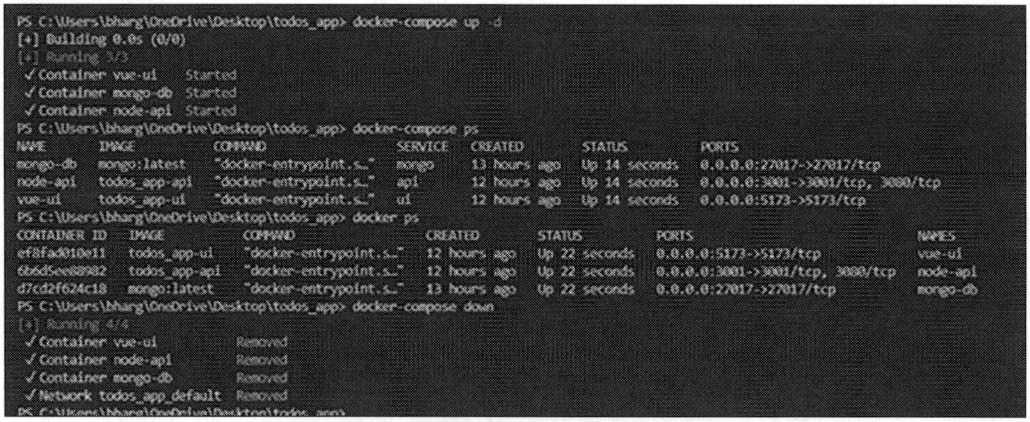

Figure 11.36: *Running Docker Compose*

The following image depicts the successful execution of a MEVN stack application within a Dockerized environment, orchestrated by Docker Compose. It demonstrates the live application interface, where the Vue.js frontend is effectively making API calls to the Node.js backend. The developer console within the browser illustrates these interactions, with network requests showing the path **/api/todos** indicating API endpoints being accessed by the frontend. This seamless integration between the UI and the backend services is a testament to the well-configured Docker Compose set up, which allows each component of the MEVN stack to communicate and function as a cohesive unit. The ability to proxy requests from the frontend to the backend without leaving the Dockerized environment streamlines development workflows and simulates a production-like setup on a local machine.

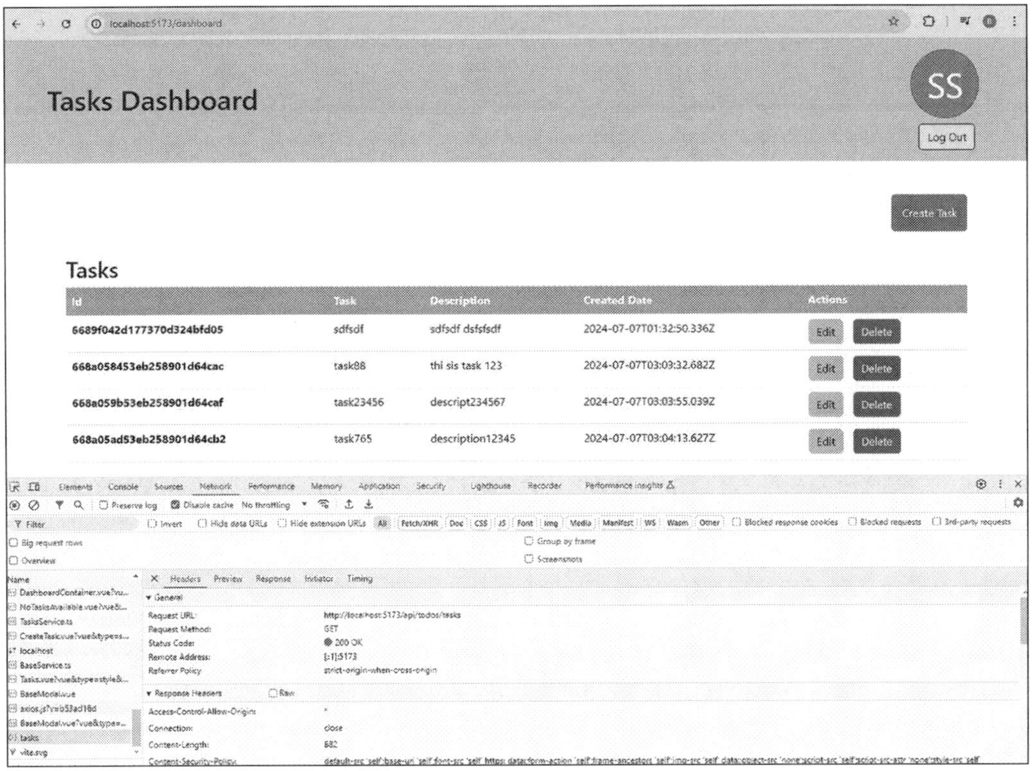

Figure 11.37: *Application Running on Docker Compose*

In the context of running applications within Docker containers, observing the logs generated by these containers is crucial for monitoring their activities and diagnosing issues. The image suggests that the user is utilizing Docker Compose to manage multiple containers, which are part of a MEVN stack application. The user retrieves the logs by executing Docker commands specifically targeting the container names defined in the Docker Compose file. For instance, **`docker logs vue-ui`** and **`docker logs node-api`** are commands used to fetch logs from the containers running the Vue.js user interface and the Node.js API, respectively. These logs provide real-time insight into the operations of each service, such as the Vite development server starting up and the Express server's database connections and request handling, which are pivotal for the iterative development and debugging process.

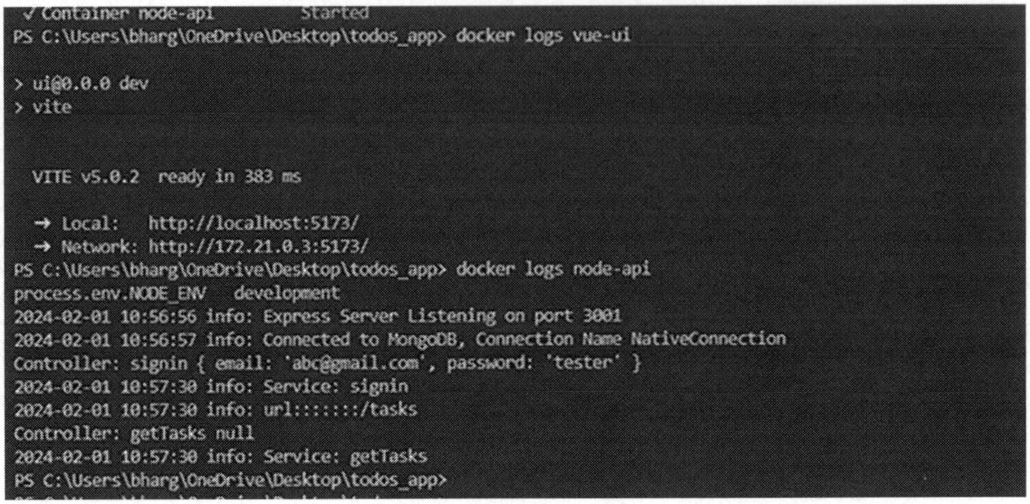

Figure 11.38: *docker logs*

As we conclude our exploration of deploying the MEVN stack using Docker Compose, it is clear that containerization brings a new level of efficiency and simplicity to the development process. Through the examples provided, we have witnessed firsthand how Docker Compose facilitates the orchestration of multiple services, ensuring that each component of the MEVN stack can be run in a consistent environment, both locally and in production.

By defining services for the Vue.js frontend, the Express backend, and the MongoDB database, Docker Compose allows us to manage the lifecycle of our full-stack application with ease. It abstracts away the complexity of starting, stopping, and rebuilding services, allowing developers to focus on what matters most – building feature-rich applications.

Publishing the Docker Image

Publishing a Docker image to a Docker registry is a crucial step in the development and deployment lifecycle of Dockerized applications. This process enables you to share your Docker images with team members, deploy them to production environments, or make them available to the public. In this chapter, we will explore how to publish a Docker image, using Docker Hub as an example registry. We will also cover best practices for versioning and managing your images effectively.

Before publishing a Docker image, ensure you have:

- Docker installed on your machine.
- An account on Docker Hub or another Docker registry.
- A Docker image to publish.

Having previously installed Docker on our system and successfully built our Docker image, the next step involves establishing an account on Docker Hub. To set up a new account, you can navigate directly to the Docker Hub signup page. Alternatively, for a more streamlined process, you have the option to sign up using your existing Google or GitHub account credentials. This flexibility allows for easy integration and access, ensuring a seamless transition to publishing your Docker image.

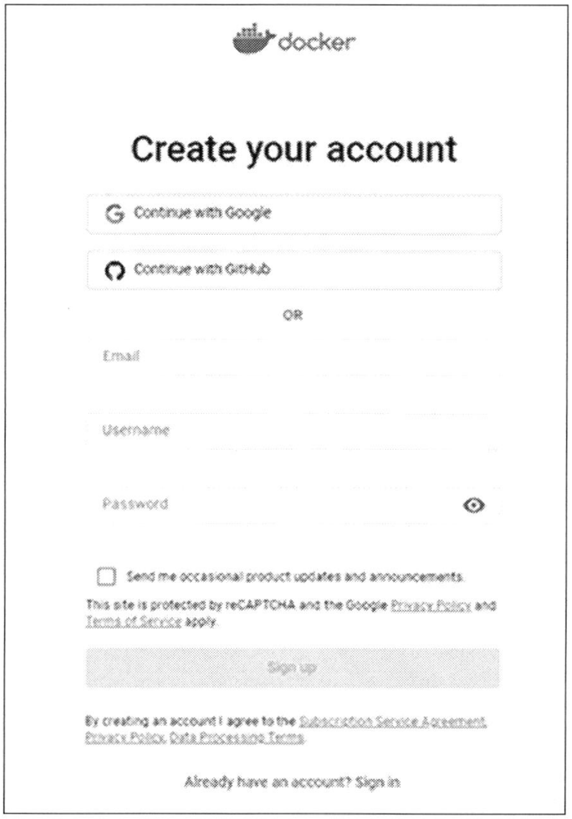

Figure 11.39: *creating a DockerHub Account*

Upon creating your account and logging in, you will be greeted with a user-friendly interface, though initially devoid of any personal repositories. Despite this, Docker Hub provides access to a vast array of public repositories hosted by other users and organizations. Your personal namespace on Docker Hub corresponds to the username you chose during the sign up process. This namespace is crucial as it will be part of the repository names for your Docker images, enabling you to manage and share your images under a unique identifier.

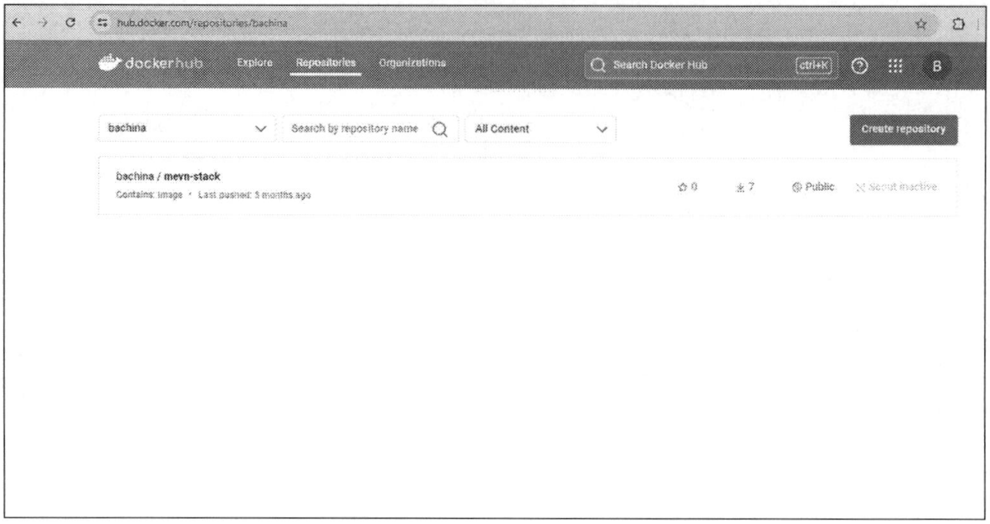

Figure 11.40: *Exploring Repositories*

Once we have logged in to DockerHub, we need to follow these steps to create one repository.

- Navigate to Repositories and click "**`Create Repository`**".
- Name your repository, set visibility (public or private), and click "**`Create`**".

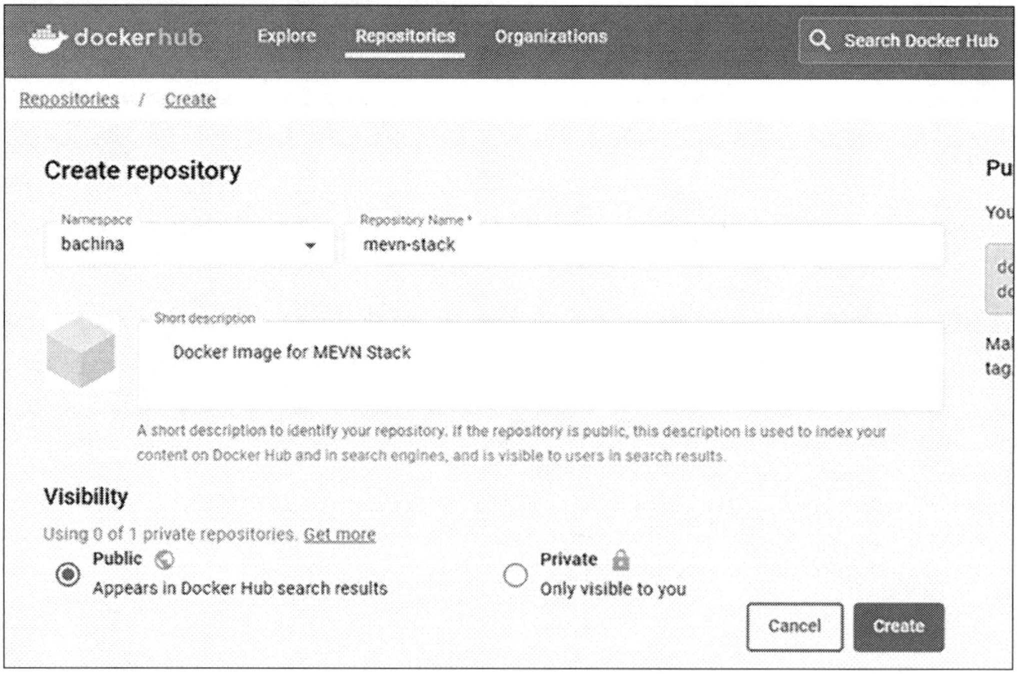

Figure 11.41: *Creating a Docker Repository*

Once you create a repository, you see the following page and you can even add an overview of the image.

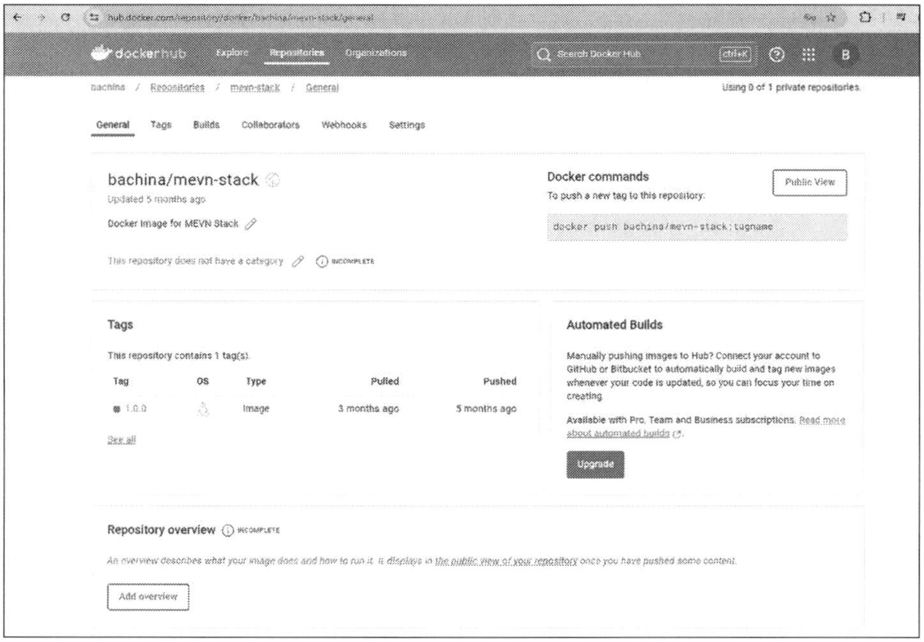

Figure 11.42: *Docker Repository*

After establishing an account on Docker Hub, it is time to tag the **`mevn-stack`** Docker image, authenticate with Docker Hub, and upload the image to your repository. The following illustration showcases the complete process, from tagging the image with the appropriate repository name to pushing it to Docker Hub.

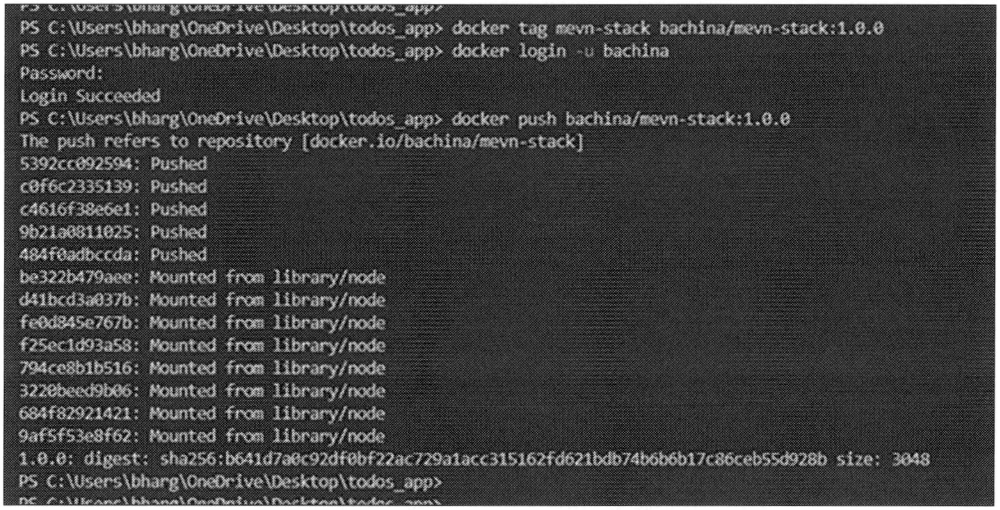

Figure 11.43: *Pushing to Docker Hub*

We can see the image on the Docker Hub now. Since it is public, anybody can clone and use it.

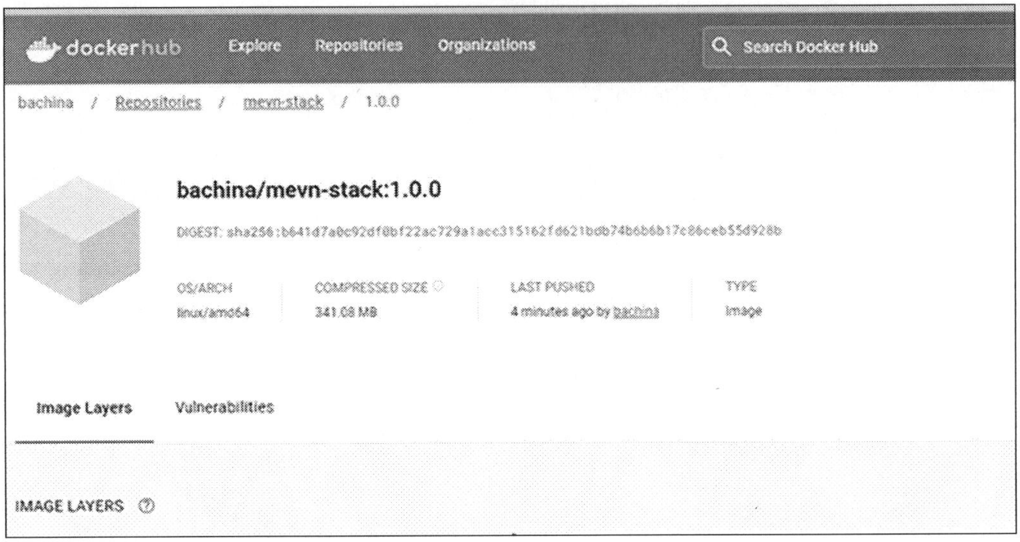

Figure 11.44: *Image Pushed to Docker Hub*

Publishing Docker images to a registry like Docker Hub simplifies the distribution and deployment of your Dockerized applications. By following the steps outlined in this chapter and adhering to best practices, you can efficiently manage your Docker images, ensuring they are accessible, versioned, optimized, and secure. This process is a cornerstone of modern container-based development and deployment strategies, facilitating collaboration and continuous delivery.

Best Practices

In reflecting on the journey through Docker and containerization, the chapter on MEVN stack deployment provides several best practices that align with the key points addressed.

Containerization Best Practices

Containerization is a critical aspect of modern software deployment strategies. Here are some best practices to ensure that your containerized applications are secure, efficient, and easy to manage:

Security

- Use official images from trusted repositories to minimize vulnerabilities.
- Regularly update images to include the latest security patches.

- Limit container privileges; avoid running containers as root whenever possible.
- Scan images for vulnerabilities as part of the CI/CD pipeline.
- Use secrets management tools instead of hardcoding sensitive information.

Efficiency

- Keep images small by using minimal base images like Alpine Linux.
- Leverage multi-stage builds in Dockerfiles to reduce final image size.
- Remove unnecessary tools and files from images to minimize the attack surface.

Configuration and Management

- Use environment variables for configuration to keep containers stateless.
- Employ orchestration tools like Kubernetes or Docker Swarm for better scalability and management.
- Implement health checks to ensure that containerized applications are running correctly.

Networking and Storage

- Define and use custom bridge networks for inter-container communication to isolate and control traffic.
- Use persistent volumes for data that needs to persist across container restarts or redeployments.

Development and Deployment

- Ensure consistency between development, testing, and production environments using the same images.
- Implement a tagging strategy for images to manage versions effectively.
- Use Docker Compose for local development to replicate production set ups.
- Automate deployment with CI/CD pipelines, integrating container build and deployment processes.

Monitoring and Logging

- Centralize logging from containers to a single service or tool for easy access and analysis.
- Implement monitoring solutions to track container performance and resource usage.

Docker Compose Best Practices

Using Docker Compose effectively involves adhering to a set of best practices that ensure maintainability, scalability, and security of your containerized applications. Here are some of the best practices for Docker Compose:

Configuration and Management

- Keep Compose files versioned and under source control to track changes and ensure consistency across environments.
- Split Docker Compose files for different environments (development, staging, production) using extends keyword or multiple Compose files to override settings.

Service Definition

- Use explicit versioning for images in the Compose file to avoid unexpected changes when newer versions are released.
- Limit each service to one responsibility (microservice architecture) to ensure that containers remain lightweight and modular.

Security

- Avoid including sensitive data in the Compose file. Use environment variables and Docker secrets for managing sensitive configuration.
- Define user and group within the Dockerfile to avoid running services as root.

Networking

- Define custom networks to facilitate secure and easy communication between services.
- Use internal network segments for backend services that do not need to be exposed to the host or the internet.

Volumes and Data Management

- Use named volumes for persistent data instead of bind mounts where possible, for portability.
- Prefer read-only volumes for data that should not be modified to protect against data corruption.

Dependencies

- Specify service dependencies using **`depends_on`** to control the order of service startup and shutdown.
- Use health checks in conjunction with **`depends_on`** to ensure that dependent services are healthy before others start.

Development Workflow

- Use **`.env`** files or environment variables for configuration parameters to avoid hardcoding values.

- Integrate Docker Compose into your development workflow for local testing that mirrors production settings.
- Utilize the build context to automate the building of custom images when starting services.

Scalability

- Prepare for horizontal scaling by designing stateless services that do not rely on local persistent data.

Performance

- Monitor resource usage and adjust service resource limits and reservations as needed.
- Prune unnecessary volumes and networks regularly to free up system resources.

Documentation

- Document the purpose and interaction of services within your Compose files for better maintainability.
- Keep your Docker Compose version updated to utilize the latest features and fixes.

Publishing Docker Images Best Practices

When it comes to publishing Docker images, following a set of best practices can ensure that your images are secure, efficient, and usable by others. Here are some key considerations for publishing Docker images:

Use Official Base Images

- Start with an official base image from Docker Hub whenever possible, as these are maintained and regularly scanned for security vulnerabilities.

Tagging Strategy

- Use meaningful tags instead of just the latest. Tags should convey information about the version of the image and its stability, such as 2.1.0, 2.1.0-alpine, stable, or development.

Minimize Image Size

- Opt for minimal base images like Alpine, which can significantly reduce the size of your images.
- Combine layers by chaining commands where appropriate and clean up in the same layer that you install temporary files or dependencies.

Security Scanning

- Regularly scan your images for vulnerabilities using tools like Docker's scanning feature or third-party services.
- Update images with patches and security fixes as they become available.

Avoid Sensitive Data

- Never include secrets or sensitive data within the image. Instead, use environment variables, Docker secrets, or external secrets management tools.

Use Multi-Stage Builds

- Multi-stage builds allow you to separate the build environment from the production environment within the same Dockerfile, minimizing the final image size.

Optimize Build Context

- Use `.dockerignore` to exclude unnecessary files and directories from your build context, speeding up the build process and ensuring that only necessary files are included in the image.

Document the Image

- Provide a well-written `README.md` in your image repository explaining how to use the image, the environment variables it accepts, and any tags available.
- Use labels within the Dockerfile for metadata such as the maintainer, version, and license.

Automated Builds

- Consider setting up automated builds with services like Docker Hub's automated builds or a CI/CD pipeline. This ensures that images are built and pushed in a consistent and controlled manner.

Provide a Health Check

- Use the `HEALTHCHECK` instruction to let Docker know how to test a container to check that it is still working.

Immutable Containers

- Avoid mutable container practices. Once an image is built, it should not change. If updates are needed, create a new image version.

Handle Initialization and Configuration

- Use `entrypoint` scripts to handle container initialization and dynamic configuration at runtime.

Version Control

- Keep the Dockerfile and related scripts in version control to track changes and maintain history.

By implementing these practices, you ensure that your Docker images are secure, lean, and maintainable, which is essential for trust and reliability in a containerized software ecosystem.

Conclusion

In wrapping up this comprehensive chapter on deploying the MEVN stack using Docker and Docker Compose, we have navigated through a journey from the basics of containerization to the intricacies of image creation, management, and deployment. We started by introducing Docker and containerization, offering a foundational understanding of the benefits and mechanisms behind Docker's approach to isolating and running applications.

We then explored Docker Compose, a powerful tool for defining and orchestrating multi-container Docker applications. With Docker Compose, we brought together the various components of the MEVN stack, ensuring each piece worked harmoniously in a simulated production environment.

Delving into the construction of Docker images, we employed best practices to build and run MEVN stack images, emphasizing the advantages of multi-stage builds. This technique not only streamlined our Docker images but also enhanced security and reduced the final image size, making our applications more efficient and faster to deploy.

We subsequently demonstrated how to run the MEVN stack on Docker Compose, showcasing how different services such as the Vue.js frontend, Node.js backend, and MongoDB database can be spun up in a cohesive ecosystem, replicable across development, staging, and production environments.

Publishing the Docker image was the next critical step, where we covered the importance of tagging, security scanning, and proper documentation. These practices ensure that the images are ready for wider consumption and meet the rigorous standards expected in a collaborative development workflow.

Finally, we consolidated our knowledge with a set of best practices that span across all areas covered in the chapter. These best practices serve as guidelines to ensure the security, efficiency, and maintainability of Docker images and containers, which are crucial for both development and operational excellence. Up to this point, we have successfully developed our entire application and deployed it using Docker. In the forthcoming chapter, we will delve into unit testing for our MEVN stack, exploring various libraries that facilitate unit testing across both the frontend and backend components.

Chapter 12
Unit Testing

Introduction

Unit testing stands as a fundamental aspect of the software development lifecycle, crucial for evaluating the functionality of individual components in isolation. This chapter delves into the array of tools and frameworks designed for unit testing, focusing on both frontend and backend aspects of application development. With practical code examples, we aim to provide a comprehensive guide to implementing robust unit testing strategies across the full stack of your application, ensuring reliability and efficiency in your development process.

For frontend testing, especially within Vue.js applications, Vue Test Utils offers a powerful and flexible API for testing Vue components. This segment introduces Vue Test Utils and demonstrates how to leverage it for comprehensive testing of Vue components, ensuring that the UI behaves as expected under various conditions. Coupled with Jest, a delightful JavaScript Testing Framework with a focus on simplicity, we explore how to set up Jest for unit testing, providing a seamless testing experience for Vue.js applications.

On the backend side, we introduce Jest in the context of Node.js, outlining steps to configure Jest for unit testing backend services. This set up ensures that the server-side logic of your MEVN stack application is tested thoroughly. Additionally, we cover Mocha and Chai, two prominent JavaScript testing frameworks known for their flexibility and assertion libraries. Mocha provides a rich API for structuring tests, while Chai offers a wide range of assertions, making it easier to validate the behavior of backend components.

Through detailed explanations and code samples, this chapter aims to equip developers with the knowledge to implement effective unit testing practices across both frontend and backend development. By embracing these tools, you can enhance the quality and reliability of your MEVN stack applications, ensuring they meet the rigorous demands of production environments.

Structure

In this chapter, the following topics will be covered:

- Introduction to Unit Testing
- Introduction to Vue Test Utils
- Introduction to Jest
- Testing Frontend
- Testing API
- Other Unit Testing Libraries

Introduction to Unit Testing

Unit testing is an indispensable practice in software development that involves testing individual units or components of code in isolation. In the MEVN (MongoDB, Express.js, Vue.js, Node.js) stack, unit testing ensures the reliability and correctness of each module, function, or method independently. By isolating units of code, developers can validate their behavior against expected outcomes, identifying and fixing bugs early in the development cycle.

Importance of Unit Testing

Unit testing plays a crucial role in software development for several reasons. Firstly, it helps identify bugs and errors early in the development process, reducing the overall cost of fixing them later. By testing individual units in isolation, developers can isolate and address issues more effectively.

Secondly, unit tests serve as documentation for the codebase, providing insights into how individual components should behave. This documentation can be invaluable for developers who need to understand existing code or make changes in the future.

Additionally, unit testing facilitates code refactoring and maintenance by allowing developers to make changes with confidence. When a codebase is well-covered by unit tests, developers can refactor or optimize code without fear of introducing regressions.

Best Practices for Unit Testing

To ensure effective unit testing, it is essential to follow best practices:

- **Test Isolation:** Each unit test should focus on testing a single unit of functionality in isolation from other components. This ensures that test results are reliable and reproducible.

- **Test Coverage:** Aim to achieve high test coverage by writing tests for all critical paths and edge cases in your code. However, prioritize quality over quantity, focusing on tests that provide the most value.
- **Test Readability:** Write clear, descriptive test cases that are easy to understand. A well-written test should clearly communicate the expected behavior of the code being tested.
- **Automation:** Automate the execution of unit tests as part of your continuous integration (CI) pipeline. This ensures that tests are run consistently and promptly after each code change.
- **Mocking and Stubbing:** Use mocking and stubbing techniques to isolate the unit under test from its dependencies. This allows you to control the behavior of external dependencies and focus on testing the unit in isolation.

Chapter Overview

In this chapter overview, we delve into the comprehensive world of unit testing within the context of the MEVN (MongoDB, Express.js, Vue.js, Node.js) stack. We explore various tools and methodologies essential for effective unit testing, offering readers a comprehensive understanding of the fundamental concepts and practices.

Introduction to Vue Test Utils

Vue Test Utils is a utility library specifically designed for testing Vue.js components. In this section, we will explore the fundamentals of Vue Test Utils, including its key features and benefits. We will learn how to leverage Vue Test Utils to write effective unit tests for Vue components, covering concepts such as mounting components, interacting with DOM elements, and asserting component behavior.

Testing Vue Components with Vue Test Utils

Once we understand the basics of Vue Test Utils, we will dive into practical examples of testing Vue components using this powerful testing library. We will explore various testing scenarios, including testing component rendering, user interactions, and component state changes. Through hands-on examples, we will demonstrate how to write comprehensive unit tests for Vue components.

Introduction to Jest

Jest is a widely used JavaScript testing framework developed by Facebook, known for its simplicity and powerful features. In this section, we will introduce Jest and its role in unit testing MEVN stack applications. We will discuss the key features of Jest and why it is a popular choice for testing JavaScript code, including Vue.js frontend components and Node.js backend services.

Setup Jest for Unit Testing Backend

To effectively test the backend logic of our MEVN stack application, we will need to set up Jest as our testing framework. In this section, we will provide a step-by-step guide on configuring Jest for unit testing backend code written in Node.js and Express.js. We will cover installation, configuration, and writing tests for Node.js modules and Express.js middleware using Jest.

Introduction to Mocha and Chai

Mocha and Chai are popular choices for unit testing JavaScript applications, offering a flexible and expressive testing environment. In this section, we will introduce Mocha as a test framework and Chai as an assertion library, explaining how they work together to facilitate unit testing in MEVN stack applications.

Set Up Mocha and Chai for Unit Testing Backend

With Mocha and Chai introduced, we will proceed to set them up for unit testing the backend logic of our MEVN stack application. We will guide you through the process of installing Mocha and Chai, configuring test suites and assertions, and writing effective unit tests for Node.js modules and Express.js middleware. Through practical examples, you will gain a solid foundation in using Mocha and Chai for backend unit testing in MEVN stack applications.

In the following sections, we will delve deeper into each of the topics covered above. We will explore advanced testing techniques, such as mocking external dependencies, testing asynchronous code, and writing integration tests for MEVN stack applications. By the end of this book, you will have a solid understanding of unit testing best practices and the tools available for testing Vue.js front-end components and backend services in a MEVN stack application.

Introduction to Vue Test Utils

Vue Test Utils is a versatile library designed to facilitate the unit testing of Vue components. Testing Vue components is essential for ensuring the reliability, functionality, and maintainability of Vue.js applications. In this chapter, we will delve into Vue Test Utils, exploring its features, advantages, disadvantages, and best practices. By understanding Vue Test Utils thoroughly, developers can streamline their testing workflow and create robust Vue.js applications.

Vue Test Utils provides a comprehensive suite of utilities for mounting, interacting with, and asserting on Vue components. Its primary goal is to enable developers to write concise and effective tests for individual Vue components in isolation. With Vue Test Utils, developers can simulate user interactions, access component state and props, and assert component behavior and output. Additionally, Vue Test Utils integrates seamlessly with popular testing frameworks like Jest and Mocha, making it a versatile choice for Vue.js unit testing.

Pros of Vue Test Utils

- **Simplicity:** Vue Test Utils offers a straightforward and intuitive API, making it easy for developers to write and maintain tests.
- **Isolation:** Vue Test Utils allows developers to test Vue components in isolation, ensuring that each component behaves as expected regardless of its context within the application.
- **Flexibility:** Vue Test Utils provides flexibility in testing various aspects of Vue components, including state changes, event emissions, and DOM interactions.
- **Integration:** Vue Test Utils seamlessly integrates with other testing tools and libraries, such as Jest and Mocha, enhancing its versatility and compatibility with different testing environments.

Cons of Vue Test Utils

- **Learning Curve:** While Vue Test Utils is relatively easy to grasp for developers familiar with Vue.js, it may have a learning curve for those new to Vue.js or unit testing in general.
- **Setup Overhead:** Setting up Vue Test Utils and configuring tests may require additional setup compared to simpler testing approaches, potentially increasing initial development time.

Best Practices

- **Maintain Component Independence:** When writing tests with Vue Test Utils, ensure that each test focuses on a specific Vue component and does not rely on the behavior or state of other components.
- **Use Shallow Mounting:** Whenever possible, prefer shallow mounting over deep mounting to isolate the component being tested from its child components.
- **Mock Dependencies:** Use mocking to replace external dependencies, such as APIs or services, with mock implementations to control test behavior and ensure test reliability.
- **Keep Tests DRY (Don't Repeat Yourself):** Avoid duplicating test code by extracting common setup logic into reusable helper functions or `beforeEach` hooks.
- **Prioritize Readability:** Write clear and descriptive test names and comments to improve the readability and maintainability of your test suite.

Practical Examples

To illustrate the usage of Vue Test Utils, let us consider some example scenarios while testing a Vue component.

Mounting a Vue Component

This example demonstrates how to mount a Vue component using Vue Test Utils' **`mount`** function. It ensures that the component renders without any errors by checking if it exists.

```
ui > src > JS App.spec.js > ...
import { mount } from '@vue/test-utils';
import MyComponent from '@/components/MyComponent.vue';

describe('MyComponent', () => {
  it('renders correctly', () => {
    const wrapper = mount(MyComponent);
    expect(wrapper.exists()).toBe(true);
  });
});
```

Figure 12.1: *Mounting a Vue Component*

Accessing Component Data

Here, we mount the component and then use the **`find`** method to locate an element with the class **`.message`.** We then access the text content of that element using the **`text()`** method and assert that it matches the expected message.

```
ui > src > JS App.spec.js > ...
import { mount } from '@vue/test-utils';
import MyComponent from '@/components/MyComponent.vue';

describe('MyComponent', () => {
  it('displays correct message', () => {
    const wrapper = mount(MyComponent);
    const message = wrapper.find('.message').text();
    expect(message).toBe('Hello, Vue!');
  });
});
```

Figure 12.2: *Accessing Component Data*

Simulating User Interaction

This example simulates a user clicking a button within the component. It uses the **`trigger`** method to simulate a click event on the button element and then awaits the asynchronous action. Finally, it asserts that the component's **`count`** data has been updated accordingly.

```
ui > src > JS App.spec.js > ...
import { mount } from '@vue/test-utils';
import MyComponent from '@/components/MyComponent.vue';

describe('MyComponent', () => {
  it('increments count when button is clicked', async () => {
    const wrapper = mount(MyComponent);
    const button = wrapper.find('button');
    await button.trigger('click');
    expect(wrapper.vm.count).toBe(1);
  });
});
```

Figure 12.3: *Simulating User Interaction*

Testing Props and Emits

In this example, we test whether a component emits a custom event when a button is clicked. After mounting the component, we trigger a click event on the button element and await the asynchronous action. Finally, we assert that the component has emitted the expected custom event.

```
ui > src > JS App.spec.js > ...
import { mount } from '@vue/test-utils';
import MyComponent from '@/components/MyComponent.vue';

describe('MyComponent', () => {
  it('emits custom event when button is clicked', async () => {
    const wrapper = mount(MyComponent);
    const button = wrapper.find('button');
    await button.trigger('click');
    expect(wrapper.emitted('customEvent')).toBeTruthy();
  });
});
```

Figure 12.4: *Testing Props and Emits*

These examples cover common scenarios encountered when writing unit tests for Vue.js components, such as accessing component data, simulating user interactions, testing Vuex store integration, and validating component props and emits. By following these patterns, developers can ensure that their Vue components behave as expected and are thoroughly tested for robustness.

While you can write tests like this, running them requires a test runner. The explanation above focuses on how you might use **`@vue/test-utils`** to interact with and assert against your Vue components. If you do not have a test runner, you will not be able to execute these tests directly. Typically, developers use Jest, Mocha, or similar tools to run the tests.

Since we went through `@vue/test-utils`, you should know that the utility primarily helps in creating instances of your components in an isolated environment, manipulating props, injecting data, simulating events, and asserting the rendered output. The actual execution of these test files and checking of assertions usually falls under the responsibilities of a test runner and assertion library.

For Vue components, you can use Jest alongside `@vue/test-utils` to test the functionality of your Vue components. `@vue/test-utils` provides utility functions to mount components in isolation, enabling you to interact with and assert on their output, like how users would interact with them in a browser. You can simulate user events, inject props, and check the DOM structure and changes in response to user actions or lifecycle events.

Introduction to Jest

Jest is a popular JavaScript testing framework developed by Facebook. It is widely used for testing JavaScript code, including React and Vue.js applications. Jest provides a simple and intuitive interface for writing tests, making it accessible for both beginners and experienced developers. With its built-in features like test runners, assertion utilities, and mocking capabilities, Jest streamlines the testing process and improves overall productivity.

Jest is designed to be easy to set up and use, offering a zero-configuration experience out of the box. It supports various testing paradigms, including unit testing, integration testing, and snapshot testing. Jest comes bundled with everything you need to write and run tests, including a powerful assertion library, a test runner, and built-in mocking capabilities. Additionally, Jest offers excellent performance with parallel test execution, making it suitable for large-scale projects.

Below are some of the advantages and disadvantages of Jest:

Pros

- **Easy to Set Up:** Jest offers a zero-configuration experience, requiring minimal set up to get started with testing. Developers can begin writing tests without the need for complex configurations, making it accessible to beginners and experienced developers alike.
- **Comprehensive Feature Set:** Jest comes bundled with a comprehensive set of features, including a powerful assertion library, a test runner, mocking capabilities, and support for code coverage reporting. These features streamline the testing process and improve productivity.
- **Fast and Efficient:** Jest is known for its speed and efficiency, with built-in support for parallel test execution. This allows developers to run tests quickly, even in large-scale projects, resulting in faster feedback cycles and improved development workflows.

- **Integration with JavaScript Ecosystem:** Jest integrates seamlessly with popular JavaScript frameworks and libraries, such as React, Vue.js, and Node.js. It provides specialized utilities and features tailored to the needs of these frameworks, enhancing the testing experience for developers.
- **Active Community and Documentation:** Jest benefits from an active community of developers and maintainers who contribute to its ongoing development and support. Additionally, Jest provides comprehensive documentation and resources, including guides, tutorials, and API references, to help developers get started and troubleshoot issues.

Cons

- **Initial Learning Curve:** While Jest is relatively easy to use, developers new to testing frameworks may encounter a slight learning curve when getting started. Understanding Jest's features, syntax, and best practices may require some initial investment in learning.
- **Browser-Specific Testing Limitations:** Jest primarily focuses on testing JavaScript code in Node.js environments. While it offers support for browser-based testing using tools like `jsdom`, it may not provide the same level of support for browser-specific behaviors compared to dedicated browser testing frameworks.

Overall, Jest is a powerful and versatile testing framework that offers numerous benefits for JavaScript developers. Its simplicity, speed, and comprehensive feature set make it an excellent choice for testing JavaScript applications of all sizes and complexities.

Best Practices

Here are some of the best practices for using Jest.

- **Use Descriptive Test Names**: Name your tests descriptively to clearly indicate what functionality they are testing.
- **Isolate Tests:** Ensure that each test case is independent and does not rely on the state of other tests. This helps in identifying and fixing issues more effectively.
- **Mock External Dependencies:** Utilize Jest's mocking capabilities to mock external dependencies such as API calls or database interactions. This helps in isolating the code under test and makes tests faster and more reliable.
- **Group Related Tests:** Organize your tests into logical groups based on functionality or the component. This improves readability and maintainability of test suites.
- **Use Matchers Wisely:** Jest provides various matchers for assertions. Choose the appropriate matcher for each assertion to make tests more expressive and readable.

- **Avoid Test Duplication:** Refactor common set up or assertions into helper functions or `beforeEach/afterEach` hooks to avoid duplicating code across tests.
- **Regularly Refactor Tests:** As the codebase evolves, ensure that tests are updated and refactored accordingly to maintain their effectiveness and relevance.
- **Monitor Test Performance:** Keep an eye on the performance of your test suite and optimize slow-running tests to improve overall efficiency.
- **Continuous Integration:** Integrate Jest tests into your CI/CD pipeline to ensure that tests are run automatically on each code change.
- **Documentation and Comments:** Provide clear documentation and comments within your tests to explain complex logic or edge cases, making it easier for other developers to understand and maintain the tests.

Jest Along with Vue/test-utils

Jest and `vue/test-utils` are commonly used together in Vue.js projects to create a robust testing environment. Each tool has a distinct role in the testing process:

- `vue/test-utils`

  `vue/test-utils` is the official library for Vue.js designed to enable developers to mount and interact with Vue components in a testing environment. It provides functions to render components in isolation, simulate user interactions, and assert various aspects of the component's behavior. It helps with creating "*wrapper*" objects around Vue components, making it easier to probe into the internal state of components, trigger events, and examine the rendered output. However, `vue/test-utils` does not have the capability to run tests by itself. It is primarily concerned with providing utilities to facilitate the testing of Vue components.

- `Jest`

  Jest, on the other hand, is a testing framework that provides the environment to execute tests written for JavaScript applications, including Vue.js projects. It comes with a test runner, assertion library, and mocking support. Jest can execute tests written for any part of your application, not just Vue components. This includes unit tests for JavaScript logic, integration tests that might involve multiple components, and snapshot tests. Jest also provides a rich set of features like code coverage reports, watch mode for re-running tests on file changes, and a mocking system that allows for more controlled and isolated testing environments.

Using Them Together

- When combined, **`vue/test-utils`** and Jest offer a comprehensive testing solution for Vue.js projects. **`vue/test-utils`** provides the necessary tools to effectively test Vue components, while Jest provides the environment in which these tests are run, along with additional tools for checking results, handling asynchronous code, and structuring test suites.
- Using Jest along with **`vue/test-utils`** allows developers to write and run tests that can inspect the rendered output, check for changes when data or props are modified, and simulate user events, all within a test suite that can be automated and integrated into continuous integration pipelines.
- This combination ensures that your Vue components work as expected and adhere to best practices, leading to more reliable, maintainable, and bug-free code.

In summary, while **`vue/test-utils`** specializes in handling Vue-specific testing scenarios, Jest provides the broader testing framework necessary to execute those tests effectively. Together, they form a powerful duo for ensuring the quality and functionality of Vue.js applications.

Testing Frontend

Now that we have completed our theoretical overview of Jest and Vue Test Utils, it is time to transition from theory to practice by setting up our testing environment. The first step in this process involves installing the necessary dependencies. These include libraries and tools that will enable us to write, run, and evaluate our tests effectively within a Vue 3 and TypeScript context.

```
// Installing Dependencies
```

```
npm install @babel/preset-env @types/jest @vue/test-utis @vue/vue3-jest
jest jest-environment-jsdom ts-jest
```

The dependencies we will install are:

- **`@babel/preset-env`**: This is a Babel preset for each environment that compiles ES6+ down to ES5 by automatically determining the Babel plugins and polyfills you need based on your targeted browser or runtime environments.
- **`@types/jest`**: These are TypeScript type definitions for Jest. They provide autocomplete and type checking for Jest's API when writing tests.
- **`@vue/test-utils`**: The official Vue.js library for unit testing Vue components. It provides methods to mount and interact with Vue components in an isolated manner.
- **`@vue/vue3-jest`**: A Vue Jest plugin specifically designed for Vue 3 components. It allows Jest to process and understand **`.vue`** files.

- **`jest`**: The main testing framework. Jest is used to write, run, and organize tests. It comes with built-in test runners and assertions to help with the testing process.
- **`jest-environment-jsdom`**: This Jest environment allows testing in a browser-like environment through JSDOM, mimicking the browser's APIs.
- **`ts-jest`**: A TypeScript preprocessor for Jest, enabling Jest to understand TypeScript syntax. This is crucial for testing Vue components, or any other code written in TypeScript.

By installing these dependencies, we set up a comprehensive testing suite that combines Jest's robust testing capabilities with the specificity of Vue Test Utils for Vue 3 components, while also ensuring compatibility with TypeScript and Babel for transpilation and type-checking. This creates a seamless and effective environment for testing Vue applications.

Let us dive into the practical aspect of our journey by beginning the implementation phase. Crafting spec files for every single component within this guide would be a considerable challenge due to time and space constraints. Instead, we will focus on creating and discussing spec files for three distinct components. This selective approach is designed to equip you with a solid understanding and foundation, allowing you to extend these principles and techniques to write unit tests for additional components on your own. This presents an ideal chance for you to gain practical experience with unit testing for Vue components. By following along with these examples, you will develop the skills necessary to apply unit testing effectively across your Vue projects, enhancing the reliability and maintainability of your applications.

The **`CreateTask.spec.ts`** file is a test specification for the **`CreateTask.vue`** component, utilizing Vue Test Utils and Jest to perform unit testing. This spec file contains two primary test cases:

- **Rendering Test**: The first test verifies that the **`CreateTask`** component correctly displays a button with text that matches the **`btnName`** prop passed to it. This ensures that the component properly receives and renders props, a fundamental aspect of its functionality.
- **Event Emission Test:** The second test checks whether the component emits the **`createTask`** event when the button (styled with **`.btn-pink`**) is clicked. This is crucial for interactive components, as it ensures that user actions, like clicking a button, result in the appropriate outcomes, such as emitting an event that could trigger other actions in the parent component or the broader application.

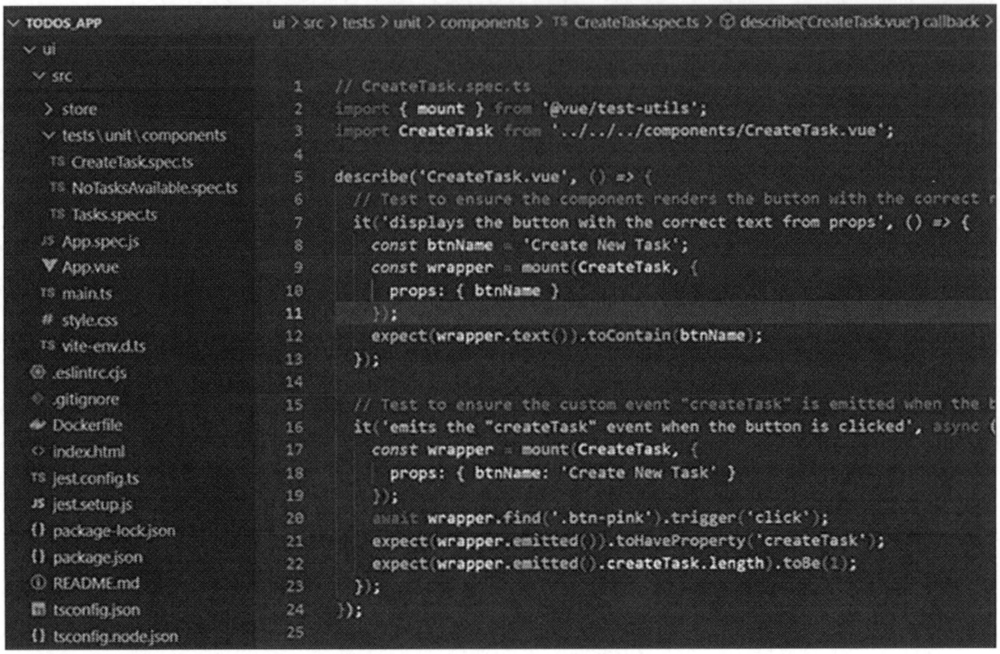

Figure 12.5: *CreateTask.spec.ts*

By conducting these tests, developers can validate both the static and dynamic aspects of the **`CreateTask`** component, ensuring it behaves as expected in isolation before integrating it into larger parts of the application. This approach exemplifies best practices in unit testing by focusing on individual components, maintaining a clear and manageable scope, and confirming both presentation and behavior.

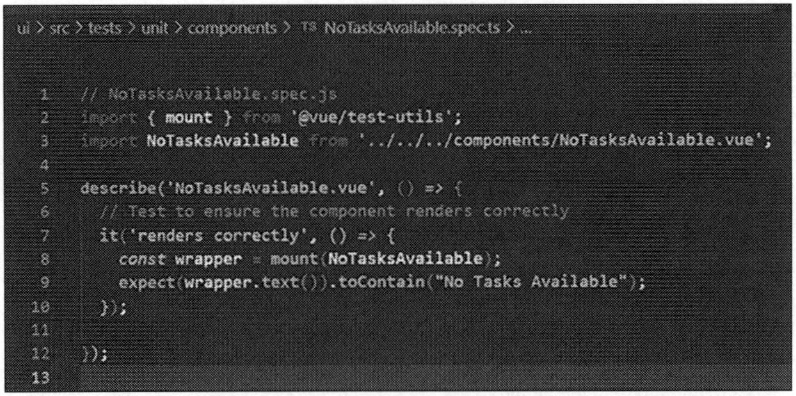

Figure 12.6: *NoTasksAvailable.spec.ts*

The **`NoTasksAvailable.spec.js`** file is a Vue component test script utilizing **`@vue/test-utils`** for the **`NoTasksAvailable`** component. In this test suite, there is a single test case defined under the description 'renders correctly'. This test case aims to verify that the **`NoTasksAvailable`** component is rendered properly by mounting the component using **`mount`** from Vue Test Utils and then checking if the rendered text includes the phrase "No Tasks Available". Essentially, this test ensures that when there are no tasks available, the component accurately displays the corresponding message, thereby confirming that the component behaves as expected under specific conditions. This kind of test is crucial for maintaining the reliability and correctness of user interface elements in Vue applications.

The **`TasksTable.spec.ts`** file is a test script written for the **`TasksTable`** Vue component, using **`@vue/test-utils`** for a more structured and comprehensive approach to unit testing. This script covers multiple facets of the component's functionality:

- **Rendering Tests:** It begins with verifying that the component correctly renders the provided tasks. By passing a predefined list of tasks as props, the test confirms whether the **`TasksTable`** component displays the correct number of task rows and the right content within those rows. This ensures that the component accurately represents data passed through its props and maintains proper structure in the DOM.

```
import { mount } from '@vue/test-utils';
import TasksTable from '../../../components/Tasks.vue'; // Adjust the import path as needed

describe('TasksTable.vue', () => {
  const tasks = [
    { _id: '1', task: 'Test Task 1', description: 'Description 1', createdAt: '2021-01-01' },
    { _id: '2', task: 'Test Task 2', description: 'Description 2', createdAt: '2021-01-02' }
  ];

  it('renders tasks correctly', () => {
    const wrapper = mount(TasksTable, {
      props: { tasks }
    });

    // Check if the component renders the correct number of task rows
    expect(wrapper.findAll('tr.tasks').length).toBe(tasks.length);

    // Check content of the first task
    const firstTaskFields = wrapper.findAll('tr.tasks')[0].findAll('td');
    expect(firstTaskFields[0].text()).toContain(tasks[0]._id);
    expect(firstTaskFields[1].text()).toContain(tasks[0].description);
    expect(firstTaskFields[2].text()).toContain(tasks[0].createdAt);
  });

  it('emits the editTask event when the Edit button is clicked', async () => {
    const wrapper = mount(TasksTable, {
      props: { tasks }
    });

    await wrapper.findAll('.btn-edit')[0].trigger('click');
    expect(wrapper.emitted()).toHaveProperty('editTask');
    const editTaskEvents = wrapper.emitted('editTask');
    // Ensure the event was emitted
    expect(editTaskEvents).toBeDefined();
    expect(editTaskEvents![0]).toEqual([tasks[0]]);
  });

  it('emits the deleteTask event when the Delete button is clicked', async () => {
    const wrapper = mount(TasksTable, {
      props: { tasks }
    });

    await wrapper.findAll('.btn-delete')[0].trigger('click');
    expect(wrapper.emitted()).toHaveProperty('deleteTask');
    const deleteTaskEvents = wrapper.emitted('deleteTask');
    // Ensure the event was emitted
    expect(deleteTaskEvents).toBeDefined();
    expect(deleteTaskEvents![0]).toEqual([tasks[0]]);
```

Figure 12.7: *Tasks.spec.ts*

- **Event Emission Tests:** The script further assesses the component's interactivity by checking if certain user actions, like clicking the `'Edit'`, `'Delete'`, or the task row itself, correctly emit the intended custom events (**`editTask`**, **`deleteTask`**, and **`detailTask`**). This aspect of testing is crucial as it ensures the component's responsiveness to user inputs and its ability to communicate actions upwards to parent components or handlers, maintaining the reactive data flow typical in Vue applications.
- **Data Integrity and Interaction**: Through simulating clicks on different parts of the component and observing emitted events, these tests validate not just the presence of interactive elements, but also their tied logic and data integrity. For example, when the '**`Edit`**' button is clicked, the test checks that an **`editTask`** event is emitted with the correct task data. This ensures that the component not only reacts visually but also sends accurate information needed for further actions or processing.

By implementing these tests, the file ensures that the **`TasksTable`** component is robust, correctly displaying passed-in data and reliably emitting events based on user interactions. This approach provides confidence in the component's reliability and functionality in a live environment, contributing significantly to the overall quality and maintainability of the Vue application.

Having explored and crafted unit tests for three distinct Vue components, we have reached a pivotal juncture in our learning journey. This marks an excellent moment for you, the reader, to apply the insights and techniques garnered to develop unit tests for your own Vue components. We are transitioning from the realm of Vue component testing into the domain of API testing, which presents a new set of challenges and learning opportunities. In our exploration, we have employed Jest as our testing framework for Vue components. Notably, Jest's versatility extends beyond just component testing; it is equally adept at handling API tests. This dual capability makes Jest a valuable tool in your development arsenal. As you proceed, I encourage you to leverage Jest for API testing as well, applying similar principles and methodologies to ensure your backend logic is as robust and error-free as your frontend.

Testing API

We have previously utilized Jest for unit testing the frontend components. Now, let us shift our focus towards API unit testing using the same framework, Jest. Since we are maintaining separate environments for the backend and frontend, we will initiate this phase by setting up the required dependencies specifically within the API directory. This approach ensures a clear separation between client-side and server-side testing, optimizing organization and maintainability. Please proceed by installing the necessary packages in the API folder, which will equip us with the tools needed to create and run our backend tests efficiently.

```
// Installing Dependencies
npm install supertest @types/supertest ts-jest @types/jest jest -save-
dev
```

- **`supertest`**: This is a Node.js library used for testing HTTP servers. **`supertest`** provides a high-level abstraction for testing Express, Koa, and other HTTP servers, making it easy to send simulated HTTP requests to test routes and API endpoints. It is commonly used in combination with a testing framework like Jest to assert the correctness of HTTP responses.
- **`@types/supertest`**: This package contains TypeScript type definitions for **`supertest`**. Installing this package allows TypeScript to understand the types used in **`supertest`**, enabling type checking and IntelliSense support in TypeScript projects when using **`supertest`**.
- **`ts-jest`**: A Jest transformer with source map support that lets you use Jest to test projects written in TypeScript. It essentially allows Jest to understand and run tests written in TypeScript by compiling TypeScript to JavaScript before tests are executed.
- **`@types/jest`**: Like **`@types/supertest`**, this package provides TypeScript type definitions for Jest. It includes types for Jest's objects, functions, and matchers, making it easier to write type-safe test code and get useful code completions in TypeScript projects.
- **`jest`**: Jest is a delightful JavaScript Testing Framework with a focus on simplicity. It works out of the box for any React project and is widely used for testing JavaScript and TypeScript applications. Jest provides a complete and integrated "zero-configuration" testing experience, supporting unit, functional, and integration testing, along with features like snapshots, test coverage, and mocking.

Together, these packages form a robust toolkit for testing JavaScript or TypeScript backend applications, such as APIs built with Node.js and Express. They provide the necessary functionalities to write, type-check, run, and assert tests effectively.

Once installed, we need to add this configuration file called **`jest.config.js`**.

```
module.exports = {
    preset: 'ts-jest',
    testEnvironment: 'node',
    testTimeout: 10000,
};
```

It is standard practice to organize our test scripts within a directory named **`__tests__`**, following common conventions. This approach helps in maintaining a clear and structured environment for our testing code. Within this designated folder, we will place our test files, such as the one for testing the user service functionalities.

This file contains tests for the **UserService** class from an application, aiming to ensure the service behaves correctly when interacting with user data. The file begins by importing the **UserService** and setting up a mock user object containing typical user information like email, password, and name. This mock user is used throughout the tests to simulate real user data.

The next section involves mocking dependencies that the **UserService** relies on – **UserRepository**, **LoggerService**, and **UserModel**. This is done to isolate the service from external factors like database calls or logging operations, ensuring that the tests are focused solely on the **UserService's** functionality. By mocking these dependencies, the tests can control the behavior of these external services. For example, whenever the **UserService** is expected to interact with the user repository, instead of making actual database calls, it uses predefined responses (the mock user data).

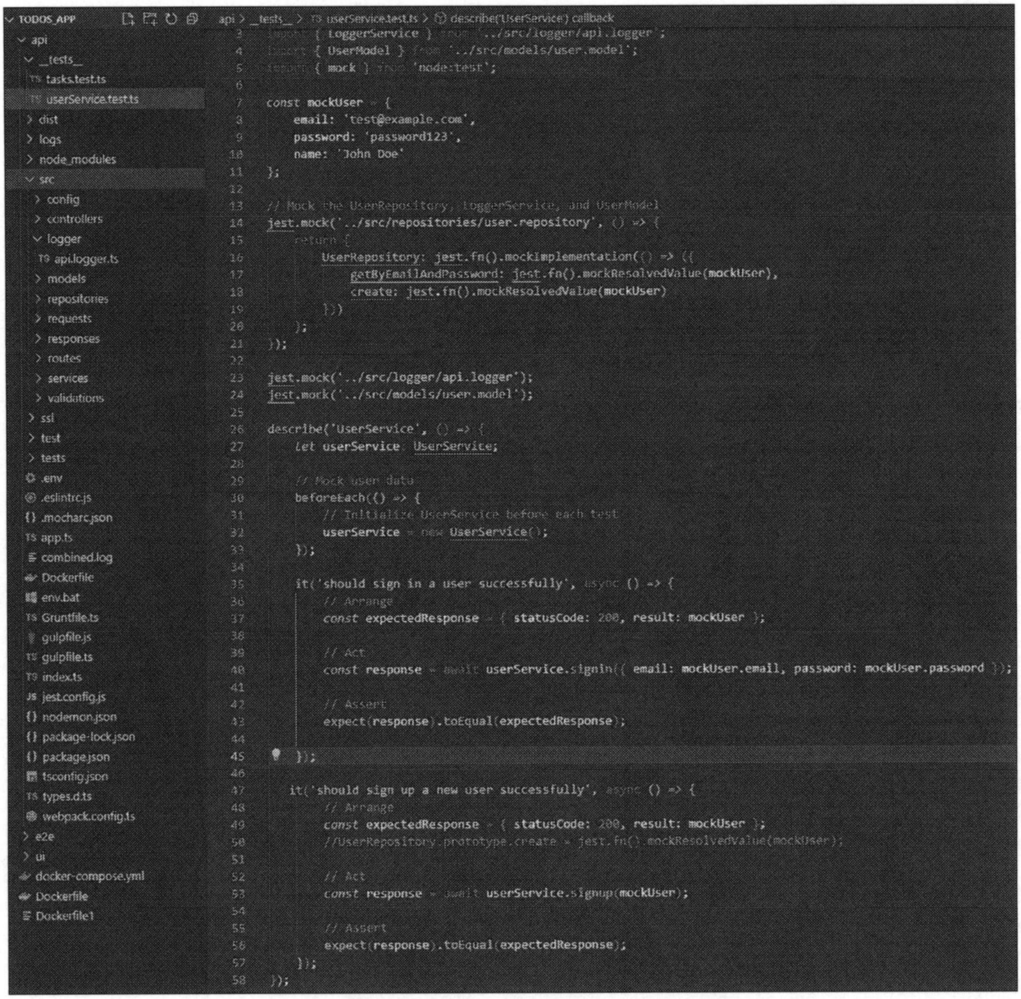

Figure 12.8: *userService.test.ts*

In the **describe** block, there are two test cases one for the **signin** method and another for the **signup** method of the **UserService**. Each test follows a similar pattern:

- **Arrange:** Set up the test conditions and expected outcomes. In this case, an expected response object is defined to match what a successful sign-in or sign-up operation should return.
- **Act:** Call the method under test with appropriate arguments. For the sign-in test, the **signin** method is called with the mock user's email and password. For the sign-up test, the **signup** method is called with the mock user's information.
- **Assert:** Check that the response from the service matches the expected response. This step verifies that the service behaves as intended, returning the correct status code and user data upon successful sign-in or sign-up.

The **beforeEach** hook is used to create a new instance of the **UserService** before each test, ensuring a fresh environment for every scenario to prevent tests from affecting each other. Overall, these tests aim to ensure that the **UserService** handles user sign-in and sign-up processes correctly, validating the functionality and reliability of critical authentication flows in the application.

Here is another test file that is designed to verify the functionality of the **'Todos'** endpoints in an Express application.

```
api > __tests__ > TS tasks.test.ts > ...
import request from 'supertest';
import app from '../app';
import mongoose from 'mongoose';

describe('Todos Endpoints', () => {

  beforeAll(async () => {
    await mongoose.connect('mongodb+srv://bhargavbook58:tester12345@todos.usujbgr.mongodb.net
  });

  afterAll(async () => {
    await mongoose.connection.close();
  });

  it('GET /tasks - should retrieve all tasks', async () => {
    const res: any = await request(app).get('/api/todos/tasks');
    expect(res.statusCode).toEqual(200);
    expect(res.body.result).toBeTruthy()
  });
});
```

Figure 12.9: *tests.test.ts*

It utilizes **'supertest'** for HTTP assertions, making it possible to simulate server requests and responses. Before all tests, it establishes a connection to a MongoDB database using Mongoose, ensuring that the database is accessible and ready for operation. After all tests have been executed, it closes the database connection to clean up resources. The core of the script tests the '**`GET /tasks`**' endpoint to ensure it responds correctly – the test sends a GET request to the endpoint and then checks that the response status code is 200 (OK), and that the response body contains a truthy 'result' field, indicating that tasks have been successfully retrieved. This test helps ensure the reliability and functionality of the application's endpoint responsible for fetching all tasks.

After setting up our test files, it is essential to integrate a test script within the **`package.json`** file of our project. This integration allows us to execute our tests effortlessly and observe the outcomes. By doing so, we facilitate a streamlined testing process, enabling us to run all our tests with a single command. This approach not only enhances efficiency but also provides immediate feedback on the test results. Once the test script is added and executed, the responses from the tests will be displayed, as illustrated in the subsequent image. This visualization aids in quickly identifying the success or failure of our tests, allowing for rapid debugging and assurance of code functionality and reliability.

```
"test": "jest"
```

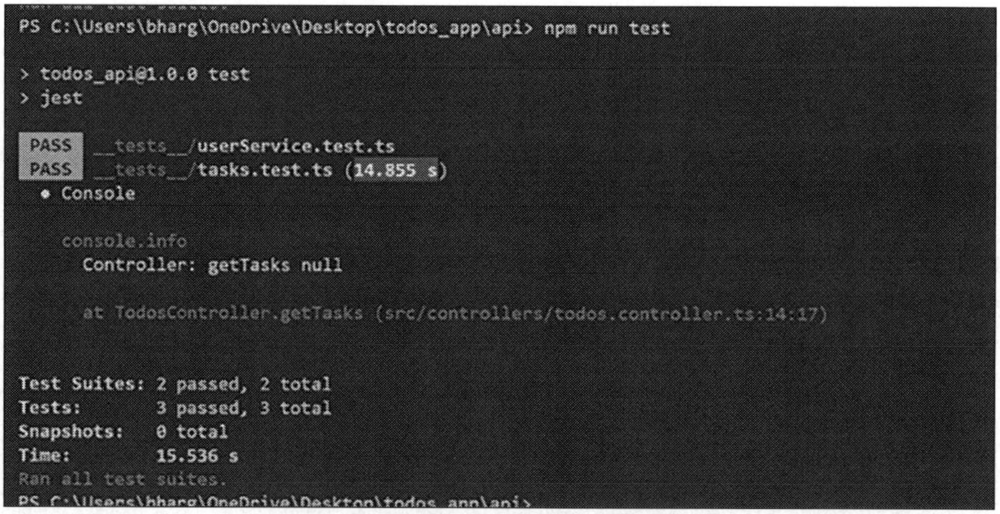

Figure 12.10: *Running Tests Successfully*

Other Unit Testing Libraries

We have delved into unit testing utilizing the Jest library, which provided a comprehensive overview of how to approach and implement tests effectively. However, the realm of JavaScript testing is vast, with other notable libraries such as Mocha, Chai, and Tap offering different approaches and functionalities. Each of these libraries has unique features and caters to various testing needs and preferences. Given the breadth of material, it is challenging to encapsulate everything within a single chapter comprehensively. This juncture presents an excellent opportunity for self-exploration and learning. Diving into these alternative libraries on your own will not only broaden your testing toolkit but also enhance your understanding of the different methodologies and practices in JavaScript testing. By exploring Mocha, Chai, and Tap, you can compare their different syntaxes, functionalities, and use cases to Jest, enriching your testing skills and knowledge.

Mocha and Chai

Mocha and Chai are popular JavaScript testing libraries used for writing and running unit tests for Node.js applications. In this chapter, we will explore the basics of Mocha and Chai, understand how they work together, and learn how to write effective unit tests for your backend code.

Mocha is a flexible and feature-rich testing framework that provides support for running both synchronous and asynchronous tests. It offers a simple and expressive syntax for defining test suites and test cases, making it easy to organize and execute tests for your Node.js applications.

Chai, on the other hand, is an assertion library that works seamlessly with Mocha. It provides a wide range of assertion styles and plugins, allowing you to write clear and concise assertions to validate the behavior of your code.

Below are some of the advantages and disadvantages of Mocha and Chai:

Pros

- **Flexible and customizable:** Mocha allows you to configure various aspects of your test suite, such as reporters, timeouts, and hooks, according to your project's requirements.
- **Extensive assertion library:** Chai offers a rich set of assertion styles, including should, expect, and assert, making it easy to write expressive and readable assertions.
- **Integration with other libraries:** Mocha and Chai seamlessly integrate with other testing utilities and libraries, such as Sinon for mocking and stubbing, enabling comprehensive testing of your backend code.

Cons

- **Learning curve:** While Mocha and Chai are relatively easy to get started with, mastering advanced features and techniques may require some time and effort.
- **Boilerplate code:** Writing set up and teardown code for test suites can sometimes result in boilerplate code, especially for complex test scenarios.

- **Configuration overhead:** Configuring Mocha and Chai for larger projects with multiple test suites and dependencies may require careful management to ensure smooth execution and accurate reporting.

Overall, Mocha and Chai are powerful testing tools that offer flexibility, extensibility, and expressive syntax for writing and running tests in JavaScript projects. However, developers should be mindful of their complexity and invest time in learning their features effectively to leverage their full potential.

Best Practices

Here are some best practices for using Mocha and Chai effectively.

Mocha

- **Organize Tests:** Structure your test suites and cases logically to improve readability and maintainability.
- **Use Descriptive Test Names:** Write descriptive test names that clearly communicate the expected behavior being tested.
- **Avoid Nested Callbacks:** Minimize nested callback functions to prevent callback hell. Utilize async/await or Promise chaining for asynchronous tests.
- **Setup and Teardown:** Utilize **`before`**, **`after`**, **`beforeEach`**, and **`afterEach`** hooks for setting up preconditions and cleaning up resources.
- **Separate Unit and Integration Tests:** Distinguish between unit tests (isolated tests of individual components) and integration tests (tests involving interactions between components) for better test organization.

Chai

- **Use Fluent API:** Leverage Chai's fluent assertion API to write expressive and readable assertions.
- **Choose Assertion Styles Wisely:** Select assertion styles (**`expect`**, **`should`**, or **`assert`**) based on personal preference and project conventions, ensuring consistency throughout the codebase.
- **Avoid Overly Specific Assertions:** Write assertions that focus on testing behavior rather than implementation details to make tests more resilient to code changes.
- **Explore Plugins:** Explore Chai plugins to extend its functionality for specific testing needs, such as testing HTTP requests or JSON structures.
- **Mocking and Stubbing:** Consider using additional libraries like Sinon.js alongside Chai for mocking and stubbing dependencies in tests.

By following these best practices, developers can harness the full potential of Mocha and Chai to write robust and maintainable test suites for their JavaScript projects.

Tap Library

The Test Anything Protocol (TAP) is a simple text-based interface between testing modules in a test harness. The Node.js library `tap` is an implementation of TAP that provides an extensive testing framework for Node.js applications. It is designed to offer a straightforward and easy-to-read testing syntax, making the process of writing tests more intuitive. With `tap`, developers can write unit tests, integration tests, and even assert the correctness of asynchronous code, making it a versatile tool for a wide range of testing scenarios.

Let us see pros and cons of the Tap Library.

Pros

- **Simplicity**: TAP's output is human-readable and easy to parse, making test results understandable without needing additional tools.
- **Asynchronous Testing**: `tap` supports asynchronous testing out of the box, catering well to Node.js's asynchronous nature.
- **Coverage Reporting**: Integrated coverage reporting helps track how much of your code is covered by tests without needing additional tools or configurations.
- **Subtests: tap** allows the creation of nested tests, known as subtests, which can help organize tests logically and improve readability.
- **Flexibility**: Being framework-agnostic, TAP can be used with any set up and integrated into various environments and build processes.

Cons

- **Popularity**: Compared to other testing libraries like Jest or Mocha, `tap` is less popular, which can lead to fewer community resources, examples, and third-party integrations.
- **Learning Curve**: Developers familiar with more conventional JavaScript testing frameworks might find `tap`'s approach and syntax less intuitive initially.
- **Debugging**: While TAP's simplicity is generally a benefit, it can sometimes make debugging more complex scenarios a bit more challenging compared to more verbose libraries.

Best Practices

Here are some of the best practices we should follow

- **Structured Testing:** Utilize subtests to structure your tests logically. This not only improves the readability of your tests but also makes it easier to identify failing tests in larger test suites.
- **Leverage Asynchronous Testing**: Take full advantage of `tap`'s support for

asynchronous tests, especially when working with Node.js applications, to ensure your tests accurately reflect your application's behavior.

- **Use Coverage Tools:** Regularly generate and review test coverage reports to identify untested parts of your application, ensuring comprehensive test coverage.
- **Keep Tests Independent**: Ensure each test is independent to avoid tests affecting each other's outcomes, leading to more reliable and understandable test results.
- **Embrace TAP's Simplicity**: Use TAP's straightforward syntax to write clear and concise tests, making your test suite easy to maintain and understand.
- **Continuous Integration:** Integrate `tap` tests into your CI/CD pipeline to ensure tests are run automatically, catching issues early in the development process.

By understanding the strengths and limitations of the `tap` library and adhering to best practices, you can effectively leverage its capabilities to ensure robust testing of your Node.js applications.

Conclusion

In this comprehensive chapter, we have delved into the essential realm of unit testing, starting with a foundational introduction that set the stage for understanding its critical role in software development. We explored Vue Test Utils and Jest, two powerful tools tailored for the Vue.js framework and general JavaScript testing, respectively. These tools enable developers to write and manage tests effectively, ensuring that individual components and functions perform as expected. We applied these concepts practically through testing frontend components, emphasizing the importance of ensuring a reliable user interface, and extended our exploration to backend API testing, reinforcing the necessity of robust server-side logic.

Moving beyond the basics, we acknowledged the diversity in the testing landscape by introducing other notable unit testing libraries such as Mocha, Chai, and Tap, offering alternative approaches and functionalities to suit different project needs. This exploration underlines the vast array of tools available to developers, each with unique advantages, and highlights the importance of choosing the right tool for specific testing requirements. As we conclude this chapter on unit testing, we pave the way for the subsequent journey into end-to-end testing. The upcoming chapter promises to expand our testing arsenal with tools like Playwright and Cypress, facilitating comprehensive testing scenarios that mimic real-world user interactions from start to finish. This shift from unit to end-to-end testing is crucial for validating the integrated performance of all components within an application, ensuring not just the functionality of individual parts, but also the seamless operation of the system.

CHAPTER 13
End-to-End Testing

Introduction

End-to-end testing is integral to the development and deployment process, ensuring the application operates as expected from start to finish. This chapter delves into the pivotal tools and frameworks that facilitate comprehensive end-to-end testing, highlighting TestCafe and Cypress for their remarkable capabilities in automating tests that mimic real-user interactions across the entire application.

We begin our exploration with TestCafe, a powerful node.js tool that allows developers to write tests in JavaScript or TypeScript. It is designed to cover the entire testing cycle, from opening the browser to executing the test and reporting the results. Setting up TestCafe is straightforward, enabling seamless integration into your development workflow. Through practical examples, we will demonstrate how to leverage TestCafe for crafting and running end-to-end tests that simulate real user behaviors and interactions within your application.

Next, we introduce Cypress, another leading end-to-end testing framework renowned for its ease of use and rich feature set. Cypress simplifies the process of setting up, writing, running, and debugging tests. Unlike many other testing tools, Cypress runs in the same run-loop as your application, providing native access to every object. This chapter will guide you through setting up Cypress in your project environment and utilizing its robust capabilities to ensure your application functions correctly under various scenarios.

By the end of this chapter, you will have a solid foundation in utilizing TestCafe and Cypress for end-to-end testing. With hands-on examples and step-by-step instructions, you will learn how to implement these tools effectively, ensuring your application delivers a flawless user experience from start to finish. Whether you are testing the frontend, backend, or the entire application flow, these tools will empower you to build more reliable, bug-free software.

Structure

In this chapter, the following topics will be covered:

- Introduction to End-to-End Testing
- Introduction to TestCafe
- Using TestCafe for E2E Tests
- Introduction to Cypress
- Using Cypress for E2E Tests
- Introduction to PlayWright
- Using PlayWright for E2E Tests

Introduction to End-to-End Testing

End-to-End (E2E) testing is a methodology used to verify the integrity and functionality of an entire software application from start to finish. Unlike unit tests that focus on individual components or integration tests that examine interactions between parts, E2E tests simulate real user scenarios to ensure the complete application flow works as intended. This includes testing the application in a scenario that mimics a real user's behavior, from interacting with the user interface, through any business logic, down to the data layer and back again.

Importance of End-to-End Testing

Let us understand the importance of E2E testing:

- **User Experience:** E2E testing ensures that the application behaves as expected in scenarios that mimic real user interactions. It helps identify issues that might not be visible through unit or integration tests but can significantly impact the user experience.
- **System Integration:** In modern applications, systems are often composed of multiple modules and services, including third-party services. E2E testing verifies that these integrated components work together seamlessly.
- **Data Integration:** By simulating real user scenarios, E2E testing ensures that data maintains integrity as it flows through the various components of the system.
- **Infrastructure and Environment:** E2E testing assesses the application's performance in an environment that mirrors the production set up, ensuring the software is compatible with the intended operating systems, devices, and browsers.

- **Regulatory and Compliance:** For applications in regulated industries, E2E testing can help ensure compliance with legal, security, and privacy standards by validating critical workflows from end to end.

Challenges in E2E Testing

Despite its importance, E2E testing can be challenging due to:

- **Complexity:** Simulating complete application scenarios can be complex and time-consuming.
- **Flakiness:** Tests can be flaky – passing at times and failing at others – especially if the test environment is not stable or if tests are not well-designed.
- **Resource Intensive:** E2E tests often require significant computational resources and time to execute, especially for large applications.
- **Maintenance:** E2E tests can be harder to maintain, particularly as the application grows and changes over time.

Best Practices

Let us look at some best practices:

- **Define Clear Test Scenarios:** Identify and prioritize key user journeys that are critical to the application's success.
- **Use Reliable Test Data:** Ensure that tests use consistent, isolated, and reliable data to reduce flakiness.
- **Automate Wisely:** Automate the most impactful scenarios to balance coverage with maintenance and execution time.
- **Continuous Integration:** Integrate E2E tests into the continuous integration/ continuous deployment (CI/CD) pipeline to catch issues early.
- **Monitor and Review:** Regularly review test results, update tests as necessary, and remove obsolete scenarios.

End-to-End testing plays a crucial role in the software development lifecycle, offering the final validation that an application meets its business and user requirements. By effectively simulating real-world scenarios, E2E testing helps teams release more reliable, user-friendly, and secure applications. Despite the challenges involved, the strategic implementation of E2E tests, combined with a balanced approach to automation and maintenance, can significantly enhance the quality and reliability of software products.

In our exploration, we have covered the fundamentals of End-to-End (E2E) Testing, laying the groundwork for understanding this critical phase in the software testing life cycle. Moving forward, we will delve into three prominent E2E testing frameworks in the upcoming sections. While it is challenging to explore each framework in exhaustive detail within the confines of this chapter, we aim to provide sufficient information to facilitate a solid starting point for utilizing these frameworks. This foundational knowledge will serve as a springboard, enabling you to commence your journey with these testing environments and apply them effectively in your projects.

- TestCafe
- Cypress
- PlayWright

Introduction to TestCafe

TestCafe is an innovative, Node.js-based end-to-end (E2E) testing framework designed for modern web applications. Unlike traditional testing frameworks that may rely on external drivers and plugins, TestCafe offers a straightforward set up and execution process, making it accessible for developers and QA engineers alike. This framework supports testing across various browsers and platforms, providing a comprehensive solution for ensuring web application integrity from the user's perspective.

Key Features of TestCafe

TestCafe sets itself apart with several distinctive features:

- **No Browser Plugins Required:** TestCafe operates directly in the browser, making it unnecessary to use browser plugins. This simplifies the interaction with the web page and enhances test stability.
- **Cross Browser Testing:** It supports testing in multiple browsers simultaneously, including modern desktop, mobile browsers, and headless browsers, facilitating cross-browser compatibility checks.
- **Built-in Test Runner:** TestCafe comes with an integrated test runner which can run tests written in JavaScript or TypeScript. It includes features like live mode for instant feedback during test development.
- **Automatic Waiting:** This eliminates the need for manual waits or timeouts in your tests. TestCafe automatically waits for page elements to load before performing actions, reducing flakiness.
- **Rich Assertion Library:** TestCafe provides a powerful and flexible assertion library, enabling you to validate test results against various conditions for comprehensive testing.
- **Easy CI/CD Integration:** TestCafe can be easily integrated into Continuous Integration and Continuous Deployment pipelines, facilitating automated testing in development workflows.

Writing the First Test with TestCafe

Creating a TestCafe test involves writing a script that navigates through the application, performs actions, and checks that the expected results occur. Here is a simple example:

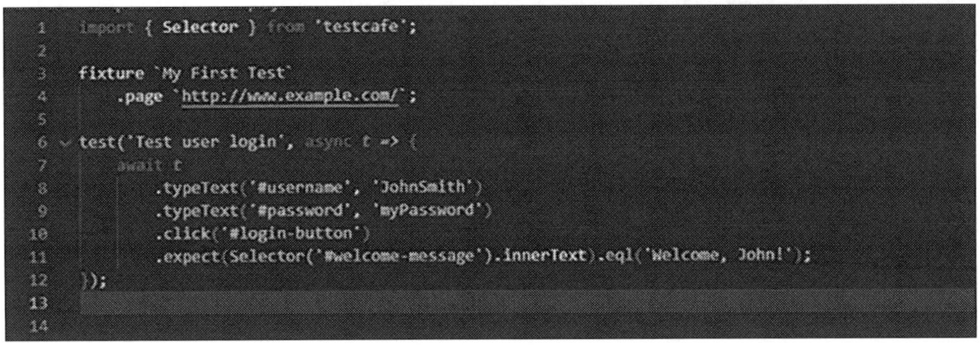

Figure 13.1: *example script*

This script performs a login action and verifies the welcome message, simulating a user's interaction with a web application.

Running TestCafe Tests

Running TestCafe tests is straightforward. You can execute tests from the command line, specifying the browsers and the test files:

```
// All the tests are under the folder my-tests
testcafe chrome /my-tests
```

This command runs all tests located in the **my-tests/** directory in the Chrome browser.

Advanced Topics and Best Practices

While TestCafe is designed to be user-friendly, mastering its advanced features can significantly enhance your testing capabilities:

- **Page Model Pattern:** Implementing the Page Model pattern can simplify maintenance and improve the readability of your tests.
- **Concurrency Mode:** Running tests concurrently across different browsers or browser instances can drastically reduce test execution time.
- **Custom Reporter Plugins:** TestCafe supports custom reporters, allowing you to format and output test results in various styles or formats.
- **Role-Based Testing:** Use TestCafe roles to simulate user roles and permissions, streamlining authentication tests.

TestCafe offers a robust, user-friendly platform for E2E testing of web applications. Its simplicity, combined with powerful features, makes it an excellent choice for teams looking to implement automated browser testing. By understanding the basics of TestCafe and exploring its advanced functionalities, developers and testers can ensure their web applications perform as expected across different environments and user scenarios.

As you become familiar with TestCafe, consider diving deeper into its documentation and community resources to fully leverage its capabilities in your testing strategy. The journey into automated E2E testing with TestCafe is just the beginning; embracing its full potential can significantly improve the quality and reliability of your web applications.

Using TestCafe for E2E Tests

Having laid the groundwork with our understanding of TestCafe, it is time to delve into the practical application of this testing framework for the E2E validation of our **`SignIn`** and **`SignUp`** screens. To ensure clarity and organization, we will establish a dedicated directory within our project structure, aptly named '*e2e*', where we will house all our E2E tests. This segregation serves a crucial purpose; it allows us to maintain a clear distinction between our E2E tests and the main codebase. As projects evolve, this separation becomes invaluable, particularly when we need to conduct regression tests. With our E2E tests neatly encapsulated within their own folder, we can effortlessly run them independently of the source code. This ensures smooth execution and easy maintenance, offering a streamlined approach to testing and validation throughout the development lifecycle.

End-to-end (E2E) testing with TestCafe involves creating automated tests that simulate real user interactions with your web application. Here is a step-by-step guide to setting up and writing E2E tests with TestCafe.

First, you need to install TestCafe. If you have not installed it yet, open your terminal and run the following command. This installs TestCafe globally on your machine, allowing you to run it from anywhere in your filesystem.

```
// Installing TestCafe
npm install -g testcafe
```

To ensure that all end-to-end (E2E) tests are organized and maintained independently from the rest of the application code, we plan to establish a distinct directory named **`e2e`**. This approach will facilitate the isolation of E2E testing concerns, including specific dependencies, configurations, and scripts. Consequently, this directory will contain its own **`package.json`** file, allowing us to manage E2E testing dependencies separately from the main application dependencies.

After setting up the **e2e** folder, we intend to employ TestCafe as our testing framework, particularly focusing on the authentication features of our application. Within this context, two specific test files will be created: `signin.test.js` and `signup.test.js`. These files will respectively contain the E2E tests for our application's sign-in and sign-up modules, enabling us to thoroughly validate user authentication flows.

Furthermore, to enhance maintainability and readability of our tests, we will also create a dedicated file for storing selectors, commonly referred to as the page model or selector file. This strategy permits us to abstract and reuse selectors across multiple test scripts, thereby reducing redundancy and simplifying future updates to our tests. By centralizing the definition of selectors, we can more efficiently manage changes in the application's UI without needing to individually update each test file. This organization not only streamlines the development and maintenance of our E2E tests but also improves their reliability and adaptability to changes in the application's user interface.

Here is the Signin Test case file. This TestCafe file defines an end-to-end test for the "`Sign In`" functionality of a web application running locally. It imports DOM element selectors from a separate file named `'selectors'`, which are used to interact with the sign-in form's email and password inputs, and the submit button. The test initiates by navigating to the application's login page at '`http://localhost:5173`'. It then performs the sign in actions by typing a predefined email address (`'abc123@gmail.com'`) and password (`'tester'`) into the respective fields, followed by clicking the `submit` button. The test waits for two seconds to allow the application to process the login and navigate or update the UI accordingly.

```
e2e > login > JS signin.test.js > test('User can sign in') callback
import { emailInput, passwordInput, submitButton, profileActions } from './selectors';

fixture`Sign In`
  .page`http://localhost:5173`;

test('User can sign in', async t => {
  // Perform sign-in actions
  await t
    .typeText(emailInput, 'abc123@gmail.com')
    .typeText(passwordInput, 'tester')
    .click(submitButton);

  // Wait for 2 seconds before asserting
  await t.wait(2000);

  // Assert that the user is logged in
  await t.expect(profileActions.exists).ok();
});
```

Figure 13.2: *signin test file*

Finally, it verifies that the sign in was successful by checking the existence of elements associated with the user's profile actions, indicating that the user has been successfully logged in and redirected to an authenticated part of the application.

Here is the signup test file. This TestCafe script automates the testing of a web application's **"Sign Up"** functionality. It utilizes predefined selectors imported from a **'selectors'** file to interact with form elements such as **first name**, **last name**, **email**, **password**, and the **submit** button.

e2e > login > JS signup.test.js > test('User can sign up') callback

```javascript
import {
    emailInput,
    firstNameInput,
    lastNameInput,
    passwordInput,
    submitButton,
    profileActions,
    verifyPasswordInput } from './selectors';
import { v4 as uuidv4 } from 'uuid';

fixture`Sign Up`
  .page`http://localhost:5173/signup`;

test('User can sign up', async t => {

  // Generate a random email address
  const randomEmail = `testuser-${uuidv4()}@gmail.com`;

  // Perform sign-in actions
  await t
  .typeText(firstNameInput, 'first')
  .typeText(lastNameInput, 'last')
  .typeText(emailInput, randomEmail)
  .typeText(passwordInput, 'tester')
  .typeText(verifyPasswordInput, 'tester')
  .click(submitButton);

   // Wait for 2 seconds before asserting
   await t.wait(2000);

  // Assert that the user is logged in
  await t.expect(profileActions.exists).ok();
});
```

Figure 13.3: *signup test file*

Unique to this test, it employs the **'uuid'** library to generate a random email address, ensuring that each test run uses a new, unique user identity to avoid conflicts with existing data. The test initiates by navigating to the sign up page of the application hosted locally at 'http://localhost:5173/signup'. It then fills out the registration form with fixed first and last names, a dynamically generated email, and a predetermined password, which it enters in both the password and verify password fields before submitting the form. After a brief pause to allow for page processing (indicated by a two-second wait), the test concludes by asserting the presence of elements related to profile actions, verifying that the user's account has been successfully created and that they are logged into the application.

In the provided screenshot, we observe the file structure and configuration set up within the **e2e** folder of a web application, aimed specifically for end-to-end testing. This directory includes distinct folders and files such as **cypress**, **login**, and **selectors.js**, alongside individual test files like **signin.test.js** and **signup.test.js**. These files and folders collectively contribute to the structured organization of end-to-end tests, segregating them from other parts of the application to enhance maintainability and clarity.

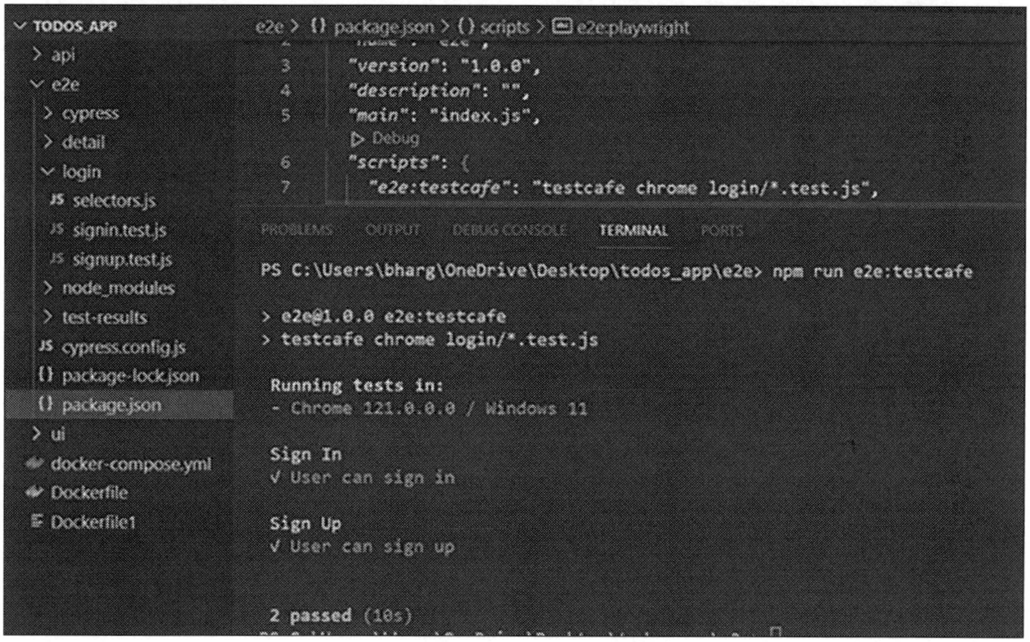

Figure 13.4: *Running Tests*

Within the **package.json** located in the **e2e** directory, a custom script named "**e2e:testcafe**" is defined, assigned to execute TestCafe tests targeting Chrome browser and filtering scripts within the **login** directory that match the pattern ***.test.js**. This approach enables the isolation of test execution to specific areas of the application, in this case, the login functionality.

Executing this script via the command **npm run e2e:testcafe** initiates the TestCafe testing process, as demonstrated in the terminal output within the screenshot. Here, TestCafe launches the Chrome browser and executes the specified tests, providing real-time feedback directly in the console. The output confirms the successful execution of two tests, labeled "`User can sign in`" and "`User can sign up`," indicating that both authentication flows are functioning as expected within the application under test conditions.

This set up exemplifies a well-organized approach to implementing end-to-end testing within a development workflow, emphasizing separation of concerns, clear organization, and efficient testing execution using dedicated scripts and directory structures. When executing TestCafe, the tests are carried out in a web browser, as illustrated below. You have the option to specify the browser in which you want the tests to be conducted.

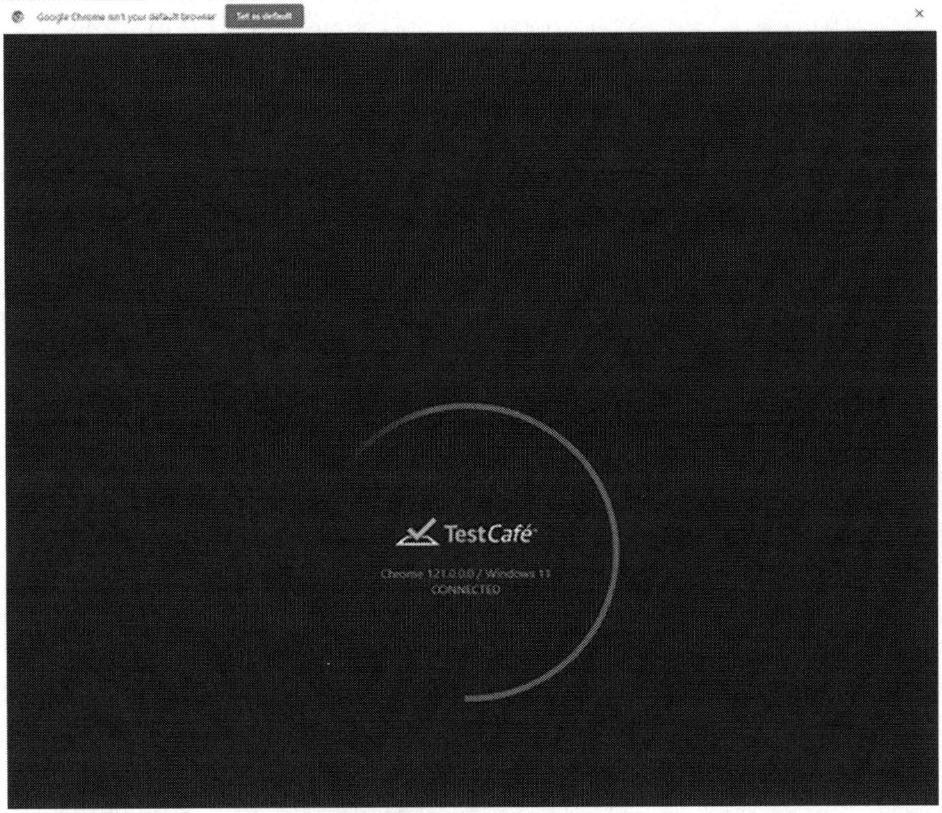

Figure 13.5: *Testcafe launching Tests*

As you become more familiar with TestCafe, continue adding more tests to cover different aspects of your application. You can test various user flows, input validations, page navigations, and more.

In conclusion, we have focused our testing efforts on the login module using TestCafe, which has provided a foundational understanding of how to apply end-to-end testing strategies to specific application functionalities. As you become more familiar with TestCafe and gain comfort with its features and workflow, it is encouraged to expand your testing to cover additional modules and user journeys within your application. Exploring further into TestCafe will help uncover more of its capabilities, enabling you to enhance the robustness and reliability of your application through comprehensive testing.

Introduction to Cypress

Cypress is a modern, all-in-one testing framework designed specifically for web applications. Built on top of a Node.js server, Cypress provides developers and QA engineers with a robust set of tools for writing, running, and debugging end-to-end tests directly inside the browser. Unlike many other testing frameworks, Cypress is not constrained by the same-origin policy, enabling more realistic user interaction testing and easier handling of network requests.

Key Features of Cypress

Cypress revolutionizes web application testing with features tailored for modern development workflows:

- **Real-Time reloads:** Cypress automatically reloads tests upon file changes, providing instant feedback to developers.
- **Time Travel:** Cypress takes snapshots as tests run, allowing testers to hover over commands in the Test Runner to see exactly what happened at each step.
- **Debuggability:** Built-in debugging capabilities let you use familiar dev tools directly from your test code or the Command Log.
- **Automatic Waiting:** Cypress automatically waits for commands and assertions before moving on, eliminating the need for manual waits or sleep commands.
- **Network Traffic Control:** Cypress allows you to stub and inspect network requests and responses, enabling easier testing of application behavior without relying on external servers.
- **Consistent Results:** Cypress runs in the same run-loop as your application, reducing flakiness compared to remote-controlled browsers.
- **Cross Browser Testing:** Supports testing across multiple browsers including Chrome, Firefox, Edge, and Electron.

Writing the First Test with Cypress

Creating tests in Cypress is straightforward thanks to its clear syntax and support for JavaScript. Here is a simple example of a Cypress test script:

```
describe('My First Test', () => {
  it('Visits the Kitchen Sink', () => {
    cy.visit('https://example.cypress.io')
    cy.contains('type').click()
    cy.url().should('include', '/commands/actions')
    cy.get('.action-email')
      .type('hello@cypress.io')
      .should('have.value', 'hello@cypress.io')
  });
});
```

***Figure 13.6**: example script*

This script checks several actions in a web application, such as visiting a page, clicking a button, checking the URL, and filling out a form.

Running Cypress Tests

Cypress tests can be run in various modes:

- **Interactive Mode:** By opening the Cypress Test Runner through the command **cypress open**, developers can run tests interactively in a browser, which is ideal for development and debugging.
- Headless Mode: For continuous integration environments, tests can be run heedlessly using the command `cypress run`.

Advanced Topics and Best Practices

To get the most out of Cypress:

- **Organize Tests:** Use `describe` and `it` blocks to structure your tests logically, making them easier to maintain and understand.
- **Custom Commands:** Extend Cypress's capabilities with custom commands, encapsulating repetitive tasks for reuse across tests.
- **Page Objects:** Implement page object patterns to abstract and encapsulate page-specific details from tests.
- **Environment Variables:** Utilize Cypress's support for environment variables to manage different configurations and secrets.

Cypress represents a significant advancement in the field of web application testing, offering a user-friendly, powerful, and comprehensive testing solution. Its direct access to both the frontend and the backend of applications, combined with real-time feedback and debugging capabilities, empowers developers and testers to write more reliable and maintainable tests. As you dive deeper into Cypress, explore its extensive documentation and community plugins to further enhance your testing practices.

Using Cypress for E2E Tests

In our testing strategy, while we have utilized TestCafe for conducting end-to-end tests on the login module, we can alternatively employ Cypress for executing end-to-end tests on the dashboard module. Employing Cypress necessitates adherence to a specific directory structure, as Cypress automatically searches for test files within predefined folders. This structured approach ensures that tests are organized and easily accessible. For effective Cypress testing, it is essential to structure your files within the Cypress designated folders, such as the **`integration`** folder for your test files, the **`fixtures`** folder for static data, and the **`plugins`** and **`support`** folders for customization and extending Cypress's capabilities. By maintaining this organized folder structure, we facilitate Cypress in identifying and running the necessary test files, thereby streamlining the testing process for the dashboard module, and enhancing the overall efficiency and maintainability of our end-to-end tests.

```
e2e\cypress\integration\dashboard\dashboard.cy.js
```

The initial step is to install Cypress either globally on your computer or locally within the **`e2e`** directory.

```
// Installing cypress

npm install -save cypress
```

Here is the cypress e2e test file. This Cypress script is structured to perform end-to-end testing specifically for a web application's dashboard functionality. It leverages imported selectors from a separate file '**`./selectors`**' to facilitate readability and maintenance, ensuring that specific HTML elements are easily identified and manipulated across different tests.

General Workflow and Setup

- The script is encapsulated within a **`describe`** block titled **`'Dashboard Tests'`**, which groups related tests for the dashboard module.
- A **`beforeEach`** hook runs before each test case, automating the process of navigating to the login page, entering user credentials, submitting the form, and verifying successful redirection to the dashboard. This set up ensures that each test starts from a consistent state.

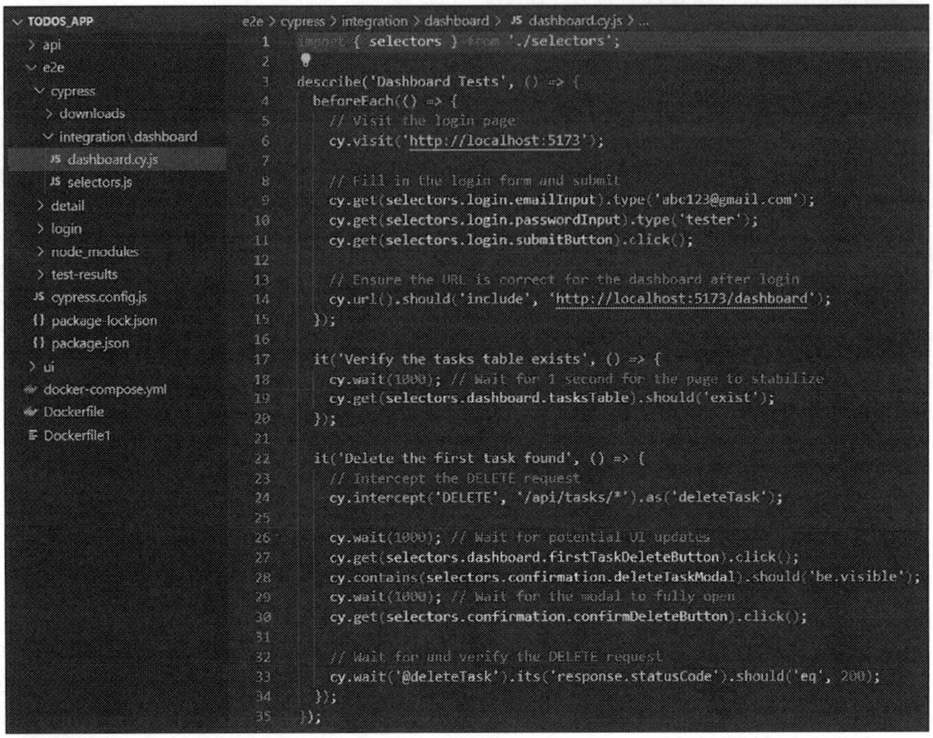

Figure 13.7: *Dashboard Tests*

Test Cases

- **Verify the tasks table exists:** This test aims to confirm the presence of the tasks table on the dashboard after a user logs in. It waits for one second to allow the dashboard to load fully and then checks if the tasks table, identified by a specific selector, is present. The existence of this table is crucial as it represents the primary feature of the dashboard, displaying tasks or other relevant information to the user.
- **Delete the first task found:** This test simulates the user action of deleting a task. It starts by intercepting any **`DELETE`** requests made to the '**`/api/tasks/*`**' endpoint, which is expected to trigger when a task is deleted. The test then proceeds to click the **`delete`** button for the first task listed on the dashboard, waits for a confirmation modal to appear (ensuring the UI has updated correctly), and confirms the deletion. Finally, it waits for the intercepted DELETE request and checks if the operation was successful by verifying that the response status code is 200, indicating a successful deletion on the server-side.

Before we run the cypress tests, we need to place the configuration file. The following snippet represents a configuration file for Cypress, a popular end-to-end testing framework. Using the **defineConfig** method provided by Cypress, the configuration is set up for end-to-end (e2e) tests. Within this configuration, the **`setupNodeEvents`** function allows for customization of Cypress's Node events, though it is left empty here, indicating no custom events are defined. The **specPattern** option specifies where Cypress should look for test files, in this case within the **cypress/integration/dashboard/** directory, accepting files with extensions **.js**, **.jsx**, **.ts**, and **.tsx**, which allows for a wide range of JavaScript and TypeScript files. Lastly, the **supportFile** option is set to **false**, indicating that there is no file for global configurations or reusable behavior to be included before the test files run, deviating from Cypress's default behavior where a support file is typically used to include global custom commands or setup code. This set up indicates a tailored approach, focusing tests specifically on the dashboard module and simplifying the global set up to potentially streamline test execution.

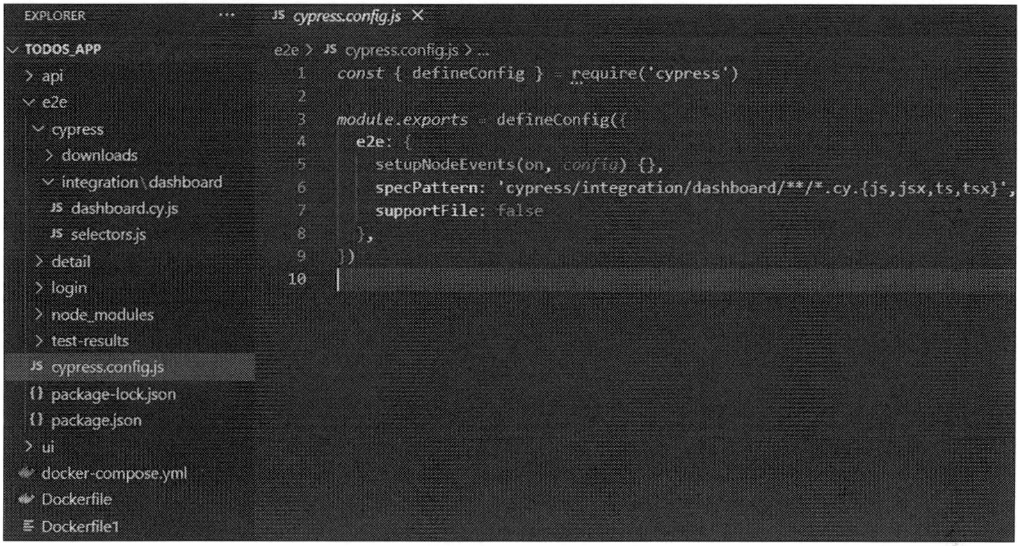

Figure 13.8: *Cypress configuration*

When the **cypress open** command is executed, Cypress initiates an interactive development environment, essentially a specialized set of development tools. Within this environment, users are presented with a user-friendly interface where they can specifically choose the component or the suite of tests they wish to execute. This selection process allows for focused testing, enhancing efficiency by allowing developers and testers to concentrate on specific areas of the application. Additionally, within the same interface, users can select the browser in which they want the tests to run. This flexibility supports cross-browser testing, ensuring that the application performs consistently across different environments. After the desired component and browser are selected, Cypress launches the tests in a separate browser window. This dedicated window allows users to observe the testing process in real-time, providing immediate visual feedback and facilitating a deeper understanding of how the application behaves under test conditions. This interactive approach not only streamlines the testing workflow but also helps in identifying and debugging issues more effectively.

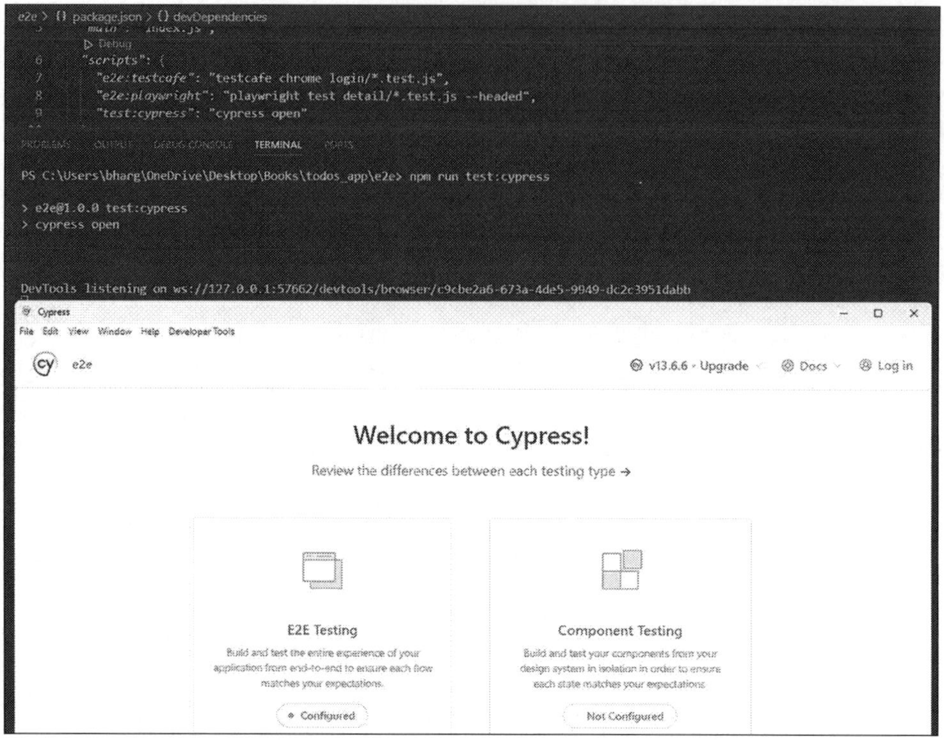

Figure 13.9: *Cypress DevTools*

Cypress Tests are running in a separate window as follows:

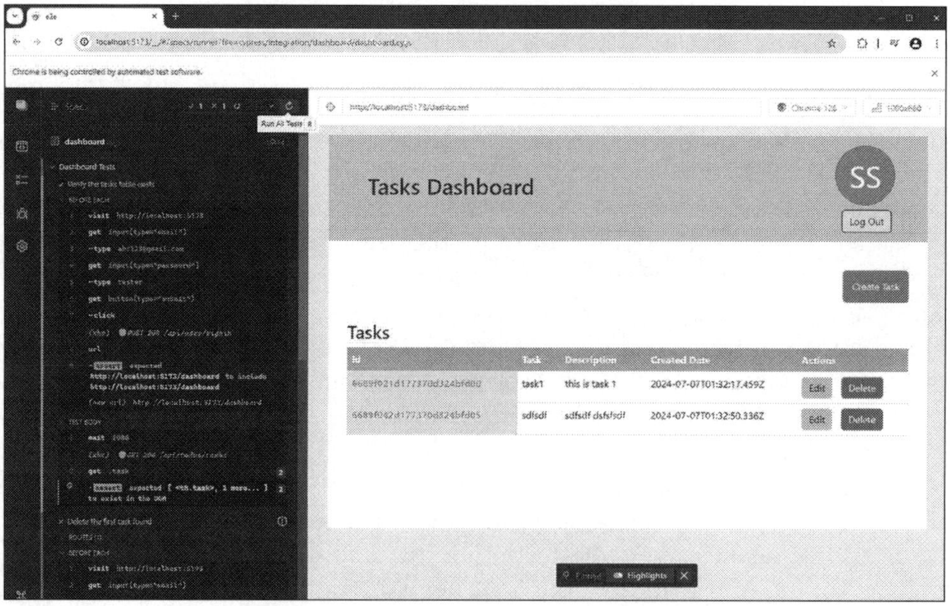

Figure 13.10: *Cypress Running Tests*

Technical Aspects and Best Practices

- The use of `cy.wait()` commands, although not recommended for simulating user wait times, is employed here to ensure the UI elements are loaded and stable before interactions or assertions are made. However, it is better to rely on Cypress's automatic waiting for elements to appear when possible.
- The `cy.intercept()` function is used to monitor and assert network requests, which helps in testing the application's integration with backend services effectively.
- Externalizing selectors to a separate file (`./selectors`) enhances the maintainability of the test code, allowing for centralized updates to selectors without modifying individual test cases.

In conclusion, Cypress provides a comprehensive and user-friendly framework for end-to-end testing, enabling developers and testers to write, run, and debug tests efficiently. By leveraging Cypress's capabilities, such as automatic waiting, real browser testing, and network traffic control, teams can significantly enhance the quality and reliability of web applications. The configuration options, like those demonstrated, allow for customization and flexibility to fit various project structures and testing requirements. As we wrap up our exploration of Cypress, it is clear that this tool is invaluable for modern web development workflows, offering a robust solution for ensuring application functionality, performance, and user experience meet the highest standards. By integrating Cypress into your development process, you can build a solid foundation for continuous testing, leading to faster releases and a more stable product.

Introduction to Playwright

Playwright is a modern automation library for testing web applications across all major browsers. Developed by Microsoft, it provides a single API to write tests that can be run on Chromium (Chrome, Edge), Firefox, and WebKit (Safari). Playwright enables reliable end-to-end testing, helping developers ensure their web applications work seamlessly across different platforms and devices.

Key Features of Playwright

Playwright boasts of several powerful features that sets it apart in the world of web automation and testing.

- **Cross Browser Testing:** Write tests once and run them across multiple browsers to ensure consistent behavior and appearance.
- **Headless Mode:** Tests can be run in '*headless*' mode without a visible UI, which is faster and ideal for CI/CD pipelines.

- **Auto-wait:** Automatically waits for elements to be ready before executing actions, reducing flakiness, and eliminating the need for manual waits.
- **Network Interception:** Intercept and mock network requests for testing different scenarios without backend dependencies.
- **Native Mobile Emulation:** Test mobile web applications by emulating mobile devices and touch events.
- **Rich set of APIs:** Offers a comprehensive API for browser context management, page navigation, and user interactions, among others.
- **Parallel Test Execution:** Supports running tests in parallel, significantly speeding up the testing process.
- **Browser Contexts:** Create isolated browser contexts for testing multi-session or multi-user scenarios.

Writing the First Test with `Playwright`

Creating a test with Playwright involves setting up the testing environment, writing the test script, and executing the test. Here is an example of a basic Playwright test script:

```
const { chromium } = require('playwright');

(async () => {
  const browser = await chromium.launch();
  const page = await browser.newPage();
  await page.goto('https://example.com');
  await page.fill('input[name="q"]', 'Playwright');
  await page.click('input[type="submit"]');
  await page.waitForSelector('text="Search Results"');
  await browser.close();
})();
```

Figure 13.11: *Example Script*

This script opens a Chromium browser, navigates to a page, performs a search operation, and checks for the presence of a result indicator before closing the browser.

Running Playwright Tests

Playwright tests can be run directly from the command line using Node.js. Additionally, Playwright integrates seamlessly with test runners like Jest, Mocha, and others, allowing for a flexible testing set up.

Advanced Topics and Best Practices

As you delve deeper into Playwright, consider exploring the following advanced features and best practices:

- **Code Generation:** Use Playwright's code generation tool to automatically generate test scripts by recording user actions.
- **Visual Comparison:** Employ Playwright's screenshot and visual comparison capabilities to catch visual regressions.
- **Authentication:** Utilize browser contexts to test scenarios involving authentication and session management.
- **Debugging:** Leverage Playwright's debugging tools and techniques to troubleshoot failing tests.
- **Continuous Integration:** Integrate Playwright tests into your CI/CD pipeline for continuous testing and feedback.

Playwright represents a significant advancement in automated web testing, providing developers and testers with a versatile tool to ensure the quality and reliability of web applications across multiple browsers and platforms. By understanding the fundamentals of Playwright and applying its advanced features, teams can build robust testing frameworks that improve the end-user experience and streamline the development process.

As you become more familiar with Playwright, continue to explore its extensive documentation and community resources to fully leverage its capabilities and stay updated with the latest features and best practices. The journey into end-to-end testing with Playwright opens new possibilities for delivering flawless web applications.

Using `Playwright` for E2E Tests

End-to-end (E2E) testing with Playwright involves simulating real user scenarios to validate the overall functionality of your Vue 3 application. Below is a step-by-step guide to writing a Playwright test for your detail page scenario:

First, you need to set up Playwright in your project. If you have not already done so, you can install it by running:

```
// Installing Playwright
npm install -save playwright@latest
npx playwright install
```

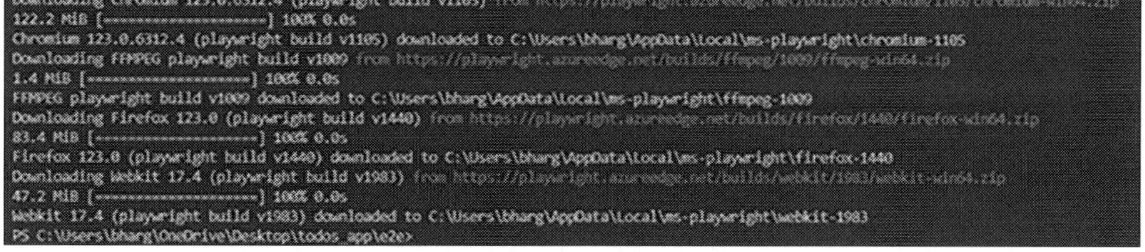

Figure 13.12: *Installing Browsers*

Here is a test file that can be executed for details page testing.

```
e2e > detail > JS detail.test.js > test('user logs in and views task details') callback
import { test, expect } from '@playwright/test';
import { selectors } from './selectors'; // Adjust the path as necessary

test('user logs in and views task details', async ({ page }) => {
  // Navigate to your application's login page
  await page.goto('http://localhost:5173');
  await page.waitForTimeout(1000); // Wait for  second

  // Fill in the email and password fields
  await page.fill(selectors.loginPage.emailInput, 'abc123@gmail.com');
  await page.fill(selectors.loginPage.passwordInput, 'tester');

  // Click the login button
  await page.click(selectors.loginPage.submitButton);

  // Wait for navigation to the dashboard
  await page.waitForURL('http://localhost:5173/dashboard', { waitUntil: 'networkidle' });
  await page.waitForTimeout(1000); // Wait for 1 second

  // Click on the first task in the dashboard
  await page.click(selectors.dashboardPage.firstTask);
  await page.waitForTimeout(1000); // Wait for 1 second

  // Wait for the task details page to load and display content
  await page.waitForSelector(selectors.dashboardPage.detailsSection);
  await page.waitForTimeout(1000); // Wait for 1 second

  // Assert various details are correctly displayed
  await expect(page.locator(selectors.taskDetails.id)).toContainText('Id:');
  await expect(page.locator(selectors.taskDetails.task)).toContainText('Task:');
  await expect(page.locator(selectors.taskDetails.description)).toContainText('Description:');
  await expect(page.locator(selectors.taskDetails.status)).toContainText('Status:');
  await expect(page.locator(selectors.taskDetails.assignee)).toContainText('Assignee:');
  await expect(page.locator(selectors.taskDetails.createdBy)).toContainText('Created By:');
  await expect(page.locator(selectors.taskDetails.createdDate)).toContainText('Created Date:');
});
```

Figure 13.13: *Detail Test file*

This file is a Playwright test script written in JavaScript, designed to automate the testing of a user's login process and subsequent viewing of task details within a web application. Initially, the script imports necessary utilities from Playwright and a set of predefined selectors from a local file to interact with the application's UI elements efficiently.

The test begins by navigating to the login page of the application, where it pauses briefly to ensure that the page has loaded. It then proceeds to fill in the login form with predefined credentials (email and password) and submits the form. After logging in, the script waits for the application to redirect to the dashboard page, ensuring the page has fully loaded before continuing.

Next, the script simulates user interaction by clicking on the first task listed on the dashboard, pausing again to allow the task details page to load fully. It then performs a series of assertions to verify that all relevant task details (such as task ID, description, status, assignee, creator, and creation date) are correctly displayed on the page. These assertions ensure that the application is functioning as expected, displaying the correct information for each task.

Overall, the script automates the process of logging into the application, navigating to the dashboard, selecting a task, and verifying that the details of the task are accurately presented, thereby ensuring the application's functionality aligns with expected behavior. This automated testing aids in identifying issues early in the development cycle, contributing to the overall quality and reliability of the web application.

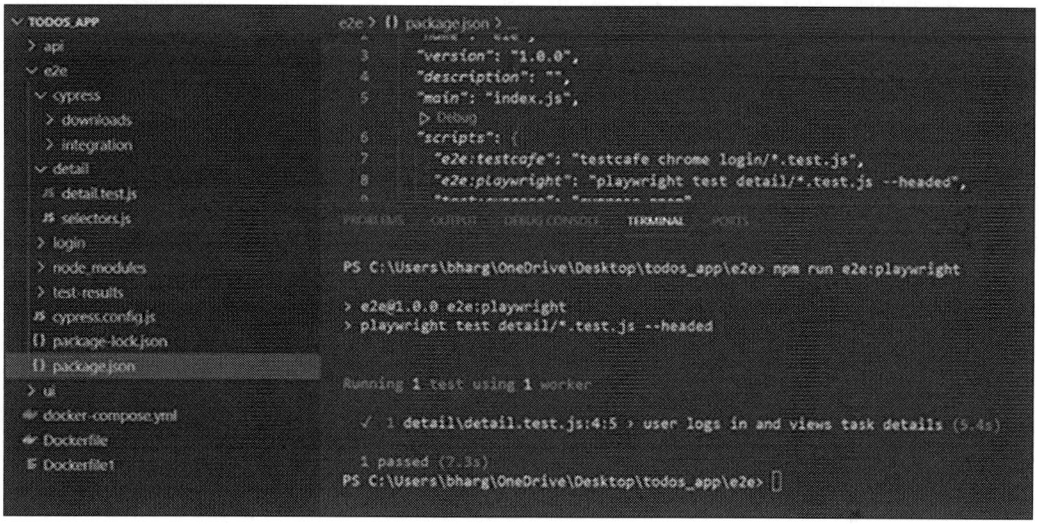

Figure 13.14: *Running Tests*

Following the successful installation of Playwright and the creation of our test scripts, we are now prepared to execute these tests. The specific command **`playwright test detail/*.test.js --headed`**, which has been conveniently included in the **`package.json`** file under the script **`e2e:playwright`**, facilitates this process. By running this command, we instruct Playwright to launch a browser in the headed mode (meaning the browser UI is visible during the test) and to execute all test files located within the **`detail`** directory that match the pattern **`*.test.js`**. As the tests run, Playwright will display the progress and results directly in the terminal, allowing us to observe the execution process in real-time and to review the outcomes immediately upon completion. This approach not only simplifies the testing procedure but also provides immediate visual feedback, enhancing our ability to quickly identify and address any issues that arise.

Playwright stands out as a comprehensive end-to-end testing framework that empowers developers to automate and validate user interactions across web applications with ease. Its support for multiple browsers, ability to handle asynchronous events seamlessly, and compatibility with modern web technologies enable thorough testing scenarios, from simple page navigations to complex user interactions. The example of automating login and task detail verification showcases Playwright's capability to ensure that applications perform reliably under varied conditions. By incorporating Playwright into development workflows, teams can streamline their testing process, enhance the quality of their web applications, and accelerate the delivery of user-centric solutions. This framework not only simplifies the creation of tests but also fosters a culture of quality and efficiency in software development.

Conclusion

This chapter provided a comprehensive overview of end-to-end (E2E) testing, a crucial phase in the software development lifecycle aimed at validating integrated software components to ensure they work as expected from the user's perspective. We introduced three prominent E2E testing frameworks – TestCafe, Cypress, and Playwright, each offering unique features and capabilities for automating browser-based tests. TestCafe stands out for its straightforward set up and cross-browser support without requiring WebDriver. Cypress offers a rich set of features for modern web applications, providing developers with a more intuitive testing process and real-time feedback. Playwright, being a newer addition, extends testing capabilities with its support for multiple browsers and advanced scenarios like mobile emulation and network conditions, enabling more comprehensive testing coverage.

By utilizing TestCafe, Cypress, and Playwright, developers can craft a robust E2E testing strategy that enhances application quality and user satisfaction. These frameworks facilitate the simulation of real-user interactions, detection of bugs, and verification of system integrity, thereby ensuring that the application performs as intended across different environments and platforms. With the knowledge gained from this chapter, teams can select the framework that best fits their project needs and integrate effective E2E testing into their development workflows. Having completed the discussion on testing, we will now progress to the deployment phase, focusing on the deployment of our MEVN (MongoDB, Express.js, Vue.js, Node.js) stack on a cloud environment, marking the next critical step in bringing our application to production.

CHAPTER 14
MEVN Stack Container Options on Google Cloud

Introduction

After constructing our MEVN stack and understanding how to execute the application within a Docker container, it is time to delve into deployment strategies for production environments, specifically focusing on cloud platforms. Embarking on the journey of deploying applications to the cloud opens a realm of possibilities for scalability, reliability, and performance. Google Cloud Platform (GCP) stands out as a comprehensive suite of cloud services that enable developers to build, deploy, and scale applications more efficiently than ever before. This chapter aims to demystify the process of leveraging GCP's robust infrastructure for deploying the MEVN Stack – a modern web application stack consisting of MongoDB, Express.js, Vue.js, and Node.js.

The journey begins with an introduction to Google Cloud, highlighting its key features and benefits that make it an ideal choice for hosting complex applications. We will navigate through the initial steps required to configure and set up Google Cloud, ensuring you have a solid foundation to build upon. As we delve deeper, we will explore the container options available on GCP, each offering unique advantages depending on your application's requirements.

Central to our deployment strategy is the Google Container Registry, where we will push our Dockerized MEVN stack image. This registry not only simplifies container management but also integrates seamlessly with other GCP services, providing a streamlined workflow for continuous delivery and deployment. Following this, we will demonstrate how to bring our application to life on Cloud Run – a fully managed platform that abstracts away infrastructure management, allowing you to focus on code. For those requiring more control and scalability, we will also cover deploying the MEVN stack on Google Kubernetes Engine (GKE), showcasing how container orchestration can be harnessed to manage complex applications with ease.

By the end of this exploration, you will have a comprehensive understanding of deploying and managing your MEVN stack application on Google Cloud Platform, equipped with the knowledge to choose the right services that align with your project's needs.

Structure

In this chapter, the following topics will be covered:

- Introduction to Google Cloud
- Getting Started with Google Cloud
- Configure and Set Up gcloud CLI
- Container Options on GCP
- Pushing Docker Image to Artifact Registry
- Running MEVN Stack on Cloud Run
- Running MEVN Stack on Google GKE

Introduction to Google Cloud

Google Cloud Platform (GCP) emerges as a prominent contender in the cloud computing arena, offering a broad spectrum of services that cater to various IT needs, from simple website hosting to complex machine learning applications. Leveraging the robust infrastructure that powers Google's own flagship products, GCP provides businesses and developers with the tools necessary to build scalable, innovative solutions. This platform encompasses a wide array of products and services, including computing, storage, networking, big data, machine learning, Internet of Things (IoT), security, and cloud management.

GCP's suite of computing services, such as Google Compute Engine, Google Kubernetes Engine (GKE), and Google App Engine, enables users to run virtual machines, manage containerized applications, and develop fully managed applications without worrying about the underlying infrastructure. Storage solutions like Google Cloud Storage offer highly available and secure storage options, catering to diverse data storage needs with ease.

A standout feature of GCP is its commitment to big data and machine learning technologies. Services like Google BigQuery and Google AI Platform provide powerful tools for data analysis, insights generation, and building complex machine learning models. These capabilities allow businesses to harness the power of their data, uncover hidden patterns, and make informed decisions.

Moreover, GCP distinguishes itself with its deeply integrated security features that ensure data protection and compliance with industry standards, making it a trusted platform for companies across various sectors. The commitment to sustainability, with the aim to run on carbon-neutral energy sources, further enhances its appeal to environmentally conscious organizations.

Getting started with GCP is facilitated by its user-friendly interface, the Google Cloud Console, and a comprehensive set of management tools and SDKs. The platform's flexible pricing model, including a generous free tier and pay-as-you-go billing, makes it accessible for startups and enterprises alike.

In summary, Google Cloud Platform offers a secure, scalable, and highly versatile cloud computing environment that empowers users to innovate and scale their applications efficiently. With its wide range of services and strong emphasis on cutting-edge technologies like machine learning and big data analytics, GCP stands as a formidable choice for developers and businesses aiming to leverage the cloud for their digital transformation initiatives.

Core Components and Services

Google Cloud Platform (GCP) encompasses a broad spectrum of services and solutions that empower developers, IT professionals, and businesses to build and scale applications, websites, and services on the same secure and reliable infrastructure that powers Google's own products. Here is an overview of the core components and services offered by GCP:

Compute Services

- **Google Compute Engine:** Offers scalable and flexible virtual machine instances. Users can customize the instance size, type, and the geographical location of their virtual machines to meet specific workload requirements.
- **Google Kubernetes Engine (GKE):** A managed environment for deploying, managing, and scaling containerized applications using Google's infrastructure. GKE is fully integrated with Kubernetes, the leading open-source container orchestration system.
- **Google App Engine:** A platform-as-a-service (PaaS) offering that allows developers to build and deploy applications without worrying about the underlying infrastructure. App Engine automatically scales your application in response to incoming traffic and supports multiple programming languages.
- **Cloud Functions:** A serverless execution environment for building and connecting cloud services. With Cloud Functions, you can write simple, single-purpose functions that are attached to events emitted from your cloud infrastructure and services.

Storage and Databases

- **Google Cloud Storage:** An object storage service for storing and serving large amounts of unstructured data. It is highly durable and available, offering various storage classes to balance cost and access speed.
- **Cloud SQL:** A fully managed database service that makes it easy to set up, maintain, manage, and administer your relational databases on Google Cloud.
- **Cloud Big Table:** A NoSQL big data database service that is suitable for both operational and analytical applications, especially those that require very high throughput and scalability.
- **Firestore:** A NoSQL document database built for automatic scaling, high performance, and ease of application development.

Big Data and Machine Learning

- **BigQuery:** A fast, economical, and fully managed enterprise data warehouse for large-scale data analytics.
- **Cloud Dataflow:** A managed service for executing a wide variety of data processing patterns including ETL, batch computations, and continuous computation.
- **Cloud Machine Learning Machine:** A managed service that enables developers and data scientists to build and bring machine learning models to production. Cloud ML Engine offers training and prediction services, which can be used together or individually.

Networking

- **Virtual Private Cloud (VPC):** Provides a private network with IP allocation, routing, and network firewall policies to deploy cloud resources.
- **Cloud Load Balancing:** A fully distributed, software-defined, managed service for all your traffic. It offers advanced capabilities like global HTTP(S) load balancing, TCP/SSL load balancing, and UDP load balancing.

Identity and Security

- **Cloud Identity and Access Management (IAM):** Defines who has access to what resources in the cloud. It helps ensure only the right individuals can access your resources.
- **Cloud Security Command Center:** Provides security management and data risk analysis for your GCP resources from a centralized dashboard.

This overview barely scratches the surface of GCP's offerings, which continue to expand and evolve, providing solutions for virtually every aspect of cloud computing. Whether you are a startup looking to innovate quickly, an enterprise seeking to leverage big data and AI, or anywhere in between, GCP has the services to transform the way you build and operate your applications.

Advantages of using GCP

Google Cloud Platform (GCP) offers a host of advantages that make it a compelling choice for organizations and developers looking to leverage cloud computing technologies. Here are some key benefits:

- **Integrated and Advanced Services**

  GCP is renowned for its integration with Google's advanced services and technologies, including artificial intelligence (AI), machine learning (ML), big data analytics, and Internet of Things (IoT) solutions. This allows users to easily implement sophisticated functionalities into their applications, enhancing capabilities and user experience without the need for significant investments in hardware or specialized expertise.

- **Global Network Infrastructure**

  One of GCP's standout features is its global infrastructure, built on the same foundation that supports Google's vast ecosystem of end-user products. This ensures that GCP services are supported by a high-performance, low-latency network, enabling applications to deliver content and services efficiently to users around the world. The platform's global network of data centres also facilitates compliance with regional regulations and policies by allowing data storage and processing in specific geographical locations.

- **Security and Compliance**

  Security is a cornerstone of GCP, offering robust protections at both the physical and digital layers. Google's commitment to security encompasses a broad range of measures, including data encryption at rest and in transit, multi-layered infrastructure security, regular audits, and transparent data usage policies. GCP complies with a wide array of international and industry-specific standards, such as GDPR, HIPAA, and ISO/IEC 27001, helping organizations meet their compliance requirements effortlessly.

- **Cost Effectiveness and Scalability**

  GCP provides a flexible and transparent pricing model, including pay-as-you-go and sustained use discounts, which helps organizations optimize their cloud expenditures based on actual usage. The platform's auto-scaling capabilities allow resources to adjust dynamically in response to changing demand, ensuring that applications remain available without incurring unnecessary costs. This scalability, combined with cost management tools, makes GCP a cost-effective solution for businesses of all sizes.

- **Developer and Operational Efficiency**

  GCP streamlines development and operational tasks with a suite of management tools and services designed to simplify deployment, monitoring, and management of applications and infrastructure. From containerized applications with Kubernetes Engine to serverless computing with cloud functions, GCP supports a wide range of computing paradigms, enabling developers to focus on innovation rather than infrastructure management. The platform's commitment to open standards and support for popular development tools further enhances productivity and flexibility.

In summary, the advantages of using GCP include access to cutting-edge technologies, a global network infrastructure, stringent security measures, scalable and cost-effective resources, and tools that boost developer and operational efficiency. These benefits make Google Cloud Platform a powerful ally for organizations navigating the complexities of digital transformation.

Getting Started with Google Cloud

Diving into Google Cloud Platform (GCP) begins with establishing a foundational Google Cloud account, a straightforward process that unlocks the vast capabilities of GCP. This initial step, accessible through Google Cloud's website, might necessitate billing details to leverage specific services or to engage with the platform's generous free tier offerings. Following account setup, users are ushered into the Google Cloud Console, an intuitive web-based interface designed for seamless navigation and management of projects, resources, and the extensive suite of services GCP offers.

For those who command a preference for the command line or need to automate tasks, the gcloud Command Line Interface (CLI) provides a powerful gateway to manage GCP's resources efficiently, allowing for automation scripts and direct command executions. Beyond this, Google Cloud's embrace of developer needs extends to providing client libraries across a spectrum of programming languages, ensuring GCP services integrate smoothly into diverse application ecosystems.

GCP's welcoming stance for newcomers is underscored by its free tier, which presents users with limited access to prevalent services, making it a risk-free playground for exploration and innovation. Additionally, a 12-month free trial featuring a $300 credit acts as a broader invitation to explore GCP's comprehensive product offerings, from computing and storage solutions to advanced machine learning and analytics services. This approach not only facilitates a gentle introduction to cloud computing for novices but also enables seasoned developers to test and deploy ambitious projects without initial financial commitment.

Let us set up a GCP (Google Cloud Platform) account to begin deploying our MEVN stack on GCP. Start by searching for 'GCP console' on Google. This will lead you to a page where you can find and click the '`Try for free`' button, allowing you to establish a free GCP Console account.

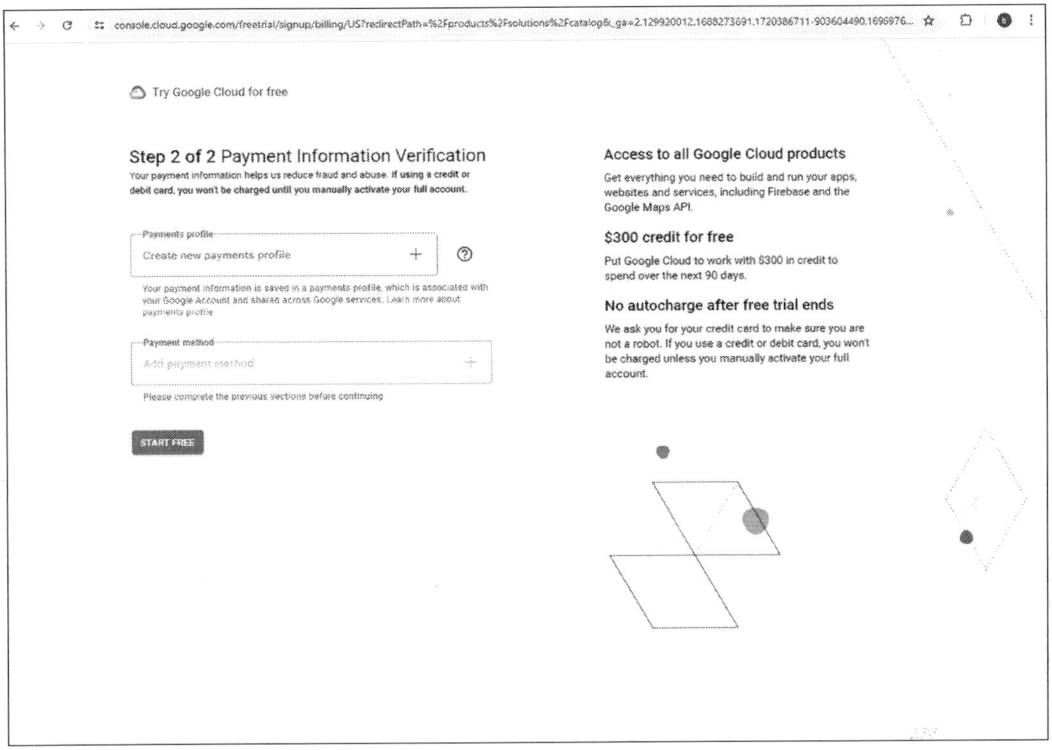

Figure 14.1: *Try Google Cloud*

After selecting the '`Try for free`' button, the process will prompt you to provide various details to set up your new GCP account. This includes specifying the type of account you wish to create, be it for personal use or for an organization. You will also be required to enter personal information, such as your name and contact details.

Furthermore, for verification purposes and to enable potential future billing, you will need to input your credit card information. Rest assured, this step is standard for confirming your identity and setting up the account's billing capabilities. Initially, you will not be charged, as GCP offers a free tier and initial credits for new users to explore and use the services without immediate cost.

Additionally, you might be asked to agree to Google Cloud's terms of service and to confirm your understanding of how Google will manage your data according to its privacy policies. It is important to review these terms carefully before agreeing to ensure you understand your rights and obligations within the GCP ecosystem.

Once you have successfully established your GCP account and logged into the console for the initial time, you will be greeted by the dashboard as illustrated below. On this dashboard, you are presented with an overview of your GCP environment. Key metrics, resource usage, and project information are prominently displayed for easy access and monitoring.

On the left-hand side of the screen, you will find the navigation pane, which lists all the available services and features offered by GCP. This pane acts as your gateway to the extensive range of GCP services, including Compute Engine, App Engine, Kubernetes Engine, BigQuery, and more. You can explore these services by clicking on their respective names, which will take you to the individual service consoles where you can configure and manage your resources.

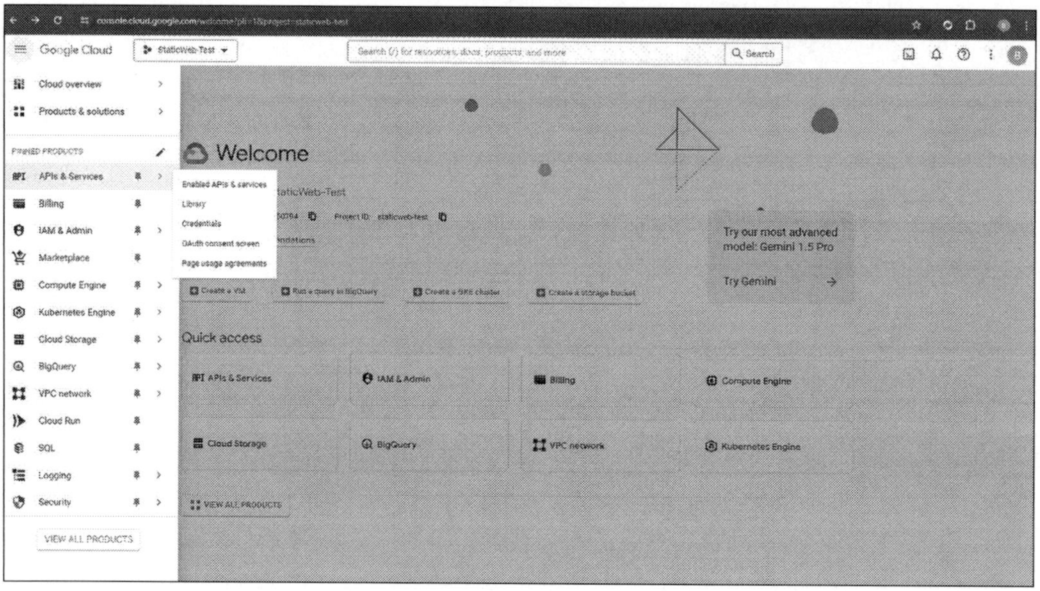

Figure 14.2: *GCP Console*

Additionally, the top of the console provides access to account settings, notifications, and support. You can use the search bar to quickly find specific services or resources within your GCP account. Remember to take advantage of the project selector to switch between different projects or to create new ones as needed.

It is advisable to familiarize yourself with the dashboard layout and the available resources. Exploring the various services and their configurations can help you better understand how to maximize the potential of your GCP environment for your specific needs.

Different Ways to Interact with GCP

There are several ways to interact with GCP services, catering to different preferences and requirements:

Google Cloud Console

- **Description:** The web-based interface provides a user-friendly way to manage GCP resources, allowing you to view and manage all aspects of your projects and accounts in a graphical interface.
- **Best For:** Users who prefer a graphical interface for managing resources, monitoring services, and deploying applications without writing code.

Cloud SDK and gcloud Command-line Tool

- **Description:** The Cloud SDK is a set of tools for the command line that includes the `gcloud` command-line tool. It allows you to create and manage resources, authenticate, and interact with many GCP services directly from the terminal.
- **Best For:** Developers and system administrators who prefer scriptable, automated interactions with GCP services.

Client Libraries

- **Description:** GCP provides client libraries in various programming languages (such as Python, Java, Node.js, Go, C#, and more), which abstract the API calls to GCP services. These libraries allow developers to interact with GCP services programmatically within their applications.
- **Best For:** Developers building applications that directly integrate with GCP services and require programmatic control.

REST and RPC APIs

- **Description:** GCP services offer REST and RPC APIs that allow you to interact with services programmatically over HTTP. These APIs can be used directly for more control over interactions with GCP services.
- **Best For:** Developers needing custom integrations or automation beyond what is provided by client libraries and who are comfortable with lower-level programming against HTTP-based APIs.

Cloud Shell

- **Description:** A browser-based shell experience provided by GCP, Cloud Shell offers a command-line interface to manage GCP resources directly from your browser. It comes pre-installed with the Cloud SDK and other utilities.
- **Best For:** Users who need quick, on-the-go access to GCP resources without the need to install the Cloud SDK locally.

Mobile App

- **Description:** The Google Cloud Console mobile app allows you to monitor and manage your GCP services from a mobile device.

- **Best For:** Administrators and developers who need to monitor resources and perform basic management tasks while away from their workstation.

Terraform and Infrastructure as Code Tools

- **Description:** Infrastructure as Code (IaC) tools like Terraform allow you to define and provision GCP infrastructure using a high-level configuration language. This enables you to manage GCP resources as code, which can be versioned and reused.
- **Best For:** Teams practicing DevOps or infrastructure as code methodologies, looking to automate the set up and management of GCP resources.

Each of these interaction methods caters to different use cases and preferences, ranging from visual and manual management through the Cloud Console to automated, scriptable interactions using the command-line tools, client libraries, or APIs. The choice of tool depends on your specific needs, technical expertise, and workflow requirements.

Configure and Set Up `gcloud` CLI

In our exploration, we examined various methods for interfacing with GCP. In this segment, we will proceed to install the Google Cloud Command Line Interface (CLI), as this tool will be instrumental in upcoming tasks. Specifically, we will use the CLI to upload Docker images to the Artifact Registry and manage Kubernetes resources.

Please follow the provided link to access the download page for the Google Cloud CLI installer. Ensure that you select the correct version tailored to your operating system. After downloading the installer, you will encounter several installation options. Navigate through these choices and complete the installation process according to your preferences and system requirements.

`https://cloud.google.com/sdk/docs/downloads-interactive`

This set up is a foundational step that will streamline our workflow, allowing for efficient management of cloud resources directly from the command line. The Google Cloud CLI is a powerful tool that facilitates a wide range of operations within GCP, enhancing our ability to deploy and manage applications seamlessly.

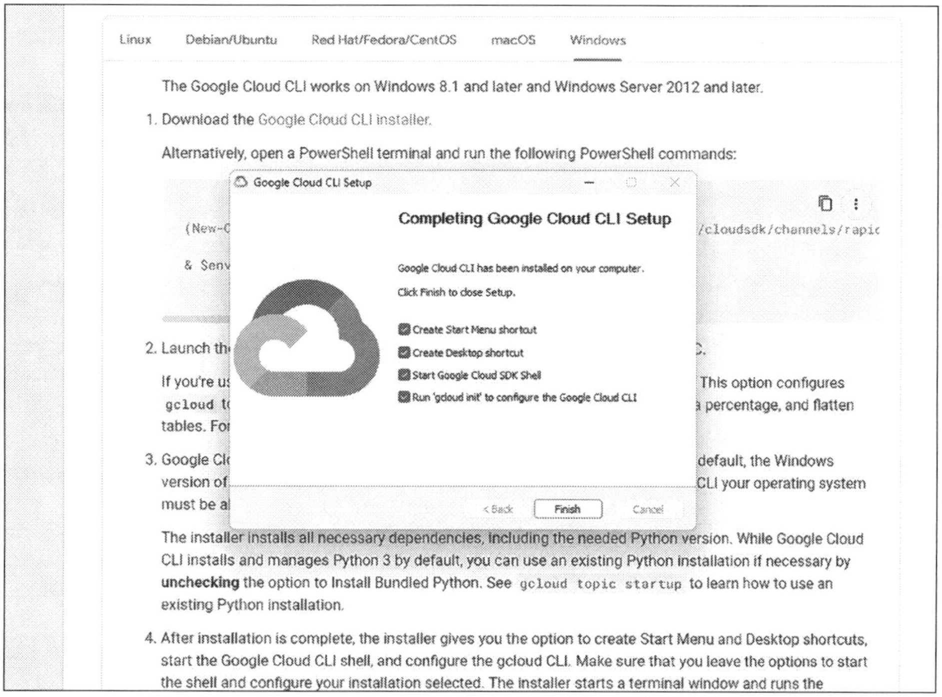

Figure 14.3: *Installing Google Cloud CLI*

After the installation is complete, a command line interface (CLI) will appear as shown in the figure that follows. Follow the instructions provided within this CLI to log into your GCP account directly from your command prompt. We can check the cheat sheet given under.

The gcloud CLI cheat sheet | Google Cloud CLI Documentation

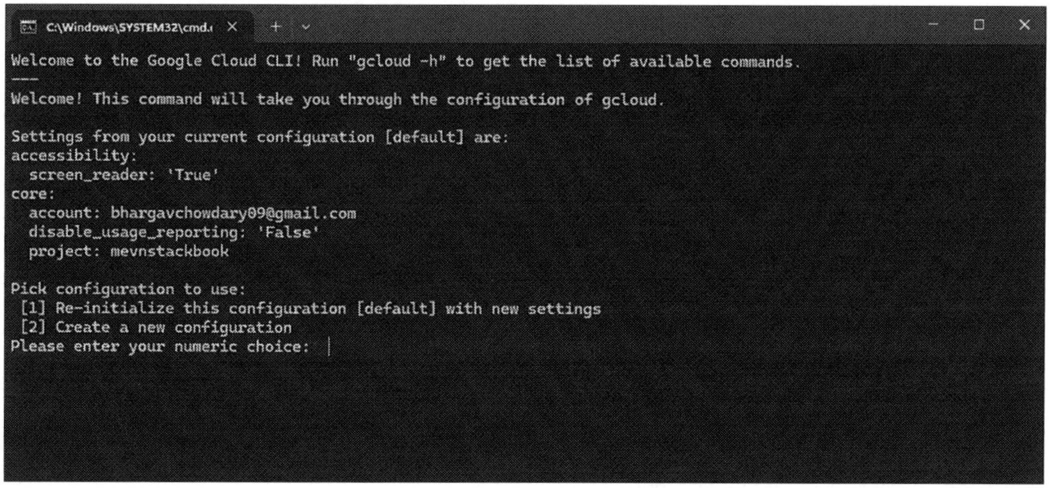

Figure 14.4: Google Cloud CLI

Container Options on GCP

In our previous discussions, we delved into the basics of getting started with Google Cloud, covering essential set up, and exploring the multiple interfaces through which we can interact with GCP's comprehensive range of services. This foundational knowledge is crucial as we move forward with our project. Now, shifting our focus to the practical application of this groundwork, we recognize that our MEVN stack (consisting of MongoDB, Express.js, Vue.js, and Node.js) has been successfully containerized. This is a significant step, as it encapsulates our application in a format that is both portable and scalable, aligning well with cloud deployment models.

With our Dockerized MEVN stack ready, the next logical step is to explore the container deployment options available within Google Cloud Platform. This exploration is vital because it will determine how our application will be hosted, scaled, and managed in the cloud environment. Each container service offered by GCP comes with its unique set of features, pricing models, and performance considerations, making it essential to understand these differences to make an informed decision. Thus, we are now poised to examine the container services provided by GCP in detail. Our goal is to identify the best fit for our Dockerized application, considering factors such as ease of deployment, scalability, operational overhead, and cost-efficiency. By understanding these options, we can ensure our MEVN stack runs optimally in the cloud, leveraging the full potential of GCP's infrastructure.

Deploying an MEVN (MongoDB, Express.js, Vue.js, Node.js) stack Docker image on Google Cloud Platform can be achieved using several container services, depending on your requirements for scalability, management, and operational overhead. Listed here are the most suitable options.

Google Kubernetes Engine (GKE)

Google Kubernetes Engine (GKE) is a managed, production-ready environment for deploying containerized applications. It is built on the open-source Kubernetes system, which automates the deployment, scaling, and operations of application containers across clusters of hosts. GKE gives you the flexibility of Kubernetes combined with the scalability and security of Google Cloud. It simplifies cluster management and eases the workload of deploying and managing applications in a distributed architecture. GKE is ideal for enterprises and developers looking for a more automated and scalable way to run applications in the cloud.

- **Best for:** Production environments, high availability, scalability, and full management of Kubernetes clusters.
- **Features:** Automated scaling, self-healing, load balancing, and a secure and managed Kubernetes service.

- **Use case:** Ideal for deploying complex applications like the MEVN stack, especially if you anticipate needing to scale the services independently or manage multiple services as part of a larger system.

Let us dive into the pros and cons of GKE service for deploying an MEVN stack Docker image:

Advantages

- **Scalability:** Automatically scales your application up or down based on traffic, with the ability to handle large-scale applications efficiently.
- **High Availability:** Offers multiple master and node configurations to ensure your application remains available and accessible.
- **Integrated Ecosystem:** Seamless integration with Google Cloud services and third-party tools, providing a robust environment for deploying microservices-based applications like MEVN.
- **Community and Support:** Extensive support from the Kubernetes community and Google Cloud, providing access to a wealth of documentation, tools, and best practices.

Disadvantages

- **Complexity:** Managing a Kubernetes cluster can be complex, requiring a good understanding of container orchestration and Kubernetes concepts.
- **Cost:** While it provides a high degree of control and flexibility, it can be more expensive than other options, especially for small-scale applications.
- **Operational Overhead:** Requires more time and resources for set up, management, and maintenance compared to fully managed solutions.

Cloud Run

Cloud Run is a fully managed compute platform that enables you to run stateless containers that are invocable via web requests or Pub/Sub events. It is built on the `Knative` platform, offering serverless execution of containerized applications. Cloud Run abstracts away all infrastructure management, so you focus solely on writing code without worrying about the underlying environment. It automatically scales up or down based on traffic and charges only for the compute resources used. This service is suitable for developers who want to build and deploy applications quickly and efficiently without managing servers.

- **Best for:** Simplicity, fast deployments, and fully managed service.
- **Features:** Auto-scaling, pay-per-use, seamless integration with Google Cloud services, and ability to run stateless containers.

- **Use case:** Suitable for stateless MEVN stack applications that can be containerized and do not require persistent connections. Great for applications with variable traffic and for users who prefer not managing infrastructure.

Let us dive into the pros and cons of Cloud Run service for deploying an MEVN stack Docker image:

Advantages

- **Simplicity:** Easy to deploy containerized applications without worrying about the underlying infrastructure.
- **Scalability:** Automatically scales up or down based on traffic, down to zero when there are no requests, which can lead to cost savings.
- **Fully Managed:** No need to manage servers or clusters, reducing operational overhead.
- **Integration:** Easily integrates with other Google Cloud services and allows for quick deployments.

Disadvantages

- **Statelessness:** Designed primarily for stateless applications, which may require additional considerations for state management in an MEVN application.
- **Performance Constraints:** There may be limitations on request processing times and concurrency, which could impact high-performance needs.
- **Limited Control:** Less control over the environment compared to VMs or Kubernetes, which might be restrictive for complex deployments.

Compute Engine

Compute Engine offers scalable and flexible virtual machine (VM) instances in the cloud. It allows you to customize the infrastructure according to your needs, providing a wide range of VM types and sizes, as well as options for disk storage and networking. Compute Engine's VMs can run the public images for Linux and Windows Server as well as custom images created or imported by users. This service is ideal for users who need full control over their virtual servers and is well-suited for applications that require persistent storage and custom virtual network configurations.

- **Best for:** Full control over VM instances, custom configurations, and persistent workloads.
- **Features:** Flexible virtual machines, custom machine types, and network settings.
- **Use case:** If your MEVN application needs specific customizations, requires persistent connections, or if you prefer managing your own VMs and network

settings. This approach requires more management but offers full control over the environment.

Let us dive into the pros and cons of Compute Engine service for deploying an MEVN stack Docker image:

Advantages

- **Full Control:** Complete control over VM instances, allowing for custom configurations and optimizations tailored to your MEVN stack.
- **Flexibility:** Can host any type of workload and is not limited to containerized applications, offering greater flexibility in terms of environment set up.
- **Persistent Workloads:** Suitable for long-running services and persistent workloads, unlike Cloud Run which is more geared towards ephemeral containers.

Disadvantages

- **Management Overhead:** Requires more management and maintenance effort, including OS patching, network configurations, and security.
- **Cost Efficiency:** Can be more expensive than fully managed options if not managed properly, especially regarding scaling and resource optimization.
- **Complexity:** More complex to set up and maintain compared to fully managed platforms, requiring a deeper understanding of cloud infrastructure.

App Engine Flexible Environment

App Engine Flexible Environment is a platform-as-a-service (PaaS) offering that allows developers to build and deploy applications without the burden of managing the underlying infrastructure. It automatically scales your application in response to incoming traffic and runs your applications in Docker containers on Google Cloud's infrastructure. Flexible Environment allows you to customize the runtime environment, network settings, and access to Google Cloud services. This is particularly useful for applications that need access to the resources of a virtual machine (VM) but also require the auto-scaling and simplified deployment model of App Engine.

- **Best for:** Application-centric management, automatic scaling, and versioning.
- **Features:** Fully managed platform, versioning, custom runtime support via Docker, and integrated Google Cloud services.
- **Use case:** Good for MEVN stack applications where you want to focus more on code rather than managing infrastructure. App Engine Flexible automatically handles deployment, scaling, and management, but with less control than GKE.

Let us dive into the pros and cons of Compute Engine service for deploying an MEVN stack Docker image:

Advantages

- **Platform Management:** Google manages the infrastructure, networking, and scaling, allowing you to focus on writing code.
- **Auto-scaling:** Automatically scales based on traffic, improving resource utilization and cost-efficiency.
- **Custom Runtimes:** Supports custom runtimes so you can containerize your MEVN stack and deploy it easily.
- **Integrated Services:** Provides seamless integration with other Google Cloud services, enhancing the overall functionality of your application.

Disadvantages

- **Limited Control:** Less control over the underlying infrastructure compared to Compute Engine or GKE.
- **Cost:** Can be more expensive than traditional hosting if not carefully monitored, especially under variable load.
- **Runtime Restrictions:** There may be limitations and constraints specific to the App Engine environment that could affect the application's architecture and performance.

Each of these services caters to different needs and operational preferences. Your choice should be influenced by the specific requirements of your MEVN stack application, such as the need for scalability, control, cost-efficiency, and operational complexity.

Pushing Docker Image to Artifact Registry

Google Cloud Artifact Registry is a fully managed service provided by Google Cloud Platform (GCP) that allows teams to manage, store, and secure their software artifacts. It is designed to replace and extend the capabilities of Google Container Registry and offers a more integrated and comprehensive solution for handling various artifact types. Here is a detailed explanation.

Artifact Registry provides a single, secure, and scalable repository for managing container images and language packages such as Maven (Java), npm (JavaScript), Python packages, and more. It is designed to support the entire lifecycle of artifacts from development to deployment, facilitating a streamlined CI/CD pipeline. Here are some of the features:

- **Unified Repository:** Store and manage different types of artifacts (Docker images, Maven, npm, etc.) in one place, eliminating the need for multiple storage solutions.
- **Fine-grained Access Control:** Utilize Google Cloud's Identity and Access Management (IAM) to set detailed permissions and roles for your team members, controlling who can access, upload, or delete artifacts.
- **Fully Managed Service:** Google Cloud handles the operations and infrastructure of Artifact Registry, including scaling, performance, and security, allowing teams to focus on development rather than infrastructure management.
- **Integration with Google Cloud Services:** Seamlessly integrates with other GCP services like Cloud Build, Cloud Run, and Kubernetes Engine, enhancing CI/CD workflows and deployment processes.
- **Global Distribution:** Configure repositories to be regional or multi-regional, optimizing access speeds and compliance with data residency requirements.
- **Security and Compliance:** Automatically scan container images for vulnerabilities, ensuring that your artifacts adhere to security standards. Artifact Registry is also compliant with common security certifications, adding an extra layer of trust.
- **Versioning and Tracking:** Keep track of different versions of your artifacts, making it easier to manage releases and rollbacks.

Use Cases:

- **Continuous Integration/Continuous Deployment (CI/CD):** Streamline your build and deployment pipelines by using Artifact Registry as the central hub for your artifacts. Automatically build, store, and retrieve artifacts as part of your CI/CD process.
- **Application Development:** Store development artifacts like libraries, packages, or container images, ensuring that all team members have access to the correct versions.
- **DevOps and Collaboration:** Improve collaboration between development and operations teams by providing a single source of truth for all software artifacts used in development, testing, and production environments.
- **Security and Compliance:** Maintain high security and compliance standards by using the built-in vulnerability scanning and access controls to manage and secure your artifacts.

In summary, Google Cloud Artifact Registry is a versatile, secure, and integrated solution for managing software artifacts within the Google Cloud ecosystem. It supports a variety of artifact formats and integrates with existing Google Cloud services, making it an essential tool for modern application development and deployment workflows.

The first thing that you need to do is click on the **`Create Repository`** button on the top, it opens a detail form where you can enter all the relevant information such as format, mode, region, and others.

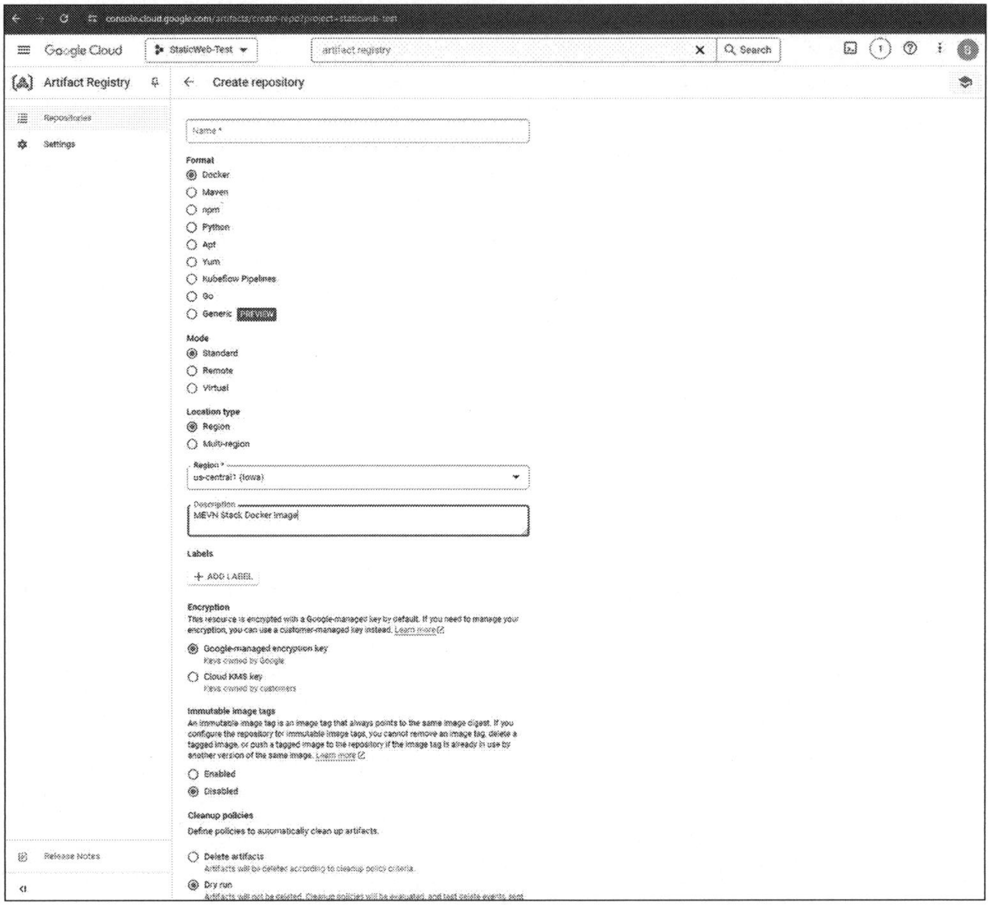

Figure 14.5: *Creating an Artifact Registry*

Upon entering the necessary information on this page and proceeding to create the repository, an Artifact Registry will be established within Google Cloud Platform. This process involves specifying several key details:

- **Name**: Assign a unique name to your repository, in this case, **`'mevn-stack'`**, which likely represents a MEVN (MongoDB, Express.js, Vue.js, Node.js) stack Docker image.
- **Format:** Choose **`'Docker'`** as the format, indicating that this registry is intended to store Docker images.
- **Mode:** Select between **`'Standard'`**, **`'Remote'`**, and **`'Virtual'`**. **`'Standard'`** is typically used for most cases, indicating that the repository will directly store and manage artifacts.

- **Location type:** Decide whether your repository should be **`'Region'`** specific or **`'multi-region'`**. Here, **`'Region'`** is selected with **`'us-central1 (Iowa)'`** as the specific location, which will affect the latency and availability of your artifacts based on geographical considerations.
- **Description:** Provide a brief description of your repository, such as **`'MEVN Stack Docker Image'`**, to give clarity on the repository's intended use or contents.
- **Labels:** Add key-value pairs as labels to help organize and identify your Artifact Registry repositories based on different criteria or environments.
- **Encryption:** Choose between Google-managed encryption keys and Customer-managed encryption keys (CMEK) for securing your artifacts. By default, Google-managed keys are used, which simplifies the encryption process.

After filling out these fields and finalizing your settings, clicking the **`Create`** button will initiate the creation of your Artifact Registry. This registry will serve as a centralized location for managing and storing your Docker images, facilitating easier deployment and version control of your MEVN Stack applications across GCP services.

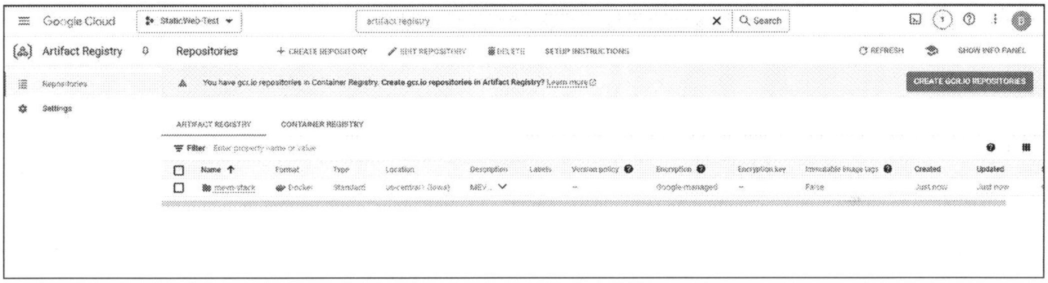

Figure 14.6: *Repository Created*

With our artifact repository now established, the next crucial step is authentication. This ensures secure communication between your command-line interface and the Artifact Registry when pushing Docker images. To do this, we will use a service account – a secure and recommended method for automated processes like continuous integration workflows. The process involves setting up a service account with the right permissions, obtaining the corresponding key, and configuring your environment to use this key for authentication. Once set up, you will authenticate with **`gcloud`**, and your CLI will be ready to push images to the registry. For complete guidance on this process, you should refer to the specific instructions provided in the Google Cloud documentation.

https://cloud.google.com/artifact-registry/docs/docker/authentication

The screenshot in *Figure* 14.7 shows the process of creating a new service account in Google Cloud Platform (GCP). In this section, you are required to fill in details such as the service account name and ID. You can also provide a description for clarity, for example, indicating that this service account will be used to push and pull images from the Artifact Registry. Once the details are filled in, you can proceed by clicking "**`CREATE AND CONTINUE`**" to configure access permissions and finalize the creation of the service account.

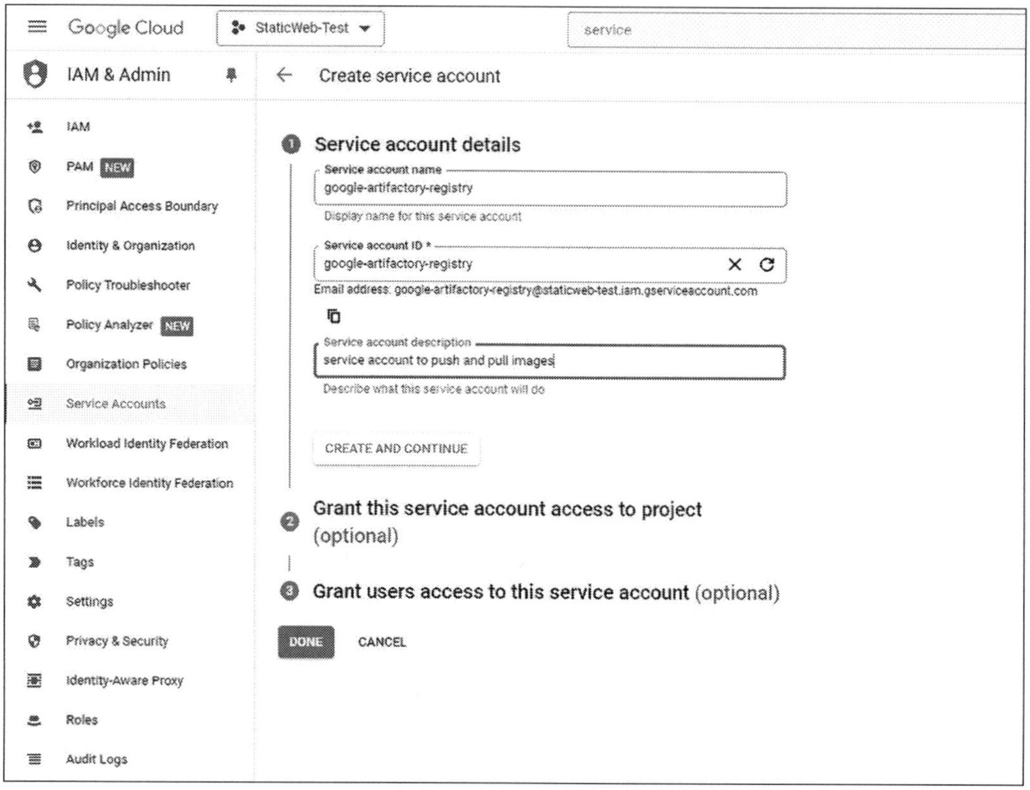

Figure 14.7: *Creating a Service Account*

The second screenshot shows the second step in creating a service account in Google Cloud Platform, focusing on granting the service account access to specific resources within the project. Here, roles such as "**`Artifact Registry Administrator`**" and "**`Cloud Run Admin`**" have been assigned, which provide the service account with the necessary permissions to manage artifact repositories and control Cloud Run resources, respectively. This step is crucial for defining the level of access the service account will have, ensuring it can perform required tasks within your GCP environment.

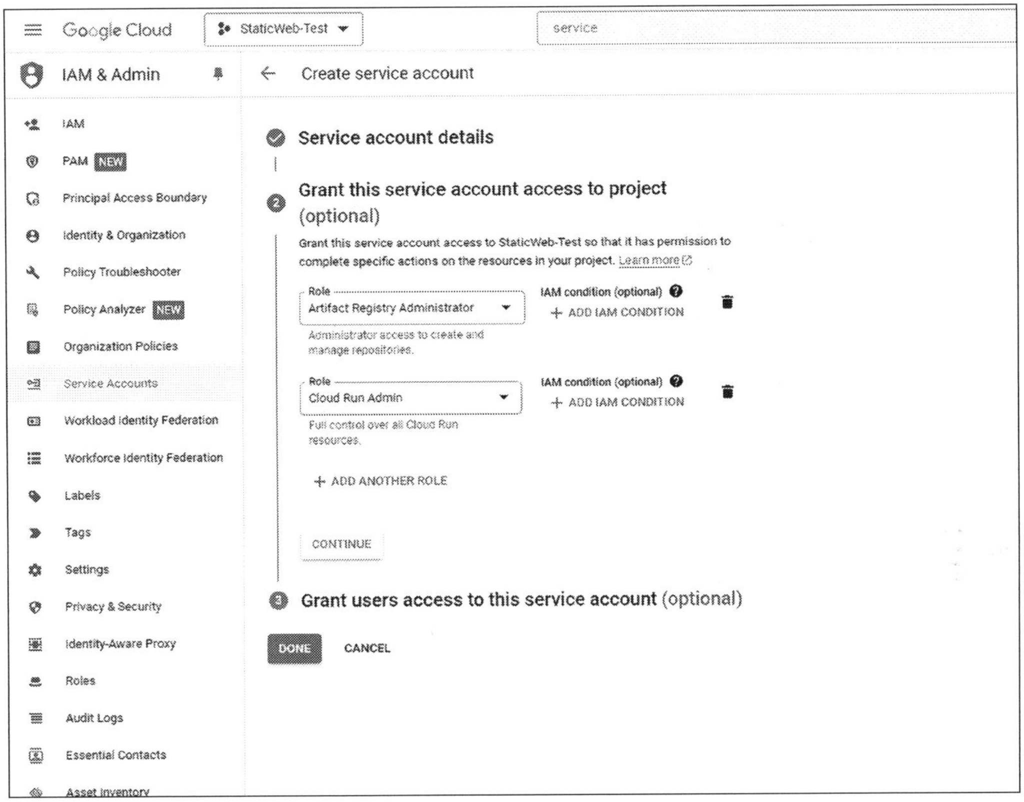

Figure 14.8: *Assigning Roles*

We can download the keys once the service account is created. The screenshot in *Figure* 14.9 pertains to the final stages of creating a service account on Google Cloud Platform, where a private key has been generated and saved to the user's computer. It is crucial to handle these keys with utmost security because they grant access to cloud resources. The dialog box in the image indicates that the key has been downloaded. Google Cloud advises against downloading keys and suggests using Workload Identity Federation for better security. If keys are downloaded, they should be stored securely, following best practices to prevent unauthorized access to GCP resources. This step is critical for enabling automated processes such as CI/CD pipelines to interact with GCP services securely.

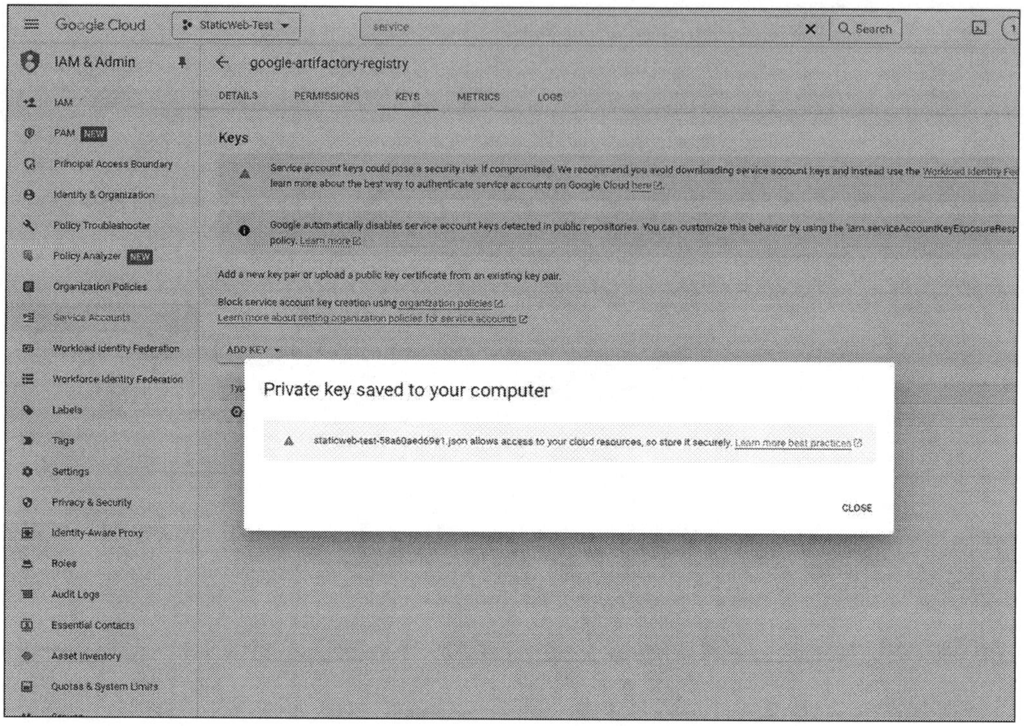

Figure 14.9: *Service Account Keys*

Having set up the Artifact Repository and configured the CLI with login credentials, we are now ready to upload our Docker image, created in *Chapter 11, Running MEVN Stack on Docker*. Before uploading, we must tag the image using the specific format: "**`LOCATION-docker.pkg.dev/PROJECT-ID/REPOSITORY/IMAGE`**". In this format, "**`LOCATION`**" refers to the Google Cloud region, "**`PROJECT-ID`**" is your unique project identifier, "**`REPOSITORY`**" is the name of your Artifact Repository, and "**`IMAGE`**" is your Docker image's name. Structured tagging is essential for organizing and retrieving your images within GCP.

```
// Format of the full mage name
LOCATION-docker.pkg.dev/PROJECT-ID/REPOSITORY/IMAGE
// format
us-central1-docker.pkg.dev/spring-display-142702/mevn-stack
```

The command **`gcloud auth configure-docker us-central1-docker.pkg.dev`** configures the Docker client to authenticate with Google Cloud's Artifact Registry located in the us-central1 region. This step is essential for allowing Docker to push and pull images from your private Google Cloud repositories.

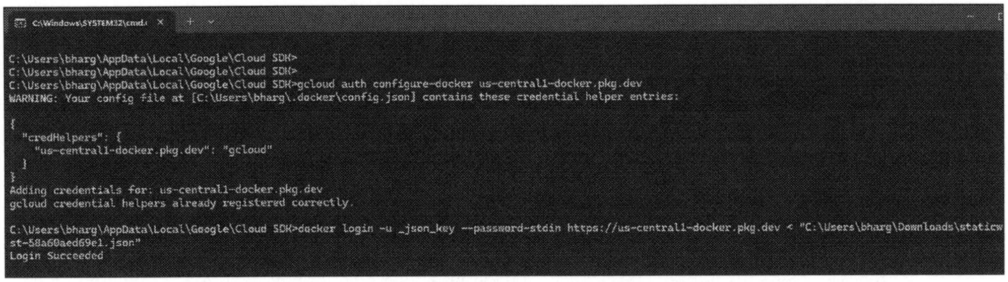

Figure 14.10: *Authentication with Google Cloud*

Tagging and pushing a Docker image involves two main steps. First, tagging assigns a unique identifier to your local Docker image, categorizing it according to version, environment, or other user-defined characteristics. This makes the image easy to recognize and manage. Pushing, on the other hand, refers to uploading the tagged image to a Docker repository, in this case, Google Cloud's Artifact Registry. This process makes the image available for deployment across various environments or for use by others within your organization. With that said, let us proceed by executing the following two commands to push the Docker image into the Artifact Registry, ensuring it is ready for deployment or further use.

```
// Tagging the Docker Image
docker tag mevn-stack us-central1-docker.pkg.dev/spring-display-142702/
mevn-stack/webapp:v1
// Pushing the Docker Image
docker push us-central1-docker.pkg.dev/spring-display-142702/mevn-
stack/webapp:v2
```

Figure 14.11: *Pushing the Docker Image*

The below image displays a section from the Google Cloud Platform's Artifact Registry interface, showing that a Docker image named '*webapp*' has been successfully pushed to the registry. It is listed under the specific project and repository path **`'spring-display-142702 > mevn-stack'`**. The image has been tagged as '*v2*' and the metadata indicates it was created and updated one day ago. This interface allows users to manage and deploy their Docker images directly within the Google Cloud environment, offering options like viewing the pull command, editing tags, and deploying to Cloud Run, GKE, or GCE directly from this page.

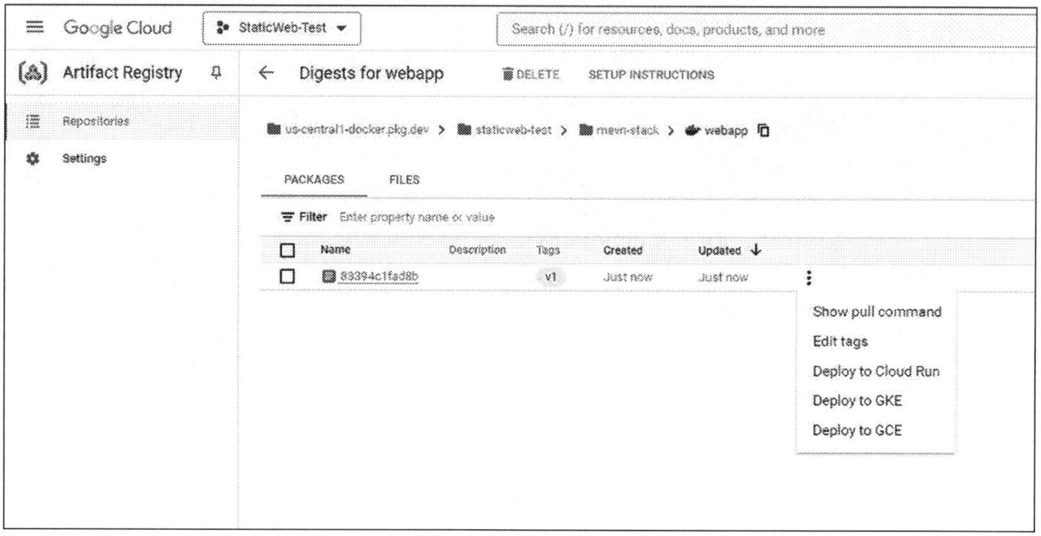

Figure 14.12: *Artifact Registry*

Concluding this section, the process of pushing a Docker image into the Google Cloud Artifact Registry is a critical step that ensures your containerized applications are efficiently managed and ready for deployment. By integrating this practice into your workflow, you leverage Google Cloud's powerful infrastructure, facilitating better version control, secure storage, and seamless integration with other Google Cloud services. This enables more agile development cycles and a more robust deployment process for your applications.

Running MEVN Stack on Cloud Run

If you aim to develop and deploy highly scalable containerized applications effortlessly on a fully managed serverless platform, GCP Cloud Run emerges as the optimal solution. With Cloud Run, you can execute your entire API using the Docker runtime without the need for intricate configurations on your part. Positioned as a service within Google Cloud Platform (GCP), Cloud Run empowers developers to craft code according to their preferences, deploying any code or container that responds to requests or events. This versatility enables you to build applications using your preferred language, dependencies, and tools, deploying them swiftly in a matter of seconds.

Whether opting for the Node.js runtime or Dockerizing the MEVN Stack, Cloud Run accommodates diverse deployment scenarios. Leveraging Docker images from the Container registry and other sources, developers can seamlessly deploy their applications. In this discussion, we will delve into the process of running the MEVN stack using the Docker runtime on GCP Cloud Run, demonstrating the platform's flexibility and ease of use for deploying containerized applications.

After successfully pushing the Docker image to the container registry, the next step is to generate a Cloud Run Service. Access the relevant service in the console to initiate the creation of the Service.

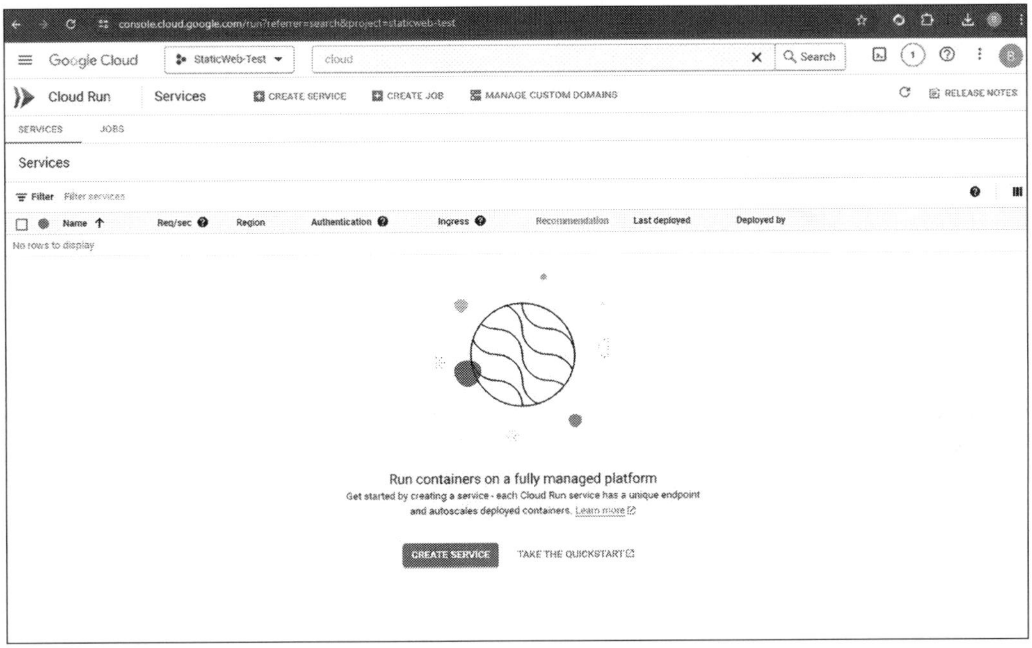

Figure 14.13: *Cloud Run Service*

The below screenshot displays the Google Cloud Run service creation page. Here, you can deploy containerized applications, choosing either a specific container from **`Artifact Registry`**, **`Docker Hub`**, or **`GitHub`**, or continuously deploy from a source repository. The form requires selecting a container image URL, setting a service name, and choosing the region. Options for authentication and CPU allocation during request processing are also provided. On the right, there is a summary of Cloud Run's pricing, including details of the free tier and information on paid tiers.

In the "**`Configure`**" section of Google Cloud Run, you assign a service name and select the geographical region where your service will be deployed. This affects latency and availability. In the "**`Authentication`**" section, you choose between allowing unauthenticated invocations, which make your service publicly accessible, or requiring authentication, which restricts access to authorized users via Cloud IAM. This is crucial for controlling access to your service based on your security and usage requirements.

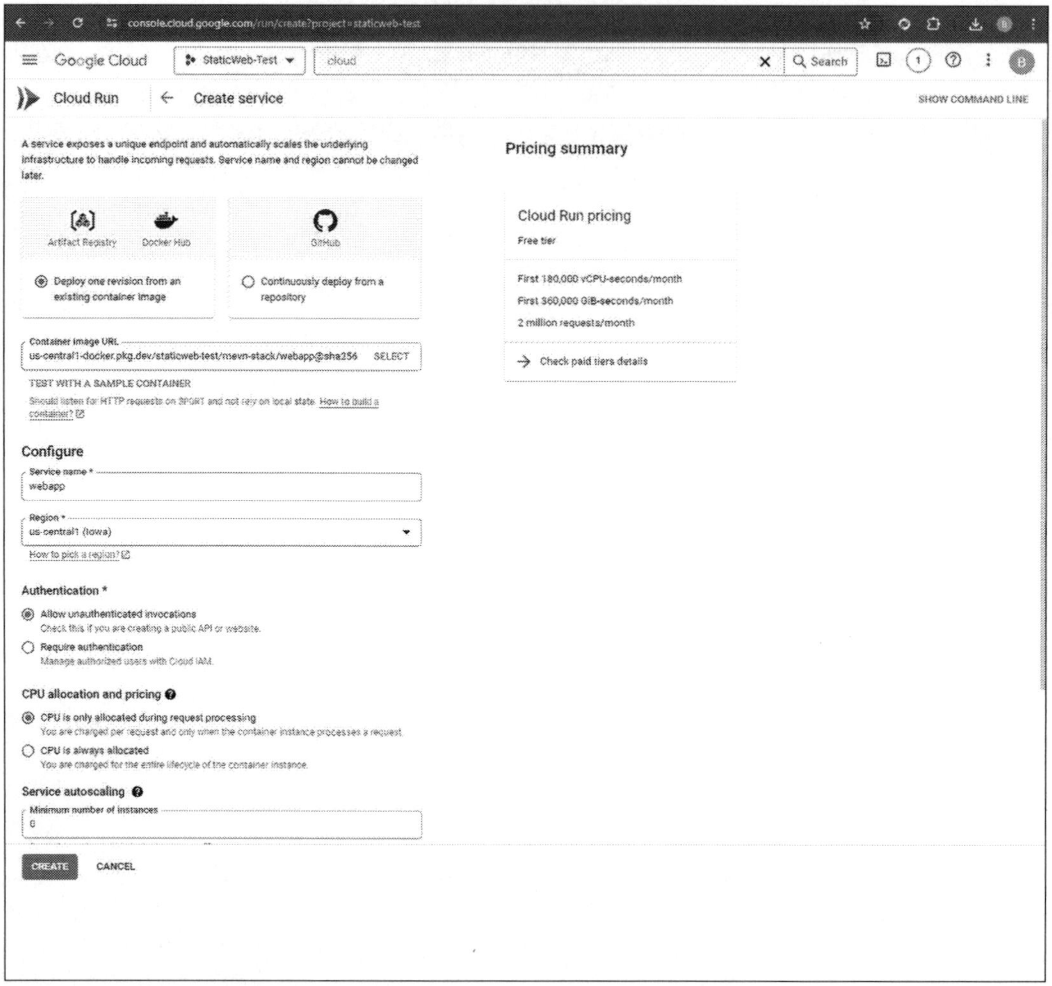

Figure 14.14: *Creating a Cloud Run Service*

We have more configuration as you can see the following screenshot.

- **`CPU Allocation and Pricing`**: You can select whether CPU is allocated only during request processing or always allocated, affecting cost and performance.
- **`Revision auto-scaling`**: Set the minimum and maximum number of instances for scaling, which helps manage traffic fluctuations efficiently.
- **`Ingress control`:** Choose between internal (only within your project or VPC) and external (open to the internet) access to control how users reach your service.
- **`Container settings`:** Specify container image URL, port, and other settings like environment variables and volume mounts for your deployed container.

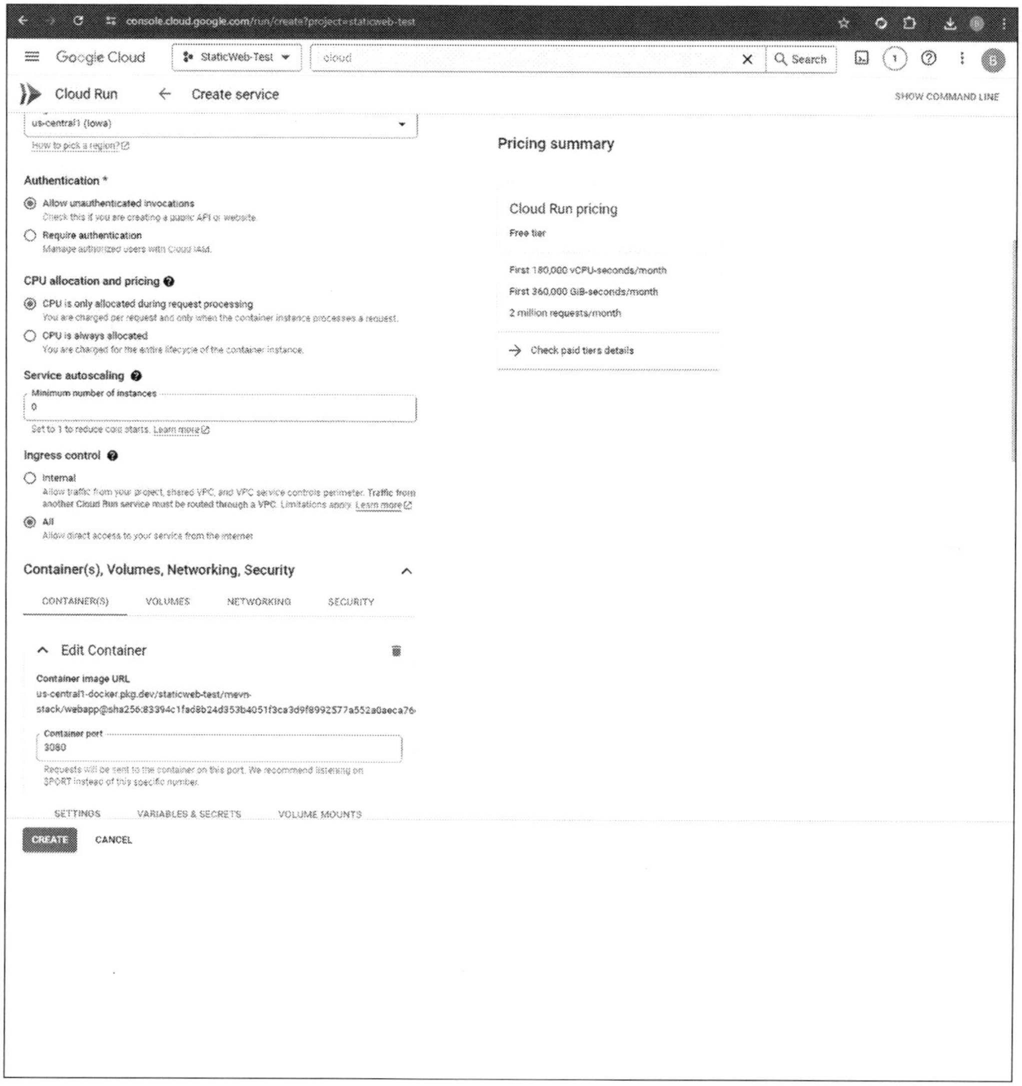

Figure 14.15: *More Configuration*

After configuring and deploying your **`Cloud Run`** service with the specified settings, the system generates a unique URL for your service, allowing web access to your MEVN stack application. The screenshot displays the service details, including the revision name, deployment status, and a pane showing the Docker image specifics, CPU allocation, and auto-scaling settings. Additional tabs like Metrics, Logs, and Triggers provide insights into the service's performance and events. This comprehensive overview aids in monitoring and managing your application's deployment on Cloud Run.

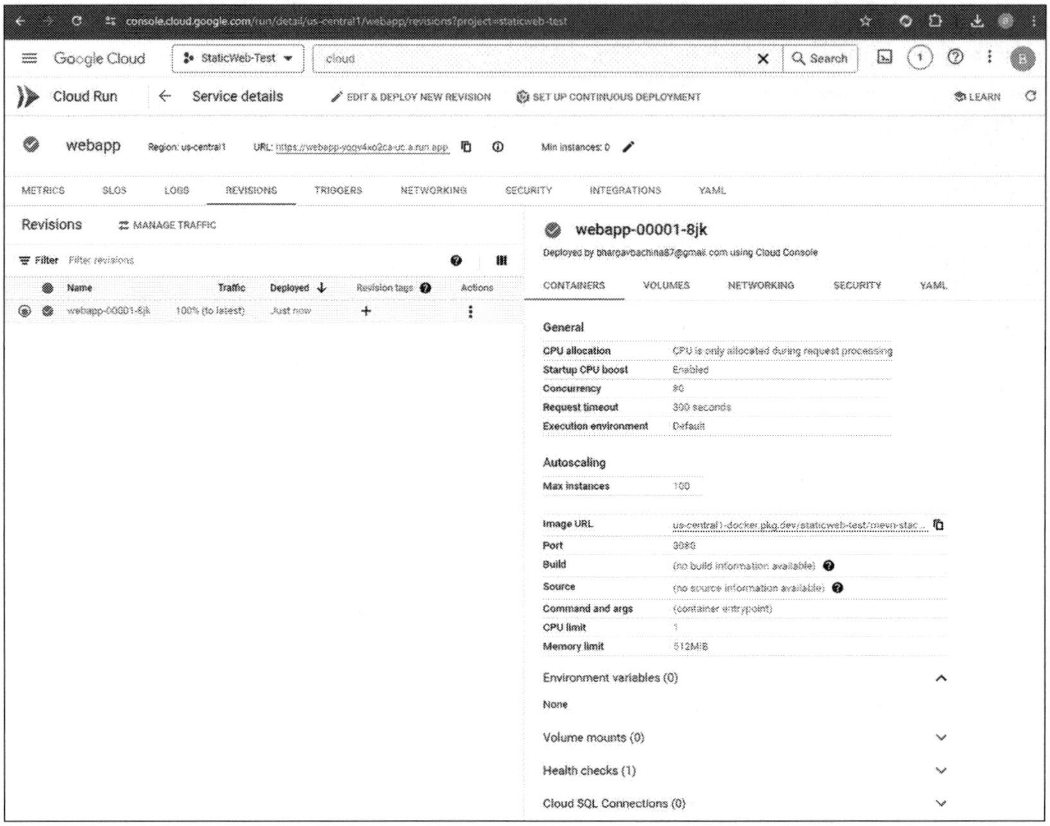

Figure 14.16: *Application Deployed*

Once the **`Cloud Run`** service is activated, the provided URL enables web-based access to your application, facilitating a direct pathway to log in and explore the dashboard functionalities. This accessibility transforms the way users interact with your MEVN Stack application, offering a seamless interface and real-time data reflection through a secure, managed platform.

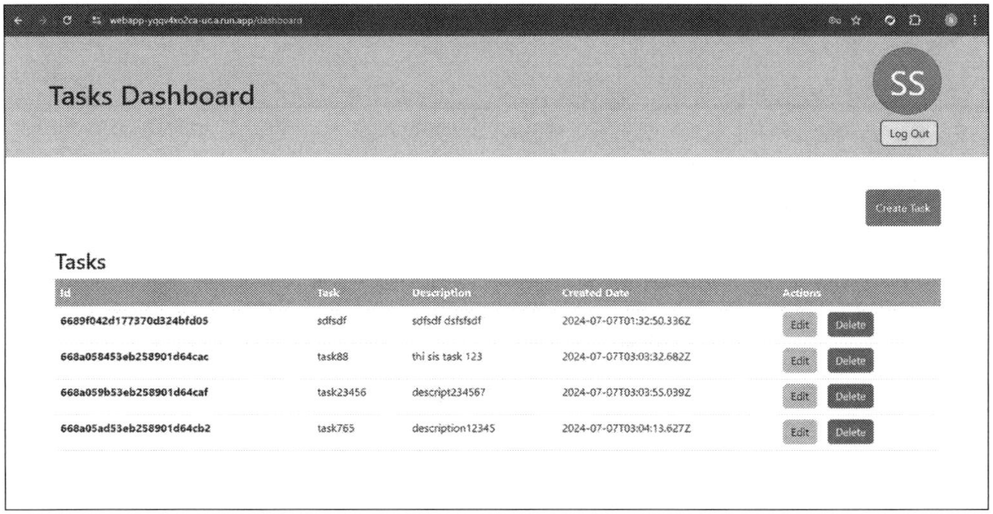

Figure 14.17: *MEVN Stack Serving through Cloud Run*

To conclude, deploying the MEVN stack on Google Cloud Run represents a modern approach to web application development and deployment, leveraging the benefits of serverless architecture. As you progress, explore integrating advanced features such as automated CI/CD pipelines, custom domain mapping, and advanced security settings. Experimenting with these features will not only enhance your application's performance but also provide deeper insights into scalable cloud-native development practices.

Running MEVN Stack on Google GKE

Google Kubernetes Engine (GKE) is a managed Kubernetes service provided by Google Cloud Platform (GCP) that enables users to deploy, manage, and scale containerized applications using Kubernetes. It offers a fully managed environment for running Kubernetes clusters, allowing developers to focus on building and deploying applications without worrying about managing the underlying infrastructure.

Key Features of GKE

- **Managed Kubernetes Clusters:** GKE abstracts away the complexity of managing Kubernetes clusters, providing automated provisioning, scaling, and updates for the cluster control plane and worker nodes. This allows users to deploy and manage Kubernetes clusters with minimal effort.
- **Integration with Google Cloud Services:** GKE seamlessly integrates with other Google Cloud services, such as Google Cloud Storage, BigQuery, and Pub/Sub, enabling users to build and deploy applications that leverage these services easily.

- **Scalability and Flexibility:** GKE enables users to scale their applications horizontally and vertically to meet varying levels of demand. It supports auto-scaling of clusters and applications based on resource utilization, allowing applications to handle traffic spikes effectively.
- **High Availability and Reliability:** GKE provides built-in features for high availability and reliability, such as automatic node repair, multi-zone clusters, and regional clusters. These features ensure that applications deployed on GKE are highly available and resilient to failures.
- **Security and Compliance:** GKE offers robust security features, including node security groups, network policies, identity, and access management (IAM), and encryption at rest and in transit. It also helps users comply with industry-specific regulations and standards, such as HIPAA and PCI DSS.
- **Developer Productivity:** GKE streamlines the development workflow by providing tools and integrations for continuous integration and continuous delivery (CI/CD), monitoring, logging, and debugging. It also supports popular development frameworks and tools, such as Docker and Kubernetes-native APIs.

GKE Architecture

GKE follows a distributed architecture consisting of several key components:

- **Control Pane:** The control plane, also known as the master node, manages the Kubernetes cluster and its components, including the API server, scheduler, controller manager, and etcd database. It exposes the Kubernetes API, which users interact with to manage the cluster.
- **Node Pools:** Node pools are groups of Compute Engine instances (virtual machines) that run the Kubernetes nodes. Each node pool can be configured with different machine types, sizes, and labels to support different types of workloads.
- **Kubernetes Nodes:** Kubernetes nodes, also known as worker nodes or minions, are Compute Engine instances that run the Kubernetes components necessary to host containers. Each node runs a `kubelet` agent, container runtime (for example, Docker), and networking components (for example, kube-proxy).
- **Load Balancers:** GKE integrates with Google Cloud Load Balancing services to distribute incoming traffic to the appropriate Kubernetes services running in the cluster. It supports external load balancers (HTTP(S), TCP/UDP) and internal load balancers for private services.
- **Persistent Storage:** GKE offers various options for persistent storage, including Google Cloud Persistent Disks, Google Cloud Filestore, and external storage solutions. Persistent volumes can be dynamically provisioned and attached to Kubernetes pods as needed.

Overall, Google Kubernetes Engine provides a powerful and flexible platform for deploying and managing containerized applications at scale. With its managed infrastructure, seamless integration with Google Cloud services, and extensive features for scalability, reliability, and security, GKE empowers organizations to build and run modern cloud-native applications with ease.

First, we need to enable the Kubernetes Engine API. The below image showcases the GKE interface for creating an Autopilot cluster. In this set up, you specify basic configurations like cluster name and region. GKE Autopilot automates node provisioning, scaling, and maintenance, among other features, simplifying Kubernetes operations.

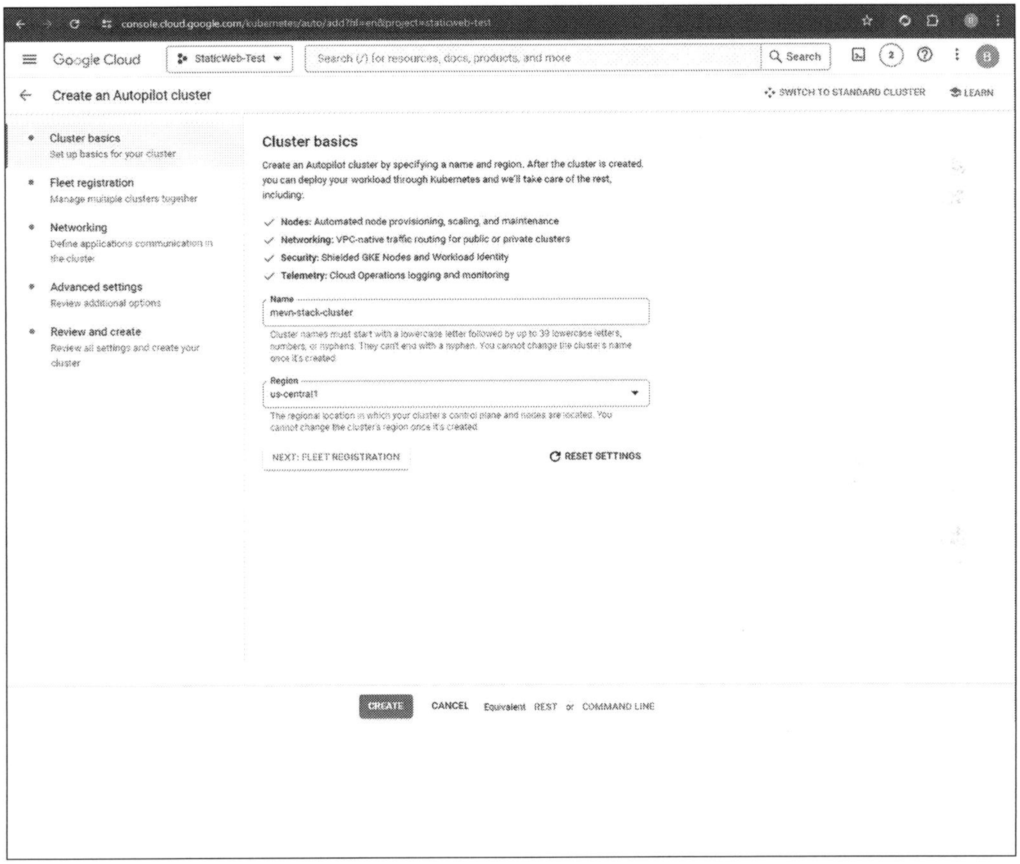

***Figure 14.18:** Creating a GKE Cluster*

After completing the set up in the GCP console, the GKE Cluster named "**`mevn-stack-cluster`**" is successfully created and visible. It is in the "**`us-central1`**" region and operates in Autopilot mode, which means Google manages the underlying infrastructure, scaling, and node provisioning automatically. The cluster currently shows zero nodes as it dynamically allocates resources based on demand in Autopilot mode. From here, you can manage the cluster by editing settings, connecting to it, or deleting it as needed.

Figure 14.19: *GKE Cluster*

The following image shows the output of a Google Cloud SDK command line interface (CLI) command **`gcloud container clusters list`**, which lists Kubernetes clusters in Google Cloud. It displays information for a cluster named "**`mevn-stack-cluster`**" in the "**`us-central1`**" region, detailing the master version, master IP, machine type (e2-small), node version, number of nodes, and status (**`RUNNING`**). This confirms the cluster is successfully deployed and operational.

Figure 14.20: *gcloud container clusters list*

If you look at the above image, we can click on that **`Connect`** button that shows the below modal window showing instructions for connecting to a Google Kubernetes Engine (GKE) cluster from the command line. It provides the specific **`gcloud`** command to configure **`kubectl`** with the credentials for the "**`mevn-stack-cluster`**" in the "us-central1" region of the "**`mevnstackbook`**" project. This set up allows command-line interaction with the cluster. Additionally, there is a link to the Cloud Console Workloads dashboard for visual management of the cluster's workloads.

`kubectl` is a command-line tool for Kubernetes, used to deploy, manage, and inspect resources in a Kubernetes cluster. It allows users to run commands against clusters to control different parts of the cluster and its workloads. Through **`kubectl`**, users can apply configurations, check the status of various resources, create, and delete resources, and manage the cluster's operational aspects.

https://kubernetes.io/docs/tasks/tools/

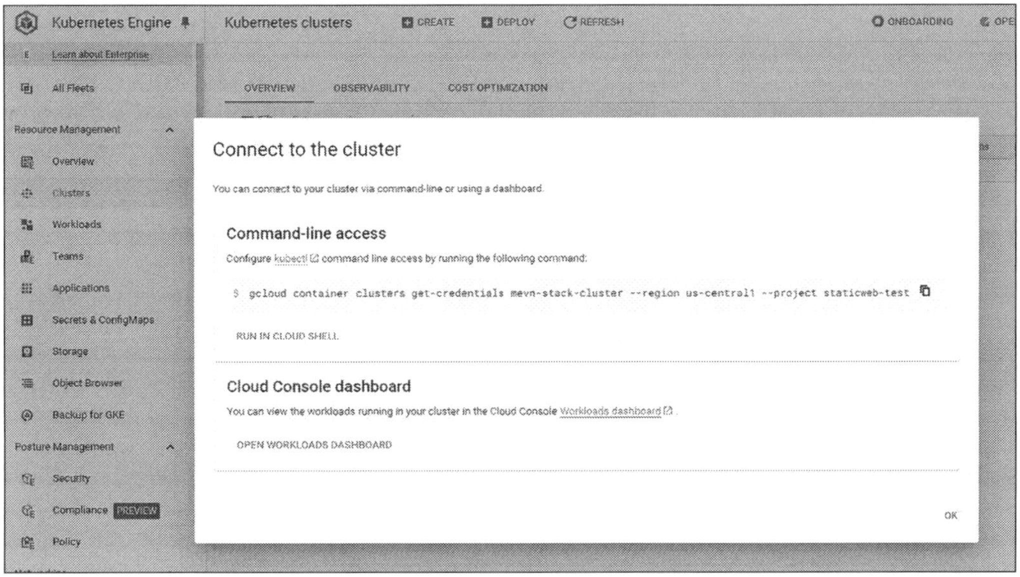

Figure 14.21: *connecting to Cluster*

Make sure we install the below plugin before we connect to the cluster from the CLI.

```
gcloud components install gke-gcloud-auth-plugin
```

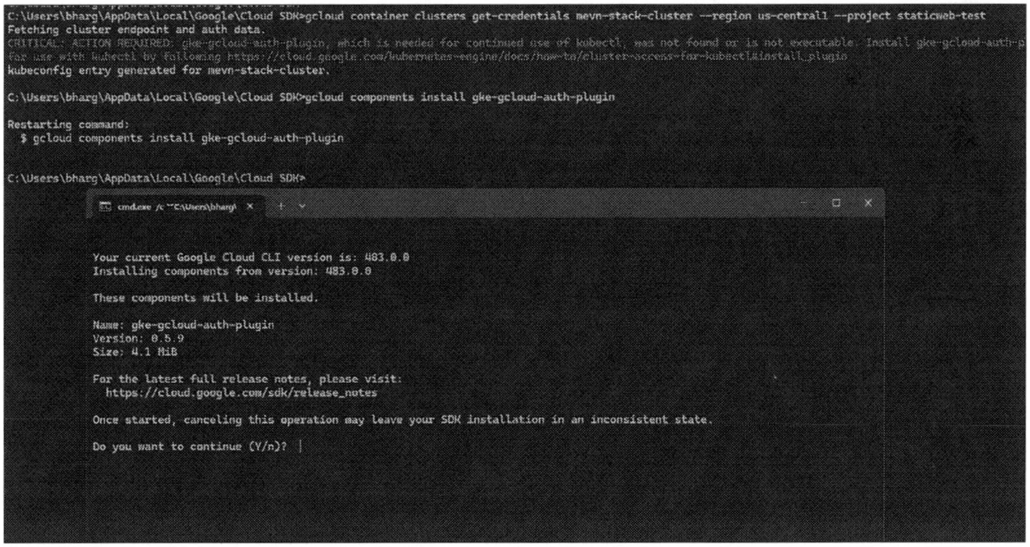

Figure 14.22: *Required components Install*

Copy and execute the provided command in your CLI to establish a connection to the GKE cluster. Once executed, you can verify the connection and the current context by using appropriate **`kubectl`** commands. This allows for direct interaction with the cluster's resources and management operations from the command line.

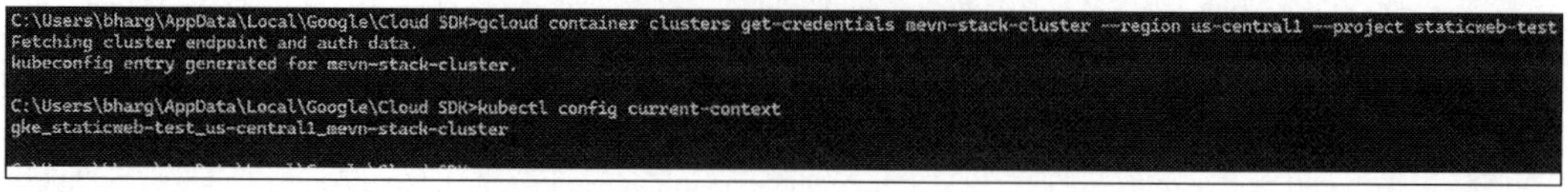

Figure 14.23: *Connected to the Cluster*

Having established a connection to the GKE cluster via CLI, the next step involves deploying Kubernetes resources. Start by visiting the Artifact Registry to obtain the pull command for the Docker image. This command is essential for referencing the image within your Kubernetes Deployment Object, ensuring the correct configuration and deployment of your containerized application within the cluster.

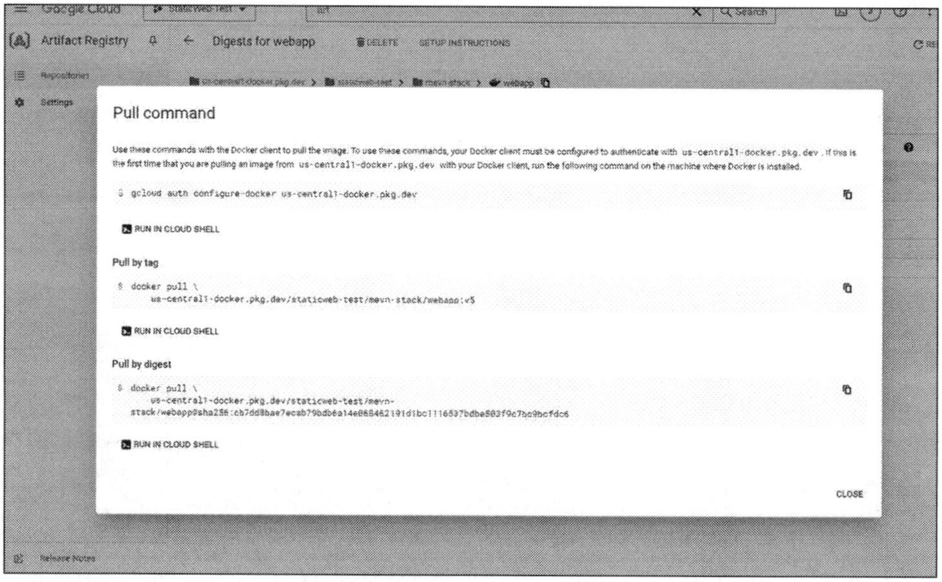

Figure 14.24: *Pull Command*

The provided Kubernetes manifest includes two parts – a Deployment and a Service. The Deployment defines how the application containers should be created, including the image to use from Artifact Registry (specified by its URL), and sets the desired number of replicas. The Service defines how to access the application, exposing container port 3080 to the external network and utilizing a **`LoadBalancer`** to distribute incoming traffic across the instances of the application. Here are the key points.

- **Kind of Resource:** The manifest defines two kinds: "**`Deployment`**" and "**`Service`**". The Deployment orchestrates container deployment, scaling, and management, using the specified Docker image from **`Artifact Registry`**. The Service, particularly of type "**`LoadBalancer`**", directs external traffic to the internal pods.

- **Docker Image URL:** Placed within the Deployment, it directs Kubernetes where to fetch the container image for deployment, specifying the MEVN stack's specific version or build.
- **Container Port:** Set to 3080, indicating the port the MEVN stack application listens on inside the container, facilitating appropriate routing of requests.
- **Service Type `LoadBalancer`:** Creates an external IP to distribute incoming traffic among pods, enabling external access to the application mapped through port **`3080`**.

```yaml
! manifest.yaml
apiVersion: apps/v1
kind: Deployment
metadata:
  creationTimestamp: null
  labels:
    app: webapp
  name: webapp
spec:
  replicas: 5
  selector:
    matchLabels:
      app: webapp
  strategy: {}
  template:
    metadata:
      creationTimestamp: null
      labels:
        app: webapp
    spec:
      containers:
      - image: us-central1-docker.pkg.dev/mevnstackbook/mevnstack/webapp:v1
        name: webapp
        imagePullPolicy: Always
        resources: {}
        ports:
          - containerPort: 3080
status: {}

---

apiVersion: v1
kind: Service
metadata:
  name: webapp
  labels:
    run: webapp
spec:
  ports:
  - port: 3080
    protocol: TCP
  selector:
    app: webapp
  type: LoadBalancer
```

Figure 14.25: *manifest.yaml*

When you run **`kubectl create`** with a YAML manifest, Kubernetes reads the manifest to understand the desired state of resources specified in the file. It then communicates with the cluster's API server to create these resources. The Deployment ensures pods are created using the Docker image and configuration specified, while the Service sets up networking to distribute incoming traffic to the pods. Kubernetes continuously monitors and maintains the resources to match the desired state defined in the YAML.

```
C:\Users\bharg\AppData\Local\Google\Cloud SDK>kubectl create -f "C:\Users\bharg\OneDrive\Desktop\todos_app_k8s\manifest.yaml"
Warning: autopilot-default-resources-mutator:Autopilot updated Deployment default/webapp: defaulted unspecified resources for c
ontainers [webapp] (see http://g.co/gke/autopilot-defaults)
deployment.apps/webapp created
service/webapp created
```

Figure 14.26: *resources created*

The following image displays results from three `kubectl` commands:

- **kubectl get deploy**: Lists deployments in the Kubernetes cluster. Here, the "`webapp`" deployment is shown as "`UP TO DATE`" and "`AVAILABLE`" with 5 replicas, all ready and operational, indicating a healthy state.
- **kubectl get po:** Shows all pods created by the deployment, listing their names, readiness, status, restart counts, and ages. Each pod from the "`webapp`" deployment is running and ready, demonstrating successful pod deployment and operation.
- **kubectl get svc:** Lists services, showing the "`kubernetes`" service (default cluster service) and "`webapp`" service. The "`webapp`" service, of type "`LoadBalancer`", provides an external IP and maps port `3080` (internal) to a port accessible from outside the cluster, facilitating access to the application.

```
C:\Users\bharg\AppData\Local\Google\Cloud SDK>
C:\Users\bharg\AppData\Local\Google\Cloud SDK>kubectl get deploy
NAME     READY   UP-TO-DATE   AVAILABLE   AGE
webapp   5/5     5            5           41s

C:\Users\bharg\AppData\Local\Google\Cloud SDK>kubectl get po
NAME                      READY   STATUS    RESTARTS   AGE
webapp-6d489d6f44-fdbjl   1/1     Running   0          45s
webapp-6d489d6f44-jnsnc   1/1     Running   0          45s
webapp-6d489d6f44-qxjq8   1/1     Running   0          45s
webapp-6d489d6f44-v96pw   1/1     Running   0          45s
webapp-6d489d6f44-x8l87   1/1     Running   0          45s

C:\Users\bharg\AppData\Local\Google\Cloud SDK>kubectl get svc
NAME         TYPE           CLUSTER-IP       EXTERNAL-IP    PORT(S)          AGE
kubernetes   ClusterIP      34.118.224.1     <none>         443/TCP          49m
webapp       LoadBalancer   34.118.229.249   34.42.87.155   3080:30998/TCP   70s
```

Figure 14.27: Resources Created

To access your web application, use the external IP address provided by the `LoadBalancer` service, appending the specified port, in this case, `3080`. This allows web-based interaction with your application deployed on Kubernetes.

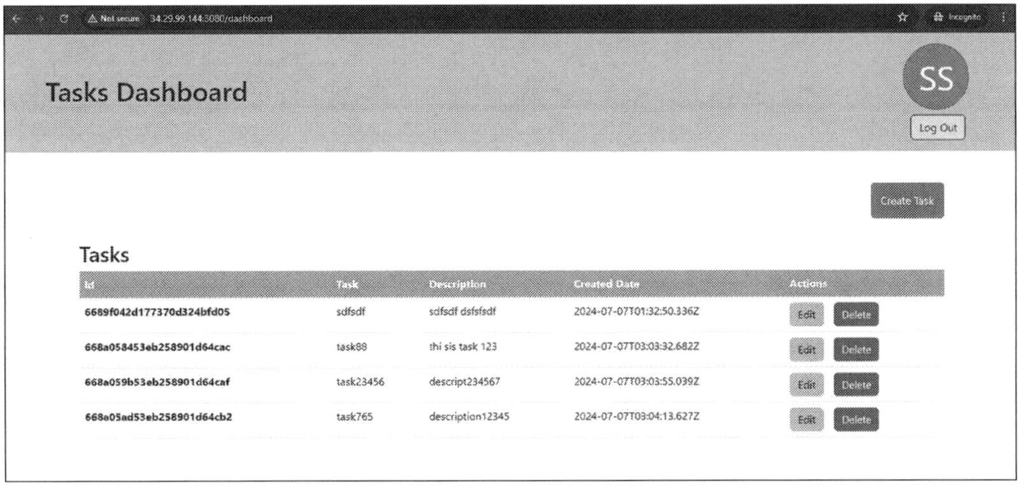

Figure 14.28: *Accessing the Application from webs*

In our journey, deploying the MEVN stack to Google Kubernetes Engine (GKE) served as an introduction to the vast capabilities of Kubernetes. This deployment, while foundational, only scratches the surface of Kubernetes' extensive ecosystem, which includes various resource types and advanced configurations.

Adding an ingress controller to our architecture would allow us to manage external access to the services more effectively, enabling URL routing, load balancing, and SSL termination. This step is crucial for applications requiring secure, controlled access from the internet.

Furthermore, for enhanced security and to ensure data integrity, implementing SSL/TLS certificates for HTTPS communication is essential. This not only secures data in transit but also builds trust with end-users by protecting their information.

Conclusion

In conclusion, this chapter provided a comprehensive overview of deploying the MEVN (MongoDB, Express.js, Vue.js, Node.js) stack on Google Cloud Platform (GCP). We began with an introduction to Google Cloud and guided readers through the initial set up, including configuring and setting up the **`gcloud`** command-line interface (CLI). Exploring container options on GCP, we discussed the process of pushing Docker images to the Artifact Registry, a pivotal step in containerized application deployment. We then delved into two deployment options – deploying the MEVN stack on Cloud Run, Google Cloud's fully managed serverless platform, and running it on Google Kubernetes Engine (GKE), Google's managed Kubernetes service. These sections offered practical insights and step-by-step instructions for each deployment method, empowering readers to leverage Google Cloud services effectively for deploying MEVN stack applications.

Looking ahead, the next chapter will extend our exploration to Amazon Web Services (AWS), where we will replicate the deployment process for the MEVN stack. We will delve into setting up AWS, configuring the AWS CLI, exploring container options on AWS, and deploying the MEVN stack on AWS Elastic Container Service (ECS) and Elastic Kubernetes Service (EKS). By comparing deployment strategies across different cloud platforms, readers will gain a comprehensive understanding of deploying MEVN stack applications in various cloud environments, enabling them to make informed decisions based on their project requirements and preferences.

CHAPTER 15
MEVN Stack Container Options on AWS

Introduction

Having successfully constructed the MEVN stack and demonstrated its operation within a Docker container locally, the next logical progression is to explore deployment strategies that harness the power and versatility of cloud services. Amazon Web Services (AWS) stands as a beacon in this journey, offering an extensive array of services that cater to deploying, managing, and scaling applications with unparalleled efficiency. This introduction aims to bridge the gap between local development and cloud deployment, focusing on AWS as the platform of choice for hosting our Dockerized MEVN stack application.

The journey on AWS begins with an essential step – configuring and setting up the AWS environment. This foundational stage involves understanding the AWS management console, setting up Identity and Access Management (IAM) roles, and configuring network access. Equipped with a properly configured AWS account, we delve into the various container services offered by AWS, such as Elastic Container Service (ECS), Elastic Kubernetes Service (EKS), and AWS App Runner. These services provide scalable and secure options to run containerized applications in the cloud, each with its unique advantages and use cases.

The process of deploying our MEVN stack on AWS involves critical steps such as pushing the Docker image to Amazon Elastic Container Registry (Amazon ECR) and then leveraging AWS services like App Runner for straightforward deployments and EKS for more complex, Kubernetes-managed environments. AWS App Runner simplifies the deployment process, offering an easy path to get web applications up and running, while EKS offers robust management features for Kubernetes applications, catering to the needs of more demanding or intricate applications. Through these steps, developers can see their MEVN stack applications transition from a local development stage to a fully fledged cloud deployment, ready to scale and perform in the vast digital expanse of AWS.

Structure

In this chapter, the following topics will be covered:

- Introduction to AWS
- Getting Started with AWS
- Configure and Set Up AWS CLI
- Container Options on AWS
- Pushing Docker Image to Amazon ECR
- Running MEVN Stack on AWS App Runner

Introduction to AWS

Amazon Web Services (AWS) revolutionized the digital landscape by introducing cloud computing solutions that significantly reduce the complexities associated with managing physical servers and data centres. Since its inception in 2006, AWS has developed into the backbone for thousands of businesses across the globe, offering over 200 fully featured services from data centres worldwide. Its comprehensive suite extends beyond traditional cloud offerings to include computing power, storage options, and networking capabilities, enabling users to scale and innovate at a faster pace.

One of the key strengths of AWS lies in its versatility. It supports various workloads, including web and mobile applications, game development, data processing, warehousing, storage, and archiving. AWS also empowers businesses to harness the power of advanced technologies like artificial intelligence (AI), machine learning (ML), Internet of Things (IoT), and more, allowing for the creation of cutting-edge applications.

Moreover, AWS's pay-as-you-go pricing model offers the flexibility to use the services businesses need without upfront costs or long-term commitments. This has democratized access to powerful computing resources, making it possible for startups and small businesses to leverage the same technologies as large corporations.

As AWS continues to innovate and expand its services, it remains at the forefront of cloud computing, offering scalable, secure, and cost-effective solutions that support the dynamic needs of modern businesses. Its global infrastructure ensures that applications run with high availability and fault tolerance, making it a preferred choice for companies looking to achieve digital transformation and accelerate growth.

Core Components and Services

Amazon Web Services (AWS) is a comprehensive and widely adopted cloud platform, offering over 200 fully featured services from data centres globally. AWS services are divided into various categories, each designed to address different aspects of cloud computing. Here are some of the core components and services provided by AWS:

- **Compute Services**
    - **Amazon EC2 (Elastic Compute Cloud):** Provides scalable computing capacity in the AWS cloud, allowing users to run and manage server instances.
    - **AWS Lambda:** Enables running code without provisioning or managing servers, charging only for the compute time consumed.
    - **Amazon LightSail:** Offers virtual private servers with easy-to-use set up and management, ideal for simpler applications.
- **Storage Services**
    - **AWS S3 (Simple Storage Service):** Offers scalable object storage for data backup, archival, and analytics.
    - **Amazon EBS (Elastic Block Storage):** Provides block-level storage volumes for persistent data storage when used with Amazon EC2 instances.
    - **Amazon Glacier:** Designed for long-term, low-cost data archival.
- **Database Services**
    - **Amazon RDS (Relational Database Service):** Simplifies set up, operation, and scaling of relational databases in the cloud.
    - **Amazon DynamoDB:** A fast and flexible NoSQL database service for applications that need consistent, single-digit millisecond latency.
- **Networking and Content Delivery**
    - **Amazon VPC (Virtual Private Cloud):** Allows users to provision a logically isolated section of the AWS cloud where they can launch AWS resources in a virtual network.
    - **Amazon CloudFront:** A fast content delivery network (CDN) service that securely delivers data, videos, applications, and APIs to customers globally.
- **Developer Tools**
    - **AWS CodeBuild:** A fully managed build service that compiles source code, runs tests, and produces software packages.
    - **AWS CodeDeploy:** Automates code deployments to any instance, including EC2 instances and servers running on-premises.

- **Machine Learning and Artificial Intelligence**
  - **Amazon SageMaker:** Enables developers and data scientists to build, train, and deploy machine learning models quickly.
  - **AWS Rekognition:** Allows adding image and video analysis to applications.
- **Analytics**
  - **Amazon EMR (Elastic MapReduce):** A cloud big data platform for processing massive amounts of data using open-source tools such as Apache Hadoop, Spark, HBase, and more.
  - **Amazon Redshift:** A fast, scalable data warehouse that makes it simple and cost-effective to analyze all data using standard SQL and existing Business Intelligence (BI) tools.

These are just a few examples of the vast range of services AWS offers. Each service is designed to work both independently and in conjunction with others, providing businesses with the tools they need to scale, innovate, and grow in the cloud computing space.

Advantages of Using AWS

Amazon Web Services (AWS) stands as a behemoth in the cloud computing domain, providing an extensive portfolio of advantages that solidify its position as the go-to platform for businesses transitioning into or expanding within the cloud. Among the multitude of benefits, scalability emerges as a pivotal feature; AWS allows organizations to scale their infrastructure up or down with ease, ensuring that they can adjust their resource allocation in real time to meet fluctuating demands. This elasticity not only optimizes operational efficiency but also significantly reduces the cost, as companies pay only for the resources they consume.

Security on AWS is paramount, with the platform offering comprehensive tools and features designed to protect data, applications, and infrastructure from potential threats. AWS's commitment to security is evident through its adherence to industry standards and certifications, providing users with peace of mind regarding their data's safety. Furthermore, AWS's global network of data centers ensures high availability and reliability, guaranteeing that services are always accessible and resilient against failures.

Innovation is another cornerstone of AWS, providing access to cutting-edge technologies such as artificial intelligence, machine learning, and Internet of Things (IoT), enabling businesses to stay ahead in their respective industries. This access to advanced tools, combined with AWS's flexible service model, empowers organizations to experiment and innovate without the need for significant upfront investments in hardware or software.

Lastly, AWS's ecosystem and marketplace offer a rich repository of applications and services that can be seamlessly integrated into any cloud-based solution, enhancing functionality and streamlining deployment processes. With AWS, companies can rapidly deploy new applications, scale existing ones, and accelerate their journey to digital transformation, all the while maintaining control over costs and compliance. These advantages collectively make AWS a formidable cloud service provider, catering to a wide array of organizational needs and driving the future of cloud computing.

- **Comprehensive Service Offering:** AWS provides a vast array of services covering almost every aspect of cloud computing, including compute power, storage options, networking capabilities, databases, machine learning, analytics, and more. This extensive portfolio allows organizations to build, deploy, and scale applications of any complexity and size.
- **Global Reach:** AWS operates 69 Availability Zones within 22 geographic regions around the world. This global presence enables organizations to deploy their applications in multiple locations with ease, ensuring lower latency and a better experience for end-users regardless of their geographical location.
- **Scalability and Flexibility:** AWS allows organizations to scale resources up or down based on demand, ensuring that they can manage growth efficiently without upfront investments in physical hardware. This scalability is complemented by the flexibility to choose the operating system, programming language, web application platform, database, and other services you need.
- **Cost-Effectiveness:** With a pay-as-you-go pricing model, AWS enables organizations to pay only for the compute power, storage, and other resources they use, without requiring long-term contracts or complex licensing agreements. This model can lead to significant cost savings compared to the expense of building and maintaining physical data centers.
- **Security and Compliance:** AWS is committed to providing a secure cloud computing environment, offering extensive security features that comply with the highest standards. This includes data encryption, network firewalls, multi-factor authentication, and compliance certifications for a wide range of industry standards and regulations.
- **Innovation and Speed:** AWS continuously innovates and introduces new services and features, allowing organizations to take advantage of the latest technologies without the burden of managing them. This fosters a culture of innovation, enabling businesses to develop new solutions and bring them to market more quickly.
- **Reliability:** AWS offers a highly reliable infrastructure with backup and redundancy built in. Their services are designed to ensure maximum uptime and continuity for critical applications and workloads.

- **Ecosystem and Community:** AWS has a vast ecosystem of partners, developers, and customers, providing a rich community for support, training, and resources. This ecosystem also includes a wide range of third-party tools and integrations that enhance and extend AWS services.

By leveraging these advantages, organizations can accelerate their digital transformation, optimize IT costs, and innovate faster, all the while maintaining high levels of security and compliance.

Getting Started with AWS

Starting with AWS involves a few structured steps to unlock the vast capabilities of AWS's cloud offerings. First, you will need to create an AWS account, which provides access to AWS services and resources. This step is straightforward: visit the AWS homepage, click on "`Create an AWS Account`," and follow the prompts. During this process, you will have to provide some basic personal information and billing details, as AWS services operate on a pay-as-you-go pricing model.

Once your account is set up, you will gain access to the AWS Management Console, a user-friendly web interface that allows you to manage your AWS services and resources. The console is designed to simplify the navigation across AWS services, offering an organized view that categorizes services by domain, making it easier to find, configure, and deploy resources.

For those who prefer working with command-line tools or need to automate tasks, AWS provides the AWS Command Line Interface (CLI). Installing the AWS CLI on your local machine enables you to control and configure multiple AWS services directly from your terminal, offering a powerful way to script operations across AWS resources.

AWS also offers Software Development Kits (SDKs) for various programming languages, including Python, Java, and Node.js, among others. These SDKs facilitate the integration of AWS services into your applications, allowing for more complex, scalable, and robust cloud-based applications.

To help new users get started and explore the breadth of AWS services, AWS offers the AWS Free Tier. This tier includes offers that are always free, 12-month free trials for certain services, and short-term trials for all new customers. It is an excellent way to experiment with and learn about AWS services without incurring upfront costs, making it accessible for individuals, developers, and businesses to start building on AWS.

To begin using AWS services, navigate to the AWS Console and start the sign-up process for a free account. This involves entering your email address, which will be used for account recovery and administrative functions, and selecting an AWS account name, which identifies your account and can be altered later in your account settings.

This initial step is crucial for establishing your identity and securing access to AWS's suite of services and products under the free tier program.

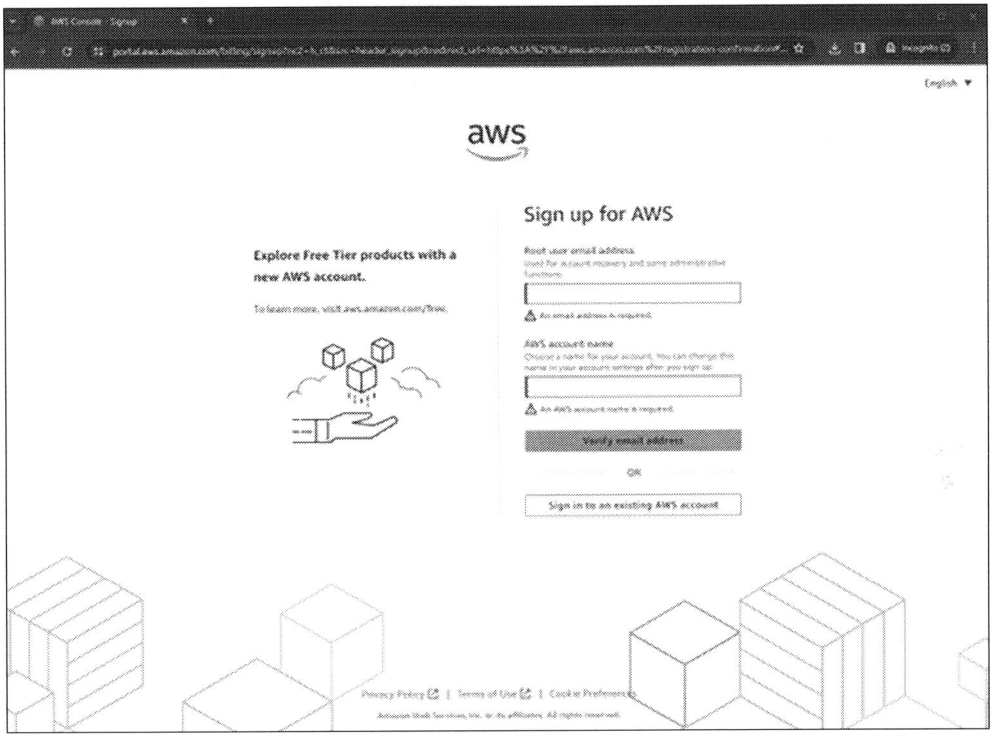

Figure 15.1: *Signing up for the free account*

The process depicted in the second screenshot involves creating a password for your new AWS account after verifying your email address. This step is crucial as it secures access to your AWS services and resources. After setting a robust password, you will proceed through the sign up process, which typically includes entering payment information and going through a phone verification step to confirm your identity. This multi-step process helps ensure the security and authenticity of AWS accounts. Once these steps are completed, you will have access to the AWS Free Tier, allowing you to explore and utilize various AWS services.

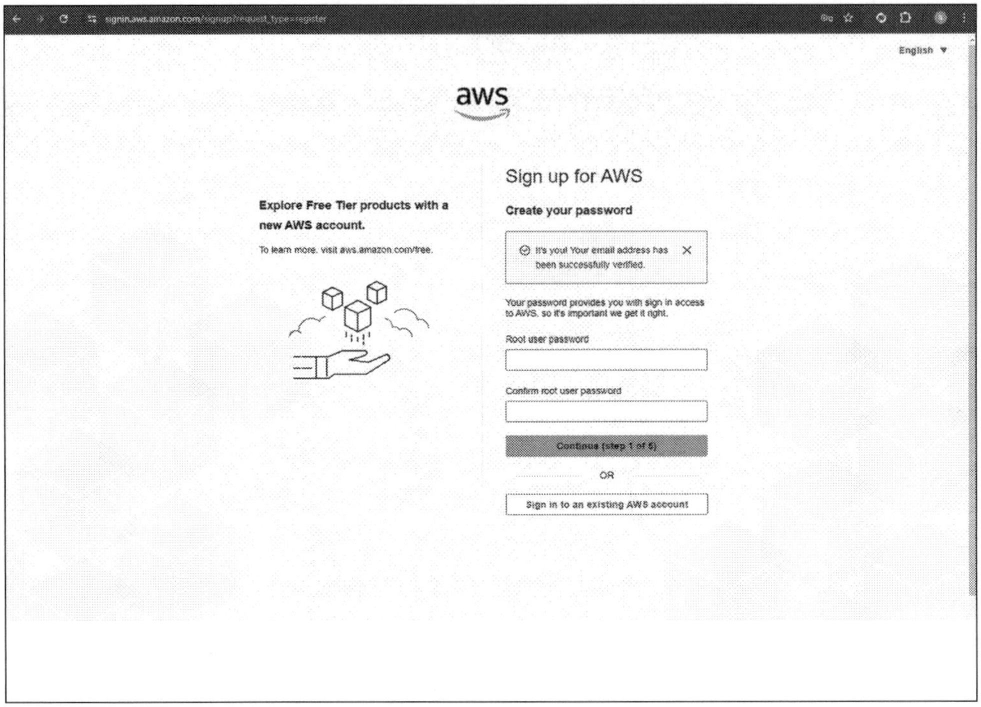

Figure 15.2: *Entering Password Information*

Once you have completed the registration and login process, you will be directed to the AWS Management Console dashboard, as illustrated in the screenshot. The dashboard serves as the central hub for navigating and managing AWS services. It provides a summary of your recently visited services, such as IAM, ECR, and EKS, allowing for quick access to frequently used tools.

The dashboard is customizable; you can add widgets to monitor various aspects such as application health, AWS cost and usage, and service status updates. The "**`Cost and usage`**" section gives a snapshot of your current and forecasted expenses, helping you track spending and manage your budget effectively. Additionally, the dashboard displays AWS Health information, including open issues and scheduled changes, ensuring you stay informed about the operational status of AWS services.

This centralized interface enhances your cloud management experience by providing key insights and easy access to your AWS resources. It is designed to help new users navigate through AWS services easily and allows experienced users to monitor their applications and resources efficiently.

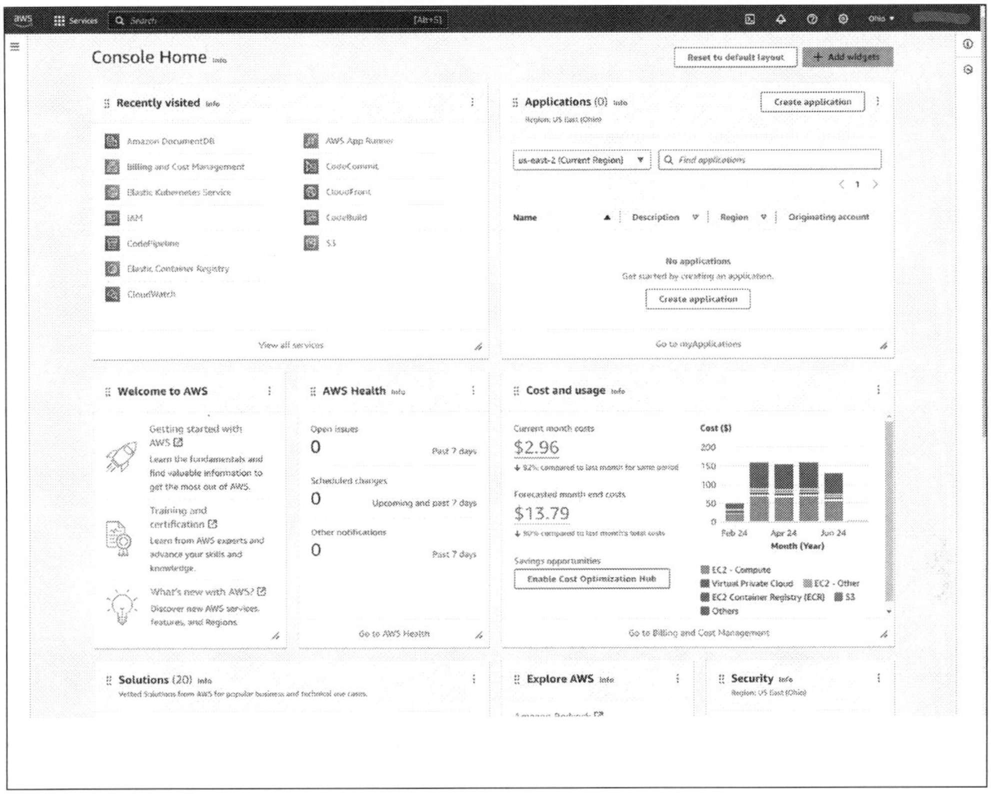

Figure 15.3: *AWS Dashboard*

It is recommended to become acquainted with the AWS Management Console and its various features. Diving into the different AWS services and their settings can enhance your understanding and utilization of the AWS infrastructure, tailoring it to meet your unique project demands.

Different Ways to Interact with AWS

Interacting with AWS can be accomplished through various methods, each catering to different use cases, levels of expertise, and operational needs. Here is an overview of the different ways to interact with AWS.

AWS Management Console

The AWS Management Console is a web-based interface that allows you to manage and monitor your AWS services. It provides a user-friendly, graphical interface to access and manage the resources.

Advantages

- Easy to use with a point-and-click interface.
- No coding required to manage services.
- Accessible from any web browser.

Disadvantages

- Can be slower than command-line tools for performing batch operations.
- May not provide the granularity needed for complex configurations.

AWS Command Line Interface (CLI)

The AWS CLI is a unified tool that provides a command-line interface to interact with AWS services. With the AWS CLI, you can control multiple AWS services directly from the terminal session on your client.

Advantages

- Allows for scripting and automation of AWS service management.
- Fast and efficient for experienced users.
- Supports almost all AWS services.

Disadvantages

- Requires familiarity with command-line tools and syntax.
- Initial set up and learning curve.

AWS Software Development Kits (SDKs)

AWS provides SDKs for various programming languages such as Python (Boto3), JavaScript, Java, .NET, and more. SDKs allow developers to integrate AWS services into their applications.

Advantages

- Programmatic access to AWS services within your application.
- Supports multiple programming languages.
- Customizable and flexible for developers.

Disadvantages

- Requires programming knowledge.
- Integration and debugging can take time.

AWS `CloudFormation`

AWS **`CloudFormation`** allows you to use programming languages or a simple text file to model and provision, in an automated and secure manner, all the resources needed for your applications across all regions and accounts.

Advantages

- Infrastructure as code helps in automating set up and replication of environments.
- Integrated with most AWS services.
- Tracks the state of your resources and can roll back changes if errors are detected.

Disadvantages

- Can be complex for beginners.
- Requires understanding of CloudFormation templates.

AWS Tools for PowerShell

For users familiar with Microsoft PowerShell, AWS provides a set of PowerShell cmdlets that allow you to manage AWS services.

Advantages

- Integrates with PowerShell scripting for Windows users.
- Suitable for automation scripts and batch processing.
- Provides a powerful toolset for Windows administrators.

Disadvantages

- Primarily for Windows users; may not be as convenient for users on other platforms.
- Requires knowledge of PowerShell scripting.

Third-Party Tools and Integrations

Numerous third-party tools and services integrate with AWS, offering additional interfaces and management capabilities, such as Terraform for infrastructure as code, or Datadog for monitoring.

Advantages

- Offers specialized functionalities and interfaces.
- Can provide features not available in native AWS tools.

Disadvantages

- May require additional costs.
- Integration and compatibility can vary.

Each interaction method has its strengths and is designed to suit different operational needs and user preferences. Your choice will depend on your specific requirements, technical expertise, and the nature of the AWS services you wish to manage.

Configure and Setup AWS CLI

Throughout our journey, we have explored different approaches to interact with AWS. In this section, we will focus on installing the AWS Command Line Interface (CLI), a critical tool for our upcoming activities. We will utilize the CLI for tasks such as pushing Docker images to the Amazon Elastic Container Registry (ECR) and managing Amazon Elastic Kubernetes Service (EKS) resources.

To begin, visit the AWS CLI installation page by following the provided link. It is essential to choose the installer that corresponds with your operating system. Upon downloading, you will be presented with various setup options. Work through these to complete the installation, tailoring the setup to fit your specific needs and system configurations.

https://aws.amazon.com/cli/

https://docs.aws.amazon.com/cli/latest/userguide/getting-started-install.html

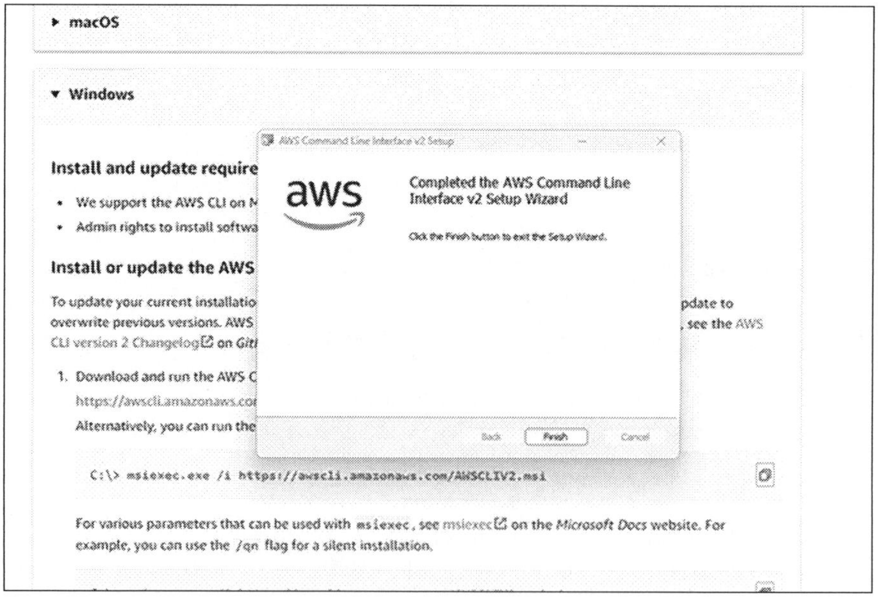

Figure 15.4: AWS CLI *Installation*

This initial configuration is a crucial step towards optimizing workflow, enabling direct command-line management of AWS resources. The AWS CLI is a versatile instrument that broadens your operational capabilities within AWS, streamlining the deployment and management of your applications.

Once the AWS CLI has been successfully installed, you will be presented with a command line interface. Follow the on-screen instructions within this CLI to sign into your AWS account directly from your command prompt. For additional commands and quick references, you can consult the AWS CLI cheat sheet provided.

https://docs.aws.amazon.com/cli/latest/

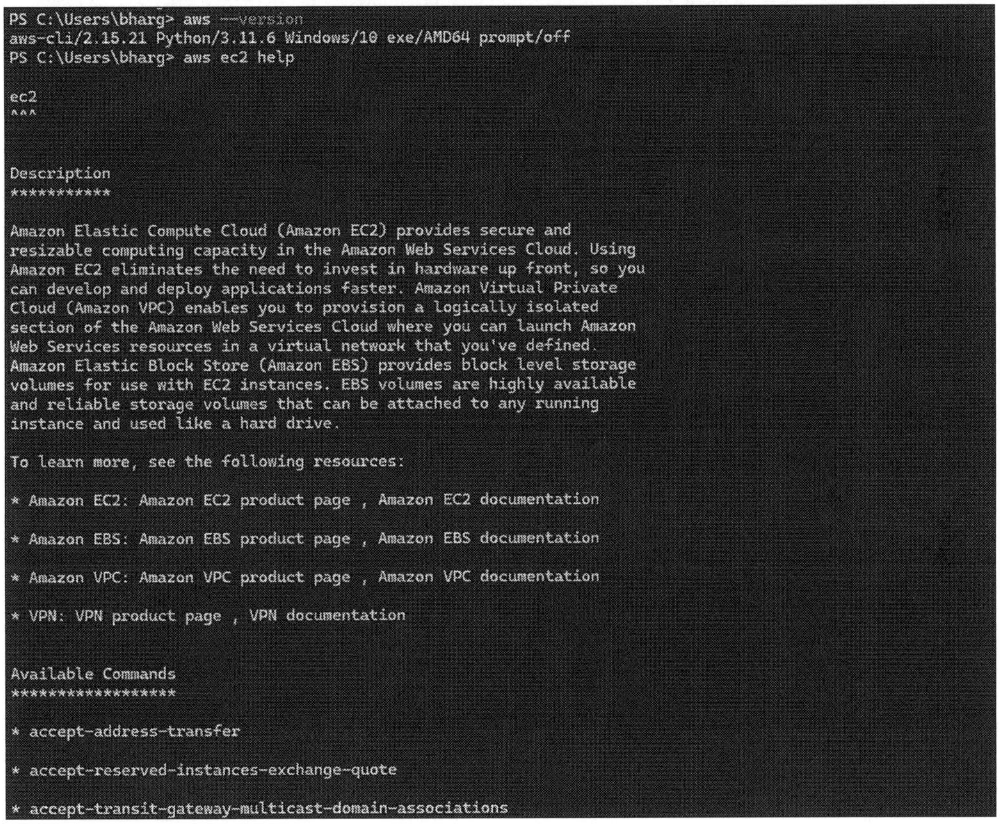

Figure 15.5: AWS CLI

After setting up the AWS CLI, we now require AWS access keys to initiate configuration through the CLI. To create an access key in AWS using the AWS CLI, you need to follow these steps:

1. Open your terminal or command prompt.
2. Use the AWS CLI command **`aws iam create-access-key`**. This command creates a new access key for the specified IAM user. If you do not specify a

user, AWS assumes the user is the one associated with the credentials used to run the command.

3. The command returns the access key ID and secret access key. Note that this is the only opportunity to view or download the secret access key, so make sure to save it securely.

4. You can then use this access key ID and secret access key to configure your AWS CLI and SDKs for accessing AWS services.

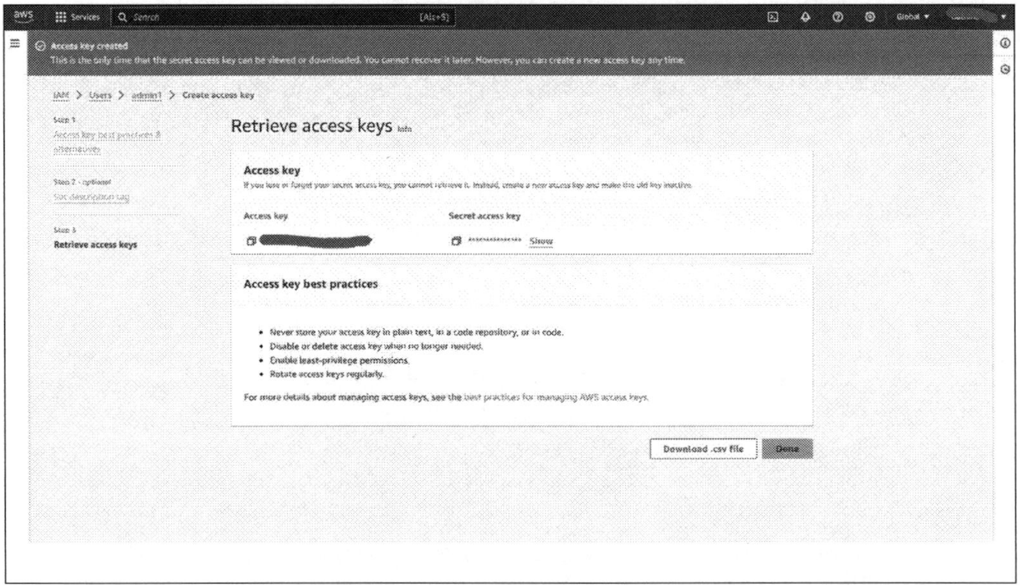

Figure 15.6: *Creating an Access Key*

Remember, it is essential to handle AWS access keys securely. Do not share your secret access keys, embed them in code, or leave them unsecured. Always follow AWS best practices for managing credentials.

With the access keys downloaded, we need to execute the **`aws configure`** command in the AWS CLI, which is essential for setting up and managing AWS services from the command line. This process involves entering the AWS Access Key ID and AWS Secret Access Key, which are crucial for authenticating and authorizing CLI operations against your AWS account. Additionally, the user specifies a default region (such as "**`us-east-1`**") and output format, which dictates how responses from AWS services are formatted in the CLI. After configuration, the user tests the setup by running commands like **`aws ec2 describe-instances`** and **`aws iam get-user`**, which fetch information about EC2 instances and IAM user details, respectively, demonstrating successful CLI setup and connectivity to AWS services.

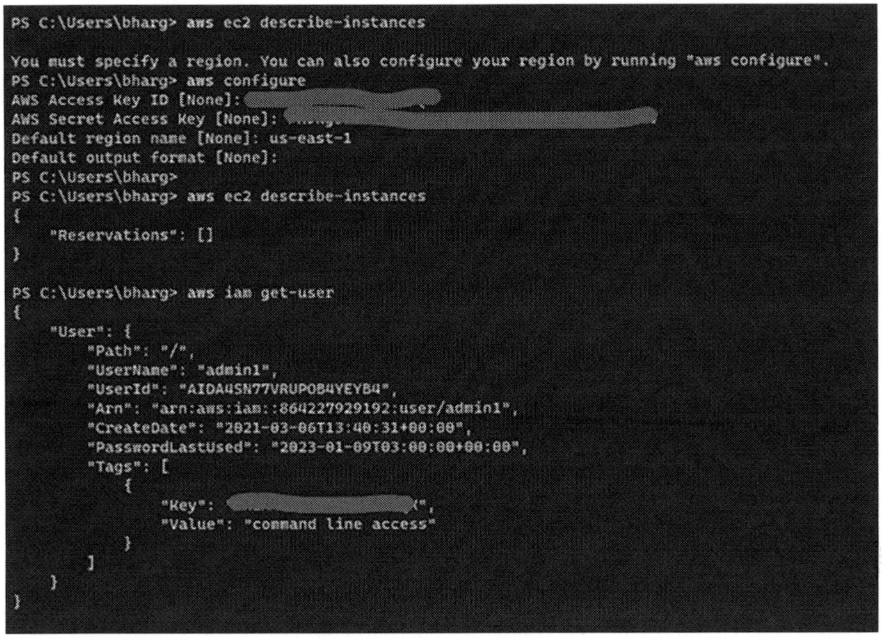

Figure 15.7: *Configuring* AWS CLI

Container Options on AWS

In our previous discussions, we explored the initial steps required to begin utilizing AWS and examined the diverse avenues through which we can engage with AWS's extensive suite of services. Given that we have successfully containerized our MEVN (MongoDB, Express.js, Vue.js, Node.js) stack, it is now pertinent to delve into the various container deployment options available within AWS to determine the most effective pathway for deploying our Docker image.

As we proceed, we will be focusing on identifying the optimal AWS container services that align with our project's needs, ensuring that our containerized application is deployed efficiently and effectively in the cloud environment. This exploration is crucial for leveraging the full capabilities of AWS, enabling us to choose the service that best matches our application's scalability, management, and operational requirements.

Amazon Web Services (AWS) provides several container management options to deploy and manage your MEVN stack Docker images. Here are the primary services suitable for such deployments:

Amazon Elastic Container Service (ECS)

Amazon ECS is a highly scalable, high-performance container orchestration service that supports Docker containers and allows you to easily run and scale containerized applications on AWS. ECS can be used to launch and stop container-based applications with simple API calls, allows you to get the state of your cluster from a centralized service, and integrates with other AWS services such as Elastic Load Balancing, VPC, and IAM.

- **Best For:** Teams that require a robust, scalable container management service that integrates deeply with the AWS ecosystem.
- **Features:** Deep integration with AWS services like IAM, CloudWatch, Load Balancer, and CloudFormation, supports both AWS Fargate and EC2 launch types, Service auto-scaling and task placement strategies.
- **Use Case:** Ideal for businesses looking to run and manage microservices, batch processing jobs, and backend services without having to operate their own cluster management and container orchestration system.

Let us dive into the pros and cons of ECS service for deploying an MEVN stack Docker image:

Advantages

- Deep integration with AWS services.
- No additional charge for ECS beyond the resources (for example, EC2 instances or Fargate) used.
- Supports both AWS Fargate (serverless compute for containers) and EC2 (manage your own cluster of servers).

Disadvantages

- Can be complex to set up and manage without prior container orchestration experience.
- Primarily tied to the AWS ecosystem, which might be a limitation if you seek portability.

Amazon Elastic Kubernetes Service (EKS)

Amazon EKS is a managed service that makes it easy to run Kubernetes on AWS without needing to install, operate, and maintain your own Kubernetes control plane or nodes. EKS is certified Kubernetes conformant, so existing applications running on standard Kubernetes can be seamlessly migrated to EKS.

- **Best for:** Businesses and developers who want to leverage Kubernetes' powerful orchestration and scalability without managing the Kubernetes control plane.
- **Features:** Managed Kubernetes service with automatic version upgrades and patching, integrates with AWS services and IAM for security, supports both AWS Fargate and EC2 nodes.
- **Use Case:** Suitable for organizations looking for the flexibility of Kubernetes to

manage complex applications with microservices architecture across hybrid or multi-cloud environments.

Let us dive into the pros and cons of EKS service for deploying an MEVN stack Docker image:

Advantages

- Fully managed Kubernetes service.
- Integrates with AWS services seamlessly.
- Automatically manages the availability and scalability of the Kubernetes control plane nodes.

Disadvantages

- More expensive than running Kubernetes yourself due to the management fee.
- Can be complex for users not familiar with Kubernetes.

AWS Fargate

AWS Fargate is a serverless compute engine for containers that works with both Amazon ECS and EKS. Fargate makes it easier to focus on building and deploying applications without having to manage the underlying infrastructure.

- **Best for:** Developers who prefer not to manage servers or clusters while deploying containerized applications.
- **Features:** Serverless compute engine for containers, Automatic scaling, and load balancing, Integrated with ECS and EKS for orchestration.
- **Use Case:** Perfect for startups and developers looking for a hassle-free deployment of containerized applications, focusing purely on application development without worrying about the underlying infrastructure.

Let us dive into the pros and cons of AWS Fargate service for deploying a MEVN stack Docker image:

Advantages

- Eliminates the need to manage servers or clusters.
- Easy to scale and integrates with ECS and EKS.
- Pay only for the resources required to run the containers.

Disadvantages

- Higher cost at scale compared to managing your own EC2 instances.
- Less control over the host environment compared to EC2.

Amazon LightSail

Amazon Lightsail provides a simpler alternative to EC2 for smaller scale applications. While it is not a traditional container service, it supports Docker and can be an easy way to deploy containerized applications like the MEVN stack, especially for developers looking for a more straightforward and cost-effective solution.

- **Best for:** Individuals, small businesses, or developers looking for a simple, quick, and cost-effective solution to deploy applications or websites.
- **Features:** Easy-to-use interface with pre-configured plans, Includes virtual machines, SSD-based storage, data transfer, DNS management, and static IP, supports Docker containers for easy deployment of containerized applications
- **Use Case:** Best suited for small-scale applications, personal projects, or for developers new to AWS looking to deploy simple web applications or websites quickly and easily.

Let us dive into the pros and cons of Amazon LightSail service for deploying an MEVN stack Docker image:

Advantages

- Simple and easy to use.
- Fixed pricing, which is great for small-scale applications and predictable billing.
- Includes everything needed to launch a project (compute, storage, and networking).

Disadvantages

- Not as scalable or flexible as ECS or EKS.
- Designed for simpler applications, so might lack some advanced features needed for more complex deployments.

AWS App Runner

AWS App Runner is a fully managed service that provides a fast, simple, and secure way to deploy containerized web applications and APIs, at scale and with no prior infrastructure experience required. App Runner automatically builds and deploys the web application and API containers to a highly available runtime environment, eliminating the need to manage the infrastructure, orchestration, load balancing, scaling, and monitoring. It is particularly suitable for developers who want to focus on their application code without worrying about the underlying infrastructure.

- **Best for:** Developers looking for the easiest way to build and deploy containerized web applications and APIs without dealing with infrastructure.

- **Features:** Fully managed service with automated deployments from source code or container images, Integrated CI/CD capabilities from GitHub repositories, Integrated CI/CD capabilities from GitHub repositories.
- **Use Case:** Ideal for small to medium-sized businesses and developers who need to deploy web applications or APIs rapidly without the complexity of infrastructure management or container orchestration. Great for quick iterations and minimal operational overhead.

Let us dive into the pros and cons of AWS App Runner service for deploying an MEVN stack Docker image:

Advantages

- **Easy to use**: Simplifies deployment and management of containerized applications with no infrastructure or container orchestration knowledge required.
- **Fully managed**: Automatically handles deployment, scaling, and monitoring, with integrated load balancing and security.
- **Fast setup**: Quickly deploy applications directly from a source code repository or a container image.
- **Cost-effective**: Automatically scales up and down based on traffic, so you pay only for the resources you use.

Disadvantages

- **Limited customization**: While it provides ease of use, there is less control over the underlying resources and configurations compared to ECS or EKS.
- **Best suited for simple applications**: While it supports containerized applications, complex architectures might require a more robust solution like EKS or ECS.
- **Vendor lock-in**: As a fully managed AWS service, moving to another provider or solution may require significant changes to your application set up and deployment process.

Each AWS container service offers different capabilities and pricing models, so your choice should depend on your application requirements, such as scale, budget, and operational complexity.

Pushing Docker Image to Amazon ECR

Amazon ECR is a fully managed Docker container registry provided by AWS that allows developers to store, manage, and deploy Docker container images. It is integrated with Amazon ECS, Amazon Kubernetes Service (AKS), and AWS Lambda, providing a secure, scalable, and reliable way to store and retrieve container images. Here are some of the features:

- **Security:** ECR integrates with AWS Identity and Access Management (IAM), allowing you to control access to your container images using IAM policies. It also provides the ability to scan images for vulnerabilities, improving the security of your application deployment workflow.
- **Scalability:** Being a managed service, ECR eliminates the need to operate your own container repositories or worry about scaling the underlying infrastructure. It handles high volumes of requests and stores images in a highly available and durable architecture.
- **Integration:** ECR is designed to work seamlessly with ECS, EKS, and Lambda, allowing for easy deployment of containers based on the images stored in ECR. It also integrates with AWS CodeBuild, AWS CodePipeline, and other CI/CD tools for automating the build and deployment process.
- **Simplicity:** ECR eliminates the need for you to set up and manage your own container repository infrastructure, providing a straightforward solution for pushing, pulling, and managing Docker images.
- **Reliability:** Backed by Amazon's robust infrastructure, ECR provides a reliable solution for storing and retrieving Docker images with high availability.
- **Cost-Effective:** With ECR, you pay only for data you store in your repositories and the data transferred to the Internet. There is no upfront fee or commitments.

Use Cases

- **Application Deployment:** Store application container images and easily deploy them across a range of AWS services like ECS, EKS, or Fargate.
- **Continuous Integration and Continuous Deployment (CI/CD):** Integrate ECR with your CI/CD pipeline for automating the build, test, and deployment phases of your application development lifecycle.
- **Microservices Architecture:** Manage and store Docker containers for microservices, allowing for easy updates and scaling of individual components of your application.
- **Environment Consistency:** By using Docker containers, you ensure consistency across multiple development, testing, and production environments, reducing "*it works on my machine*" problems.
- **Private Image Hosting:** Host your private Docker images securely in the AWS cloud, ensuring that only authorized users or services can access them.

In summary, Amazon ECR provides a secure, scalable, and efficient way to manage Docker container images, facilitating streamlined development and deployment workflows, particularly in environments that leverage containerized applications.

Creating a repository on AWS involves a few straightforward steps, as demonstrated by the Amazon Elastic Container Registry (ECR) service in the provided screenshot. Here is how the process typically unfolds:

- **Access Amazon ECR**: Navigate to the Amazon ECR section within your AWS Management Console. This is where you manage your Docker container images.
- **Create a New Repository**: Click on the **`"Create repository"`** button, typically located at the top right corner of the interface. This initiates the creation process.
- **Configure Repository Settings**: In the creation window, you will be prompted to provide details such as the repository name. In the example, the repository is named **`'webapp'`**. You may also configure other settings like tag immutability, scan frequency for vulnerabilities, and encryption type (for example, AES-256 for enhanced security).
- **Review and Create**: After configuring the settings, review them to ensure accuracy, then confirm and create the repository.

Once the repository is successfully created, as indicated by a notification like "**`webapp has been successfully created in private registry`**" in the screenshot, you can then use it to push, pull, and manage your Docker images. The repository's URI, provided on the dashboard, is crucial for these operations, serving as the address for image storage and retrieval.

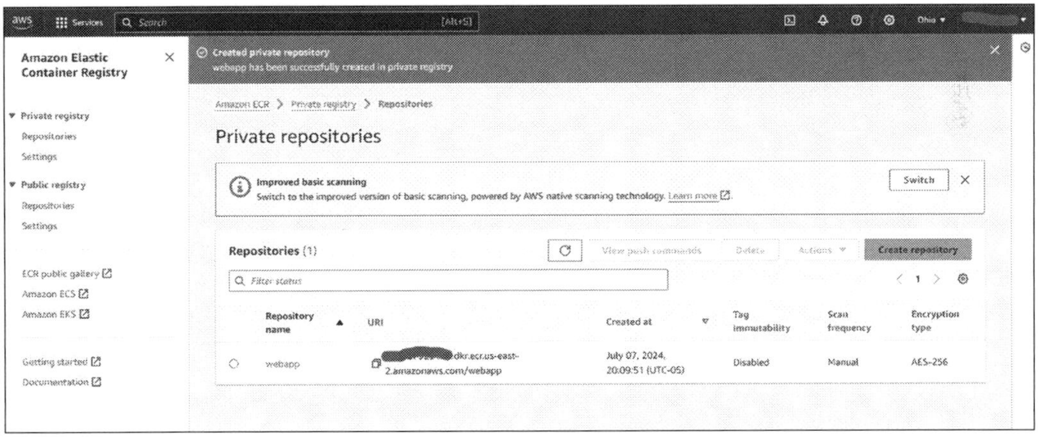

Figure 15.8: *Creating AWS Repository*

In the provided scenario, the repository **`'webapp'`** is now ready for use, with details such as creation date and encryption settings displayed on the dashboard. This set up allows for organized, secure management of container images within AWS.

Pushing a Docker image to AWS ECR involves several steps. First, authenticate your Docker client with your AWS account to ensure secure communication with ECR. This is done via the AWS CLI, which retrieves an authentication token used by Docker. After authentication, build your Docker image locally if you have not done so. Then, tag the built image with the ECR repository URI, which identifies the remote repository where the image will be stored. Finally, push the tagged image to the ECR repository using the Docker push command. This makes your Docker image available in ECR for future deployment to AWS services.

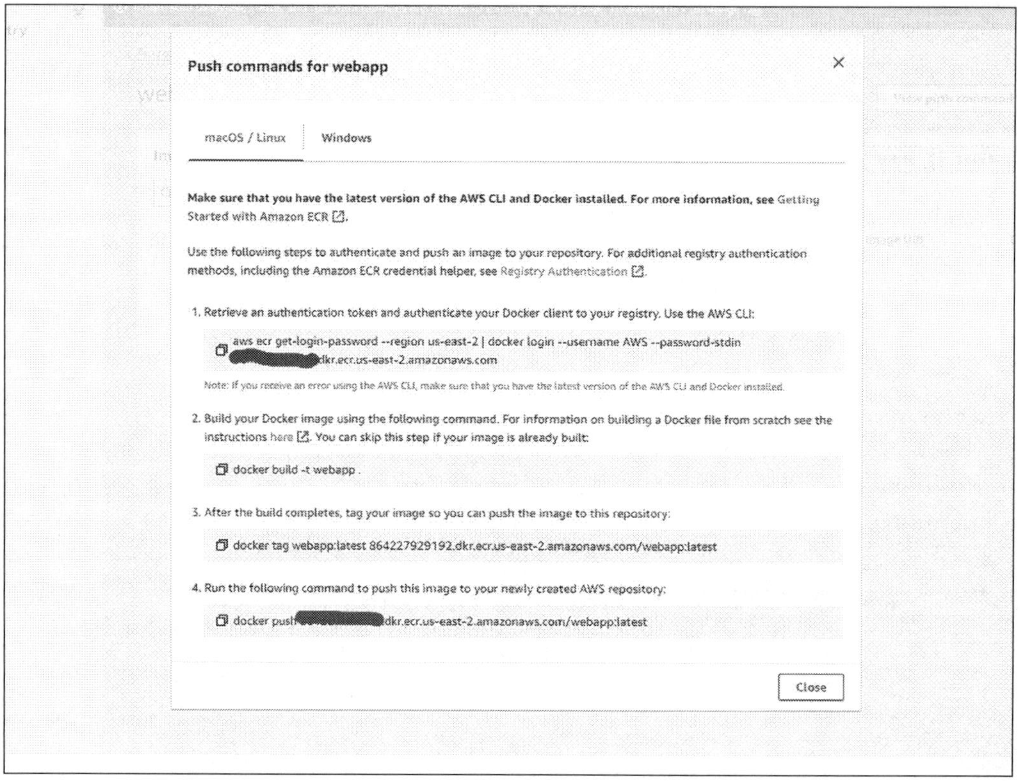

Figure 15.9: *ECR Push Commands*

The screenshot in Figure 15.10 depicts the process of authenticating and pushing a Docker image to AWS ECR using Windows PowerShell. First, we need to execute the AWS CLI command **`aws ecr get-login-password`** to retrieve an authentication token, which is then used to log into the ECR repository with Docker. Following successful authentication indicated by "**`Login Succeeded`**," the user employs the `docker tag` command to tag a local image for ECR. Finally, they push the tagged image to the ECR with `docker push`, successfully uploading it as shown by the "**`Pushed`**" statuses for various image layers. This sequence demonstrates the end-to-end process of preparing and transferring a Docker image to be stored and managed within AWS's managed container registry service.

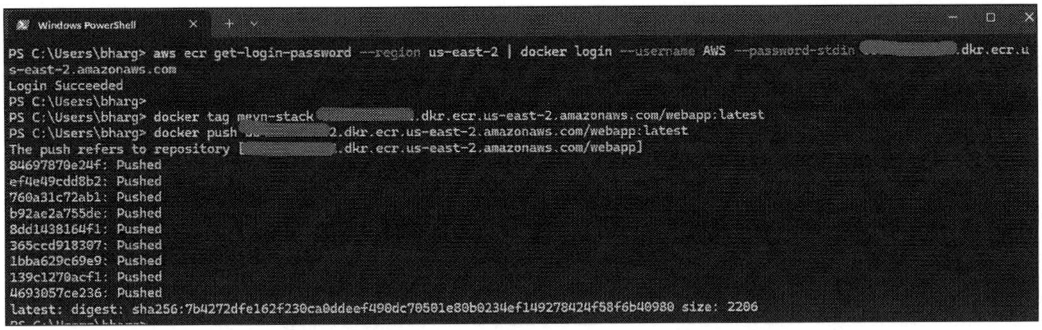

***Figure 15.10**: docker image pushed successfully*

Following the successful execution of commands from the CLI, the Docker image is now visible within the AWS Console under the Amazon ECR section. This confirmation in the AWS Console showcases the newly pushed Docker image, displaying its details such as the image tag "`latest`," its size, and the time it was pushed.

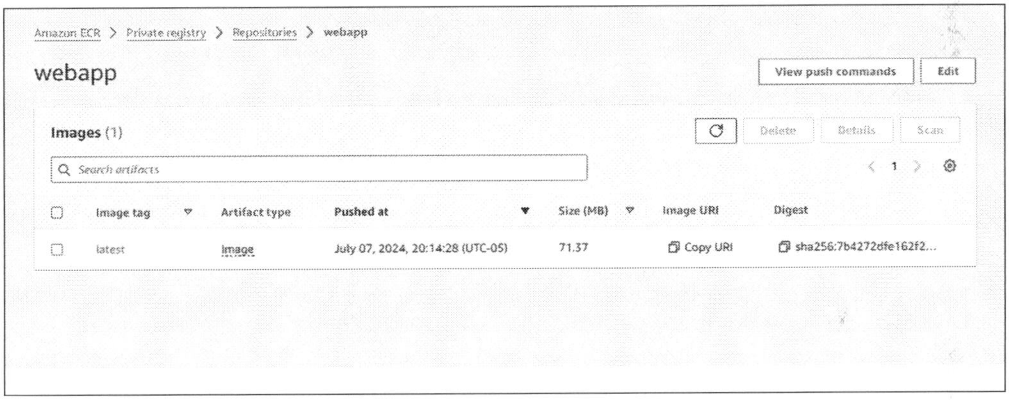

***Figure 15.11**: ECR Repository*

This visual representation in the console serves as a confirmation of the successful upload and allows for further actions such as scanning for vulnerabilities, reviewing image details, or managing image tags and settings.

Running MEVN Stack on AWS App Runner

AWS App Runner is a fully managed containerized application service provided by Amazon Web Services (AWS). It allows developers to deploy containerized web applications and APIs quickly and easily without needing to manage the underlying infrastructure. App Runner handles all the operational aspects of application deployment, scaling, and management, allowing developers to focus on building and improving their applications.

Key Features of AWS App Runner

- **Fully Managed Service:** AWS App Runner abstracts away the complexities of infrastructure management, such as provisioning, scaling, and monitoring, allowing developers to focus on writing code.
- **Container Support:** App Runner supports containerized applications built with Docker. Developers can specify the Docker image for their application, and App Runner will automatically deploy and run it.
- **Auto Scaling:** App Runner automatically scales the application in response to changes in traffic, ensuring optimal performance and cost-efficiency. It can scale both up and down based on demand, helping to maintain consistent performance and minimize costs during periods of low traffic.
- **Integration with AWS Services:** App Runner seamlessly integrates with other AWS services, such as Amazon RDS for databases, Amazon S3 for storage, and Amazon CloudWatch for monitoring and logging, providing a comprehensive platform for building and deploying applications.
- **Simple Deployment:** Developers can deploy their applications to App Runner using the AWS Management Console, AWS Command Line Interface (CLI), or AWS Software Development Kits (SDKs). The deployment process is straightforward and requires minimal configuration.

Overall, AWS App Runner simplifies the process of deploying and managing containerized applications, enabling developers to quickly bring their ideas to production without worrying about infrastructure management. It is well-suited for a wide range of use cases, including web applications, APIs, and microservices.

Following the successful upload of your Docker image to AWS's container registry, the subsequent phase involves deploying your application using AWS App Runner. In the AWS Management Console, navigate to the AWS App Runner service to start the set up of your new service. This process will enable you to configure and launch your application directly from the image stored in the container registry.

The screenshot in *Figure* 15.12 shows the set up process for a service in AWS App Runner, focusing on the "*Source and deployment*" section. This part is crucial as it defines the origin of the Docker image that will be used to run your application. Here is how the process breaks down:

- **Repository Type:** You have the option to select the type of repository where your container image is stored. In this case, "`Container registry`" has been chosen, indicating that the service will deploy using a container image from a registry rather than source code.
- **Provider:** The selected provider is Amazon ECR (Elastic Container Registry), specifying that the Docker image is hosted in AWS's own private container registry service.

- **Container Image URI**: This field is filled with the unique resource identifier of the Docker image within Amazon ECR. This URI is crucial as it directs App Runner to the exact image to pull and deploy.

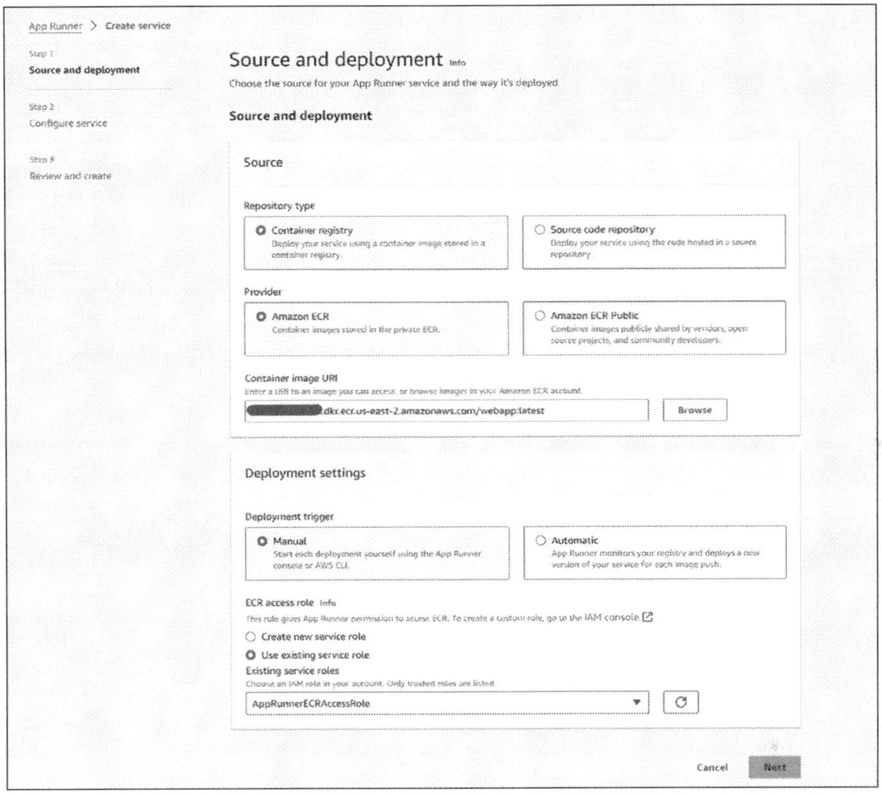

Figure 15.12: *Creating an App Runner*

- **Deployment Settings**: You can choose between manual and automatic deployment triggers. Manual requires you to start each deployment through the App Runner console or AWS CLI, while Automatic means App Runner will watch your ECR repository for new image pushes and automatically deploy new versions of your service.
- **ECR Access Role Info**: Defines whether to create a new service role or use an existing one. This IAM role gives App Runner permission to access resources from ECR. In this instance, an existing service role named `AppRunnerECRAccessRole` is selected.

This part of the set up focuses on detailing the service configuration, including:

- **Service Settings**: Here, you can specify the '`Service name`' and set the `'Virtual CPU'` and `'Virtual memory'` for your service. These settings determine the computing resources available to your application, affecting performance and cost.

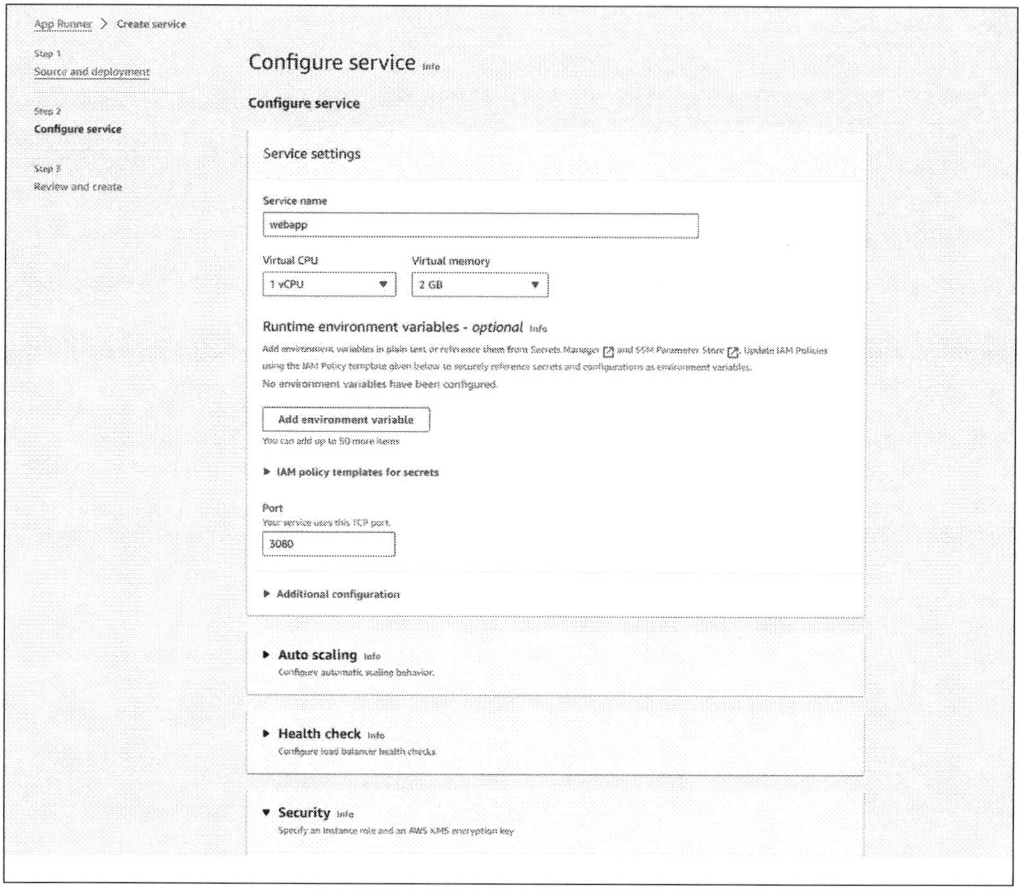

Figure 15.13: *Configuring AWS App Runner*

- **Service Settings:** Here, you can specify the '**`Service name`**' and set the '**`Virtual CPU`**' and '**`Virtual memory`**' for your service. These settings determine the computing resources available to your application, affecting performance and cost.
- **Runtime Environment Variables**: This optional section allows you to add environment variables for your service. These can be key-value pairs that your application can use to modify its behavior without changing the code. AWS also enables secure integration with Secrets Manager and SSM Parameter Store for sensitive configurations.
- **Port:** Specifies the TCP port your service uses. For web applications, the default is often set to 80 or 8080, but here, it is set to 3080, which should match the port your containerized application is designed to listen on.
- **Additional Configuration**: Expands into more detailed settings like logging and metrics.

- **Auto Scaling:** This section allows configuring the auto-scaling behavior of your service based on request traffic, ensuring that your application scales up or down to maintain performance and minimize costs.
- **Health Check**: You can configure health checks for your service to ensure AWS App Runner monitors the health of your application and can act if it becomes unresponsive.
- **Security:** This is where you specify an IAM role, and any AWS KMS encryption keys used to secure access to your service and protect your data.

Following the set up, AWS App Runner has successfully launched the service, as indicated by the operational status and the availability of a public URL. This URL provides web access to the deployed application, allowing for immediate and global reachability.

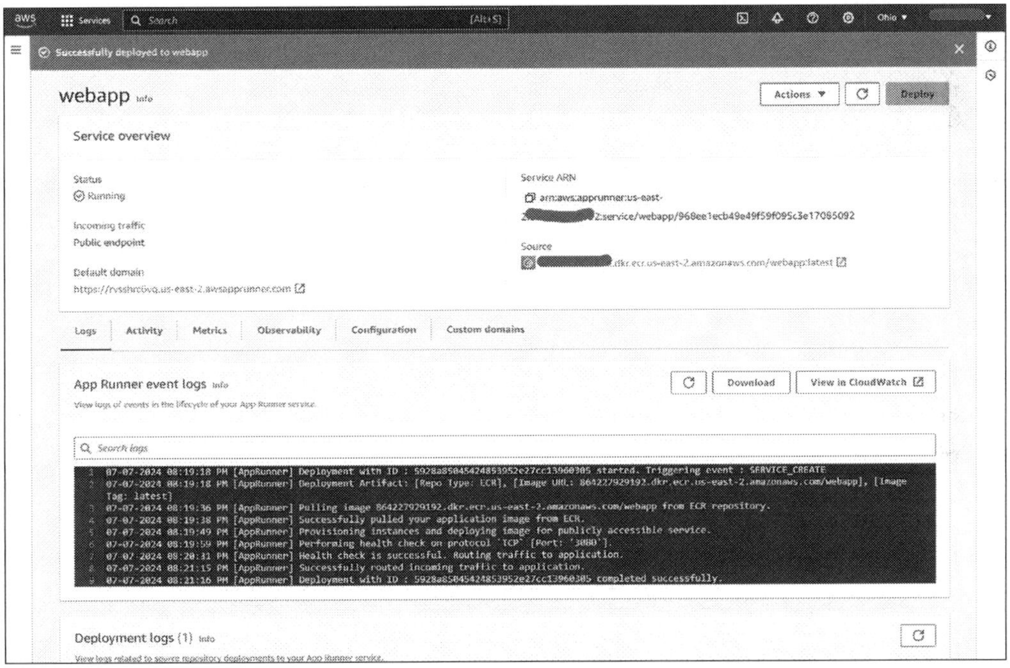

***Figure 15.14**: Configuring AWS App Runner*

Additionally, the service dashboard offers a log section where you can review the deployment process. These logs confirm the successful completion of the deployment, detailing each step taken by App Runner to build, deploy, and start the service, ensuring transparency and traceability of the deployment lifecycle.

The following image illustrates how effortlessly you can view application logs directly in AWS CloudWatch from the AWS App Runner service, without the need for any additional setup or configuration. This feature underscores one of App Runner's significant benefits – the ability to get your application up and running quickly, along with streamlined monitoring capabilities. By simply clicking on the "**View in CloudWatch**" button, users can access detailed logs of their application's performance, errors, and other runtime activities, facilitating immediate insights into the application's operational status and helping in quick troubleshooting and analysis. This integration with CloudWatch enhances the operational efficiency of maintaining and monitoring web applications deployed through App Runner.

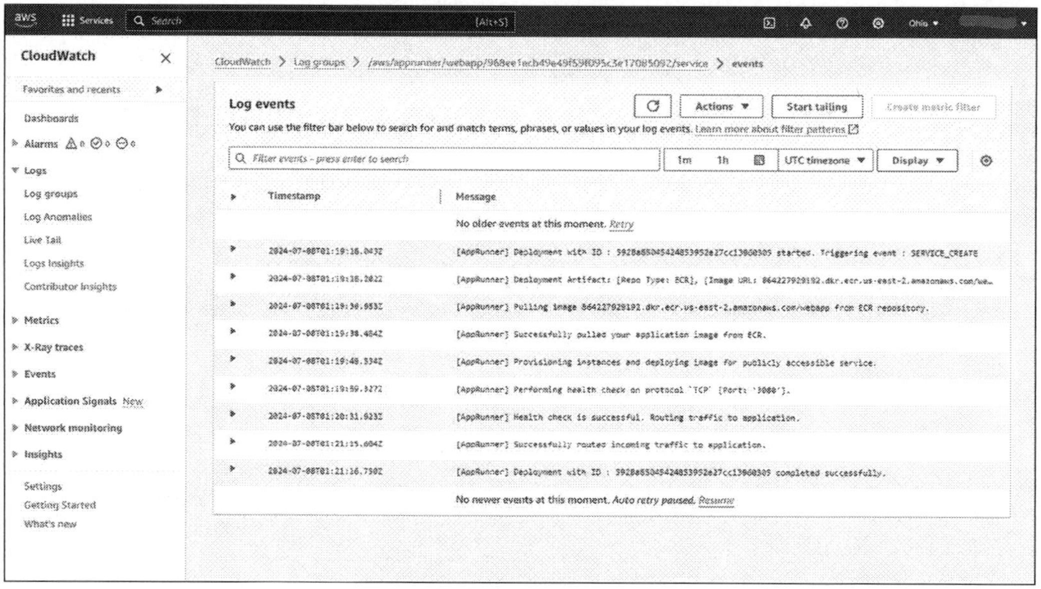

Figure 15.15: *CloudWatch Logs*

Amazon CloudWatch is a monitoring and observability service from AWS that provides data and actionable insights for AWS, on-premises, and hybrid applications and infrastructure. The service enables users to collect and track metrics, logs, and event data, helping you gain system-wide visibility into resource utilization, application performance, and operational health. CloudWatch facilitates various functionalities including setting alarms, visualizing logs and metrics, and reacting automatically to changes in your AWS resources.

After deploying the MEVN Stack application and acquiring the URL from AWS App Runner, you can enter it into your web browser to access the application online via HTTPS. This showcases the application's live functionality and secure accessibility from any web-enabled device, demonstrating the successful deployment and public accessibility of your MEVN stack application hosted on AWS infrastructure. The "**Tasks Dashboard**" as visible in the screenshot is a part of this MEVN application, showcasing tasks with options to edit or delete, highlighting the interactive and user-friendly interface of your web application.

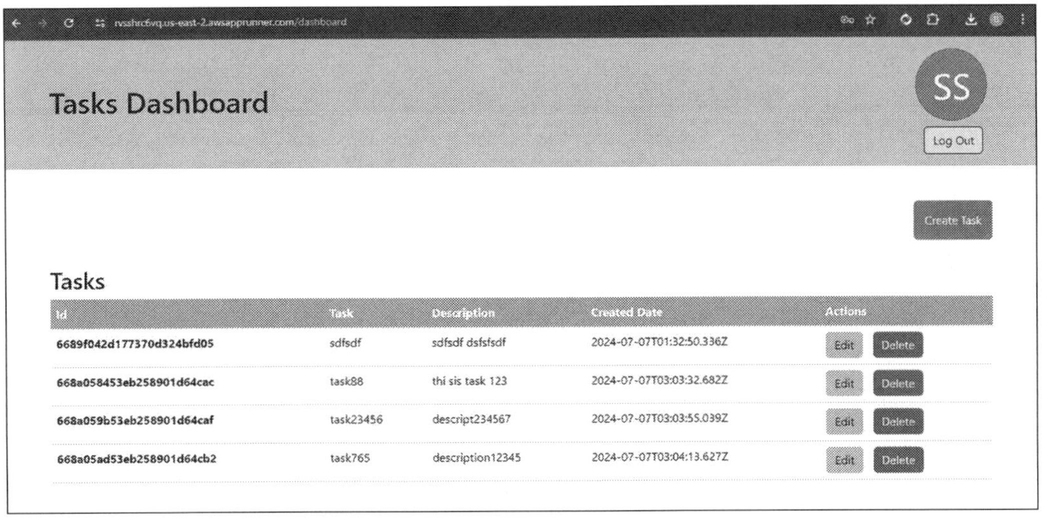

Figure 15.16: *Application Running on AWS AppRunner*

With the successful deployment of the MEVN stack on AWS App Runner, we have demonstrated the streamlined process of bringing a web application to a global audience using AWS's managed services. This achievement marks a significant milestone in leveraging cloud capabilities for efficient, scalable, and secure application delivery.

Moving forward, consider exploring additional AWS services to enhance your application's functionality, security, and performance. Incorporating services like AWS Lambda for serverless computing, Amazon RDS for managed database solutions, and Amazon CloudFront for content delivery can further optimize your application. Additionally, implementing AWS Identity and Access Management (IAM) will provide fine-grained access control to your AWS resources, enhancing security.

Remember to monitor your application's performance and usage with Amazon CloudWatch to gain insights and maintain operational health. Regularly reviewing your architecture and adopting AWS best practices will ensure that your MEVN stack application remains robust, secure, and cost-effective.

By embracing the full spectrum of AWS services and tools, you can continue to evolve your application to meet changing demands and seize new opportunities in the cloud computing landscape.

Conclusion

Throughout this chapter, we have embarked on a comprehensive journey through AWS, starting from an introductory overview, advancing through the initial setup, and diving deep into its extensive suite of services. We have covered the essentials of getting started with AWS, setting up the AWS CLI for streamlined command-line interactions, and explored various container solutions provided by AWS. Further, we illustrated the steps to push a Docker image to Amazon ECR, followed by deploying the MEVN stack application using AWS App Runner demonstrating the versatility and power of AWS for modern application deployment.

As we transition from AWS to Azure, the upcoming chapter will mirror this journey within Microsoft's cloud environment. We will explore Azure's foundational concepts, the configuration of the Azure CLI, container solutions such as Azure Container Instances (ACI) and Azure Kubernetes Service (AKS) and demonstrate the deployment of containerized applications. This parallel exploration will offer insights into the distinct features and advantages of Azure, enabling you to make informed decisions based on your project's needs and preferences. Stay tuned as we continue to unfold the world of cloud computing, this time through the lens of Azure.

CHAPTER 16 MEVN Stack Container Options on Azure

Introduction

After constructing the MEVN stack and demonstrating its functionality within a Docker container on a local environment, the next step in our journey is deploying this application to the cloud. Microsoft Azure emerges as a compelling choice for this venture, offering a wide array of services designed for modern cloud architectures. This section aims to guide you through the deployment of the Dockerized MEVN stack application on Azure, highlighting the platform's capabilities and services that facilitate seamless application deployment and management.

The initial phase involves configuring and setting up Microsoft Azure. This process includes creating an Azure account, setting up resource groups, and configuring Azure services for deployment. A well-configured Azure environment is crucial for the successful deployment of containerized applications, providing the foundation upon which our application will thrive.

Azure offers several container services, such as Azure Container Instances (ACI), Azure Kubernetes Service (AKS), and the integration of Docker containers with Azure App Service. Each service caters to different deployment and management needs, from simple container deployments with ACI to orchestrated container management with AKS. This flexibility allows developers to choose the most suitable environment for their application's requirements.

The deployment process further involves pushing the Docker image to Azure Container Registry (ACR) and leveraging Azure's services like App Service for hosting web applications and AKS for managing Kubernetes clusters. Azure App Service simplifies the deployment of web apps, enabling automatic scaling and patching, while AKS offers comprehensive Kubernetes management, allowing for complex application deployments that require scaling and orchestration. Through these steps, developers can efficiently transition their MEVN stack applications from local development to a scalable, cloud-hosted environment, taking full advantage of Azure's robust cloud infrastructure.

Structure

In this chapter, the following topics will be covered:

- Introduction to Microsoft Azure
- Getting Started with Azure
- Configure and Set Up Azure CLI
- Container Options on Azure
- Pushing Docker Image to Azure Container Registry
- Running MEVN Stack on Azure App Service

Introduction to Microsoft Azure

Microsoft Azure is a comprehensive collection of cloud services offered by Microsoft, enabling the building, deployment, and management of applications through Microsoft's global network of data centres. Launched in February 2010, Azure has evolved into one of the leading cloud platforms, competing directly with Amazon Web Services (AWS) and Google Cloud Platform (GCP), providing scalable and reliable cloud computing resources.

Azure caters to a wide range of computing needs, offering services that encompass not only traditional cloud offerings such as virtual machines (VMs) and storage but also newer technologies like AI, machine learning, and Internet of Things (IoT) solutions. The platform is designed to support applications that can scale from small projects to global product launches, providing a flexible environment that supports multiple programming languages, tools, and frameworks, including both Microsoft-specific and third-party software and systems.

One of Azure's strengths lies in its integration with Microsoft's software and services ecosystem. For organizations already using Microsoft solutions, such as Windows Server, Active Directory, and SQL Server, Azure offers a seamless transition to the cloud, with direct integrations that simplify operations and reduce the learning curve. Moreover, Azure supports a wide range of operating systems, databases, and developer tools, making it a versatile choice for a variety of application development and deployment scenarios.

Azure is committed to security, privacy, compliance, and transparency, providing a secure foundation upon which businesses can build and run their services. With a global footprint, Azure's infrastructure is designed to deliver high availability and performance at scale, offering a robust platform for businesses to innovate and grow in the digital era. Whether you are a small business, a large enterprise, or somewhere in between, Microsoft Azure provides the tools and services necessary to meet your cloud computing needs.

Core Components and Services

Microsoft Azure is a comprehensive cloud computing platform created by Microsoft to build, deploy, and manage applications and services through Microsoft-managed data centres. Azure provides a wide range of cloud services, including those for computing, analytics, storage, and networking. Users can pick and choose from these services to develop and scale new applications, or run existing applications, in the public cloud.

Compute Services

- **Azure Virtual Machines (VMs):** Scalable on-demand VMs for running applications.
- **Azure Kubernetes Service (AKS):** Managed Kubernetes service for deploying and managing containerized applications.
- **Azure Functions:** Event-driven, serverless computing service for running applications in response to events.

Storage Services

- **Azure Blob Storage:** Massively scalable object storage for unstructured data.
- **Azure File Storage:** Managed file shares for cloud or on-premises deployments.
- **Azure Queue Storage:** A data store for queuing and reliably delivering messages between applications.

Database Services

- **Azure SQL Database:** Managed relational SQL Database as a service.
- **Azure CosmosDB:** Globally distributed, multi-model database service.
- **Azure Database for MySQL and PostgreSQL:** Fully managed database services for MySQL and PostgreSQL.

Networking Services

- **Azure Virtual Network:** Provision private networks, optionally connect to on-premises data centres.
- **Azure Load Balancer:** Provides high availability and network performance to your applications.
- **Azure Content Delivery Network (CDN):** A global CDN solution for delivering high-bandwidth content.

AI and Machine Learning Services

- **Azure Machine Learning:** A cloud service for training, deploying, automated machine learning, and tracking ML models.
- **Azure Cognitive Services:** APIs for AI services like computer vision, text analytics, and speech.

Internet of Things (IoT) Services

- **Azure IoT Hub:** Centralized management of IoT devices.
- **Azure IoT Central:** IoT app platform that provides global connectivity, monitoring, and security.

Developer Tools

- **Azure DevOps:** Services for teams to share code, track work, and ship software.
- **Visual Studio Code:** A lightweight but powerful source code editor which runs on your desktop.

Azure's vast array of services supports a broad range of industry standard protocols and technologies, offering solutions for all sectors and industries. With Azure, businesses can quickly scale up or down to meet demand, paying only for what they use, making it a flexible and cost-effective solution for cloud computing.

Advantages of Using Microsoft Azure

Microsoft Azure presents an extensive array of benefits that solidify its position as a leading cloud computing platform, catering to a diverse range of needs for businesses and developers alike. This vast cloud ecosystem is designed to support the deployment, management, and scaling of applications with unparalleled efficiency and reliability. The advantages of Azure stem from its robust architecture, innovative service offerings, and Microsoft's long standing expertise in enterprise software, all of which contribute to its growing appeal among organizations of all sizes.

One of Azure's most compelling advantages is its deep integration with existing Microsoft products and services. Organizations that rely on Microsoft's software ecosystem, including Windows Server, Active Directory, SQL Server, and Office 365, find Azure to be a natural extension that offers seamless interoperability. This integration simplifies the migration of on-premises systems to the cloud and enables a cohesive environment that enhances productivity and collaboration.

Azure's commitment to supporting hybrid cloud configurations allows businesses to retain their on-premises data centers while extending their capabilities into the cloud. This flexibility is crucial for organizations that require a gradual cloud migration strategy or need to comply with data residency regulations. Azure's hybrid solutions, such as Azure Arc and Azure Stack, enable applications and data to seamlessly operate across multiple environments, providing the agility needed to respond to changing business requirements.

The platform's global footprint, with an extensive network of data centers across the globe, ensures that applications are delivered with minimal latency to users anywhere in the world. This global reach, combined with advanced networking services, makes Azure a robust solution for deploying high-performance and scalable web applications, IoT solutions, and global enterprise systems.

Furthermore, Azure prioritizes security and compliance, offering a comprehensive set of features that protect applications and data at every layer. With advanced threat detection, network security, and identity management services, along with a vast array of compliance certifications, Azure meets the stringent security requirements of industries such as finance, healthcare, and government.

Innovation is at the heart of Azure, with continuous investment in emerging technologies like artificial intelligence, machine learning, blockchain, and Internet of Things (IoT). These services empower developers and businesses to build next-generation solutions that can transform industries and create new market opportunities.

In summary, Microsoft Azure provides a powerful, flexible, and secure cloud platform that supports the diverse and evolving needs of modern organizations. Its comprehensive suite of services, global infrastructure, and seamless integration with Microsoft's ecosystem make Azure an indispensable tool for businesses seeking to innovate and grow in the digital age.

- **Comprehensive Integration with Microsoft Products:** For organizations already using Microsoft software such as Windows Server, Office 365, or SharePoint, Azure provides seamless integration, allowing for a unified environment that reduces complexity and improves efficiency in operations.
- **Hybrid Capability:** Azure stands out with its strong support for hybrid cloud environments. It allows businesses to integrate their on-premises datacenters with the cloud, leveraging the best of both worlds. Azure's hybrid capabilities enable applications and data to work across on-premises, cloud, and the edge, enhancing flexibility and scalability.
- **Global Presence:** Azure's infrastructure spans over 60 regions worldwide, more than any other cloud provider. This global reach ensures that applications can be deployed close to users, reducing latency, and improving performance while adhering to local regulatory requirements.
- **Security and Compliance:** Azure is known for its commitment to security, offering a wide range of built-in security features and compliance certifications. Azure adheres to a rigorous set of compliance standards and is trusted by enterprises, governments, and startups alike for managing and protecting data.

- **Scalability and Flexibility:** Azure services are highly scalable, providing resources on-demand to accommodate any workload size. This scalability, coupled with a pay-as-you-go pricing model, ensures that businesses only pay for the resources they use, allowing for cost-effective scaling of applications as needed.
- **Innovative Services:** Azure continuously invests in the development of new and innovative services, particularly in areas like AI, machine learning, Internet of Things (IoT), and analytics. These services empower businesses to build cutting-edge solutions that can transform industries and create new opportunities.
- **Strong Developer Ecosystem:** Azure provides a rich set of tools and services that cater to developers, including Azure DevOps for continuous integration and delivery, Visual Studio Code for development, and a plethora of SDKs for different programming languages. This robust ecosystem accelerates the development and deployment of applications.
- **Enterprise-Grade Support:** Azure offers enterprise-grade support options, including direct access to Azure engineers, 24/7 technical support, and a comprehensive set of documentation, tutorials, and forums. This support ensures that businesses can confidently run critical applications with the backing they need.

By leveraging these advantages, organizations using Microsoft Azure can accelerate their digital transformation, innovate faster, and efficiently scale their operations in the cloud.

Getting Started with Azure

Embarking on the journey with Microsoft Azure, Microsoft's premier cloud computing platform, marks the beginning of exploring a vast landscape of possibilities for deploying, managing, and scaling applications. Azure is not just about offering computing power; it is a comprehensive suite that includes services for analytics, storage, databases, networking, developer tools, and more, designed to meet the needs of modern businesses and developers.

The initial step towards leveraging Azure's capabilities involves creating a Microsoft Azure account. You can sign up for an account through the Azure website, where Microsoft provides a generous starting offer – a free trial that includes $200 in Azure credits for the first 30 days and limited free services for 12 months. This allows you to experiment with Azure's various offerings without upfront costs. The sign up process is straightforward, requiring some personal and billing information to set up your account.

Once your account is active, you will gain access to the Azure Portal, an intuitive web-based user interface designed for efficient cloud resource management. The portal serves as your central hub for deploying, monitoring, and managing Azure services. It is designed to be user-friendly, offering a comprehensive dashboard view of your resources, and is where you will interact with Azure's extensive catalogue of services.

For those who prefer command-line tools or need to automate Azure service management, installing the Azure Command-Line Interface (CLI) is a crucial next step. The Azure CLI is a powerful tool that allows you to manage Azure resources directly from the terminal, providing a flexible way to script and automate your cloud infrastructure. Additionally, Microsoft offers Software Development Kits (SDKs) in various programming languages, enabling seamless integration of Azure services into your applications. With these tools at your disposal, coupled with Azure's rich documentation and tutorials, you are well-equipped to begin building and deploying your projects on one of the world's leading cloud platforms.

In this section, we delve into the process of creating a Microsoft Azure account, a fundamental step for developers and IT professionals looking to leverage Azure's vast array of cloud services. The journey begins with visiting the Azure sign-up page, where new users are prompted to create an account, starting with basic details such as an email address. The sign up process is streamlined and user-friendly, guiding you through several stages including account creation, profile set up, and identity verification.

We can create the Azure Account here.

https://azure.microsoft.com/en-us/free

The first image highlights the initial step where you enter your email to start forming your new Azure identity. This is your gateway to accessing and managing Azure services.

Moving to the next step, as illustrated in the second image, users fill in more detailed information including name, phone number, and address. This information is crucial for setting up your Azure profile and ensuring that the services align with your location's regulations and available offerings.

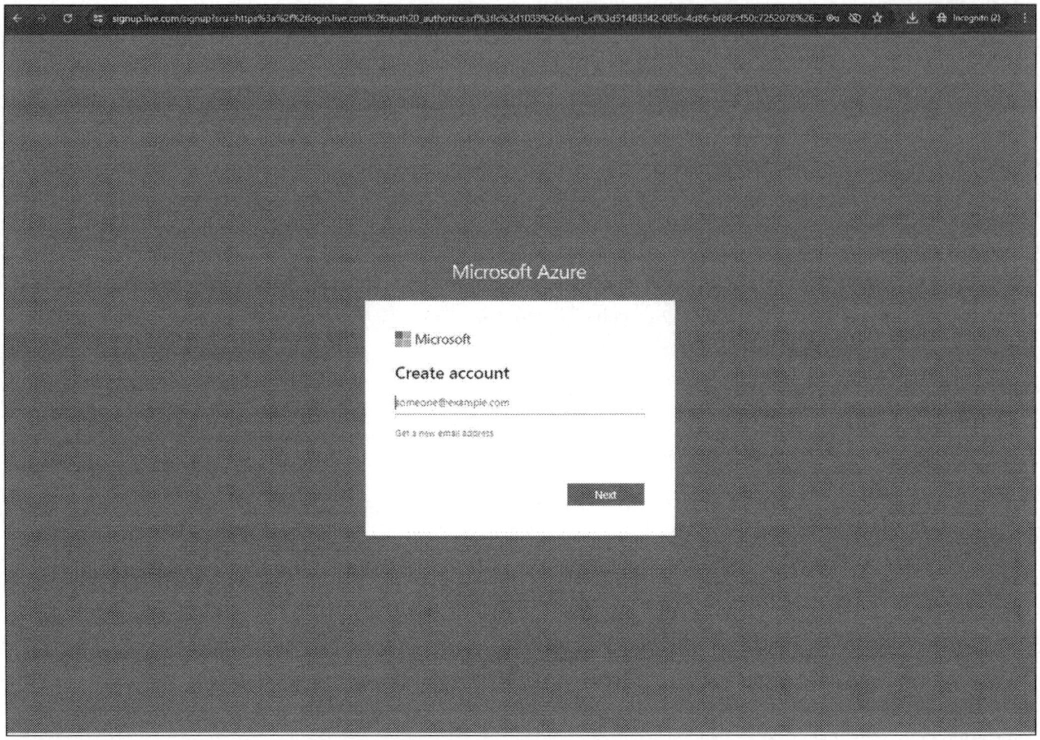

Figure 16.1: *Creating an Azure Account*

The final image encapsulates the verification process by requesting credit or debit card details. This step is essential for identity verification and engages the Azure free account offer, which includes free services for 12 months, a set amount of monthly credit for the first 30 days, and access to more than 55 always-free services. Importantly, Azure assures users that there will be no automatic charges; payment methods are only charged if the user decides to upgrade to paid services after the initial free period.

Creating an Azure account opens a realm of possibilities in cloud computing, from developing and hosting web applications to managing large-scale databases and machine learning models. As users step into Azure, they embark on a path filled with opportunities for innovation, scalability, and efficiency in their projects or business operations.

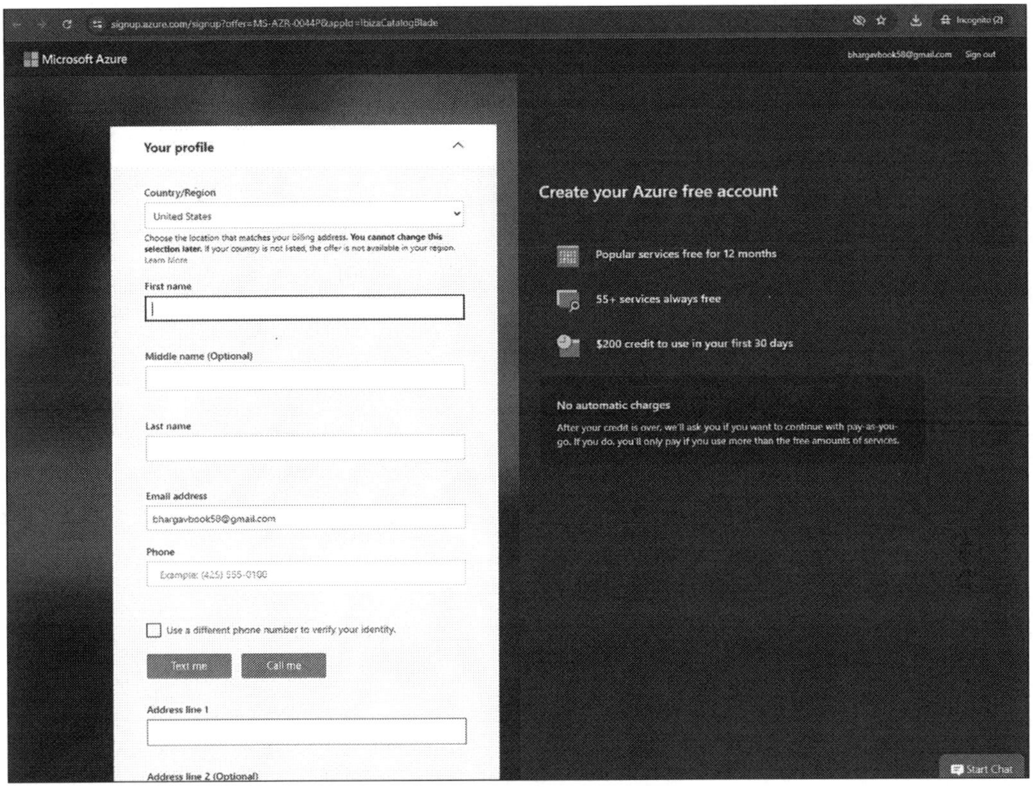

Figure 16.2: *Signing up Azure Account*

Once you have successfully created an Azure account, logging in will bring you to the Azure portal dashboard as illustrated in the image. The dashboard provides a streamlined, user-friendly interface, showcasing various Azure services and features that are available to you. From this initial screen, you can begin your Azure journey by starting with an Azure free trial, which offers $200 credit towards Azure products and services, along with access to popular free services for 12 months.

The portal highlights key services such as virtual machines, app services, and SQL databases, allowing for easy navigation and management of your cloud resources. Additionally, the dashboard offers quick access to resource creation, subscriptions management, and a QuickStart Centre for new users. The Azure portal is designed to provide a comprehensive view of all your resources and services, enabling efficient management and monitoring of your cloud environment. This organized approach aids in exploring the full potential of Azure, setting the stage for your cloud computing projects.

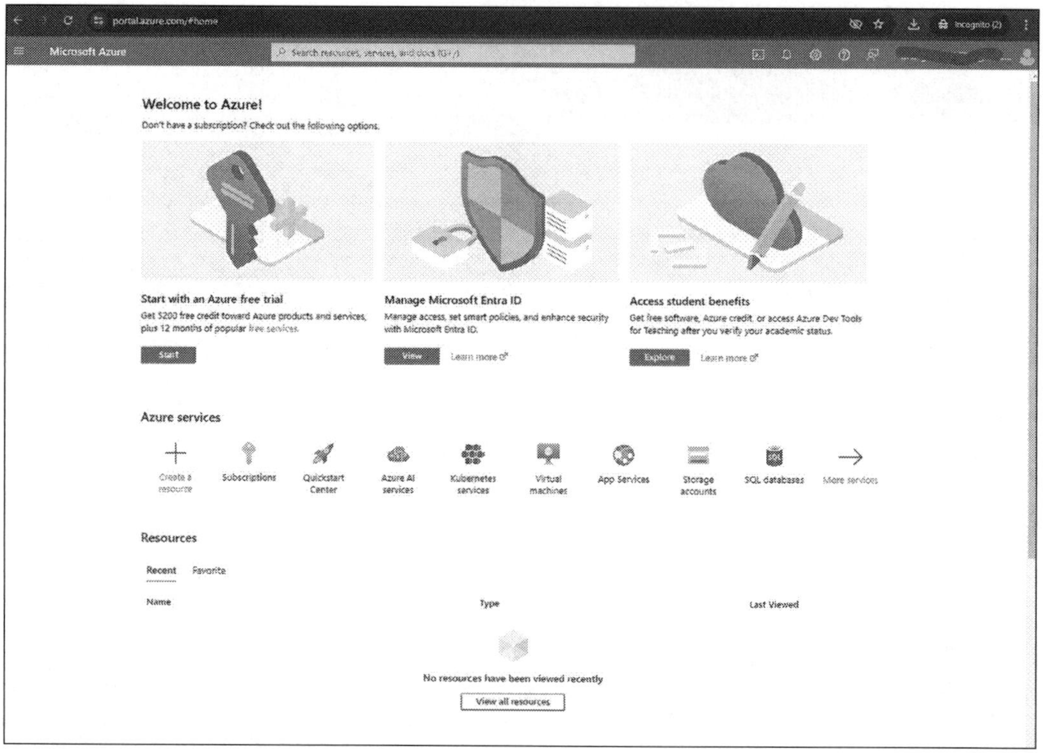

Figure 16.3: *Azure Portal*

After successfully establishing an Azure account and accessing the Azure portal, the next step involves creating a subscription. In Azure, a subscription acts as a logical container used to group your resources for billing purposes. Every resource you use or create in Azure must be associated with a subscription, which enables you to organize costs and billing in a way that aligns with your budget and project management needs.

Within the Azure portal, as depicted in the screenshot, you are presented with three primary subscription options:

- **Free Trial:** This option offers full access to all Azure services with certain limitations, providing a set number of free credits to explore and test different Azure products and services. The Free Trial is ideal for users new to Azure, allowing them to learn and experiment without incurring costs.
- **Pay-As-You-Go:** This flexible payment plan requires no upfront costs and no long-term commitment. Users pay only for the resources they consume, making it suitable for businesses or individuals looking to scale their operations according to demand.
- **Azure for Students**: Tailored for educational purposes, this offer provides students with credits and access to select free products for 12 months,

promoting innovation, exploration, and learning in a cloud environment without financial barriers.

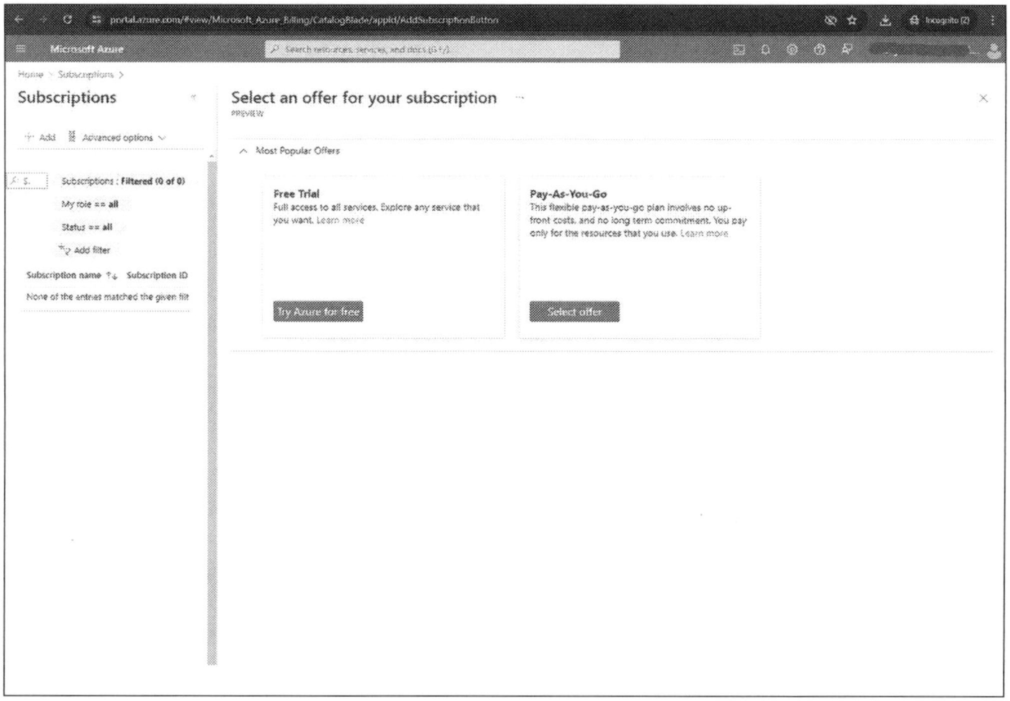

Figure 16.4: *Different Subscription Offers*

In addition to selecting a subscription, you will also work with resource groups within Azure. A resource group is a collection of resources that share the same lifecycle, permissions, and policies. They provide an efficient way to manage and organize Azure resources such as virtual machines, databases, and more, within a particular subscription. By effectively managing subscriptions and resource groups, you can streamline your Azure infrastructure, optimize costs, and enhance organizational efficiency.

After choosing the appropriate Azure subscription that fits your needs, the platform will prompt you to choose a billing method to manage your account's expenses. Upon completing this step, your subscription will be successfully established, as indicated in the Azure portal. Within this subscription, you will organize your Azure resources into resource groups. These resource groups serve as containers that hold related resources for an Azure solution, ensuring structured management and billing under the umbrella of your chosen subscription. This hierarchical structure facilitates efficient resource and cost management, allowing for streamlined project organization and budgeting within Azure's cloud environment.

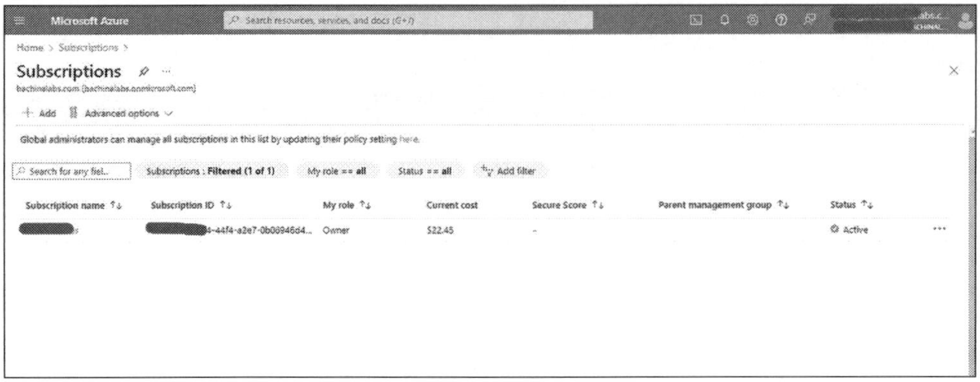

***Figure 16.5:** Subscription Created*

It is advisable to familiarize yourself with the Azure Portal and its myriad functionalities. Exploring the diverse Azure services and their configurations can deepen your comprehension and leverage of the Azure ecosystem, customizing it to fulfil the specific requirements of your project.

Different Ways to Interact with Azure

Interacting with Microsoft Azure can be achieved through various interfaces and tools, each catering to different preferences, operational needs, and technical expertise levels. Here is an overview of the different ways to interact with Azure:

Azure Portal

The Azure Portal is a web-based, user-friendly interface that allows you to manage Azure services and resources.

Advantages

- Intuitive graphical user interface (GUI) that is easy to navigate.
- No need for script or code knowledge to perform most actions.
- Accessible from any browser and any device.

Disadvantages

- Can be slower than command-line options for batch operations or complex tasks.
- Some advanced configurations might require scripting or CLI commands.

Azure CLI (Command-Line Interface)

The Azure CLI is a set of commands used to manage Azure resources from the command line or in scripts.

Advantages

- Enables scripting and automation of Azure resource management.
- Cross-platform support (Windows, macOS, Linux).
- Quick execution of commands and can be integrated into deployment pipelines.

Disadvantages

- Requires familiarity with command-line interfaces and Azure command syntax.
- Steeper learning curve compared to the Azure Portal.

Azure PowerShell

Azure PowerShell is a module offering cmdlets to manage Azure resources directly from the PowerShell command line.

Advantages

- Powerful scripting capabilities that integrate with Windows PowerShell.
- Ideal for automation scripts and batch processing.
- Rich set of commands and consistent with PowerShell syntax.

Disadvantages

- Primarily tailored for Windows users, though it can be used on other platforms via PowerShell Core.
- Requires knowledge of PowerShell scripting.

Azure SDKs (Software Development Kits)

Azure provides SDKs for various programming languages, including .NET, Java, Python, JavaScript, and more, allowing developers to interact with Azure services programmatically.

Advantages

- Enables integration of Azure services directly into applications.
- Supports multiple programming languages.
- Ideal for developers building cloud-native applications.

Disadvantages

- Requires programming knowledge and understanding of Azure services.
- Integration and debugging can be time-consuming.

Azure ARM Templates (Azure Resource Manager)

ARM templates are JSON files that define the resources you need to deploy for your solution, allowing you to automate and replicate deployments.

Advantages

- Enables infrastructure as code, improving consistency and repeatability.
- Integrates with CI/CD pipelines for automated deployments.
- Supports complex deployments through declarative syntax.

Disadvantages

- JSON syntax can be verbose and complex.
- Requires understanding of Azure resources and dependencies.

Azure Cloud Shell

Azure Cloud Shell is an interactive, browser-accessible shell for managing Azure resources. It provides a choice of Bash or PowerShell and is preconfigured to use with your account.

Advantages

- Accessible directly in the Azure Portal.
- No need to install or configure the Azure CLI or PowerShell locally.
- Persistent storage for files across sessions.

Disadvantages

- Requires internet access and browser.
- May be less responsive than local CLI or PowerShell environments.

Terraform for Azure

Terraform can be used with Azure to manage and provision resources in a predictable, consistent manner. By writing configuration files, users can set up the entire Azure infrastructure without having to manually click through the Azure Portal. Terraform integrates with Azure through the Azure Provider, which allows Terraform to manage and interact with Azure resources and services.

Advantages

- Allows for clear and concise description of resources in human-readable configuration files.
- Running the same configuration multiple times results in the same state, preventing duplication and inconsistencies.

- Tracks state of resources, enabling complex changesets with minimal human intervention.

Disadvantages

- Requires understanding of Terraform syntax and concepts, as well as an understanding of Azure's architecture and service offerings.
- While powerful, managing state files (especially in a team environment) can be complex and requires careful handling to avoid conflicts.
- Setting up Terraform and writing the initial configuration files can be time-consuming.

Configure and Set Up Azure CLI

The Azure Command-Line Interface (CLI) is a powerful toolset that allows you to manage Azure resources quickly and efficiently directly from the command line. To begin using the Azure CLI, you must first download and install it. The installation process is straightforward and well-documented on the official Azure website. The CLI is available for installation on various operating systems, including Windows, macOS, and Linux. We can check the following URLs for the installation instructions.

https://learn.microsoft.com/en-us/cli/azure/get-started-with-azure-cli

https://learn.microsoft.com/en-us/cli/azure/install-azure-cli-windows?tabs=azure-cli

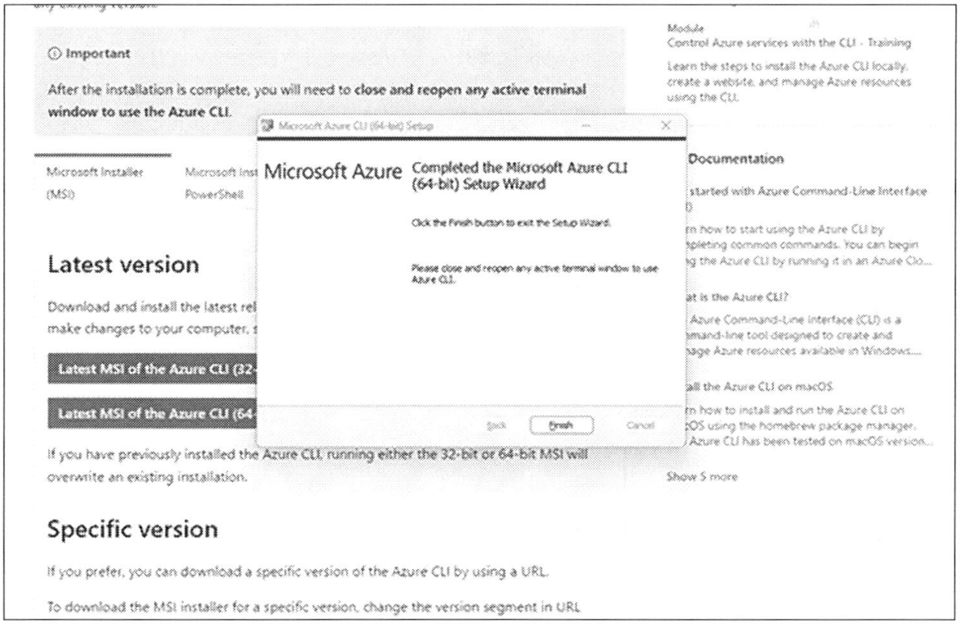

Figure 16.6: *Installation Completes*

As depicted in the accompanying image, once the Azure CLI installation on a Windows machine is complete, it is crucial to restart any active terminal windows. This ensures that the updated system path settings are recognized, allowing the Azure CLI commands to be executed from any new command line session. Upon finishing the setup, a prompt will confirm the successful installation of the Azure CLI.

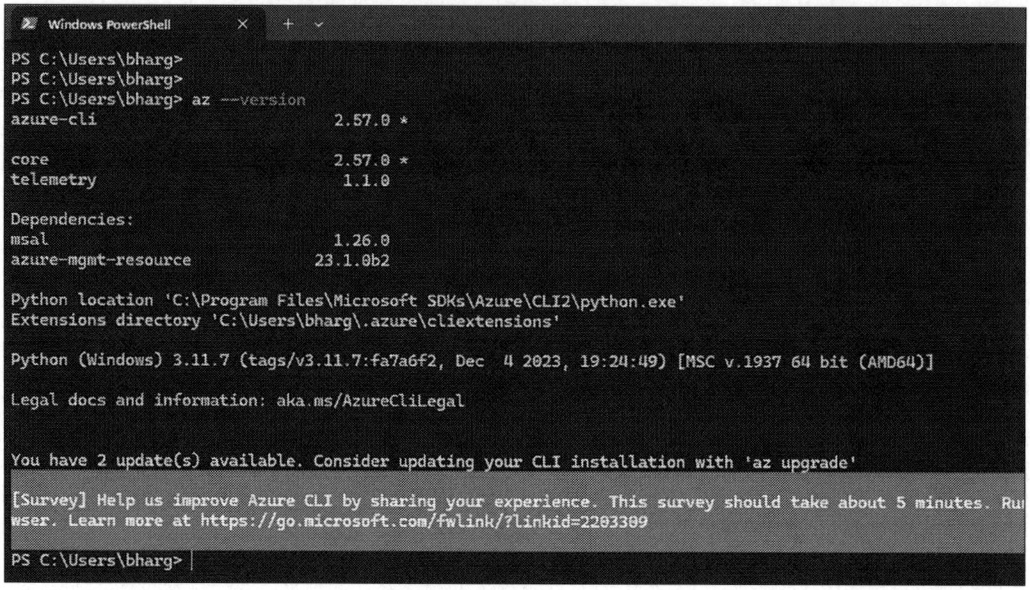

Figure 16.7: Azure CLI

After installation, you can open a new command line window and run **`az login`** to sign into your Azure account. This will open a browser window where you can enter your Azure credentials to authenticate. Once logged in, you can begin to execute commands to manage your Azure resources.

The Azure CLI is designed to be idempotent, allowing you to run commands multiple times with the same result, which is essential for scripting and automation tasks. Whether you need to manage virtual machines, set up cloud services, or handle storage accounts, the Azure CLI provides a comprehensive set of commands for all your Azure management tasks.

For more advanced configurations, you can customize your CLI experience by setting up default parameters for frequently used commands, enabling logging to monitor the CLI activity, or even writing scripts to automate complex tasks.

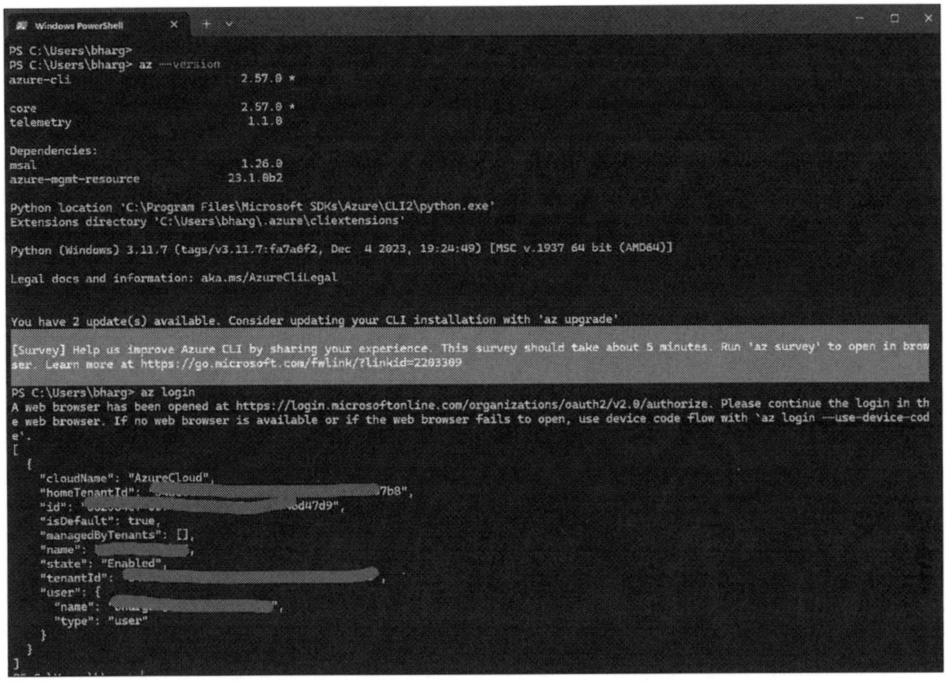

Figure 16.8: *Azure Login Successful*

In the next section, we will delve into container services provided by Azure, demonstrating how to manage and deploy containerized applications using Azure's suite of tools and services. Stay tuned to learn how Azure simplifies container management, offering scalable and reliable solutions for modern application deployment.

Container Options on Azure

In our previous sessions, we embarked on an educational journey to understand the foundational steps necessary for leveraging Microsoft Azure, covering the various methods available for interacting with Azure's comprehensive array of services. Now, considering our MEVN (MongoDB, Express.js, Vue.js, Node.js) stack has been successfully encapsulated within a Docker container, our next strategic move involves exploring the container deployment solutions offered by Azure. This step is essential for determining the most suitable environment for executing our Dockerized application.

As we proceed, our focus will shift to dissecting the different container services provided by Azure. This examination is pivotal, as it will enable us to identify the platform that not only aligns with our application's architectural demands but also optimizes our deployment strategy in the cloud. By understanding these options, we aim to harness the full potential of Azure's infrastructure, thereby ensuring our application is deployed in the most efficient, scalable, and manageable manner possible.

Microsoft Azure offers a range of container services suitable for deploying your MEVN stack Docker image. Here is an overview of the container options available on Azure:

Azure Kubernetes Service (AKS)

Azure Kubernetes Service (AKS) is a managed container orchestration service based on Kubernetes, which simplifies the deployment, management, and scaling of containerized applications across a cluster of machines.

- **Best for:** Enterprises and developers looking for a scalable, managed Kubernetes environment for complex applications.
- **Features:** Fully managed Kubernetes service, reducing the complexity of deployment and management, Integrated with Azure DevOps, Azure Active Directory, and other Azure services for seamless operations, Auto-scaling, self-healing, and load balancing capabilities.
- **Use Case:** Ideal for deploying and managing containerized applications with complex architectures, requiring scalability and high availability. Suitable for both development and production environments.

Let us dive into the pros and cons of AKS service for deploying an MEVN stack Docker image:

Advantages

- **Managed Service:** AKS reduces the complexity of your Kubernetes deployment since Azure handles critical tasks like health monitoring and maintenance.
- **Scalability:** Easily scales resources to meet demand without manual intervention.
- **Integration:** Seamless integration with Azure services and Azure DevOps tools.

Disadvantages

- **Complexity:** Despite being managed, Kubernetes can still be complex to newcomers.
- **Cost:** While the management feature of AKS is free, the underlying compute resources can be expensive as you scale.
- **Overhead:** Requires a good understanding of Kubernetes concepts for effective management and optimization.

Azure Container Instances (ACI)

Azure Container Instances (ACI) provides the easiest and quickest way to run a container in Azure, without having to manage any virtual machines or adopting additional services.

- **Best for:** Quick deployments and short-lived containers, ideal for simple applications or task-based workloads.
- **Features:** Offers the fastest and simplest way to run a container in Azure without having to manage servers or adopt additional services, per-second billing and no additional overhead costs, Can be used with Azure Logic Apps for event-driven applications.
- **Use Case:** Best suited for scenarios requiring isolated containers, batch jobs, or situations where you need to quickly start and stop containers without the overhead of orchestration.

Let us dive into the pros and cons of ACI service for deploying an MEVN stack Docker image:

Advantages

- **Simplicity:** ACI is straightforward to use, making it ideal for single containers.
- **Speed:** Rapid deployment and startup times.
- **Per-second Billing:** You only pay for the exact amount of compute resources your container uses.

Disadvantages

- **Limited Capabilities:** Not suitable for complex applications that require orchestration.
- **Networking:** Limited network configuration options compared to other services.
- **Scalability:** More suited for individual containers rather than large-scale deployments.

Azure Web App for Containers

Azure Web App for Containers allows you to deploy and run containerized web applications on a scalable and managed platform.

- **Best for:** Developers who need to deploy web applications quickly and easily, with the flexibility to scale and integrate with Azure services.
- **Features:** Allows you to deploy web apps packaged as containers, Supports custom domains, SSL, and autoscaling, Integrated environment with built-in CI/CD, authentication, and monitoring capabilities.
- **Use Case:** Suitable for deploying and managing web applications or APIs that are containerized, with seamless scaling and management features. Ideal for developers seeking PaaS capabilities with custom container deployments.

Let us dive into the pros and cons of Azure web app for containers for deploying a MEVN stack Docker image:

Advantages

- **Integrated Environment:** Built-in features such as CI/CD, authentication, and custom domain support.
- **Simplicity:** Easy to deploy and manage without deep containerization knowledge.
- **Scalability:** Automatic scaling and performance tuning features.

Disadvantages

- **Flexibility:** Less control over the underlying infrastructure compared to IaaS solutions.
- **Cost**: Can become costly at scale, especially with additional service integrations.
- **Platform Limitations:** Certain advanced container functionalities might not be supported.

Azure Service Fabric

Azure Service Fabric is a distributed systems platform that makes it easy to package, deploy, and manage scalable and reliable microservices and containers.

- **Best for:** Running microservices or containerized applications that require orchestration and management at scale.
- **Features:** A distributed systems platform that facilitates packaging, deployment, and management of scalable and reliable microservices and containers, supports both stateless and stateful services, Advanced networking, monitoring, and continuous deployment capabilities.
- **Use Case:** Designed for applications that are composed of microservices or need to maintain state across multiple instances. It is suitable for complex, large-scale applications requiring a high level of control over deployment and management processes.

Let us dive into the pros and cons of Azure Service Fabric for deploying a MEVN stack Docker image:

Advantages

- **Microservice Architecture:** Tailored for complex, large-scale applications based on microservices.
- **Stateful Services:** Supports both stateless and stateful microservices.
- **Mature:** Provides advanced features for application lifecycle management and monitoring.

Disadvantages

- **Learning Curve:** Complex and requires significant time to understand and use effectively.
- **Overhead:** More infrastructure and orchestration to manage compared to other PaaS offerings.
- **Transition:** Might be overkill for simpler applications or single-container deployments.

Azure Functions

Azure Functions is a serverless compute service that enables you to run event-triggered code without explicitly provisioning or managing infrastructure.

- **Best for:** Developers and businesses looking for an event-driven, serverless compute solution to simplify complex orchestration problems, automate small tasks, or create scalable microservices architecture without managing infrastructure.
- **Features:** Event-Driven execution, serverless architecture, scalability, cost effectiveness, and so on.
- **Use Case:** Ideal for scenarios like processing orders, analyzing logs, or managing inventory levels, where actions are triggered by data changes or specific events, Suitable for building lightweight APIs that respond to web requests and can scale automatically with demand.

Let us dive into the pros and cons of Azure Functions for deploying a MEVN stack Docker image:

Advantages

- **Cost Efficiency:** You only pay for the compute time you consume, which can significantly reduce costs for intermittent workloads.
- **Scalability:** Automatically scales based on demand.
- **Event-Driven:** Seamlessly integrates with other Azure services and external systems for a wide range of scenarios like data processing, web APIs, and automation tasks.

Disadvantages

- **Execution Time Limit:** There are time limits on function execution, which might not be suitable for long-running tasks.
- **Cold Start:** Can experience latency during the initial run when the function is idle for a long period.
- **Complexity in Large Applications:** While great for small pieces of logic,

managing a large application entirely on Azure Functions can become complex due to the nature of serverless architecture.

Each of these Azure services offers different features and capabilities, so the choice of service depends on your specific application requirements, such as scalability, manageability, and the complexity of the services you are deploying.

Pushing Docker Image to Azure Container Registry

Azure Container Registry (ACR) is a managed Docker container registry service provided by Microsoft Azure. It allows developers to store and manage container images across all types of Azure deployments. ACR provides a secure, scalable, and reliable hosting environment for container images, making it easier for teams to store, manage, and deploy their Docker and Open Container Initiative (OCI) images in Azure. Here are some of the features.

- **Private Registry:** ACR offers private Docker image storage, enabling teams to maintain the confidentiality and integrity of their container images. It is integrated with Azure Active Directory (Azure AD), allowing fine-grained access control based on user identity and group membership.
- **Geo-Replication:** This feature enables the replication of container images across multiple Azure regions, improving the speed of image download and deployment while providing a higher level of availability and redundancy.
- **Automated Image Builds and OS & Framework Patching:** ACR Tasks provide automated container image builds from source code repositories. This feature can also automate OS and framework patching for your Docker containers, ensuring that they are always up to date with the latest security patches.
- **Integration with Azure Services:** ACR seamlessly integrates with Azure Kubernetes Service (AKS), Azure Web Apps, and other Azure services, facilitating continuous integration and continuous deployment (CI/CD) workflows.
- **Security and Compliance:** ACR provides features like content trust, image scanning, and private link to help maintain security and compliance standards. It supports automated image scanning to identify vulnerabilities and integrates with Azure Policy to enforce compliance rules.
- **Helm Chart Support:** In addition to Docker images, ACR supports the storage of Helm charts, which are packages for Kubernetes applications. This allows for the centralized management of Kubernetes application definitions along with their corresponding container images.

Use Cases

- **Container Image Storage and Management:** Store and manage Docker and OCI images in a central registry, with support for tagging and versioning to track different iterations of images.
- **DevOps CI/CD:** Integrate ACR with Azure DevOps, GitHub Actions, or other CI/CD tools to automate the build, test, and deployment pipeline for containerized applications.
- **Global Distribution:** Utilize geo-replication to distribute container images across global Azure regions, ensuring faster deployment and high availability of applications.
- **Security Application Development:** Implement secure development practices by controlling access to container images, scanning for vulnerabilities, and ensuring that only trusted images are deployed.
- **Multi-environment deployments:** Use ACR to manage and deploy container images across various environments, such as development, testing, and production, ensuring consistency and reliability.

In summary, Azure Container Registry provides a robust and secure platform for storing and managing Docker and OCI container images, integrating well with Azure's ecosystem and supporting a range of deployment strategies and DevOps practices.

In *Chapter 11, Running MEVN Stack on Docker* we delved into the creation of a Docker image, which is a crucial step before deployment. As we transition to deploying our Docker image to Azure Container Registry (ACR), a preliminary step involves setting up the necessary infrastructure on Azure. This set up includes creating a resource group, which acts as a logical container in which all related resources, such as our container registry, will reside.

To initiate this process, we employ the Azure CLI tool, which facilitates direct communication with Azure services through your local command line or terminal. The first command in this sequence is:

```
// Creating a Resource Group
az group create –name rg-mevn-stack –location westus
```

This command creates a new resource group named **`rg-mevn-stack`** in the **`westus`** Azure region. Resource groups are fundamental for resource management in Azure, allowing you to organize and aggregate Azure services for effective management and billing.

Following the creation of the resource group, the next step is to establish our Azure Container Registry (ACR) instance where our Docker image will be stored:

```
// creating a ACR Repository
az acr create –resource-group rg-mevn-stack –name webapp –sku Basic
```

Here, **az acr create** initiates the creation of a new container registry within the **rg-mevn-stack** resource group. The registry is identified by the name **webapp**, and we select the **Basic** service tier (SKU), which provides a cost-effective solution for storing Docker images.

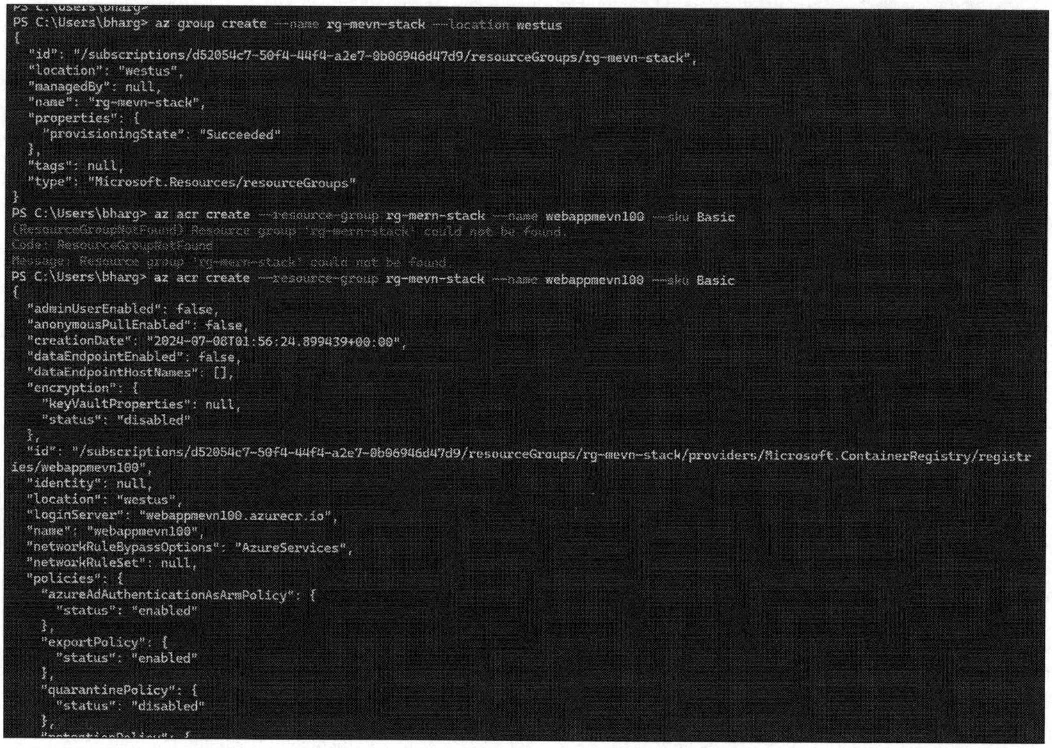

Figure 16.9: *Creating a Repository*

By executing these commands, we lay the groundwork required for storing and managing Docker containers in Azure. Once the ACR is set up, we can proceed to build and push our Docker image to this registry, making it available for deployment within our Azure infrastructure. This process exemplifies the integration between Docker containerization technologies and Azure's cloud services, paving the way for the streamlined deployment and scaling of web applications.

The command executed successfully establishes an Azure Container Registry (ACR) repository, as reflected in the Azure portal's interface depicted in the screenshot. This visual confirmation within the portal indicates that the ACR repository, named **'webappmevn'**, has been properly created and is now accessible. The Azure portal provides a comprehensive overview, including details such as the associated resource group **'rg-mevn-stack'**, the location set to **'West US'**, and the subscription information. This integrated registry serves as a private storage and management facility for your Docker images, streamlining container lifecycle management across Azure services. The registry's status, as shown, confirms successful provisioning and readiness for storing and managing container images and artifacts, facilitating efficient deployment workflows.

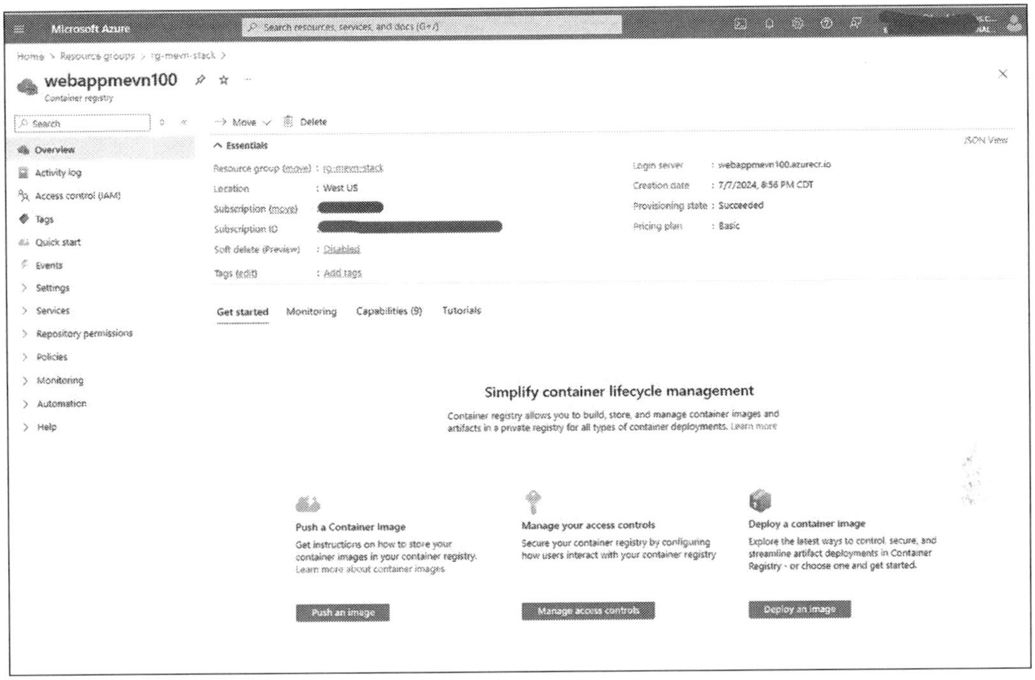

Figure 16.10: *Repository Created*

With the Azure Container Registry (ACR) set up, we can proceed to deploy our Docker image. This step is essential for storing and managing the container images in the cloud, facilitating easy access and deployment across various Azure services. To achieve this, we utilize the Azure CLI to build and push the Docker image directly to our ACR.

```
// Building and Pushing the Docker Image
az acr build -image webappmevn/web-app:v1 -registry webappmevn -file
Dockerfile .
```

Here is the breakdown of the command:

- **`az acr build`:** This command tells Azure to start a build task within your ACR.
- **`--image webappmevn/web-app:v1`:** This option specifies the name and tag for the image. In this case, **`webappmevn/web-app`** is the name of the image, and **`v1`** is the tag representing the version of the image.
- **`--registry webappmevn`:** This option specifies the name of your Azure Container Registry where the image will be stored.
- **`--file Dockerfile`:** This option tells Azure which Dockerfile to use for the build. The Dockerfile contains all the commands a user could call on the command line to assemble an image.

- The final **.** specifies the build context to the current directory. This means all the files in the current directory are available to the build process.

Figure 16.11: *Building and Pushing Docker Image*

Executing the above command initiates the process of building the Docker image based on the instructions in the Dockerfile and then pushing the newly created image to the specified registry in Azure. This integrated build and push operation streamlines the workflow, reducing the steps required to deploy containerized applications to Azure. Once the image is pushed, it can be used to run containers in various Azure services like Azure Kubernetes Service (AKS), Azure App Service, or others that support Docker containers.

In the displayed screenshot, we observe the successful upload of a Docker image to the Azure Container Registry (ACR). This registry, identified as **`'webappmevn'`**, now houses the repository **`'webappmevn/web-app'`** where our Docker image resides. The presence of the image in ACR signifies that our build and push process was successful, as indicated by the tag count and manifest count within the repository details.

The **`'Tag'`** section lists **`'v1'`**, denoting the version or specific iteration of the Docker image we have pushed. This tagging mechanism is crucial for version control and ensures that the correct iteration of the image is deployed to container services.

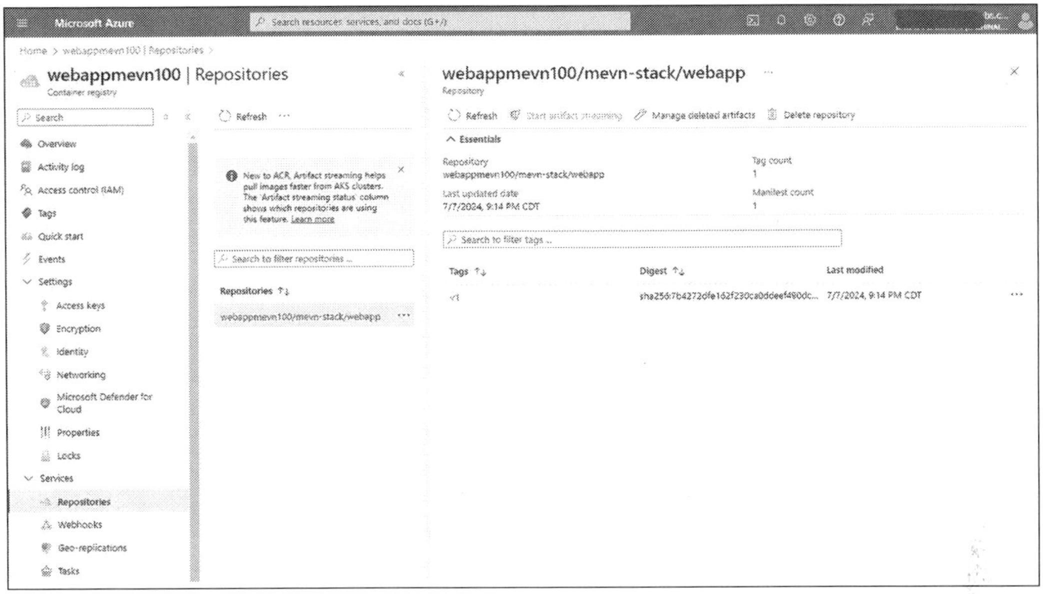

Figure 16.12: *ACR Repository*

With the Docker image now securely stored in ACR, it becomes readily accessible for deployment across various Azure container services such as Azure Kubernetes Service (AKS), Azure Web Apps for Containers, or Azure Container Instances. This integration facilitates seamless deployment processes, allowing for scalable, efficient, and reliable hosting solutions for your applications within the Azure ecosystem.

This set up exemplifies a crucial step in modern cloud infrastructure deployment, enabling rapid, consistent, and automated deployments. The ability to store and manage container images in ACR simplifies development workflows and enhances the collaboration between development and operations teams, paving the way for more sophisticated containerized application architectures.

Running MEVN Stack on Azure App Service

Azure App Service is a fully managed platform provided by Microsoft, designed to help developers quickly deploy web applications, REST APIs, and mobile back ends without the complexity of infrastructure management. This service streamlines the process of building, deploying, and running applications, offering an easy path from source code to global high-availability solutions.

Here are some of the key features.

- **Easy Deployment:** Deploy your applications directly from your favorite development tools, whether it is Visual Studio, GitHub, BitBucket, Docker

Hub, or Azure DevOps. Azure App Service simplifies the deployment process, allowing for continuous integration and continuous delivery pipelines, and provides out-of-the-box support for a wide range of languages and frameworks.

- **Automatic Scaling:** The service automatically scales your applications based on their traffic patterns, ensuring they perform consistently without the need for manual scaling. This feature helps maintain application responsiveness and reduces costs by adjusting resources dynamically.
- **Integration with Azure Services:** Azure App Service is deeply integrated with other Azure services, enabling a seamless connection to databases, caching, messaging, and more, enhancing the functionality and scalability of your applications.
- **Security:** Azure App Service provides built-in security and compliance features, supporting secure connections with TLS/SSL certificates, identity service integration for authentication, and ISO, SOC, and PCI compliance standards to protect your applications and data.
- **Cost-Effectiveness:** With Azure App Service, you only pay for the compute resources you need. The service offers multiple pricing tiers to suit different needs, from lightweight development and testing scenarios to high-volume, global-scale applications.
- **Simplified Operations:** The platform handles infrastructure maintenance, such as patching and load balancing, allowing developers to focus on writing code and improving their applications instead of managing underlying servers or infrastructure.

Azure App Service is particularly beneficial for developers seeking to leverage the power of cloud computing while minimizing the operational overhead associated with traditional web hosting environments. It is ideal for a range of applications, from simple websites to complex, scalable web applications and APIs. For more detailed information, you can explore the Azure App Service documentation provided by Microsoft. https://learn.microsoft.com/en-us/azure/app-service/

Let us embark on the process of constructing a web application via the Azure portal, which will include deploying our Docker image. This task involves navigating through the Azure portal to establish a new Web App, a service that enables the building, deployment, and scaling of enterprise-grade web, mobile, and API apps on any platform. By leveraging Azure's App Service Web Apps, we benefit from robust performance, scalability, and compliance requirement handling while operating within a fully managed platform, thus eliminating the need for extensive infrastructure maintenance. This approach simplifies the deployment of our Docker containerized applications, ensuring a smooth and efficient development and deployment workflow.

Creating a web application in Azure involves a series of steps that start with logging into the Azure Portal and navigating to the App Services section. Here, users can create, manage, and deploy web applications. The process begins with setting up the project details, such as choosing a subscription for billing purposes and organizing resources within a resource group. Users must then provide instance details, including a unique name for the web app, the type of publishing method (code, Docker container, or static content), the operating system (Linux or Windows), and the geographic region where the app will be hosted.

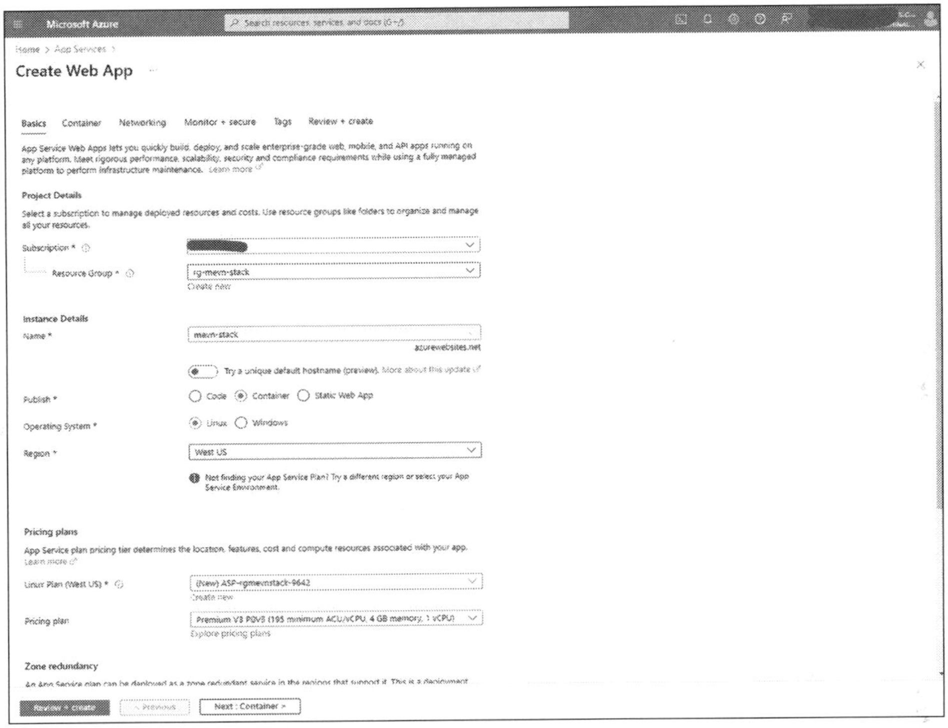

Figure 16.13: *Creating a webapp*

After configuring these settings, users must select an appropriate pricing plan, which will affect the app's available features and overall cost. Once all settings are reviewed and validated, the web app can be created. Following creation, the app can be deployed using various methods, such as direct code upload, using continuous integration and deployment pipelines, or through Docker container deployment. This streamlined process in the Azure Portal makes it accessible for developers to set up and launch web applications with minimal hassle.

On the next screen, we need to select the Docker Image that we have pushed in the previous section. The error message in the image suggests that Azure cannot perform credential operations for the specified container registry due to the admin user being disabled.

The command **`az acr update -n webappmevn --admin-enabled true`** is used in Azure CLI to update the settings of an ACR instance. Specifically, this command enables the admin user account for the container registry named **`'webappmevn'`**.

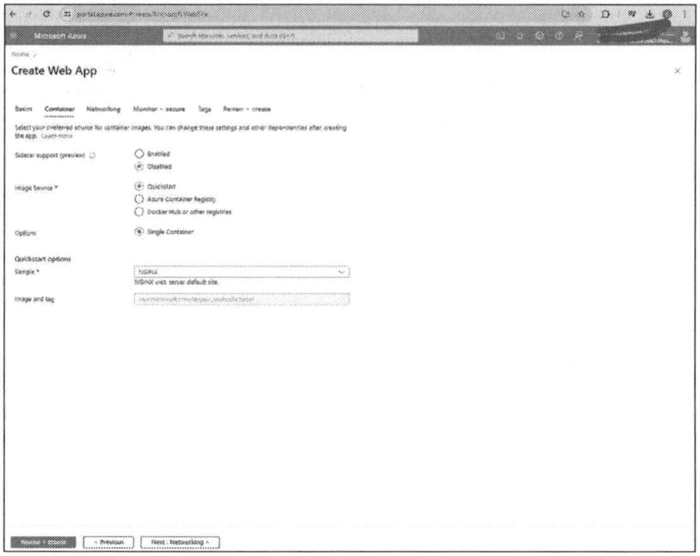

Figure 16.14: *Admin Access Disabled*

By executing the command **`az acr update -n webappmevn --admin-enabled true`**, you enable the admin account for the **`'webappmevn'`** container registry. This operation allows Azure to access the registry with an admin-level account, thereby resolving the credential issues and enabling the web app service to pull the specified container image from the registry. Once the admin account is enabled, you can obtain the access keys for the registry, which can then be used to authenticate from the Azure web app service, allowing the deployment of the containerized application.

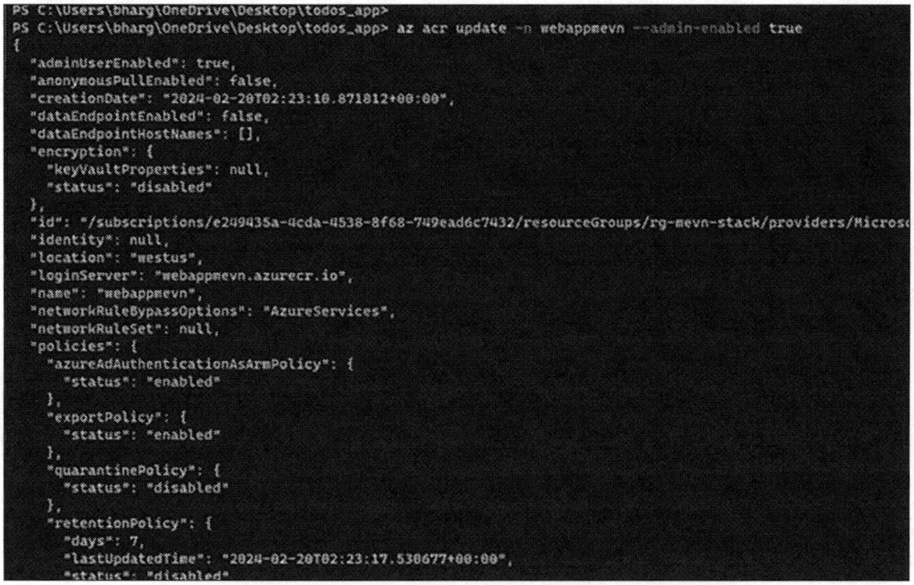

Figure 16.15: *Running the command*

Once the command is executed successfully, it will enable the admin user for the Azure Container Registry, allowing us to proceed with the selection of the desired container image. This step is crucial for moving forward with the subsequent stages in the process. With the admin user enabled, the Azure Web App service gains the necessary permissions to access and pull the specified container image from the registry.

After selecting the container image and completing the remaining steps in the Azure Web App creation process, we can finalize the setup and deploy our web application. Upon successful deployment, we will be directed to the overview page of the newly created Azure Web App.

The overview page of a Microsoft Azure Web App named "**`mevn-stack`**." This page acts as the central hub for managing the web app, displaying critical information such as the app's status, which is "**`Running`**," indicating that the app is active and operational. It also shows the app's default domain name (mevn-stack.azurewebsites.net), allowing users to access the web app through this URL. Additional details include the geographic location of the web app hosting (East US), the operating system (Linux), and the associated Azure subscription details. The App Service Plan listed suggests the pricing tier and capabilities available to the web app.

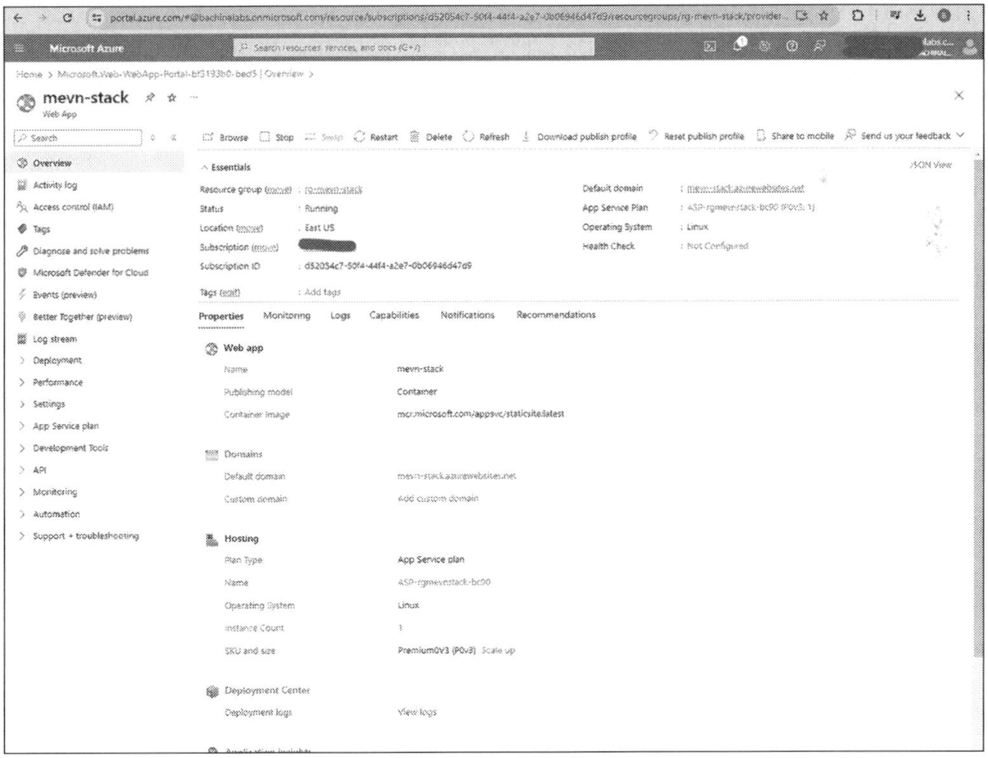

Figure 16.16: *WebApp Overview Page*

The overview page provides various management tools and settings, including options for browsing the app, stopping, restarting, or deleting it. The web app is deployed as a container, indicated by the publishing model and the container image details (**webappmevn.azurecr.io/webappmevn/web-app:v2**). This shows that the app is using a Docker container for deployment, which is sourced from the Azure Container Registry. Users can manage domain names, monitor performance, and configure settings directly from this dashboard, making it a comprehensive tool for web app administration in Azure.

The URL https://mevn-stack.azurewebsites.net mentioned in the above image refers to the default domain provided by Azure for the web application named "`mevn-stack`." This URL is automatically generated by Azure when you create a new Web App and is unique to this specific application. The structure of the URL typically follows the pattern `[app-name].azurewebsites.net`, where `[app-name]` is replaced with the name of your web app, in this case, `'mevn-stack'`.

You can access the application from this URL by simply entering it into the browser's address bar and pressing Enter. This action will direct your browser to the web application hosted on Azure's cloud infrastructure. If the web app is running (as indicated by the status "`Running`" in the Azure dashboard), the browser should display the application's home page or its default landing page.

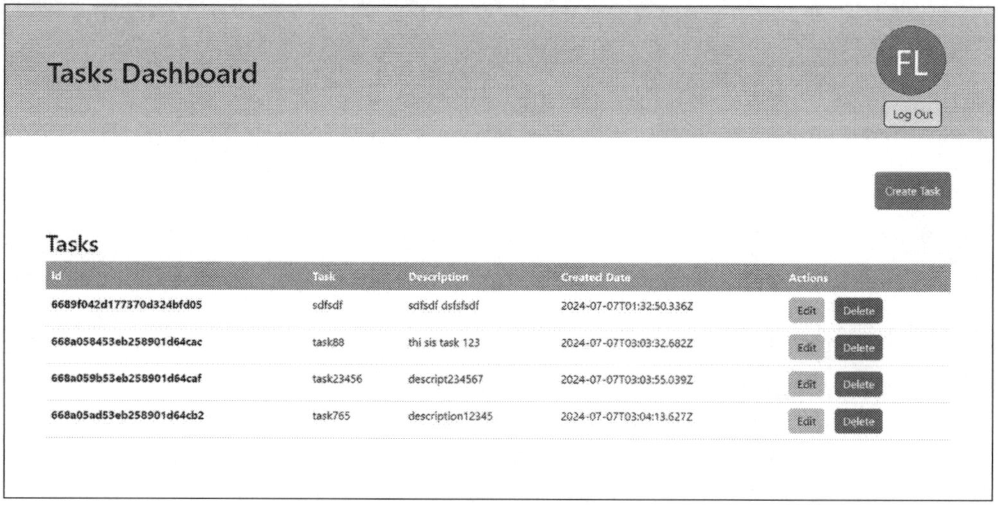

Figure 16.17: *Accessing the MEVN Stack*

This default domain is part of the Azure App Service and allows developers to quickly deploy and access their web applications without the need for purchasing and configuring a custom domain. However, for production environments, it is common practice to map the Azure app to a custom domain to maintain branding and ensure trust with users. But for development, testing, or internal applications, accessing the app via this default Azure-provided URL is a straightforward and effective method.

Deploying an MEVN (MongoDB, Express.js, Vue.js, Node.js) stack application on Azure Web App is a significant step towards leveraging cloud capabilities for your application. Once deployed, your application, accessible via the default URL provided by Azure (such as https://mevn-stack.azurewebsites.net), is up and running on a highly scalable, managed environment. This set up not only simplifies the deployment process but also offers robust features for application management and performance optimization.

Beyond just deployment, Azure Web Apps provide a suite of powerful features to enhance, monitor, and manage your application:

- **Monitoring**: Azure offers comprehensive monitoring tools through Azure Monitor and Application Insights. These tools allow you to track performance, diagnose issues, and understand the traffic patterns of your web app. You can set up alerts for specific metrics or incidents to stay informed about the health and performance of your application.
- **Logging:** Azure provides detailed logging capabilities, including application logs, web server logs, and database logs. These logs are invaluable for troubleshooting and understanding the behavior of your application. You can access these logs directly from the Azure portal or download them for offline analysis.
- **Adding a Custom Domain**: While Azure provides a default domain (`yourapp.azurewebsites.net`), you can also configure your web app to use a custom domain name. This enhances your brand identity and makes your application appear more professional. You can purchase a domain through Azure or use an existing one, and then configure DNS settings to point to your Azure web app.
- **Security and Compliance:** Azure ensures your application is secure by providing features like authentication services, managed SSL certificates, and compliance standards. You can also integrate with Azure Active Directory for secure and seamless sign-in experiences.
- **Scalability:** Azure Web Apps support auto-scaling, allowing your application to handle varying loads efficiently. You can configure scaling rules based on metrics such as CPU usage or request rates, ensuring that your app remains responsive under different load conditions.
- **Backup and Restore:** Azure offers automatic backups for your web applications, allowing you to restore your app to a previous state in case of issues. This feature is crucial for maintaining data integrity and minimizing downtime.
- **Continuous Integration/Continuous Deployment (CI/CD):** Azure supports CI/CD pipelines, enabling you to automate the deployment process from code check-in to production. This ensures that updates to your application are smoothly rolled out, reducing manual errors and downtime.

By leveraging these features, you can ensure that your MEVN stack application on Azure Web App is not only running smoothly but also optimized for performance, security, and user experience. This holistic approach to application management allows developers to focus more on feature development and less on infrastructure management.

Conclusion

In this chapter, we have introduced Microsoft Azure, a comprehensive cloud platform that provides a wide range of services from web applications to AI and machine learning tools. We began by guiding you through the initial steps of getting started with Azure, including setting up an account and familiarizing yourself with the platform's core services and interface. Following that, we covered the configuration and set up of the Azure Command-Line Interface (CLI), a powerful tool that enables you to manage Azure resources directly from the command line.

We delved into the various container options available on Azure, highlighting the flexibility and scalability that these services offer for containerized applications. We walked through the process of pushing a Docker image to the Azure Container Registry, an essential step in managing and deploying containerized apps. Lastly, we explored running a MEVN (MongoDB, Express.js, Vue.js, Node.js) stack application on Azure App Service, demonstrating the ease with which modern web applications can be deployed and managed on the Azure platform.

Concluding this chapter, it is important to recognize that while we have covered substantial ground, the container options and capabilities within Azure are vast and continually evolving. Due to the expansive nature of Azure's services, it is challenging to cover all container options comprehensively in this book. However, this chapter serves as a solid foundation for understanding Azure's key concepts and starting your journey. We encourage you to explore beyond these basics, experiment with different services, and tailor solutions to fit your specific needs. Azure's extensive documentation and community resources can provide further guidance as you continue to explore and harness the full potential of the platform.

Index

Symbols

<BaseModal> 262

A

AEFE, advantages
  auto-scaling 498
  platform, managing 498
  runtimes 498
  service, integrating 498
AEFE (App Engine Flexible Environment) 497
AEFE, disadvantages
  cost 498
  limited, controlling 498
  runtime, restrictions 498
Amazon ECR
  about 539
  concepts 541-543
  features 540
  use cases 540
API
  about 362
  CORS, implementing 365-367
  CSRF, implementing 367
  Helmet, implementing 363-365
  Rate Limit, implementing 368-373
API, key areas
  authenticating 362
  authorizing 362
  CORS (Cross-Origin Resource Sharing) 362
  CSRF 363
  encryption, hashing 362
  Helmet 362
  rate, limiting 363
API Structure, building 175-181
API Structure, directory files
  app.ts 151
  index.ts 151
API Structure, purpose
  controllers 151
  requests 151
  responses 151
  routes 151
  services 151
Artifact Registry 498
Artifact Registry, features
  fine-grained access, controlling 499
  global, distributing 499
  security, compliance 499
  service, managing 499
  services, integrating 499
  unified, repository 499
  version, tracking 499
Artifact Registry, key points
  description 501
  encryption 501
  format 500
  labels 501
  location, type 501
  mode 500
  name 500
Artifact Registry, use cases
  app, developing 499
  CI/CD 499
  DevOps, collaborating 499
  security, compliance 499
Atlas CLI 197, 198

Atlas CLI, setting up
  data, deleting 198
  data, fetching 198
  data, inserting 198
  data, querying 198
  data, uploading 198
  features, automating 198, 199
AWS (Amazon Web Services)
  about 522
  advantages 524-526
  project, utilizing 526-529
AWS App Runner
  about 543
  concepts 544, 545
  features 544
  process, managing 544
  setup, configuring 545-549
AWS CLI
  about 530
  advantages 530
  disadvantages 530
  setup, configuring 532-534
AWS CloudFormation
  about 531
  advantages 531
  disadvantages 531
AWS, container
  Amazon ECS 535, 536
  Amazon EKS 536, 537
  Amazon Lightsail 538
  AWS App Runner 538, 539
  AWS Fargate 537
AWS, core components
  compute, service 523
  data, analytics 524
  database, service 523
  developer, tools 523
  machine, learning 524
  network, content delivery 523
  service, storage 523
AWS, interact ways
  AWS CLI 530
  AWS CloudFormation 531
  AWS Management Console 529
  AWS SDKs 530
  PowerShell 531
  Third-Party Tools 531
AWS Management Console
  about 529
  advantages 530
  disadvantages 530
AWS SDKs 530
Axios 272, 273
Azure App Service
  about 577
  features 577, 578
  key aspects 583
  structures, analyzing 578-582
Azure CLI 565-567
Azure Container Registry (ACR)
  about 572
  command, utilizing 575
  concepts 573-575
  features 572, 573
  structures, analyzing 576, 577

B

Backend With Webpack,
    building 347-354
Bootstrap 5 244
Bootstrap 5, advantages
  accessibility 246
  consistency 245
  cross-browser, compatibility 246
  customizing 246
  document, community 246
  JavaScript, components 246
  mobile-first, responsiveness 246
  rapid, developing 245
  utility, classes 246
Bootstrap 5, benefits 246-248
Bootstrap 5, concepts
  accessibility, improving 245
  card decks, dropping 245
  components, utilities 245
  customization, enhancing 245
  droppe, supporting 245
  Forms, updating 245
  grid system, improving 245
  JQuery Dependency,
    removing 245
  Navbar, updating 245
  SVG Icons 245

Buffer
about 85
creating 86-88
data, manipulating 88
operations, utilizing 88, 89
Buffer, uses
binary data, handling 85
binary data, manipulating 86
encode, decoding 86
files, interacting 85
native libraries, interfacing 86
network, communicating 85
performance, efficiency 86
streams, integrating 86
built-in log, rotating 322
Bunyan 328
Bunyan Library, advantages
child, loggers 327
community, supporting 327
external system, integrating 327
high, configuring 327
readable logs, developing 327
structure, logging 327
Bunyan Library, disadvantages
complexity 327
curve, learning 327
file size, considering 327
performance, overhead 327
requirement, managing 327

C

callback function, arguments
Request Object (req) 116
Response Object (res) 116
Callback Hell 121
Callback Hell, approaches
Async/Await 122
modularization 121
promises 121
Callback Hell, characteristics
code, nesting 121
error, handling 121
maintenance, challenges 121
readability, issues 121
Callbacks 120
Callbacks, error handling 120
Child Processes 89
Child Processes, methods
exec() 91, 92
execFile() 92, 93
fork() 93, 94
spawn() 90, 91
Child Processes, use cases
concerns, separating 90
CPU-bound, tasks 90
shell commands, executing 90
Cloud Run 495
Cloud Run, advantages
fully, managing 496
integrating 496
scalability 496
simplicity 496
Cloud Run, disadvantages
limited, controlling 496
performance 496
statelessness 496
Cluster Module
about 94
benefits 94
process, implementing 94
Cluster Module, CPU cores
Master Process Logic 95
Worker Process Logic 95
Composition API
about 63
approach, utilizing 64, 65
components, analyzing 63, 64
properties, utilizing 63
Composition API, advantages
large, components 65
logic, reusing 66
TypeScript, supporting 66
Compute Engine 496
Compute Engine, advantages
flexibility 497
full, controlling 497
persistant, workloads 497
Compute Engine, disadvantages
complexity 497
cost, efficiency 497
overhead, managing 497
Containerization 392

Containerization, best practices
configure, managing 433
development, deploying 433
efficiency 433
log, monitoring 433
network, storage 433
Containerization Docker, role
continuous integrate, deploying 393
orchestration, managing 393
portability 393
createRouter function 240
CSRF Protection, reasons
stateless 367
Token-Based, authenticating 367
Cypress 471
Cypress, best practices
custom, commands 472
environment, variables 472
organize, test 472
page objects 472
Cypress, key features
automatic, waiting 471
cross browser, testing 471
debug, ability 471
network traffic, controlling 471
real-time, reloading 471
results, consistency 471
time, travelling 471
Cypress, mode
headless 472
interactive 472
Cypress With E2E, using 473-477
Cypress With First Test, writing 471

D

DefinePlugin 355
Docker
about 391
history 391
image, building 398
image, running 399, 400
project, utilizing 395-398
Docker Compose
about 400
complex application, simplifying 400
development, ensuring 400
file, writing 402, 403
process, utilizing 400
project, utilizing 403-407
Docker Compose, best practices
CI/CD Pipelines, composing 408
compose file, optimizing 408
data persistence, managing 408
log effectively, monitoring 408
service, isolating 408
updation, maintaining 408
variables, configuring 408
version, controlling 407
Docker Compose, key features
build, configuring 401
extensibility/scalability 402
network, communicating 401
service, isolating 401
volume, managing 401
workflow, simplifying 401
Docker, core concepts
Docker Client 394
Docker Compose 394
Docker Containers 393
Docker Daemon 394
Dockerfile 394
Docker Image 393
Docker Network 394
Docker Registries 394
Docker Volumes 394, 395
Docker, installing 36-40
dotenv 346
dotenv, alternatives
configstore 346
convict 346
cross-env 346
dotenv-expand 346
env-cmd 346
nconf 346
node-config 346
rc 346

dotenv, best practices 345, 346
Duplex Streams
about 103
Backpressure, handling 104
cleanup, error handling 105
creating 103
reading 104
use cases 105
writing 104
Duplex Streams, characteristics
channels, independency 103
Two-way, communicating 103

E

E2E (End-to-End) Testing 462
E2E Testing, best practices
continuous, integrating 463
review, monitoring 463
test data, reliablity 463
test scenarios, defining 463
wisely, automating 463
E2E Testing, challenges
complexity 463
flakiness 463
maintenance 463
resource, intensive 463
E2E Testing, importance
data, integrating 462
environment, infrastructure 462
regulatory, compliance 463
system, integrating 462
user, experience 462
EventEmitter, creating 113
Exception
about 124
Asynchronous Code, handling 126
Synchronous Code, handling 125
Unhandled, handling 127
Exception, types
assertion, errors 125
JavaScript, errors 124
Promise, rejection 125
System, errors 124
User-Defined, errors 125
ExpressJS
about 20
application, generating 25
key features 20, 21
setting up 23, 24
use cases 21, 22
Express Server, setting up 156-162

F

final zip file, steps
backend, building 386
frontend, building 387
frontend, copying 387
scripts, combining 387, 388
SSL, copying 387
zipping 387

G

GCP, advantages
cost effectiveness, scalability 487
global network, infrastructure 487
operational efficiency, developing 488
security, compliance 487
service, integrating 487
GCP CLI, configuring 492, 493
GCP Container, options
AEFE (App Engine Flexible Environment) 497
Cloud Run 495
Compute Engine 496
GKE (Google Kubernetes Engine) 494
GCP, core components
big data, machine learning 486
compute, services 485
databases, storage 486
networking 486
security 486
GCP (Google Cloud Platform) 484, 485
GCP, interact ways 490-492
GCP With Google Cloud, utilizing 488-490

GKE, advantages
community, supporting 495
ecosystem, integrating 495
high, availability 495
scalability 495
GKE, disadvantages
complexity 495
cost 495
operational, overhead 495
GKE (Google Kubernetes Engine) 494
Global Exception Handler 373-376
Global Exception Handler, benefits 373, 374
Google GKE
about 511
concepts 513-516
key, components 512
key, features 511, 512
key, points 516, 517
kubectl commands, utilizing 518
Grunt 386
Gulp 385
Gulp/Grunt, benefits 386

H

Helmet, vulnerabilities
Clickjacking, preventing 363
HSTS 363
XSS, protecting 363
HTTP, methods
DELETE 153
GET 153
HEAD 153
OPTIONS 153
PATCH 153
POST 153
PUT 153
HTTP Server 115
HTTP Server Client, building 118
HTTP Server, error handling 119
HTTP Server, request handling
request method, handling 117, 118
URL, parsing 116, 117
HTTP Server, usage
callback functions, utilizing 116
server, setup 115
Husky Pre-Commit Hooks, configuring 383
Husky Pre-Commit Hooks, setup
Git Hooks, enabling 383
Hook, adding 383
Hook Execute, making 384
Husky, installing 383
test, committing 384, 385

J

Jest 445
Jest, best practices 446, 447
Jest, cons
browser-specific, testing 446
curve, learning 446
Jest, pros
documentation, community 446
easy, setup 445
fast, efficient 445
feature, comprehending 445
JavaScript Ecosystem, integrating 446

L

Large Files Streams, advantages
efficiency, increasing 112
memory usage, r educing 112
performance, optimizing 112
scalability 112
Lifecycle Hooks 66
Lifecycle Hooks, stages
onBeforeMount 66
onBeforeUnmount 68
onBeforeUpdate 67
onMounted 67
onUnmounted 69
onUpdated 68

Linting 376
Linting, categories
  Linting API 381-383
  Linting UI 377-380
Linting, reasons
  automating 377
  best practices 377
  code, quality 377
  consistency 377
  error, preventing 377
Logger Service
  about 311, 312
  class, defining 312
  console, logging 313-315
  public log, methods 313
Logger Service, functionality
  centralize log, managing 311
  log levels, controlling 311
  performance, scalability 311
  security, compliance 311
  structured, logging 311
Logger Service With Bunyan, setting up 323-326
Logger Service With Pine, setting up 316
Logger Service With Pino, setting up 319-321
Logger Service With Winston, setting up 328-331
Logging 309
Logging, importance
  app health, monitoring 309
  error track, debugging 309
  performance, optimizing 309
  security, compliance 309
Logging, strategies
  Correlation IDs, debugging 310
  log, levels 310
  structured, logging 310
  what to log 309
Logging Tools, best practices
  centralize, logging 310
  log, libraries 310
  log rotation, managing 310

M

MEVN HTTPS, running steps
  application, accessing 360-362
  Node.js Server, configuring 359, 360
  SSL certificate, generating 358, 359
MEVN Stack 270, 271
MEVN Stack Cloud, running 506-511
MEVN Stack, components
  Express.js 2
  MongoDB 2
  Node.js 2
  Vue.js 2
MEVN Stack Docker Image, running 409-415
MEVN Stack, reasons
  cancellation 272
  ease use 271
  ecosystem, community 272
  HTTP Request, progressing 272
  interceptors 271
  JSON, transforming 271
  promise-based 271
  server-side, usage 272
  timeouts 271
  web browser, supporting 271
MEVN Stack, use cases 2-4
MEVN Stack With Docker Compose, running 421-428
Microsoft Azure
  about 552, 553
  advantages 554-556
  core, components 553, 554
  portal, subscripting 560
  project, optimizing 556-562
Microsoft Azure, container
  Azure Container Instances (ACI) 568, 569
  Azure Functions 571, 572
  Azure Kubernetes Service (AKS) 568
  Azure Service Fabric 570, 571
  Azure Web App 569

Microsoft Azure, interact ways
  Azure CLI 562
  Azure Cloud Shell 564
  Azure Portal 562
  Azure PowerShell 563
  Azure SDKs 563, 564
  Terraform 564, 565
Middleware 154
Middleware, components
  Next Function (next) 154
  Request Object (req) 154
  Response Object (res) 154
Middleware, tasks 155
Middleware, types
  Application-level 155
  Built-in 155
  Error-handling 155
  Router-level 155
  Third-party 155
Mocha and Chai 457
Mocha and Chai,
    best practices 458
Mocha and Chai, cons
  boilerplate, code 457
  curve, leaning 457
  overhead, configuring 458
Mocha and Chai, pros
  flexible, customizing 457
  libraries, integrating 457
  library, asserting 457
Mongo Aggregation 199
Mongo Aggregation,
    capabilities
  composition 200
  filter, projecting 200
  group, summing 199
  performance,
    aggregating 200
  pipelines, aggregating 199
Mongo Compass
  about 230
  data filter, querying 232
  data, importing 234
  document view, editing 233
  installing 230
  pipelines, aggregating 234
  structures, navigating 232
MongoDB 195
  about 4
  CRUD Operation, using 10-12
  Docker, running 43
  history 4
  installing 41, 42
  setting up 6-8
  SQL, utilizing 5, 6
  use cases 5
MongoDB Atlas, advantages
  alerts, monitoring 44
  automatic, scaling 44
  backup, restoring 44
  cost, managing 45
  data migration, tools 45
  ease, use 44
  global, distributing 45
  high, availability 44
  security, features 44
  service, managing 44
MongoDB Atlas,
    setting up 44-47
MongoDB Database, types
  Admin 9
  Config 9
  Local 9
MongoDB, key features
  document model, flexibility 4
  framework, aggregating 5
  high, performance 4
  scalability 4
MongoDB, use cases
  environment variables,
    security 196
  performance, pooling 197
  replica set,
    connecting 196, 197
  scenarios, connecting 195, 196
  Standard Connection
    String (URI) 195
Mongoose
  about 201
  CRUD Operations,
    implementing 218-222
  models, implementing 208-210
  MongoDB, configuring 203-205
  repository pattern 210

Mongoose, advantages
boilerplate code, reducing 203
facilitates, developing 203
readability, improving 203
streamlines object, mapping 203
Mongoose, concepts
instance, methods 202
Middleware 202
model, creating 202
plugins 203
pool, connecting 203
population 202
query, building 202
schema, defining 202
static, methods 202
transactions 203
validating 202
multi-stage image, building 416-421

N

Node.js 14, 15
Node.js Backend, setting up 138-144
Node.js Event System 112
Node.js Event System, use cases 115
Node.js Event System, working
error, handling 114
events, emitting 113
listeners, removing 114, 115
methods, listening 113
Node.js File System
about 107
directories, working 110, 111
files read, writing 109, 110
file, streaming 111, 112
Node.js, key features
asynchronous, event driven 17
no buffering 18
single-threaded, looping 18
Node.js, methods
Asynchronous 108
Synchronous 108, 109
Node.js, phase
callbacks 16
check 17
idle/prepare 16
poll 17
timers 16
Node.js REPL (Read-Eval-Print Loop) 19, 20
Node.js, use cases
API, developing 18
applications, backend 18
command line, tools 18
data, streaming 18
Internet of Things (IoT) 18
microservices, architecture 18
network, applications 18
real-time, applications 18
server-side web, applications 18
web applications 18
Node.js With NVM, installing 28
Nodemon Setup, installing 144-147
NVM Environment, tasks
current version, installing 31, 32
Node.js, uninstalling 32
On Mac, installing 30, 31
On Windows, installing 29, 30
versions, listing 32
versions, switching 32

O

Options API
about 60
limitations 63
use cases 62, 63
Options API, components
computed 61
data 61
lifecycle, hooks 61
methods 61
props 61
watch 61
Options API With Vue, using 61, 62

P

Pine Library, advantages
customizable log, formatting 318
log levels, supporting 318
log, readability 318
Node.js, integrating 318
performance 318
simplicity ease, use 318
Pine Library, disadvantages
built-in log, rotating 319
complex log, requirements 319
features, comparing 318
less community, supporting 318
tools, integrating 319
Pine Library, functionality
custom format 317
initialization 317
Pinia Store
about 281
dashboard/tasks module, implementing 290-296
error, handling 287, 288
login module, implementing 285-289
rehydrating state 301
task detail module, implementing 297-300
Pinia Store, advantages
Composition API, compatibility 282
developer, experience 282
DevTools, integrating 282
hot module, replacing 282
modularity 282
Plugin, supporting 282
simplicity 282
Pinia Store, best practices
DevTools 284
modularity 284
naming 284
persistence 284
testing 284
TypeScript 284
Pinia Store, effects
cancellation 284
error, handling 284
modularization 284
state, loading 284
Pinia Store, set up 282, 283
Pinia Store, structure
actions 284
getter 284
state 284
state mutations, avoiding 284
Pino 322
Pino Library, advantages
child loggers 322
customizing 322
ecosystem, compatibility 322
high, performance 322
pretty, printing 322
structured, logging 322
Pino Library, disadvantages
built-in, transports 322
curve, learning 322
log process, complexity 322
too verbose, setting 322
Playwright 477
Playwright, best practices
authenticating 479
code, generating 479
continuous, integrating 479
debugging 479
visual, comparing 479
Playwright E2E Tests, using 479-481
Playwright, key features
APIs Rich, set 478
auto-wait 478
browser, contexts 478
cross browser, testing 477
headless, mode 477
mobile, emulating 478
network, intercepting 478
parallel test, executing 478
Playwright Tests, running 478
Playwright With First Test, writing 478

Postman With APIs, steps
todos routes,
testing 225-229
user routes, testing 223, 224
Postman With APIs,
testing 222, 223
Promises
about 122
Async/Await,
simplifying 123, 124
chaining 123
creating 122
resolution, consuming 122
Promises, states
fulfilling 122
pending 122
rejecting 122
proxy, core issues 280
proxy, setting up
configuring 279
export, configuring 279
path, rewriting 279
vite, plugins 279
proxy setup, advantages
endpoint, managing 280
environment,
flexibilty 281
experience, enhancing 281
performance,
optimizing 281
security 281
Publishing Docker
Image 428-432
Publishing Docker Image,
best practices 435-437

R

Readable Streams
about 99
creating 99
data, consuming 100, 101
use cases 101
Readable Streams, modes
Flowing Mode (Non-Paused) 99
Paused Mode (Buffered) 99
rehydrating state 301
rehydrating state, best practices
data, validating 304
persistence 304
security 304
synchronizing 304
versioning 304
rehydrating state, key point
consistency 301
offline, supporting 301
performance 301
user, experience 301
REPL, core features
Eval 96
Loop 96
Print 96
Read 96
REPL (Read-Eval-Print Loop) 95
REPL, usage
access, modifying 96
custom commands,
adding 97
environment,
customizing 97
load sessions, saving 98
variables/functions,
optimizing 97
repository pattern, advantages
concerns, separating 210
flexibility 211
maintainability 211
testability 211
repository pattern, interface
ITaskRepository 212
IUserRepository 211
TasksRepository 214
UserRepository 212, 213
Request Validation 184
Request Validation, aspects
compliance 185
database errors, reducing 185
data, integrity 184
easy, maintaining 185
error, handling 184
logic, assurance 184
resource misuse, preventing 184
security 184
user, experience 184

Request Validation, frameworks
  Express-validator 186, 187
  Joi 185, 186
RESTful APIs, advantages
  easy, communicating 154
  flexibility 154
  independence 154
  portability 154
  scalability 153
  simplicity 154
  standardd-based 154
  tools, debugging 154
RESTful, constraints
  HATEOAS 153
  resources-based 152
  resources, manipulating 152
  self-descriptive, messaging 152
RESTful, core principles
  cacheable 152
  Client-Server, separating 152
  Code on Demand 152
  layer system 152
  stateless 152
  uniform, interface 152
REST (Representational State Transfer) 151

S

Streams 98, 99
Streams, types
  Duplex 99
  Readable 99
  Transform 99
  Writable 99
Styling 70

T

TAP, best practices
  asynchronous, testing 459
  continuous, integrating 460
  simplicity, embracing 460
  structure, testing 459
  test, independency 460
  tools, coverage 460
TAP, cons
  curve, learning 459
  debugging 459
  popularity 459
TAP, pros
  asynchronous, testing 459
  coverage, reporting 459
  flexibility 459
  simplicity 459
  subtests 459
TAP (Test Anything Protocol) 459
Task Runners 385
TasksRepository, methods
  create(item: T) 214
  delete(id: string) 215
  getAll() 214
  getByID(id: string) 214
  update(id: string, item: ITask) 215
TestCafe 464
TestCafe, capabilities
  mode, concurrency 465
  page model, pattern 465
  plugins, reporting 465
  role-based, testing 465
TestCafe, key features
  automatic, waiting 464
  browser, plugins 464
  built-in test, runner 464
  CI/CD, integrating 464
  cross browser, testing 464
  library, asserting 464
TestCafe Tests, running 465
TestCafe With E2E, using 466-470
TestCafe With First Test, writing 465
Testing API 452-456
Transform Streams
  about 105
  creating 106
  error, handling 107
  uppercase, using 106, 107
  use cases 107
Transform Streams, characteristics
  data, transforming 105
  dual, nature 105

U

UI Development
  about 248
  dashboard module, implementing 256, 257
  edit/delete task modal, implementing 265-270
  header, visualizing 257-259
  login module, implementing 250-253
  sign up, component 253-256
  task modal, implementing 262, 264
  task presentation, component 260, 261
Unit Testing
  about 439
  frontend, utilizing 448, 449
  functionality, analyzing 451, 452
  importance 439
  test cases, optimizing 449-451
Unit Testing, best practices
  automating 440
  mock, stubbing 440
  Test, coverage 440
  Test, isolating 439
  Test, readability 440
Unit Testing, concepts
  Jest 440
  Mocha and Chai 441
  Vue Test Utils 440

V

Vite 33-35
Vite, actions
  compilation 335
  optimization 335
  output 335
  ready for deploying 336
Vite CLI Frontend, using 135-137
Vite CLI, project structures 133-135
Vite CLI Typescript Template, creating 130-133
Vite, installing 33
Vite UI Assets, serving 337-340
VSCode, installing 33
Vue 3 TypeScript, directories
  App.vue 306
  components 305
  containers 305
  layouts 305
  main.ts 307
  modals 306
  routes 306
  services 306
  store 306
Vue.js 25
VueJS
  about 54
  events 59
  Forms 80
  Lifecycle Hooks 66
  props 59
  reactivity system, utilizing 56, 57
  Slots 75
  Styling 70
  Template Refs 78
VueJS, advantages
  community, supporting 56
  component-based, architecture 55
  data, binding 55
  ease, learning 55
  ecosystem, tooling 55
  flexibility, integrating 55
  performance, optimizing 55
VueJS Communication, patterns
  EventBus, replacing 60
  Provide/Inject 60
  Teleport 60
  Vuex State, managing 60
VueJS, components
  Script 58
  Styles 58
  Template 58
VueJS, concepts
  community, supporting 55
  performance, optimizing 55
  reactive, composable 54
  robust, tooling 55
  simplicity, learning 54

VueJS, directives
DOM, elements 73
dynamic 75
global 74
hooks, arguments 74
VueJS, disadvantages
barrier resources, community 56
challenges, integrating 56
ecosystem, dependency 56
limited, resources 56
risk, flexibility 56
SEO, challenges 56
share to rivals, comparing 56
Vue.js, key features
component-based, architecture 26
developer, tools 26
DOM, rendering 26
integrating 26
reactive data, binding 25
VueJS, slots
default 75
named 76
props, destructuring 77, 78
scoped 76
slot fallbacks 77
VueJS, styles
class, binding 71
global 72, 73
scoped 72
Vue Test Utils 441
Vue Test Utils, best practices
component, maintaining 442
mock, dependencies 442
prioritize, readability 442
shallow, mounting 442
tests, dry 442
Vue Test Utils, component scenarios
component data, accessing 443
props/emits, testing 444, 445
user interaction, simulating 443
Vue Component, mounting 443
Vue Test Utils, cons
curve, learning 442
setup, overhead 442
Vue Test Utils, pros
flexibility 442
integrating 442
isolating 442
simplicity 442

W

Webpack 163
benefits 347
considering 348
Webpack, ability
graph, dependency 163
loaders, plugins 163
module, bundling 163
Webpack, key aspects
runtime, configuring 347
uniformity 347
Webpack, key components
configuring 166
entry, point 166
loaders 166
mode 166
modules 165
output 166
plugins 166
resolve 166
target 166
Webpack, key features
code, splitting 163
customizing 164
hot module, replacing 164
loaders 163
optimizing 164
plugins 164
server, developing 164
Webpack, reasons
analytics, monitoring 169
API, reliability 169
error, handling 169
maintainability 169
professionalism 169
security 169
user, feedback 169

Webpack Routes,
defining 168, 169
Webpack TypeScript,
setting up 164, 165
Webpack, use cases
Large Web Applications 164
Single Page Applications
(SPAs) 164
Transpiling 164
Winston 333
Winston Library, advantages
flexible log, formatting 332
log levels, customizing 332
multiple loggers,
supporting 332
rich, integrating 332
stream, integrating 332
transport manage,
versatility 332
Winston Library, disadvantages
complexity 332
curve, learning 332
dependency, managing 333
file, managing 332
performance, overhead 332
Writable Streams
about 101
creating 101, 102
use cases 102
Writable Streams, modes
Buffered Mode 101
Drain Mode 101

Made in United States
Orlando, FL
04 November 2026

90201504R00343